THE JEWS: THEIR ROLE IN CIVILIZATION

The original preparation of this book was made possible by funds generously made available by the American Jewish Committee.

This is the third volume of a three-volume work.
Its companion volumes are:

THE JEWS:

THEIR ROLE
IN CIVILIZATION

FOURTH EDITION

Edited by

Louis Finkelstein 1895

CHANCELLOR

THE JEWISH THEOLOGICAL SEMINARY OF AMERICA

SCHOCKEN BOOKS · NEW YORK

First SCHOCKEN PAPERBACK edition 1971

Published by arrangement with Harper & Row, Publishers
Copyright © 1949, 1955, 1960, 1971 by Louis Finkelstein
Library of Congress Catalog Card No. 74-107615
Manufactured in the United States of America

To

IRVING LEHMAN

(1876–1945)

Who in life and precept

integrated the ancient tradition

of the Hebrew prophets with the

spirit of American democracy

CONTRIBUTORS AND MEMBERS OF
THE PLANNING COMMITTEE[1]

William Foxwell Albright, *The Johns Hopkins University*, Emeritus Professor of Semitic Languages

Alexander Altmann, *Brandeis University*, Philip W. Lown Professor of Jewish Philosophy

Hillel Bavli, *The Jewish Theological Seminary of America*, Seminary Professor of Hebrew Literature[2]

Itzhak Ben-Zvi, *The State of Israel*, President (December 8, 1952–April 23, 1963)[2]

Elias J. Bickerman, *Columbia University*, Professor Emeritus of Ancient History

Arturo Castiglioni, *Yale University*, Professor of the History of Medicine[2]

David Daiches, *University of Sussex*, Dean, School of English and American Studies

Moshe Davis, *The Jewish Theological Seminary of America*, Research Professor of American Jewish History

Ben Zion Dinur, *The Hebrew University*, Professor Emeritus of Modern Jewish History

Jessica Feingold, *The Jewish Theological Seminary of America*, Director, The Institute for Religious and Social Studies

Louis Finkelstein, *The Jewish Theological Seminary of America*, Chancellor, Solomon Schechter Professor of Theology

Eli Ginzberg, *Columbia University*, Hepburn Professor of Economics

Nahum N. Glatzer, *Brandeis University*, Professor of Jewish History

Judah Goldin, *Yale University*, Assistant Professor of Classical Judaica, Advisor in Jewish Literature in the University Library, and Fellow of Davenport College

Bernard R. Goldstein, *Yale University*, Assistant Professor of the History of Science

Robert Gordis, *The Jewish Theological Seminary of America*, Seminary Professor of Bible

Simon Greenberg, *The Jewish Theological Seminary of America*, Vice-Chancellor, Vice-President of the Faculties, Professor of Homiletics and Education

Abraham S. Halkin, *The Jewish Theological Seminary of America*, Stuart E. Rosenberg Professor of History

Israel Halpern, *The Hebrew University*, Rosenbloom Professor of Jewish History

Abraham J. Heschel, *The Jewish Theological Seminary of America*, Professor of Jewish Ethics and Mysticism

[1] As of July 1970
[2] Deceased

Oscar I. Janowsky, *City College of The City University of New York*, Professor of History, and Director, New York Area Studies

Mordecai M. Kaplan, *The Jewish Theological Seminary of America*, Professor Emeritus of Philosophies of Religion

Milton R. Konvitz, *Cornell University*, Professor of Industrial and Labor Relations and Professor of Law

Anita Libman Lebeson, formerly Instructor in History, *University of Illinois*, College of Jewish Studies

Frederick Lehner, *West Virginia State College*, Professor of German and French[2]

Shmuel Leiter, *The Jewish Theological Seminary of America*, Associate Professor of Modern Hebrew Literature

Saul Lieberman, *The Jewish Theological Seminary of America*, Rector, Distinguished Service Research Professor of Talmud, and Louis Ginzberg Professor of Palestinian Institutions

R. M. MacIver, *Columbia University*, Lieber Professor Emeritus of Political Philosophy and Sociology

Ralph Marcus, *The University of Chicago*, Professor of Hellenistic Culture[2]

Yudel Mark, *Jewish Education Committee of New York*, Consultant for Yiddish Schools; *YIVO Institute for Jewish Research*, Chief Editor, *"Yiddishe Sprakh"*

Alexander Marx, *The Jewish Theological Seminary of America*, Jacob H. Schiff Professor of History[2]

Abraham Menes, *Zukunft*, Coeditor; *Jewish Daily Forward*, Columnist

Jacob J. Rabinowitz, *The Hebrew University*, Associate Professor of Jewish Law

Cecil Roth, *University of Oxford*, Reader Emeritus in Jewish Studies; Editor-in-Chief, *Encyclopaedia Judaica*[2]

Harry A. Savitz, M.D., *Hebrew Rehabilitation Center*, Physician-in-Chief Emeritus; *Beth Israel Hospital*, Boston, Staff Member

Charles Singer, *University of London*, Professor Emeritus; *University College*, London, Fellow; *Oxford University*, Magdalen College, Honorary Fellow; *History of Technology*, Joint Editor; *American Philosophical Society*, member[2]

Shalom Spiegel, *The Jewish Theological Seminary of America*, William Prager Professor of Medieval Hebrew Literature

Bernard D. Weinryb, *Dropsie College*, Professor of History and Middle East Economics

Eric Werner, *Hebrew Union College*, Professor Emeritus; Chairman, Department of Musicology, *University of Tel-Aviv*, Israel

Rachel Wischnitzer, *Yeshiva University*, Stern College, Professor Emeritus of Fine Arts

CONTENTS

CONTENTS

INTRODUCTORY NOTE

This book is the first comprehensive description of Judaism and the Jews. While avoiding the anatomical structure and purely alphabetical organization of an encyclopedia, it is designed as a readable and unified sketch of a singular human phenomenon. The principal relevant facts concerning the people of Israel and its faith are summarized in a succession of essays, which form an ordered whole and afford penetrating glimpses into particular aspects of the subject. This book includes the first compact history of the Jews written by scholars specializing in the several fields; an appreciation of the role of Judaism in world culture, seen from a wide variety of disciplines and skills; an initial effort toward a demography of the Jews in America; and a brief outline of the Jewish religion.

The complexity of the work, despite all efforts to achieve simplicity and uniformity, indicates the difficulty and intricacy of the subject. The history of Israel opens with the birth of Abraham, some 120 generations ago in the Mesopotamian bronze age, the period of Hammurabi, and since that time there has been scarcely a civilized dialect which does not contain some record bearing on the chronicle of this ancient people and its faith. One might almost say that no inhabited land but has witnessed Jewish heroism and martyrdom.

To compose a history of the Jews requires erudition and command of method, rarely, if ever, combined in one individual. It is one thing to reconstruct a living record of prebiblical and biblical Judaism from archaeological and literary records, and quite another to discern in an inexhaustible mass of documents, record books, living monuments or institutions, the pattern of modern Jewish life. Few scholars could master both techniques. And the sort of research that enables a man to interpret a prolix medieval work (its confusion of fact and legend, its reliance on hearsay evidence, its extravagance and vagueness) is completely different from that required for the exegesis of an obscure, but pregnant, biblical or talmudic or philosophical text.

In the course of its long, tortuous history, Judaism has profoundly affected, and been deeply affected by, cultural phenomena covering the whole range of human experience. To understand fully the place of Judaism in civilization it would be necessary to master philosophies and mental outlooks of cultures as varied as those of the ancient Canaanites, the Egypt of the Pharaohs, the Mesopotamia of the Assyrians, the Baby-

Ionians, and the Persians, the Seleucid and the Ptolemaic empires of the Greeks, the world empire of the Romans, the deserts of the Arabs, pre-Christian and Christian Europe, as well as the chaotic and complex world of our own day.

In turn, the faith and tradition of the Jews have left an indelible stamp on Western music, art, science, mathematics, medicine, philosophy, letters, education, philanthropy, law, public administration, manners, morals, and religion. The extent of this influence is not yet fully understood, for there are few scholars who know Jewish lore and, at the same time, enough of any field in Western culture to discover mutual relationships. Histories and anthologies of Western philosophy are still necessarily written with scant reference to such towering figures as Maimonides and Crescas, and none at all to the penetrating insights of the Talmud. The reconstruction of talmudic mathematics, and the analysis of its influence on that of the medieval period, are still in their initial stages; only the merest beginning has been made in the study of the relation of talmudic legal principles to the Canon Law and through it to later norms. The educational technique of the ancient Rabbinic schools, which might be of great practical value today, remains unknown except to the preoccupied, completely dedicated talmudic scholar. Students have still to describe the literary forms of Rabbinic Judaism that directly—and indirectly, through the Gospels—exerted so profound an influence on later composition. The Jewish conception of the whole of life as a work of art, a pageant of worship, in which every action must follow the score set down in the codes, yet may reflect individual ingenuity and piety, is only now beginning to be expounded. The essays in the present volumes can but suggest vast areas of research in these and other fields.

The three paperback volumes are being issued for distribution separately and in one set. Therefore certain material will be repeated in each, such as the introductory note, the list of contributors and member of the planning committee, the contents of all three volumes, and the list of abbreviations. An index will apply only to the volume in which it appears.

The physical size of the present paperback edition was determined by practical problems of manufacture and binding. The difficult choice of chapters from the hardcover edition was made by representatives of the respective publishers, Harper & Row and Schocken Books, necessarily on the basis of the material most needed by a mass audience. Ten excellent chapters had to be omitted; perhaps some readers of this paperback edition will be encouraged to seek that information in previous editions.

The paperback edition contains new material in several areas. "The Modern Renaissance of Hebrew Literature" by the late Hillel Bavli has been expanded by Shmuel Leiter. The contribution of the Jews to medicine described by the late Arturo Castiglioni has been expanded by Harry A.

Savitz, M.D. The chapter on science and Judaism by the late Charles Singer has been expanded by Bernard R. Goldstein. Authors in the original edition who have generously brought their chapters up to date are Moshe Davis, Simon Greenberg, Yudel Mark, Cecil Roth, and Eric Werner. Previous bibliographies have also been enriched by William F. Albright, Alexander Altmann, Elias J. Bickerman, David Daiches, Judah Goldin, Abraham S. Halkin, Israel Halpern, Mordecai M. Kaplan, Milton Konvitz, Anita Libman Lebeson, Bernard Weinryb, and Rachel Wischnitzer.

The bibliographies are not uniform either in their comprehensiveness or in their selectivity. Similarly, the various writers are by no means uniform in their use of footnotes for detailed discussion. In some chapters the notes are numbered by sections of the chapter, notably in the articles by Judah Goldin and Alexander Altmann. In others, the numbering is continuous for the whole chapter.

While grateful for the material provided in the current volume, and realizing that the authors are pre-eminent, the editor can take no responsibility for the views expressed, and is indeed in actual disagreement with a number of them. Some authors disagree with others. Each was invited to write his own chapter because of the special contribution he had to make, regardless of whether it would contradict the views of others or of the editor.

Despite all efforts to bring about common approaches and common standards, a collection of essays inevitably remains an assembly of differing styles, as well as points of view. The editor has made no effort to overcome inconsistencies among the authors; on the contrary, he has drawn attention to them. He has also made no effort to persuade writers to address themselves, necessarily, to the same audience. Some essays are technical; others, without diminution of scholarly integrity and insight, are popular in presentation. Some writers have considered it their task to present merely the consensus of present scholarship, and have avoided reference to their own theories and hypotheses. In other essays, the student will find bold insights and theories, together with references to the commonly accepted views.

The problem of anti-Semitism is dealt with only tangentially in this edition. The editor was persuaded to omit the chapters intended to cover that subject in detail. A number of studies, specifically dedicated to this problem, are now being conducted by various institutions; and the comprehensive works to emanate from them would doubtless make superfluous any summary statement in these volumes.

The English translation of the Hebrew Scriptures issued by the Jewish Publication Society of America (1943) has been used, in general, for quotations from the Bible. However, several authors, for example, Dr. Robert

Gordis, were permitted to substitute their own renderings, because these seemed basic to their argument. Similarly, in specialized articles, such as that by Professor Shalom Spiegel, diacritical marks and technical forms of transliteration have been used, whereas in the book generally transliteration has followed the system set up for popular works by the Jewish Publication Society of America. The names of modern settlements in Palestine have been cited in the spelling commonly used in Zionist English publications, though that may be out of accord with the transliteration system employed in the rest of the book. Hebrew words which have become part of the English language are spelled according to the standard English dictionaries and encyclopedias, as *Cabbala* instead of *Kabbalah*. Because of the fact that the papers were prepared at different times and in different countries, it has been impossible to achieve real consistency in spelling or transliteration. Because of the difference in pronunciation, no effort has been made to reconcile the transliteration of Hebrew with that of Yiddish. In some cases popular pronunciation has determined the transliteration, as in *Agudas* (for *Agudat*) and *kosher* (for *kasher*).

Foreign words and transliterations of foreign phrases are italicized. However, the titles of talmudic treatises are printed in Roman letters in the text, notes, and bibliographies. The abbreviation "R." is used for Rabbinic Sages, who bore the title Rabbi or Rab, and lived in talmudic times. Those who lived after the close of the Talmud are described as "Rabbi."

The notes in brackets, further distinguished by the use of letters of the alphabet, were added by the editor and his associates to guide the reader, particularly where a subject mentioned in one passage is more fully discussed in another essay. The reader will find a number of individuals and organizations mentioned in more than one place. This duplication has been allowed because each of the various authors treats a given subject differently, and the repetition seemed valuable. Sometimes chapters overlap considerably, such as those of Dr. Arturo Castiglioni and Professor Charles Singer, or those of Dr. Moshe Davis and Mrs. Anita Libman Lebeson. However, the reader should find the overlapping helpful to a complete study of the subject.

All royalties will continue to be earmarked for subsequent improved editions, in hopes that the work may become a classic worthy of its subject and useful to generations yet unborn.

And now, having ended this task, I follow the example of R. Nehuniah be Hakkanah, great Sage of the first century, who when he entered the House of Study prayed that no error should occur through him, and when he left gave thanks for his portion.

Louis Finkelstein

The Jewish Theological Seminary of America
New York City, July 1969

THE JEWS: THEIR ROLE IN CIVILIZATION

CHAPTER I

THE INFLUENCE OF JEWISH LAW ON THE DEVELOPMENT OF THE COMMON LAW

By Jacob J. Rabinowitz

1. INTRODUCTION

The Jews came to England in considerable numbers after the Norman conquest.[1] They were able to establish themselves under the protection of the king, who welcomed them as a source of income and ready cash. Their financial transactions were numerous and involved large amounts of money. For some time they had a virtual monopoly of the moneylending business, because the taking of interest was prohibited to Christians by the Church.[2] Many a castle was built with funds advanced by Jews to the nobleman who built it, and even some monasteries were built with money borrowed from the Jews.[3] When Aaron of Lincoln—probably the richest Jew in their midst—died, a special branch of the Exchequer was required to handle his financial affairs, so that the king's share of the estate might be collected.[4]

Justice in civil matters between Jew and Jew was administered by the Chapters of the Jews, that is, by Rabbinical courts, in accordance with Jewish law.[5] A special court, the Exchequer of the Jews, which at one time consisted of Jews and Gentiles, had jurisdiction over disputes arising between Jew and Gentile.[6, 6a]

For many centuries before their settlement in England Jews had cultivated the study of law with great devotion and religious fervor. *Dine mamonot, i.e.,* that branch of the law which deals with matters relating to property, contract, and torts, as distinguished from ritual law, was particularly favored by men of acute intellect among them. "He who wishes to acquire wisdom should study *dine mamonot,*" reads an early talmudic text.[7] Throughout the lands of their dispersion justice was administered among them by Rabbinical courts in accordance with talmudic law as interpreted by leading Rabbis.[8] As a result of centuries of study and practice there developed among them a body of law, and with it a large number of legal forms and devices, far more mature and complex than anything that was known to English lawyers of the twelfth century. Under these circumstances it would be very strange indeed if the Jews did not use the legal forms with which they were familiar, and which were elaborately discussed in their legal literature.

That so little attention has been given to the possible influence of Jews upon the development of the law of the creditor-debtor relationship, a field where their influence should have made itself felt more effectively than in any other legal field, is probably due to the fact that most sources of Jewish law are not available in English. Even where available, it takes years of study to master their intricacies.

Pollock and Maitland have this to say about the possible influence of Jewish law upon English law:

Whether the sojourn of the Jews in England left any permanent marks upon the body of our law is a question that we dare not debate, though we may raise it. We can hardly suppose that from *Lex Judaica*, the Hebrew Law which the Jews administered among themselves, anything passed into the code of the contemptuous Christians. But that the International *Lex Judaismi* perished in 1290 without leaving any memorial of itself, is by no means so certain.[9]

While it may be conceded that cases of deliberate and conscious adoption by English lawyers of rules and doctrines from the Hebrew law were rare —although this is by no means certain—the adoption of security devices used by the Jews falls into an entirely different classification. Their origin is extrajudicial, they are born of the exigencies and necessities of trade and commerce, where Jew meets Gentile on more or less equal terms, and where religious prejudices are thrust into the background. The judiciary but passes on their effect and validity and is in a limited sense only a party to their creation.

The researches conducted by the present writer have revealed that the *lex judaismi* did leave some important memorials of itself in English law, but that these had come to be so integrated in the English legal system that their origin was completely forgotten.

In the following pages an attempt will be made to present some of the highlights of Jewish influence upon the development of English law.

2. THE JEWISH GAGE

The form of security most frequently used by the Jews in England was known as the "Jewish gage." The nature of this gage has never been fully understood by historians of English law,[10] for the simple reason that its roots are to be found in Hebrew law, with which these historians were totally unfamiliar. The form of security represented by the "Jewish gage" was, as Pollock and Maitland[11] point out, a completely novel institution in England, in that it gave rights in land to a creditor who was not in possession of the land. It was introduced by the Jews and was patterned by them after devices which they had used for many centuries prior to their settlement in England. Only a reference to Hebrew law can give us a clue to its understanding.

The Hebrew device that gave rise to the Jewish gage is not a mortgage in the sense of a pledge of specific property as security for the payment of a debt. It does not form part of the Hebrew law of mortgages, but is rather an integral part of the Hebrew law of execution.[12] It is a general lien in favor of the creditor upon all the real property owned by the debtor at the time the debt is incurred. By virtue of this lien the creditor may follow the property into the hands of a transferee who acquired the property after the lien had attached to it.[13] The lien is implied in law as an incident of every debt evidenced by a *shtar* bond, signed at the instance of the debtor by two witnesses and accompanied by sufficient publicity,[14] and of every judgment of a court of competent jurisdiction.[15] Although a stipulation to the effect that the debtor binds his property for the payment of the debt is usually incorporated in the bond, its omission has no legal effect. In the language of the Talmud,[16] the omission is presumed to be an error of the scrivener.

There is, however, one important limitation upon the right of the creditor to follow the debtor's property into the hands of a transferee. As long as the debtor has free assets sufficient to satisfy the debt in full, the creditor cannot proceed against the property in the hands of a transferee.[17] This limitation of the creditor's right under the lien of the Hebrew *shtar* is an important characteristic of this lien and distinguishes it from a mortgage. The debtor's land, according to Hebrew law, stands surety for the payment of his debts, and just as the surety's liability, under ordinary circumstances, is secondary—that is, he is liable only in case the principal debtor does not possess sufficient assets to satisfy the debt—so the liability of the debtor's land is only secondary.

Originally, the creditor's lien attached only to the debtor's immovable property.[18] At a later period it was held that by inserting a special provision to that effect in the *shtar*, the lien could be extended to the debtor's movable property.[19] At an earlier period the question was raised by the Babylonian scholar, "Master Samuel," as to whether or not the debtor could subject his future acquisitions to the lien of the creditor.[20] By analogy with conveyance of property, some argued that a lien on property to be acquired in the future by the debtor should be ineffective, just as a sale of such property would be ineffective. The conclusion of the Talmud, however, is that the creation of a lien is not to be likened to a conveyance.

In the posttalmudic period the practice became almost universal to incorporate in every *shtar* a lien on the maker's property *movable and immovable, present and future*.[21] This standardized lien clause was introduced by the Jews of England into the bonds they used when advancing money to Gentiles, and was apparently given full force and effect by the English courts. The Latin formula used was *obligo omnia bona mea, mobilia et immobilia.*[22] The legal effect given to this formula by the Exchequer of the Jews was substantially the same as that given to it by Jewish law. The lien of the creditor upon the debtor's land was enforced by the Exchequer of the Jews not only against the debtor himself, but also against a transferee.[23] Similarly, the rule of Jewish law that the lien is enforceable against the transferee only where the debtor does not possess free assets sufficient to satisfy the debt was followed by the Exchequer.[24]

From the Jewish bonds the lien clause found its way into general use; in the thirteenth and fourteenth centuries we find that almost every bond made in England contains the formula: *Obligo omnia bona mea, mobilia et immobilia.*[25] The provision for the binding of the debtor's future acquisition occurs less frequently, but it, too, is found in several bonds in Madox's *Formulare,*[26] and elsewhere,[27] where the lien clause reads: *Obligo omnia bona mea, mobilia et immobilia, presentia et futura.*

The Jewish gage, which, as we have seen, is part of the Hebrew law of execution, the fundamental idea of which is that the entire property of the debtor, movable and immovable, is bound for the payment of his debts, had a profound influence upon the development of English economic life and English law. It was this idea, which gradually gained a foothold in feudal England with its fixity of ownership of land, that resulted, on the economic side, in broadening the base of credit by making land, the principal source of wealth, readily available as security, and, on the legal side, in making land in possession of the debtor liable for the payment of his debts. As Pollock and Maitland have already noted,[28] the statute creating the *writ of elegit,* enacted in 1285, was patterned after the Jewish gage. This writ gave a judgment creditor, or a creditor upon a recognizance, the right to collect his debt from the debtor's real property, to the extent of one-half thereof, by seizing the property through judicial process and holding it until the debt had been paid by the debtor, or until the creditor had satisfied himself out of the rents and profits. The limitation of the creditor's right to one-half of the debtor's property followed an earlier enactment, during the reign of Edward I, which put a similar limitation upon the Jewish creditor.

The idea of the Jewish gage gradually gained a foothold in England, for, contrary to the view of Pollock and Maitland, the *statute of elegit* was not altogether an innovation. According to Pollock and Maitland, prior to 1285 the only remedies available to a creditor against a defaulting debtor were the writs of *fieri facias* and *fieri levare,* the former directing the sheriff to seize the debtor's chattels and make the debt therefrom, and the latter directing him to make the debt from the fruit of the debtor's land.[29] It was only in 1285, these writers assert, that the creditor was given a right in the debtor's land. However, it appears from certain bonds made some twenty-five years before the enactment of the *statute of elegit* that provision was already made then for seizure of the debtor's land by the creditor upon default. Thus in a bond[30] executed about 1260 we find the formula *obligo omnia bona mea, mobilia et immobilia* followed by the clause giving the obligee the right, upon default by the obligor, to seize the latter's land and receive the profits therefrom until the obligation had been fully satisfied, a procedure which was invariably followed in the case of the Jewish gage in which the formula *obligo omnia bona mea*, etc. originated. A similar provision is found in several other bonds[31] enrolled upon the Close Rolls during the reign of Henry III. In still another bond[32] of about the same time we find a specific provision to the effect that the obligation shall constitute a charge upon the obligor's land even in the hands of a transferee. Obviously, then, the creditor's right in the debtor's land was not unknown in England before 1285. What was new in the *statute of elegit* was the extension of this right to all judgment creditors. It may therefore be said that this statute and the practices preceding it, which are the basis of the modern law of execution in England and the United States, are an outgrowth of the *Jewish gage*.

3. The Hebrew Odaita and the English Recognizance

Although under Hebrew law a bond attested by two witnesses gave the creditor a lien on the entire property of the debtor, good against the whole world except prior lienors, creditors very often sought further means to facilitate collection of their debts and to overcome procedural difficulties in their enforcement. One of these was the so-called *Odaita*, literally, confession or recognizance. It consisted of a formal declaration by the debtor, before a court of competent jurisdiction, acknowledging the existence of the debt. The declaration was embodied by the court in a document attested by it, and had the force of a judgment.[33]

According to the Talmud, the principle upon which the validity of this device is based is this: an admission against interest is as good as the testimony of "a hundred witnesses."[34] A rule of evidence was thus converted into a means of effecting and initiating jural relationships between the parties, instead of merely proving the existence of such relationships.

The debtor's declaration was sometimes made before two witnesses, rather than before a court, and in such case it was necessary either for the creditor or the debtor to address the witnesses and ask them to bear witness to the declaration about to be made.[35] This safeguard was intended to remove the possibility of the declaration having been made in a jocular manner.

In the twelfth century Maimonides, the great Hebrew philosopher[35a] and codifier of Hebrew law, introduced an innovation into the Hebrew law of recognizances or, perhaps, codified an innovation introduced earlier. He maintained that the requirement for the debtor to address the witnesses with the words "ye be my witnesses, etc." applies only to cases where the declaration is made in the course of a casual conversation. Where the debtor, on the other hand, makes a true or genuine recognizance—*hodaah gemurah*, in Hebrew—this requirement may be dispensed with.[36] As a result of this innovation the phrase "make a true or genuine recognizance" was incorporated in almost every Hebrew recognizance document.

From a certain passage in the Talmud it appears that *Odaita* was in frequent use among Jews during the talmudic period.[37] In the post-talmudic period this form of security became still more frequent, because, according to some authorities,[38] when the debt was evidenced by an *Odaita* the consideration for it could not be inquired into by the court. A totally gratuitous promise, when made in the form of a declaration of a debt, is valid and enforceable, according to these authorities; by his declaration the debtor has precluded himself from attacking the validity of the debt on any ground. Although the prevailing opinion[39] is that a gratuitous promise is valid when accompanied by sufficient formality and solemnity, whether made in the form of a declaration of debt or in the form of an assumption of an obligation, practical draftsmen sought to remove all doubt by drafting most of their documents in the form of a declaration. Only where the declaration form was not feasible, as in the case of a conditional obligation, or of an obligation which could not be reduced to a sum certain (such as the promise to support a child for five years) was the form of an assumption of an obligation used.[40]

The Jews of medieval England used the *Odaita*—recognizance form—in practically all documents written in Hebrew and evidencing transactions between Jew and Jew or Jew and Christian.[41] The Hebrew starrs of acquittance, which are the most numerous of all available Hebrew documents of medieval England, and which the writer will discuss later in more detail, all take the form of a recognizance. The introductory phrase in these documents usually reads: "X recognizes a true recognizance"—a phrase which, as we have seen, is characteristic of the Hebrew *Odaita* and is directly traceable to the rule about the formal requisites for the validity of a recognizance. In the Calendar of the Plea Rolls of the Exchequer of the Jews there are virtually hundreds of entries of starrs of acquittance, and in all of these the recognizance form is used. One of the earliest extant documents evidencing a debt by a Christian to a Jew takes the form of a recognizance.[42] In the thirteenth century all the documents evidencing debts owed by Christians to Jews, take the form of a recognizance. These are found either in full or in abbreviated form in the published records of the Exchequer of the Jews. In a British Museum collection of Hebrew documents, published by the Jewish Historical Society of England, we find a document containing two parallel texts, one in Hebrew and the other in Latin, where the Hebrew phrase *Mode Hodaah Gemurah* is translated *recognosco veram recognicionem*.[43] The Norman-French equivalent of this phrase *reconnusse verreye reconusaunce* is found in Madox's *Formulare Anglicanum*[44] in a document of recognizance, made by a Jew and dated 1275, and in several documents in the Calendar, etc. In the Madox document the introductory phrase reads: *Jeo ke suy ensele de suz reconnusse verreye reconusaunce et testemoine*. The word *testemoine*—testify—is indicative of the procedural origin of the recognizance. As has already been remarked, the recognizance takes the place of testimony by witnesses, on the principle that an admission against interest is as good as the testimony of a hundred witnesses.

On the origin of the Hebrew recognizance, a document found in the Public Records Office in London and published in Meyer D. Davis's collection of Hebrew documents is particularly illuminating. The document reads: "I, the undersigned, recognize a ṭrue recognizance that what is written above in the Latin tongue is true and that I made this starr of acquittance to Prior Alexander so that it may be in his hands and in the hands of his assigns as proof of their rights even as a hundred witnesses. And what I have acknowledged I have signed, Jacob, son of Samuel."[45] The phrase "even as a hundred witnesses" is clearly an allusion to the talmudic dictum that an admission against interest is as good as the testimony of a hundred witnesses. From this the recognizance derives its force and validity.

The close resemblance between the form of the Hebrew *Odaita* and that of the recognizance of English law is quite obvious. But the resemblance is not only one of form; it extends to the most fundamental feature of these devices. In the earliest reported cases of recognizances the debtor not only confesses the debt, but also binds his property as security for its payment, a feature which is characteristic of the Hebrew *Odaita*, as well as of other forms of obligation in Hebrew law. Thus in Select Civil Pleas[46] pl. 25 (Hilary Term, 1201), we find: "Miles de Hastings owes to Brian, son of Ralph twenty marks; to wit, ten marks on the Octave of Easter and ten marks at the Nativity of St. Mary the Virgin; and thereof [Miles] places in pledge to him his land of Hokinton, which he holds of the fee of William de Hastings." And again in pl. 174 (Octave of Michaelmas, 1202), it is recorded: "John the vintner demands against Ralph the priest of Elmham thirty-six shillings and four pence; and they make a concord to the effect that Ralph shall give (John) two marks of silver (now), and shall pay him one mark within the octave of S. Edmond, and another within the Octave of Mid-lent; and in case he shall not have paid (them) he has put in pledge to (John) all the lands which he holds as of lay fee in Suffolk."

Further, more direct evidence of the Jewish origin of the recognizance and of its effect in giving the creditor a right in the debtor's land, is found in an entry in the Close Rolls[47] which contains the full text of the instrument executed by the obligor, not just a notation of its tenor and import. Both, the obligor and obligee, were Christians, yet the instrument is a perfect specimen of a Jewish bond, giving the creditor the fullest protection possible under Hebrew law and practice. In the first place, it contains the clause *obligo omnia bona mea, mobilia et immobilia, presentia et futura* which, as we have seen, is characteristic of every kind of Hebrew obligation. Secondly, it contains a provision that in case of default by the debtor the creditor shall have the right to seize the debtor's land and hold it until he had been fully paid, a right which was in all respects identical with that of the Jewish creditor under the "Jewish gage." Thirdly, the provision contained in the instrument, that the surety who guaranteed performance be bound as a principal debtor, is one which is found in Jewish bonds in England, and which goes back to early talmudic times. In an early talmudic text (*c.* second century) we read: "If a man lent his fellow money on a guarantor's security, he may not exact payment from the guarantor [in the first instance]; but if he said, 'on the condition that I may exact payment from whom I will,' he may exact payment from the guarantor [in the first instance]."[48] Later on the two types of undertaking to answer for another's debt, the one imposing upon the accommodating party a primary liability and the other imposing upon him a secondary liability, became so far standardized that they were referred to by two different names, the former being called *Kabblanut* and the latter *Arabut*, very much as these same types of undertaking later came to be called in English and American law by two different names, *suretyship* and *guarantee*. When the Jews came to England they applied this distinction, which had become elementary in Hebrew law, to their transactions with Christians, and wherever possible they made provision that the accommodating party be primarily liable.[49] This provision, which is very convenient from the creditor's point of view, was adopted by Christian creditors, together with the other features of the Jewish bond, when they entered the business of moneylending.

That Jewish security devices should have been adopted by the English is not at all surprising. It must be borne in mind that when the Jews came to England they did not find fixed and established forms of security which they could use. Moneylending on a large scale was unknown in England before the arrival of the Jews. It was the Jew who developed this business, and with it the instruments through which it was carried on. Under these circumstances it was almost inevitable that he used forms of security with which he was familiar, and that these should later be adopted by money-lenders generally.

In this connection it is interesting to note Pollock and Maitland's observations on the nature and origin of the recognizance: "The parties go into the chancery or the exchequer and procure the making of an entry upon the close roll or some other roll. The borrower confesses that he owes a certain sum which is to be paid upon a certain day, and grants that, if default be made, the money may be levied by the sheriff. This practice, which is of some importance in the history of the chancery may have its origin in the fact (for fact it is) that some of its officers were money-lenders on a great scale."[50] The close connection between the Exchequer and the Jews is well known. It was a special branch of the Exchequer, the Scaccarium Judeorum, that had jurisdiction over the financial affairs of Jews and over disputes arising between Jew and Gentile. The money-lending barons of the Exchequer apparently adopted the convenient device of the recognizance from their Jewish wards whose business affairs they were charged with supervising. For convenient it certainly was, since it afforded the easiest way of proving the debt and at the same time bound the debtor's property for its payment.

4. THE GENERAL RELEASE AND THE HEBREW STARR OF ACQUITTANCE

The General Release is a legal form used by lawyers throughout the United States and England whenever a settlement between the contending parties to a controversy is effected out of court. It is one of the most widely used legal forms.

This form contains some very peculiar language to which hardly anyone pays attention. It states, for instance, that the party giving the release releases and discharges the party to whom the release is given from all claims, demands, etc., "from the beginning of the world" to the day when the release is executed; an obvious exaggeration which calls for explanation. Yet no one, as far as the writer is aware, has ever attempted to trace the origin of this form or to account for its peculiarities. It has become part of the daily routine of office practice, and is taken for granted by those using it without arousing their curiosity.

It can be shown that the General Release is an adaptation of an old Hebrew form, introduced by the Jews of medieval England into their dealings with their Christian neighbors; and this accounts for some of its quaint phraseology.

One of the forms most frequently used by the Jews in England was the so-called Starr of Acquittance, the word "starr" being an Anglicized form of the Hebrew word *shtar*. The starr would be executed by the Jewish creditor and delivered by him to his Christian debtor upon payment of the debt owed by the latter to the former.

A large number of such starrs is found in the collection of Hebrew *Shtarot* published by M. D. Davis. Most of these starrs were written in Hebrew, and even when written in Latin or Norman-French they were endorsed in Hebrew by the Jewish creditor, to prevent forgery by the debtor or a plea of forgery by the creditor. In these starrs the creditor, after specifying the debt or claim to which the starr related, would proceed to release the debtor from all other debts "from the creation of the world" to the date of the execution of the instrument, or, sometimes, "to the end of the world." The following is a translation from the Hebrew original of a typical starr of acquittance: "I, the undersigned, recognize a true recognizance that Roger fil. Godward de Sewenington and his heirs are quit from me and my heirs of ten marks and one measure of wheat and of all debts, pledges and challenges from the creation of the world until Pentecost in the 43rd year of the reign of our Lord the King Henry fil. John, and what I have recognized I have signed."[51] The pattern of this starr is exactly like that of the General Release found in fourteenth century documents written in Latin, and in our own time may be found in every formbook used by lawyers through the length and breadth of the United States and England. Both have this outstanding characteristic in common: in addition to specifying the claim or debt immediately preceding the execution of the instrument they include all debts, claims, etc., from the beginning or the creation of the world.

The question naturally arises, who copied from whom? Did the Jewish creditors follow a pattern set for them by English draftsmen, translating it into Hebrew, or did the latter copy from the Jews?

Were there no other evidence as to the origin of the starr of acquittance, the fact that Jews for a long time occupied the position of principal financiers in England, and that they had a highly developed system of law and legal forms of their own, would make it reasonable to suppose that, at least in documents written in Hebrew, they used their own forms rather than adaptations of English forms. But one need not rely solely on this circumstantial evidence. The internal evidence from documents used in England, and the evidence from Hebrew sources outside England, is so abundant and convincing as to leave no doubt of the Hebrew origin of the Starr of Acquittance and its counterpart, the General Release.

To begin with, the phrase "from the beginning of the world" suggests a Jewish origin. It is well known that the Jews count the years of their calendar from the creation of the world. The present year [1959-1960], for example, is 5720, according to Jewish tradition. When the Jewish draftsman wanted to set down a date as far back as possible, it was natural for him to go back to the beginning of his calendar. The exaggeration implicit in this phrase was apparently overlooked because of the absolute certainty it afforded in removing all possible future controversies as to the debts and claims to which the acquittance related, including possible claims against the releasee's predecessors in interest.

Secondly, the starrs, as has already been remarked, were usually written in Hebrew, and even when written in Latin they were endorsed by the creditor in Hebrew. The Hebrew equivalent of the phrase, "from the beginning of the world," found in the modern General Release, is *"mibriat ha-olam,"* literally, from the creation of the world. This phrase occurs uniformly in all the Hebrew starrs, while in the Latin releases there are variations. Along with *a creatione seculi,*[52] which is the exact equivalent of the above Hebrew phrase, we find *a principio seculi,*[53] *ab initio seculi,*[54] *a principio mundi*[55] and *ab origine mundi.*[56] The uniformity of the Hebrew phrase, on the one hand, and the variations in the Latin versions, on the other, suggest that the former was the model and the latter were the copies.

Finally, the essential characteristics of the General Release are found in a Hebrew form occurring in a whole series of Hebrew formbooks and responsa of leading Rabbis, beginning with the tenth century—that is, long before the Jews came to England—down through the centuries almost to our own day. In the earlier sources this form is called *Shtar Abizarya*—the word *abizarya* meaning acquittance—and a distinction is drawn between it and the *Shtar Mehila,* the latter being a release of a specific claim or debt. In the later sources it is called *Mehila Kolelet,* which is the exact Hebrew equivalent of the English term "General Release." Under its former name it is found in a recently published fragment of the formbook of Rab Saadia Gaon[57, 57a] where the creditor releases the debtor from all claims and demands *"from the days of the world until now."* Under the same name it appears in the formbook of Rab Hai Gaon,[58, 58a] where it is very elaborate, and very nearly approaches our modern General Release. It also appears, still under the name of *Shtar Abizarya,* in the formbook of Rabbi Judah Barzillai,[59] and in the *Sefer Haittur* of Rabbi Isaac b. Abba Mari of Marseilles.[60]

In a thirteenth-century case in the responsa of Rabbi Solomon b. Adreth a similar form was apparently used, but it is no longer referred to as *Shtar Abizarya.* From this responsum it is evident that the form under discussion was in general use, and that it was very comprehensive in scope. Indeed, in the table of contents it is called *Mehila Kolelet*—general release. The responsum reads, in part, as follows: "Question: R sold a field to S with warranty. Many years thereafter R and S had again dealings between them, and S released R from everything and every obligation, as is customary, and he did not remember the obligation of the warranty at the time when he executed the release. Is the obligation of the warranty included in the release?"[61]

A little later in the thirteenth century, in the responsa of Rabbi Asher b. Yehiel,[62] we find reference to a form, the substance of which is that the creditor releases the debtor "from all demands he had against him to this day," the form itself not being quoted by the Rabbi, but only its import stated. In the fourteenth century, in the responsa of Rabbi Nissim Gerondi[63] and in those of Rabbi Isaac b. Shesheth[64] there is reference in the text itself to a release which is called *Mehila Kolelet.*

Finally, in a sixteenth-century formbook, compiled by Rabbi Solomon Jaffe[65] in accordance with the usages prevailing in the Jewish communities of Constantinople and Salonica, we find a most polished specimen of this form under the name *Shtar Mehila.*

In order to show concretely the close resemblance between the form of the General Release now in use in England and in the United States, and the Hebrew forms that have just been mentioned, the writer will quote the material portions from the former and from some of the latter.

The General Release reads, in part, as follows:

Know all men by these presents, that I . . . have remised, released and forever discharged, and by these presents do for myself and my heirs, distributees, executors and administrators, remise, release and forever discharge the said . . . his heirs, distributees, executors and administrators, of and from all manner of action and actions, cause and causes of action, suits, debts, dues, sums of money, accounts, reckonings, bonds, bills, specialties, covenants, contracts, controversies, agreements, promises, variances, trespasses, damages, judgments, extents, executions, claims and demands whatsoever, in law and in equity, which against the said . . . I ever had, now have, or which I or my heirs . . . hereafter can, shall or may have for, upon or by reason of any matter cause or thing whatsoever *from the beginning of the world* to the date of these presents, and more particularly . . .

The *Shtar Abizarya* in the formbook of Rab Hai Gaon reads, in part, as follows:

X son of Y said to us: Ye be my witnesses and accept *"Kinyan"* [a symbolical delivery of some object, ordinarily a kerchief, which confirms the transaction and imparts to it binding legal force] and hand over [the document attesting the transaction] to A son of B, that of my own free will, without duress, [I have made this declaration] that I have received and accepted and have been fully paid everything he owed me, growing out of all there was between us *from the days of the world* until now. . . . And in accordance with what preceded between them, whether partnership or a loan, business transactions or purchase and sale, inheritance or things other than these, one is to specify accordingly, and then generalize and write of everything that transpires among men: of partnership, of joint venture, of business transactions, of inheritance, of purchase and sale, of deficit and surplus, of profit and loss, of loan and bailment, of pledge and of suretyship, of trespass and of fraud and of all manner and fashion of things in the world. And I cleared and acquitted the above named and his heirs, for myself and my heirs for all generations, of all *claims, challenges and demands* which men may demand of one another.

The introductory paragraph of the *Shtar Mehila* contained in the form-book of Rabbi Samuel Jaffe reads as follows:

Before us, the undersigned witnesses, X, of his own free will, without duress, but wholeheartedly and willingly, made a true, valid and effective recognizance that he has received total and complete satisfaction of all the demands, rights and complaints that he had, or might have had, against Y and his representatives, *from the day the world was created* to the present day, and particularly of such and such a debt, and such and such a demand.

The similarity between the pattern of the General Release, on the one hand, and that of the two Hebrew forms quoted above, on the other, is obvious and needs no further elaboration. But the similarity is not only one of pattern; it extends to some of the most significant terms and clauses of these forms. In his chapter on Releases, sec. 508, Littleton says: "Also, if a man release to another all manner of demands, this is the best release to him to whom the release is made, that he can have, and shall enure most to his advantage." To this Coke, fol. 291 b, adds: "Demand, *demandum*, is a word of art, and in the understanding of the common law is of so large an extent, as no other one word in the law is, unless it be *clameum*, whereof Littleton maketh mention, sect. 445."

A mere glance at the Calendar of the Plea Rolls of the Exchequer of the Jews will reveal that both of these terms, *claims* and *demands*, occur in starrs found on almost everyone of its pages, while the Hebrew equivalents of these terms may be found in numerous documents in M. D. Davis's collection of Hebrew *Shtarot*. As in the case of the form itself, and perhaps more convincingly, the question as to which was the model and which the copy, the Hebrew terms or their equivalents in Latin and Norman-French, is answered by a reference to the Rab Hai Gaon form quoted above which dates back to the tenth century, and in which the same Hebrew terms signifying claims and demands, as those found in the Hebrew *Shtarot* in England, occur.

5. THE COMMON LAW WARRANTY OF REAL PROPERTY[66]

The warranty clause, commonly used in the United States and England in the conveyance of real property, is also of Jewish origin. The modern warranty clause reads substantially as follows: "The grantor, his heirs and assigns will warrant, defend and acquit the grantee, his heirs and assigns against all men." In English deeds of conveyance of the Middle Ages the last phrase of the above clause often reads, "against all men and women"; sometimes it reads, "against all men and women, Christians and Jews."

A comparison of the medieval warranty clause, of which our modern version is obviously a direct offspring, with the standard Jewish warranty clause used by Jews in the various lands of their dispersion from the Middle Ages down almost to our own day, reveals that the former is an abbreviated adaptation of the latter. The Jewish warranty clause reads substantially as follows:

And whoever shall come from the four winds of the world, man or woman, Jew or Gentile, son or daughter, heir or legatee, near or far, who shall arise and contrive and make any claim or requisition whatsoever on the said William, or his heirs or representatives, regarding the said house with the court and appurtenances, it will be obligatory upon me, my heirs and representatives, to free them and protect them against those claimants, and to maintain their possession of the house, court and appurtenances aforesaid, in peace and comfort (peaceably and quietly), on the surety of all my property, landed or movable, which I now possess or may in future acquire.

It is fairly obvious that the phrase "against all men and women, Christians and Jews" of the medieval English clause was taken almost verbatim from the above Jewish clause. What is more, the terms *defend* and *acquit* also seem to have been taken from the Jewish formula. The Hebrew equivalent of *defend* is found in a number of Hebrew documents from Angevin England and also in the formulary of Rabbi Jehudah Barzillai (eleventh century, Spain). The equivalent of *acquit* is likewise found in many Hebrew documents from Angevin England and in a portion of a warranty clause quoted in the Talmud.

Together with the warranty clause itself, some of the important rules of law connected with warranty were adopted by the English from the Jews. The extension of the benefit of the warranty to the assigns of the grantee is one of these rules. Thus, where A conveys a parcel of real property to B who, in turn, conveys it to C, and X evicts C by virtue of a paramount title, C has an action for breach of warranty not only against B, his immediate grantor, but also against A, his grantor's grantor. The reason for this is that C, who is B's assign, is included within the scope of the warranty given by A to B. The inclusion of assigns within the scope of the warranty was copied by the English from the Jews, together with the other features of the warranty clause.

Another rule in medieval English law of warranty which seems to have been adopted by the English from the Jews was that all real property remaining in the hands of the grantor at the time of the conveyance becomes bound for the warranty, defense and acquittance of the grantee. This rule of law is traceable to the Hebrew legal concept of *ahrayut* which, freely rendered, means that a man's property stands surety for the obligations he assumes in writing, whether the obligation grows out of a loan of money, a warranty incidental to the conveyance of real property, or the endowment of wife by husband. In virtually every Hebrew deed of conveyance in medieval England, as elsewhere, there is a stipulation for a warranty binding the grantor's property, movable and immovable, present and future. The idea of *ahrayut* was apparently taken over by the English together with the Hebrew warranty clause; this resulted in the rule, which prevailed in medieval England, that the obligation of a warranty constitutes a charge upon all the real property remaining in the hands of the grantor at the time he makes the conveyance.

6. The Hebrew Ketubah and Anglo-American Dower[67]

The origin of the Anglo-American institution of dower, whereby the married woman, upon the death of her husband, is entitled to a life estate in one-third of the real property that the deceased husband owned at any time during the marriage, is shrouded in mystery.

However, certain rules with regard to dower, as well as the formula that was used in medieval England when the husband endowed his wife at the church door, appear to be of Jewish origin.

The outstanding characteristic of dower in Anglo-American law is that it constitutes a charge upon all the real property that the husband owned at any time during the marriage, regardless of who the owner of the property may be at the time of the husband's death. As a result of this rule the practice grew up in England and the United States to have the wife release her dower rights whenever the husband conveys a parcel of real estate. For without such a release the property would be subject to the wife's claim of dower if the husband should predecease her.

The important effect of this rule of law, and of the practice that grew out of it, upon family life and the relations of husband and wife throughout the ages need hardly be emphasized. It served as an effective counterbalance to the rather low position to which the *feme coverte* or married woman was relegated in English law.

The rule that dower constitutes a charge on the husband's property did not become firmly established in English law until about the beginning of the thirteenth century. Glanvil, in his treatise on the laws of England, written about 1187, still hesitates to concede to the widow the right of claiming dower in property transferred by her husband during his lifetime. However, while Glanvil was still hesitating about the rule of law, the common practice, as shown by deeds of conveyance of the time, was to have the wife join in the conveyance, or release her dower rights whenever a conveyance was made by the husband. Legal practice, as is often the case in the early stages of the development of a legal system, preceded legal theory in this respect.

This practice of having the wife join with her husband in the conveyance of real property prevailed among the Jews for at least a thousand years prior to their settlement in England. It grew out of a rule, ascribed by the Talmud to Simeon b. Shatah, which subjected all of the husband's property to a lien in favor of the wife for the payment of her *Ketubah*. A release by the wife of her dower rights is already mentioned in the Mishna. In later times this practice became almost universal among the Jews. In all the available Hebrew documents from Angevin England, evidencing conveyances of real property by Jew to Jew and by Jew to non-Jew, there is not a single instance where there is not a release by the wife of her dower rights.

This practice alone, which the English apparently copied from the Jews, might have been sufficient to give rise to the rule that where the wife fails to release her dower rights the property remains subject to such rights. But there is also evidence that the English endowment formula was copied from the Hebrew *Ketubah* formula. The most definite trace of Hebrew influence upon the development of the English endowment document is found in the medieval English dower *de la plus belle*, which originated in a provision in the Hebrew *Ketubah* giving the wife the right to collect her dower from the best part of her husband's property.

7. The Common Law Mortgage[68]

The form of mortgage used in the United States and England also is of Jewish origin. This form is at variance with both the true economic significance of the transaction and the intention of the parties. Since a mortgage is a pledge of property to secure a debt, one would expect the mortgage instrument to read that if the mortgagor fails to pay the debt on the due date the mortgaged property is to be forfeited to the mortgagee. Instead, the mortgage is, in form, an immediate conveyance of the property by the mortgagor to the mortgagee, with a condition that if the former pays the debt when due the property is to revert back to him.

In the modern form of the mortgage the conveyance and the condition are incorporated in one single instrument. However, in the early stages of the development of the mortgage the conveyance and the condition were incorporated in two separate instruments, and both instruments were delivered to a third, neutral, party to be turned over to the mortgagor should the debt be paid, or to the mortgagee in case it was not paid.

A device identical in all respects with the English mortgage in its earlier stage of development was used by the Jews throughout the Middle Ages.

and was designed to overcome a certain rule of Hebrew law known as *asmakta*.

Briefly stated, in accordance with the doctrine of *asmakta*, where a conveyance is made, or an obligation is assumed, as a penalty for the non-compliance with an undertaking to which it is collateral, the conveyance or the obligation is not valid. There is lacking that finality of determination which is requisite for the validity of an act in law, since the intention of the party purporting to make the conveyance, or to assume the obligation, is to fulfill his main undertaking, and not to effect a transfer of his property, or an assumption of an obligation other than his main obligation. In a mortgage with a forfeiture clause, for example, the intention of the mortgagor is to undertake to pay the mortgage debt, and not to effect a conveyance of his property. The forfeiture clause is intended as a penalty for the nonpayment of a debt, and therefore it is not valid. Only where there is a present conveyance of the property with a condition making the conveyance void in case of repayment of the money by the grantor is the transaction valid.

As a result of this doctrine, the practice grew up among Jews that whenever a transaction in the nature of a mortgage took place, it took the form of an outright conveyance of the property by the mortgagor to the mortgagee and an agreement by the mortgagee that the conveyance shall be void if the borrower returns the money to the lender on the due date. In order to remove all appearance of *asmakta* from the transaction, the conveyance by the mortgagor and the agreement by the mortgagee were delivered to a third party (*shalish*).

The Jews of medieval England used this device in their transactions with non-Jews, and through them it came into general use in England. For a long time the mortgage was used in England in exactly that form in which it had been used by the Jews; that is, two separate instruments were employed and both instruments were delivered to a third party. It was not until the beginning of the fifteenth century that conveyance and condition began to be incorporated in the same instrument and the mortgage assumed the form in which it is still used in the United States and England.

8. THE CONDITIONAL OR PENAL BOND[69]

The conditional or penal bond is a device similar in conception and design to the mortgage in the form of a conveyance with a condition subsequent.

It contains the same logical twist as that involved in the common law mortgage. Instead of the conditional obligation it is intended to be, with the obligation emerging upon the happening of a certain contingency, it takes the form of an absolute obligation which is to become void in case of the nonoccurrence of the contingency upon which the obligation is made to depend.

Thus where a fidelity company undertakes to guarantee the faithful performance of his duties by a person entrusted with the administration of some fund, the company's bond will usually read somewhat like this: "X company is bound to pay $1,000, but the condition of this bond is such that if Y will faithfully perform his duties the obligation of this bond shall be void; otherwise it shall remain in full force and effect."

This device, too, is of Jewish origin and was designed by the Jews to overcome the difficulty of the doctrine of *asmakta* mentioned above.

Maimonides in his Code of Hebrew Law cites the following device which was used by the "sages of Spain" to remove the flaw of *asmakta* from conditional obligations: The obligor would undertake an immediate and absolute obligation, and the obligee, on his part, would undertake to release the obligor upon the nonoccurrence of the contingency upon which the obligation was to depend. The doctrine of *asmakta* not being applicable to releases and defeasances, this device accomplished the purpose of a conditional obligation in a legally valid manner by inverting the condition and attaching it to the release instead of the obligation.

The Maimonides device, in the form of two separate instruments—one an absolute obligation and the other a conditional avoidance of the obligation—is mentioned in the responsa of Rabbi Solomon b. Adreth and is found in a Hebrew document from Angevin England, evidencing a transaction between two Jews and dated 1251. As in the case of the mortgage, both instruments were delivered to a third party. Numerous examples of the use of this device by English Jews in their transactions with non-Jews are found on the rolls of the Exchequer of the Jews.

From the Jews the device passed into general use among Englishmen, who used it for the purpose of overcoming a rule known in English law as the rule against penalties, which is similar to the Hebrew doctrine of *asmakta* and which, there is reason to believe, was developed through the influence of that doctrine.

The English device, in its original form, was in every detail identical with its Hebrew counterpart. Two instruments were used and both instruments were delivered to a third party. The modern form in which both, the obligation and the condition, are incorporated in a single instrument came into use at the beginning of the fifteenth century, about the same time that the mortgage assumed its present form.

9. Trial by Jury

The generally accepted view of the origin of trial by jury is that it developed from the inquest that was used by the Frankish kings on the

Continent for the purpose of determining questions of ownership of land to which the king laid claim and other disputed issues, relating mainly to fiscal matters, between the king and his subjects. It was the royal prerogative to have such questions decided by a verdict of the *best men* of the neighborhood, instead of by the then prevailing modes of trial, such as the ordeal, combat, or the oath with oath helpers.

The first important step in the development of the jury system in England, according to this view, was a series of ordinances, known as assizes, by which Henry II extended to his subjects, in certain specified types of cases dealing with possession of land, the royal prerogative of trial by inquest. Another important step was taken when judges began to allow the parties, in cases not covered by the assizes, to have their case decided by a verdict of their neighbors or, as the phrase went, to *put themselves upon the country*. The final step was to compel the parties to *put themselves upon the country*.[70]

Pollock and Maitland were apparently aware of the break in the continuity of the story, which is presented by the transition from trial by jury in a few selected types of cases, as a result of an ordinance, to trial by jury in nearly all cases, by consent, real or fictitious, of the parties. In their *History of English Law*, they say:

> Trial by jury, in the narrowest sense of that term, trial by jury as distinct from trial by an assize, slowly creeps in by another route. The principle from which it starts is simply this, that if in any action the litigants by their pleadings come to an issue of fact, they may agree to be bound by the verdict of a jury and will be bound accordingly. In course of time the judges will in effect drive litigants into such agreements by saying, "You must accept your opponent's offer of a jury or you will lose your cause"; but in theory the jury only comes in after both parties have consented to accept its verdict. In course of time the jury, which has its roots in the fertile ground of consent, will grow at the expense of the assize, which has sprung from the stony soil of ordinance.[71]

But the question still remains, how did it happen that "the fertile ground of consent" was substituted for "the stony soil of ordinance." Where did the principle of consent, which apparently developed simultaneously with the assizes,[72] or, perhaps, even preceded them, come from?

An indirect answer to this question is contained in the following passage from Pollock and Maitland:

> We have seen . . . that the verdict of jurors becomes a common mode of proof only because litigants "put themselves" upon it, and that the summons of a jury . . . is always in theory the outcome of consent and submission. Both litigants have agreed to be bound by a verdict of the country. They

might perhaps have chosen some other test. We may, for example, see a plaintiff and a defendant putting themselves upon the two witnesses named in a charter, or upon the word of some one man.[73]

The similarity, in principle as well as in idiom, between *putting oneself* upon a jury and *putting oneself* upon some witness or witnesses seems to be significant. This similarity not only points to the broad principle upon which trial by jury was based, namely, that parties may choose the means of deciding the issues between them and that they will be bound by such choice, but it also furnishes a clue to a hitherto unknown influence upon the development of the jury system in England.

An institution which is quite similar to the jury system in medieval England is found among the Jews at a very early time. It is the lay court, usually consisting of three judges, which derives its jurisdiction from the fact that the parties voluntarily submitted their controversy to it. The binding effect of the decision of such a court is based not on its inherent power, but on the agreement of the parties to be bound by its decision. Moreover, according to Jewish law, parties may agree to be bound by the testimony of certain witnesses, and they will be bound by such testimony, even if the witness happens to be one who would ordinarily be considered incompetent. In other words, the principle of consent in Hebrew law, as in medieval English law, applies to judge and witness alike. Indeed, we find the same term used in the Mishna to signify agreement to be bound by the decision of a judge and by the testimony of a witness. In Mishna (Sanhedrin 3, 2), we read:

If one suitor said to the other, "I accept my father as trustworthy," or "I accept thy father as trustworthy," or "I accept three herdsmen as trustworthy," R. Meir says: He may retract. But the sages say: He cannot retract.

The rule of the Mishna is interpreted by the leading posttalmudic authorities as applying to witnesses and judges alike.[74] The Talmud,[75] commenting on the phrase "I accept three herdsmen as trustworthy," says that although herdsmen are ignorant of the "affairs of the world," their decision is binding, if the parties accepted them as judges.

The similarity between the principle enunciated in the above Mishna and that underlying the binding effect of a jury's verdict in medieval England is obvious. This similarity, coupled with the fact that the same principle was also applied to the testimony of a witness, both by the Jews of early talmudic times and by Englishmen in the Middle Ages, appears to be of great significance.

What is most significant, however, is that the Hebrew equivalent of the phrase *se ponere super* or *put oneself upon* is found in a responsum by a famous thirteenth-century German rabbi in connection with the submission of a controversy to a lay court. In this responsum, after citing Mishna (Sanhedrin 3, 2), quoted above, the learned Rabbi says:

> The same rule applies to two parties who took upon themselves to abide by the decision of the heads of the community. And if the plaintiff says: "We didn't put ourselves upon them," let the defendant affirm his allegation upon oath . . . In such a case where they put themselves upon the "best men of the town" and the heads of the community it is the custom in our entire realm that whatever one takes upon himself before the heads of the community, who were chosen with the consent of the community, he cannot retract therefrom."[76]

The idiom in this quotation, used by the Rabbi to express the idea of submission of a controversy by the parties, is identical with that used in medieval England to express the same idea in connection with a jury. The combination of similarities between the ideas and between the idioms expressing them makes the possibility of a mere coincidence very remote.

Another indication of the relationship between the English jury and the Jewish lay court is found in an entry on the rolls of the Exchequer of the Jews, dated 1244. This entry reads, in part, as follows:

> . . . and that this is true she puts herself upon the township of London. The Jew does likewise; wherefore let inquest be had on the morrow of the Ascension.[77]

The parties *put themselves* upon the township of London, that is, upon representatives of the community, exactly as in the responsum of the thirteenth-century German Rabbi, quoted above.

A further parallel between the English jury and the Jewish court may be seen in the fact that, as in the case of the members of the jury, an oath was administered to the members of the Jewish lay court in England each time they were selected to try a case or to discharge some other judicial function, such as the assignment of dower to a woman. The oath was administered in the form of an adjuration in the presence of ten persons (a *minyan*), a procedure which is mentioned by Rashi,[78] the famous eleventh-century commentator of the Talmud. Reference to such an oath by the members of a lay court is found in three Hebrew documents from medieval England. The opening sentence in these documents reads: "We were selected and adjured in the presence of ten persons to constitute a *bet din* (a court)."[79] There seems to be no authority in Hebrew law, talmudic or posttalmudic, for an oath to be administered to members of a Jewish lay court. Nor is there any evidence of such practice among the Jews outside of England. It seems likely that this is a case of non-Jewish practice having been adopted by the Jews. This further strengthens the assumption of a close relationship between the two institutions, the Jewish lay court and the English jury, for it seems to indicate that in the

thirteenth century, when trial by jury had hardly passed beyond its formative stage, the Jews regarded it as being so much akin to their lay court that
they copied a procedure from the jury and applied it to the lay court.

The historical connection between the Jewish lay court and the English
jury appears in certain aspects of the history of the Jews in medieval
Europe.

As soon as the Jews became an important element in medieval Europe
new methods of trial had to be developed in order to meet the case of
litigation between Jew and non-Jew. The mode of trial that prevailed in
Europe at that time, the ordeal by fire or by water, was entirely alien to the
Jew, repugnant to his concept of proof, and altogether unsatisfactory to
him. He needed some rational legal framework under which his business
undertakings might achieve a degree of security and stability. He could not
afford to allow his business transactions to be regulated by totally in-
adequate archaic rules of substantive and procedural law. One is not likely
to be willing to risk his money on the outcome of an ordeal by fire or
by water.

In one of the earliest extant charters granted to the Jews in Europe, in
addition to provisions of a substantive nature, is a provision that the Jew
is not to be subjected to the ordeal by fire or hot water.[80] Substitutes for
trial by ordeal had to be provided in litigation between Jews and non-Jews.
One of these was to submit the controversy to a body of neighbors, similar
to the Jewish lay court. In order to secure impartiality, these bodies were
made up of Jews and non-Jews.[81]

In England we find throughout the thirteenth century that cases between Jews and non-Jews are tried by mixed juries, usually six Jews and
six non-Jews.[82] There is also good reason to believe that the trial of cases
between Jews and non-Jews by mixed juries goes well beyond the
thirteenth century. In a charter granted by King John to the Jews in
1201 there is the following provision: "And if a Christian shall have cause
of action against a Jew, let it be tried by the Jew's peers."[83] A similar
provision is found in a charter by King Richard I, dated 1190,[84] and one
of like nature was probably also contained in the charter granted to the
Jews by Henry I.[85] This provision for trial by the Jew's peers, *per pares
judei*, can hardly have reference to anything else but trial by a mixed
jury, for, so far as the writer knows, not a single recorded instance has
been found of a case between a Jew and a non-Jew having been tried by a
court consisting wholly of Jews.[86]

It seems likely that submission of controversies between Jews and non-
Jews to mixed juries had its origin in a charter granted to the Jews by
Henry I, and that, consequently, it antedated the assizes of Henry II. In
addition to the numerous cases, recorded on the rolls of the Exchequer
of the Jews, in which the parties *put themselves* upon a mixed jury, one

finds on these rolls a large number of cases in which they *put themselves* upon some witness or witnesses, arbitrators, officials, etc. The following are typical examples:

Elias de Abbacia and Vives, son of Isaac of Stanford, *put themselves upon three Christians and three Jews* of Northampton for the determination of a question relating to 40s. of chattels of commendise and 100s. claimed by the one of the other. The arbitrators are to notify their award to the Justices of the quindene of St. Martin.[87]

Manser of Huntingdon, attached to answer Peytevin of Bedford, for that he will not suffer three of his chirographs to be placed in the Chest according to the Assize, comes before the Justices, and says that the said chirographs were made *sub poena*, and that therefore it was that he would not permit them to be placed in the Chest. Peytevin avers that this is false, and that his real reason was that there was a dispute between them as to a certain debt which Manser demands of him; and that this is true, *he puts himself upon the oath of Master Moses*, and gives ½ mark to have his oath; and Manser does likewise. Master Moses, being summoned, comes before the Justices and, being sworn, says, that the said dispute, and nought else, stands in the way of the chirographs being placed in the Chest . . .[88]

The idea of *putting oneself upon*, *i.e.*, of the parties voluntarily selecting a method of deciding a disputed issue between them, was deeply ingrained in the Jew's mind, as a result of his many centuries of experience with the lay court. The Jew's commercial and financial activities also contributed to the development of this idea, since a simple and expeditious method of resolving disputes is a necessary concomitant of a high degree of business activity. It is therefore not unlikely that the Jews, who frequently had occasion to resort to litigation, had something to do with the shaping of the ideas that led to the establishment of trial by jury.[89]

10. The Thirty-ninth Clause of Magna Carta

One of the basic principles of the Anglo-American system of law, and an important component of democracy, as it is understood and practiced in the United States and England, is that of the supremacy of the law. The law is supreme; the ruler and those whom he rules are alike subject to it and bound by its dictates. Government by rule of law, rather than by the arbitrary will of any individual or group of individuals, is the corollary of this principle.

In the United States this principle finds expression in the famous *due process of law* clauses of the Fifth and Fourteenth Amendments to the United States Constitution declaring that no person shall be deprived "of life, liberty, or property, without due process of law."

Through various intermediate stages, the due process clause of the

United States Constitution is traceable to the thirty-ninth clause of Magna Carta, which reads:

Nullus liber homo capiatur, vel imprisonetur, aut disseisiatur, aut utlagetur, aut exuletur, aut aliquo modo distruatur, nec super eum ibimus, nec super eum mittemus, nisi per legale judicium parium suorum vel per legem terrae.

No freeman shall be taken or imprisoned, or disseized, or outlawed, or exiled, or in any way destroyed, nor will we go upon him, nor send upon him, except by the lawful judgment of his peers or by the law of the land.

A whole literature has been written on the meaning of the phrase *or by the law of the land*. Some historians of the English Constitution are of the opinion that the phrase is to be interpreted, rather narrowly, as having reference to matters of judicial procedure. The clause is interpreted by these historians as embodying a guarantee that the then prevailing modes of trial will be observed in cases involving the liberty or property of freemen. The more widely accepted view, however, is that the phrase has reference to both substance and procedure, and that the clause was intended as a guarantee against the arbitrary infringement by the king of the personal liberty and property rights of freemen.[90]

The great principle embodied in the thirty-ninth clause of Magna Carta is found in the medieval legal literature of the Jews, which deals quite extensively with the problem of the limitations of royal power. We shall begin with the *Mishna Torah*, the Code of Hebrew Law, written by Maimonides several decades before Magna Carta was signed by King John.[90a] In the 5th chapter of *Gezela Va-abeda*, sections 13 and 14, it is stated:

13. And in like manner where a king was angered against one of his serfs or servants (*abadav ve-shamashav*) among the inhabitants of the realm and took away his field or court, it is not robbery, and its enjoyment is permitted. He who purchases it from the king acquires title to it, and the original owner cannot reclaim it from him. For, such is the rule with regard to all kings that they may take to themselves the property of their servants when angered against them . . . But where a king took away a court or a field from one of the inhabitants of the realm, not in accordance with the laws which he had enacted, he is a robber, and if a purchaser acquires the property from the king, the original owner may reclaim it from such purchaser.

14. The general rule is: Every law which the king enacts for all, and which is not intended for one person alone, is not robbery. But where he takes away from one person alone, not in accordance with the law known to all, committing an act of brigandage against that person, it is robbery.

It would be hard to find a more forthright statement of the limitation of royal power. Simply stated, Maimonides's rule is, that a law, the effect of which is to deprive an individual of his property rights, is not valid, unless it is regularly promulgated, of general application and known at the time it is sought to be applied. The similarity between this rule and the principle of *the law of the land* of Magna Carta, or of *due process of law* of the United States Constitution, is quite obvious and needs no elaboration. What is more, the exception made by Maimonides to his rule limiting the validity of royal acts, namely, that it does not apply where such acts are directed against the king's *serfs or servants*, is also clearly implicit in the words of Magna Carta, which limits the application of the thirty-ninth clause to freemen.

Maimonides's statement with regard to the limitation of royal power is predicated upon a Talmudic maxim, as interpreted by the leading Jewish jurists of the Middle Ages, which reads: "The law of the kingdom is law."[91] Rabbi Joseph ibn Migas, a leading Jewish authority of the early twelfth century in Spain, expounding this maxim, places the emphasis on the word "law" and says: "The law of the kingdom is law, but the robbery of the kingdom is not."[92]

Nahmanides, the famous thirteenth-century Jewish philosopher and jurist, places the emphasis on the word "kingdom," saying that the law of the *kingdom* is law but not the law of the *king*.[93]

Similar views are expressed by Rabbi Judah, or Sir Leon, of Paris who cites Ri (R. Isaac b. Meir) and Rabbenu Tam (R. Jacob b. Meir), the famous French Tosafists of the twelfth century as his authorities.[94]

The doctrine of the limitation of the royal power was common learning among the Jews of the Middle Ages and was certainly well known among the Jews of England. In fact, Mordecai b. Hillel cites a decision by an unnamed London Rabbi in which this doctrine was involved.[95] The case arose between two Jews and the decision turned on the validity in law of a certain levy by the king. The Rabbi decided that the levy in question was not valid, distinguishing between regular taxes, which are valid, and so-called "dona," or forced gifts, which were often exacted from the Jews of England by the king and which, the Rabbi held, were not a valid exercise of the royal power.

In 1215 the Jews had good reason for offering to the barons advice on how the royal power should be limited. They had but recently been subjected to a veritable reign of terror by a rapacious king whose depredations could not bring but, home to them with particular vividness the distinction between *the laws of the kingdom* and the *robbery of the king*. It was in 1210 that John threw the whole Jewish community of England into prison and extorted from them, by the most ruthless and cruel means, the then enormous sum of 66,000 marks.[96] It is, therefore, not at all unlikely that the Jews had some part in the formulation of clause thirty-nine of Magna Carta.

NOTES

[1] Pollock & Maitland, *History of English Law*, I, p. 468 (2nd. ed.); J. M. Rigg, *Select Pleas, Starrs & Other Records from the Rolls of the Exchequer of the Jews. A.D. 1220-1284.* Selden Society Publications, XV, p. x.

[2] Pollock & Maitland, *op. cit.*, I, p. 473.

[3] J. Jacobs, *The Jews in Angevin England*, p. xiv.

[4] *Ibid.*, p. xvii.

[5] Rigg, *op. cit.*, p. xiii. n. 1.

[6] *Ibid.*, p. xx.

[[6a] Cf. Cecil Roth, "The European Age in Jewish History (to 1648)," this work, Vol. I, p. 239.]

[7] *Ibid.*, Mishna, Baba Batra, end.

[8] See Finkelstein, *Jewish Self-Government in the Middle Ages*, pp. 6-7.

[9] Pollock & Maitland, *op. cit.*, I, p. 475.

[10] *Ibid.*, p. 473.

[11] *Ibid.*, p. 469.

[12] Shulhan Aruk, Hoshen Mishpat, ch. 111, sec. 1.

[13] Mishna Baba Batra 10.8; Hoshen Mishpat, ch. 39, sec. 1, and ch. 111, sec. 1.

[14] *Ibid.*

[15] *Ibid.*, ch. 372, sec. 8.

[16] Baba Mezia 15b.

[17] Mishna Gittin, 5.2; Hoshen Mishpat, ch. 111, sec. 8.

[18] Baba Batra, 44b; Hoshen Mishpat, ch. 113, sec. 1.

[19] *Ibid.*

[20] Baba Batra, 157 a-b; Hoshen Mishpat, ch. 112, sec. 1.

[21] See *e.g.*, Sefer Hashtarot (Formulary) of Rabbi Judah Barzillai, No. 34.

[22] Rigg, *op. cit.*, pp. 33, 93, 94, n. 1.

[23] *Ibid.*, pp. 18, 53, 63.

[24] *Ibid.*, p. 65; *Calendar of the Plea Rolls of the Exchequer of the Jews*, I, p. 73; *Calendar of the Close Rolls*, Edw. I, I, p. 389.

[25] Pollock & Maitland, *op. cit.*, n. 1, II, p. 2, n. 2, & p. 225, n. 6; *Madox Formulare Angelicanum*, Nos. 159, 640, 644.

[26] *Madox, op. cit.*, Nos. 119, 643, 645.

[27] *Calendar of the Close Rolls*, 1268-1272, pp. 243, 258, 300, 410-411.

[28] Pollock & Maitland, *op. cit.*, I, p. 475, n. 1.

[29] *Ibid.*, II, p. 596.

[30] *Madox, op. cit.*, n. 25, No. 635.

[31] *Calendar of the Close. Rolls*, 1259-1261, pp. 463-464; 1264-1268, pp. 395, 504.

[32] *Ibid.*, 1264-1268, p. 521.

[33] Sanhedrin, 29b; Hoshen Mishpat, ch. 39, sec. 7, and ch. 250, sec. 3.

[34] Gittin, 40b.

[35] Hoshen Mishpat, ch. 81, sec. 6.

[[35a] Cf. below, Alexander Altmann, "Judaism and World Philosophy: From Philo to Spinoza," pp. 84 f.]

[36] Hoshen Mishpat, ch. 81, sec. 8; Yad Hahazakah, Toen, ch. 7. The phrase "*Hodaah Gemurah*" does not appear in the printed editions of Maimonides's Code. It appears in Tur's quotation of the passage from Maimonides. A comparison of a large number of quotations from Maimonides's Code, as found in Tur, has convinced the writer that the author of Tur had before him a revised and corrected version of the code. Certain evidence recently found by the writer points to the conclusion that the phrase *Hodaah Gemurah* did not originate with Maimonides and that it is of considerably earlier date than his Code.

[37] Baba Kamma, 84b.

[38] Ketubot, 101b, Rashi's commentary *ad loc.;* see also the commentary of Rabbi Asher b. Yehiel *ad loc.*

[39] Hoshen Mishpat, ch. 40, sec. 1.

[40] See Hoshen Mishpat, ch. 60, sec. 2.

[41] See, *e. g.,* Meyer D. Davis, ed., *Hebrew Deeds of English Jews,* Nos. 1, 7, 8, 9.

[42] John H. Round, ed., *Ancient Charters,* Pipe Roll Society Publ., X, p. 82.

[43] Abrahams, Stokes and Loewe, *Starrs & Jewish Charters in the British Museum,* pp. 4-5 (1234).

[44] No. 689.

[45] Davis, *op. cit.,* n. 41, No. 193.

[46] Selden Society Publications, III.

[47] *Calendar of Close Rolls,* 1256-1259, p. 493.

[48] Mishna Baba Batra, 10.7.

[49] Davis, *op. cit.,* n. 41, No. 54. This is an assignment of a debt in which it is recited that William de Huneworth is the debtor and Roger Michael of Holt Market is the *kabblan, i.e.,* the surety with primary liability.

[50] *Op. cit.,* II, p. 204, n. 1.

[51] Davis, No. 118.

[52] Rigg, *Select Pleas,* p. 42.

[53] *Ibid.,* p. 72.

[54] *Madox, op. cit.,* No. 142.

[55] *Ibid.,* No. 702.

[56] *Ibid.,* No. 703.

[57] Supplement to *Tarbiz,* publication of the Hebrew University of Jerusalem, I, No. 3, p. 70; (Additional note by Professor Saul Lieberman—On the exact meaning of the term see *ibid.,* p. 22, n. 1; Geiger *apud* Kraus, Additamenta ad librum Aruch completum, p. 2).

[57a] On Saadia Gaon, cf. Judah Goldin, "The Period of the Talmud," this work, Vol. I, pp. 202 ff.]

[58] *Tarbiz, op. cit.,* p. 22.

[58a] On Hai Gaon, see Abraham S. Halkin, "Judeo-Arabic Literature," this work, Vol. II, pp. 137 ff.]

[59] No. 4.

[60] S. v. Mehilah. See *Tarbiz, ibid.*

[61] Responsa of R. Solomon b. Adret, *sub nomine* Toledot Adam, No. 217.

[62] Ch. 76, sec. 3 & 4.

[63] No. 22.

[64] No. 404.

[65] Tikkun Soferim, No. 50.

[66] For a full discussion and citation of authorities, see J. Rabinowitz, "The Origin of the Common Law Warranty of Real Property and of the Inchoate Right of Dower," in *Cornell Law Quarterly*, XXX, 1944, pp. 77-94.

[67] *Ibid.*

[68] For a full discussion and citation of authorities see Rabinowitz, "The Common Law Mortgage and the Conditional Bond," in *University of Pennsylvania Law Review*, XCII, 1943, pp. 179-194.

[69] *Ibid.*

[70] Pollock & Maitland, I, p. 140 f. J. B. Thayer, *A Preliminary Treatise on Evidence*, p. 47 f.

[71] I, p. 149.

[72] See Glanvil, 13, 2. See also, n. 19, *infra*.

[73] II, p. 623.

[74] Maimonides's Code, Sanhedrin 7, 2; Hoshen Mishpat 23, 1.

[75] Sanhedrin 25b.

[76] Teshubot Maimonyot, Shoftim No. 10, quoting a responsum of R. Meir b. Baruch of Rothenburg.

[77] *Calendar of the Plea Rolls of the Exchequer of the Jews*, I, p. 156. Cf. Pollock & Maitland, *op. cit.*, II, p. 624, n. 1. "The verdict of the jurors is not just the verdict of twelve men; it is the verdict of a *pays*, a country, a neighborhood, a community."

[78] Rashi, *Commentary to Shebout* 38b, catchword *Be-Sefer Torah*.

[79] Davis, *Hebrew Deeds* (*Shtarot*), Nos. 3, 15, 156.

[80] ". . . . Et nullatenus volumus, ut praedictos Judeos ad nullum judicium examinandum, id est nec ad ignem nec ad aquam calidam seu etiam ad flagellum, nisi liceat eis secundum illorum legem vivere vel ducere." Aronius, *Regesten zur Geschichte der juden im fraenkischen und deutschen Reiche*, No. 81; Rozière, *Recueil Général des Formules*, I, No. 27 (Charter of Louis the Pious, before 825).

[81] See S. W. Baron, *The Jewish Community*, I, pp. 249-250.

[82] See *e. g.*, *Calendar of the Plea Rolls of the Exchequer of the Jews*, I, pp. 127-128, 145, 169. See also Jacobs, *The Jews in Angevin England*. p. 201, quoting an early case of an inquest by twelve Christians and twelve Jews from the rotuli de Ablatis, ed. Roberts, p. 92 (1199-1200).

[83] Rigg, *Select Pleas*, etc., p. 1.

[84] Rymer, *Foedera*, ed. Clarke, I, 51.

[85] In the preamble to John's charter reference is made to a charter granted to the Jews by his father's grandfather, Henry I. John's charter is stated there to be a confirmation of the one granted to the Jews by Henry I.

[86] In his essay entitled *"Per Judicium Parium vel. per Legem Terrae,"* *Magna Carta Commemoration Essays* (p. 102), Professor F. M. Powicke, compares the *per judicium parium* of Magna Carta with the *per pares judei* of John's charter to the Jews, and arrives at the conclusion that neither refers to trial by jury. In support of this conclusion he cites Bracton's *Note Book*

(II, p. 706, case 918), in which a Jew objected to the jurisdiction of the court on the basis of King John's charter, although he was offered to have his case decided by a mixed jury. However, the Jew's objections did not rest upon the *per pares judei* clause of the charter, but upon another clause in the same charter which reads: "And as often as cause of action shall have arisen between Christian and Jew, let him who shall have appealed the other for the deraignment of his cause have witnesses, to wit, a lawful Christian and a lawful Jew." See Selden Society Publication, LX, Introduction, p. clxl.

[87] *Calendar ... of the Exchequer of the Jews*, I, pp. 11-12 (1219).

[88] *Ibid.*, pp. 106-107 (1244-1245).

[89] It is true that the generally accepted view is that trial by jury as a result of ordinance preceded trial by jury as a result of voluntary submission by the parties. However, it is not at all certain that this was so. Professor Haskins (*Norman Institutions*, p. 224, n. 109) quotes a document from Normandy, dated 1182, in which it is stated that a certain controversy was voluntarily submitted by the parties to twelve sworn men. Also, in a document of considerably earlier date (1124-1130), found in the Cartulary of Ramsey (p. 143), there is reference to submission of a controversy to *twelve* sworn men —the usual number of men on a jury. Incidentally, this number may be of some significance. Stobbe (*Die Juden in Deutschland waehrend des Mittelalters*, p. 143) cites a charter granted to the Jews of Worms in 1312, according to which the Jewish Council (*Judenrath*), consisting of *twelve* members, was to administer justice among the Jews in accordance with Jewish law. He also cites evidence to the effect that already at the time of the first Crusade (1096) the Jewish council of Worms consisted of *twelve* members. It is quite likely that the number of members on the council was deliberately made to correspond to the number of princes of Israel of old (No. 1:16). Indeed, in *Masseket Soferim* 19, 10, a seventh century Rabbinic source, there is reference to "twelve good men of the town [town councilors] corresponding to the twelve tribes of Israel." If the Jews had some part in the development of trial by jury, it may well be that the number of men on a jury was adopted from the Jews.

It should be noted that the number—twelve—of the Jewish community councilors may also be of significance as indicative of the influence of Jewish community organization upon the development of town government in the later Middle Ages in Europe. The same number of town councilors is found in Montpelier in the beginning of the thirteenth century. The *Coutume* of Montpelier of the year 1204 refers to "*duodecim probi et legales viri, jam electi ad consulendum communitatem Montispessulani*" (twelve honest and lawful men just elected to counsel the community of Montpelier). *Thalamus Parvus, Le Petit Thalamus de Montpelier* (Montpelier, 1836), p. 52.

In addition to the number of councilors in Montpelier, their description as *probi et legales viri* also points in the direction of Jewish influence. The meaning of the term *homo* or *vir legalis* (lawful man), which also occurs quite frequently in English medieval records after the Norman Conquest (cf. "a lawful Christian and a lawful Jew" in the clause of King John's charter quoted above, n. 86), has given rise to considerable speculation and differences of opinion among the leading authorities on English institutional history. See Ch. E. Odegard, Legalis Homo, *Speculum,* XV, 1940, pp. 186-193. The writer believes that *homo legalis* is a literal translation of the Hebrew *ish kasher—a worthy man.* The Hebrew word *kasher* ordinarily means that which is in accordance with the law—*lawful.* Thus, meat from an animal slaughtered in accordance with Jewish ritual law, and otherwise not unfit for consumption according to the same law, is said to be *kasher;* a *sukkah* built in accordance with the rules of the law is similarly said to be *kasher.* But when the adjective *kasher* qualifies the noun *ish* or *adam* (a man) it means *worthy.* Cf. Mishna, *Berakot* 2, 7; B. *Moed Katan* 25a; Maimonides, Code, Nahalot 4, 6. Cf. also M. Jastrow, *A Dictionary of The Targumim, The Talmud Babli and Yerushalmi, and the Midrashic Literature,* pp. 677b-678a. It seems that *homo legalis* is a Hebraism which, in the form of *homme loyal,* first found its way through the Jews into the French vernacular and thence, in its Latin form, into the language of official documents.

[90] See McIlwain, "Due Process of Law in Magna Carta," *Columbia Law Review,* XIV, pp. 27f.

[[90a] Cf. Halkin, *op. cit.,* pp. 139 ff.]

[91] Gittin 10b.

[92] See Sefer Haterumot 47, 8.

[93] *Ibid.*

[94] Haggahot Mordecai, Baba Batra ch. 1, No. 659, s.v. Heshiv. There is some evidence that R. Judah of Paris settled in England about the year 1182. Cf. Jacobs, *The Jews in Angevin England,* p. 76.

[95] Mordecai, Baba Kamma, ch. 10, No. 152.

[96] Rigg, *Select Pleas,* etc., p. xxiv.

BIBLIOGRAPHY

ABRAMS, I., STOKES, H. P., and LOEWE, H. (eds.), *Starrs and Jewish Charters in the British Museum.* Cambridge, 1930-1932.

BARON, SALO W., *The Jewish Community.* (2 vols.) Philadelphia, 1942.

BIGELOW, M. M., *History of Procedure in England from the Norman Conquest.* Boston, 1880.

DAVIS, MEYER D. (ed.), *Hebrew Deeds of English Jews before 1290.* London, 1888.

FINKELSTEIN, LOUIS, *Jewish Self-Government in the Middle Ages.* New York, 1924.

JACOBS, JOSEPH, *The Jews in Angevin England.* New York, 1893.

MALDEN, H. F. (ed.), *Magna Carta: Commemoration Essays.* London, 1917.

POLLOCK, FREDERICK, and MAITLAND, FREDERIC W., *History of English Law before the Time of Edward I.* (2 vols.) Cambridge, 1923.

RABINOWITZ, JACOB, "The Origin of the Common Law Warranty of Real Property and of the Inchoate Right of Dower," in *Cornell Law Quarterly.* XXX, 1944.

———, "The Common Law Mortgage and the Conditional Bond," in *University of Pennsylvania Law Review.* XCII, 1943.

RABINOWITZ, JACOB, "The Origin of Representation by Attorney in English Law," *Law Quarterly Review*, LXVIII, 1952.

RIGG, J. M. (ed.), *Select Pleas, Starrs & Other Records from the Rolls of the Exchequer of the Jews, A.D. 1220-1284*. London, 1902.

ROUND, JOHN H. (ed.), *Ancient Charters, Royal and Private prior to A.D. 1200*. London, 1888.

THAYER, JAMES B., *A Preliminary Treatise on Evidence at the Common Law*. Boston, 1898.

CHAPTER 2

A PHILOSOPHY OF JEWISH ETHICS

By Mordecai M. Kaplan

Introduction

The wide range of subject matter discussed in this book as germane to Judaism* testifies to a far broader conception of Judaism than the conventional one which would limit it to a particular set of religious dogmas, practices and institutions. The very fact that religion as such occupies only one section of the book, whereas the greater part of the book is devoted to a variety of subjects such as law, poetry, art, science, literature and social welfare, implies that Judaism is a many-faceted, dynamic civilization, the civilization of the Jewish people. Once we realize this truth about Judaism, we naturally come to the conclusion that it is impossible to understand Judaism without knowing a great deal about the Jewish people. A knowledge of its history, sociology and demography is indispensable for an understanding of Judaism. These considerations indicate the approach in this chapter to the study of Judaism as a contribution to world ethics.

A comparative study of the different ethical systems, or normative patterns of human conduct, reveals an infinite variety of practices approved by some peoples and condemned by others. But the underlying distinctions of right and wrong, and the accompanying inner inhibitions that we associate with conscience, can be found in every human society, even the most rudimentary. Even those high principles which are often referred to as the consummation of ethics are not monopolized by any one religion, culture or ethical system.

Judaism, however, is unique in being the first civilization consciously and deliberately to recognize the primacy of the ethical good in human life. It is unique in being the creation of a people which was the first to dedicate itself to the furtherance of what we generally speak of as the good life. Whatever acceptance and prevalence the good life owes to Judaism are the result of the fact that for centuries there has lived a people which did not merely produce a few religious leaders or thinkers who uttered some startling and inspiring ideas of ethical import, but which had the

* When this chapter was written, the title of the book was to have been *Judaism and the Jews*, as explained in the Preface.

highest interests and purposes of its entire population organized around the assumption that the ethical idea is fundamental to living as human beings. Judaism's contribution to the good life was made possible because Judaism, not merely as a religion but as the living historical civilization of the Jewish people, is the product of a new and original emphasis on the place of the ethical in human life. What that emphasis was, it is the purpose of this chapter to set forth.

1. THE RELATION OF ETHICS TO RELIGION

Human beings in their mutual relations feel and act on the basis of what they expect of one another. These expectations, which assume a certain uniformity in human behavior, may be divided into natural and ethical. A natural expectation is one formed on the assumption that the person, with whom we have dealings, will feel and act toward us on the basis of the power we possess to help or harm him, to satisfy his wants or to cause him pain. We expect, for example, that one who owes us money should pay his debt. This is a natural expectation, provided we are in a position to enforce payment. But if, despite our inability to enforce our claim and his ability to deny it, we still expect him to pay his debt, we are entertaining an ethical expectation. No human society could exist for any length of time if it had to depend entirely upon coercion. No social machinery can be so devised as to exert pressure ubiquitously. There are numerous occasions when the individual can manage to elude all law enforcement. This would mean that on all such occasions, if we could not rely on people to act ethically, we would never know what to expect of them. Such a state of uncertainty would lead to anarchy and chaos in social life.

The tendency in present-day apologetic literature of religion is to convey the impression that the combination of ethics and religion is an original contribution of the Judeo-Christian tradition. The truth is that all human societies in one way or another look to their gods as the chief guardians of moral behavior. It could not be otherwise, since no external authority can possibly be adequate as a means of getting people to live up to moral requirements. A god's gaze is always assumed to be capable of penetrating the most secret recesses of the heart. To quote but a few instances—in describing the ancient Mexican religion, Andrew Lang says that "the prayers, penances and confessions . . . indicate a firm belief that even these strange deities 'made for righteousness,' loved good, and, in this world and the next, punished evil."[1] In the mythology of the Inca race the sun god is represented as addressing the parents of that race, as follows: "My children, when you have brought the peoples of these lands to our obedience, you should have care to maintain them therein by the laws of reason, of piety, of clemency and equity. . . . In this you will follow my example, for, as you know, I cease not from doing good to mortals . . ."[2]

James Henry Breasted devotes his entire book *The Dawn of Conscience* to proving the unmistakable emergence of a moral order among the Egyptians as far back as five thousand years ago. One of the tomb reliefs of the Memphite cemetery reads: "I did that which men loved and the gods approved, that they may make my eternal house (tomb) endure and my name flourish in the mouths of men."[3] Likewise the inscription on the tomb of the first known great explorer, Harkhup of Elephantine, bears testimony to the assumption, present in all human societies, that God demands obedience to the moral law. That inscription reads: "I desired that it might be well with me in the great God's presence."[4] Similar examples of this intimate bond between morality and religion could be multiplied *ad libitum*.

It is tempting to evaluate the character of a civilization on the basis of its ethical maxims. Even so high an authority as Breasted yields to that temptation. "As a young orientalist," says Breasted, "I found that the Egyptians had possessed a standard of morals far superior to that of the Decalogue over a thousand years before the Decalogue was written."[5] In this he speaks not as a scientist but as a special pleader. If ever there was a case where comparisons are odious it certainly is this one. There are times when it is far more scientific to be puzzled by what is unique in a phenomenon than to see in it only the familiar. The truth is that there is nothing in any ancient civilization which can compare with the ethical implications of believing in a God Whose claim to allegiance and obedience is based on His having redeemed a people from bondage to a tyrant, or that can compare with the duty on the part of an entire population to set aside one day in seven to physical and spiritual recreation. No text should be torn out of its historical context, even in preaching, much less in objective science.

To ascertain Judaism's contribution to world ethics it is necessary to ascertain the historical background of mankind at the time that the influence of Judaism made itself most felt. That was unquestionably the case when the classic world order began to break up. It is, furthermore, necessary to establish the particular context of Judaism as a whole, in order to discover what in its ethic was distinctive and therefore most likely to strike the attention of the Gentiles who came in contact with it.

2. THE DIMENSIÓN OF THE ETHICAL

The study of human life has by this time made it clear that man's deliberate efforts to better his lot and to improve himself lie in more than the one dimension of those vital needs, or vitalities, which man shares with other living beings. As manifestations of physical and mental life, the vital needs are manifestations of power, for life is inherently power. Those needs are governed by nature or necessity; yet in satisfying them, man must reckon with something more than their inherent necessity. Always something asserts itself that clearly lies outside that dimension. So insistent have been those transnatural factors in human life that they have succeeded in winning recognition for themselves as constituting the human differential. All living beings are, to be sure, governed by natural forces or impulses. These may even be the source of those higher developments in man that mark him off from the rest of creation; but only in man do those natural forces or impulses achieve self-consciousness. Self-consciousness introduces a new quality into the content of human life. That new quality impels man to live in other dimensions beside the one of the vitalities or of power. One such dimension is that of the rational, or the universal, and the other is that of the spiritual, or the eternal. The dimension of the rational may be said to give *form* to the content of human life; the dimension of the spiritual may be said to give to it *purpose*.

To the dimension of the rational or the dimension of the universal belong all the interests and values that center around truth, or the knowledge of reality for its own sake, together with all those interests and values which center around moral goodness, or the practice of the right for its own sake. Since in ancient times the development of reason was for the most part limited, except in the case of Hindu and Greek philosophers, to the interests and values of moral goodness, tne term "rational" will here be used interchangeably with "ethical," and *vice versa*. To the dimension of the spiritual, or the eternal, belong the three groups of interests and values that center respectively around (1) personality, or the self as a responsible being, (2) the social group, which is the medium of man's physical and mental life and growth, and which evokes his loyalty, and (3) the totality of things, or cosmos, as divine, or as contributing to man's salvation or self-fulfillment, and as evoking his piety.

The significant fact about any human society, from the most rudimentary to the most civilized, in which the integrative forces are stronger than the disintegrative, is that the rational and the spiritual values not only figure in the mutual relations and expectations of its members but are also regarded as original and autonomous instead of as derived from, or ministering to, the vitalities. To be sure, health, prosperity and social approval are generally considered rewards for ethical conformity, and for deference to the interests of personality, society and God; but those rewards are only incidental. In fact, the rationality or spirituality of any act is impugned as soon as it is believed to be motivated by the prospect of reward.

From the foregoing we can realize what is meant by the universality of ethics and religion. The diversities in ethical and religious thought and practice result from the differences in the opportunities to achieve knowledge and social contact with other groups and ways of life. The scope of life possible to a rudimentary society like that of a nomad tribe which wanders from oasis to oasis is far narrower than that possible to an urban community which engages in trade and commerce. That narrowness is bound to be reflected in its ethics and religion. Except when under the influence of some individual or collective passion, human beings normally reckon, according to their lights, with the 'rational and the spiritual interests. So long as any human group is sufficiently integrated to know itself as a unit, and is not subject to extraordinary pressure or influence, it manifests an unmistakable regard for rational and spiritual considerations. Every normal society reflects some sensitiveness to the universal values of reason and to the eternal values of the spirit.

3. WHEN ETHICAL VALUES ARE QUESTIONED

Societies of men—families, tribes, clans, federations of clans, and city-states—have always been in a condition of flux, due to the pressure of populations on the food supply. In the struggle for existence, the weaker societies are broken up by the stronger. The survivors of the weaker society, finding their inherited way of life unable to provide them with the necessary protection and maintenance, become reconciled to their conquerors' way of life. But there are societies which fall victim to disintegration, not as a result of direct assault from without but of intrigue and struggle within. Then the very assumptions on which social solidarity is based begin to be questioned. Those assumptions will generally be found to belong to the ethical and the spiritual dimension of life.

Such a questioning attitude, however, never achieved the articulation and self-consciousness potent enough to act as a disruptive force on a large scale until the appearance of the Greek Sophists. Their activity was part of the general disintegration of the Greek spirit. The scientific progress, which had prepared the way for them, became in their hands a means of undermining all faith in the rational and spiritual foundations of society. By making a business of training young men for political careers, they succeeded in developing in those who were to be entrusted with authority a cynicism toward the very moral values that were essential to conscientious exercise of power. The morally corrosive influence of the Sophists reached down to the period of the Roman Empire and had no small share in its final disintegration.

Skepticism, whether intellectual, ethical or spiritual, thrives on social decay. Its procedure generally consists in proving that the higher values, which are upheld as the special distinction of man, are in effect nothing more than indirect or disguised means of gaining power over others. The yearning for truth and the passion for righteousness are shown to be merely a form of self-delusion. The undermining of faith in the intrinsic reality and worth of man's higher values is aided by the prevalent diversity in laws, customs and moral expectations. That diversity was played up by the Sophists as evidence that all ethical standards were nothing more than subjective and without any inherently obligatory character. The very ideal of justice became in their hands a mere honorific term for the cunning exercise of power which the strong wielded over the weak, or for the vindictive urge of the weak against the strong. Such reasoning led to the nihilism that threatened to paralyze man's efforts to transcend his selfishness.

The initial impulse to counteract this menace of moral nihilism came from Socrates. He succeeded in transmitting to subsequent generations the deep conviction that there ought to be a way of recapturing the faith in fundamental principles of truth and goodness as universally valid and as independent of their partial and distorted embodiments in actual life. Three schools of thought, the Platonic, the Aristotelian and the Stoic, which flourished during the Greco-Roman period, sought to retrieve the recognition of the inherent otherness of rational and spiritual values, an otherness that renders their essence independent of all considerations of power. Thus Plato discovered the nature of the idea as something other than any of its embodiments. He maintained that the highest idea of all, the Idea of the Good, was identical with God. Aristotle saw the danger of assigning complete otherness to the good and true; it was likely to lead to a final separation of the idea from the tangible realities of existence. He tried, therefore, to hold on to Plato's discovery without having to sever connections with the dimension of power and the vitalities in which we live and have our being. The Stoics attained the clearest and most emphatic enunciation of duty, and the consciousness of the "ought" as the very essence of reason which men share with cosmic reason. They expressed their intuitive awareness of the distinctive ethical dimension by stressing duty as an imperative of reason. Their emphasis upon the originality, independence and otherness of the ethical is so much like Judaism's assumption concerning the nature of the good life that Philo of Alexandria[6a] was able to regard Stoicism as little more than a Greek version of the teachings of Moses.

With the prominent role of the great philosophic schools in those days, and especially with the great influence wielded by the Stoics in high social and governmental circles, one would imagine that they should have succeeded in checking the progressive social disintegration and the moral disorientation of their day. Their learning had a marked influence on Roman jurisprudence, but their teachings had no effect on the inner life of those who controlled the destinies of the state. It did not even touch the masses, which were becoming increasingly demoralized. The military campaigns carried on by Rome contributed to the supplanting of vast populations. The number of human beings transported and sold into slavery and thus left culturally and spiritually rootless kept growing. The intellectualized ethics of the philosophic schools had no message for these forgotten people. The Stoics became, as it were, private chaplains of the well-to-do, with never a thought for the underprivileged who constituted the bulk of the population.

4. The Western World Saved from Moral Disintegration by Judeo-Christian Tradition

Within this mass of confused and disintegrating humanity, the Jewish people appeared as a strange and inexplicable phenomenon. Despite the most cruel blows of fate, this pe ple clung desperately to its group life and managed to survive by virtue of its confidence in its way of life as the only one certain to bring salvation to mankind. The Jewish people lived in a state of dispersion far beyond the borders of its own land; yet all its scattered communities regarded themselves as bound together by a common destiny. So contagious was the example of the Jews that many Gentiles, noting the inner sense of security that Judaism afforded its adherents, joined the Jewish people.

Before long a new wave of religious enthusiasm swept from Palestine to all Jewish communities in the Diaspora, in the form of the Christian gospel. That gospel not only retained the confidence the Jews had had in their own way of life, as well as the original emphasis upon the primacy and the divine character of the ethical, but it also possessed the irresistible vigor and impetus of a new revelation. Thus did the long stored-up moral energy of the Jewish people sweep across the Western world like a tidal wave. In the same way that Paul saved the personality of Jesus from oblivion, so did Christianity save the ethical emphasis of Judaism from being confined to the Jewish people. In both instances, however, transmission of values from one civilization to another resulted in their refraction.

The fact, however, that the Judeo-Christian way of life called forth astonishment and admiration among the spiritually uprooted and disoriented in the Greco-Roman world does not mean that they had a clear idea of what was most significant in that way of life. They were scarcely aware of the distinctive character of the ethical teachings and ideals in the Judeo-Christian tradition. They did not weigh the ethical precepts of Judaism or Christianity against those of Stoicism. They merely found in that tradition an answer to the question that then troubled all who sought some means of overcoming their sense of frustration: What is salvation, and how can one attain it? The conviction that accompanied the answer given by Judaism and Christianity brought into sharp relief the ethical teachings that were included in the answer. In a world in which all ethical values and assumptions were in danger of being swept away, the sincerity with which the Jewish people affirmed the divinely revealed nature of its own way of life, provided the only safe anchorage.

No philosophy, however consistent and edifying, could hope at that stage of human development to restore the confidence in the inherently independent and underived character of the difference between right and wrong. Philosophic thinking had destroyed that confidence. Only supernatural revelation could restore it. The Jews were the only people who, at that critical period in the life of Western mankind, were convinced that God had revealed to them the true way of life. Moreover, the ardent conviction that the God Who had revealed to them their way of life was the only true God, reinforced the validity of the claim that their way of life was divinely revealed and therefore unquestionably true. By affirming the oneness of God and prohibiting the worship of Him under any conceivable image, Judaism was able to hold its own against the philosophies of the day, not only in the ethical aspect of reason but also in the metaphysical. This rendered its teachings acceptable to the sophisticated as well as to the unlettered. The same is true of Christianity. Accordingly, *the service that the Jewish people rendered to human civilization may be said to consist in having restored confidence in the original and underived character of the ethical values and in their independence of the considerations of expediency and self-interest.*

Undoubtedly the assertion that the Ten Commandments were spoken by God at Sinai, taken literally, conveys a fact which is in conflict with the modern man's outlook. But a knowledge of the workings of the ancient mind and of the way it was wont to report its profoundest experience has taught us to penetrate beneath the surface of a tradition and to get the functional significance of that tradition, from the standpoint of the attitudes and behavior it was intended to call forth. There is a large area of feeling and experience for which even the most articulate lack the right expression. Suppose an ancient people, untutored in philosophic speculation, had the irresistible intuition that the ethical values stemmed from a source other than that of individual expediency—by no means incredible—how could they put that intuition into words other than those recorded in the Jewish tradition? As what else than a revelation from God could they possibly describe this experience of compelling certainty? The sense of inner compulsion which a highly important truth always carried with it led the ancients to ascribe that truth to a source which belonged to a different dimension of being from that of normal experience. Such a source could only be Divine Revelation.

5. MORAL VALUES GIVEN FOUNDATION OF CERTAINTY BY JUDAISM

In the light of these considerations, Judaism's contribution to world ethics consists in having reaffirmed the objective character and cosmic significance of the difference between good and evil, right and wrong, at a most critical juncture in the history of Western mankind. That affirmation by itself did not determine the content of the ethical values. It did not, for example, actually answer the question whether slavery and polygamy were morally right or wrong. But it helped to re-establish the certainty that a moral standard was part of the very nature of reality, and that to function as human beings we must always strive to approximate it in all our relations with one another.

Because the modern era is also one of social confusion and disintegration, there has been a recrudescence of the nihilist notion that the only function of power is to be successful, regardless of the claims of reason and spirit. The first sensational formulation of such nihilism in modern times is to be found in Machiavelli's *The Prince*. It finally attained rodomontade swagger in Nietzsche. Many thinkers have sought to restore the rational foundations of ethics, but none with as much acumen as did Kant. His great contribution to the understanding of the nature of the moral law consists in the rediscovery of its intrinsic rationality and worth, independently of any empirical consequences to which its application may lead. He stresses again and again the need of its being observed for its own sake and not for the sake of happiness or any other good. In describing the moral law as a categorical imperative, which is the expression of the autonomy of the practical reason, Kant definitely assigns to it a different dimension from that in which man lives out his vital needs and powers. This fact, which Kant points out as true of the moral law, is what human beings normally experience in the form of intuition, and what the Jewish people with its tradition, which it regarded as divinely revealed, helped to conserve for Western civilization. But what the Jewish people accomplished no individual thinker or school of philosophers could have accomplished.

How liable human beings are to lose their normal intuition concerning the objective and underived character of the moral law, has been amply demonstrated in the 1930's by the spread of fascism. Fascism is essentially moral nihilism. In its lethal effect on human life it outstrips by far the moral nihilism of the philosophic hedonists, who declare that pleasure is the only criterion of the good. According to fascism, virtually the only thing worthwhile in human life is the possession of power over other people's lives and happiness. Nietzsche's nihilism can be practiced only by the individual who possesses extraordinary cunning and prowess. But fascism goes much further and makes it possible for every Tom, Dick or Harry to act out the tendency to nihilism. This tendency is no less innate than the tendency to reckon with the moral law, even as the death-wish is as innate as the will-to-live. If mankind will recover from its contemporary partial relapse into moral nihilism, it will be only through some extraordinary reassertion of its will-to-live. Some rightly choose to call such a reassertion a manifestation of Divine Grace.

6. The Area of Human Relations the Principal Object of Jewish Ethics

From the standpoint of ethical theory, it may be sufficient to establish the autonomy, the otherness or the different dimensionality of the moral law of ethical values. But from the standpoint of everyday living and the betterment of human relations, it is necessary to know to which of the needs or vitalities of human life the moral law is to be applied. This involves specifying the particular vital functions which are most prone to moral evil, or to the violation of the moral law. If we divide the vitalities into two main areas, one harboring the physical desires and the other the various strivings and ambitions which function through the mutual relations of human beings, the tendency in certain ages and civilizations, like the Hindu and the medieval Western, has been to regard the physical hungers as man's chief stumbling block. This has been especially true in relation to the sex hunger.

Judaism, on the other hand, may be said to have been the first civilization to insist that the field of human relations is the area most in need of being brought within the dimension of the moral law. The tendency of the strong and the clever to exploit the weak and the simple is, in the estimate of Judaism, the source of man's undoing. To be sure, Judaism abounds in taboo and restrictions intended to restrain the physical hungers from running riot. But whatever provision it makes for such restraint it does essentially in the same spirit as modern society provides for the social health of the community, as a kind of hygienic measure. Only to the extent, however, that human relations are implicated in those physical hungers do those hungers become subject to moral law.

Since the main evil in the area of human relations, which has ever brought in its wake chaos and disaster to human life, is the lust to dominate (directly, when one is strong enough to do so, or indirectly by identifying oneself with the leader or his mob in whom such strength resides), that is the evil against which Judaism principally invokes the moral law. This distinctive note in the ethics of Judaism is quite unmistakable. A summary of the ethical teachings in Israel's Torah might well be the famous scripture in Zechariah: "Not by might nor by power but by My Spirit, saith the Lord of Hosts" (Zech. 4:6), or even the less well known scripture in Samuel: "For not by strength shall man prevail" (I Sam. 2:9).

7. THE ETHICAL IMPLICATION OF TORAH AS A CONSTITUTIVE PRINCIPLE OF PEOPLEHOOD

"Torah" is often used, in a limited sense, to designate the Pentateuch together with the mass of Rabbinic tradition based on it. As such "Torah" consists of the Written and the Oral Law.[7a] The term "Torah" may also be used in a wider sense, to designate all that we understand by Judaism. To grasp, however, the essence of what that term conveys in this wider sense, it is necessary to study carefully what it represents in its more limited sense. The Torah as the Written and the Oral Law is not a book or a code but a people-making instrument. It was the charter of the Jewish people. This function of Torah throws much light upon Judaism's contribution to what has been described as "the ethical seriousness in our Western culture." As an idea, therefore, "Torah" may be said to represent the principle that made the Jews into a people.

Rab Saadia[8a] uttered a most penetrating truth when, in referring to the Jews, he said, "The only thing that makes us into a people is the Torah." By that he probably meant to negate the idea that it was kinship, blood or race that made the Jews into a people, and to affirm the fact that the particular pattern of living or way of life unfolded in the Torah formed the bond of ethnic unity. There is another possible negation involved in Rab Saadia's statement. It may justly be interpreted as implying that the constitutive principle of Jewish peoplehood is not the power the group has over its individual members, as in the case of all other peoples, but the opportunity which the Jewish group affords the individual Jew to share the way of life promulgated in the Torah. This amounts to saying that, in so far as the Jews felt that the Torah was the constitutive principle of their peoplehood, it precluded the machinery of state from being that principle.

The state as a political entity is essentially the organization of the force inherent in a nation. A state-constituted nation is therefore the product of force, regardless of moral law as such. The machinery of the state has all too often been directed against the underprivileged within the nation itself as well as against other nations. Franz Oppenheim, in his book *The State*, proves that, historically, the state is the product of the same *force majeure* which enables the invader to conquer and take away the lands and goods of the conquered. It is therefore intrinsically the antithesis of morally constituted organization. Those who compiled the Torah, and had it adopted as the basis of Jewish unity, had no such sociological awareness of the origin and true character of the state, yet intuitively they must have sensed these facts about the state.

Likewise, the spiritual leaders of the Jewish people seem to have been eager to prevent Israel from being completely identified with the state and dependent upon it for survival. To mention only a few striking examples of this negative attitude: the early preference for divinely sent instead of popularly chosen leaders, the resistance which the prophet Samuel is said to have displayed toward the people's demand for a king, the Torah's casual reference to the appointment of a king as optional instead of as an expected procedure, the prophet Hosea's allusion to the institution of kinghood as irritating to God, and above all, the greater judicial and legislative authority which Pharisaism[9a] conferred upon the spokesman of the Torah than upon the representatives of the state. All these instances point to a conscious deprecation of organized force as the basic principle of peoplehood. The ethical implications of that attitude to the state are, indeed, far reaching. The significance of this attitude in our day may be inferred from the fact that it is the very antipode of that implied in the Hegelian conception of the state as "the Divine Idea as it exists on earth." What that conception implied, and what happened when it was acted on by some nations, was frankly expressed in the well known epigram of H. V. Treitschke: "The essence of the state is in the first place power, in the second place power, and in the third place, once more, power" ("*Bundesstaat und Einheitstaat*").

Since, according to the idea of "Torah," the authority of the people as a whole over the individual who is a member of it does not stem from the collective force which it can bring to bear upon him, that authority must stem from another source. That source is none other than the Will of God, which the people mediates for the individual. Torah thus came to represent the articulation of the Will of God as it manifested itself, first, in the career of the people and, secondly, in the particular way of life to which the people was committed. The Jews thus evolved the principle that the basis of society, or its main cohesive influence, was not the power the strong might wield over the weak, but the common submission of both strong and weak to the Will of God. The Will of God is not the will of a mighty potentate who can intimidate human beings into obedience, but the principle of righteousness conceived in cosmic terms and become articulate in the people's philosophy of life and in the precepts and commandments that set forth the norms that guide its life.

The unity which the Jewish people, through its Torah, held up as the only kind that may legitimately bind men together, coincides with what Josiah Royce interpreted to be the motivating influence of all ethical living. Royce identified loyalty to a cause as the most potent factor for the good life. He defined a "cause" as "*some conceived, and yet also real, spiritual unity which links many individual lives into one, and which is therefore essentially superhuman, in exactly the same sense in which we find the realities of the world of reason to be superhuman.* Yet the cause is not, on that account any mere abstraction. It is a live something. 'My home,' 'my family,' 'my service,' 'mankind,' 'the church,' 'my art,' 'my science,' 'the cause of humanity,' or once more 'God's Will'; such are the names for the cause . . . This cause is not a mere heap or collection of human beings; it is a life of many brethren in unity . . . Such a principle does not mean, 'lose yourself,' or even simply 'sacrifice yourself.' It means 'Be as rich and full and strong a self as you can, and then with all your heart and your soul and your mind and your strength, devote yourself to this cause, to this spiritual unity, in which individuals may be, and (when they are loyal) actually are, united in a life whose meaning is above the separate meanings of any or all natural human beings.' "[10] Every word in the foregoing passage brings out most sharply the implications of that section of the Torah known as the *Shema*, which it has been the sacred duty of every Jew to read twice daily. There everyone in Israel is invoked to love God with all of his being and to express that love by being ever mindful of God's behests and communicating them to his children. The love of God which the Israelite is called upon to foster is the exact equivalent of the loyalty to a cause which Royce so warmly urges as indispensable to salvation.

8. THE RATIONALE FOR THE GOOD LIFE SUPPLIED BY THE TORAH NARRATIVE

How did the Will of God, according to the Torah, reveal itself in the career of Israel? In answer, the Torah unfolds the panorama of the creation of the world and the spread of mankind, and it indicates the place of Israel in that panorama. This gives to the Torah a function which very few suspect, since to most people Torah is only a synonym for law. That function is to convey to the individual an orientation that is expected to motivate loyalty to his people and love for his God, and to arouse in him an eagerness to perform God's Will as revealed in His people's code of law and ethics. This means that on a par with legal and ethical precepts is the narrative that serves as their background and rationale. The Jew is not expected to obey God's Will blindly. Such obedience might be prompted by fear, or by the awareness of God's overwhelming power. That would destroy the very essence of the ethical deed. A deed is ethical, as has been shown, only to the extent that it is a free act. It is a free act when motivated by the love of God. The reason for loving God, which the Torah advances to the Jew, is not the success or prosperity he might enjoy, or share with his people, but the divinely guided career and the God-appointed destiny in which he should participate as a member of that people. This accounts for the importance the Torah attaches to having the Jew oriented as definitely as possible concerning the place of his people in God's world.

Seldom are the foregoing facts regarded as having any ethical significance. The truth, however, is that Judaism has made a far greater contribution to the good life by means of this indirect emphasis upon the need, on the part of every individual, for an ethico-spiritual orientation to life as a whole than if it had developed in elaborate form some abstract argument concerning the nature of the moral good. Judaism could not have stressed more strongly the principle of the dignity of the human person than by this recognition of the right of the individual to know the general pattern and meaning of life and the place of his own group in that pattern. It is like honoring a soldier who is a mere private with information not only about the tactics of the battle but also about the strategy of the war.

The comprehensiveness of the narrative portion of the Torah and the brilliance with which its significant points are highlighted have probably done more to foster both cosmic and group consciousness, first in the Jews and then in the adherents of Christianity and Islam, as a rationale for ethical attitudes and conduct, than all the systematic thinking of the philosophers. It matters not that, from a scientific viewpoint, the narrative of the origin and early beginnings of Israel is on the whole legendary. That very fact is perhaps all the more reason for regarding the narrative section of the Torah as ethically significant, because it points to the existence of definite ethical assumptions as having shaped, if not actually having created, the narrative material.

In this discussion only the merest mention can be made of what renders the Torah narrative so conspicuously important, from the standpoint of the good life. The career of Israel is there shown to owe its beginnings to God's purpose of having a people that would fulfill His Will. What God wills concerning man is clearly stated in the reason given for God's choice of Abraham as the founder of a people: "For I have known him to the end that he may command his children and his household after him, that they may keep the way of the Lord, to do righteousness and justice" (Gen. 18:19). That choice fell upon Abraham because he happened to be the first human being to obey God implicitly. He fulfilled the Divine behest to be *tamim* ("simple" or "perfect") which, to judge from the various contexts in which that term is used, implies acting in a spirit of implicit obedience to God. Thus Abraham is represented as the foil, setting off by contrast the character of Adam, who symbolizes man in general and who in the allegory of the Garden of Eden is represented as having through his sin brought toil, suffering and death on the human race. How far Abraham was willing to make God's Will the dominant purpose of his own life is indicated by the unquestioning faith he displayed—a faith which God "accounted it to him as righteousness" (Gen. 15:6)—and the readiness to sacrifice his only son at God's bidding. His very self-surrender to the Will of God, which is synonymous with righteousness and justice, impells him paradoxically enough to take God to task for threatening to carry out a seeming act of injustice. "Shall not the Judge of all the earth do justly?" (Gen. 18:25) asks Abraham, when learning of the doom that was to befall the wicked cities of Sodom and Gomorrah.

The descendants of Abraham were to grow into a people that was to live not by might nor by strength but by the spirit of God, or the spirit of righteousness. How was that to be compatible with the realities which called for the acquisition of a land? All the habitable lands the ancients knew of had already been occupied. No new people could have arisen without displacing some existing people. Such displacement could not apparently take place without involving the unrighteous use of force. The Torah resolves this dilemma by pointing out that the peoples which inhabited the land of Canaan had made themselves unworthy of it, by reason of their moral corruption. During Abraham's life, however, and for a number of centuries after him, the iniquity of the Amorite was not yet full (Gen. 15:16). His descendants had therefore to wander about for a long time. When they finally did find temporary domicile, they had to pay for it by becoming slaves in a land that was not theirs (Gen. 15:13), and by submitting to harsh treatment. All this, in order not to commit the injustice of dispossessing a people before it had become completely undeserving of its land! However dangerous we now know such rationalization of conquest to be, nevertheless, in its unsophisticated form, it undoubtedly expresses a new kind of group sensitivity to ethical values.

To proceed with the Torah narrative: in the meantime the events, which culminate in the redemption of the Israelites from Egypt and the revelation of the laws by which they are to order their lives, help to emphasize the ethical implications of God's relation to man. That relation was experienced by the Israelites in their miraculous redemption from Egyptian bondage. From beginning to end, that redemption, as well as the journeying through the wilderness and the final occupation of the land, is depicted as having been made possible entirely through God's intervention. Everywhere in the telling of those stories we note the unmistakable purpose of stressing the weakness and the helplessness of the Israelites and their complete dependence upon God.

The key to the understanding of the narrative portions of the Torah and of the other books of the Bible is to be found in statements like the following: "The Lord will fight for you and ye shall hold your peace" (Ex. 14:14), or, "(Beware of saying to yourselves), 'My power and the might of my hand hath gotten me this wealth'" (Deut. 8-17). The sin to which the Torah ascribes Israel's wanderings in the desert is not the sin of having worshiped the Golden Calf, but that of having refused to rely upon God's power to enable them to overcome the strongly fortified natives of Canaan. That refusal implied that the Israelites had not abandoned the prevalent assumption that whatever force man wielded was entirely his own, and being his own he could do with it what he pleased. This, according to the Torah, is man's cardinal sin. The one unvarying theme in all of ancient Judaism's teachings concerning Israel's career is the deprecation of the possible claim that whatever success Israel achieved in its struggle for existence, for freedom, or for possession it owed to its own prowess. All such success must be ascribed only to God.

The power of God is always directed against strong peoples which act insolently. They generally defy God's Will, which is essentially the same as what we mean by the moral law. This fact stands out most conspicuously in the case of the redemption from Egypt. As is well known, that event figures as the main point of reference in Israel's religious career. It is the seminal or archetypal event in its history. From it the Jew is expected to draw the principal inspiration for fulfilling God's Will. The commemoration of it is given as a rationale for the Sabbath. It is the main rationale for the Passover festival, which had been transformed from a nature festival to a historical one, and which came to be celebrated with far greater *éclat* than the two other pilgrim festivals. The main experience of God's intervention in Israel's career is thus associated with an event in which God redresses the wrong done to those who have been oppressed and rescues them from the power of their oppressor. This fact could not but contribute to the conception of God as the champion of the weak against the strong. That conception of God is a corollary of the intuition that the distinction between right and wrong belongs to a different dimension of existence from that of the physical vitalities and powers.

9. POWER ENTRUSTED BY GOD TO MAN FOREVER SUBJECT TO ABUSE

It is doubtful whether the comparative study of religion can yield a parallel instance of such unmitigated insistence on treating force or power as something with which it is dangerous to entrust man. It is as though traditional Judaism affirmed of power, whether exercised over things in the environment or over other human beings, what the ancient Greeks said about fire, when they spoke of it as stolen from heaven by Prometheus. In common with the rest of the world, the Jews naturally identified power as the very essence of Godhood. On the other hand, they fully realized that man's avoidable sufferings were, for the most part, the result of the abuse of power. That is the abuse described in Scriptures as violence, a term for that which caused God to regret that He had created man (Gen. 6:6).

In the Middle Ages many mystics believed that by proper invocation of the different appellations of God and His angels they might achieve control over nature. Those who held that belief realized fully the dangers their very success might bring on them and on the rest of the world. They feared that they might become so intoxicated with their newly acquired power as to use it for selfish ends. They therefore prescribed numerous restrictions which would permit only those of pure and unselfish character to engage in mystic lore, and they themselves underwent the most exacting routines in self-discipline. In our own day likewise, we have come to dread the possible consequences of entrusting the knowledge of modern science and invention to all and sundry. Remembering the possible abuses of force, we are afraid to consent even to the enforcement of international peace.

Fear of the abuse of force led all those who had a hand in the shaping of the Jewish consciousness—priests, prophets and sages—to emphasize the existence of a sharp antithesis between force and spirit, between power and moral law. That was one of the ways in which the ancients tried to articulate the profound intuition that spirit and moral law constituted a different dimension of existence from, and were entirely other than, considerations of utility or expediency which have to do with whatever force or power man has at his command. When Plato discovered the fact that ideas as such belonged to an entirely different order of existence from the things we know through the senses, he was able to articulate that fact only by emphasizing the impassable gulf that divided ideas from things. Had he not gone to extremes in stressing the otherness of idea, philosophy would probably have made little progress. Similarly, if Judaism had not gone to extremes in maintaining that force was incommensurate with spirit, or that power could not be equated with moral law, man would never have understood why all his achievements in the domain of power turn to dust and ashes, unless they are based on the moral law and unless they conform to the demands of the spirit.

10. Torah Law as a Means of Channeling Power into Moral Conduct

But if Judaism had stopped at the deprecation of man's use of power, it would have done what many other civilizations and religions tried to do when they sought to prevent man's involvement in material things and physical desires. Instead it sought to channel man's use of force within a way of life according to the Will of God. The way of life detailed in the Torah includes for the most part such laws, customs and mores as were on the whole common to the ancient civilizations of the Nile and the Euphrates. In the form in which those laws are found in the traditional Torah, they are the result of modification, first, as a result of differences in local conditions that obtained in Eretz Yisrael and, secondly, as a result of a uniquely ethical outlook on life. The general effect of thus directing whatever power man legitimately possesses into the channel of law has been to foster what may be considered the most important ethical principle underlying the use of power. That principle is that the exercise of power must be accompanied by the assumption of a commensurate degree of responsibility. Responsibility is modern man's equivalent for the traditional concept of Divine law for man.

It may well be that even despite the ethical refinement of the law and custom which had thus come down from Israel's prehistoric days, or would have been taken over from other civilizations, the laws and customs still fall below accepted standards of the best in modern life. That fact, however, is entirely irrelevant from the standpoint of Judaism's role in the ethical development of mankind. *That development was determined not by the particular content of the law but by the spirit that permeated the law.* The laws in the Torah dealing with slavery assume the institution of slavery to be normal, and in addition discriminate between a Hebrew and a Gentile slave in a manner that would now be regarded as definitely unethical. There are, to be sure, many laws which, even in the light of the highest standards of what is best in our own day, are ethically unimpeachable. But this method of appraising each particular law to determine how much of it is standard and how much is above standard is misleading from the standpoint of the question: How did the Torah influence the ethical consciousness of the Western world? That influence does not derive from any particular law or laws, but from the spirit that permeates all of them. We should, therefore, recognize that spirit and analyze its essential character if we want to know in what way the Torah as law contributed to world ethics.

The purpose to be served by the laws of the Torah is unmistakably set forth again and again. That purpose is declared to be that of rendering Israel a holy people. During the preparations for the theophany on Mt. Sinai, Moses was commanded to tell the Israelites that they were to be "a Kingdom of priests and a holy nation" (Ex. 19:6). In the very midst of what is known as the "Book of Covenant," which contains most of the laws that have served as the basis of civil jurisprudence in traditional Judaism, we read, "And ye shall be holy men unto me" (Ex. 22:30). The collection of laws known as the "Holiness Code"[11a] is called such because of the opening behest, which seems to represent the spirit intended to animate the whole of that code: "Speak unto all the congregation of the children of Israel, and say unto them; ye shall be holy; for I the Lord your God am holy" (Lev. 19:2). That the keeping of the commandments is to be the means of rendering Israel holy is stressed in numerous passages (cf. Lev. 22:31; Num. 15:40; Deut. 14:2, 14:21, 23:15, 28:9).

11. HOLINESS IN GOD AND MAN AS HARMONIOUS SYNTHESIS OF POWER AND GOODNESS

The meaning of holiness has been explored by students of both rudimentary and highly developed religions. They have invariably found that holiness was used in two senses, a physical and an ethical. In addition, they have found that "holy" and "divine" are generally used interchangeably. A god is a holy being, and a holy being is one that possesses something of the attribute of godhood. These discoveries of the scientific study of religious phenomena do not justify us in interpreting those phenomena as though those who were aware of them were students of religion. But they do help us penetrate into the religious consciousness of the ancients and reconstruct their ways of thought and their emotional responses.

These two conceptions of holiness as physical and as ethical are found in the Bible, though it is not always easy to draw the line between them. When God was about to descend on Mt. Sinai, He ordered Moses to warn the Israelites not to go near the mountain, lest they be stoned or shot through. When Uzza touched the Holy Ark for fear that it might fall off the wagon, as the cattle which drew it slipped, he was smitten. In both instances, holiness is conceived as a powerful physical force that shocks the human being to death when he ventures too close to it. However, there are equally unmistakable evidences of the use of the term "holiness" in a spiritual or ethical sense, as when God is said to have blessed the Sabbath and to have hallowed it (Ex. 20:11). The nature of the commandments imparted to Israel, after they are urged to be a holy nation, is entirely of a spiritual and an ethical character. The same is true of most of the behests in the Holiness Code.

The inference to which the foregoing facts point is that the purpose of the Torah, in that phase of it which deals with law, is to answer the question that its narrative section raises: Since whatever power man wields, and that reveals itself in his desires and ambitions, is not his own but entrusted to him by God, to Whom it actually belongs, how is man to know whether he employs it as he should? The answer furnished by the Torah is the following: The only way you can be sure that you are employing properly the God-given power entrusted to you is by using it in accordance with the prescribed testimonies, judgments and statutes. In the words of the Torah itself, "And ye shall remember all the commandments of the Lord and do them; and that ye go not about after your own heart and your own eyes, after which you use to go astray: that ye may remember and do all my commandments and be holy unto your God" (Num. 15:39-40).

The assumption is that the laws or commandments emanate from the moral or spiritual dimension in the nature of God, a dimension of holiness which is other than the one of force or power. The prophet Isaiah says: "The Lord of Hosts is exalted through justice, and God the Holy One is sanctified through righteousness" (5:16). A further assumption is that the nature or holiness of God is such that the dimension of force and the dimension of goodness abide in Him in perfect harmony, though those two attributes exist in Him on a scale beyond human computation. To the degree that they exist in man in a state of harmony, man is godlike, or holy. To achieve that godliness, or holiness, he has to obey the law of God. When man deliberately transgresses or ignores God's law, the assumption is that he does so because he imputes to himself all or most of the power he needs for the fulfillment of his desires and ambitions. If he credits himself with, and takes glory in, all the power he happens to possess, he dispenses with worship entirely; if he leaves some margin to supernatural sources, he tends to worship God in the wrong spirit, or to worship false gods.

If space allowed, it would have been interesting to note how differently the Greek philosophers developed the aim of God-likeness as the animating principle of ethical behavior. All that need be mentioned at this point is that the meaning of God-likeness is necessarily determined by that in human life which is considered as of supreme value and, therefore, as a reflection of divinity. To the Greek thinkers, a life of contemplation was of supreme value. Therefore to be Godlike meant to them to be like God in the ability to see life as it really is, to excel in *theoria*. For the creators of Judaism, what mattered most was the existence of a people that ordered its life in accordance with the principle of holiness, as it was assumed to exist in God. The apotheosis of Torah implies that the harmony of power and goodness is achieved by a people when it organizes its life around laws which have as their purpose the striving to be holy, even as God is holy.

12. THE SIGNIFICANCE OF THE ARCHAIC CHARACTER OF TORAH LAW

As a result of the tendency to incorporate ancient forms of thought into our own universe of discourse, we may be using the same words as did the ancients, but we seldom speak the same language. Ancient concepts taken out of their original context are desiccated and devitalized and have about as much of the original taste to the intellectual palate as dried-out vegetables have to the physical. Thus the traditional doctrine of the Torah as divinely revealed loses its functional significance when dissociated from the ancient universe of discourse and, in losing that significance, is reduced to a theological dogma devoid of any ethical connotation. To recapture what the conception "divinely revealed" meant in its original setting, we have to find in our own universe of discourse some conception that bears as close a resemblance to it as possible in terms of pragmatic significance. Such a modern analogy, it seems, is offered by the conception "back to nature." If that is true, a second ethical implication of the Torah as divinely revealed becomes apparent, the first being the one discussed above, namely, the otherness and autonomy of the moral law.

With the aid of that analogy we can understand what motivated those who compiled the various writings which go by the name of Pentateuch. They who "handled the Torah" (*tofse ha-torah*, Jer. 2:8) were people who seemed to have sought out whatever ancient fragments contained law or narrative which they regarded as furthering the purpose of giving moral and spiritual character to Israel's life as a people. They took for granted that the archaic laws, which were part of the original tribal life of Israel, were inherently more moral and spiritual than those which obtained in their own day. This was in line with the prevalent tendency to idealize Israel's sojourn in the wilderness as having been a period when the people was assumed to have been governed by the very presence of God in its midst (Ex. 25:8). In the words of Jeremiah: "Thus saith the Lord: I remember for thee the affection of thy youth, the love of thine espousals; how thou wentest after me in the wilderness, in a land that was not sown" (2:2). Since the archaic laws in the Torah were known to have come down from what were already then olden times, and were viewed as the embodiment of the ethical principles by which power was to be regulated, they were inevitably regarded as having emanated from God. By the time those laws were integrated into Israel's Torah they were for the most part already obsolete. But they served the all-important purpose of emphasizing the need of submitting every exercise of human power to the Will of God as manifest in the law of righteousness. It is, indeed, significant that the prophetic writings close with the words: "Remember ye the law of Moses My servant, which I commanded unto him in Horeb for all Israel, even statutes and ordinances" (Mal 3:22).

13. TORAH AS BACKGROUND OF PROPHECY IN ISRAEL

Only on the assumption that the Jews had been sensitized to moral and spiritual interests through the medium of Torah, which, in outline at least, was a forerunner of the Torah as we have it, can we view the prophetic contribution to Judaism in its proper perspective.[12a] The biblical scholars, who have assumed that the prophetic writings represent the emergence of a new spiritual force completely alien to the environment in which it appeared, make far greater demands upon credulity than the traditional view which looks upon the prophets as having functioned entirely in line with long existing ethical trends. It is inconceivable that the prophets would resort to violent denunciation of their people's ignorance of God's true character, or that they would engage in bitter condemnation of the social injustice that prevailed among their contemporaries, unless those whom they addressed might be expected to know better and to act more ethically. Already Hosea alludes to some kind of Torah which God had written for Israel, but which had remained a dead letter (8:12). In the parable of the vineyard, Isaiah states that after all that God had done for the House of Israel and the men of Judah, "He looked for justice, but behold violence" (5:7). Apparently those whom Isaiah addressed must have been familiar with the stories we read in the Pentateuch and with the laws that form part of the traditional Torah. Otherwise his bitter denunciation would have been entirely unwarranted. Only people familiar with the story of Sodom and Gomorrah could have grasped the invective implied in being called "Rulers of Sodom and people of Gomorrah" (1:10). Only on the assumption that new moons, Sabbaths and holy convocations were strictly observed—which indicates the existence of priestly Torah—has Isaiah's reference to their futility any meaning.

We must therefore conclude that not only do the prophets themselves owe their passion for righteousness to a moral climate which had been deliberately fostered, but that their very mission must be understood as an application to new and bewildering situations of the ethical principles which were accepted in their day as of long standing. Moreover, only this intrinsic relation between Torah and Prophecy can account for the fact that the writings of the prophets attained a canonicity second in authority and sanctity only to that of the traditional Torah. Such canonicity is another one of those unique elements in Judaism which have had a greater influence on the world than even some of its most important ethical principles. We can well understand that anciently recorded tradition or law should be raised to the status of a high ethnic possession. But that a collection of the most vehement censure of a people's policies and way of life should be given the same high rank as its organic law marks a new stage in the ethical development of human societies.

Such moral censures abound in the writings of all great civilizations, but they merely point to the existence of a few moral critics who refused to reconcile themselves to the evils of the life around them. Their protests generally remained voices in the wilderness. In the case of Israel's prophets, however, their most denunciatory charges against their people were incorporated into the body of that people's sacred writings. Thus the trait of group self-criticism came to be an ethical requirement or expectation. This is something entirely new in the ethical consciousness of mankind and should be set down as a further contribution of Judaism to world ethics. A long time will probably elapse before nations, churches or even lesser groups will be able to overcome their collective vanity and acquire the ability to submit to criticism. Without such ethical maturity, collectives are bound to neutralize whatever virtues or moral excellences some of their individual members may attain. "Moral man in immoral society" is not merely the title of a book; it describes the present universal condition of man.

14. THE ETHICAL IMPLICATIONS OF THE PROPHETIC CONCEPTION OF GOD

There is an integral relation between the spirit of prophecy and the spirit of Torah. This is evident from the fact that the main provocation for the prophets' rebuke is the people's failure to live up to the fundamental teaching of the Torah. The people is denounced for not acting on the principle that whatever power man possesses is entrusted to him by God, and must be employed in accordance with God's ethical traits which find expression in His laws. This underlying principle of the Torah may be viewed either as derived from or as the source of the Jewish conception of God. According to that conception, God combines in Himself in perfect harmony infinite power and unqualified righteousness. In the conduct, however, which the prophets beheld in people about them, and in the political intrigues carried on by the governments of Israel and Judah, this conception of God was consistently ignored. God was regarded in much the same light as the other peoples regarded their respective deities. He was to them the main source of power, and was therefore to be appealed to and, if need be, even cozened, in the hope that He would grant some of that power to them for the fulfillment of their own wants. In this attitude toward God, all moral issues were ignored. The sacrificial cult and the ritual practice were observed with meticulous care, but all those laws which sought to protect the weak against the strong were completely overlooked.

This is the refrain of so much of the prophetic writings that one typical passage from the Book of Jeremiah should suffice to illustrate the point:

Trust ye not in lying words, saying: "The temple of the Lord, the temple of the Lord, the temple of the Lord, are these." Nay, but if ye thoroughly amend your ways and your doings; if ye thoroughly execute justice between man and his neighbor; if ye oppress not the stranger, the fatherless, and the widow, and shed not innocent blood in this place, neither walk after other gods to your hurt; then will I cause you to dwell in this place, in the land that I gave to your fathers, for ever and ever. Behold, ye trust in lying words, that cannot profit. Will ye steal, murder, and commit adultery, and swear falsely, and offer unto Baal, and walk after other gods whom ye have not known, and come and stand before Me in this house, whereupon My name is called, and say: "we are delivered," that ye may do all these abominations? Is this house, whereupon My name is called, become a den of robbers in your eyes? Behold, I, even I, have seen it, saith the Lord. (Jer. 7:4-11.)

In this indictment we hear echoes of the Ten Commandments which must have been generally known at that time.

In all the prophetic indictments, the worship of false gods, as well as of the true God in the wrong spirit, is an outstanding charge. As in the Torah, so in the prophets, unethical conduct is always closely associated with idolatry. The reason for this association of ideas can easily be surmised. Unethical conduct was considered as stemming from the failure to use, according to prescribed law, the power that God entrusted to man. This failure is part of the general tendency of man to view as his own whatever power he happens to possess and to resort to some deity for whatever additional control he may want to exercise over things or fellow men. When an Israelite sought superhuman aid in that spirit, he was bound either to misconceive the character of Israel's God or to turn to other gods. There are two ways in which men appeal to Deity, either as a power that sanctions and grants their uncriticized wants—such is the popular conception—or as a power helping them to discover and fulfill their true but unrecognized needs—such is the prophet's conception of God.

The foregoing pattern of ideas seems to underlie the characteristic attitude of the prophets toward the political intrigues and maneuverings of the royal households both in Israel and in Judah. The prophets took very literally and very seriously both the historical perspective and the way of life which were regarded as constituting "the Torah of God." They were certain that, if the Israelites had lived in accordance with the true way of life as formulated in that Torah, they would have been secure from attack and invasion by foreign foes. The fundamental principle of all the ancient narratives expressed in the verse, "The Lord will fight for you, and you shall hold your peace" (Ex. 14:15), is at the basis of the unvarying political policy of the prophets.

Thus in denouncing the alliance with Egypt, Isaiah says:

Woe to the rebellious children, saith the Lord, that take counsel, but not of me; and that form projects, but not of My spirit, that they may add sin to sin . . . it is a rebellious people, lying children, children that refuse to hear the teaching of the Lord, that say to the seers, "See not" and to the prophets. . . . "Cause the Holy One of Israel to cease from before us." Wherefore saith the Holy One of Israel: Because ye despise this word and trust in oppression and perverseness and stay thereon . . . For thus said the Lord God, the Holy One of Israel: In sitting still and rest shall ye be saved, in quietness and in confidence shall be your strength; And ye would not (30:1-15).

The prophet condemns the resort to military force and diplomatic intrigue, instead of relying upon God's miraculous power, as a grievous sin. God, however, cannot come to the aid of His people unless they conform to His law of righteousness. If they want to avoid disaster they must repent of their evil ways. "Therefore," continues Isaiah, "will the Lord wait, that He may be gracious unto you, and therefore will He be exalted that He may have compassion upon you; for the Lord is a God of justice; happy are all they that wait for Him" (30:18).

It is amazing with what persistence Judaism held on to the twofold principle until modern times, first, that the miraculous manifestation of Divine power is the only means of man's salvation and, secondly, that God would manifest His power as soon as man would repent and submit to God's law of righteousness. The pietist movement known as Hasidism,[13a] which flourished in Eastern Europe during the nineteenth century and still numbers many adherents, proves that Judaism, in some Jewish circles, still prefers to rely upon Divine miracle, in disregard even of the realities of life, rather than trust to man's initiative. So fearful is Judaism of man's use of power. Such a defiance of the realities of life flared up almost two thousand years ago, when the Jews experienced the full weight of the Roman yoke. In those days there was a much better chance for such defiance to spread and to become the rallying cry for multitudes of men than there is today. Among the Jews as a people, this determination to live by the letter as well as the spirit of the Torah and the prophets led to the gradual severance of their inner life from the state. This made it possible for R. Johanan ben Zakkai[14a] and his successors to reconstitute the Jews into the *Kenesiah*, or the synagogue. In addition to being a people, Jews were now also the *Kenesiah*. At the same time, among a small section of Jewry, the renewed determination to live by the teachings of the Torah and the prophets found embodiment in the Messianic movement of Jesus of Nazareth, the movement which Paul succeeded in developing into Christianity and which found embodiment in the *ecclesia*, or church.

The foregoing twofold principle, which is at the basis of both traditional Judaism and traditional Christianity, seems at first to belong to the domain of theology, in that it expresses a particular view with regard to God's way with man. But viewed functionally, it is a most revolutionary ethical idea. It accentuates what is involved in the problem of human conduct and men's relation to one another. It makes clear that human nature tends to be corrupted by the possession of power. Consequently, the only way to overcome that tendency is to subordinate the use of power to the moral law. *This cardinal doctrine concerning power furnishes the best clue to Judaism's contribution to world ethics.*

The prophets did not have to create this cardinal doctrine. They absorbed it from the tradition of Torah, which had been of long standing. Without the prophets, however, that tradition would have died out; they put new life into it by emphasizing the potency of the moral law, and its categorically imperative character. Jeremiah refers more than once to the moral law as integral to the very constitution of the universe and of man. Such reference implies that only by conforming to the moral law can man be true to his innermost essence. Thus Jeremiah tells his people to stand by the ways and look and ask for the ancient paths: "Where is the good way, and walk therein and ye shall find rest for your souls" (6:16). Elsewhere we read: "Yea the stork in the heaven knoweth her appointed

times, and the turtle and the swallow and the crane observe the time of
their coming, but My people know not the ordinance of the Lord. How
do ye say 'We are wise, and the Law of the Lord is with us?' " (Jer. 8:7).
Man's distinction, accordingly, is in the achievement neither of worldly
wisdom, strength nor wealth, but in the realization of the moral law as
inherent in the very nature of God. "Thus saith the Lord: Let not the
wise man glory in his wisdom, neither let the mighty man glory in his
might, let not the rich man glory in his riches; but let him that glorieth
glory in this, that he understandeth, and knoweth Me, that I am the
Lord who exercise mercy, justice, and righteousness, in the earth" (Jer.
9:22-23).

15. THE THREE CARDINAL PRINCIPLES OF PROPHETIC ETHICS

A further contribution which Judaism has made to world ethics through
the prophets is the specific formulation which the moral law received at
their hands. That formulation helps to identify and motivate the particular
laws or expectations which embody the moral law. Such a formulation of
the moral law is that given by the prophet Micah who was a contemporary
of Isaiah during the latter half of the eighth century (B.C.E.). "What
the Lord doth require of thee; only to do justly, and to love mercy, and
to walk humbly with thy God" (Mic. 6:8).

When we study the history of the various attempts to formulate ethics
into a normative science, free from a religious or theological basis, we note
very little, if any, advance on the theories to be found in Plato's and
Aristotle's writings. The reason for the failure to make any headway in
ethical theory is that it is as difficult to motivate the good life by means
of reasoning based on other than intrinsic grounds, as it is to prove the
worth-whileness of life itself by means of such reasoning. Two outstanding
modern thinkers recognized this truth, each in his own way, Immanuel
Kant and M. Guyau. How, then, is the good life to be motivated?
Judaism's answer has been: By sharing the life of a people which is conse-
crated to the furtherance of the good life as defined by the prophet Micah.
Not intellectual speculation concerning the good life, but the actual expe-
riencing of it in the give-and-take of human intercourse can motivate it
and channel out for it the proper laws, customs and moral standards.

The good life as an object of experience may be described, in terms
of the modern universe of discourse, as doing the best of which we are
capable and being at our best in both prosperity and adversity. Evidently
everything depends upon what we mean by "best." According to the
prophet Micah, to do one's best is to practice justice and lovingkindness,
and to be at one's best under all circumstances is to walk humbly with
God. What this implies may be inferred from what Judaism regards as

the central problem of human conduct. We have seen that problem to be, how to prevent man from misusing the power entrusted to him by God. The laws given in the Torah, which are regarded as commanded by God, are intended as specific means of solving that problem. It should not be difficult to group those laws under the categories of justice, lovingkindness and walking humbly with God. By noting how each of these three categories is related to the problem of power, we can get at the ethical purpose underlying virtually all the laws in the Torah.

a. Justice

Justice is that aspect of human behavior which seeks to prevent anyone from being deprived of that measure of power with which God has entrusted him. This, of course, assumes that the power so entrusted is to be used in accordance with God's Will. It is obvious that the ultimate in the defiance of God is the fratricide associated with the name of Cain, because murder is an absolute and irrevocable extinction of a human life, which is the sum total of the power entrusted to a human being. To destroy a human life is thus also an act of *lèse majesté* against God, in whose image man is made (cf. Gen. 9:6), or whose harmonious combination of power and goodness must be reflected in human life. To inflict suffering upon a fellowman without justification is to rob him of such power as God has bestowed upon him. To deprive anyone of whatever rightly belongs to him is to deprive him of legitimate power, and therefore to commit an act of injustice. Whatever abilities we naturally possess and whatever is necessary to enable those abilities to function are ours by *divine* right. Justice thus precludes all manner of oppression, exploitation and deceit, as well as all forms of theft, slander and assault. Moreover, native and alien are alike in respect to justice.

The foregoing prophetic conception of justice limits its scope merely to negating what is wrong. This limitation stands out in strong contrast to the conception of justice in Greek ethics. In Greek ethics, justice is conceived as coextensive with the good life as a whole, whereas in Jewish ethics it occupies only one of three areas of the good life, the other two being lovingkindness and walking humbly with God. In Greek ethics, justice is essentially an aesthetic aspect of human behavior; it is harmony and sense of proportion. It is the harmony and proportionate functioning of conflicting tendencies and interests within the individual himself and among those of different individuals. Plato studied justice as it might be realized in the state, because it could be seen there on a sufficiently large scale to illustrate the principle of harmony in the individual.[15] Justice, to be sure, is a quality pertaining both to the state and to the individual. But in neither instance is it conceived as being conformity to a human or divine standard which is autonomous or independent of aesthetic or utilitarian considerations. The fact that justice is approached from a purely humanist standpoint enables one to examine it analytically and to differentiate it into such categories as distributive and corrective justice. But when justice is removed from the religious synthesis in which it is seen in Judaism it ceases to have that new dimensionality, or that otherness, which renders any extraneous sanction superfluous or irrelevant. From the standpoint of power as God's gift to man, justice as the obligation to do nothing that might rob man of that gift is inherently understandable.

b. Lovingkindness

Lovingkindness, from the standpoint of its effect on the power to which man is entitled, is the particular behavior in human relations which elicits and activates that power in others. To love one's neighbor as oneself is to call forth in him the fullest use of whatever powers God has endowed him with. All consideration shown to the unfortunate, all humane treatment of those who are dependent, all provisions for the needy enable human power, otherwise unused, to come into play, and therefore belong to the category of lovingkindness. So also does the act of forgiveness. When, instead of bearing a grudge against our neighbor, we air our grievance frankly and come to an understanding with him (Lev. 19:17) we help him to make use of his legitimate powers; whereas, if we vent our anger upon him, we are bound to inhibit his use of them.

To express the basic intuition that justice and lovingkindness constitute a dimension of reality which is self-existent, other and underivable from the dimension of the vital needs, Judaism projects them into the very being of God. God is, accordingly, represented throughout all stages of Judaism as a God of both justice and lovingkindness. In His capacity as a God of justice, He is the author of those laws which tell man what he must do to guard against depriving his fellow man of the power wherewith God has endowed him. In that same capacity, God punishes those who transgress His laws. In His capacity as a God of lovingkindness, He not only teaches man how to conduct himself so as to elicit the best in his fellow, but He also calls upon the transgressor to repent. When man repents, God forgives, and by His forgiveness enables man to use his own powers as God would have him do. A frequently repeated principle in the Rabbinic writings is the application of *imitatio dei* to the divine attributes of lovingkindness ascribed to God. Commenting on the verse in Ex. 15:2, Abba Saul, who read it to mean, "I will be like Him," added: "Be thou like Him. Just as He is gracious and compassionate, so be thou gracious and compassionate."[16]

c. Humility

"To walk humbly with God," the third item in Micah's summary description of the good life, is rendered most significant, like the other two items, in the light of the central problem of human conduct and human relations. How we bear ourselves amid the vicissitudes of fortune, which affect the amount of power over which we have control, determines our character and our share in the good life. Prosperity, or the possession of all those instruments which augment one's power, easily turns one's head and gives rise to a sense of self-sufficiency and insolence. Such an attitude must lead to the disregard of God's laws of justice and lovingkindness. This is a danger to which nations are even more subject than individuals. "Jeshurun waxed fat, and kicked— Thou didst wax fat, thou didst grow thick, thou didst become gross— And he forsook God who made him, And contemned the Rock of his salvation" (Deut. 32:15).

The villain in the divine drama of human life, as portrayed in Jewish Scripture, is not a demonic or satanic being which tempts man to defy God, but man himself who, having come into great power through conquest, wealth or fame, tries to play the god. He is the *rasha*, the wicked one. The *rasha* acts as a foil to God's purpose with man. He tries to thwart that purpose by denying God, either openly or in his heart, and he attempts to order the world according to his own arrogant will-to-power. "For the wicked [the *rasha*] boasteth of his heart's desire, and the covetous vaunteth himself, though he contemn the Lord. The wicked [the *rasha*], in the pride of his countenance saith: 'He will not require' . . . His ways prosper at all times . . . He saith in his heart: 'I shall not be moved' " (Ps. 10:3-6). At the very opposite pole of the wicked one (*rasha*) is the humble one (*ani* or *anav*), who walks humbly with God. When Abraham interceded with God in behalf of Sodom, he said: "I am mere dust and ashes." His humility was not confined to his attitude toward God. It also found expression in his attitude toward Lot, to whom he said: "Let there be no strife, I pray thee, between me and thee" (Gen. 13:8), although as the head of the clan Abraham might well have resorted to the prerogative of authority and power. Likewise it is said of Moses, when he was assailed by Miriam and Aaron, that he was "very meek [*anav*] above all the men that were upon the face of the earth" (Num. 12:3).

To walk humbly with God, however, is a virtue which is by no means intended to be limited to a life of prosperity. It has its place also under conditions of adversity. Misfortune, whether due to natural causes or to human viciousness, leaves one bereft of power. It often leads to bitterness and despair, which are bound to lead to moral deterioration of the sufferer. Such an attitude is a kind of inverted pride and rebellion against God. The Sage whose words are recorded in the Book of Proverbs prayed that he be tempted neither to deny God by reason of prosperity nor to repudiate Him by reason of adversity (Pr. 30:8). But not always are men spared either temptation. Occasions of adversity are by far the more prevalent. The advice to walk humbly with God even under those circumstances is, therefore, always timely. When Job sat upon the ash heap and scraped himself with a potsherd, his wife said to him: "Dost thou still hold fast thine integrity? blaspheme God, and die." His answer to her is Judaism's conception of walking humbly with God in time of adversity: "Thou speakest as one of the impious women speaketh. What? shall we receive good at the hand of God, and shall we not receive evil?" (Job 2:8-10) In the Book of Psalms we get an insight into the soul of the humble one who, despite suffering, knows how to walk humbly with God.

16. GOD IN HISTORY AS VIEWED BY THE PROPHETS

The prophets express the conviction that had the Israelites followed the principles of justice, lovingkindness and walking humbly with God, as embodied in God's Torah, they would have enjoyed peace and security. They were equally certain that invasion, enslavement and exile were God's punishment for the violation of these principles by relying upon the manipulation of power politics, and by mere lip worship to God and His law. The political and social crises which began to come in fast succession, as one or another of the neighboring empires or of invading hordes threatened to overwhelm Israel, led the prophets to achieve a larger world orientation than had been possible under the dispensation of Torah. Torah had taught Israel's spokesmen to think in historical terms, but their mental horizon scarcely extended beyond the immediate neighboring peoples. The events amid which the prophets lived changed all that. The rise and fall of empires had to be fitted into the traditional conception of the God of Israel, the God Who is the source of all power, and whose main attributes are justice and lovingkindness. This led the prophets to give universal scope to their ethical intuitions and assumptions.

The main concept by which the prophets succeeded in universalizing the ethical teachings of Judaism was that of "the day of YHWH."[17a] This concept, it appears, was originally promulgated by the zealots of YHWH and the "success prophets" of an earlier era. It was used by them as a slogan of victory for mobilizing the armed forces in battle against the enemies of Israel. The great prophets, however, reinterpreted the concept of "the day of YHWH." They employed it as a means of getting their people to think in terms of world events as a manifestation of God's power, a power that is not arbitrary or subject to whim, but one dominated by justice and love. Thus did the ethical principles pass beyond the stage of individual reflection or inspiration. Had they remained in this stage, they would have been of as little influence as those of the philosophers. Only by being given the impetus of a profoundly moving religious idea—such as that which enabled men to behold the hand of God in the shaping of human history—did those ethical principles finally permeate the consciousness of the greater part of mankind.

In the course of time, the concept of the Day of YHWH came to express the hope that God would establish His Kingdom on earth. This assurance grew out of the deep conviction according to which the world was inherently so constituted that, despite the prevalence of evil and the repeated setbacks in man's moral progress, the good life would be achieved by man in ever-increasing measure. The prospect of such a future is always needed, but never more than in times of crisis like our own.

It is not too much to say that Judaism's contribution to world ethics consists in having called attention to the truth that, for men to learn the art of living together, the one problem they must seek to solve is how to tame their will-to-power. To discover the specific character of that contribution we have to interpret the ethical teachings of Judaism as they functioned in solving that problem. The conclusions we then arrive at are: First, that Judaism has always affirmed in the most vigorous fashion the inherent truth and the categorical and imperative character of the moral law, apart from all considerations of expediency, aesthetic interest or any other source of validation. The fact that it promulgated that principle at a morally crucial period in ancient times enabled it to save Western mankind from moral disintegration. Secondly, as a result of this intrinsic and underived character of the moral law, the problem of the good life cannot be *why* we should live the good life, but *how* we should live it. It is no more possible to prove why we should live the good life than why we should live at all, especially when life bears down hard on us. The answer that Judaism gives to the question of *how* to live is contained in Micah's description of the good life as consisting of justice, lovingkindness and walking humbly with God. This summary, properly understood, points to the only possible means of taming our will-to-power.

The assumption of traditional Judaism, that the specific laws and social arrangements which incarnate justice, lovingkindness and walking humbly with God were supernaturally revealed to ancient Israel, is for many no longer tenable. But, interpreted functionally, that assumption implies that *all* human laws and social arrangements must be subjected to the moral test of being effective as a means of taming man's will-to-power. Otherwise they are only pretentious disguises for selfish exploitation of power and its antisocial use.

Never since the days of Rome's decline and the disintegration of the classic order has mankind been so threatened, as it is today, by moral nihilism. Never since then has it been in such need of the reaffirmation of the moral values as the only means of saving human life from impending doom. Together with all other bodies which are in a position to forestall a world cataclysm, the Jewish people, by reason of its enduring moral tradition, can play once again an important role in the salvation of mankind.

Notes

1 See the article "Ethics and Morality," by H. B. Alexander in the *Encyclopedia of Religion and Ethics* (New York, 1912), Vol. V, p. 440.

2 *Ibid.*, p. 441.

3 J. H. Breasted, *The Dawn of Conscience* (New York, 1939), p. 124.

4 *Ibid.*, p. 126.

5 *Ibid.*, p. xi.

[6a Cf. below, Alexander Altmann, "Judaism and World Philosophy: From Philo to Spinoza," pp. 66 ff.; cf. also Ralph Marcus, "Hellenistic Jewish Literature," this work, Vol. II, pp. 73 ff.]

[7a Cf. Robert Gordis, "The Bible as a Cultural Monument," this work, Vol. II, pp. 10 ff.; cf. also Louis Finkelstein, "The Jewish Religion: Its Beliefs and Practices," this work, Vol. II, p. 469.]

[8a Cf. Judah Goldin, "The Period of the Talmud (135 B.C.E.-1035 C.E.)," this work, Vol. I, pp. 202 ff.]

[9a Cf. *ibid.*, pp. 121 ff.]

10 Josiah Royce, *Sources of Religious Thought* (New York, 1914), pp. 199-201.

[11a Cf. William Foxwell Albright, "The Biblical Period," this work, Vol. I, pp. 13-14.]

[12a Cf. Gordis, *op. cit.*, pp. 15 ff.]

[13a Cf. Yudel Mark, "Yiddish Literature," this work, Vol. II, pp. 426 f.]

[14a Cf. Goldin, *op. cit.*, pp. 150 f.]

15 *The Republic*, 368-369.

16 Shabbat, 133b.

[17a On the use of the Tetragrammaton, YHWH, cf. Elias J. Bickerman, "The Historical Foundations of Postbiblical Judaism," this work, Vol. I, pp. 98-99.]

Bibliography

Aristotle, *Nicomachean Ethics*. London, 1926.

Breasted, James H., *The Dawn of Conscience*. New York and London, 1933.

Cohen, Abraham, *The Teachings of Maimonides*. London, 1927. Ch. XI.

Finkelstein, Louis, *The Pharisees*. Philadelphia, 1938. Chs. X, XIV-XVIII.

Hastings, James, (ed.), *Encyclopedia of Religion and Ethics* (New York, 1910-1922): "Righteousness," Vol. X, pp. 777-811, "Conscience," Vol. IV, pp. 30-47, "Ethics," Vol. V, pp. 415-436.

Herford, R. Travers, *Pharisaism*. London and New York, 1912. Ch. VI.

Lazarus, Moritz, *The Ethics of Judaism*. Philadelphia, 1901.

Moore, George F., *Judaism in the First Centuries of the Christian Era*. Cambridge, 1927-1930. Vol. II, pt. V.

PORTER, N., *Kant's Ethics*. Chicago, 1886.

ROYCE, JOSIAH, *The Sources of Religious Thought*. New York, 1914.

SCHECHTER, SOLOMON, *Aspects of Rabbinic Theology*. New York, 1909. Ch. XIII.

STRONG, T. B., "Ethics," *Dictionary of the Bible* (James Hastings, ed.), New York, 1902. Vol. I, pp. 777-789.

ADDENDUM

CADBURY, HENRY J., *National Ideals in the Old Testament*. New York, 1920.

GINGER, MILTON J., *Religion, Society and the Individual*. New York, 1957.

LASSWELL, HAROLD D., and CLEVELAND, HARLAN (eds.), *The Ethic of Power: The Interplay of Religion, Philosophy, and Politics*. New York, 1962.

CHAPTER 3

JUDAISM AND WORLD PHILOSOPHY: FROM PHILO TO SPINOZA

By Alexander Altmann

It would be futile to attempt a presentation of Judaism as a philosophic system, or to speak of Jewish philosophy in the same sense as one speaks of American, English, French or German philosophy.[1] Judaism is a religion, and the truths it teaches are religious truths. They spring from the source of religious experience, not from pure Reason. There can, therefore, be no purpose in treating Judaism and world philosophy as two manifestations of the philosophic spirit, the one in a specific and the other in its generic form.

Yet while one must be careful not to confound Judaism with philosophy, one must not ignore the fact that many of the leading religious concepts of Judaism (such as the Unity and Incorporeality of God, *Creatio ex nihilo*, a universal Law for all mankind) were evolved in opposition to the mythical world view, and are therefore imbued with a high degree of rational and abstract thought.[2] They do not for this reason become in themselves philosophic, for they never lose touch with the springs of religious imagination; their whole tenor and significance remain religious. At the same time, their rational character places them in direct proximity to the Greek philosophic tradition, which grew up independently from a different stem of civilization. That tradition, too, developed in marked defiance of mythology, the traces of which it still bears in the classical, medieval and Renaissance periods.

Both the Jewish religious and the Greek philosophic traditions have, then, this in common that they are grappling, each in its own way, with the problem of mythology. It should, therefore, not be surprising if they had something to tell each other. The fact is that they did communicate with each other, and that they profited by their mutual contacts. The influence of philosophy on the development of Jewish thought, both rational and mystic, forms an important chapter in the history of the Jewish mind. World philosophy, likewise, was stimulated and enriched by the influence of Judaism. Our task will be to trace the various forms that this mutual interpenetration of Judaism and philosophy assumed in the course of history.

The importance of the contribution Judaism has made to the evolution of Western civilization can hardly be exaggerated. Ever since the entrance of the Jewish element into the world of Western thought—an entrance largely effected through the gateway of Alexandria—Judaism has become a potent factor in the intellectual realm of Western civilization. This is true in a double sense: not only has a considerable volume of Jewish thought been absorbed into that civilization through the medium of Christianity, but direct Jewish influence, too, has been strong and persistent, a fact to which E. Troeltsch has rightly drawn attention.[3]

It may be hard, in the modern age of emancipation and secularization, to separate the Jewish from general Western traits in the contributions of individual Jewish philosophers. In many cases no distinctly Jewish tradition may be traceable. Yet there can be little doubt that, in some way or other, a Jewish "quality" asserts itself. This applies not merely to the intensely Jewish Hermann Cohen, but also to thinkers on the extreme periphery of Judaism like Samuel Alexander and Henri Bergson. Alexander's "Taking Time Seriously"[4] is essentially Jewish and opposed to the Platonic-Christian tradition. Bergson's Comprehension of Reality and Being, under the symbols of purpose, creation, realization, insistence, progress, power, energy and life, has its origin in prophetic teaching, as Nathan Soederblom has emphasized.[5]

As we shall endeavor to show, there is an unbroken line of Jewish influence from the Hellenistic period down to the Middle Ages, and leading to the modern period of philosophy. We hope our historical survey will demonstrate how intimate is the fusion between Judaism and world philosophy, and how well founded is the Jewish claim that, through its contribution, Judaism has become an integral part of the intellectual and spiritual make-up of Western civilization.

1. HELLENISTIC JEWISH PHILOSOPHY

Hellenistic Jewish philosophy derives from the influence of Stoic, Platonic and Neopythagorean thought on the Greek-speaking Jews of Alexandria in the period between the second century B.C.E. and the first century C.E. At its mature stage, it joins the movement of the Platonic "Renaissance," inaugurated by Posidonius (b. c. 135 B.C.E.), the great Stoic teacher and tutor of Cicero, who has been termed "the first Neoplatonist," although a distance of more than three hundred years separates him from Plotinus, the founder of the Neoplatonic School.[1] The revival of Platonism must have been of particular interest to Hellenistic Jews because it broke the spell of Stoic materialistic pantheism and paved the way for a spiritual concept of God, more in line with the Jewish tradition. Both the unknown author of the *Wisdom of Solomon* (first century B.C.E.) and Philo of Alexandria[1a] (c. 30 B.C.E.-40 C.E.) are greatly indebted to Posidonius.[2] But in many respects Philo pursues the Platonic trend much more resolutely, and with infinitely deeper appreciation, than Posidonius,[3] and it has been rightly said that he merits the title of "the first Neoplatonist" with greater justification than his Stoic master.[4]

The process of Hellenization—the universal characteristic of the epoch —produced, so far as philosophy is concerned, a frame of mind which was different in Alexandria from what it was in Rome. Whereas the Romans adopted the scientific and "humanist" outlook of Greek philosophy, and regarded themselves, unreservedly, as the disciples of the Greeks,[5] the Alexandrian Jewish writers, and the Orientals in general, were inclined to employ science and philosophy in the service of religion.[6] Cicero, through the mouth of Pontifex C. Aurelius Cato, refuses to be guided in matters of religion by the Stoic philosophers, and accepts his ancestral faith "even without proof."[7] Philo and his Jewish predecessors introduce philosophy into the very heart of religion, and try to uphold the authority of the Bible by claiming that the Greek thinkers were in fact the disciples of Moses.

Analogous claims were made by other Orientals such as the Egyptians and Persians.[8] The Christian Fathers were eager to repeat these claims at a time when they had to defend themselves against attacks from the Neoplatonic pagan philosophers. It was a favorite contention of theirs that Plato had been a disciple of the prophets. According to one particular legend, he had met the prophet Jeremiah during his stay in Egypt and received from him the Mosaic doctrine of monotheism.[9] Eusebius devotes the twelfth book of his *Praeparationes Evangelicae* to proving "the accord of Plato's doctrines with the oracles of the Hebrews."

The theory of the Hebraic origin of Greek philosophy persisted throughout the Middle Ages down to the Cambridge Platonists.[10] It is quoted approvingly by Judah Ha-Levi and alluded to by Maimonides.[11] Its chief historic significance lies in the fact that it enabled Christian thinkers in the early Middle Ages to "admit the pagan Plato to the realm of the *doctrina Christiana*." It can hardly be assumed that Plato would have achieved the position in Christian thought which Augustine and the School of Chartres assigned to him, without the belief that he had known and used the Scriptures.[12]

At first sight, the attitude of the Hellenistic Jewish writers, who, in addition to absorbing the dominant philosophy of the age, claimed its identity with the "deeper" meaning of the Bible, seems to be a novel one in the history of Jewish thought. In reality, it is in basic accord with the earlier tradition of Jewish Wisdom literature. It exhibits the same pattern of mind, and is in fact the continuation of the older movement on a new level.

There is an unbroken line from the canonical Wisdom literature (Proverbs, Job, Ecclesiastes) to the Wisdom of Ben Sira (about 200 B.C.E.), which the author's grandson translated into Greek shortly after 132 B.C.E., and from that work to the pseudonymous Wisdom of Solomon, which was produced a little later by a Diaspora Jew of Alexandria. While Ben Sira shows no trace of philosophic influence, the Wisdom of Solomon is considerably influenced by Posidonius's *Protreptikus*.[13] It thus represents the historic link between the earlier Hebrew Wisdom movement and Hellenistic Jewish philosophy.

The pattern of thought, which underlies the whole of postbiblical Wisdom literature, is best described as a persistent effort to equate Torah and Wisdom. Whereas the canonical writers make no attempt to interpret Wisdom (*Hokmah*)[13a] in terms of specifically Jewish religious teachings and observances—their concept of Wisdom has rightly been defined as belonging to an essentially "humanist" tradition—Ben Sira[13b] is the first to affirm the identity of Torah and *Hokmah*. When the Divine Wisdom was seeking for a place on earth where she might alight and make her home, God directed her to the Temple in Jerusalem (Ecclus. 14:9-12). "Divine wisdom and the Law are coextensive and coeternal." The national possession of Israel is "a universally and eternally valid expression of truth, because it is the word of the only God, the Creator of all."[14] The same equation occurs in the Wisdom of Solomon[14a] and the Book of Baruch (probably written after 70 C.E.), and pervades the whole of Rabbinic Torah mysticism. It underlies as a preformed structural pattern the thought of Philo as well. In endeavoring to discover the sum total of Greek wisdom in the Bible, Philo merely applies the principle that the Wisdom literature had firmly established, namely, that of the identity of Torah and Wisdom. It is a natural corollary of this theory that any true wisdom found in the possession of the heathens must derive from the Bible.

The fusion of the two streams of Greek and Jewish tradition, which characterizes Hellenistic Jewish philosophy, has its *raison d'être* not merely in the particular frame of mind just described, but also in the fact that there existed certain affinities of outlook which suggested spiritual kinship. The stern rejection, from Xenophanes onward, of Homeric mythology and anthropomorphism in the Greek philosophical schools (except the Epicureans) is relative to this point. It had found classical expression in Plato's *Republic*, which banishes mythology, chiefly on account of its unethical character.[15] The tradition is upheld by the Stoa. The older school had endeavored to bridge the gulf between philosophy and mythology by employing the method of allegorical interpretation. The younger Stoa, from Panaetius onward, rejected mythology altogether. In Posidonius's telling phrase, which Augustine was to quote almost verbally, "Homer is to blame because he ascribed human qualities to the gods rather than derive divine excellencies upon man."[16] The Septuagint does not attempt to introduce philosophic concepts into its rendering of the biblical text. But it meticulously seeks to avoid anthropomorphism.[17] Aristobulus first offered allegorical interpretations of difficult passages in the Bible, and Philo follows in this tradition. His contempt of mythology is derived as much from Platonic-Stoic "enlightenment" as from the scorn which the biblical writers pour on the false pagan gods. The very term "mythology," which for Plato still retained an air of solemnity,[18] is used by him as synonymous with fancy, lie and falsehood.[19] Whereas the Stoics could afford to criticize the allegorization of myths,[20] Philo, to whom the Bible possesses undisputed authority as a divinely inspired Book, is compelled to allegorize at least those passages which, in their literal sense, appear mythical.

Another aspect which Judaism and certain trends in Greek philosophy had in common was the notion of the "moral God." As Werner Jaeger has shown, there are many facets in Plato's approach to the Divine; but primarily it is the Socratic, *i.e.*, ethical, approach: What is the nature and unity of virtue? His answer is: The divine Good, the "measure of all things." The philosopher's life thus becomes an assimilation to the Divine standard, *Imitatio Dei*.[21]

The same can be said of the Stoic ideal of the Wise, which places the practice of virtue above theoretical knowledge, and teaches that following the "unwritten law" of nature is tantamount to following God. The younger Stoa had emphasized the need for training in the arts and sciences (the so-called "Encyclical Studies"), but, as Seneca made it clear, they were not ends in themselves but steppingstones to a virtuous life.[22]

The moral character of this teaching must have struck Hellenistic Jews —and, no doubt, Palestinian Jews as well—as fundamentally akin to Judaism. The Rabbinic *Ethics of the Fathers*, and Jewish ethics in general, though not appreciably influenced by Stoic moral philosophy, show indeed many affinities in both thought and expression.[23] Philo shows himself keenly aware of this spiritual kinship. A large proportion of his philosophy is taken up by the concept of the Wise and its implications. In one of his earliest treatises he elaborates the famous Stoic paradoxes which declare the wise to be the only free, rich, noble and beautiful. He is emphatic that the Encyclical Studies are not ends in themselves, but preliminaries to virtue, "the greatest of all themes." Like the Stoics, he describes them as "handmaids" of philosophy.[24] He accepts the Platonic-Stoic doctrine of the Four Virtues,[25] but, characteristically, adds two more, piety and humanity.[26] Of great significance to him is the notion of Natural Law. He sees in the biblical figures of the Patriarchs living embodiments of that Law, and the legislation of the Torah is to him the unfolding, in all essential details, of its principles.[27] Moreover, the "ideal state," which

Plato had outlined in his *Republic* and *Laws*, he considers to be realized in the shape of the Mosaic legislation. Here he is in complete agreement with the sentiments expressed in the *Letter of Aristeas* and in Josephus's *Antiquities*.[28]

Finally, the Platonic-Stoic belief in Divine Providence as a benevolent and just power must have impressed Hellenistic Jews as yet another evidence of spiritual kinship with Judaism. Cicero makes the point that Divine beatitude is incompatible with idleness, and Seneca in his treatise *On Providence* seeks to prove the just rulership of Divine Reason in the world. It was this belief which formed one of the main planks of the Stoic doctrine *vis-à-vis* the Epicureans, who considered the gods "a privileged class of society in the universe, yet powerless to interfere with the scheme of things."[29] In Plato's *Laws* the gods are represented as sternly just rulers of the cosmos like earthly rulers, steersmen, and guards, and the same metaphors reappear in Stoic theology. Philo, both as a Stoic and as a Jew, is unable to conceive of an idle deity. To ascribe inactivity to God is to him tantamount to blasphemy. Many of the expressions he uses in describing God's world-ruling functions are borrowed from the Platonic-Stoic vocabulary.[30]

It is the great achievement of Philo not only to have grasped the essential points of contact between Jewish and Greek thought, but to have created a metaphysical system which combined important elements of the two traditions, and paved the way for Neoplatonism. Moreover, it is due to his transformation of Platonic philosophy that, as we have noted before, "Platonism could be considered as having an affinity with Judaism or with Christianity so that 'Platonic' doctrines could be made to appear as consonant with Scripture, and passages from the Bible could be interpreted in a 'Platonic' sense."[31]

In speaking of God's transcendence, Philo sometimes uses Platonic terms. God is "the measure of all things"; "the Good and Beautiful"; "the best Being"; "the first Good"; "the sun of suns."[32] No doubt, in his interpretation, Plato's Idea of the Good was meant to be identical with God, a view which has since been held by a great many scholars.[33] But Philo seems to outbid Plato when, in other passages, he calls God "better than the Good, purer than the One, and more primordial than the Monad."[34] God's essence is unknowable, and the only statement that can be made of Him is "that He is, not what He is."[35] The biblical phrase (Ex. 3:14), "I am that I am," he interprets to mean "My nature is to be, not to be spoken; no personal name may be properly assigned to the truly Existent."[36] Through him, this verse has become a *locus classicus* for scholastic ontology. He was also the first to interpret in the sense of "negative theology" the biblical passage (Ex. 33:13 ff.) in which Moses implores God to manifest His glory, and receives the answer, "Thou shalt see what is behind Me, but My face thou shalt not see." Philo explains it, like Maimonides after him, by distinguishing between the knowledge of God's "essence" and that of his "actions."[37]

Philo's negative theology is a blend of biblical and Platonic motives. Negative theology is implied in two passages of Plato (*Parm.* 142 A; *Epist.* VII 341 C-D) which, in the Neopythagorean and Neoplatonic school traditions, were understood to refer to the supreme God.[38] The passage in the *Parmenides* reads: "The one cannot have a name or be spoken of, nor can there be any knowledge or perception or opinion of it. It is not named or spoken of, not an object of opinion or of knowledge, not perceived by any being." The similarity of this utterance of Plato's to some of the Philonic passages quoted above is striking enough. Nor is there any difficulty in assuming that the *Parmenides* passage could have served as a starting point for Philo's negative theology, seeing that it reappears with but slight variation in the Neoplatonic treatise of Pseudo-Dionysius Areopagita as characteristic of the Godhead, and has had a decisive influence on the rise of medieval mysticism.[39]

On the other hand, in calling God "better than the Good and purer than the Monad," Philo goes much beyond Plato and the Neopythagoreans. His source appears to be the Jewish prophetic teaching that God is beyond comparison. "To whom will you liken Me, that I should be equal?" (Is. 40:25).[40] Philo never fails to stress the gulf that divides the created from the Uncreated. "God has no likeness even to what is noblest of things born"; "He Himself resembles none of the things which have come into being."[41] He is the absolute, transcendent Being Which, at the same time, fills the world.[42]

The most celebrated of Philo's notions is that of *Logos*. Philo knew Plato's *Timaeus* both from the original and from Posidonius's Commentary. In his own account of creation, he adopts the figure of *demiurge*; but whereas in Plato's cosmology the pattern of Ideas, the model, in whose likeness the world is framed, is independent of the Divine Craftsman, standing as it does in its own right,[43] it now becomes the "thoughts" of the God-Creator. The Ideas become the ideas of God, a concept which can also be found in Seneca,[44] and has played an important part in philosophical speculation from Plotinus down to Augustine, Anselm of Canterbury, the School of Chartres, Malebranche and Kant. As Philo puts it, "When God willed to create this visible world He first fully formed the intelligible world, in order that He might have the use of a pattern wholly God-like and incorporeal. This 'intelligible world,' 'the universe that consisted in ideas' has 'no other location than the Divine Reason which was the Author of this ordered frame.' "[45]

But Philo apparently hesitates to describe the "intelligible world" in terms of "Divine Reason." Since it is but the ideal abstract of the visible

world and as such accessible to contemplation and knowledge, it cannot
be identical with the Mind of God, Which is assumed to be beyond human
approach. Philo, therefore, distinguishes between the hidden mystery of
God and the Divine Mind in process of creation. Posidonius had already
identified the Platonic *Ideas* with the Stoic *Logos*. Philo goes a step further
by placing the Ideas in the Mind of God; but he makes it clear that they
represent only God's relation to the world, not His essence. The *Logos*
doctrine is thus introduced not so much in order to bridge the gulf between
God and the world, as is often asserted, but rather to create that gulf.
Philo is emphatic that those who know the *Logos* know only the "Shadow"
or "Image" of God; the *Logos* is "the God of the Imperfect," and "those
who regard the Image of God, the *Logos*, as His very self are like people
who take the gleam of the perihelion for the sun or the halo of the moon
for that luminary itself."[46]

Apart from the Stoic and Platonic elements of Philo's *Logos* concept,
there is in it also the biblical notion of "angel" as well as a number of
mythological features. The figure of "divine man," which goes back to
Iranian mythology and plays an important part in Gnosis, is sometimes
associated with the *Logos* as the Image of God.[47] Of special significance
is the close affinity between the *Logos* and the biblical figure of *Wisdom*,[48]
since it illustrates the historic connection between Philo and the ancient
Jewish Wisdom literature. The question whether Philo's *Logos* may
have derived from the biblical notion of the "Word of God" has been
answered in the negative.[49] But occasionally Philo does suggest that the
"*Logos of God*" through which the world was made was the "Word of
God" in the biblical sense: "God spake and it was done"; "His Word was
deed."[50]

Echoing Plato's famous image of the Cave (*Rep.* VII 514 ff.), Philo
compares those who are unable to rise to the contemplation of the Ideas to
"dwellers in perpetual night" who "disbelieve those who live in the
daylight."[51] In terms which are borrowed from the descriptions of Eros
in the *Symposium* and *Phaedrus*, he speaks of the "winged and heavenly
yearning" for the "Forms of good" when, "smitten by its ideal beauty,"
the mind follows the archetypal pattern of all virtue and "beholds with
ecstasy its most divine loveliness." The mind of the "genuine philosopher"
is "borne upward, insatiably enamoured of all holy Natures that dwell on
high."[52] Like Plato, Philo sees the motive power of philosophic Eros
in the divine nature of the soul. But he gives this thought a biblical turn:
the Spirit of God inbreathed into man is the force that calls him up to
God. Thus Moses is "called up above" (Lev. 1:1) to behold the archetypes
whereas Bezalel merely fashions the "shadows."[53] Moreover, the Platonic
concept of Eros is blended with the biblical idea of the Love of God. The
"delight in the Lord" (Ps. 37:4) which the Psalmist experiences is

interpreted as the "ecstasy of love" and "divine frenzy" which Plato described. But whereas in Plato's view the Eros finds fulfillment only in the vision of the One pure Being to which the Mind, albeit "with difficulty," is able to rise, Philo's Love of God is an end in itself since, belonging to the order of created beings, the soul can only "love God but not behold Him." "With Lovers of God, then, in their quest of the Existent One, even if they never find Him, we rejoice, for the quest of the Good and the Beautiful, even if the goal be missed, is sufficient of itself to give a foretaste of gladness."[54]

Philo approaches the problem of "knowing God" from yet another angle. The younger Stoa had revived the Socratic maxim of "Know thyself" and interpreted the Self as the divine soul, the *daemon* in man. Then it went a stage further: "He who knows himself knows the Divine."[55] Philo gives this trend of thought a Jewish coloring: Self-knowledge reveals man's "nothingness" before God, "and the man who has despaired of himself is beginning to know Him that is."[56] But he also interprets the Socratic-Stoic maxim in a mystical sense. We have to learn "to live in the soul alone"; to migrate from body, sense and even speech in order to find God in the peace of our mind.[57] The Divine Spirit abides only in those who "having disrobed themselves of all created things and of the innermost veil and wrapping of mere opinion, with mind unhampered and naked will come to God." Their symbol is the High Priest who, once a year, in solitude enters the Holy of Holies.[58] In words and images which seem to be directly borrowed from Philo, Plotinus expresses a similar view.[59]

Philo's doctrine of the "knowledge of God" culminates in his theory of prophetic ecstasy. Plato had distinguished between three kinds of "divine frenzy": that of the prophet, the poet, and the philosopher who is transported by Eros.[60] Philo assigns the highest rank to the divine possession "to which the prophets as a class are subject."[61] The phenomenon of ecstasy—he is the first to introduce the term in its technical sense into philosophic literature[62]—can therefore be studied best in the prophet. Philo does not distinguish between the ecstatic character of early Hebrew prophecy (Nebiism) and its classical form.[62a] To him all prophecy, including that of Moses, is ecstatic. It means that "the mind is evicted at the arrival of the divine Spirit."[63] This view seems to be borrowed from Posidonius.[64] But Philo's concept has a depth of its own. Prophetic inspiration he describes as something akin to the mystical experience of illumination from above. In its most elaborate form, this view is expressed in Philo's mystical theory of the "Light Stream" which emanates from God and is perceived by the "Eye of the soul," a theory which is deeply steeped in Greco-Egyptian mythology and cannot be pursued here.[65] But the concept of an illumination from above has its root in Philo's own experience of "inspiration" which he occasionally describes with remarkable psychological insight.[66]

A matter of particular interest is Plotinus's indebtedness to Philo. Whereas it is generally admitted that the forerunners of Plotinus bear unmistakable traces of Philonic influence, scholars have been reluctant to agree that the same is the case with Plotinus himself.[67] Yet this conclusion can hardly be avoided. Numenius, who stands midway between Philo and Plotinus, knew and appreciated Philo's work. It was he who said, "Either Philo platonizes or Plato philonizes." Traces of Jewish doctrines, probably through Philo's mediation, have also been found in Ammonias Saccas, the teacher of Plotinus and Origen, whose personality seems to have impressed itself deeply on his disciples.[68] Origen is decisively influenced by Philo.[69] Should, then, his fellow student, Plotinus, have had no knowledge of the Jewish thinker, as some scholars have ventured to suggest? In fact, H. Guyot's painstaking study has revealed abundant evidence of Plotinus's indebtedness to Philo. Guyot's conclusion is that Plotinus had read Philo and made use of his writings, notwithstanding the fact that he nowhere mentions his name.[70] This view has been endorsed by Fritz Heinemann who sees in Philo the most important factor, next to Plato himself, in the evolution of Neoplatonism.[71]

Philo's share in the development of the Neoplatonic doctrine is matched, if not surpassed, by the influence he has exercised on Christian·theology. It is widely assumed that the *Logos* in the Fourth Gospel is indebted to Philo, but it may as well be that we move here in the general atmosphere of nascent Gnosis or are faced merely with a simple and straightforward exegesis of text of Genesis.[72] Philonic influence is, however, clearly attested in patristic literature, both in Greek and in Latin, where Philo is not only an accepted authority in the field of allegorical exegesis, but also highly regarded on account of his *Logos* doctrine. His influence is recognizable as early as in the Apologists of the second century C.E. and gains depth in the Christian Platonists of Alexandria (Clement, Origen). The very preservation of his writings is due to the ample use to which they were put by the Church Fathers who even came to consider their author a convert to Christianity, a legend which was propagated by Eusebius. As late as in the fourth century, St. Ambrose and St. Jerome show close acquaintance with his teachings. So numerous are the echoes and reminiscences of Philo scattered through the writings of St. Ambrose that very often successful attempts have been made to reconstruct from the works of Ambrose the much-corrupted text of Philo.[73] Literal borrowings from Philo have been found in Nemesius of Emesa (*c.* 400), and an analysis of John of Damascus's (d. *c.* 749) famous *De fide orthodoxa* leads to the same result.[74]

The question as to how far Jewish mysticism and philosophy are shaped by the legacy of Philo constitutes one of the most fascinating problems of modern research in the history of Jewish thought. It seems that Philo's influence in this respect is much wider and more effective than previously assumed. A number of Philonic motifs are echoed not only in talmudic and midrashic literature,[75] but, as Samuel Poznański has shown, extend to the Jewish sectarians in Persia and Babylonia in the tenth century c.e. The angel doctrine of Nahawandi (middle of ninth century) and of the Maghariya sect is closely akin to the *Logos* of Philonic tradition. The "Alexandrian" whose writings Karkassani records among the books of the Maghariya is identical with Philo.[76] From these circles the *Logos* concept has traveled to the early Jewish mystics in medieval Germany.[77] Moreover, traces of Philonic influence can be found in the Jewish Neoplatonists of the Middle Ages (Gabirol, Judah Ha-Levi).[78] Seeing that the cabbala is evolved chiefly from Neoplatonic sources—in some measure through the mediation of Gabirol[79]—it can be stated that Philo has a certain share in its evolution. A comparison, moreover, of the basic doctrines of cabbala and Philo's philosophy reveals striking resemblances to which Erwin R. Goodenough has drawn attention. David Neumark's endeavor to reclaim Philo as a Jewish philosopher of considerable influence on Jewish thought[80] has been increasingly vindicated.

2. MEDIEVAL JEWISH PHILOSOPHY

Medieval Jewish philosophy is an offspring of the Arabian culture, which, as a result of the Hellenization of Islam, took its rise under the Abassid caliphs in the ninth century c.e. The fascinating story of the transmission of Greek science and philosophy to the Middle Ages cannot be told here in any detail. Only the salient points need be recalled in order to help us to appreciate the character of medieval Jewish philosophy, and the role it was destined to play in that process of transmission.[1]

At the time when Saadia Gaon[1a] inaugurated medieval Jewish philosophy, the homogeneous unity of the ancient Hellenistic civilization, which had embraced the Middle Eastern and European centers of culture, had ceased to exist. It had broken up into three, more or less distinct, civilizations, *i.e.*, the Latin, Byzantine and Islamic spheres. Of the three, the one least connected with the ancient legacy of Greece was the Latin West. The sources of Greek thought available to Latin readers in the early Middle Ages were, apart from a few translations of original texts, such accounts and casual references as could be found in the works of Latin writers, like Cicero, Seneca, Macrobius and the Latin Fathers. The development of Western thought would have taken a different course had Boethius (*c.* 470-*c.* 525) been allowed to carry out his great project of translating into Latin the whole of Plato's and Aristotle's writings. Unfortunately, his execution by order of Theodoric in 524 deprived the Latin West of an opportunity that was not to recur until the thirteenth century.

The result was that medieval Christian philosophy in the Latin West remained almost exclusively dependent on the Platonic and Neoplatonic traditions which were reinforced by the authority of Augustine, the dominant figure in Latin Christianity. From the end of the Academy (forcibly closed by Justinian in 529) until John Scotus Erigena (c. 810-c. 877) there is an almost complete gap in the philosophy of the West. From the ninth century onward, the writings of Pseudo-Dionysius Areopagita give a powerful impulse to Latin thought through a series of translations reaching down to the Renaissance period. Scotus Erigena, the first Christian scholastic, bases his thought chiefly on the Neoplatonic mysticism of Pseudo-Dionysius. Then there is a further gap from Scotus to Béranger de Tours (d. 1088) and Anselm of Canterbury (1033-1109). The Christian scholasticism of the thirteenth century (Albertus Magnus, Thomas Aquinas) bears the full impress of the influx of the writings of Aristotle and of the Arabian Commentaries and is greatly indebted to medieval Jewish thought, notably Gabirol and Maimonides.

In Eastern Christianity, the legacy of Greece had remained much more alive than in the Latin West. Synesius, bishop of Ptolemais (c. 410), had been brought up in the Neoplatonic School of Alexandria, and Nemesius of Emesa is deeply steeped in Neoplatonic thought. The closing of the Platonic Academy in Athens by Justinian did not disrupt the continuity of the philosophic tradition. Not only did pagan Neoplatonists, such as Simplicius, devote themselves to the writing of learned commentaries on Aristotle—thus following a line of activity which had already been in vogue among earlier members of the school (Plutarch, Syrianus)—but Christian scholars were no less eager to develop the study of Plato's dialogues and Aristotle's lecture courses. John Philoponus (485-555) is outstanding among Christian commentators on Aristotle in the sixth century.

Moreover, Neoplatonism penetrated into Christian theological speculation through the influence of Pseudo-Dionysius Areopagita, a Christian thinker of the school of Proclus (410-485), the great pagan Neoplatonist at Athens. The pious fraud that ascribed the mystical teachings of Proclus's disciple to Paul's convert at Athens (Acts 17:34), facilitated their absorption into Christian thought. John of Damascus, the spokesman of the Eastern Church, shows himself deeply influenced by the negative theology of Pseudo-Dionysius. As he spent part of his life at the Umayyad court, it is probable that through his intermediacy negative theology was transmitted to Islamic and Jewish thought. As has been stressed by Wensinck, a great deal of Stoicism also was absorbed into the rising Islamic and Jewish philosophy through his mediation. The philosophic interest evinced by Christian scholars in Alexandria was shared by the Syriac Church, which sponsored the translation from Greek into Syriac of a large number of Greek pagan and patristic works. It is against this background of the Eastern Christian tradition in the early Middle Ages that the magnificent rise of Islamic culture must be viewed.

The Arab conquest of the Eastern centers of learning did not put an end to the continuity of the ancient civilization. On the contrary, thanks to the remarkable tolerance and generosity displayed by the Islamic rulers, it led to a powerful revival of Greek science and philosophy. Under the patronage of the Caliph Mamun (813-833), a school for translations was established in Bagdad. The Arabic Nestorian Hunain ibn Ishak, the head of the school, was possibly in personal contact with the Byzantine civilization. His excellent knowledge of Greek enabled him to base his translations on the original texts of the manuscripts, of which he possessed a large collection. In the tenth century, when the knowledge of Greek had faded in Arab lands, translations into Arabic were based on Syriac intermediate renderings. A very considerable part of the scientific and philosophic literature of classical and Hellenistic Greek thought down to the Neo-platonists was thus made accessible to the Islamic world. It included complete translations of many of Plato's *Dialogues*; Galen's *Synopsis of Plato*; practically the whole corpus of Aristotle's writings, together with their more important commentators; over a hundred medical and philo-sophic works of Galen; several Plato commentaries by Proclus, and parts of Porphyry's *History of Philosophy*.

Then there are two outstanding Neoplatonic works which made their reappearance in disguise: the "Theologia Aristotelis," a Syrian forgery, which is a recast of the last portion of Plotinus's *Enneads*; and the "Book on the Pure Goodness" (*Liber de causis*), which is based on Proclus's *Elements of Theology*.

It was inevitable that the acquisition of this vast treasure of Greek thought should initiate a period of profound scientific and philosophic activity. While the Latin West was confined to a small segment of the Greek legacy, the Islamic world, being in almost complete possession of the ancient tradition, assumed the leadership in the cultural sphere. The Jews living under Islamic rule took a prominent part in all branches of science,[2] and soon evolved a philosophic movement of their own, which persisted throughout the Middle Ages and reached down into the Renaissance period.

For nine centuries—from Philo to Saadia (882-942)—Jewish phil-osophic activity had ceased. Alexandrian Jewry had lost its creative impulse, and the Academies of Palestine and Babylonia felt little in-clination toward philosophy;[3] only faint traces of Platonic, Neopythagorean and Stoic thought, probably through the intermediacy of Philo, can be found in talmudic and midrashic literature. Even so, they proved to be of some importance for the subsequent evolution of medieval Jewish philosophy. But they do not represent any philosophic effort. What there existed of speculative endeavor in the religious field was attracted by Gnostic thought, the influence of which is reflected in apocalyptic literature, scattered talmudic and midrashic references, the ecstatic hymnology of *Hekalot* mysticism and kindred mystical tracts.[4]

The first systematic treatise of Jewish mysticism is the *Sefer Yezirah* (Book of Creation)—written probably between the third and sixth centuries —which approaches the problem of cosmology from a background of "late Hellenistic, perhaps even late Neoplatonic mathematical mysticism" combined with Rabbinic *Merkaba* speculation.[5] In the view of Leo Baeck, the book is a Jewish version of Proclus's Neoplatonic philosophy and, in a way, a Jewish parallel, in miniature, to the writings of Pseudo-Dionysius.[6] Whether or not Baeck's thesis is correct—G. G. Scholem doubts it[7]—the *Sefer Yezirah* seems to have originated from some Neoplatonic or Neopythagorean source, as is evidenced by the terminology employed; it suggests, as Scholem points out, a paraphrase of some Greek text.[8] When Jewish philosophy re-emerged in the tenth century, the authority of the book, which claimed the Patriarch Abraham as its author, was already established. The first literary attempt of the newly awakened philosophic impulse is Saadia's Commentary on the *Sefer Yezirah* (931 C.E.). It would, however, be mistaken to infer from this fact that medieval Jewish philosophy inherited the Gnostic and mystical traditions of the period intermediate between Philo and Saadia as an essential feature of its character. These traditions play some part in medieval Jewish thought, particularly when they are reinforced by similar trends in the Islamic tradition, but, on the whole, medieval Jewish philosophy is cast in a rationalistic mold.

The rationalistic bent of medieval Jewish philosophy is largely inspired by the intellectual climate of Islamic thought, but has a temper and quality of its own which derives from the rational character inherent in the Jewish religion. It must also be borne in mind that many of the problems with which Islamic religious philosophy was confronted for the first time as a result of the influx of Greek thought were not entirely new to Jewish thinkers. Judaism had already faced them, in some measure, at a previous stage in the history of Jewish thought, when it had its first experience of the Hellenistic civilization. The process of rationalization through which Islam was passing had long before left its impress on the body of Jewish thought. Thus, the nature of the Law—a problem on which the Arabian theologians fought violent battles—is defined by Saadia in accordance with an earlier talmudic distinction between rational and revelational laws, a distinction which clearly reflects the Greek concept of the Written and Unwritten Laws. Another instance is the "purification of the idea of God," which had, in Judaism, already resulted in the Philonic and targumic avoidance of anthropomorphic references to God. Here and in many other fields of speculation, medieval Jewish philosophy had only to link up with the Jewish theological tradition.[9] Moreover, the "humanist" element preserved in the canonical Wisdom literature offered some authoritative basis for speculative thought.

In its initial phase, medieval Jewish thought is not yet committed to any particular philosophic system, but reflects, with rational theology as its focal point, the influence of the various schools of Greek philosophy that had become known through the fresh translations. Its Arabic model is the movement of Kalam, which had been stimulated, to some extent, by the theological discussions in the Eastern Church, particularly by John of Damascus. As M. Schreiner has emphasized, some credit for the rise of Kalam is due to the influence of Jewish thought.[10] Through the intermediacy of Origen, the legacy of Philo plays a not inconsiderable part in the development of Kalam. As has been pointed out, John of Damascus preserved a great deal of Philonic thought. The word "Kalam" denotes, in the first place, speech, and later assumed the meaning of dogmatic theology; it is, however, significant, as Wensinck points out, that the *mutakallimun* (speakers, disputants) were by their very name characterized not as theologians but as rationalists and philosophers, which is a clear indication of the rationalistic direction that Islamic theology took from its inception.[11]

Saadia Gaon, the outstanding representative of Jewish Kalam,[11a] follows in his *Book of Doctrines and Beliefs* the lead of the Mutazilite wing of Kalam, with which the movement of Islamic Kalam gradually came to be identified. But unlike some of the Karaite[11b] adherents of Kalam (Josef al-Bassir, Joshua ben Yehudah) he is not merely a Mutazilite clothed in a Jewish garb. His dependence on the Mutazila, though far from inconsiderable, has often been overstated. He freely employs Platonic, Aristotelian, Stoic, and Neoplatonic elements of thought as they suit his trend of argument. He shows himself intimately acquainted not only with Greek philosophy, but also with Gnostic schools, Indian thought, and Christian theology. Despite his eclecticism, Saadia was able to give a powerful lead to subsequent Jewish philosophy, and to imbue it with the rationalistic and "humanist" traditions that he had absorbed through his invigorating experience of the rising Islamic culture, nowhere struggling harder to find its true expression than in the bewildering atmosphere of Bagdad in the tenth century with its immense variety of religious sects and philosophic schools.[12]

Saadia emphatically states that the doctrines of the Jewish religion can be verified by rational inquiry. There is, in his view, no conflict between Reason and Revelation. Speculative reason is able to work out, by its own independent effort, the truths of revelation. Yet revelation is necessary for pedagogical reasons. Since the process of rational inquiry involves time and is exposed to error, man has to be guided by the authority of revelation

before he is able to rely on the results of his speculation. But while defending the need for Divine Revelation, Saadia is no less insistent in his demand
that man should try to understand rationally what religion teaches him.
He implies that the duty of philosophizing is a religious commandment.
His distinction between rational and revelational laws in the Torah was
accepted by Jewish Kalam philosophers and Neoplatonists such as Josef
ibn Saddik. It was rejected, on Aristotelian grounds, by Maimonides, but
has been of considerable importance for the evolution of the doctrine of
natural law. Its identification of natural and rational law, which goes back
to the Stoa, is upheld by Thomas Aquinas and Hugo Grotius.

Saadia's arguments for Creation, which are deduced from the principles
of Aristotelian physics, follow the Kalam. By refuting the various cos-
mologies in vogue at his time and by stressing the significance of the
biblical concept of *Creatio ex nihilo*, he clearly showed the incompatibility,
at this vital point, of Jewish and Platonic-Aristotelian thought. His viewpoint was adopted by practically all Jewish philosophers in the Middle
Ages.

Equally important is his doctrine of the Divine attributes. The conception of God as Creator implies the three attributes of Life, Power and
Wisdom, which are not separate aspects of the Divine Essence, such as the
Christian notion of trinity suggests, but really one and identical with the
essence of God.

The philosophy of Kalam remained the guiding star for Oriental Jewry.
Samuel ben Hofni (d. 1013),[12*] Gaon of the Academy of Sura (Baby-
lonia) like Saadia, is deeply influenced by Kalam. The same applies to
Nissim ben Jacob, of Kairouan in North Africa, and to a lesser degree to
Hai Gaon (d. 1038), the last rector of the Academy of Pumbedita (Baby-
lonia).

The Karaites, in particular, follow in their theology the pattern of
Kalam in its Mutazilite form. As late as in the fourteenth century Karaite
Kalam is still prevalent, and reaches its culminating point in Aaron ben
Elijah, whose work, *Tree of Life*—written in 1346—attacks Maimonides
from the standpoint of Kalam.[13] It may be noted that the Latin West
became acquainted with Islamic Kalam chiefly through the account given
of it by Maimonides, who strongly rejects its principles and method of
argument. Leibnitz, *e.g.*, knew the Kalam theory of continuous creation
from Maimonides's *Guide*. In his (unpublished) dialogue, *Pacidius
Phillethes seu prima de motu philosophia*, a Mutakallimun appears at the
end of the discussion, a hymn in praise of God's continuous creation.[14]

The second phase of medieval Jewish philosophy is characterized by the
influence of the Islamic tradition of Neoplatonism, and by al-Kindi's, al-
Farabi's and Avicenna's attempts to combine it with Aristotelianism. As
Renan has shown, Aristotle's authority dates from the last phase of Neo-

platonism when, after the closing of the Academy, the Neoplatonic professors devoted themselves almost exclusively to the study of Plato's great disciple.[15] They tried to prove his concord with Plato, and this tradition is followed by al-Kindi and al-Farabi. The former, in his *Liber de intellectu*, pretends to discuss the intellect "secundum sententiam Platonis et Aristotelis"; and one of the latter's works is entitled *Concordance of Plato and Aristotle*.[16] This tendency is not confined to the medieval Islamic tradition, but is also characteristic of early Latin thought; Boethius intended to show the essential concord between Plato and Aristotle.[17]

A recent discovery, by M. Guidi and R. Walzer, of an Introduction to Aristotle by al-Kindi[18] has thrown some light on his ultimate Greek source. He is, as Walzer suggests,[19] apparently nearer to some Christian variant of Proclus's Athenian Neoplatonic school than to the Neoplatonic Christian school of Alexandria, with which al-Farabi, and through him Averroës, are ultimately connected. The introduction of Divine Revelation into an otherwise predominantly Aristotelian system of thought constitutes the main evidence for the link between al-Kindi and Proclus. There are parallels to al-Kindi's theology in Christian theologians like John of Damascus. Al-Farabi, on the other hand, had his immediate spiritual ancestors in Alexandria and is obviously nearer to classical Greek philosophy than al-Kindi. Walzer assumes his ultimate Greek source to be the Christian Neoplatonist, Synesius, who tried to reconcile philosophy and Christian faith by interpreting the dogma as "a sacred and mysterious allegory," which the philosopher need not take too seriously; he held himself free to "be a priest, fond of wisdom at home and fond of myths outdoors." His belief in the supremacy of philosophy as the final arbiter over the truths of revelation makes him indeed a forerunner of Averroës through the intermediacy of al-Farabi. Saadia, though a contemporary of al-Farabi (d. 950), is not yet touched by the Neoplatonic Aristotelianism of the Islamic thinker, nor should it be possible to derive his thought from the influence of al-Kindi.

The first Neoplatonist in medieval Jewish philosophy is Isaac ben Solomon Israeli (*c.* 850-950), whose *Book of Elements* and *Book of Definitions*—both preserved in Hebrew and Latin translations, the Arabic originals having been lost—are largely inspired by Aristotle and Galen. His definition of philosophy as *imitatio dei* follows the Neoplatonic commentators of Aristotle, and may have been adopted under the influence of Nemesius.[20] In medieval Jewish philosophy Israeli's reputation as a philosopher was considerably less than his fame as an author of medical writings. Christian Schoolmen were, however, impressed by his importance as a philosopher as well.

Of great significance in the history of both Jewish and Christian medieval thought is Solomon ibn Gabirol[20a] (*c.* 1020-1050, possibly 1070), the first Jewish philosopher in Spain. His writings became known to the Latin world through the translation of the *Mekor Hayyim* (*Fons Vitae*)[20b] by Dominicus Gundissalinus in collaboration with Avendeath, a baptized Jew of Toledo (*c.* 1090-*c.* 1165). Owing to the corruption of Gabirol's name into Avicebron or Avicembrol, he was considered by the Scholastics to have been a Christian. His philosophy is less faithful to Aristotle than al-Kindi's, al-Farabi's, and Avicenna's, and makes an original attempt to break the dualism inherent in the Aristotelian concept of the universe. Its key notions are the unity of matter as the common element subsistent to all being and the concept of form as the principle of differentiation. Fundamentally, there is no gulf between the spiritual and the material since both share in the same matter. All created beings, including the angels, are composed of matter and form. From the Will of God proceeds the dynamic activity of form and from His essence the element of matter.

Gabirol's Neoplatonism is derived chiefly from Plotinus and Proclus, most probably also from Philo. His position in the world of Arabian and Jewish thought has been rightly compared to that of Duns Scotus in Latin Scholasticism.[21] His work exercised a profound influence on the Schoolmen of the thirteenth and fourteenth centuries, notably on Albertus Magnus and Duns Scotus.[22] It also influenced Jewish Neoplatonists like Abraham ibn Ezra (*c.* 1092-1167) and the Jewish mystics of Gerona in the thirteenth century.[23] His great hymn, *The Royal Crown*, which expresses the essence of his philosophy in the language of religious exaltation has found its way into the Jewish liturgy.

The most popular of medieval Jewish thinkers is the Neoplatonist Bahya ben Joseph ibn Pakudah whose book *The Duties of the Heart* (written between 1080 and 1090) has become the standard work of Jewish moral philosophy. The "duties of the heart," such as sincerity of faith, humility, and love of God, should inspire the "duties of the limbs," *i.e.*, the ceremonial observances. There is a sprinkling of asceticism in Bahya's ideal of the devotional life, which is due to the influence of Islamic mysticism and has its ultimate source, as I. Heinemann has shown,[24] in Hermetic literature. The much-debated question as to whether or not Bahya was influenced by al-Ghazzali (1059-1111), the great Islamic philosopher and mystic, seems to be decided in the negative. The passages which Bahya has in common with al-Ghazzali are based on an earlier Christian source, as has been evidenced by D. H. Baneth.[25]

The influence of Islamic mysticism, chiefly in the form given to it by the "Faithful Brethren" of Basra, is also pronounced in the treatise *On the Nature of the Soul*, which has been wrongly attributed to Bahya, and probably belongs to about the same period. In describing the descent of the soul through the celestial spheres and zones of elements until it reaches earth and enters the body, the book shows itself to be strongly influenced by Gnostic sources, especially of Hermetic origin.[26] Similar views were expressed, within the orbit of Latin thought, by Macrobius in his Commentary on the *Somnium Scipionis* (third-fourth century).[27]

Abraham bar Hiyya, of Barcelona (beginning of the twelfth century), the first medieval Jewish philosopher who wrote his works in Hebrew, adopts the usual Neoplatonic triad of World, Soul, and Intellect, but adds to it two more stages, *i.e.*, the Worlds of Light and Dominion (Speech). The latter is possibly a variant of the *Logos*, as Julius Guttmann has suggested.[28]

Of great interest is Abraham bar Hiyya's attempt to establish a Jewish philosophy of history, which goes back for its sources to talmudic, Gnostic, Christian, and Islamic concepts. The periods of the world historic process correspond to the seven days of Creation; man's corruption through the fall of Adam has been remedied in one particular line of the descendants of the First Man, *i.e.*, the "chosen people" of Israel, in whom the rational soul is preserved in its original purity.[29] This concept is decisively influenced by the Islamic version of the Gnostic Anthropos myth, and has been adopted by Judah Ha-Levi.[30]

Joseph ibn Saddik (d. 1149) combines Neoplatonic, Aristotelian and Mutazilite teachings in his *Microcosm*, which may have been inspired by Nemesius of Emesa, the Christian Neoplatonist of the fifth century.[31]

Judah Ha-Levi, the celebrated poet[31a] and thinker (*c*. 1085-*c*. 1141), is hardly a Neoplatonist in the strict sense, and could be termed a Jewish follower of Kalam with some justification. Like al-Ghazzali, his Islamic counterpart and model, he seems to have passed through a more or less radically philosophic phase, from which he emerged as a mystic and theologian rather than a philosopher.[32] His famous dialogue, *Kuzari*, is a glowing tribute to Judaism. It bears, in the Arabic original, the title *Book of Arguments and Proofs in Defense of the Despised Religion*, and is almost contemporary with Abelard's *Dialogue between a Jew, a philosopher, and a Christian* (written about 1141). Judah Ha-Levi, like al-Ghazzali, places the intuitive knowledge of the prophet above the speculative knowledge of the philosopher. The "God of Aristotle" is the God of rational theology, a mere "First Cause"; the "God of Abraham" is the personal, living God of religious experience, the God of revelation. The prophet is endowed with a suprarational disposition which enables him to reach the "angelic" stage, and to commune with God.

It appears that at about the middle of the twelfth century the Aristotelian component of Jewish Neoplatonism became predominant, a tendency which Judah Ha-Levi's attack upon Aristotelianism was intended to combat. The first work, in which the new trend of thought found expression, Abraham ibn Daud's *The Exalted Faith*, did not appear until a few decades after *Kuzari*. But, as Julius Guttmann surmises, Judah Ha-Levi's polemic would have been pointless if the new trend toward a more consistent Aristotelianism had not been fairly strong as early as in his day.[33] It is no easy matter to draw a hard and fast line to demarcate the new Aristotelianism from the earlier type of Neoplatonism, which had also been shot through with Aristotelian elements. Both Abraham ibn Daud and Maimonides, who represent the new phase of development, still contain a great deal of Neoplatonism, if this term is at all permissible in denoting the peculiar character of early medieval thought. Raymond Klibansky has made the point that the medieval Platonic tradition as a whole is much too complex to be described indiscriminately as either Platonism, as was formerly, or Neoplatonism, as is now the rule.[34] It is much easier to distinguish between the Neoplatonic Aristotelianism of Abraham ibn Daud and Maimonides, on the one hand, and the strict Aristotelianism of Averroës, on the other.

Although Maimonides (1135-1204) was a younger contemporary of Averroës, there is no evidence that Maimonides was acquainted with the works of the Islamic philosopher at the time when he wrote the *Guide of the Perplexed*.[34a] He mentions Averroës at some later date in a letter to Samuel ibn Tibbon, but from Maimonides's previous silence it appears that the *Guide* was written "in complete ignorance of the works of Averroës." Moreover, "on all the points at issue between Avicenna and Averroës, Maimonides follows the views of the former and restates them without the slightest suggestion of his knowledge of the views of the latter."[35]

Maimonides, like his predecessor, Abraham ibn Daud (d. *c.* 1180) recognizes in Aristotle the principal philosophic authority. His proofs for the existence of God follow the Aristotelian pattern. In addition, he develops an argument, first suggested by Avicenna, which postulates, on logical grounds, a necessary being whose existence follows from its essence, and is transcendent to all contingent being. This necessary being is an absolute unity. Following the Neoplatonic tradition of "negative theology," Maimonides explains in his famous doctrine of attributes that no positive statement, except that of existence, can be made of God. Two kinds of attributes only are admitted, those of "negation," which exclude imperfections from God, and those of "action," which describe His relation to the world. The latter, which include God's moral attributes, matter most from the aspect of religion. Maimonides's conflict with Aristotle concerns the problem of Creation. The alternative between the Aristotelian doctrine of the eternity of the world and the Jewish concept of *Creatio ex nihilo* is tantamount to the choice between an impersonal God, from Whom the world emanates by necessity, and a personal God, endowed with will, Who creates the world freely. Neither of these doctrines can be rationally demonstrated, and the decision is therefore to be left to the authority of prophecy. Maimonides argues against Aristotle that the law of causal necessity which operates within the created world does not apply prior to creation. God remains in control of the physical laws of nature. The possibility of miracles is thus safeguarded, but Maimonides tends to allegorize the miracles narrated in the Bible.

The core of Maimonides's philosophy is his theory of prophecy. The prophet is superior to the philosopher, but not, as Ha-Levi had it, on account of a suprarational disposition. There exists no faculty higher than the rational, but as a result of supreme intellectual training and moral conduct a person whose mind is concentrated on "God and the angels" may receive flashes of intuition, which illumine both the rational and imaginative faculties of his soul and give it insight into metaphysical truths denied to the discursive thinking of the ordinary philosopher. The over-powering vision of the prophet requires for its expression the use of symbolic images. Hence the pictorial character of prophetic speech and the necessity to interpret it allegorically. In addition to being a perfect phi-losopher, the prophet is also the lawgiver of the ideal state, and thus represents Maimonides's version of Plato's "philosopher-king," following the precedent of al-Farabi and, ultimately, of Philo.

Maimonides's *Guide*, the most important work of Jewish philosophy, achieved a notable synthesis of Judaism and Neoplatonic Aristotelianism. It exercised a powerful influence on Jewish philosophic thought and, to some extent, also on Jewish mysticism (Abraham Abulafia),[36] although Maimonides's treatment of cosmology and theology hardly contains the mystic themes attributed to it in cabbalistic thought.[37] Through its popular presentation in his famous code (*Mishne Torah*),[37a] the essential outline of Maimonides's philosophy became accessible to large sections of the community. His statement of the "Thirteen Principles" of the Jewish faith,[37b] formulated in his Commentary on the Mishna, was the first attempt of its kind and gave rise to a prolonged discussion. It soon found its way into the Daily Prayer Book. Of considerable importance is Maimonides's influence on the Christian Schoolmen of the thirteenth century (Albertus Magnus, Thomas Aquinas, Duns Scotus).[38]

The last phase of medieval Jewish philosophy is dominated by the more radical Aristotelianism of Averroës. Maimonides's endeavor to bridge the gulf between Aristotle and the Bible by whittling down their differences had not won the day, as is evidenced by the embittered controversy that divided Jewry during the thirteenth century.[39] In the end, the orthodox opponents of Maimonides helped to swell the rising cabbalistic movement, while the rationalists accepted the lead of Averroës.

The Jewish struggle over the legacy of Maimonides's rationalism is, in a way, an echo of the great controversy that had arisen in the Christian world of the Latin West.[40] There had grown up in the university of Paris a school of Averroists, whose philosophic doctrines were considered to be contrary to the teaching of the Church. It was Thomas Aquinas's endeavor to vindicate the truths of Christianity against heretical teachings of the Averroists, and Maimonides furnished him, in some respect, with the methods to be employed in achieving a synthesis between Aristotle and the Bible. The famous altarpiece by Francesco Traini, in St. Catarina at Pisa, and many similar paintings depict the triumph of Thomas over Averroës, who lies prostrate before the Christian philosopher.[41] Characteristically enough, Averroës wears the Jewish badge upon each shoulder.

There is poetic truth in his presentation as a Jew, seeing that Jewish commentators and translators had a large share in making Averroës known to Latin Christianity. As has been pointed out by Steinschneider, the preservation of Averroës's Commentaries on Aristotle is due almost entirely to Jewish activity. Averroës's popularity among Jews is best illustrated by the fact that of his extensive writings almost all were translated into Hebrew, some of them more than once, and that a host of Hebrew commentaries were written on them.

The influence of Averroës's teachings on Jewish thought varies in degree. Isaac Albalag (thirteenth century) represents, like Siger of Brabant, and John of Jandun on the Christian side, the more extreme form of Averroism, which is known as the doctrine of the double truth. Jewish Averroists of a more moderate outlook are Samuel ibn Tibbon, the translator of Maimonides's *Guide*, and Jacob Anatoli (1194-1256), the chief representative of the Hebrew translators in Sicily, who translated Averroës into Hebrew; Joseph Caspi (1279-c. 1340); Hillel ben Samuel of Verona (d. c. 1291); Moses ben Joshua of Narbonne (d. 1362); and Judah Messer Leon (fifteenth century).

The outstanding Jewish Averroist of the late medieval period is Levi ben Gerson (Gersonides, 1288-1344), whose *The Wars of the Lord*—by its cabbalistic opponents mockingly called "The Wars against the Lord"[42] —attempts the reconciliation of Judaism and philosophy on a strictly Aristotelian basis. Gersonides abandons the Neoplatonic concept of the unity of God, which excludes positive attributes, and affirms, like Thomas Aquinas, that positive terms may be attributed to God. Creation means that the plurality of forms, which is contained in God, is released and imparted to the *prima materia*, the substratum of becoming. Gersonides thus upholds the concept of creation in Time, but not in the sense of *Creatio ex nihilo*. The activity of God is spent in the act of creation; the governance of the world is regulated by natural causality. Prophecy is knowledge of causal necessity applied to a concrete situation.

The extreme rationalism of the Averroists is made the target of attack by Hasdai ben Abraham Crescas (c. 1340-1410), which recalls Judah Ha-Levi's criticism of Neoplatonic Aristotelianism three centuries earlier. Crescas's religious philosophy is based on a *reductio ad absurdum* of

Aristotelian metaphysics as a whole. His critique of Aristotle demolishes such basic Aristotelian notions as Matter, Space and Time, and foreshadows the approaching Renaissance. Pico della Mirandola quotes him extensively, and Spinoza, possibly also Giordano Bruno, are indebted to him. Crescas's demonstration of the infinity of Space and Time renders Aristotle's proof for the existence of God (that of the "Prime Mover") invalid. But even an infinite world requires as its ground a necessary Being. Creation need not be interpreted as an act in Time, but must be understood as *Creatio ex nihilo*. Like Gersonides, Crescas admits positive attributes of God. But God is essentially not a pure intellect; He is essentially pure love. It follows that man achieves communion with God not through knowledge but through love. Prophecy is a result of such communion in love.

Crescas's successors continue more or less the Aristotelian tradition of Jewish philosophy, but the steady deterioration in the political fortunes of Spanish Jewry during the fifteenth century is reflected in a decline of the philosophic spirit and in a trend toward religious dogmatism.

Simon ben Zemah Duran (1361-1444) reverts essentially to the position of Maimonides, and resumes the discussion of "principles" of faith. He reduces them to three, *i.e.*, Existence of God, Revelation, Reward and Punishment, principles which Averroës had declared to be essential to all revealed religion, and from which, in the opinion of Duran, the whole system of Judaism could be derived.

Joseph Albo (d. 1444) makes Duran's triad the basis of an elaborate dogmatic system. His philosophy seeks to harmonize the essential elements of earlier Jewish thought, notably Maimonides and Crescas. In combining Saadia's and Maimonides's views on natural law, he distinguishes between natural, conventional, and divine laws. Hugo Grotius knew his work, and may have derived from it his distinction between rational and revelational laws.

The last great Spanish-Jewish thinker is Don Isaac Abrabanel (1437-1509), whose philosophy marks a complete return to religious dogmatism in the garb of philosophy. In his son, Judah Abrabanel (Leone Ebreo, c. 1460-c. 1521), the philosophic impulse comes to life again through his contacts with the leaders of the Platonic Academy of Florence. His *Dialoghi d'Amore*[42a] was the most successful philosophic work of the Italian Renaissance, and transmitted its spirit to other countries as well. Medieval philosophy had ignored the aesthetic elements of Plato's philosophy. In Leone's concept of the universe God is the source of both truth and beauty, and the universe a living organism animated by love. Leone's theory of knowledge is essentially Averroistic.[43]

Elijah Delmedigo (1460-1493), another Jewish philosopher of the Italian Renaissance, translated Averroës's writings, at the request of Pico della Mirandola, from Hebrew into Latin. His *Examination of the Faith* strikes a balance between the doctrine of the double truth and the philosophic interpretation of religion, as attempted by Maimonides.[44] Delmedigo is the last Jewish Averroist of importance.

From the thirteenth down to the end of the fifteenth century, Averroism had been the dominating influence in Jewish philosophy, but concurrently, Christian Scholasticism had also begun to exercise some influence on a number of Jewish philosophers, in both Spain and Italy. Hillel of Verona makes ample use of Averroës's refutation by Thomas Aquinas, without, however, following Thomas in his complete rejection of Averroës. Gersonides's scholastic method obviously emulates the procedure in vogue among Christian Scholastics. Certain Christian traits are also unmistakable in Crescas's thought, and Judah Messer Leon, too, exhibits some dependence on Christian Scholasticism. The transition of medieval Jewish philosophy from the Arabian to the Latin sphere of influence is reflected in the abandonment of Arabic in favor of Hebrew as a medium of expression for Jewish philosophy. The replacement of Arabic by Hebrew coincides with the gradual recession of Islam from Spain. A new terminology and style was created in the Hebrew tongue, which proved itself plastic enough to express in lucid and graceful terms the subtle notions and distinctions of philosophic speculation. Harry A. Wolfson has pointed to the interesting fact that Jewish thinkers, especially the commentators, introduced into the study of philosophy an attitude toward texts and a method of interpretation similar to that adoped by Rabbinic scholars toward the Talmud, and continued in the Rabbinic novellae upon the Talmud. The French school of the Tosafists, which began to flourish in the twelfth century, marked the climax of this development in the Middle Ages, and undoubtedly led to the introduction into the philosophic literature of the form of novellae upon standard texts, "resembling the talmudic novellae in their external literary form even to the extent of using the same conventional phrases by which questions and answers are introduced." Crescas's work is an instance of that type of novellae literature in medieval Jewish philosophy.[45]

While medieval Jewish philosophy, in its latest phase, is somewhat indebted to Christian Scholasticism, the latter movement owes a great deal to Jewish philosophic activity, especially to the Jewish translators who helped to make Aristotle and Arabian philosophy accessible to the Latin West. The rediscovery of the lost works of Aristotle, as well as the newly established contacts with the philosophic speculations of Arabians and Jews, revolutionized the outlook of Latin Christianity.[46] The result was the recognition of philosophic truth as independent of Divine Revelation, and the rise of Christian Averroism with its radical separation of philosophy and faith. The new development was made possible chiefly through the translations from the Arabic into Latin, a process in which intermediate Hebrew translations formed an integral part.

One must, however, not underrate the significance of the translations made by Christian scholars in the twelfth and thirteenth centuries from the original Greek into Latin. As Klibansky has emphasized, the intellectual development of the Latin West was not completely unrelated to that of the Greek world. It is most likely that the close political and economic connection between East and West from the earlier Middle Ages was accompanied by a marked influx of Byzantine ideas into the Occident.[47] Thus Greek patristic literature was translated into Latin in the twelfth and thirteenth centuries. The translation of Aristotle's *De anima* from the Greek into Latin is older than the Arabic-Latin one which was made by Michael Scot in 1217. Whereas Thomas of York interprets Aristotle invariably *secundum expositionem Averrois*—following as he does the Arabic-Latin translations—Thomas Aquinas quotes the *exemplaria Graeca*. Most of the Aristotelian works used by him had been rendered from the Greek into Latin, or had been revised, by William of Moerbeke, who had also translated Simplicius's Commentaries on some of Aristotle's works.[48]

But the important activities of the Christian translators, notably William of Moerbeke, Robert Grosseteste, and Gerard of Cremona, were amply supplemented by the works of their Jewish opposite numbers. They were in that age the chief intermediaries between the Islamic and Latin civilizations. A more detailed description of this aspect of medieval Jewish effort has been given by Charles and Dorothea Singer in *The Legacy of Israel*.[49] The motives that prompted Jewish translators were varied. We know of generous Jewish patrons of literature such as Meshullam of Lunel, who was, perhaps, the first medieval Jewish Maecenas of his kind, and of Benveniste ben Solomon ibn Labi (fourteenth century). A number of Christian rulers such as Frederick II, his son Manfred, Robert of Anjou, and Don Pedro III, sponsored translations of Greek, Arabian and Jewish works into Latin. The ultimate motive, however, was, according to Moritz Steinschneider, a genuine interest in the spread of learning,[50] and due credit must be given to the numerous Jewish translators who, through their work, saved many of the literary treasures of the past from oblivion.

3. MEDIEVAL JEWISH PHILOSOPHY IN ITS BEARING ON THE WORLD

The final disintegration of the close-knit unity of medieval Scholasticism must be considered a natural process, seeing that the elements of which it was composed were of a heterogeneous nature. Renaissance and Reformation liberate the religious spirit of the biblical tradition; Machiavelli renews the Roman concept of power; Grotius, Descartes and Spinoza rediscover, on the basis of Stoic thought, the autonomy of reason in the spheres of both practical and theoretical philosophy. This natural process, by which the three principal elements of the Latin civilization break away from their more or less artificial harmonization, has far-reaching effects on the evolution of the modern world. Human energies are set free which for centuries had been harnessed to the labors of subtle reconciliation. The abounding vitality of the Renaissance, which Burckhardt so vividly describes, is a direct result of this release of energy. Important changes take place in the social and political spheres, in the development of commerce and industry. The new discoveries and inventions of the period greatly enhance man's self-consciousness. The individual citizen begins to assert his human rights *vis-à-vis* feudal pressure and ecclesiastic regimentation. The idea of religious tolerance emerges as one of the leading concepts of the modern age.[1, 1a]

It would be idle to pretend that in this complex and universal process, which extends from the Renaissance down to the Enlightenment of the seventeenth and eighteenth centuries, Judaism, or for that matter medieval Jewish thought, played a dominant role. The inferior social and political status of the Jews in the period concerned renders any such assumption meaningless. It would, however, be equally mistaken to ignore the contribution of Judaism, and medieval Jewish philosophy in particular, to the development of the modern outlook. As we shall see, this contribution is marked and has a quality of its own. It assumes considerable depth in the religious field; many of the heterodox movements of the Middle Ages, including the Reformation in its various forms, owe a great deal to Judaism. But Jewish influence extends to the purely philosophical realm as well.

At first sight, it may seem paradoxical to attribute to medieval philosophy any significance for the evolution of modern thought. Are we not justified in contrasting medieval Scholasticism with the free spirit of inquiry that characterizes modern philosophy? In answering this objection, it may be pointed out that, notwithstanding its "modern" outlook, modern philosophy is much more indebted to medieval thought than is commonly realized. It did not, like Minerva, spring full grown—from its father's head—clad in glittering armor, and chanting a triumphant song of victory. Rather, did it arise as a result of a long process, stretching from the Renaissance down to the philosophy of Enlightenment in the eighteenth century. Throughout this period of transition and growth, the medieval legacy was never extinct; on the contrary, it formed the ever-present background of thought and exercised an appreciable influence. How considerably Descartes is shaped by Christian Scholasticism has been demonstrated by Etienne Gilson, and re-emphasized by Jacques Maritain in his fascinating book on Descartes.[2] A parallel case is Spinoza, who is as much heir to medieval Jewish philosophy as Descartes is to Christian. As Manuel Joel, Leon Roth and Harry A. Wolfson have shown—the latter with overwhelming evidence—medieval Hebrew literature is a basic element in Spinoza's thinking.[3]

With Leibnitz, the most erudite man of his century, the position is essentially the same. He is steeped in medieval thought, both Christian and Jewish. We owe to a French baron, A. Foucher de Careil, the publication of two manuscripts by Leibnitz, one containing a précis of, and observations on, Maimonides's *Guide*; the other commenting on a contemporary attempt to harmonize Spinoza and the cabbala.[4] Judging from his opening remarks in the first of the two manuscripts, Leibnitz was very much impressed by the profundity of Maimonides, of whom he says that he was "a distinguished philosopher, mathematician, physician and expositor of Holy Scripture" (*"fuit in philosophia, mathematicis, medica, arte, denique, sacrae scripturae intelligentia insignis"*). His acquaintance with both Maimonides and the cabbala are not without influence on his own philosophy, as Foucher de Careil and, more recently, Joseph Politella have shown.[5] Needless to say, he is even more thoroughly familiar with the Christian Scholastic tradition. In answering John Toland's *Christianity not Mysterious* he reverts to the Scholastic thesis that nothing is allowed in theology which is contrary to reason, but that what is above reason is not therefore excluded.[6]

Spinoza and Leibnitz are by no means isolated instances of medieval Jewish influence on seventeenth-century thought. In 1629 the appearance of Buxtorf's Latin translation of Maimonides's *Guide* (replacing the older translation by Justinian) had given rise to an intensified study of the Jewish philosopher.[7] Leibnitz drew his knowledge of Maimonides from this translation.[8] In addition to Leibnitz, Hugo Grotius, John Selden, Pierre Bayle, John Spencer, and the Cambridge Platonists read Maimonides.[9]

The cabbala, too, exercised considerable influence.[9a] As early as in the Renaissance period, cabbalistic thought had fascinated thinkers like Pico della Mirandola, the first Christian student of the cabbala, at whose suggestion Pope Sixtus IV had arranged the translation into Latin of Recanati's cabbalistic Commentaries on the Pentateuch, and of other works besides.[10] The cabbala held a special attraction for Milton, some of whose most original notions Denis Saurat has traced back to the *Zohar*. Saurat's arguments have been disputed by Martin Alfred Larson, but without venturing to pass a verdict on this very intricate problem it does appear that there is a considerable measure of evidence for Milton's indebtedness to the cabbala.[11] It also seems from Harris Francis Fletcher's work on *Milton's Rabbinical Readings* (Urbana, University of Illinois Press, 1930) that Milton made ample use of Rabbinical commentaries on Scripture.

The role of cabbala in the philosophy of the Cambridge Platonists (Henry More, Cudworth) has not yet been sufficiently clarified.[12] Ernst Cassirer, in his excellent monograph on *The Platonic Renaissance in England and the School of Cambridge* (Berlin, 1932) ignores it entirely, but there can be little doubt that cabbalistic influence was pronounced. On the other hand, one must not be misled by the use of the word "cabbala" in the works of this school, seeing that, *e.g.*, Henry More's *The Defense of the Threefold Cabbala* (London, 1662) lavishly employs that term without offering a single quotation from cabbalistic writings. His philosophy is a curious mixture of Plotinus, patristic thought, Descartes, Rabbinic exegesis and medieval Jewish philosophy. He is familiar with Maimonides, whom he calls "the most rational of all the Jewish Doctors."[13]

Of great significance is Maimonides's influence on John Spencer, whose famous work, *De legibus Hebraeorum ritualibus et eorum rationibus* (first published in Cambridge, 1685) elaborates Maimonides's historical interpretation of the ceremonial laws in the Bible. To the rationalists of the seventeenth century the ceremonial laws appeared most awkward, if not offensive. Spencer is glad to use the historical argument and thus to maintain the "wisdom" of the Divine Lawgiver. Robertson Smith said of Spencer's work that "it created the foundations of the science of comparative religion." As Julius Guttmann remarked, this title to fame can be claimed, in the first place, by Maimonides.[14] The subject excited great interest, which did not abate in the eighteenth and the early nineteenth centuries. Pierre Bayle's review of the second edition of Spencer's work (1688) thoroughly approves of the author's aim to show that one need not resort, for the solution of all difficulties, to the inscrutable Will of God, but could demonstrate the reasonableness of the ceremonial laws of the Bible by reference to historical circumstances.[15] In the eighteenth century, Moses Lowman, the author of *A Rational of the Ritual of the Hebrew Worship; in which the wise designs and usefulness of that Ritual are explain'd, and vindicated from objections* (London, 1748) seeks to apply the "principles of true religion stated by Herbert of Cherbury" to the Mosaic law in order to show "their real virtue and worth," but in fact goes back to Maimonides, whom he calls "the most learned and judicious Hebrew Doctor."[16] He also wrote *A Dissertation on the Civil Government of the Hebrews* (London, 1740).

As late as 1827, James Townley published a book entitled *The Reasons of the Laws of Moses from the "More Nevochim" of Maimonides with notes, dissertations, and a life of the author* (London). It shows how persistent was the interest in Maimonides's interpretation of biblical law. Townley quotes Clavering, bishop of Peterborough, the ardent admirer of Maimonides, who had said, "The memory of Maimonides has hitherto flourished and will continue to flourish forever." His references, in the preface of the book, to earlier publications on the subject, accessible to English readers, again show how deep and widespread was the interest in the discussion that Maimonides had started. He mentions, apart from

Lowman, Fergus's *On the Reasonableness of the Laws of Moses*; Michaelis's *Commentaries on the Laws of Moses* (4 vols., translated from the German by Smith); and Woodward's *On the Wisdom of the Egyptians*, which tries to refute the opinions of John Spencer.[17]

A great deal of medieval Hebrew literature had been translated into Latin, and thus made accessible to a wider public of scholars. As an interesting example we may quote the edition both of the Hebrew original and of its Latin translation of Maimonides's *Hilkot Aboda Zara* under the title *R. Mosis Maimonidae De Idololatria Liber, cum interpretatione Latina & Notis Dionysii Vossii* (Amsterdam, 1641). But it appears that the knowledge of Hebrew among scholars and philosophers was fairly widespread. The humanists of the Renaissance had rediscovered not only the Greek, but also the Hebrew language. In the seventeenth century it was quite fashionable to quote from Hebrew Rabbinic and philosophic literature in the original language. The works of Hugo Grotius and John Selden are steeped in Hebrew learning. The same applies to Paul Fagius, Sebastian Muenster, Joseph Scaliger, John Buxtorf, Wilhelm Schikard and others.[18] Wilhelm Schikard's *Mishpat ham-Melek, Jus Regium Hebraeorum, e Tenebris Rabbinicis erutum & luci donatum* (1625) is another instance of interest in the biblical legislation, and betrays great Hebrew erudition.

Rather significant, from a philosophic point of view, is William Wollaston's *The Religion of Nature Delineated* (London, 1722). The book, whose first two editions appeared anonymously, ran into eight editions, and enjoyed an exceptionally wide circulation. Queen Caroline, who held the author in great esteem, commissioned John Clarke to translate its learned notes with their quotations in Latin, Greek and Hebrew into English. A French translation of the work by Garrigne appeared at The Hague in 1726.[19] This scholarly and well-reasoned book, which shows also great gifts of literary grace, is in very large measure influenced by medieval Jewish philosophy, particularly by Maimonides. The "Religion of Nature" which it advocates is but a replica of Maimonides's negative theology, but makes also ample use of other Jewish writers, such as Saadia, Abraham ibn Ezra, Joseph Albo, and medieval commentators as well as talmudic and midrashic sources. The notes abound in Hebrew quotations side by side with quotations from Plato, Cicero, and Chrysostom; the latter's hatred for the Jews, so violently expressed in his Sermons, did not save him from being cited in close proximity with Jewish writers.

The foregoing literary survey will have made it plausible that acquaintance with medieval Jewish thought in the postmedieval period down to the nineteenth century was significant enough to influence the development of philosophy. The next question we have to answer concerns the nature of that influence.

Wilhelm Dilthey sees the two principal aspects of the evolution of modern thought in what he terms European pantheism, on the one hand, and the idea of a universal, natural religion, on the other. In masterly fashion, he traces the history of European pantheism from Nicholas Cusanus over Giordano Bruno to Spinoza and Hegel, Schelling and Goethe. In even greater detail, he describes the line of development that leads from the "universal theism" of the Renaissance philosophers to the Natural Law School (Grotius and Selden) and the movement of Deism in the seventeenth century, and, further down, to the concept of natural religion in the eighteenth century philosophy of Enlightenment. Dilthey is emphatic that in both these lines of development great influence is exercised by the legacy of Stoic thought which the Renaissance had rediscovered.[20] He may have overrated the role played by the Stoic revival.[21] There can, however, be little doubt that from Francis Petrarch (b. 1304) onward the awakening interest in human character and temperament creates a literature which goes back for its model to the Roman Stoics (Cicero, Seneca, Marcus Aurelius, Epictetus). From Petrarch and the Florentine writers, the movement spreads to Vives, Cardano, Scaliger, Telesio, Montaigne, and reaches its climax in the scientific anthropologies of the seventeenth century.

It is from this literature with its new awareness of the human will and that will's immanent power that the philosophy of the age receives its most stimulating impulse. It strengthens the belief in the moral autonomy of man, and helps to disrupt the Christian dogma of original sin; it stands diametrically opposed to the asceticism and defamation of the body which characterizes the Middle Ages. To live in the full consciousness of power and beauty, to be sensitive to the passions and affections operating in private and political life, this was the overwhelming experience that manifested itself in the new literature on man.[22] It went hand in hand with a pantheistic trend in metaphysics as we meet it in the Platonism of the Florentine Academy. In all this development a great deal of Stoicism asserts itself. It penetrates the Platonism of the age, and communicates to it the monistic and pantheistic tendency of the Stoa. It infuses the spirit of humanism into the general outlook of the period. In a way, the whole movement represents a revival of ancient paganism, all the more pronounced for its rehabilitation of Epicurus. Thinkers such as Giordano Bruno and Laurentius Valla are marked by a decidedly pagan outlook, not to speak of Machiavelli.[23]

But whilst Dilthey is justified in stressing the Stoic and generally pagan background of Renaissance philosophy, it must be pointed out that the transition from the Scholastic philosophy of the Middle Ages to modern thought is not one from Christianity to paganism. The philosophy that emerges as the new European philosophy is still Christian, though shorn of some of the dogmatic elements of Christianity. As Erich Przywara remarked, the absolutist philosophies of the modern age are "de-theologized theologies." Hegel's system cannot be divorced from his theological background.[24] Descartes's rationalism is a kind of secularized Scholasticism,[25] and Spinoza's logical schematism is "shot through and enlivened by a religious awe in presence of the Infinite, which must be traced, not so much to his system and its effect, as to his upbringing in a Jewish family and to a transference to *Deus-substantia* of the psychological attitude that an orthodox Jew would manifest toward the Creator-God of Judaism."[26] Franz Rosenzweig put the position in a nutshell when he said that Descartes, Leibnitz, Kant and Hegel were no longer pagan Greek philosophers, but Christian heretics. In them, a new, postmedieval, synthesis between biblical religion and Greek philosophy is achieved.[27] Our thesis is that this new humanist synthesis is decisively aided and promoted by the influence of medieval Jewish philosophy, in which the humanist trend had been much stronger than in Latin Christianity.

The humanist element, as represented by the Stoic tradition, which the Renaissance rediscovered for the Latin West, had been at the bottom of medieval Jewish philosophy right from its inception. One of the essential differences between Jewish and Christian medieval thought lies in the fact that, while both share in the Neoplatonic and Aristotelian traditions, the Stoic legacy had been much more alive in Judaism than in Latin Christianity. It had remained a potent factor also in the Eastern, Greek Church, as is evidenced by the writings of Clement, Origen, Nemesius of Emesa, and John of Damascus; all of whom are greatly indebted to Philo. It is due to the Philonic heritage that the humanist tradition was much stronger in the Eastern than in the Western Church.[28] John of Damascus seems to have exercised some influence in the rise of Arabian Kalam, and in this way, besides other channels, Stoic notions may have made their entrance into Islamic theology and philosophy.[29] It was S. Horovitz who first drew attention to the Stoic elements in Kalam,[30] and the matter is at present (1946) being further investigated.[31] The evidence available is enough to suggest that Stoicism played a decisive role in the evolution of Islamic philosophy. Medieval Jewish Scholasticism which takes its rise from the Arabian Kalam, bears, from the outset, eloquent testimony to this fact.

That medieval Jewish philosophy is influenced by the pantheistic trend of the Stoa can hardly be denied. We know that the Philonic *Logos* plays some part in Gabirol's and Judah Ha-Levi's thought.[32] The affinity of Philo's *Logos* to the Stoic *Logos* is obvious, and it appears that the pantheistic outlook which informs Gabirol's attack upon Aristotle is inspired not merely by the intrinsically Jewish concept of unity, but by Stoicism as well. Gabirol sees in matter the matrix of all being, both corporeal and spiritual.[33] It is interesting that, while Duns Scotus adopted his notion of *materia universalis*, Roger Bacon rejected it as leading to pantheism.[34] There is some truth in this observation, but remarkably enough, medieval Jewish thinkers such as Abraham ibn Ezra[35] and the mystics of Gerona, showed themselves amenable to this pantheistic trend of thought, which also dominates some of the cabbalistic systems.[36] As Gerhard Scholem remarks, Spinoza could have claimed Moses Cordovero as his spiritual ancestor.[37] It is the Stoic legacy, in addition to its Neo-platonic tradition, that is largely responsible for the monistic outlook of cabbala. Renaissance Neoplatonism differs from original Neoplatonism chiefly on account of the influence of the cabbala. The Renaissance view that matter, the flesh and nature are not a degradation, but an expression of the Divine, is first brought forward by Pico della Mirandola as derived from cabbalistic thought.[38]

In this connection, mention must be made of a further contribution of medieval Jewish philosophy to the emergence of the modern view of the universe. Giordano Bruno rediscovered the infinity of space, and thus helped to lay the foundations of the new European pantheism. He was preceded by Hasdai Crescas (*c.* 1340-1410), whose critique of Aristotle anticipates, in all essentials, the Renaissance view.[39] Crescas's arguments are largely determined by his immanent criticism of the absurdities to which Aristotle's concepts of matter and space lead. But they are also guided by the influence of positive Jewish teaching. He quotes the famous Rabbinic dictum which calls God "the Place of the World,"[40] an utterance which Philo and, following him, John of Damascus, had paraphrased, and which played an important part in cabbala.

Two things are implied in this concept. It breaks with the idea of God's transcendence in a spatial sense, so characteristic of the medieval view of God beyond the spheres; and it gives a new meaning to space as a metaphor for the Infinite. The infinity of God becomes the symbol of space. It is in this sense that Newton understood the Rabbinic utterance that had become known to him through the Cambridge Platonists.[41] His famous phrase which describes space as *sensorium Dei* thus goes back to Jewish influence. Space is no longer a mere attribute of body or motion. Newton's absolute space has since been replaced by Kant's phenomenal space and by the functional space of modern physics, but this development was initiated, or at least heralded, by Crescas's critique of Aristotle, which was ex-tensively quoted by Pico della Mirandola, and probably known to Giordano Bruno.[42]

The Stoic element in medieval Jewish thought is even more pronounced when we come to consider the medieval Jewish contribution toward the development of the Natural Law School and of the modern view of religion. The idea of natural law and natural religion is deeply ingrained in medieval Jewish thought. Saadia declares that human reason is able to work out the truths of revelation, by its own independent effort, provided it avoids the pitfalls of impatience and error. There is no essential difference between the truths of reason and those of revelation. The problem is thus not so much one of reconciliation as one of explaining why revelation is at all necessary. Of his three answers to this question, the most significant is the one which assigns to revelation a pedagogical function; it foreshadows Lessing's theory of revelation as an educational force in the history of the human race.[43] Saadia's view is influenced by the Kalam concept of natural religion (fitra) which, in turn, goes back to Stoic sources, as has been shown by Arent Jan Wensinck. It is reason, divinely implanted in man, that enables him to work out his own salvation.[44]

Saadia's concept of *rational laws* as distinct from *revelational laws* arises from the same consideration.[45] It is adopted not only by the Jewish followers of Kalam, but also by Jewish Neoplatonists like Joseph ibn Saddik.[46] Its rejection by Maimonides is in line with the Aristotelian tradition which reserves the aspect of rationality to theoretical truths only.[47] As Leo Strauss has shown, Judah Ha-Levi, too, admits the existence of a law of reason as the framework of every code, and identifies it with the law of nature. It includes the indispensable minimum of morality required for the preservation of any society, and the demands of natural piety as well.[48] Joseph Albo, toward the close of the medieval period, speaks of "two divine laws existing at the same time," the reference being to the Noachic and Mosaic revelations. With the Talmud he affirms that "The pious of all nations have a share in the world to come."[49] No doubt, the biblical concept of the Noachic laws with its implication of a basic morality common to all mankind greatly facilitated the acceptance by medieval Jewish thinkers of the Stoic notion of natural law.

It is not surprising that the evolution of the idea of natural law and religion in the sixteenth and seventeenth centuries should have followed the Stoic pattern, as Dilthey emphasized, seeing that medieval Jewish philosophy had preserved the Stoic legacy so effectively. It is no mere coincidence that the elaboration of natural law by Grotius and Selden goes hand in hand with biblical exegesis and makes frequent reference to medieval Jewish sources. Grotius quotes Saadia's distinction between rational and revelational laws, but seems to attribute it to Maimonides.[50] He knew Albo, and may have derived his knowledge from that source.[51] What seems to have most impressed both him and Selden is the tolerant outlook implied in the concept of the Noachic law. "Among the Hebrews there were always living some strangers, persons devout and fearing God. ... These, as the Hebrew Rabbis inform us, were obliged to observe the laws given to Adam and Noah, to abstain from idols and blood, and other things that were prohibited; but not in the same manner to observe the laws peculiar to the Jewish people."[52]

Selden, in the preface to his great work, *De Jure Naturali et Gentium, juxta Disciplinam Ebraeorum, Libri septem* (1665), draws attention to the novelty, introduced by him, of identifying the *Jus Naturale et Gentium* with the Noachic laws. The frontispiece of the book shows a group of bearded men, one of whom, obviously a Jew, wears headgear. The group is assembled round an altar of stone which bears the Hebrew inscription, *Mizvot Bene Noah* ("the commandments for the descendants of Noah"). Two tablets of stone are leaning against the altar, the one containing the First, the other the Second Commandment. The Jew points with his finger to the tablet, on which the words *Lo Yihyeh Leka* ("Thou shalt have no other gods besides Me") are clearly visible. He seems to insist that in addition to the seven Noachic laws the concept of the Unity of God is entitled to universal acceptance.

One may say that the frontispiece chosen by Selden is symbolic of a trend of thought that can be traced throughout the periods of the Renaissance and Enlightenment. The universal theism and, arising from it, the concept of natural religion draw much of their inspiration from Jewish sources. Nicholas Cusanus opens the long and impressive series of humanists who advocate a universal religion of reason. As we shall see, in most of them medieval Jewish thought represents an important element. His adoption of Maimonides's doctrine of negative attributes compels Cusanus to give a new interpretation to the Christian concept of trinity as denoting not the essence, but the activity of God.[53] This transformation of the Christian dogma enables Cusanus to plead for a universal religion; he feels that both Jews and Mohammedans could accept his modified notion of trinity. In his *De pace fidei*, he claims that all religions are essentially one.

Georgios Gemistos Plethon (1385-1450), the spiritual begetter of the Florentine Academy, radically upholds the unity of God, and rejects the doctrine of trinity outright. His concept of the Divine Will is influenced by Gabirol. As Gennadios reports, he was a disciple of the Jew Elissaios. His religion of humanity has many affinities to Judaism.[54] His avowed aim was "the foundation of a universalist theism as a new religion, different from Christianity."[55]

Marsilius Ficinus, the leader of the Florentine Academy, is likewise free from dogmatism, and deeply touched by medieval mysticism, including cabbala. He knew Gabirol, and his concept of love, in which Platonic and biblical motifs are blended, may owe some inspiration to Crescas.[56]

Pico della Mirandola, tutored in medieval Jewish thought by Elijah del Medigo, and introduced into cabbala by Johanan Aleman, sees in cabbala a confirmation of Christianity; but, in fact, little is left of Christian dogmatism in his universalist theory of salvation through knowledge of God.[57]

It is in this atmosphere of humanism that Leone Ebreo, the Jewish Renaissance philosopher, finds his spiritual home. Had he remained in Spain, where Catholic Christianity was firmly entrenched, he would probably, as Carl Gebhardt suggests, have shunned closer contact with the Gentile world. In Italy he entered into an environment that was dominated, not by exclusiveness, but by a keen desire to absorb the humanist ideas of ancient paganism and of Jewish as well as Islamic thought. In his *Dialoghi d'Amore*, the most successful literary work of the Renaissance —it was translated into several languages and transmitted the spirit of the age to the whole of Europe—Leone boldly underlines the fact that he writes as a Jew for the non-Jewish world; something revolutionary, and surely indicative of the new universalism that the Renaissance had created.[58]

In France, Jean Bodin had a deep understanding of Judaism, and a good knowledge of medieval Jewish thought.[59] He lavishly quotes Philo, Saadia, Maimonides and other Jewish thinkers. In 1593 he wrote his *Hetaplomeres* which purports to be a religious disputation in Venice between a Catholic, a Lutheran, a Reformer, a Jew, a Mohammedan, a representative of natural religion, and a pagan universalist. Both Solomon, the Jew, and Toralba, the spokesman of natural religion, do credit to Judaism. Solomon is a full-blooded Jew, convinced of the superiority of Judaism; stressing the unity and incorporeality of God; and placing the emphasis on practical morality rather than on theology. Toralba represents natural religion in terms of the Adamitic and Noachic revelations. He rejects the Christian dogmas of incarnation and trinity. He subscribes to Solomon's objections against the dogma of original sin. Thus, in Bodin's view, Judaism and natural religion go very well together.

It is not clear which of the conflicting religions Bodin accepted for himself. Dilthey thinks that he suspended judgment, and was prepared to recognize the relative truth of each religion, provided it fulfilled the condition of tolerance. Readers of the *Hetaplomeres* in the seventeenth century, however, accused Bodin of being inclined toward Judaism. His treatment of Solomon is indeed exceedingly sympathetic, and Judaism is portrayed as much more consistent than Christianity.[60]

The universal theism of the Renaissance was attacked by the Reformation. Luther vigorously renewed the Christian dogma of original sin and the exclusiveness of the Christian claim to holding the key to salvation. He denounced Erasmus's courageous plea for the freedom and essential goodness of the human will. But the evolution of the modern spirit could no longer be suppressed. The development of modern thought follows in the footsteps, not of Luther, but of Erasmus, Reuchlin, and Sebastian Franck.[61] They are the heralds of the philosophic movements of the

seventeenth century; and they are shaped by the legacy of the Renaissance
in which so much of the biblical and medieval Jewish heritage had come
to life again. From Erasmus there goes a straight line to Coornhert, the
great Dutchman who helped to make Holland the home of freedom of
conscience and speech; to the heterodox movements of Socinianism and
Arminianism, and to the Deists.[62]

Another school of modern speculative theology, which culminates in
Friedrich Schleiermacher, arises from the mystical tradition of medieval
and Renaissance philosophy,[63] and is also somewhat indebted to medieval
Jewish thought, seeing that its spiritual ancestors (Eckhart, Cusanus)
were influenced by Maimonides.[64] It is inspired by the same universalist
theism which we met in the Renaissance.[65]

The sixteenth and seventeenth centuries are filled by a longing for
religious peace and tolerance, for the establishment of natural religion,
and for freedom of conscience.[66] But the hopes cherished for the establishment of a universal religion of reason remained unfulfilled. The heterodox
movements suffered defeat. The Cambridge Platonists were unable to
stem the advance of Puritanism and orthodox Calvinism. Nevertheless,
Cassirer assures us, the labors of these thinkers did not remain without
result; they paved the way for the "Enlightenment" of the eighteenth
century, in which the struggle between Luther and Erasmus was resumed
and decided in favor of the latter.[67] The weapons for this struggle had
been forged in the seventeenth century. Bayle's Dictionary became the
arsenal of the whole philosophy of Enlightenment. Bayle was emphatic
that religion was primarily morality, and that the literal sense of the Bible
must be discarded if it offends against the moral sense.[68] This seems a
modern version of Maimonides's exegetical rule that Scripture must be
interpreted in conformity to reason. Bayle knew Maimonides, whose
doctrines of free will and providence he quotes.[69] Bayle's work is followed
up by Voltaire, who declares that religion is to be judged according to its
moralizing influence, and postulates tolerance as "the fundamental claim
of reason" and "the very essence of the philosophic spirit."[70]

A similar tendency prevails in English Deism. John Locke attempts to
prove the *Reasonableness of Christianity*. Toland's *Christianity not Mysterious* and Tindal's *Christianity as Old as the Creation* make the point
that the essential criterion for the genuineness of any revelation is its universality and independence of time and space. Universality belongs to
the moral law only. Religion is the knowledge of our moral duties *qua*
divine laws. The primacy of practical reason is the guiding principle in all
these moralistic interpretations of religion, a tendency which may have been
fostered from Jewish sources. Maimonides's negative theology culminates
in the idea of God as the Divine standard for man's practical duties. In
the famous last chapter of the *Guide*, the "hidden God" of the mystic

becomes the "revealed God" of the moralist. We do not know the essence of God, but we know His moral attributes. Ultimately, the God of theology and the God of ethics are one, but as Maimonides's thesis implies, the idea of God as the "moral God" is meaningful in itself. The significance of morality is independent of metaphysics. This separation, in a sense, of ethics from ontology is the first step in a direction which was to be followed by the philosophers of modern Enlightenment down to Kant.

The influence of Deism was decisively broken by Hume's analysis of human nature, which destroyed the rational basis of natural religion. According to Hume, the *raison d'être* of religion is neither logical nor ethical, but psychological; religion arises from the emotional states of hope and fear and other psychic phenomena which lie at the root of even the higher religions. Natural religion has thus to be discarded; what remains is, in the phrase which forms the title of Hume's book, a "Natural History of Religion."[71]

This radical attack upon the rationality of religion did not make its influence felt during the eighteenth century; least of all in Germany, where the influence of Leibnitz's harmonizing tendency prevailed. It left room for the claims of both reason and revelation. Leibnitz, as we have noted before, knew and admired Maimonides, whose synthesis of faith and reason he must have felt to be akin to his own trend of thought.

Moses Mendelssohn follows in the footsteps of Leibnitz. The basic ideas of religion—the existence of a personal God and the immortality of the individual soul—are universal possessions of mankind by dint of their reasonableness. They need not wait for revelation to be announced, since they are manifest at all times and everywhere. In his famous phrase, Judaism is not a revealed religion, but a revealed law. Mendelssohn's importance as an apostle of tolerance in the eighteenth century is considerable, and enhanced by his friendship with Lessing, who essentially shared his outlook. The difference between him and Lessing concerns the nature of reason in relation to history. Mendelssohn believes in the constancy and immutability of reason; Lessing holds it to be dynamic, not static. It is only in the historical process that the fullness of reason manifests itself. Man's failures are necessitated by the dialectic nature of the historical process, and it is for this reason that we must be tolerant and sympathetic toward them.[72]

While Lessing is heir to the humanist tradition and a herald of Hegel, Mendelssohn is in intimate touch with both the humanist tradition and the legacy of medieval Jewish thought, particularly Maimonides. It is a testimony to the persistence of Maimonides's influence that Moses Mendelssohn could consider himself a disciple both of the medieval Jewish thinker and of the rationalists of his period. An interval of almost three centuries separates Mendelssohn from the close of medieval Jewish philosophy. During that long interval Jewish philosophic activity had almost completely ceased. Yet when, after this period of silence, broken only by Spinoza, Mendelssohn opened the new era of modern Jewish philosophy, he took up his position in a manner which suggested that he was in complete accord with the tenor both of his time and of medieval Jewish philosophy. That he was able to do so is in large measure due to the influence that medieval Jewish philosophy, posthumously, as it were, had exerted on the evolution of modern thought.

Our analysis would be incomplete if we omitted reference to Spinoza's great contribution to European thought which began to exercise its influence from the late eighteenth century onward. The revival of interest in Spinoza in the nineteenth century means that a great deal of the medieval Jewish legacy which he preserved came to be appropriated by modern thought. The "Jewishness" of Spinoza consists in much more than in his knowledge of medieval Jewish philosophy and the influence it had on the processes of his thinking. It is of the very essence of his approach to the problems of philosophy. Santayana hardly exaggerates when he calls Spinoza's pantheism a faithful expression, in logical terms, of the biblical concept of the omnipotence of God.[73]

There is at work in Spinoza's thought a Jewish passion for unity which the medieval systems had failed to satisfy. As H. A. Wolfson has shown, the medieval attempt to derive the material world from a God wholly spiritual, can hardly be regarded as successful.[74] Spinoza certainly refused to regard it as such, and although his concept of *Deus sive Natura* destroys the biblical notion of the personality of God, it preserves the religious fervor of the biblical spirit. As Frederick Pollock put it, "God has not been reduced to nature, but Nature exalted to God."[75] Moreover, in full conformity with Judaism, Spinoza stresses the activity of God. "It is as impossible for us to conceive of God as non-existing as to conceive of him as not acting" (Eth. II, 3 sch.). It is this concept of God as the active source of all things, as the power that pervades and animates the universe, which so deeply impressed Jacobi, Herder and Goethe.

There has been a great deal of controversy as to the indebtedness of Goethe to Spinoza. But dispute could only arise through a mechanistic interpretation of Spinoza's system, an interpretation which is historically wrong and certainly in flagrant contradiction to Herder's and Goethe's views of Spinoza.[76] They rightly saw in Spinoza's Substance the *ens realissimum*, the active power of the universe. They welcomed enthusiastically the radical pantheism of this new "world religion," as Jacobi termed it, as an expression of the monistic trend of the age. Neither Descartes's nor Leibnitz's pluralistic systems could satisfy the overwhelming yearning for unity that had taken hold of the post-Kantian schools of Idealism. Both Hegel and Schelling are deeply influenced by Spinoza.

There is yet another aspect of Spinoza's Jewish quality. He comes to philosophy, as Leon Roth observes, not from physical science or mathematics or logic, but from the problem of conduct as an eminently practical problem.[77] He is primarily a moralist, and for that matter, a Jewish moralist. His saying that "Blessedness is not the reward of right living, but the right living itself" is reminiscent of a famous passage in the Rabbinic *Ethics of the Fathers*.[78] His advice not to pursue the things perishable—riches, honor, sensual pleasures—but to love the object that is eternal and infinite, recalls a well-known passage at the end of Maimonides's *Guide*. Spinoza's concept of *Amor Dei Intellectualis* derives from the same source. Like Maimonides, Spinoza affirms that man is the more perfect the greater the object of his knowledge and love, a phrase which seems to be echoed in a beautiful utterance of Kierkegaard: "Not one shall be forgotten who was great in the world; but each was great in his own way, according to the greatness of the things he loved. For he who loved himself became great for himself, and he who loved others became great through his devotion, but he who loved God became greater than any of these."[79]

Spinoza's ethics has met with fierce opposition, and was rejected by Herbart and others as irreconcilable with the moral consciousness. But Nietzsche showed deep insight into the Jewish character of Spinoza's attitude when he remarked that Spinoza had restored to the world its innocence.[80] Spinoza's view is the complete antithesis to the doctrine of original sin, which from Augustine over Luther to Pascal, Kierkegaard and Karl Barth has dominated the Christian consciousness.

NOTES

[1] Cf. Julius Guttmann, *Die Philosophie des Judentums* (Munich, 1933), pp. 9-11; Felix Weltsch, "Mahi Pilosofiah Yehudit?" in *Eyoon,* ed. S. Ucko, Vol. I (Jerusalem).

[2] Cf. Hermann Cohen, *Die Religion der Vernunft aus den Quellen des Judentums* (Leipzig, 1919).

[3] Cf. E. Troeltsch, *Gesammelte Schriften*, IV (1925), 820-821; Albert Lewkowitz, *Das Judentum und die geistigen Stroemungen des 19. Jahrhunderts* (Breslau, 1935). On the "Hebrew Consciousness" as an essential element of Christianity cf. John MacMurray, *The Clue to History* (London, 1938).

[4] Cf. Samuel Alexander, *Space, Time and Deity* (1920); *Spinoza and Time* (1921).

[5] Cf. Nathan Soederblom, *The Living God* (Oxford University Press, 1939), p. 311, n. 1.

I

[1] Cf. W. W. Jaeger, *Nemesios von Emesa,* Quellenforschungen zum Neuplatonismus und seinen Anfaengen bei Poseidonios (Berlin, 1914).

[[1a] Cf. Ralph Marcus, "Hellenistic Jewish Literature," this work, Vol. II, pp. 73 ff.]

[2] Cf. I. Heinemann, *Poseidonios' Metaphysische Schriften,* I (Breslau, 1921), II (1928).

[3] Cf. I. Heinemann, in *Monatsschrift fuer Geschichte und Wissenschaft des Judentums* (Breslau), Vol. 64, (28), 1920, pp. 101-122.

[4] Cf. F. Heinemann, *Plotin, Forschungen ueber die plotinische Frage, Plotins Entwicklung und sein System* (Leipzig, 1921), p. 8.

[5] Horace's famous line (*Epist.* II, 156-157) is typical of the Roman attitude in this respect.

[6] H. H. Schaeder, "Der Orient und das griechische Erbe," in *Die Antike*. ed. W. W. Jaeger (Berlin, 1928).

[7] Cicero, *De natura deorum*, III, ii; cf. K. Kerényi's interpretation of this passage in *Die antike Religion* (Amsterdam, 1942), pp. 123-126.

[8] Cf. Theodor Hopfner, "Orient und griechische Philosophie," in *Beitraege zum "Alten Orient,"* No. 4 (Leipzig, 1925).

[9] Cf. Hopfner, *loc. cit.*, p. 8, n. 1.

[10] Cf. Solomon Munk's article in *Dictionnaire des Sciences Philosophiques*, ed. A. Franck (Paris, 1875), II, 834 ff.; J. Burnet, *Early Greek Philosophers* (London, 1920), pp. 17-19.

[11] Cf. Kuzari, I, 63, II, 66; *Moreh Nebukim*, I, 71.

[12] Cf. Raymond Klibansky, *The Continuity of the Platonic Tradition during the Middle Ages* (London, 1939), p. 34.

[13] Cf. I. Heinemann's work quoted above, I, 136 ff.

[13a On *Hokmah* and the Wisdom literature, cf. Robert Gordis, "The Bible as a Cultural Monument," this work, Vol. II, pp. 28 ff.]

[13b Cf. Elias J. Bickerman, "The Historical Foundations of Postbiblical Judaism," this work, Vol. I, pp. 97 ff.]

[14] Cf. J. Coert Rylaarsdam, *Revelation in Jewish Wisdom Literature*, (Chicago, 1946), p. 38; chapters I and II of this book give a valuable survey of the historical development of Jewish Wisdom literature.

[14a Cf. Marcus, *op. cit.*, pp. 67-69.]

[15] Cf. W. W. Jaeger, *Paideia, The Ideals of Greek Culture*, II (Oxford, 1944), pp. 213, 217.

[16] Cf. I. Heinemann, *loc. cit.*, p. 117; Augustine, *Confessions*, I, 16.

[17] Cf. J. Freudenthal, in *The Jewish Quarterly Review* (London), Vol. 2, 1890, pp. 205 ff.

[18] Cf. Kerényi, *loc. cit.*, p. 18.

[19] Cf. *De Cher.*, 125; *De Gig.*, 58-59; *De Post*, 2-9.

[20] Cf. Cicero, *De natura deorum*, III, xxiv ff.

[21] Cf. Jaeger, *loc. cit.*, p. 415.

[22] Cf. I. Heinemann, *loc. cit.*, p. 76, n. 2.

[23] Cf. J. Bergmann, "Die stoische Philosophie und die juedische Froemmigkeit," in *Judaica, Festschrift zu Hermann Cohens Siebzigstem Geburtstage* (Berlin, 1912), pp. 145-166.

[24] Cf. *De Congr.*, 11 ff.; I. Heinemann, *op. cit.; Monatsschrift*, Vol. 64 (28), 1920, pp. 18 ff.

[25] Cf. *De Mut.*, 153; *Leg. All.*, L. 63.

[26] Cf. *Philo*. Loeb Classical Library, ed. F. H. Colson-G. H. Whitaker, VIII, x-xi. It was Panaetius who first introduced the concept of *humanitas* into philosophical ethics. Cf. R. Reitzenstein, *Werden und Wesen der Humanitaet im Altertum* (1907).

[27] Cf. *De Abr.*, 5; also in many other places. Cf. E. R. Goodenough, *By Light, Light, The Mystic Gospel of Hellenistic Judaism* (1935), pp. 72-94.

[28] Cf. Leon Roth, *Paganism,* Ahad Ha'am Memorial Lecture, 1934 (Jerusalem, 1934).

[29] Cf. A. H. Armstrong, *The Gods in Plato, Plotinus, Epicurus,* in *Classical Quarterly* (London), Vol. 32, 1938, pp. 192-195.

[30] Cf. *De Dec.*, 53; *Quod Deus,* 30.

[31] Cf. R. Klibansky, *loc. cit.,* pp. 33-34.

[32] *De Somn.*, II, 193; *De Post.,* 21; *De Fuga,* 131; *De Sacr.,* Ab. 92; *De Sacrifiant,* 4.

[33] Cf. J. A. Stewart, *Plato's Doctrine of Ideas* (Oxford, 1909), p. 59; a brilliant advocacy of this view has been recently put forward by W. W. Jaeger, *loc. cit.,* pp. 285-286; p. 414, n. 39b.

[34] Cf. *De Vita Contempl.,* 2; *De Praem.,* 40.

[35] Cf. *De Praem.,* 39; *Quod Deus,* 62.

[36] Cf. *De Mut.,* 11; *De Post.,* 167.

[37] Cf. *De Mut.,* 9; *De Post.,* 169.

[38] Cf. E. R. Dodds, *Proclus, The Elements of Theology* (Oxford, 1933), pp. 310 ff.

[39] Cf. Raymond Klibansky, *Plato's Parmenides in the Middle Ages and the Renaissance,* Medieval and Renaissance Studies, I.2 (London, 1943), pp. 284-286.

[40] Cf. Emile Bréhier, *Les Idées philosophiques et religieuses de Philon d'Alexandrie* (Paris, 1925), p. 73.

[41] *De Gig.,* 42; *De Somn.,* 75; *Leg. All.,* II, 1.

[42] Cf. *De Conf.,* 136; *De Post.,* 14; 20; 30; *De Fuga,* 75.

[43] Cf. F. M. Cornford, *Plato's Cosmology* (London, 1937), pp. 34 ff.

[44] Cf. *Ep.,* 65, 7.

[45] *De Op.,* 16; 20.

[46] Cf. *Leg. All.,* III, 96; 207; *De Somn.,* I, 239.

[47] Cf. Goodenough, *loc. cit.,* p. 366; R. Reitzenstein, *Zwei religionsgeschichtliche Fragen* (1901), pp. 83-92.

[48] Cf. Goodenough, *loc. cit.,* pp. 22 ff., 58, 161, 273.

[49] Cf. Leopold Cohn, "Zur Lehre vom Logos bei Philo," *Judaica, Festschrift zu Hermann Cohens Siebzigstem Geburtstage* (Berlin, 1912).

[50] Cf. *De Sacr.,* Ab. 8; 65; *De Fuga,* 95.

[51] Cf. *Quod Omn.,* 5; *De Migr.,* 10; 13; *De Ebr.,* 136.

[52] Cf. *De Ebr.,* 136-137; *De Plant.,* 24-5.

[53] Cf. *De Plant.,* 26-27; one will notice the etymological interpretation of the name "Bezalel" (In the shadow of God).

[54] Cf. *Phaedrus,* 247c; *De Plant.,* 39; *De Mut.,* 7; *De Post.,* 21.

[55] Cf. I. Heinemann, *loc. cit.,* pp. 69-70.

[56] Cf. *De Somn.,* I, 60; *De Sacr.,* Ab. 55; *Quis. Rer.,* 74; elsewhere he affirms that from the spiritual nature of the mind we may infer God's own spirituality, and that in this sense self-knowledge leads to the knowledge of God. Cf. *De Mig.,* 192-193.

[57] Cf. *Quis Rer.,* 71.

[58] Cf. *De Gig.,* 52-53.

[59] Cf. *Enn.*, VI, 9. 11; W. R. Inge, *The Philosophy of Plotinus* (1929), II, 146.

[60] Cf. *Phaedrus*, 244.

[61] Cf. *Quis Rer.*, 249.

[62] Cf. the article "Ekstasis" in G. Kittel, *Theologisches Woerterbuch zum Neuen Testament.*

[62a Cf. Gordis, *op. cit.*, pp. 15 ff.]

[63] Cf. *Quis Rer.*, 265.

[64] Cf. I. Heinemann, *Monatsschrift*, Vol. 64 (28) 1920, pp. 26 ff.

[65] Cf. Goodenough, *loc. cit.*

[66] Cf. *De Migr.*, 35.

[67] Cf. Charles Bigg, *The Christian Platonists of Alexandria* (Oxford, 1913), pp. 123, 242; Thomas Whittaker, *The Neo-platonists* (Cambridge, 1918), p. 33; Inge, *loc. cit.*, I, 37.

[68] Cf. F. Heinemann, "Ammonias Sakkas und der Ursprung des Neuplatonismus," in *Hermes, Zeitschrift fuer Klassische Philologie*, ed. R. Heinze and A. Korte, Vol. 61 (Berlin, 1926), p. 11, 21-25.

[69] Cf. P. Aloisius Lieske, S.J., *Die Theologie der Logos-mystik des Origenes* (Muenster i.W., 1938).

[70] Cf. H. Guyot, *Les Reminiscences de Philo le Juif chez Plotin* (Paris, 1906).

[71] Cf. F. Heinemann, *Plotin*, pp. 6-9, 189.

[72] Cf. Carl Siegfried, *Philo von Alexandria als Ausleger des Alten Testaments* (Jena, 1875), pp. 317-321. R. Bultmann, *Zeitschrift fuer Neutestamentliche Wissenschaft*, Vol. 24 (1925); F. C. Burkitt, *Church and Gnosis* (Cambridge, 1932), pp. 92-99.

[73] Cf. Otto Bardenhewer, *Patrology*, transl. Thomas J. Shahan (Freiburg i. Breisgau, 1908), pp. 431-436; Hans Lewy, "Neue Philontexte in der Ueberarbeitung des Ambrosius, mit einem Anhang: Neu gefundene Philonfragmente," in *Sitzungsberichte d. preuss. Akademie der Wissenschaften, Phil.-Hist. Klasse*, 1932, pp. 1-64.

[74] Cf. Jaeger, *Nemesius of Emesa*, pp. 139-143; John of Damascus, *De fide orthodoxa*, ed. Migne, col. 852 (quoted by A. J. Wensinck, *The Muslim Creed* [Cambridge, 1932], p. 69); *De Somn.*, I. sec. 65-70.

[75] Cf. J. Freudenthal, *Hellenistische Studien*, vol. 1, (Breslau, 1874), I, 67 ff.; Leo Baeck, "Zwei Beispiele midraschischer Predigt," in *Monatsschrift*, Vol. 69, 1925, pp. 258 ff.

[76] Cf. W. Bacher, *The Jewish Quarterly Review*, Vol. 7, 1894, p. 703; S. Poznański, *Revue des Etudes Juives* (Paris), Vol. 50, 1905, pp. 12-23.

[77] Cf. G. G. Scholem, *Major Trends in Jewish Mysticism* (Jerusalem, 1941), pp. 113-114.

[78] Cf. M. Bieler, *Der Goettliche Wille (Logosbegriff) bei Gabirol* (1933); I. Heinemann, *Zion*, Vol. 9, p. 168.

[79] Cf. G. Scholem, *"Ikbotav shel Gabirol ba-Kabbalah,"* in *Meassef Sofre Erez Yisrael*, 5700 [1940].

[80] Cf. David Neumark, *Geschichte der juedischen Philosophie des Mittelalters*, Vol. 2, 1 (1910). pp. 465-467.

2

¹ Cf. for the following account R. Klibansky, *The Continuity of the Platonic Tradition during the Middle Ages* (London, 1939); R. Walzer, "Arabic Transmission of Greek Thought to Medieval Europe," in *Bulletin of the John Rylands Library* (Manchester), Vol. 29, No. 1 (1945), pp. 160-183; Thomas Whittaker, *The Neo-Platonists* (Cambridge, 1918), pp. 154-215; Etienne Gilson, *La Philosophie Au Moyen Age* (Paris, 1944); A. J. Wensinck, *The Muslim Creed* (1932); *The Legacy of Islam*, ed. Sir Thomas Arnold and Alfred Guillaume (Oxford, 1931); A. Mez, *Die Renaissance des Islams* (1922).

[¹ᵃ Cf. Judah Goldin, "The Period of the Talmud," this work, Vol. I, pp. 202 ff.]

² Cf. J. Finkel, "An Eleventh Century Source for the History of Jewish Scientists in Mohammedan Lands," in *Jewish Quarterly Review*, N.S. 8 (1927-1928), pp. 45 ff.; S. Poznański, "Die juedischen Artikel in Ibn al-Qifti's Gelehrtenlexikon," in *Monatsschrift fuer Geschichte und Wissenschaft des Judentums*, N.F. 13 (49), 1905, pp. 41 ff.

³ Cf. N. N. Glatzer, *Geschichte der Talmudischen Zeit*. (Berlin, 1937), pp. 167-169.

⁴ Cf. G. G. Scholem, *Major Trends in Jewish Mysticism* (Jerusalem, 1941), pp. 39-74; see also the present writer's articles, "Gnostic Themes in Rabbinic Cosmology," in *Essays in honour of the Very Rev. Dr. J. H. Hertz* (London, 1942), pp. 19-32, and "The Gnostic Background of the Rabbinic Adam Legends," in *Jewish Quarterly Review*. N.S. Vol. 35, No. 4 (1945), pp. 371-391; also "Kedushah Hymns in the Earliest Hekalot Literature (from an Oxford Manuscript)," in *Melilah*, ed. Edward Robertson and Meir Wallenstein (Manchester, 1946), II, 2-24.

⁵ Cf. Scholem, *loc. cit.*, p. 75.

⁶ Cf. Leo Baeck, "Zum Sepher Jezira," in *Monatsschrift fuer Geschichte und Wissenschaft des Judentums*, N.F. 34 (70), 1926, pp. 371-376.

⁷ Cf. Scholem, *loc. cit.*, p. 363, n. 128.

⁸ Cf. Scholem, *loc. cit.*, p. 75.

⁹ Cf. *Saadya Gaon, The Book of Doctrines and Beliefs, Abridged Edition, Translated from the Arabic, With an Introduction and Notes*, by Alexander Altmann (Oxford, 1946), pp. 17-18.

¹⁰ Cf. M. Schreiner, *Der Kalam in der juedischen Literatur* (Berlin, 1895).

¹¹ Cf. Wensinck, *loc. cit.*, p. 79.

[¹¹ᵃ Cf. Abraham S. Halkin, "Judeo-Arabic Literature," this work, Vol. II, pp. 142 f.]

[¹¹ᵇ On Karaism cf. Goldin, *op. cit.*, pp. 199 f.]

¹² Cf. *Saadya Gaon, loc. cit.*, pp. 12-14.

¹²* Cf. Jacob Mann, "The Last Geonim of Sura," *JQR*, N.S., XI (1920-1921), p. 419.

¹³ Cf. Julius Guttmann, *Die Philosophie des Judentums* (Munich, 1933), pp. 85-96.

¹⁴ Cf. A. Foucher de Careil, *Leibniz, la Philosophie Juive et la Cabale* (Paris, 1861), pp. 33-40.

¹⁵ Cf. E. Renan, *Averroes et l'Averroisme*, pp. 92-93, quoted by Thomas Whittaker, *loc. cit.*, p. 183.

[16] Cf. R. Klibansky, *loc. cit.*, pp. 16-22; Gilson, *loc. cit.*, pp. 346-347.

[17] Cf. R. Klibansky, *loc. cit.*, p. 22.

[18] Cf. M. Guidi and R. Walzer, "Uno scritto introduttivo allo studio di Aristotele," in *Reale Accademia Nazionale Dei Lincei* (1940).

[19] Cf. R. Walzer, *Arabic Transmission*, etc., pp. 174 ff.

[20] Cf. Gilson, *loc. cit.*, p. 73.

[20a] On his poetry see Shalom Spiegel, "On Medieval Hebrew Poetry," this work, Vol. II, pp. 104-105.]

[20b] Cf. Halkin, *op. cit.*, p. 144.]

[21] Cf. C. R. S. Harris, *Duns Scotus* (Oxford, 1927), p. 231; W. Kahl, *Die Lehre vom Primat des Willens bei Augustinus, Duns Scotus und Descartes* (Strassburg, 1886), p. 55 (quoted by C. R. S. Harris).

[22] Cf. C. R. S. Harris, *loc. cit.*, *passim*.

[23] Cf. Julius Guttmann, *loc. cit.*, pp. 135-136; G. Scholem, "Ikbotav shel Gabirol ba-Kabbalah," in *Meassef Sofre Eretz Yisrael*, 5700 [1940].

[24] Cf. I. Heinemann, "Die Lehre von der Zweckbestimmung des Menschen im griechisch-roemischen Altertum und im juedischen Mittelalter," in *Bericht des Juedisch-theologischen Seminars* (Breslau, 1926), pp. 37-48.

[25] Cf. D. H. Baneth, "The Common Teleological Source of Bahye ibn Paqoda and Ghazzali," in *Magnes Anniversary Book* (Jerusalem, 1938) pp. 23-30.

[26] Cf. Julius Guttmann, *loc. cit.*, pp. 126-128.

[27] Cf. Gilson, *loc. cit.*, p. 116.

[28] Cf. Julius Guttmann, *loc. cit.*, p. 383, and his Introduction to *Abraham bar Hija, Megillat ha-Megalle*, ed. A. Poznański and Julius Guttmann, (Berlin, 1924); see also G. Scholem, *Monatsschrift*, N.F., 39 (75), pp. 172 ff.

[29] Cf. Julius Guttmann, *loc. cit.*, pp. 130-131.

[30] Cf. R. A. Nicholson, *Studies in Islamic Mysticism* (Cambridge, 1921); H. H. Schaeder, "Die islamische Lehre vom Vollkommenen Menschen," in *Zeitschrift der Deutschen Morgenlaendischen Gesellschaft*, N.F. 4 (79), 1925, pp. 192 ff.; see also the present writer's articles, "Saadya's Theory of Revelation: its Origin and Background," in *Saadya Studies*, ed. E. I. J. Rosenthal (Manchester, 1943), pp. 22-25, and "The Climatological Factor in Yehudah Hallevi's Theory of Prophecy," in *Melilah*, Vol. 1, ed. E. Robertson and M. Wallenstein (Manchester, 1944), Vol. I, p. 16.

[31] Cf. Gilson, *loc. cit.*, pp. 72 ff.

[31a] Cf. Spiegel, *op. cit.*, pp. 105-106.]

[32] Cf. Leo Strauss, "The Law of Reason in the Kuzari," in *Proceedings of the American Academy for Jewish Research*, XIII (1943), pp. 52, 62.

[33] Cf. Julius Guttmann, *loc. cit.*, p. 153.

[34] Cf. R. Klibansky, *loc. cit.*, p. 36.

[34a] Cf. Halkin, *op. cit.*, pp. 148-149; see also, below, Charles Singer, "Science and Judaism," pp. 229 ff.]

[35] Cf. H. A. Wolfson, *Crescas' Critique of Aristotle* (Cambridge, Harvard University Press, 1929), p. 323.

[36] Cf. G. G. Scholem, *Major Trends of Jewish Mysticism*, pp. 124 ff.

[37] Cf. the present writer's article, "Das Verhaeltnis Maimunis zur juedischen Mystik," in *Monatsschrift*, N. F., 44 (80), 1936, pp. 305 ff.

[37a] Cf. Halkin, *op. cit.*, pp. 139-140.]

[37b] Cf. Louis Finkelstein, "The Jewish Religion: Its Beliefs and Practices," this work, Vol. II, p. 485.]

38 Cf. Jacob Guttmann, "Der Einfluss der maimonidischen Philosophie auf das christliche Abendland," in *Moses Ben Maimon,* ed., W. Bacher, M. Brann, D. Simonsen (Leipzig, 1908), Vol. 1, pp. 135 ff.; E. Koplowitz, *Die Abhaengigkeit Thomas von Aquins von R. Moses ben Maimon* (1935).

39 Cf. Joseph Sarachek, *Faith and Reason: The Conflict over the Rationalism of Maimonides* (Williamsport, Pa., 1935), Vol. 1.

40 Cf. J. L. Teicher, "Maimonides, Christian Theology and the Jewish Opposition," in *Journal of Theological Studies* (Oxford, 1942), XLIII, pp. 69 ff.

41 Cf. *The Legacy of Israel,* ed. Edwin R. Bevan and Charles Singer (Oxford, 1928), p. 265.

42 Cf. M. Joel, *Lewi ben Gerson (Gersonides) als Religionsphilosoph* (Breslau, 1862), p. 12.

[42a Cf. Spiegel, *op. cit.,* pp. 108 f.]

43 Cf. Carl Gebhardt, *Leone Ebreo, Dialoghi d'Amore* (1929), p. 51.

44 Cf. Julius Guttmann, "Elia del Medigos Verhaeltnis zu Averroës in seinem Bechinat ha-Dat," in *Jewish Studies in Memory of Israel Abrahams* (New York, 1927), pp. 192 ff.

45 Cf. H. A. Wolfson, *Crescas' Critique of Aristotle,* pp. 24-31.

46 Cf. C. R. S. Harris, *loc. cit.,* p. 70, and *passim.*

47 Cf. R. Klibansky, *loc. cit.,* p. 20.

48 Cf. Martin Grabmann, *Mittelalterliches Geistesleben* (Munich, 1926), pp. 16-18, 276-295.

49 Cf. *loc. cit.,* pp. 173 ff.

50 Cf. M. Steinschneider, *Die hebraeischen Uebersetzungen des Mittelalters und die Juden als Dolmetscher* (Berlin, 1893), pp. xvi-xx.

3

1 Cf. Wilhelm Dilthey, *Gesammelte Schriften* (Leipzig and Berlin, 1921), Vol. II; Jacob Burckhardt, *The Civilization of the Renaissance in Italy,* Transl. by S. G. C. Middlemore (London-New York, 1928 [9th impression]).

[1a Cf. Cecil Roth, "The Jews of Western Europe (from 1648)," this work, Vol. I, Chap. 5.]

2 Cf. E. Gilson, *Etudes sur le Rôle de la Pensée Mediévale dans la Formation du Système Cartésien* (Paris, 1930); Jacques Maritain, *The Dream of Descartes,* Transl. by M. L. Andison (London, 1946).

3 Cf. Leon Roth, *Spinoza* (London, 1929); H. A. Wolfson, *The Philosophy of Spinoza,* 2 vols. (Cambridge, Mass., 1934).

4 Cf. A. Foucher de Careil, *Leibniz, la Philosophie Juive et la Cabale* (Paris, 1861); The first part of this work contains "Leibnitii observationes ad Rabbis Mosis Maimonidis librum qui inscribitur Doctor Perplexorum." By the same author: *Refutation inédite de Spinosa par Leibniz* (Paris, 1854); contains "Leibnitii Animadversiones ad Georg. Wachteri librum de recondita hebraeorum philosophia."

5 Cf. Foucher de Careil, *Leibniz,* pp. 33, 37, and *passim*; Joseph Politella, *Platonism, Aristotelianism and Cabalism in the Philosophy of Leibniz* (Philadelphia, 1938), pp. 13-16; 25-26; 29-34.

[6] Cf. F. H. Heinemann, "Toland and Leibniz," in *Philosophical Review* (New York, 1945), pp. 437 ff., 443.

[7] Cf. David Kaufmann, "Der 'Fuehrer' Maimûni's in der Weltliteratur," in *Gesammelte Schriften*, Vol. II, ed. M. Brann (Frankfort a.M., 1910), pp. 174 ff.

[8] Cf. Foucher de Careil, *Leibniz*, p. 2; David Kaufmann, *loc. cit.*, p. 175.

[9] For evidence see further below in the text.

[9a For the tenets of Cabbala cf. Abraham J. Heschel, "The Mystical Element in Judaism," this work, Vol. II, Chap. 5.]

[10] Cf. Israel Abrahams, "Pico della Mirandola," in *Hebrew Union College Jubilee Volume* (Cincinnati, 1925), pp. 317 ff.

[11] Cf. Denis Saurat, *Milton, Man and Thinker* (London, 1944); M. A. Larson, *The Modernity of Milton* (Chicago, Ill., 1927).

[12] Certain attempts in this direction have been made by Flora Isabel MacKinnon, *Philosophical Writings of Henry More,* ed. with Introduction and Notes (New York, 1925); Politella, *loc. cit.*

[13] Cf. Henry More, *The Defense of the Threefold Cabbala* (London, 1662), p. 80.

[14] Cf. Julius Guttmann, "John Spencers Erklaerung der biblischen Gesetze in ihrer Beziehung zu Maimonides," in *Festschrift Professor David Simonsen* (Copenhagen, 1923), pp. 259 ff.

[15] Cf. Pierre Bayle, *Oeuvres Diverses*, I (1727), 537.

[16] Cf. *loc. cit.*, pp. 3, 27.

[17] Cf. *loc. cit.*, pp. iii-iv, vii.

[18] Cf. the list of Christian talmudical scholars given by John Selden in his *De Jure Naturali et Gentium, juxta Disciplinam Ebraeorum, Libri septem* (1665), pp. 34-35.

[19] Cf. *British Museum Catalogue of Printed Books* (London, 1884); *Dictionary of National Biography*, ed. Sidney Lee (London, 1909); *Nouvelle Biographie Générale,* ed. Firmin Didot Frères (Paris, 1866).

[20] Cf. Dilthey, *loc. cit.*, pp. 107-108, 315-316, and *passim*.

[21] Cf. Leo Strauss, *The Political Philosophy of Hobbes* (Oxford, 1936), p. 4.

[22] Cf. Dilthey, *loc. cit.*, pp. 16-89.

[23] Cf. Dilthey, *loc. cit.* pp. 326 ff.; J. H. Whitefield, *Petrarch and Renascence* (Oxford, 1943).

[24] Cf. Erich Przywara, S.J., *Analogia Entis* (Munich, 1932), p. 41.

[25] Cf. Maritain, *loc. cit.*

[26] Cf. F. C. Coplestone, "Pantheism in Spinoza and the German Idealists," in *Philosophy,* Vol. XXI, No. 78 (1946), p. 45.

[27] Cf. The present writer's article, "Franz Rosenzweig and Eugen Rosenstock-Huessy: An Introduction to their Letters on Judaism and Christianity," in *Journal of Religion* XXIV (1944), (Chicago, Ill.), p. 262.

[28] Cf. W. W. Jaeger, *Humanism and Theology* (The Aquinas Lecture, Milwaukee, 1943); R. Walzer, "Arabic Transmission of Greek Thought to Mediaeval Europe," in *Bulletin of the John Rylands Library* (Manchester), Vol. 29, No. 1, pp. 168-171.

[29] Cf. A. J. Wensinck, *The Muslim Creed* (Cambridge, 1932).

[30] Cf. S. Horovitz, "Ueber den Einfluss der griechischen Philosophie auf

die Entwicklung des Kalam," in *Jahres-Bericht des Juedisch-theologischen Seminars* (Breslau, 1909).

[31] Cf. Simon Van den Bergh, *Epitome der Metaphysik des Averroes* (Leyden, 1924); an annotated translation of Averroës's *Destructio destructionis,* by the same author, is to be published by the trustees of the Gibb Memorial Fund, Oxford. It will deal with the influence of Stoic thought on Moslem theology, which Van den Bergh thinks to be very considerable. (Letter to the present writer.)

[32] Cf. M. Bieler, *Der goettliche Wille (Logosbegriff) bei Gabirol* (1933); I. Heinemann, *Zion* (Hebrew), Vol. 9, p. 168.

[33] Cf. Julius Guttmann, *Die Philosophie des Judentums* (Munich, 1933), pp. 105 ff.; Abraham Heschel, "Der Begriff des Seins in der Philosophie Gabirols," in *Festschrift fuer Dr. Jakob Freimann* (Berlin, 1937); by the same author: "Das Wesen der Dinge nach der Lehre Gabirols," in *Hebrew Union College Annual,* Vo. XIV, 1939, pp. 359 ff.

[34] Cf. C. R. S. Harris, *Duns Scotus* (Oxford, 1927), I, 126 ff.

[35] Cf. Julius Guttmann, *loc. cit.,* pp. 135-137.

[36] Cf. G. Scholem, "Ikbotav shel Gabirol ba-Kabbalah," in *Meassef Sofre Eretz Yisrael,* 5700 [1940].

[37] G. G. Scholem, *Major Trends in Jewish Mysticism* (Jerusalem, 1941), pp. 249, 402.

[38] Cf. Denis Saurat, *Milton,* p. 231.

[39] Cf. Julius Guttmann, "Chasdai Creskas als Kritiker der aristotelischen Physik" in *Festschrift Jakob Guttmann* (Leipzig, 1915), pp. 28-54; H. A. Wolfson, *Crescas' Critique of Aristotle* (Cambridge, Harvard University Press, 1929), pp. 34-37.

[40] Cf. H. A. Wolfson, *loc. cit.,* pp. 123, 201.

[41] Cf. Flora Isabel MacKinnon, *Philosophical Writings of Henry More,* pp. 293-295; see also Leibnitz, *Nouveaux Essais sur l'Entendement,* II, 17 (ed. C. J. Gebhardt, Vol. V, Berlin, 1882, pp. 136). Leibnitz attacks the doctrine of real space as "an idol of some modern Englishmen," "Since space," he writes to Samuel Clarke, "consists of parts, it is not a thing which can belong to God" (Collection of Papers, Leibnitz to Clarke, 3rd paper).

[42] Cf. H. A. Wolfson, *loc. cit.,* pp. 34-37.

[43] Cf. the present writer's article, "Saadya's Conception of the Law," in *Bulletin of The John Rylands Library* (Manchester), Vol. 28, No. 2 (1944), pp. 320 ff., 331.

[44] Cf. A. J. Wensinck, *loc. cit.,* pp. 214-216.

[45] Cf. the present writer's article quoted above.

[46] Cf. S. Horovitz, "Die Psychologie bei den juedischen Religionsphilosophen des Mittelalters von Saadia bis Maimuni," in *Jahres-Bericht des Juedisch-theologischen Seminars* (Breslau, 1906), p. 159.

[47] Cf. the present writer's article quoted above, p. 334.

[48] Cf. Leo Strauss, "The Law of Reason in the Kuzari," in *Proceedings of the American Academy for Jewish Research,* XIII (1943), 47 ff.

[49] Cf. Joseph Albo, *Sefer Ha-Ikkarim,* ed. Isaac Husik (Philadelphia, 1929), IV, 355.

[50] Cf. Hugo Grotius, *The Rights of War and Peace, including the Law of Nature and of Nations* (transl. A. C. Campbell), 3 vols., 1814, Book I, ch. I, 9. See Leo Strauss, *loc. cit.,* p. 48, n. 4.

[51] Cf. the present writer's article quoted above, p. 335.

[52] Cf. Hugo Grotius, *loc. cit.*, Book I, ch. I, 16.

[53] Cf. Albert Lewkowitz, *"Das Judentum und die geistigen Stroemungen der Neuzeit,"* in *Bericht des juedisch-theologischen Seminars* (Breslau, 1929), p. 44-49.

[54] Cf. Lewkowitz, *loc. cit.*, pp. 16-21.

[55] Cf. Dilthey, *loc. cit.*, p. 45.

[56] Cf. Lewkowitz, *loc. cit.*, p. 26.

[57] Cf. Lewkowitz, *loc. cit.*, pp. 26-32.

[58] Cf. Leone Ebreo, *Dialoghi d'Amore* (ed. Carl Gebhardt), pp. 35-37; 94-96.

[59] Cf. Jacob Guttmann, "Ueber Jean Bodin in seinen Beziehungen zum Judentum," in *Monatsschrift fuer Geschichte und Wissenschaft des Judentums* (1905), pp. 477 ff.; Lewkowitz, *loc cit.*, pp. 72-86.

[60] Cf. Dilthey, *loc. cit.*, p. 147.

[61] Cf. Dilthey, *loc. cit.*, pp. 73 ff.

[62] Cf. Dilthey, *loc. cit.*, p. 77.

[63] Cf. Dilthey, *loc. cit.*, pp. 77, 80, 109.

[64] Cf. Lewkowitz, *loc. cit.*, p. 45; Joseph Koch, "Meister Eckhart und die juedische Religionsphilosophie des Mittelalters," in *Jahresbericht der Schlesischen Gesellschaft fuer vaterlaendische Kultur* (Breslau, 1928).

[65] Cf. Dilthey, *loc. cit.*

[66] Cf. Dilthey, *loc. cit.*, pp. 90-108.

[67] Cf. Ernst Cassirer, *Die Philosophie der Aufklaerung* (Tuebingen, 1932), pp. 182-188.

[68] Cf. Cassirer, *loc. cit.*, p. 223.

[69] Cf. Pierre Bayle, *Oeuvres Diverses,* III, 792.

[70] Cf. Cassirer, *loc. cit.*, p. 225.

[71] Cf. Cassirer, *loc. cit.*, pp. 238-244.

[72] Cf. E. Cassirer, "Die Idee der Religion bei Lessing und Mendelssohn," in *Festgabe zum Zehnjaehrigen Bestehen der Akademie fuer die Wissenschaft des Judentums* (Berlin, 1929), pp. 22-41.

[73] Cf. George Santayana in his Introduction to Spinoza's *Ethics,* in Everyman's Library, ed. Ernest Rhys (1910).

[74] Cf. H. A. Wolfson, *The Philosophy of Spinoza,* I, 79 ff.

[75] Cf. Pollock, *Spinoza* (1912), p. 331; the phrase is quoted by Leon Roth, *loc. cit.*, p. 72.

[76] Cf. F. H. Heinemann's Review of Franz Koch's "Goethe und Plotin," in *Deutsche Literaturzeitung,* 1927, No. 11.

[77] Cf. Leon Roth, *loc. cit.*, p. 43. On Spinoza's "Jewishness" see also A. E. Taylor's *The Faith of a Moralist* (1932), p. 221.

[78] Cf. *Abot,* IV, 2.

[79] Cf. Soeren Kierkegaard, *Fear and Trembling,* transl. by Robert Payne (Oxford, 1939), pp. 13-14.

[80] Cf. Friedrich Nietzsche, "Zur Genealogie der Moral," in *Nietzsches Werke,* Taschen-Ausgabe (Leipzig, 1905), VIII, 377-378; David Baumgardt. "Spinoza und der deutsche Spinozismus," in *Kant-Studien* (Berlin), Vol. XXXII, No. 1 (1927), p. 191.

BIBLIOGRAPHY

The materials suggested below for further reading are listed under headings that correspond to those used in the body of the chapter. They contain books and articles that have appeared since 1946, the year in which the chapter was written. The literary material used by the author and referred to in the Notes has not been relisted below.

GUTTMANN, JULIUS, *Philosophies of Judaism: The History of Jewish Philosophy from Biblical Times to Franz Rosenzweig.* Translated by David W. Silverman. New York, Chicago, San Francisco, 1964.

VAJDA, GEORGES, *Introduction à la pensée juive du Moyen Age.* Paris, 1947.

WOLFSON, HARRY AUSTRYN, *Philo: Foundations of Religious Philosophy in Judaism, Christianity, and Islam.* 2 vols. Cambridge, Mass., 1947; 4th printing, rev., 1962.

I. HELLENISTIC JEWISH PHILOSOPHY

BAER, YITZHAK FRITZ, *Yisrael ba-amim.* Jerusalem, 1955; see also articles in *Zion*, XXIII-XXIV (Jerusalem, 1958-1959).

GOLB, NORMAN, "The Qumran Covenanters and the Later Jewish Sects," *The Journal of Religion*, XLI (Chicago, 1961), pp. 38-50.

LEWY, HANS, *Philo: Selections.* Oxford, 1946; reprinted in Lewy, Hans, *et al.*, *3 Jewish Philosophers.* New York, 1965, 1969.

LIEBERMAN, SAUL, "How Much Greek in Jewish Palestine?," in *Biblical and Other Studies*, edited by Alexander Altmann (Cambridge, Mass., 1963), pp. 123-141.

RICHARDSON, W., "The Philonic Patriarchs as *Nomos Empsychos*," in *Studia Patristica*, edited by Kurt Aland and F. L. Cross (Berlin, 1957), pp. 515-525.

WOLFSON, HARRY AUSTRYN, *Philo, op. cit.*

———, *The Philosophy of the Church Fathers*, Vol. I. Cambridge, Mass., 1956; 2d ed., rev., 1964.

———, "The Preexistent Angel of the Magharians and Al-Nahawandi," *JQR*, LIII (1960), pp. 101-124.

———, *Religious Philosophy: A Group of Essays.* Cambridge, Mass., 1961.

II. MEDIEVAL JEWISH PHILOSOPHY

ALTMANN, ALEXANDER (ed.), *Biblical and Other Studies.* Cambridge, Mass., 1963. Contains, among others, Arthur Hyman, "Spinoza's Dogmas of Universal Faith in the Light of Their Medieval Jewish Background"; Alexander Altmann, "The Delphic Maxim in Medieval Islam and Judaism."

——— (ed.), *Jewish Medieval and Renaissance Studies.* Cambridge, Mass., 1967. Contains Georges Vajda, "Le Problème de l'unité de Dieu d'après Dawūd Ibn Marwān al-Muqammiṣ"; Herbert Davidson, "Saadia's List of

Theories of the Soul"; Arthur Hyman, "Maimonides' Thirteen Principles"; S. D. Goitein, "Abraham Maimonides and His Pietist Circle"; A. S. Halkin, "Yedaiah Bedershi's Apology"; Sara O. Heller Wilensky, "Isaac Ibn Latif—Philosopher or Kabbalist?"; Alexander Altmann, "Moses Narboni's 'Epistle on Shi'ur Qoma' "; Lawrence V. Berman, 'Greek into Hebrew: Samuel ben Judah of Marseilles, Fourteenth Century Philosopher and Translator."

————, *Studies in Religious Philosophy and Mysticism*. London and Ithaca, N.Y., 1969.

ALTMANN, ALEXANDER, and STERN, S. M., *Isaac Israeli: A Neoplatonic Philosopher of the Early Tenth Century*. Oxford, 1958.

DAVIDSON, HERBERT, *The Philosophy of Abraham Shalom*. Los Angeles, 1964.

MIHALY, EUGENE, "Isaac Abravanel on the Principles of Faith," *HUCA*, XXVI (1955), pp. 481-502.

PINES, SHLOMO, *Ha-Scholastiqa she-aharē Thomas Aquinas u-mishnatam shel Hasday Crescas ve-shel qodemav*. Jerusalem, 1965.

————, *Moses Maimonides: The Guide of the Perplexed*. Translated with an Introduction and Notes . . . With an Introductory Essay by Leo Strauss. Chicago, 1963.

REINES, ALVIN J., "Abrabanel on Prophecy in the *Moreh Nebukhim*," *HUCA*, XXXI-XXXVIII (1960-1967).

ROSENBLATT, SAMUEL (trans.), *Saadia Gaon: The Book of Beliefs and Opinions*. New Haven, 1948.

ROSENTHAL, ERWIN I. J., *Griechisches Erbe in der juedischen Religionsphilosophie des Mittelalters*. Stuttgart, 1960.

SERMONETTA, J. B., "La dottrina dell'intelletto e la 'Fede filosofica' di Jàhudah e Immanuel Romano," *Studi Medievali*, 3ª Serie, VI, 2 (Spoleto, 1965), pp. 1-76.

SIRAT, COLETTE, "Mar'ōt Elōhīm (Les Visions divines) de Hanokh Ben Salomon Al-Qostantini," *Rev. études juiv.*, Quatrième série, I (CXXI), 1962, pp. 247-354.

STERN, S. M., "The First in Thought Is the Last in Action: The History of a Saying Attributed to Aristotle," *Journal of Semitic Studies*, VII (1962), pp. 234-252.

————, "Ibn Hasdāy's Neoplatonist," *Oriens*, XIII-XIV (1961), pp. 58-120.

VAJDA, GEORGES, *L'Amour de Dieu dans la théologie juive du Moyen Age*. Paris, 1957.

————, *Isaac Albalag: Averroïste Juif, traducteur et annotateur d'Al Ghazâlî.*

————, *Recherches sur la philosophie et la Kabbale dans la pensée juive du Moyen Age*. Paris, 1962.

WERBLOWSKY, R. J. ZWI, "Faith, Hope and Trust: A Study in the Concept of *Bittahon*," *Papers of the Institute of Jewish Studies, London*, edited by J. G. Weiss, I (Jerusalem, 1964), pp. 95-139.

WILENSKY, SARA O. HELLER, *Rabbi Yishaq 'Arāmā u-mishnato*. Jerusalem and Tel-Aviv, 1956.

WOLFSON, HARRY AUSTRYN, "Asilut ve-yesh me-'ayin eşel Crescas," in *Sefer Assaf* (Jerusalem, 1953), pp. 230-236.

————, "Judah Halevi on Causality and Miracles," in *Meyer Waxman Jubilee Volume* (Chicago, 1966), pp. 137-153.

————, "Maimonides and Gersonides on Divine Attributes as Ambiguous Terms," in *Mordecai M. Kaplan Jubilee Volume* (New York, 1953), pp. 515-530.

————, "Maimonides on the Unity and Incorporeality of God," *JQR*, LVI (1965), pp. 112-136.

————, "The Meaning of *ex nihilo* in the Church Fathers' Arabic and Hebrew Philosophy, and St. Thomas," in *Medieval Studies in Honor of Jeremiah Denis Matthias Ford* (Cambridge, Mass., 1948), pp. 355-367.

————, "The Meaning of *ex nihilo* in Isaac Israeli," *JQR*, L (1959), pp. 1-12.

————, "Saadia on the Trinity and Incarnation," in *Studies and Essays in Honor of Abraham A. Neuman* (Leiden, 1962), pp. 547-568.

III. MEDIEVAL JEWISH PHILOSOPHY IN ITS BEARING ON THE WORLD

ALTMANN, ALEXANDER, "Moses Mendelssohn on Leibnitz and Spinoza," in *Studies in Rationalism, Judaism and Universalism in Memory of Leon Roth,* edited by Raphael Loewe (London, 1966); reprinted in Alexander Altmann, *Studies in Religious Philosophy and Mysticism,* London and Ithaca, N.Y., 1969.

————, *Tolerance and the Jewish Tradition.* Robert Waley Cohen Memorial Lecture, 1957. London, 1957.

————, "William Wollaston (1659-1724): English Deist and Rabbinic Scholar," *Transactions of the Jewish Historical Society of England,* 1948, pp. 185-211; reprinted in Alexander Altmann, *op. cit.*

BLUMENKRANZ, BERNHARD, *Juifs et chrétiens dans le monde occidental.* Paris, 1960.

HEIDRICH, PETER, *Maimunizitate bei Meister Eckhart.* Diss. Rostock, E. Germany, 1959. Reviewed in *Theologische Literaturzeitung,* LXXXV, 6 (Leipzig-Berlin, 1960), pp. 469-470.

LIEBESCHUETZ, HANS, "The Significance of Judaism in Peter Abaelard's Dialogus," *The Journal of Jewish Studies,* XII (1961), pp. 1-18.

SCHOLEM, GERSHOM, "Zur Geschichte der Anfaenge der christlichen Kabbala," in *Essays Presented to Leo Baeck* (London, 1954), pp. 158-193.

TEICHER, J. L., "The Latin-Hebrew School of Translators in Spain in the Twelfth Century," *Homenaje a Millás-Vallicrosa,* Vol. II (Barcelona, 1956), pp. 403-444.

VAJDA, GEORGES, "Un Abrégé chrétien du 'Guide des Egarés' de Möise Maimonide," *Journal Asiatique,* 1960, pp. 117-136.

WOLFSON, HARRY AUSTRYN, "Causality and Freedom in Descartes, Leibniz, and Hume," in *Religious Philosophy: A Group of Essays,* pp. 196-216 (see esp. pp. 204-205).

————, "Philosophical Implications of the Pelagian Controversy," *Proceedings of the American Philosophical Society,* CIII (1959), pp. 554-562.

————, "The Twice-Revealed Averroes," *Speculum,* July, 1961 and January, 1963.

CHAPTER 4

THE JEWISH CONTRIBUTION TO MUSIC

By Eric Werner

Preface

Laudamus veteres, sed nostris utimur annis.

Any attempt to evaluate the Jewish contribution to the world of music will, at the very outset, be confronted by a number of controversial premises. These premises must first be clearly defined or at least circumscribed. Hence, we shall distinguish in the following pages between the musical contributions of Judaism, and those of individual Jews. In a few cases these accomplishments coincide, but certainly not always. Furthermore, it would be a misuse of an otherwise fruitful method to abstract certain elements of style from the works of composers like Mahler, Mendelssohn and Schoenberg—to name only a few—and then to pose these personal mannerisms as general criteria in a discussion of Judaism's musical accomplishments. Aside from the purely hypothetical character of all conclusions arrived at in this way, we must bear in mind two important, yet antithetic facts:

The musical contributions of Judaism lie chiefly in the realm of collective and anonymous *folk music*, the basis of its musical culture. On the other hand, individual composers of Jewish birth concerned themselves, naturally, with the *art music* of their time and environment. Considered together, it is obvious that the former aspect (folk music) far surpasses and outweighs the latter (individual works of art). Yet we must not disregard the efforts of individual composers and musicians, for they form a characteristic part of that involved mosaic known as the Jewish-Gentile symbiosis. It must be remembered that these composers speak for themselves rather than for the Jewish group.

This study endeavors to implement such general theses with essential and concrete details.

The Time of Royal Singers

Judaism originated in the Near East and migrated to the West. So simple a fact accounts for the unique position of Jewish culture, the gigantic bridge spanning the gulf between Orient and Occident. This bridge was to bear the traffic of Babylonian astronomy, as well as Greek philosophy, songs of the desert along with legalistic discussions of the academies.

Even in biblical times the Jewish people must have enjoyed an outstanding reputation as a musical nation. That is known from Jewish sources as well as from those of their hostile neighbors. An Assyrian document tells us that King Sennacherib demanded and received as tribute from King Hezekiah many Jewish musicians, male and female.[1] During the Exile, the Babylonians mockingly asked the Jewish captives to entertain them with music they brought out of Palestine. "Sing us one of the songs of Zion!" (Ps. 137). Musicians as tribute, and interest in a vanquished enemy's folk music, was unusual indeed.

Nor is it a coincidence that the idolized King David became the patron saint of Jewish music. Even if only a small fraction of the psalms attributed to him are in fact his, he would still tower above all ancient rhapsodists, except possibly Homer. David is the perfect embodiment of that unforgettable age of seers, poets and rhapsodists, which so many subsequent centuries ardently admired. Quite aside from the many legends that adorn his story in the Bible, the historical facts remain clearly to demonstrate his significance for the history of music. It was he who organized the cult music of the Levitical orders, as we learn from various biblical passages. If we understand I. Sam. 19:18-20 correctly, David combined in his person the gift of the professional prophet with that of the born poet and musician. We are entitled to assume that he was actually the author of Psalm 18, which is included *in toto* in II Sam. 22. Here is a psalm quite detached from the style of primitive folk song, as the Hebrew text will reveal. This would mean that with David artistic poetry and art music entered the history of Judaism. A great king, a brilliant soldier, and a highly gifted poet and musician! Small wonder that posterity saw in him the ideal of all pious men. Byzantine Christianity identified him with Jesus, the "faithful shepherd," and with Orpheus, the divine singer.

The biblical period, in general, created an abundance of musical forms and institutions which, later on, through Christianity, became the adored and incessantly imitated standards of Western civilization. The principal form, of course, was the psalm and the principal institution was the musical service of the Temple in Jerusalem.

A Sacred Ensemble

The literary parallelism so characteristic of the Psalms demands a corresponding musical rendition. Here is the origin of the manifold formal types we encounter in the Psalter. In the simple solo psalmody, one person alone sings its prayer (Ps. 3-5). In the response psalm, the congregation answers the chanting soloist with short and concise formulae (Ps. 48, 100, 118). The antiphon has two groups chanting alternately (Ps. 136, 148), while in the refrain psalm a refrain verse is sung by a group and interjected into the singing of the full text, as rendered by a soloist (Ps. 135: 1-3). The very acclamations "Hallelujah" and "Amen" and even the often misunderstood "Selah," have themselves become texts of thousands of compositions, following the call "Sing unto the Lord a new song!" We shall see later how, through constant use of the Psalter by Christians and Jews, the parallelism of the Psalms (which all translations retained) contributed greatly to the universality of certain musical forms.

Perhaps even more important than the psalm forms was the ideal of Temple music. It was here that a permanent example was set, and music became an integral and indispensable part of solemn worship. Up to this very day, the conception of cult music, as first represented in the Temple, has closely associated the art of music with the spirit of true religion. Musical services are described in the passages of II Chron. 15:16-24; 16: 4-7; 25:1-7, and the minute, meticulous organization of such services became the ideal of cult music for all Christianity. Many Popes—latterly Pius XI—in decrees and constitutions have praised the musical service of the Sanctuary as the model *par excellence* of all truly sacred song.

Two facts pertaining to the Psalms and the music of the Temple should not be forgotten, for they disclose the continuity of musical practice and rendition: the usage of the so-called *contrafact*, and the function of the organ.

A contrafact is the use of a familiar melody for a new text. Thus, the anthem, *America* (*My Country, 'tis of Thee*) is a contrafact of the older *God Save the King*; the hymn beginning "Rock of ages, let our song praise Thy saving power," is a perfect contrafact of the older *Maoz Tzur*. This practice is long established in the history of liturgy. Upon the idea of the contrafact the Roman Church built many of its greatest hymns and sequences. Martin Luther made quite a point of his policy "to take the songs from the streets and to use them [with sacred texts] in the church. Why should the devil have all the fine tunes?" The use of the contrafact is probably as old as mankind, yet the first records of its being employed are found in the Psalms. Some of them bear superscriptions which have nothing whatever to do with their contents, *e.g.*, Psalm 22, "To the chief musician upon the 'Hind of the Morning,' a psalm of David"; or Psalm 56, "To the chief musician upon 'Mute Dove far away' by David"; and so on. These odd superscriptions gave the first lines of folk songs, then familiar to the Psalmist. They indicated that the respective psalms were to be sung to particular tunes which, unhappily, have long since been lost.

The organ was used regularly in the Second Temple and is called *Magrepha* in talmudic literature. The tractate *Arachin* gives us a fairly good description of the *Magrepha*. We learn that it was an instrument somewhat between a siren and a primitive organ with ten pipes. It seems that its sound was powerful enough to be heard far outside of Jerusalem proper. Just how this organ worked is not quite clear. We know that it cannot have been operated by water power, for the Greek water organ, *hydraulis,* is mentioned in the Talmud, and its use in the Temple was expressly prohibited.

All these facts come to us from a time which rarely recorded the names of inventors, composers or organizers. Thus almost all Jewish musical contributions of this period are necessarily anonymous. However, they are not, for this reason, any less important. Quite the contrary! They must be considered the core of Jewish musical lore.

The Establishment of Musical Tradition

If, in a rather rough simplification, we call the biblical period one of naïve creativity, we must consider the following thousand years—(200 B.C.E. to 900 C.E.)—as the epoch of creative reflection. The external events that give meaning to these terminal dates are the beginning of Hellenism[1a] and the decline of the Gaonate (the Babylonian talmudic academies).[2a] These years encompass the period when Judaism lived in close relationship with the Greeks, the Romans, the Persians and the Arabs. The civilizations of these peoples were, at that time, not too distantly related to the Jewish orbit. Then, about 900 C.E., the great Jewish migrations from the Near East westward began. To the cultural history of Judaism this event is of even greater importance than the catastrophe of the Temple's destruction in the year 70 C.E. and the severance of Christianity from the mother religion at the Council of Nicea in 325 C.E. For as long as Israel lived and worked among kindred civilizations the perpetual problem of its culture, the problem of positive and negative assimilation, was not essentially acute. Jewish contributions to music during that period grew organically out of the germ cells firmly implanted in previous centuries. Especially noteworthy is the fact that cultic music flourished proudly, resisting the fate that had doomed the Sanctuary itself.

A direct remnant of that glorious Temple music was the melismatic element. This is the technical term for expanded coloratura singing. We know this technique to have been a distinctive feature of Temple worship and it has never since ceased to be characteristic of the Jewish chant. Melismatic practice was borrowed by the church; it became a principal attraction of its music in the famous Jubili or Alleluias, of which we shall hear more later. The idea to envelop, as it were, the priestly blessing in a rich array of musical ornaments was probably common to all Semitic peoples, but it was through Judaism that the practice became so characteristic of all devoutly exalted music. To this very day, certain parts of the Jewish prayers, especially the *Avoda* of the Day of Atonement, are adorned with these ancient forms of pious ecstasy.

Vehakohanim tune. Ashkenazic Tradition

78

Ve-ha-ko-ha-nim   ve-ho-om   ho-om-dim

bo-a-zo-ro,   ke-she-ho-yu sho-me-im es ha-shem ha-nich-

hod   ve-ha-no-ro,   ha-nich-

hod   ve-ha-no-ro ve-ha-no-ro.   *etc.*

We see in this illustration how some melisms are built up to quite impressive chain coloraturas. Such an effect can be achieved only when certain musical motifs are retained and varied. This principle of motif technique conquered the music of the church and thereby the music of the Occident. There is no doubt that the ancient Greeks, and probably the Egyptians too, knew the technique and made full use of it. But it so happened that it was through the Bible and the Judeo-Christian liturgy that this form structure became common property and was eventually systematized by musical theory.

How does a motif penetrate the memory and imagination of the listener? Obviously, it must bear certain characteristic features either in melody or in rhythm. (Harmony is excluded, since it came into being much later.) Apparently, the melodic element is by far the most effective "carrier," being easily variable, in contradistinction to rhythm, which soon loses its identity through variation. Frequent recurrence of the same motifs leads eventually to the establishment of so-called modes. The basic term "mode" is best explained as a melodic pattern which consists of two or three motifs and retains its identity through all kinds of variations.

Traditional music of the synagogue is based upon numerous modes, well known to every cantor. Most of old Jewish melodies are derived from these basic modes of the tradition. One example may illustrate this important point:

Magen - Abot - Mode

Vayekulu

The numbers indicate the
"standing tones" of the mode.

'Va-ye- ku -lu ha-sho... o-retz; vekol tze-vo-om, va-ye- kal..ha-shvi-i me-lach-to

a - shero-so, va-yish-bos ba-yom hash vi – i mi-kol me-lach-to a-sher o-so.

Sephardic Tune for the Tal-prayer

after Idelsohn

Lech le-sha-lom ge-shem u-vo le-sha-lom tal ki rav le-ho -shi-a u – mo-rid ha

tal a-shir shi-ra-ti ve-a-sim di -vra-ti v'ag-bi-ra se -fa-ti le-tzur ye-shu-a-ti.

Hatikvah

Spanish Cancion
("Virgen de la Cueva")

after Idelsohn

German Catholic Hymn
("Der Himmel jetzt frohlocken soll" 16th Century)

The first is the bare framework of the so-called *Magen Avot* mode, termed after the responsorial prayer on Friday evening; the following three tunes are melodies based upon that mode. First, is the *Vayekulu* of the Friday evening service, second the well-known "*Tal*" and *Hallel* of the Sephardic Jews, third, the familiar *Hatikvah* tune. It is easy to recognize the *Hatikvah* as just an extended version of the older *Hallel* and *Tal* tune. (Is any further evidence required to dismiss the widespread notion that the *Hatikvah* was borrowed from Smetana's *Moldau*? As a matter of fact, we have here one of the many "itinerant tunes" that permeate the folk music of several European and American nations.)

The principle of modality, common to the music of the entire Near East, is not a result of theoretical speculation but of the incessant reiteration or variation of living melodies, which, in the course of centuries, finally crystallized into a series of melodic skeletons. These skeletons were adorned with individual embellishments, melisms and other accessories. The finished (individual) product is a modal melody. Every musician knows some modes from his studies in counterpoint, where the so-called *church-tones* usually form his raw material. Both Jews and Greeks bequeathed their systems of modality to the incipient church, which combined them into magnificent musical synthesis.

Here the question arises: Who promoted this remarkable development? Fortunately, we can answer this question exactly and in detail, supported by many ancient sources. The institution of the cantor (*hazan*) is old and venerable. Although his functions changed somewhat in the course of centuries, it was the *hazan* who, from the sixth century to the end of the nineteenth, originated innovations of the liturgical music, and yet strove assiduously to preserve elements of the old tradition. It was definitely to the *hazan's* credit that in the period between 400 and 1000 the music of the synagogue attained an organic unity.

In the most critical part of this period—during the Babylonian Gaonate —it must have been a commanding personality, indeed, who with the full weight of his authority supported the *hazanim*. This man, according to various old sources, seems to have been R. Yehudai Gaon, a great Rabbi of the eighth century in Babylonia. It was he who officially introduced the "ternary" form (ABA) into the sphere of our religious music. He recommended that the opening eulogy (*berakah*) and the closing eulogy (*hatimah*) be chanted in the same mode, the prayer between them in a different, but "not too divergent" tune. We know also that he introduced the chanting of the *Kol Nidre* into the synagogue. Moreover, two ancient documents state that the "first *hazanim* received the authentic tradition from him." The ternary form, a part of that tradition, prevailed in European art music from the late Middle Ages down to Bach and Handel, thereby assuming an importance which cannot be overrated. In written form it occurs first in the *ballades* of the French *trouvères* (twelfth century). Its recommendation and sanction by Yehudai Gaon, three centuries earlier, should therefore be appreciated to a far greater extent than heretofore. Be it noted, Yehudai's endorsement of the ternary form was the first utterance (to my knowledge) of a rational and artistic sense of form in medieval music, and it was the music of the synagogue to which it was first applied.

ATTEMPTS AT MUSICAL NOTATION

At about the same time (eighth-ninth century) the problem of musical notation was at least temporarily solved by Jewish scholars and musicians. Art music was almost nonexistent and instrumental music had been forbidden since the fall of the Temple. What remained was a traditional chanting of the prayers and the cantillation of the scriptural lessons, according to certain ancient modes. The Rabbis felt the urgent need of a codified system, consisting of mnemonic signs which would facilitate the study and ensure the preservation of those modes. These symbols did not purport to give a precise code of musical notation; such was incompatible with other aims of these rhetoric signs. Actually, they had to serve grammatical, exegetic and musical purposes simultaneously. Consequently, the individual marks—the accents or the *teamim* of Scripture—do not indicate *single tones*, as does modern notation, but each sign stands for a *whole musical phrase*. These semimusical devices existed since the sixth century in rudimentary form; their perfection was accomplished around 900 by the masoretes.[3a] The modes of cantillation that these accents symbolize are, of course, much older, and some of them might go back to the time of Jesus and even earlier. It should be emphasized that this rather primitive kind of notation has little musical value without the indispensable support of oral tradition and personal teaching. Yet, through personal instruction, the system has worked very efficiently, as the following facts demonstrate. In 1518 the great Christian scholar Johannes Reuchlin, with some assistance by Jews, managed to transliterate the ancient Jewish signs into the musical notation of his time. Since that day this procedure has been emulated by a good many scholars whose musical transcriptions show but negligible differences from each other. Moreover, when we compare our contemporary practice of scriptural cantillation with Reuchlin's text, we find that in all essential points there has been little change in the more than four hundred years that have elapsed since Reuchlin.

Where did these mysterious signs or accents originate? A definite answer has, thus far, not been furnished, but all indications point to southern Syria, where early Christianity, Judaism and other sects faced the same problem, *viz.*, how to preserve the musical modes of the public recitation of the Scriptures. Hence it is not surprising that both the Eastern and the Western Church employed a system closely akin to the Jewish. Out of the system of the Roman Church evolved slowly, in the course of many centuries, our modern musical notation. Thus, while we may say that Judaism was one of the pacemakers of our notation, we must add that its own markings remained in a somewhat primitive state. The illustration on the next page shows the similarity of the so-called ekphonetic signs of the Greek Church compared to Hebrew scriptural accents.

THE CHURCH SINGS HEBREW TUNES

The musical interrelation between synagogue and church, while not entirely unknown, is still frequently overlooked or disregarded. Yet, it was through the church that Judaism made its lasting, its strongest and its most characteristic musical contribution. As a matter of fact, it is no exaggeration to state that about sixty per cent of the Gregorian chant, the authentic music of the Catholic Church, is of Jewish origin. Considering the tremendous authority of the Roman Church in all musical matters up to the eighteenth century, it is not difficult to appreciate the indirect Jewish legacy to the music of the Western world. Nor is this a recent discovery or claim; the attitude of the church on this question is quite unequivocal. The principle covering all ecclesiastical activities has been expressed in these terms: The Christian church is the sole legitimate heir of the synagogue both *de jure* and *de facto*. This statement, repeated innumerable times by the Church Fathers, explains why the church has always made open claim that both its liturgy and its music are of Hebrew origin.

Aside from theology, the outstanding musicologists all agree upon the close connection between early Christian and ancient synagogue music. Most outspoken are two great authorities on the Gregorian chant, Peter Wagner and Father Dechevrens, both priests. The latter goes so far as to maintain that "the Gregorian chant is the music of the Hebrews, and there is for the totality of the Roman Catholic melodies but one modal system, not that of the Greeks, but that of the sacred nation of the Hebrews."

FORMS OF CHURCH MUSIC

The central elements of the Christian liturgy, *viz.*, the Psalms, the Doxology, the Thrice Holy and the Lord's Prayer, all originate in the Hebrew language. With the exception of the Lord's Prayer, they form the core of synagogue liturgy to the present day. However, they were not used to the same extent in the service of the Temple.

Early Christianity, a movement of the poor and the meek, was born in the rural sections of the country, and opposed the rigid service and the hierarchy of the metropolitan Temple in Jerusalem. This was an institution

8–9th century

EARLY MEDI-EVAL GREEK	EKPHONETIC NAME	LATIN NEUMES	HEBREW NEGINOT IN THE ('ת"מ"א–BOOKS)
⌒	ὀξεῖα	Acutus (Virga)	Tifha
\	βαρεῖα	Gravis	Legarmeh
ﻻ	ὑπόκρισις	Quilisma descendens	Darga or Shalshelet
⌒	καθίστη	Circumflexa	Zarqa
/\	κρημαστὴ ἀπ' ἔξω	Flexa	Atnach
⌒	συρματική = περισπωμένη	Circumflexa	Zarqa-silluq

Later development
11th–12th Centuries

EARLY MEDIEVAL GREEK	BYZANTINE	LATIN NEUMES	HEBREW NEGINOT ('ת"מ"א)
⌒	ὀξεῖα	Virga	Tifha or Yetib
—	ὀλίγον (ἴσον)	Virga iacens	
∧	κρημαστή ἀπ' ἔξω	Flexa or clivis	Atnach
∨	κρημαστή ἀπ' ἔζω	Podatus	Shofar or baby-lonian Tifha
+	τέλεια	Punctus	Sof Pasuq

The most frequent combinations of accents at the close of sentences are:

I. ⌒⎯⎯⎯ + ⎯⎯ = …

II. ⌒⎯⎯⎯ + ⎯⎯ = … (∧)

of the priestly aristocracy, whereas Christianity concentrated upon the
ideology of the Kingdom of Heaven and did not recognize the rule of
priestly dynasties. It was the forms of synagogue worship that presented
the pattern for the liturgy of the young church. Hence the Christian
hostility to instrumental music through the first eight centuries. For the
Temple employed a large priestly orchestra and a trained choir, while the
provincial synagogue had available only a lay cantor and no accompaniment, except congregational response.

Five forms of musical liturgy, all born of the Hebrew genius, constituted the worship of the synagogue and later became integral parts of
the ecclesiastical service: Simple Psalmody, Response, Antiphone, Litany
and Lesson.

The *simple psalmody* was the usual chanting of the Psalms by one
precentor; here the congregation did not participate actively. The *response*
divides one or several verses in halves, of which the first part is rendered
by the cantor, the second by the congregation; *e.g.*:

CANTOR: Blessed be the name of the Lord;
CONGREGATION: Forever and ever.

Or:

CANTOR: Praise ye the Lord, to whom all praise is due;
CONGREGATION: Praised be the Lord, to whom all praise is due forever and
   ever.

The *antiphon* divides not only the verses, but also the performers into
two groups; *e.g.*:

> 1st GROUP: O give thanks unto the Lord, for He is good.
> 2nd GROUP: For His mercy endureth forever.
> 1st GROUP: So let Israel now say:
> 2nd GROUP: For His mercy endureth forever.

In this special example the second group reiterates the same verse, which
is not necessarily the general practice; this refrain-antiphon is a type closely
related to the *litany*, in which the cantor chants a short stanza, and the
entire congregation responds with one or two refrain verses; *e.g.*:

CANTOR: Give us thy protection; deliver us from danger; grant us joy and
   honor as the closing hour draws nigh.
CONGREGATION: O Lord, we stand in awe before thy deeds (or:) Help us,
   O Lord.
CANTOR: All their sins forgiving, show favor to thy chosen as the closing
   hour draws nigh.
CONGREGATION: O Lord, we stand in awe before thy deeds (or:) Help us,
   O Lord.

All these are poetic forms, inviting music, and therefore all Christian churches made full use of such structures. The reasons for retaining the cantillating rendition of the lesson, as practiced frequently in the Roman and regularly in the Greek Church, are less of a practical and more of a traditionalist nature. Here emphasis is laid upon the continuity with the spirit and expression of the Near East, the cradle of every church. Usually the cantillation as practiced in the church is more primitive than that of the synagogue. But there is one remarkable exception: In the Lamentations, which are chanted during Holy Week, Catholicism has preserved what is probably its oldest stratum of Jewish origin. The numbers of the verses are sung in Hebrew to this day, and the body of the verse is cantillated in a tune which has many a parallel in synagogue tradition. This mixture of psalmody and cantillation is a form characteristic of the most ancient and venerable portions of Catholic liturgy. In the examples on the next page, a few analogous cantillations and melodies are given, together with the tune of the Lamentations.

THE WORDLESS HYMN

Most of the Church Fathers, especially St. Augustine, considered the Hallelujah and its solemn rendition the pinnacle of ecclesiastical music. From earliest Christianity, the Hallelujah displayed a propensity toward disembodiment, that is, to being sung without the actual word "Hallelujah," even without its consonants. Such obviously mystic, ecstatic practice led first to the omission of the consonants, and later the vowels A E U I A were replaced by those of the doxology: E U O U A E-*seculorum amen*. This "wordless hymn" was called Jubilus and praised as the kind of glorification most appropriate to the Divine Being.

There are many indications that triumphant laudation of this manner, too, is of Jewish origin. The Talmud speaks most eloquently about the glorious chanting of the Hallel, of which the Hallelujah is the very epitome. Numerous passages compel us to infer that the wordless hymn was an ancient Jewish custom. During the Middle Ages a number of Rabbis raised their voices against wordless chanting, a practice they deemed cabbalistic and devious. In the sphere of Hasidism,[4a] however, the form of the wordless hymn achieved new and vigorous life. Among the Hasidim it was called *Niggun*, and many of these ecstatic, wordless tunes have come down to us. They were frequently composed by the Hasidic *Saddikim* (Saints) as means to attain the highest transport, *hitpashtut hagashmiut*, disembodiment. Innumerable are the tales in which, through the *Saddik's* musical intercession, fallen souls were purified, sick ones healed, and frenzied men soothed and led back to sanity. The famous

The Mode of Lamentations in the Roman Church

Lamentations I, 1.

A — — — leph quo-mo-do se-det so-la ci-vi-tas ple-na po-pu-lo:

fac-ta-est qua-si vi-dua do-mi-na Gen-ti-um.

Some Catholic and Jewish Chants in Comparison

Lamentations   Yemenite Jews, after Idelsohn

(1) Na-ha-mu, na-ha-mu 'a-mi, yo-mar esh-kol ko-fer, le-na-hem nimtzo ko-tub ba-se-fer.

Lamentations III, 1.   Gregorian (Naples version)

(1a) E-go vir vi-dens, pau-per-ta-tem me-am, in vir-ga indignatio-nis e-ius.

Tonus Peregrinus Ps. 114.   Gregorian

(2) In exitu Israel ex E-gyp-to, Domus Jacob de po-pu-lo bar-ba-ro.

Sephardic   after Consolo and Aguilar

(2a) Ka-ra-ti shim-cha A-do-nai mi-bor tach-ti-yot.

Ps. 81, 1.   Yemenite Jews, after Idelsohn

cf.
with { (3) La-me-na-tze-ach al ha-gi-ttit, mi-ze-mor l'-A-saph.
A

Ps. 45, 2.   Gregorian

(3a) Eruc-tavit cor meum ver-bum bo-num, di-co e-go: lin-gua mea...ca-la-mus scribae.

Priestly Blessing.   Yemenite Jews, after Idelsohn

cf.
with { (4) Ye-vo-re-che-cho A-do-nai   etc.
A

Invitatorium Sixti Toni (Ps. 95, 1-2)   Gregorian

(4a) Ve-ni-te exsultamus Do-mi-no, prae-oc-cu pamus..fa-ciem e-ius.   etc.

Barchu of the High Holidays.   Ashkenazic Jews

(5)   etc.

Hymnus: Iste confessor.   Gregorian

(5a) I ste con-fess-or, Do-mi-ni co-leu-tes.

Saddik Shneour Zalman indicated clearly his preference for wordless tunes, stating: "The songs of the soul . . . consist of tones only, dismantled of words."

Such conceptions of the ethical power of music, whose roots are as old as mankind itself, display a striking affinity to the musical philosophy of the Church Fathers. In the latter milieu, the rich synthesis of Hebrew and classic spirit tended toward Neoplatonism. In the Hasidic realm, the infiltration of mystic lore into traditional Judaism likewise created an atmosphere of esoteric speculation. These two philosophies of religion, although separated by a millennium, ran parallel in many respects.

MUSICAL PHILOSOPHY IN JERUSALEM AND ATHENS

All too often we forget that man not merely experiences emotions but insists upon contemplating them as well. Music, acclaimed as the most expressive of the arts, was early to become a favorite subject of these reflections. Now, some ideas on music were to a certain degree common to all peoples of the Near East. When we probe into the earliest history of these notions, we find that they originated in a magical conception of music. The art supposedly possesses powers which surmount the ordinary faculties of man. Countless legends of the magic of music show clearly the primeval functions of music. Such ideas are met with all over the world, and they found their way even into the guarded enclosure of biblical lore, as may be seen in various narrations, *e.g.*, in the stories of the battle of Jericho, David and Saul, Elisha before the king, and so on.

Greek philosophy sublimated the magic ideology and explained the powers of music in a more rational way. According to the Greek theories, each musical mode, each tune even, is endowed with a particular *ethos* of its own, expressing its character and, conversely, attuning the listener to its individual spirit. When this principle merged with certain Oriental ideas on the harmony of the spheres and the basically cosmic order of music, a grandiose, universal concept was established which influenced the entire theory of music up to the eighteenth century.

Some of the Church Fathers championed this Greek philosophy of music and added biblical, that is, Jewish elements to it. With Clement of Alexandria, of the late second century, this *ethos doctrine* assumed a very practical character. He ordered the devout and faithful Christians not to emulate, in their chants, the sensuous tunes of the voluptuous and decadent Greeks. Christians should praise God in a classical mode of ancient Greece which was, according to him, identical with the Hebrew mode of certain psalms. This *Tropos Spondeiakos*, for which Clement found most eloquent words of praise, has come down through the writings of Greek music theorists. Being identical with ancient Jewish tunes, it is almost the only concrete source from which we may draw reliable information on Jewish music in the time of Jesus and shortly afterward. Indeed, while investigating this mode, the writer found certain old Jewish parallels to the originally Greek melody. In the illustration on the next page, the mode, as we know it from Greek sources, is compared with some Hebrew chants. The similarity is obvious. Moreover, we can perceive how this mode made its way into the traditional and authentic music of the Roman and the Greek Catholic Church.

TRANSFUSION OF TUNES

In what way were Hebrew melodies carried over into the Christian cult? All sources tell us that the road over which the liturgical music traveled westward was paved by Judeo-Christians, the Apostles and their disciples. The bearers of the Jewish musical tradition in the Diaspora were the lay ministers and cantors of the great communities in Asia Minor and Greece. These men sympathized openly or secretly with the new Messianism of Christianity and, when they joined the new church, brought with them as gifts their old "hymns, psalms and spiritual songs," as St. Paul called them. In Palestine, the situation was somewhat different. There the Christian community consisted almost exclusively of Jews, and the transition from the old to the new ritual was a slow, gradual, organic process—going on for centuries—as we learn from the Acts of the Apostles, and Eusebius's *History of the Church*. Although the entire problem bristles with difficulties, it is possible to state that for the liturgical texts created before the eighth century more than half the corresponding tunes are of Jewish origin. The church borrowed from the synagogue up to the ninth century. Then the relationship gradually reversed itself and, at the time of the Renaissance and later, Jewry was heavily indebted to the church for many of its melodies. Nor was Jewry entirely unaware of the age-old interrelation of church and synagogue music. The famous Jewish poet, Immanuel of Rome, wrote: "What does the art of music say to the Christians? 'Indeed I was stolen out of the land of the Hebrews' " (Gen. 40:15).

JEWISH TUNES IN WESTERN MOLD

The first wave of the great Jewish migration westward broke on the shores of North Africa, Spain, southern France, and Italy. Soon two spiritual centers took shape in Spain and northern France. In these countries two forms of intellectual activity evolved, attracting like magnetic fields all neighboring communities until they included, respectively, a good deal of the Arab countries and the entire Rhineland.[5a] Each cultural

Tropos Spondeiakos

center developed a poetic and musical style of its own, in many respects differing from the other. Not only divergent physical and moral climates account for this bipartition of an originally uniform tradition. Various other factors contributed to the partition. What hitherto had been a whole—the music of Jewry in general—now began to break up into art and folk music. That this cleavage did not result in two completely different styles, as it did four centuries later in European music, was due to the unifying force of a new musical element.

This binding force was what we have come to call the technique of the "leading motif." Although the designation is borrowed from Richard Wagner's vocabulary, the practice was many centuries older, and was a remarkable contribution to European musical structure. The basic idea is to associate a particular holiday, or a particular text characteristic of this holiday, with a special tune or mode, which is used on no other occasion [*neima* or *lahan*]. This principle of leading motifs, assigned to special days or texts, evoked in the listeners clearly defined associations and emotions, even when the tune was detached from its original text or ritual environment. Thus, every Jew will immediately be reminded of the Day of Atonement when he hears the *Kol Nidre*, and, what is more, he will respond emotionally to this experience. The Christian, too, knows certain hymns which are reminiscent of particular occasions and produce corresponding sentiments. It can be proved that this practice of musical association, or leading motif, was borrowed from the medieval synagogue and has since pervaded the liturgies of all churches.

The same centuries (twelfth-fourteenth) also witnessed the opposite interaction, namely, the filtration of Spanish and German elements into Jewish tradition. This musical exchange resulted, especially in the Rhineland, in the creation of some of the most beautiful and noble Jewish melodies. A later generation, ignorant of their syncretistic origin, named these tunes *Missinai, i.e.,* brought from Mt. Sinai, in praise of their outstanding significance and value.

An example of each (see next page) may illustrate these converse trends. First we have the leading motif, originating in Judaism, entrenching itself in the practice of the church. The opposite direction is shown in a Jewish melody of the same time, demonstrating the adoption of German and French elements.

The Sanctus is a rather late addition to the Gregorian chant and serves as a leading motif for a whole Mass of the Virgin. The *Tal Kaddish* of our illustration is broken up into its constituent parts, some of which have their roots in German folk song, others in the *chansons* of the *trouvères* in northern France. It should be noted that these foreign elements have undergone a considerable transformation, having been adapted to the basic Jewish background and admirably integrated into an organic unit.

Olenu of the High Holidays

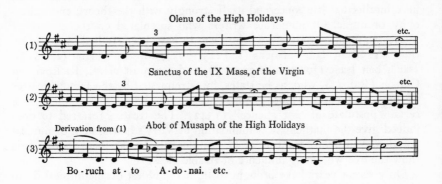

(1)

Sanctus of the IX Mass, of the Virgin

(2)

Derivation from (1)   Abot of Musaph of the High Holidays

(3)

Bo - ruch at - to   A - do - nai. etc.

Tal-Kaddish

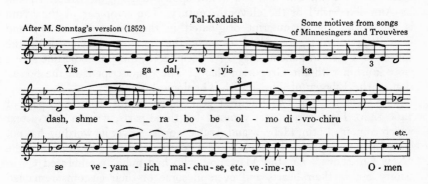

After M. Sonntag's version (1852)   Some motives from songs
                                                     of Minnesingers and Trouvères

Yis _ _ _ ga - dal, ve - yis _ _ _ ka _

dash, shme _ _ _ ra - bo be - ol - mo di - vro-chiru

se   ve - yam - lich mal - chu - se, etc. ve - ime - ru   O - men

Some Parallel Passages in Medieval Music

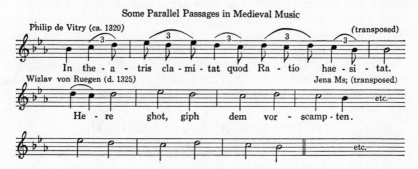

Philip de Vitry (ca. 1320)   (transposed)

In the - a - tris cla - mi - tat quod Ra - tio hae - si - tat.

Wizlav von Ruegen (d. 1325)   Jena Ms; (transposed)

He - re   ghot, giph   dem   vor - scamp - ten.

The Spanish-Arabic center was not quite so rich in fine melodists, but here intellectual life concerned itself strongly with the theory and philosophy of music. Of numerous writers who speculated on the essence of music, we mention only a few who seem to have been studied by Christian theorists: Shem Tob Falaqera (c. 1225-1295), Moses Abulafia (c. 1250), Isaiah ben Isaac (fourteenth century), and foremost of all, R. Levi ben Gerson (Ralbag), who, as he states, "was requested by the famous master of musical theory, Monseigneur Philippe de Vitry, to demonstrate a certain postulate of that science" (1342). The treatise referred to does indeed give the mathematical foundation of Vitry's new system of musical notation. With the exception of Gersonides, all Jewish theorists of music show the overwhelming influence of Arabic ideas.

Only recent years have brought to light the oldest extant musical documents of Judaism. The first is a hymn upon the death of Moses, a poem by Amr ibn Sach'l of the eleventh century. The composer of the hymn is unknown. The manuscript originated in the thirteenth century and is written in what are called *neumes*, the notation developed by the church and then in general usage. As deciphered, their melodic line shows close kinship with the Gregorian chant.[6] The manuscript is in the possession of the Library of The Jewish Theological Seminary.

The second, about two hundred years later, comes from the Spain of 1460-1480. Here is a masterly motet for three parts, written over a text which contains Latin, Hebrew and Arabic words. As yet its wording has not been fully deciphered. It seems to be a composition for the liturgy of the "New Christians," *i.e.*, the Marranos, who had publicly embraced Christianity but in their hearts and even in some of their customs remained devout and faithful Jews.[7a] The most remarkable feature of this manuscript is the juxtaposition of an ancient Jewish tune—which corresponds to the text (a *Kedusha*, Sanctification)—with a Gregorian hymn, set against the Hebrew tune. One is inclined to believe that the Marrano composer used the extremely enigmatic language as well as the Gregorian tune to camouflage the Jewish character of the piece before the eyes of the dreaded Inquisition.

THE DECLINE OF ANONYMOUS COLLECTIVITY

Approaching the dawn of the sixteenth century, we cannot fail to notice a gradual, but clearly discernible decline of general creativity in the Jewish world. Yet it cannot be said that, from the sixteenth century on, the number of Jewish thinkers or artists decreases or that their accomplishments do not measure up to those of previous generations. Actually, what was languishing was not the creative power itself, but its agency. While anonymous and collective expression of the Jewish group diminishes, individual contribution grows stronger. Judaism had, in the previous ages, conserved its creative vitality through its excellent faculty of transformation and active assimilation. Speaking of music, it had absorbed many elements of non-Jewish origin, but, capable of complete integration, it had assimilated them, as a plant assimilates air and light into its system. The spirit of the Renaissance, with its emphasis upon the individual, filled the intellectual air of Southern and Western Europe, and its Jewry was not untouched by it. On the contrary, where the opportunity arose, Jews responded powerfully and positively to the new conception of man and his intellectual freedom. Italy, fatherland of the Renaissance and of its frequent concomitant, political tolerance, offered the first opportunity for spontaneous creation by musicians of Jewish birth. The contributions of Judaism cease, those of Jews begin and accumulate. No wonder, then, that the fruits of this new era testify to the irresistible attraction of authors to the culture of their environments, and the gradual loss of Jewish cultural autonomy. Creative power of the individual still remains intact, but in its expression the traditional Jewish substance wanes and weakens.

JEWISH COMPOSERS IN NORTHERN ITALY AND VENICE

The dukes of Mantua and Ferrara, the dynasties of Gonzaga and Bardi, patronized contemporary composers more readily than did the equally music-minded, but conservative courts of the church. Moreover, in a number of cases, the Gonzagas demonstrated a tolerance with regard to Jews which surpassed by far the friendly indifference that was general among Italian nobility. Thus, we find at their court in Mantua a number of Jewish musicians with the high standard of ability demanded by their times. Some of them may be mentioned: Abramo d'all Arpa Ebreo (1525-1566); Isacchino Massarano (1560-1599); Davit da Civita, a composer of madrigals (about 1615), and Allegro Porto, likewise a composer of vocal pieces. The first Jewish composer to reach truly historic stature was Salomone Rossi il Ebreo (1565-1628). For more than forty years he served as court musician at Mantua, and the great number of his compositions demonstrates a prolific creativeness by no means common even in those times. Rossi's significance for the history of music has been clearly established by the great historian, Hugo Riemann, who says: "Rossi is one of the most important representatives of the *stile nuovo* [style of the late Renaissance] in the instrumental field; he was perhaps the first who cultivated the trio-sonata, and his way of treating this form has remained exemplary for a long time . . ."

Rossi was a descendant of an old aristocratic family which traced its ancestry back to King David. As a composer, he enjoyed a great reputation among his contemporaries. Monteverdi, then Italy's outstanding master, held him in such high esteem that he accepted him as collaborator in the writing of portions of the oratorio *Maddalena*. The fields of vocal and instrumental music were tilled by Rossi with equal diligence. He wrote chamber music, suites, madrigals, operatic pieces and music for the church and for the synagogue.

In the Jewish realm, he set a precedent by introducing into the synagogue, hitherto the jealously guarded court of archaic tradition, the style and the technique of his time. This meant four- to eight-part polyphonic choruses without accompaniment, full of the enchanting beauty of the late Palestrina style, and of the same admirably rounded form. It is understandable that soon a sharp reaction against so revolutionary an innovation arose, the more so since, fifty years before, orthodox Catholic circles had raised very similar objections against Palestrina's music. At that time the Council of Trent granted to Palestrina the needed artistic latitude. Now the famous Rabbi Yehuda Leon de Modena, in the company of certain other rabbis, went out of his way to sign an official opinion that there could not be a prohibition of choral art music in the synagogue.

Rabbi Leon de Modena deserves our attention in more than one respect. His incredible versatility—he admits that he succeeded in mastering more than thirty occupations—brought him into closer contact with the general spirit of his time than was heretofore considered befitting a rabbi. A well-trained musician, he founded the first artistic choir in synagogal history, a group of fine singers, named by him *Bezochrenu et Zion* (In Remembrance of Zion). The concerts of this choral society, which he conducted, attracted wide circles of the Venetian nobility.

Rabbi de Modena induced Rossi to write a set of thirty-three liturgical pieces for his synagogue, all of them choral compositions from three to eight parts. The music, though noble in style and beautiful in expression, shows but little trace of Jewish tradition. It deviates in no way from the then current idiom of the Venetian school.

Yet the chain of tradition was not completely broken in northern Italy. Strangely enough, it is other than a Jewish source which documents this fact. The interest in synagogue music displayed by Venetian noblemen in de Modena's time was a contributing factor in the appearance of a famous musical work eighty years later. The *Estro Armonico Poetico*, a collection of fifty psalm compositions for chorus and orchestra, became Benedetto Marcello's *magnum opus*. This talented non-Jewish composer included eleven melodies of Jewish tradition, quoted together with their original Hebrew texts. He made use of these tunes as *cantus firmi*, *i.e.*, as nuclei for his own compositions, intending thus to add a certain flavor of authenticity to them.

The first part of our illustration is an old German-Jewish tune of *Maoz Tzur* which displays a certain kinship to the Gregorian chant; but in this case it is wise to exercise utmost caution before assuming Jewish authorship, for here the synagogue seems to have borrowed from the church. The second part shows an old Sephardic song, which, in sharp contrast to the simple German march rhythm, has the intricate, rhythmical pattern usually found in classical Arabic music. Marcello indicated in all eleven cases whether the origin of the piece was Sephardic or Ashkenazic.

The *Maoz Tzur* quoted above is definitely older than the melody with which we are familiar today. Our familiar melody consists of three different German folk songs, the last of which was written around 1620.

In his preface to the *Estro*, Marcello gives a brief history of music in the Bible, expounding the manifold merits of Jewry in the field of musical endeavor. He concludes: "It seems to me most probable (which some Jews assiduously confirm) that the melodies quoted in this work lingered in the memories of the first Jews exiled from Palestine, and that they handed down these tunes by oral tradition to succeeding generations." We see here that Marcello included the traditional tunes for their authenticity and age, not for their beauty. This is the attitude of a scholar, rather than of an artist. In his scholastic concern for the music of the Bible, Marcello by no means stood alone. Since Reuchlin and Boeschenstein edited the first musical transcription of scriptural cantillation, the active interest of theologians had produced many an attempt at reconstructing the ancient, long-forgotten tunes and chords of the Temple.

CHRISTIAN THEOLOGY AND THE MUSIC OF THE BIBLE

A concomitant result of these studies was a revival of the dormant interest in Jewish customs, ritual and history. The masoretic accents of Scripture, as the hypothetical basis of synagogal chant, soon became a favorite topic of Christian scholars. Polyhistors like Bottrigari, Valdensis, Muenster, theologians like Athanasius Kircher, Vitringa, August Pfeiffer, musicologists like Burney, Forkel and the famous Gerbert, all struggled with the problem of scriptural accents, synagogal chant and the Temple music of old.

Their learned endeavors in the field of biblical music were closely watched by many contemporary composers. Time and again we meet the suggestion to reconstitute the music of the Protestant Church after the pattern of an imaginary Temple cult. These intentions frequently led to tortuous and not always unbiased arguments. Thus we need not be astounded to find titles of music collections like *Musae Sioniae, Hymnodia Sionia, Fontana d'Israel* (J. H. Schein, 1586-1630), etc.

Efforts of the scholars to bring the ancient music of Judaism into clear relief were matched by the accomplishments of composers, engaged in the gigantic work of interpreting Scripture in the musical idioms of *their* time. This mutual stimulation reached its glorious climax in the works of Johann Sebastian Bach, George Frederick Handel and a host of lesser, yet still shining luminaries of musical history.

While Judaism cannot claim a share in those extraordinary accomplishments, we should understand that it was the spirit of Hebrew literature as recovered by Protestant ardor that functioned as a catalytic agent, so to speak, between the forces of religion and those of music. Alas, this creative phenomenon was then—in the midst of the eighteenth century—totally remote from the Jewish people.

TWILIGHT BEFORE THE EMANCIPATION

During the decades preceding Emancipation, we notice signs of cultural and spiritual decline in all Jewries of Europe. Not a few Jews, attracted by the glamour of European civilization and eager to participate in it, were convinced that they would have to abandon their ethnic and religious identities before entering the larger world. This might explain why, of the few Jews connected with the history of music shortly before 1800, not one remained faithful to his religion. On the other hand, these individuals demonstrated by their remarkable understanding of all things musical that their original Jewish background, far from being an obstacle, actually deepened their appreciation of the intensive musical culture of their time.[8] We mention here only two converted Jews who made significant contributions to European music: Lorenzo da Ponte and Adolf B. Marx.

Da Ponte (1749-1838), the librettist of Mozart's *Marriage of Figaro*, *Don Giovanni* and *Così fan tutte*, was a Jew of Trieste who, early in life, adopted Christianity and became a priest—"Abbate," as he called himself. Not taking his ecclesiastical vows too seriously, he led the life of a Casanovalike adventurer. Nevertheless, he was a brilliant and, in some respects, an ingenious poet, who fully understood Mozart's genius; and he merits ample credit for the excellent dramatic structure of *Figaro* and *Don Giovanni*.[9]

Marx (1794-1866), son of a wealthy physician, friend of Felix Mendelssohn, founded the *Berliner Allgemeine Musikalische Zeitung*, and later was appointed professor of the history of music at the University of Berlin. He was one of the first representatives of modern musicology, a keenly logical student of musical theory and an outstanding teacher. His creative attempts, the oratorios *Moses* and *John the Baptist*, were failures. His chief merit lies in his clearly defined methodology and in his championship of the great contemporary composers.

These two personalities can be considered typical exponents of the centrifugal forces within Judaism, before the great wall collapsed, that wall which hitherto had separated the old people from its neighbors.

OUTSTANDING JEWISH COMPOSERS IN FIVE GENERATIONS

It is not the purpose of this study to present a complete list of Jewish musicians since 1800. (This must remain the thankless task of a special bibliography to be compiled by an apologete.) Since the musicians of Jewish birth cultivated the style and the forms determined by their

environment, it is impossible to trace a consistent line of organic development in their works. Therefore it seems of doubtful value to apply the
rigid method of musicology. The general import of these composers has
been fully expounded in books on musical history and in monographs.

Instead of a long dull list or a strictly historical disquisition we shall
present thumbnail sketches of eight of the most significant Jewish composers, representative of the five generations since Emancipation.

First Generation: Giacomo Meyerbeer (1791-1864)
              Felix Mendelssohn-Bartholdy (1809-1847)

An anecdote in lieu of a preface: Abraham Mendelssohn, Moses
Mendelssohn's son and Felix's father, was a prototype of the radical
assimilationist whose only link with Judaism was forged by his generous
philanthropy. Nonetheless, Felix's teacher, old Zelter, Goethe's friend,
announced the forthcoming visit of his twelve-year-old pupil to the
Olympian of Weimar with the jest: "Indeed, it would be 'some ting raire'
[spelled in Yiddish slang *eppes Rores*] if a Jew's son would become an
artist." Then he added wistfully, "It is true, he is a Jew's son but not
a Jew."

Meyerbeer, son of Jacob Herz Beer, founder of the first Reform
synagogue of Berlin, was essentially a showman of genuine dramatic
instinct and explosive power. Yet, Richard Wagner, his flatterer to his face
and most vicious critic under pseudonyms, was right when he stated that
Meyerbeer's music seeks mere effect, and it is "effect without cause."
On the other hand, the merits of Meyerbeer in the fields of orchestration
and operatic style are undeniable. Often his melodies lack *noblesse*, and
his style goes too eagerly after the current fashion. Still, in the history of
opera he was a powerful influence to which even his violent critic, Wagner,
was heavily indebted, as *Rienzi* and *Tannhaeuser* demonstrate most clearly.

In sharp contrast to the theatrical Meyerbeer, Mendelssohn represented
the introvert and aristocratic type of artistry fostered by romanticism. His
propensity toward retrospection led him to the study of the great masters
of the baroque, chiefly Johann Sebastian Bach. He ardently championed
the work of that greatest of all Protestant composers and conducted the
first performance of his *St. Matthew's Passion* after the composer's death.
By that signal action he started the revival of Bach's then almost forgotten
art. In spite of his somewhat archaic inclinations, Mendelssohn was a
composer of distinct originality. The ingenious *Midsummer Night's
Dream*, especially the overture written in his seventeenth year, the fiery
Violin Concerto, his once tremendously popular *Songs without Words*
display supreme mastership. No less famous are his oratorios, especially
Elijah and *St. Paul*. The latter work may, with good reason, be considered
his declaration of faith, glorifying the message of Christian universalism.

His fine organ compositions, cantatas and choruses are not so well known, perhaps because of a certain lack of genuine power conditioned by his aristocratic tendencies. Only German racial theorists were able to discover traces of Jewishness in his music. Although from the Jewish point of view such a demonstration would not be unwelcome, there is no real basis for such a thesis. As organizer and first director of the famous Leipzig conservatory, he established the most renowned musical academy of Central Europe. Teacher, organizer, reviver, creative composer, all his activities made him a truly venerable figure in German cultural history— up to 1933.

Second Generation: Jacques Offenbach (1819-1880)

Son of the meritorious cantor, Isaac Judah Eberscht of Cologne, Offenbach showed little if any interest in the musical legacy of his ancestors. He is not unjustly called the "father of the modern operetta." Actually this title reflects but one facet of his complex personality. He was essentially of a polar nature—demonic satirist as well as demonic tragedian. His masterpieces of musical satire, contemporary with and akin to the drawings of Daumier, hold up a merciless mirror to the corruption of the Second French Empire. To this category belong his sharp-witted *Orpheus in Hades, Beautiful Helen, The Duchess of Gerolstein* and many others. The tragic genre is represented only by his unforgettable *Tales of Hoffmann*, his last work. The mocking satirist shed a tear, and it became the fairest memory of him. A charming jester all his life, he showed the profound side of his music only shortly before death took the pen from his untiring hands. While most of his operettas have long since been forgotten, a few live on vigorously, and many of his catchy and witty melodies have lost nothing of their charm in eighty years.

Third Generation: Gustav Mahler (1860-1911)

None of the three composers mentioned thus far can be considered as an embodiment of Jewish ideas or ideals. This is certainly regrettable. The case of Mahler, however, borders on the tragic and must be understood as a woeful symptom of the inner disintegration of the Jewish community. This is so, not only because of the monumental stature of Mahler's genius, which towers far above that of all other Jewish composers, but chiefly because his real spiritual sources ran deeply in emotional and intellectual Jewish terrain.

In many respects he must be viewed as a living anachronism: a prophet burning with the ethical fanaticism of an Amos, a God-seeker of the ecstatic *Saddik* type. A sensitive spirit uttering the words "I shall die to live again for God," though unaware of the Psalmist's similar exclamation, a composer who mysteriously shows distinct kinship with Hasidic tunes,

Mahler, an embodiment of the noblest concepts of Judaism, was entirely estranged from his own people, his own faith!

And yet he felt something of the cleavage in the depths of his being. His ardent love for German folk song, which bore splendid fruit in his first four symphonies, did not fully satisfy his searching soul. He had to go back to medieval poetry (*veni creator spiritus*) and to the mysticism of the second part of Goethe's *Faust*. And in the end he sought and found the real source of his feelings in the poetry of the ancient Far East. In his farewell to life, the immortal *Song of the Earth*, he sings: "I will go home to my abode. No more of roaming far away. Still is my heart, awaiting now its hour."

His influence upon the following generations was extraordinary. Not even now (1946), thirty-five years after his death, can we really measure the full impact of his genius upon modern music. Suffice it to say that no contemporary composer of stature has been left wholly untouched by Mahler's style and technique.

Fourth Generation: Arnold Schoenberg (1874-1951)
Ernest Bloch (1880-1959)

Both of these composers, while vastly different from each other, bear the imprint of Mahler's influence. Schoenberg, the most controversial figure in modern music, shows the keenly logical and technical discipline of a true heir of Mahler, while Bloch represents the "voice crying in the wilderness" of modern musical business; he has not compromised with the concessions generally made to the purely ephemeral demands of the musical market. There is common ground between Bloch and Schoenberg. Both are primarily concerned with the autonomy of melody, and their techniques, despite differences, render harmony almost as a function and a development of melody. Both composers stand today in the forefront of contemporary music. Schoenberg's work began with the consistent disintegration of Wagner's Tristan style and led him to the borders of tonality and beyond them. He was probably the first "atonal" composer, a designation which Schoenberg himself justly abhors. It is interesting to state that this composer has recently found his way back to his people, as the works *Moses* and *Kol Nidre* demonstrate.

Bloch was early attracted by Jewish conceptions: his cello rhapsody *Shelomo* (1912), his great Sabbath liturgy for the synagogue, his inspired *Baal-Shem* suite, his symphony *Israel*, all bear proud witness to Bloch's love of Judaism. He was the first musician of real stature, after the Emancipation, publicly and unmistakably to identify himself with Israel's cause.

Fifth Generation: Darius Milhaud (1891-   )
George Gershwin (1898-1937)

The social and musical background of these two composers, even their geographic preconditioning, could not be more completely antithetic. Milhaud is the product of the complex, refined and sometimes decadent tradition of western Europe, Gershwin, the son of plain eastern Jewish immigrants. And yet, in one respect, they are alike: in their love for the folk song of the common man. Both composers erected monuments to the musical lore of their native countries: Milhaud in his numerous Provençal pieces, Gershwin in his *Porgy and Bess,* glorifying Negro lore of the deep South. It was Gershwin's merit to span the gulf between "classical" and "popular" music. By incorporating jazz elements into serious music and by introducing the "classical" technique into popular and dance music, he enriched both realms. Alas, his early death interrupted a promising development; and in the absence of a legitimate heir, the gulf between serious and popular music is widening again. Yet Gershwin's masterpiece, his *Porgy and Bess,* the first truly American opera, will live on as long as America loves her own songs.

Milhaud, the descendant of an old Avignon family, entered on his career soon after the First World War as a strong anti-Wagnerian. A member of the "Group of Six," in the early twenties, he assiduously followed its motto: "Return to simplicity." Later, to his own advantage, he left that narrow path. Moreover, he has become increasingly conscious of his Jewish musical heritage. He has written articles on Jewish folk song, and, what is more, his artistic work has been greatly enriched by this interest. His *Zions-Hymn,* his exultant psalms, his magnificent *Israel Lives* and many other compositions put him in the first line of living composers. That the three greatest living composers of Jewish birth are paying heed and homage to their people's musical tradition is a gratifying sign of the trend of our times.

Thus, lightly etched, we behold the eight most significant Jewish composers since the Emancipation. To say that their importance cannot equal that of a Bach or a Mozart is no indictment or disparagement of their accomplishments. We need only stop for a moment to remember that for fifteen hundred years the Jewish people was excluded from the general growth of music. Nonetheless, this small minority was able in the course of a hundred and fifty years to produce a score of outstanding musicians whose efforts well-nigh reach the highest attainments of creative genius.

On the other hand, not all Jewish composers have wrestled with the highest ideals. The history of popular music, of the operetta, of the "hit song," is replete with Jewish names. It depends upon the reader's system of values as to whether or not he considers this a matter of pride. Musical art may not have experienced any serious advance through their efforts; yet these composers have certainly brought many joyous hours to millions.

Since Offenbach, literally hundreds of operetta composers have flooded the markets of America and Europe with their products. We mention only a few names of that numerous host: Oscar Straus, (1870-1954), E. Kalman (1882-1953), L. Fall (1873-1925), L. Ascher (1880-1942), Sigmund Romberg (1887-1951), Jerome Kern (1885-1946), Irving Berlin (1888-   ). These are genuine talents, and each of them is being imitated and "emulated" by scores of followers. The fashions of popular music change often and unexpectedly. Yet, this kind of composition follows paths of its own, and what was good business yesterday may be a loss tomorrow. Thus, purely commercial music had a course of its own, somewhat removed from the principal thoroughfares of the realm of serious music.

Interpretive Musicians

Even more numerous and at least as well known as the composers are the names of Jewish interpretive musicians. A few outstanding instrumentalists might well be mentioned, for in many cases they have enriched the musical life of entire generations and countries. We list here only those outstanding artists who have influenced the whole course of their art.

Conductors: Ferdinand von Hiller (1811-1885), intimate friend of Felix Mendelssohn, highly meritorious conductor in western Germany, gifted composer and writer. It is interesting to note that this convert had to find an outlet for his Old Testament nostalgia in his oratorios, though none of them attained lasting success.

Hermann Levi (1839-1900), the famous champion of Richard Wagner's work. He was the first conductor of *Parsifal* (!), presumably the reward for his unswerving loyalty to Wagner, in spite of the master's anti-Semitic writings and opinions.

Gustav Mahler (1860-1911), the famous composer. Here it must suffice to note that he was the first representative of a type of conducting since his day frequently imitated. He was an obsessed, demonic idealist, often given to despotic fanaticism. To be sure, he was not an endearing conductor, but proved nonetheless, an ingenious and altogether faithful interpreter of the composer's intentions.

Leo Blech (1871-1958), general music director of the Berlin State Opera, the prototype of fine craftsmanship and reliable solidity.

Bruno Walter (1876-   ), inspiring champion of Bach, Mozart and of the works of his mentor and teacher, Gustav Mahler.

Arthur Bodanzky (1877-1939), disciple of Mahler, conductor at the Metropolitan Opera, a fascinating conductor of fiery temperament.

Fritz Reiner (1888-   ), at present director of the Pittsburgh Symphony; another of the Mahler heirs.

Otto Klemperer (1885-   ), revolutionary director of the Kroll-opera, Berlin; at his best as opera conductor; protagonist of contemporary music.

Eugene Ormandy (1899-   ), director of the Philadelphia Symphony;

a conservative interpreter of a slightly didactic, but intelligent and in-spiring nature.

Leonard Bernstein (1918-   ), the youngest in the galaxy of prominent conductors; as a composer displaying creative interest in Jewish matters; for example, his symphony, *Jeremiah.*

Most of these conductors come from Central or Western Europe. When we turn to violinists and pianists, virtuosi of the concert stage, we find the overwhelming majority to be of Eastern Jewish origin. One reason for this seems to lie in the fact that the tradition of Jewish fiddlers (*klezmorim*) in the Eastern countries was still alive in the middle of the nineteenth century, whereas it was completely forgotten and obsolete in Central and Western Europe. These fiddlers functioned as dance bands, and as teachers, furnishing the cultural life of East European Jewry with a strongly artistic element.

Violinists

Most of the outstanding violinists of the past hundred years were directly or indirectly disciples of the two superb teachers of violinistic style: Joseph Joachim (1831-1907), the intimate friend of Brahms, eminent artist and teacher, finally director of the States Academy of Music of Berlin; and Leopold von Auer (1845-1925), the unforgettable master who transplanted the best European tradition to America. Of renowned violinists there are only three who developed outside the orbit of these two great pedagogues: Arnold Rosé (1863-1946), concertmaster of the Vienna State Opera and primarius of a famous string quartet; Fritz Kreisler (1875-   ), the well known interpreter of the works of the classics. His antagonistic, or at best indifferent, attitude toward con-temporary music stands in sharp contrast to the style of the third of this group, Joseph Szigeti (1892-   ), the versatile advocate of modern litera-ture for the violin. Bronislaw Hubermann (1882-1947), most inspiring and noble interpreter of serious music, a virtuoso of first magnitude, but ruthless enemy of virtuosity for its own sake, was a *rara avis* among violinists. He had, moreover, the great merit of having founded the Palestine Orchestra at the time Hitler ousted the Jewish members of German orchestras. Hubermann defended, proudly and unyieldingly, the honor of Jewish musicians in a revealing correspondence with Wilhelm Furtwaengler, then director of the Berlin Philharmonic Orchestra. As an artist he belongs in the Joachim orbit.

Of Auer's disciples we mention here Mischa Elman (1891-   ) and Jascha Heifetz (1901-   ), the great virtuosi; Yehudi Menuhin (1916-   ), one of the younger among the eminent violinists, may be considered a spiritual grandchild of Auer, since his training lay in the hands of Auer adepts.

Pianists

The briefest list of pianistic artists reflects the countless facets of the development of European style. Paraphrasing a Latin bon mot: *Quot digiti tot styli!* Beginning with Ignace Moscheles (1794-1870), the elegant friend and epigone of Mendelssohn, there is not one field of piano playing where men of Jewish extraction have not carved out their more or less significant niches. Joseph Fischhoff (1804-1857) and Stephen Heller (1814-1888) belong to the adherents of the Schumann-Chopin romantic school. Anton Rubinstein (1829-1894), friend and champion of Liszt and Wagner, seems to have been of a nature not unlike Mahler's, though scarcely of his depth. Theodor Leschetitzky (1830-1915), master teacher, and Leopold Godowsky (1870-1931), both had a flair for virtuoso style, occasionally neglecting the more rigid demands of classic diction. Moritz Moszkowski (1854-1925), a fine pianist and composer of charming miniatures, and Moritz Rosenthal (1862-1946) are both exponents of late romanticism. So was Ignace Friedman (1882-1947), the great interpreter and editor of Chopin's work, one of the noblest artists of our time. In certain contrast to these neoromanticists stands the figure of Arthur Schnabel (1882-1951), stanch champion of Mozart, Beethoven and Schubert, at the same time a radical modern composer. To the same ultraclassic category belongs Rudolf Serkin. A remarkable attempt at synthesizing the virtuoso style of the Liszt school with the more severe idiom of the classicists is undertaken by the ingenious and brilliant Vladimir Horowitz (1904-   ). Modern and ultramodern music has found its faithful and subtle interpreter in Eduard Steuerman (1902-   ).

As for vocalists, their number is legion. We will not even begin to list them, for in a very real sense the evaluation of singers is largely a matter of personal taste. Nor did singers contribute independently to music's development, being more often the instruments of composers and conductors than autonomous interpreters. Of some significance were the singers of the stage; their story belongs rather to the history of the theater than to that of music.

The Science of Musicology and Its Jewish Students

In antiquity and the Middle Ages music was considered more as a science than an art, and its study was part of the *quadrivium educationis,* together with algebra, geometry and astronomy. This connection with the astronomic-mathematical branch of natural science came to an end when humanism and the Renaissance proclaimed the freedom of the individual and his scientific research. The forms of the opera and of the oratorio, with their emphasis upon spontaneous emotions of the individual, stressed the purely *artistic* side and disregarded the scientific approach of musical endeavors. The ensuing centuries and their characteristic ideologies raised this emotional attitude (at least, where secular music was concerned) to an almost antiscientific individualism. On the other hand, it was emotional romanticism, with its archaic tendencies, that gave new impetus to musical science. The history of music was given a solid standing in the academic curricula of Germany, Austria and, later, of France and England. Mendelssohn and his school consistently cultivated the music of past centuries, especially of the baroque period. Thus, it was hardly a coincidence that Mendelssohn placed A. B. Marx as the first professor of musical history at the University of Berlin. Marx was the forerunner of a group of distinguished musicologists, of whom not a few were of Jewish birth. Bypassing Eduard Hanslick (son of a Christian and a Jew), Richard Wagner's deadly adversary, the name of Guido Adler (1855-1942) and his Vienna school will for all time be linked with the establishment of musicology based upon sound historic-philological methods. This venerable Nestor of musical science had trained a host of younger scholars, of whom E. Wellesz is of outstanding significance. The Berlin school, meanwhile, had produced such able students as the late O. Abraham, one of the founders of comparative musicology, and Curt Sachs, of New York University (d. 1959), the greatest authority on musical instruments and their history and at the same time a foremost scholar in the field of the music of antiquity. A specialist in Asiatic music was the late Robert Lachmann, who also published some studies on the music of Oriental Jews. The universalistic tradition of the Riemann school is upheld by so profound a scholar as Alfred Einstein, of Smith College (d. 1952). We should add here the pioneers of the science of Jewish music, Eduard Birnbaum (1855-1920) and Abraham Z. Idelsohn (1882-1938) who, while in every respect universal scholars, applied the methods of general musicology to the particular problems of the music of Judaism and synagogal tradition. They set an inspiring example for the Jewish musicologists of today.

Epilogue

> "History is change."
> (J. Burckhardt)

A critical evaluation of the Jewish contribution to world music must, of necessity, expound its results in restrospective terms. Nor is it the historian's task to prophesy, however wide the vistas he has opened. The present moment, however, still belongs to the historian; and from this narrow point between past and future we may venture to estimate accomplishments yet to come. We may expect significant attainments in music only where a valuable musical tradition is already in existence. Thus, Jewish contributions may be looked for in Russia, America, perhaps in

Western Europe and Palestine. Individual creations of Russian or French Jews will be acclaimed—and claimed—by their native countries, and the Jewishness of the composers will be of little, if any, significance. Not quite so simple is the American situation, where composers of international stature have drawn originality and power from the eternal sources of their Jewish tradition. Nevertheless, they will remain exceptions rather than become the rule.

Palestine, on the other hand, has no art-music tradition of long standing; but it is building one speedily and, once this prerequisite of musical culture is fulfilled, we may expect significant contributions. Vigorous Jewish life in the Holy Land has already generated a remarkable musical folklore. Art music takes longer than the fifty years Hebrew folk song has had for its new life; a certain intellectual and spiritual homogeneity is likewise required. When this standard will be reached Palestinian compositions will be considered, rightly or wrongly, as the typical output of the Jewish spirit, as an accomplishment characteristic of Judaism, rather than of the personal style of its particular composer. This, then, may become the beginning of a chapter yet unwritten: the role not of Jews, but of Judaism in modern music.

POSTSCRIPT

The discovery of the Dead Sea Scrolls, beginning in 1948, has added some important new facts to our knowledge of ancient forms. We know now that the Gregorian form of the antiphone was anticipated by the monkish inhabitants of Qumran, who composed a number of such hymns. Furthermore, it is established that the trumpets used before the destruction of the Temple could produce clear tones with definable pitches. Finally, some of the Dead Sea Scrolls contain signs which might possibly be the forerunner of a descriptive musical notation.

With regard to music in Israel, my prediction in the original chapter above, written over twenty years ago, has in general come true, with only one exception, albeit a weighty one: the expected growth of genuine popular song in Palestine has not occurred; quite a contrary event has been noted: it has ceased ever since statehood was achieved. The mass immigrations of European and Oriental Jews, undertaken as emergency measures, upset the growing homogeneity of the Palestinian songs, so promisingly initiated by the previous, more orderly waves of immigration. The new immigrants were themselves unwilling to or incapable of filling the vacuum with songs of their own. The situation of the first Zionist settlers repeated itself, but under totally different, and for the genesis of popular chants decidedly unfavorable, conditions. Thus it happened that the folksong or popular song, as we encountered it in 1945, was in a way frozen—it did not grow, nor did it wither; it was kept in a state of suspended development. Folksong was enlarged, but neither homogenized nor improved by the absorption of Near Eastern-Oriental lore; if anything, it was vulgarized. This is the present situation, and no end of it is in view, especially since an uncritical eclecticism, championed in the Westernized kindergartens of Israel, has imported for children a mass of Teutonic and French nursery songs, which have left considerable traces in the popular chants of the adults. Thus if the development of popular song in Israel has left its seemingly predetermined path and has become somewhat chaotic, musical research has followed its erratic course and taken good account of its various movements. Israeli musicologists have watched carefully over the changing manifestations of popular expression.

Israel's Main Institutions of Music

After an initial period of experimentation, Israelis have taken the lead in the field of Jewish music. Actually, they began by cultivating music exactly like musicians in any Western country would; but soon certain important differences began to emerge. In the midst of the Arabic orbit, the Jewish musician felt himself to be either a bridgebuilder or a straightforward representative of Western music. Accordingly, Israeli musical institutions fall into the patterns delineated by these two possibilities for music in the Near East: either they deal, sometimes in a naive and uncritical way, with folklore, especially Jewish folklore, or they cultivate entirely Western art music. To the latter category belongs the Israel Philharmonic Orchestra, founded by Bronislaw Hubermann and first directed by Arturo Toscanini. It has remained to this day a rather conservative institution. The younger ensembles, especially the chamber orchestra under the direction of Gary Bertini, have contributed more to the advancement of art music in Israel, if less to publicity. The big choruses, the regular chorus festivals (*Zimriah*) cultivate more the popular or folkloristic music of Israel. The big music libraries of the Hebrew University and of the cities of Tel-Aviv and Haifa, the many conservatories and music schools, the two academies of music (in Jerusalem and Tel-Aviv), and most recently the two departments of musicology at the universities of Jerusalem and Tel-Aviv, all testify to the extremely vivid interest in music in the State of Israel.

Yet, neither the identity of Jewish music nor its tradition has really been strengthened in Israel. While the Orthodox organizations pay the usual lip service to Jewish musical tradition, little, if anything, has been done to further it.

The Jerusalem organization of "religious music" under the Ministry of Religion is a group of well-meaning but, however pious, rather inept music-lovers. Art music in the Synagogue is prohibited now just as it was fifty years ago, and no change of this sterile attitude is in sight.

Against this unsatisfactory state of affairs must be set the excellent work on Hebrew folklore in progress for the past twelve or fifteen years. In trying to examine and cultivate the folklore of the many Oriental Jewish communities, the scholars run against time, but even so they have accomplished many fine results. The Central Institute of Jewish Music, attached to the Hebrew University in Jerusalem, under the able leadership of Israel Adler, is an outstanding research institute of Hebrew folklore, the finest and greatest in the world. Its records and documents are of major importance for musicology.

Another bright spot in this uneven image is held by the new composers of Israel. It is too early to speak of a distinct style of art music that is characteristic of Israel, but certain elements of a distinctive style have begun to crystallize. The best known of the new Israeli composers, most of whom enjoy an international reputation, are J. Tal, P. Ben-Chayim, Oe. Partos, and B. Orgad.

The American Situation

The organizing efforts in the United States have been no less eagerly conducted than in Israel. Yet, exactly as in Israel, organization *per se* does not replace original and creative work. Since 1948 no less than four major institutions have come into being to sponsor and cultivate work and training in Jewish music. Three of them specialize in Synagogue music: the schools of liturgical or sacred music established by the Hebrew Union College-Jewish Institute of Religion, The Jewish Theological Seminary, and the Yeshiva University, all in New York City. They have succeeded in graduating a considerable number of well-trained cantors for American congregations. A certain elevation of musical standards, if not of taste, in the Synagogue is undeniable. It must be regretted, though, that the serious efforts of these institutions are ignored or at least not appreciated by the rabbinical bodies, which still look upon them with the traditional distrust characteristic of the relations between rabbis and cantors for the past thousand years. On the secular side, the Hebrew Arts School for Music and Dance, under the inspired leadership of Tziporah H. Jochsberger, is doing outstanding work in the musical education of Jewish children and adolescents.

Another institution is the National Jewish Music Council in New York, a purely promotional organization. It champions the cause of Jewish music in the press, through radio and other mass media, all over the country. It is enterprising and energetic, but its zeal is not always matched by its taste, which often lacks discrimination and artistic standards. Much more significant for the representation of the music of Judaism are those recognized composers who have identified themselves before the world with Judaism and its principles. In their forefront stood—and his memory is still green—Arnold Schoenberg (d. 1951), who in many of his late works identified himself unreservedly with Judaism and Israel. His major work, the monumental opera *Moses und Aron*, has been performed posthumously in Switzerland, Germany, England, the United States (in Boston, not New York!) and France, each time with great acclaim and success. His posthumous *Modern Psalms* were left unfinished but his moving *Survivor of the Warsaw Ghetto* and the symphonic work *Kol Nidre* have already attained the status of classics (although the latter has not yet been performed in New York) and remain musical monuments of lasting value. Next to this imposing figure even such fine composers as Ernest Bloch (d. 1959) or Ernest Toch (d. 1964) lose some degree of artistic merit. Turning to the living, the Nestor of Jewish composers, Darius Milhaud, has most eloquently testified to the love for his Jewish patrimony in his opera *David* written for the Termillennary of the City of Jerusalem (nonscenic première in Jerusalem, 1954). In his autobiography he memorializes his Judaeo-French-Provençal ancestry.

Of American composers with a positive Jewish attitude Lucas Foss represents the lyric and experimental vanguard, while Aaron Copland and Y. Wyner have abstained from electronic or aleatoric ventures. Leonard Bernstein, vacillating between the prophetic and the theatrical, has once again shown his talent in his *Chichester Psalms*, an attractive setting of several Psalms. His use of liturgical concepts of Judaism (as in *Kaddish Symphony*) or biblical ideas (as in *Jeremiah Symphony*) may not have been clearly defined, but his *Chichester Psalms* are clear-cut compositions of the original texts.

The output of learned studies in the field of Jewish music has been quite impressive, though still attributable to a very few able scholars: the ambivalence of taking a position between studies on Jewish folklore and on the musical aspects of Jewish history has resulted in a tendency for scholars to specialize in one or the other of these fields. In this sphere the efforts of Israeli scholars are almost parallel to those of the Americans, and the interchange of ideas and personal visits is quite intense. Most of them have worked in both countries. Of Israeli students we mention here I. Adler, B. Bayer, Gerson-Kivi, Avenari, H. Shmueli, Mrs. M. Smora-Cohn, P. Gradenwitz, and S. Hofmann; of Americans, J. Newman, the late S. Rosowsky, whose extensive study on cantillation deserves to be read with much attention and just as much caution, Johanna Spector, Judith Eisenstein, and this writer.

One is tempted to conclude this short survey with a somewhat curious observation: Jewish musical tradition seems to be better cared for by individuals, be they composers or scholars, than by organizations or institutions.

NOTES

[1] *Keilinschriftliches Textbuch zum Alten Testament,* 3rd ed., Leipzig, 1909, p. 45.

[1a Cf. Elias Bickerman, "The Historical Foundations of Postbiblical Judaism," this work, Vol. I, Chap. 2.]

[2a Cf. Judah Goldin, "The Period of the Talmud," this work, Vol. I, pp. 194, 208-209.]

[3a Cf. Robert Gordis, "The Bible as a Cultural Monument," this work, Vol. II, pp. 3-4.]

[4a Cf. Yudel Mark, "Yiddish Literature," this work, Vol. II, pp. 427-428.]

[5a Cf. Cecil Roth, "The European Age in Jewish History (to 1648)," this work, Vol. I, Chap. 4, *passim.*]

[6] This oldest document of Hebrew music has been recorded according to the transcription of the writer and its first public rendition is part of the record-album, "Israel Sings," available at the Union of American Hebrew Congregations.

[7a Cf. Roth, *op. cit.,* pp. 245 f.]

[8] This was especially the case of the *Hazanim*: composers and singers with the ability of a Wolf Bass, Leon Singer (Leoni), A. Beer, etc., absorbed and integrated the musical style of their time.

[9] Da Ponte spent the last thirty years of his life, a miserable pauper, in this country; his American activities deserve new treatment in the light of late research. (Krebiehl's meritorious study of that subject ought to be revised and enlarged.)

SELECT BIBLIOGRAPHY

This is not a complete bibliography; such an undertaking would easily fill a large volume. Only such works are mentioned here as are based upon original research and contain numerous bibliographical notes.

FRIEDMANN, ARON, *Lebensbilder beruehmter Kantoren.* Berlin, 1921-1927.

HOEEG, CARSTEN, "La notation ekphonétique," in *Monumenta Musicae Byzantinae.* Copenhagen, 1935.

IDELSOHN, ABRAHAM Z., *Jewish Music in Its Historical Development.* New York, 1929.

——, *Thesaurus of Oriental-Hebrew Melodies.* 10 vols. New York and Berlin, 1921-1933.

The Jewish Encyclopedia, New York and London, 1901. Articles on Jewish Music, Accents, Psalms, etc.

SACHS, CURT, *The Rise of Music in the Ancient World, East and West.* New York, 1943.

SALESKI, GDAL, *Famous Musicians of a Wandering Race.* New York, 1927.

SCHONBERG, JAKOB, *Die traditionellen Gesaenge des israelitischen Gottesdienstes in Deutschland.* Nuernberg, 1926.

WAGNER, PETER, *Einfuehrung in die Gregorianischen Melodien.* Leipzig, 1921, Vol. III.

WERNER, ERIC, and SONNE, ISAIAH, "The Philosophy and Theory of Music in Judaeo-Arabic Literature," in the *Hebrew Union College Annual*, XVI, 251-319. Cincinnati, 1941.

WERNER, ERIC, "Preliminary Notes for a Comparative Study of Catholic and Jewish Musical Punctuation," in the *Hebrew Union College Annual*, XV, 335-367.

——, "Manuscripts of Jewish Music in the Edward Birnbaum Collection," in the *Hebrew Union College Annual*, XVIII, 397-429.

——, "Prolegomena to a Bibliography of Jewish Music," in *Historia Judaica*, pp. 175-188. New York, 1944.

ZUNSER, ELYOKUM, *A Jewish Bard* (Autobiography), edited by A. H. Fromenson. New York, 1905.

CHAPTER 5

JUDAISM AND ART

By Rachel Wischnitzer

In contrast to the general conception of gods in antiquity, Israel saw in the Deity not simply one aspect of nature in preference to others, or an incorporation of a number of gods. The God of Israel transcended the world scene. He was the cause of events in nature and in history. And, being invisible, He could not be identified with any form in "heaven, earth or sea."

The attribute of invisibility was thus fundamental to the Jewish conception of God. To identify Him with any material form whatever would be to confuse the Creator with His creature.

Graven and molten images are usually associated in the Bible with idol worship; but it is quite conceivable that attempts were occasionally made by some dissidents to fashion images of the God of Israel, too. Therefore, the invisibility of God had to be stressed over and over again. When Deuteronomy recalls the circumstances of the Revelation it repeatedly insists that "Ye heard the voice of words, but ye saw no form; only a voice" (4:12). "For ye saw no manner of form on the day that the Lord spoke unto you in Horeb out of the midst of the fire" (4:15).

It is from the imagery of Creation that the Second Commandment (Ex. 20:3-4) drew its vocabulary. Nothing of the created, visible world can possibly represent God, and since "likenesses" of the visible world actually are worshiped in various cults as manifestations of God, they are particularly distasteful.[1]

The Second Commandment in the Book of Exodus reappears in chapter five of Deuteronomy without changes. In chapter four, however, the issue of image making and idol worshiping is taken up more specifically, and there the principal concern of the Lawgiver appears to be over figures "male or female" (Deut. 4:16), not "heaven, earth and sea" and "what is in them." William F. Albright[2] has suggested that the Lawgiver, in pointing to figures, wished to denounce the infamous bloody rites associated with the Canaanite god Baal and the goddess Ashthoreth. The sun was proclaimed the principle of life in Egypt; sex was the principle of life adored in the Asiatic cults. The statues of the human-bodied gods in wood and stone cast a magic spell upon the soul of the people and this spell had to be broken at all cost. Hence again and again it is pointed out that these statues can neither see nor listen to the worshiper, for they are only the works of human hands (Deut. 4:28).

Next the Lawgiver enumerates the animals, birds, snakes and fish (4:17-18). Significantly last come the celestial spheres. The sun, moon, stars and the host of heaven are individually mentioned, the astral cults strictly forbidden. But there is no reference to images associated with the astral cults. The astral cults consisted chiefly in stargazing and incense burning on altars raised on roofs. What was prohibited was "lifting up thine eyes unto heaven" (Deut. 4:19) for purposes of adoration, a practice obviously less offensive than the sanguinary ritual connected with some image cults. The motivation for the prohibition of astral cults reveals the new attitude clearly. Ikhnaton had conceded the celestial Nile as a common possession to all mankind, but the two other Niles, the actual river and the subterranean stream on which the sun was supposed to travel by night back to the east, he reserved as the exclusive property of the Egyptian Empire. But the Lawgiver tells us that the celestial bodies were "divided" by the Lord "unto all nations under the whole heaven" (4:19) and do not belong to the religious sphere of any particular nation.

The attitude of Judaism toward the arts was also affected by the changing function of the arts themselves.

The symbolic significance of an image is not an inherent quality of the image. If in the eighth century B.C.E. ivory plaques with portrayals of Egyptian deities—Horus, Re, Isis, Nephtys—and various symbols were used in Samaria as inlays in furniture, we can be sure that the owners of such furniture did not bother about the significance of the ivory carvings. The few panels that have survived the destruction of Samaria and have been excavated appear to be Phoenician ware. The Phoenician carvers who copied Egyptian models probably did have a vague idea of the subjects depicted, but the Israelite customers in Samaria hardly knew what or whom the small inlay figures were meant to represent.[3] It is interesting to note that the Prophet Amos, when denouncing the upper classes of Samaria for reclining on "beds of ivory" (3:15; 4:4), probably aimed at idleness and luxury rather than the impropriety of the Egyptian figure decoration of the couches. He does not even mention the carvings.

With this in mind, we can better comprehend the cultural background of King Solomon's time (second part of the tenth century B.C.E.) and more easily evaluate the significance of the decoration of the royal palace and the Temple of Jerusalem built by the King.[3a]

The ivory throne in the palace hall was overlaid with gold and flanked by lion statues (I Kings 10:18-20). Lion figures standing guard at a palace gate or a throne were no objects of worship in the Near East; rather they were intended to exalt the authority of the ruler. The winged cherubim in the Holy of Holies of the Temple, carved in wood and paneled with gold (I Kings 6:23 ff.; II Chron. 3:10), were placed on top of the Ark as its crowning part (I Kings 8:6 f.). There is no indication that these cherubim were regarded as cult objects. The interior walls of the main hall of the Temple, the Sanctuary, were decorated with a relief of alternating cherubim, palm trees and open flowers (I Kings 6:29; II Chron. 3:7). There is no suggestion in the Bible that these wall reliefs were associated with any ritual.

Edward B. Tylor has pointed out that the motif of cherubim flanking a palm tree in the Solomonic Temple was derived from Assyrian art, where the palm tree is found flanked by winged human or animal figures.[4] The design is familiar from the ancient Assyrian seals and later wall reliefs in royal palaces in Nineveh. Tylor has been able to interpret the scene. The winged male figures on either side of the tree, carrying a basket and what was supposed to be a fir cone, actually are pollinating the date palm. The fertilization of the date tree in the Near East was described by Herodotus, Theophrastus and Pliny the Elder in his *Natural History*. The Assyrians apparently saw in the achievement of their palm growers an evidence of the assistance of supernatural forces and therefore represented the gardeners as fantastic beings, winged, eagle-headed men, griffins or winged horses. The palm tree became converted into a ceremonial object, a kind of standard set with palmettes or palm-leaf clusters, a symbol of the Tree of Life. Behind the picture there may have been the idea of an actual liturgical performance.

We must determine just what was the relationship of the cherub-palm motif of I Kings 6:29 to the Assyrian ceremonial scene. Since we know that the Temple was built with the help of Tyrian artisans, we have to take into account Phoenician influences in the elaboration of the motif. In Phoenician art the Assyrian "gardeners," who are treated as winged sphinxes, appear in most conventionalized postures, while the tree is simplified and considerably reduced in its form—so much so that it seems rather doubtful that the subject meant the same there as in the original conception. The Phoenician limestone seal from Megiddo[5] may give us an idea of what the design of the cherub-palm tree decoration was like in the Temple at Jerusalem. Since the eatable date fruit is not frequently mentioned in the Bible, we are probably not wrong in assuming that the original meaning of the motif had been lost.[6]

Not before talmudic times do we find reference to the motif of the cultivation of the date palm, that is, to its artificial fertilization. Max Gruenbaum[7] cites Pesahim 56a and records the romantic story of the barren palm tree in Chamtan, wistfully "looking" toward Jericho, which was known from biblical times as the palm city (Deut. 34:3; II Chron. 28:15). A palm grower, the story goes, advises the people how to make the tree bear fruit. Josephus (*Bell. Jud.* IV:8:3) mentions a syrup of a palm fruit, apparently dates, produced in Jericho. The question is, however, was the date a popular foodstuff in biblical times in Palestine? Even more important, what role did fertilization of the date tree play in popular imagination in biblical times? It seems that the poet's mind was inspired by the general symbolism of a tree, its growth, its blossoming, its fruitfulness and beauty, rather than by any specific aspect of its cultivation.

The national tree was the olive. It is this tree which the prophet Zechariah uses as a political metaphor in his fifth vision. The king, Zerubbabel, and the High Priest, Joshua, who are expected to establish firmly the new commonwealth after the return of the exiles in 519 B.C.E., are seen as two olive trees flanking a seven-branched candlestick and furnishing it with oil (4:3 ff.). Here the original Oriental conception underlying the picture can easily be recognized, but the olive substitutes for the date palm.

It is the olive tree again which is used as a metaphor in Psalm 52:8, where the righteous is compared with a "leafy olive-tree in the house of God." In Psalm 92:12 the righteous is promised that he shall "flourish like the palm tree" and the cedar. The reference to the Temple is repeated: Those "planted in the house of the Lord . . . shall flourish in the courts of our God. They shall still bring forth fruit in old age" (vss. 13, 14).

The metaphors used in the Psalms show that the tree had become the symbol of the godly. The cult of the reproductive capacities of mother nature, practiced in Assyria, has been sublimated in Palestine into a figure of speech serving to exalt the faithful. The palm tree flanked by cherubim on the reliefs of the Temple at Jerusalem represents one of the stages in this process of spiritualization; perhaps it is the direct prototype for the literary figure.

H. T. Obbink, the Utrecht scholar,[8] has similarly attempted to explain the purpose of the "golden calves" of Jeroboam. Contrary to the palm-and-cherub reliefs in the Temple, the golden calves erected in the sanctuaries of Beth-el and Dan are expressly said to have been intended as cult objects. Jeroboam, when proclaimed king of the seceded Northern Kingdom after Solomon's death, promptly restored the two ancient sanctuaries in order to prevent pilgrimage to Jerusalem (1 Kings 12:26, 27) and gave each sanctuary a golden calf. Suspecting a disparaging tendency on the part of the Judean recorder toward the schismatic king, Obbink doubts that the bulls were actually intended as cult statues. He believes rather that they were meant as supports for the invisible YHWH comparable to the cherubim of the Temple at Jerusalem. For prototypes he points to Near Eastern bull statues used as pedestals for deities.

We know statues of the Sumerian-Acadian Anu and the ancient Semitic god Hadad were represented standing or walking on animals. Hittite deities are found standing on pedestals set on the back of a lion or a bull.

But would a wingless animal of the pedestal type be likely to suggest to the worshiper the invisible presence of God and thus be comparable in its effect to the cherubim of the Temple at Jerusalem? The cherubim set up on the top of the Ark were regarded as flying creatures of the heavenly region, rather than as supports set up on the ground. God communed with Moses "from between the two cherubim" (Ex. 25:22). He "sitteth between the cherubim" (Ps. 99:1). The conception of an uplifted position, a raised throne, seems to be fundamental to the image of the cherubim. It is this idea of an exalted position which inspired the comparison of Tyre, before its fall, with a cherub (Ez. 28:14, 16).

If, then, Jeroboam wished to imitate the cult of Jerusalem he would not have chosen as a model the wingless pedestal type of bull. The suggestion of the Divine Presence produced by a pair of cherubim was hardly possible with a wingless bull. There is, however, a different category of bulls, which fits better into the picture: it is the winged bull of Assyrian art, which can be visualized as a flying creature although it stands on the ground. But George Ernest Wright has pointed out that those huge Assyrian bulls are practically nonexistent in Palestine and Syria.[9]

Assyrian art became an influence in Jewish imagery much later, when the Jews were brought into direct contact with Mesopotamian civilization. It was noticeable in Zechariah's vision and, earlier, in Ezekiel's vocabulary. "By the river of Chebar" in Babylonia, Ezekiel had his vision which carried him back to Jerusalem into the Temple. The Lord appears to the prophet on a "seat" (Ez. 1:1 ff.) placed above four creatures which resemble the cherubim in their function, but possess distinct features of their own. Although winged, these creatures are also wheeled and thus suggest a chariot which can be driven on the ground. The "chariot" actually goes down and up in the interior of the Temple.

While the appearance of the Temple cherubim is not described in the Bible (we can imagine them either as winged sphinxes of Phoenician art, or as winged ethereal angel-like figures of Egyptian divinities, of which a Phoenician version is seen in the ivories of Samaria)[10] Ezekiel's "living creatures" are elaborately described as hybrid figures combining characteristics of a man, a lion, a bull and an eagle. The mystical quaternion implies that Ezekiel had speculated on the meaning of the colossi set up at the gates, and actually carrying the arches of the portals of Assyrian palaces. Assyria at that time was no longer a foe, but a comrade in misfortune, for she had been conquered by the Babylonians a decade before. The composite animals combining the body of a lion and a bull with the head of a man and the wings of an eagle appeared to Ezekiel as similar to the cherubim of the Temple, and the qualities symbolized by the four creatures, the strength of the lion, the virility of the bull, the swiftness of the eagle and the intelligence of man, seemed to offer a key to the comprehension of the mystical nature of the cherubim.

Flying and moving on the ground, Ezekiel's creatures are a blending of two conceptions. The seat of the Lord of Ezekiel's vision is an uplifted throne and at the same time a chariot, a *Merkabah* riding on the floor of the Temple.

The personifications of the four ideal qualities survive in a somewhat modified form in the well-known saying in *Pirke Abot* (V:20): "Be fierce as the leopard, swift as the eagle, fleet as the deer and strong as the lion to perform the will of thy Father in heaven." Originally symbolizing the qualities of faithful doormen guarding royal palaces, the Assyrian animals became converted in Ezekiel's vision into drivers of the Lord's throne-chariot and finally symbols of the pious Jew. The process of spiritualization is strikingly similar to what we observed in the development of the date tree motif.

What do these shiftings in symbolism mean in terms of Jewish art?

On a fragment of a Jewish marble sarcophagus from Rome (in the Berlin Museum)[11] we see a seven-branched candlestick flanked by palm-trees and liturgical symbols, the *etrog*, the *lulab* and some dishes. Ernst Cohn-Wiener, who dated the sarcophagus in the second century C.E., associated it with Zechariah's vision of the leaders of the Restoration. The interpretation is tempting and might be correct in a general sense. However, there are more than two trees flanking the Menorah on the relief, and if we set the date in the late third or fourth century C.E., which is more plausible, a vaguely Messianic interpretation will appear more proper. The *etrog* and *lulab* may allude to a Messianic Feast of Tabernacles in which the pious hopes to have his part.

In a sarcophagus found in a Jewish catacomb on the site of the Villa Torlonia[12] in Rome, the palm-tree motif is abandoned; the Menorah stands alone in the center, flanked by the symbols of Tabernacles. These symbols remain the permanent companions of the candelabrum in Jewish art.

The four animals of *Pirke Abot* became extremely popular in Jewish art. We know them chiefly from the folk art of the eighteenth and nineteenth centuries; they are common in the carved or painted decoration of Torah shrines and *almemars* in Poland, and appear printed on paper flags which children used to carry in the synagogue processions on Simhat Torah. In Germany they were frequently embroidered or painted on linen wrappers of the Torah Scroll.

However, the practice of portraying the four animals symbolic of the pious must be of older origin, since they appear in the magnificent *Arha*

Turim codex of the Vatican (Cod. de Rossi 555) executed by a scribe, Isaac ben Obadiah, in 1436 in Mantua.[13] The manuscript is beautifully illuminated by a first-rate artist of the school of Pisanello. The style, the color scale, the facial types and costumes are extremely close to what we find in the paintings and drawings of this great master of the Italian *quattrocento*.

Among the four larger miniatures of the manuscript there is a synagogue scene with the worshipers in the background and the reader at the *almemar* in the foreground. To the right of the desk, members of the congregation are seen taking out the Scroll from a beautifully carved Torah shrine. In the corner rectangles of the painted frame that encloses the scene are displayed the four animals, the leopard, the eagle, the deer and the lion, in the sequence adopted in *Pirke Abot*, and each animal is accompanied by the appropriate clause written on a scroll. It was a particularly fine idea to frame the synagogue scene with the symbols of piety.

Ezekiel's throne-chariot of God gave rise to esoteric speculations which constitute what is known as the lore of *Maasse Merkabah*. We do not know when the first attempt at pictorial representation of Ezekiel's vision was made by Jews. According to the Talmud (Rosh Hashanah 24b) it is forbidden to portray the four living creatures together. However, the interest in the subject was so great that it could not be entirely ignored. In the thirteenth century prayer book of the Bodleian Library in Oxford (cod. 2373) the *Merkabah* is pictured as an illustration to the portion recited at Pentecost (Mahzor Shabuot).[14] The Divine chariot is treated as a portal carried by two of the fabulous creatures, a twin bull and a twin lion. The eagle and the man are displayed inside the portal, where they are accompanied by other fantastic animals. The inclusion of the *Merkabah* symbolism in the prayer book for Pentecost was not arbitrary since the first chapter of the Book of Ezekiel where the chariot vision is recorded constitutes the *Haftarah* for the first day of Pentecost.

The association with Pentecost brought about an interesting modification in the conception of the *Merkabah*, for in the miniature the "man" of the Ezekiel vision is Moses. Since Pentecost is the Feast of Commemoration of the "Giving of the Torah," the reference to Moses is quite justified, all the more as Moses is depicted in the monologue of the Torah in the prayer book for Pentecost, as the ideal man superior to any biblical figure. In order to emphasize the central motif of the festival, the Revelation on Sinai, the Giving of the Torah is represented on the top of the picture, above the Divine canopy.

The four mystical creatures appear again, this time associated with the prayers for the Day of Atonement. In this conception the portal is literally the "Open Gate of Mercy." In a miniature of the early fourteenth century

Mahzor of the Breslau University Library, the Gate of Mercy is designed as a portal with open wings.[15] The four Merkabah figures are painted on the capitals and bases of the archway which have the form of round medallions. The motif of the archway still retains a relation to the throne-chariot concept, a relation pointed out in the medallions in which the living creatures are displayed. The medallions are meant, of course, to recall the wheels of Ezekiel's vision.

The four wheels, or medallions, enclosing the four mystical figures eventually lose every relationship with the portal which still gave the illusion of a canopied throne. In the *Mahzor* of the Leipzig University Library (second half of the fourteenth century) the four medallions stand unmotivated in a rectangular frame.[16] Rendered in a sort of shorthand style, the four creatures are merely intended to remind us of the Temple, as the text deals with the Temple tax. A pair of scales for weighing the *shekalim* is shown beside the medallions. Beasts and grotesques complete the picture.

The evolution of the chariot motif in Jewish medieval book illustration reveals, then, a tendency to dissolve the visual forms, already considerably disintegrated owing to the talmudic prohibition and the vagueness of *Merkabah* philosophical conceptions. They become immerged in patterns of beasts, foliage and interlaces. The animal decoration of Romanesque and Gothic art afforded a congenial vocabulary for these unrealistic elaborations.

After a glimpse into medieval prayer-book illustration, which uses the nostalgic visions of the Babylonian Exile[16a] as a hieratic background for synagogue liturgy, the contrast with Jewish art in antiquity becomes particularly striking. The climate of the Middle Ages seems much closer to the exalted mood of the Babylonian deportees than to the more realistic attitude of the Jews of the Hellenistic period. The beginnings of the synagogue are still shrouded in obscurity, and we do not know much about the trends in Jewish art before the third century B.C.E. when, suddenly, we meet with synagogue inscriptions.

Judaism was confronted with Hellenism all over the Diaspora, in the West and in the East, and some aspects of Hellenistic culture were necessarily felt by the Jews to be a challenge to their beliefs.[16b] Clashes between what we may call two strongly opposed conceptions of life were unavoidable. It should not be overlooked, however, that a steady process of dissociation of Hellenism from mythology was taking place, a process which made art, in some of its phases at least, tolerable to uncompromising monotheism. Typical of the more realistic and humane approach toward life were, for instance, the late Hellenistic Pergaminian sculptures in Athens, which portray enemy warriors as men endowed with a sense of dignity and pride rather than as mythological monsters.

In Roman art the scope of interests reaches further and portrait, landscape, idyllic animal scenes, subjects of current history, become increasingly important. Reliefs showing the emperor distributing largess to the populace, publicly displayed, were used as means of political propaganda.

Since art, therefore, was shifting toward secular aspects, the Jewish position had to be reconsidered. Jews had their own political concerns, too, and it may be gathered from Rabbinical writings that they were actually re-examining their historical experience in the light of contemporary events, and their discussions of an ideal leader reflected most real political aspirations. And along with the acuteness of political thinking a keener understanding of the culture and the arts of the surrounding population developed.

There is a story in the Mishna which can be regarded as typical of the new attitude. Rabban Gamaliel, the Patriarch (died before 114 c.e.), we are told, once attended the *termae* of Aphrodite at Acco. When asked how he could reconcile his conduct with the Jewish attitude toward pagan art, the Sage dismissed the question with a joke: "I did not come into her domain," he said, "she came into mine," for nobody will maintain that the bathhouse was built for Aphrodite, while it can be said that the statue was set up as an adornment of the bathhouse (Aboda Zara 44b). The debate is striking, for it reflects a most uninhibited attitude of the leading groups of Jewry toward an art which obviously was felt to be no longer a temptation to the Jewish believer.

In discussing the precedent established by the Palestinian Patriarch, a Jewish authority in Babylonia, Rabbah b. bar Hanah (latter part of the third century), ruled that a statue set up for decorative purposes—as may be the case in a large city—would not be objectionable. What was to be avoided were images in smaller places which were likely to be worshiped by the populace (Aboda Zara 41a). The distinction made in this decision is clear. To the educated classes in the big centers, art no longer meant crude idol worship.

Within the more sophisticated Roman civilization, then, emerges a Jewish art. The most important monument of Jewish antiquity is no doubt the synagogue at Dura-Europos on the middle Euphrates in Syria dated by inscription 245 c.e.[17] The entire walls of the synagogue have been found covered with biblical scenes. Dura was a Roman city of recent standing captured from the Persians. The population lived in expectation of a recapture. This actually happened before the decoration of the synagogue was completed. Nothing could possibly reflect more faithfully the feelings of the Jews of Dura than the paintings of their prayer house with their special emphasis on the good old Persian king, Ahasuerus, portrayed seated on Solomon's lion throne (the famous throne which, according to

Rabbinical views, nobody was worthy of inheriting, except possibly the Persian king), and a most detailed rendering of Ezekiel's "Vision of the Dry Bones," showing the scattered tribes reunited and gathered under one king, the resurrected King David.[18] The meaning of the biblical episode portrayed was unmistakable to the members of the congregation who knew that Davidic descendants were still alive, out of reach of the Roman invaders and under the protection of Sapur.

Were these extraordinary paintings unique?

From the mosaic decoration found in synagogues of the fourth to sixth centuries in North Africa[19] and Palestine it can be inferred that this representational art, biblical in content, talmudic in interpretation, was fairly well spread over a large area. The Jerusalem Talmud (Aboda Zara 3, 42d) records that the Samaritans made images of Jacob and Joseph, regarding the latter as their direct ancestor. It would thus appear that in the art of the Jews of the ancient period all the different traditions due to the Judaic, Israelitic and mixed popular elements were represented. The Samaritans revered Joseph as their ancestor and emphasized his story in their art, the synagogue of Dura likewise cherished the memory of Joseph, but was anxious to stress the unity of the nation, the emblem of which—the Temple of Jerusalem—was depicted above the Torah niche. This emblem is common to the floor mosaics of the synagogues at Naaran[20] and Bet Alpha[21] in Palestine, as well as to the gold glasses from Jewish catacombs in Rome. (A fine specimen of the latter can be seen at the Metropolitan Museum in New York.)[22]

It would take us too far afield to discuss the decoration of the ancient synagogue in detail. One more motif should be mentioned, however, because of its controversial character: the signs of the Zodiac, the *mazalot*. The ceiling tiles of the Dura synagogue were decorated with these signs, the floor mosaics of Palestinian synagogues display them. What was the attitude of the Rabbinical authorities toward this pictorial motif, intended to evoke the image of heaven?[23] On the whole, it would appear that they were opposed to its use. However, in the Babylonian Talmud (Aboda Zara 42b) we have a curious concession: pictures of the planets are permissible, but not those of the sun and moon. And the same source (43a) records that Rabban Gamaliel "had a picture of lunar diagrams in his upper chamber in the form of a chart hanging on the wall." There are other talmudic references to astronomical studies carried on by the Rabbis. The prohibition of images has no apodictic character in the sources of the time. What we have in the Talmud are records of discussions, of debates. Thus, in the Babylonian Talmud (Aboda Zara 41a) we find side by side two strictly opposed statements. According to one opinion, all images are prohibited; according to another, an image is not prohibited except when the figure holds a staff or a bird in its hand. What is discussed here is

pagan rather than Jewish art, and in particular statues of divinities. Jewish
art is also referred to and, significantly, without comment. In the Jerusalem Talmud it is related that "at the time of Rabbi Johanan (third
century C.E.) they began to have paintings on the walls and the Rabbis
did not hinder them." Are we to suppose that the paintings on the walls
were meant to be synagogue paintings? In a fragment of the Jerusalem
Talmud (Aboda Zara 3.3) preserved in the Public Library in Lenin-
grad[24] we read: "In the days of Rabbi Abun [first half of the fourth
century C.E.] they began to depict designs of mosaics and he did not
hinder them." Pavement mosaics referred to in this text can safely be
taken to be synagogue mosaics, since such mosaics have actually been
excavated in Palestine and the Diaspora.

From the point of view of Judaism it is important to discover that the
art practiced by Jews was a national, popular art dedicated to problems
of Jewish interest. This art offered a counterpart to the Rabbinical interpretation of Jewish history and Jewish behavior. Art, a companion of
literature, shared in the responsibility for the cultural and political education of the community.

Although the Rabbinical leaders seem on the whole to have tolerated
art with some misgivings or, at best, without taking issue for or against it,
in the case of the Dura murals—of which thirty panels have survived—we
have to assume an active part of the spiritual head of the congregation
in the planning of the decoration. The murals reveal throughout an intimate knowledge of the vast field of tradition.

As for style, the paintings have the "descriptive" quality of late Roman
art, particularly of the provinces. What the synagogue artist was striving
for was to convey the meaning, the point of a story, rather than to give the
illusion of figures moving and acting in a three-dimensional space. Pom-
peian paintings had that plastic, illusionistic quality, but it was from later,
more vehemently meaningful art that medieval Bible illustration developed. Christian art students evaluate the Dura synagogue paintings
particularly from that point of view.

Examining the synagogue mosaics, we notice in the sixth century a
tendency to depict liturgical objects rather than figure scenes, and a more
conventional, rigid style which reflects restraint, introversion, an attitude
due to the deteriorating political and social status under Byzantine domination. There are also to be taken into account general ideological trends,
the controversy provoked in the Christian church by the Monophysite
doctrine, and later on, in the seventh century, the powerful propaganda of
Islam. How the mere threat of an Arab avalanche could affect the cultural
policy of a country may be gathered from the bloody iconoclastic campaign
initiated by Leo the Isaurian in Byzantium. Aiming at the power of the

monastic orders, the emperor, who was of Asiatic origin and spoke Arabic, had understood the signs of the times and knew how to make use of the new slogan.

The East was definitely becoming iconoclastic, and we can safely assume that Jewish art adjusted itself without misgivings to the uncompromising attitude of Islam, which agreed with the moods prevailing in the Jewish community. The *hadit*, in which the Prophet is reported to have declared that those to be punished most severely on the Day of Judgment are the portrayers, was probably approved by the Jews, although they had never denounced art so harshly.

In the earliest preserved Hebrew manuscripts of the tenth and eleventh centuries, executed in Syria, Palestine and Egypt, the process of ornamentalization and geometrization of real objects of the visible world is found to be completed, and the pictures of the seven-branched candlestick and the Temple utensils appear in Bible illumination, immerged in ornamental design.[25] Nothing is left of other representational topics and the skill of the artist exerts itself in penmanship. Dedications to patrons in huge gold lettering on diapered backgrounds became an outstanding feature of the magnificent parchment codices, and the masoretic notes of the Bible—a running grammatical commentary—in minuscule writing were arranged in marginal and full-page ornamental pieces.

The synagogue walls were decorated in a similar style and were hung with textiles; so, for example, the prayer house in which Maimonides prayed. It is reported that he felt distracted by the ornamental designs on tapestries and synagogue walls and therefore covered his eyes at prayer in order to achieve greater concentration.[26]

Meanwhile, in the European settlements, beasts and birds and all sorts of plants began to creep into the interlaces of the arabesques of the Jewish manuscript decoration. The synagogues were affected by a similar change of style.

The new departure seems to have been made first in the treatment of the masoretic notes, which were now written in animal and floral outlines. Rabbi Judah ben Samuel of Speyer and Regensburg condemned this practice in his *Sefer Hasidim* (twelfth century).[27] A scholar is bound to pay strictest attention to a clear disposition and legibility of the text, while the scribe is too readily inclined to neglect the text for the sake of an elegant flourish. Much of the friction between the writers and the scribes in the Middle Ages was due to this basic conflict. No concerted efforts were made to restrain art in book or synagogue decoration, however, and we cannot even speak of a united front of the Rabbinical authorities on this question.

Very significant is the fact that one of the great authorities of the twelfth century, Ephraim ben Isaac, Rabbi of Regensburg, declared himself a partisan of art.[28] He was consulted by R. Joel b. Isaac Ha-Levi of Bonn about some textiles used in the synagogue, the design of which—birds, fish and horses—seemed to him controversial; and R. Ephraim ruled in favor of animal decoration, pointing to its absolute harmlessness at a time when animal worship was no longer a problem.

The role of animal symbolism in Hebrew manuscript illumination has been touched upon in our discussion of the *Merkabah* motif. We cannot deal with this problem at any length. Suffice it to say that the famous medieval animal book, the *Physiologus,* was much influenced by the Bible and is even traced by some scholars to a Jewish source.

To understand the interest in animals, their habits and appearance, we must also take into account the role of hunting in the Middle Ages. Legend has it that Rabbi Judah ben Samuel spent his youth at archery and at the age of eighteen realized that he wished rather to study Jewish lore.[29] We cannot take this tale too literally; however, it reveals an interest in this sport, at least on the part of the recorder and his public. We do know that Rabbi Ephraim ben Isaac discussed hunting with hound and falcon in a matter-of-fact way, without any unfavorable comment.[30]

It seems that objections to animal decoration appear only after a certain period of toleration, and not as a warning against a newfangled fashion. Thus, Rabbi Isaac ben Moses Or Zarua of Vienna (*c.* 1200) recalled the verdure decoration—foliage with birds—of the Meissen synagogue from his boyhood days. In his old age he felt compelled to disapprove of that sort of thing.[31]

In the Cologne synagogue a controversy was started over some stained-glass windows which Rabbi Eliakim ben Joseph (first half of the twelfth century) wished removed.[32] His attack is particularly interesting because the Cistercian Order had prohibited stained-glass windows in their churches in 1134. The interdict aimed at the luxurious indulgence in colored glass, and was a measure of self-imposed restraint of the senses, proper for a fraternal community. Bernard of Clairvaux (d. 1153) particularly condemned animal decoration (*Patrologia Latina,* vol. 182, cols. 913 ff.). But what was in order for a monastic association was hardly right for a community of men, women and children, and we have Rabbi Judah ben Samuel's words to show that this was actually the Rabbinical view. "Do not say," he warned, "that you want to put on the hairy cloth of the Christian monk, for this would be a sinful way, as you have to deny yourself only what the Scriptures forbid you to enjoy."[33] In fact, Rabbi Eliakim's attitude was dictated by "political anxiety," rather than by religious scruples. He was fearful lest the Jews be accused of worshiping the lions and snakes depicted on those windows, the more so as the windows happened to be on the side the congregation faced at one particular prayer. It may be recalled that the Second Crusade had swept over the Jewish settlements in 1146 and the victims of the first, of 1096, were not yet forgotten. Although the Rabbi tried to associate his objections with some reservations voiced here and there in the Talmud, it was evident that these references were meant only to add some dignity to a restriction provoked by a situation beyond his control.

The last refuge of the artist was the book, for it was less exposed to the public eye than the synagogue. It is true that the Rabbinical authorities did not directly favor book decoration, not to speak of illustration; however, it is significant that while Rabbi Meir of Rothenburg (d. 1293) mildly criticized the animal-and-bird decoration of the prayer books, he did not base his criticisms on religious considerations.[34] The considerable number of prayer books from the thirteenth and fourteenth centuries decorated in this manner is proof that there was no marked opposition to be reckoned with. Perhaps the best evidence of the rather tolerant attitude prevalent is found in the illustrated prayer book (Breslau University Library) executed by a disciple of the Rothenburg Sage.[35]

It is with a sense of profound respect that we examine the huge medieval prayer books, the Bibles and the smaller Haggadas admirably written and illuminated on parchment and exquisitely bound.

Attempts at Bible illustration are found in all the types of Hebrew writings: here it may be an Esther scene, there the "Giving of the Law," or "Abraham in the fiery furnace," an episode from postbiblical literature.

Continuous biblical picture cycles are rare, however, and there is not one Bible illustrated throughout. Strange to say, an illustration beginning with Adam and Eve is found in Haggadas rather than in Bibles, the most beautiful of them (Codex Add. 27210 of the British Museum) exhibiting an immaculate thirteenth-century French Gothic style.[36] The somewhat later Haggada of the Sarajevo Museum, executed in Spain, opens with the scenes of the six days of Creation—each day represented by the disk of the earth showing the successive improvements, and the seventh day illustrated by the Lord seated on a bench and enjoying His rest.[37] Such a thing would not be possible in a Bible. The Haggada was allowed some measure of freedom and informality. There must have been a certain reluctance to illustrate the Bible codex throughout either because of the immensity of such a task or for religious reasons. At any rate, the most magnificent Bible codex, (Cod. Kennicott I of the Bodleiana completed in La Coruña in Spain in 1476) shows only a few figures: David, Phineas, Balaam and Jonah.[38] Its decoration is chiefly animal and floral.

This particular attitude toward Bible illustration may account for the behavior of Moses Arragel, the Rabbi of Guadalajara, who in 1430 compiled a Castilian translation of the Old Testament for the Order of Calatrava of which he was a vassal.[39] When asked to supervise the work of the illustrators also, Arragel declined, referring to the Decalogue. Did he fear to be involved in problems of interpretation? Possibly so, although in the Bible commentary he furnished he shows an admirable tact in giving credit to Christian and Jewish exegesis alike and siding with none.[40] The alternative is that he honestly opposed Bible illustration as something even the most liberal-minded Jew could not wholeheartedly approve.

With the expulsion from Spain (1492)[40a] the fine Hebrew manuscript production of that country was brought to a standstill. The deterioration of the position of the Jews in Germany throughout the fifteenth century was accompanied by a marked decline in the quality of their books, and the sketchy colored drawings found in their manuscripts of that time reflect haste and carelessness. In Italy alone Hebrew book illumination and, especially, illustration remain on a high level during the fifteenth and sixteenth centuries and show an unparalleled variety and wealth of vocabulary and finesse of execution.[40*] In this art, with its emphasis on balance and mellowness of color—an Italian contribution—there is to be noted also a considerable strain of influences imported by refugees from Spain and Germany.

It has often been said that the Jews had experienced no renaissance, and some students of Jewish history are inclined to extend the medieval period down to the Enlightenment and Emancipation of the eighteenth century. However, the attitude of the Jews toward art in the Renaissance seems to have outgrown the medieval pattern to such an extent that a consideration of that period in distinct terms seems imperative.

The retarding elements that make themselves noticeable during the later Middle Ages in book illumination in Germany and even in Spain are not to be discounted in the appreciation of manuscripts produced in Italy, furthermore, most important is the role of the printed book and the new techniques of illustration, the woodcut and the engraving.

The Jewish scribe and illuminator had no permanent contact with his Christian colleagues, monks or laymen organized in guilds. In the printing presses, however, Jews and Christians were bound to work together. The Jews, frequently forbidden to run presses, had their books printed in Christian printing shops, where Jewish composers had to be employed for Hebrew prints.

The practice of the printers for economy's sake to use the same cuts for various publications and to exchange cuts among themselves, had an effect upon Hebrew printing, too. The new border pieces, title pages and even illustrations turned up in the Hebrew books; and we are not surprised to discover in the Mantua Haggada of 1560 a woodcut from Holbein's Lyons Bible of 1538 as an illustration for the "son who does not know how to ask questions," and Michelangelo's Jeremiah of the Sistine ceiling in the Vatican as one of the Rabbis of Bene Berak.

If this is plagiarism, then we also have to dismiss as plagiarism the famous Renaissance church, St. Francesco in Rimini, since Alberti used the Roman gate of Rimini as a model for the church façade. What we are driving at is not to demonstrate that the whole Renaissance movement was imitative, but to point out the enthusiastic interest in research, in copying and reproducing in various techniques and adapting to various purposes of art works greatly valued. Jews and Christians alike were carried away by this artistic enthusiasm. Jewish and Christian artisans alike reproduced on faïence dishes the biblical scenes of the Loggias in the Vatican painted by pupils of Raphael. Adorned in addition with Passover symbols and illustrations from a Venetian Haggada (first printed in 1609), the Jewish plates were used for the *Seder* meal.[41] Holbein, Michelangelo, Raphael had thus become the teachers of the budding Jewish artist. And later developments were to show how these new influences affected his outlook and sensitivity.

Unfortunately the rapprochement so conspicuous in the keen interest in Hebrew language and literature among the humanists, and the emergence of the Jewish author in Italian literature—one may recall the *Dialoghi d'Amore,* a philosophical treatise by Leone Ebreo,[41a] the son of the Sephardic refugee from Spain, the great Isaac Abrabanel—did not last. That rapprochement was built on an unstable political foundation, and who could better sense the changing "climate" than a native, Italian Jew? It was the poet and grammarian Samuel Archevolti (d. 1609) who uttered the all-familiar warnings. It was clear to him that the first target for anti-Jewish attacks would be refugees, and he was alarmed by what in their customs might irritate the native Jew-baiters. There was that German synagogue at Venice with its quaint interior decoration, nothing particularly disturbing since the Ashkenazic rabbis tolerated it, but somehow inappropriate, perhaps outmoded, not in line with the fashion of the day. Archevolti objected to the "trees and plants" in that decoration, more suited for an inn or a theater, he thought, than a prayer house.[42] He went so far as to admit that he really worried lest the non-Jews accuse Jews of worshiping those images. Had not Apion, centuries earlier, slanderously accused the Jews of worshiping an ass's head?

Another story may illustrate the sense of insecurity and frustration typical of the Jews in the later sixteenth and the seventeenth century. The Jews of Ascoli, when expelled in 1569, went to Pesaro. Among the things they took with them was their synagogue Shrine. In 1639 Rabbi Moses of Trani raised the question whether the lions that adorn the Shrine were compatible with the Jewish view of plastic arts.[43] The rabbi could not know, of course, that someday lion statues carved in the round would be excavated on the site of antique Palestinian synagogues. (I refer to the finds in Chorazin and Kfar Birim.)[44] So he decided in the negative. His view was adopted by Rabbi David ibn Abi Zimra.[45] The argument brought forth was the usual reference to the diverting effect upon the worshiper. However, Abraham Joseph Solomon Graziano of Modena, the great book collector, was of a different opinion. He pointed out (*c.* 1670) that the lions set at the foot of the Shrine could not be well seen from the seats of the congregation and were hardly liable to disturb anyone. Graziano's liberal attitude calls for an explanation. It was Graziano's own great-grandfather, we learn, who had moved the Ascoli Shrine to Pesaro. This Shrine meant something to the man. He gave vent to his indignation in marginal remarks jotted down in his copy of Rabbi Joseph Caro's *Shulhan Aruk.* That is where David Kaufmann found them.[46]

Archevolti's summons to refrain from decorating synagogues was confirmed by the rabbinical court at Safed with some reservations regarding already existing decorations which were not to be obliterated.[47] Every new wave of persecution was followed by pious exhortations to abstain from display of any sort which might bring discredit upon the community. But no wholesale condemnation of art was pronounced by any responsible body in the name of the synagogue.

The Renaissance had released the forces of the individual, Jew and Christian alike, and there was no way back into the narrowness and isolation forced upon the Jews in the Middle Ages. Here and there emerges a name of a Jewish artist associated with some unusual achievement.

Meanwhile in the East, too, there were stirrings. In the medieval period, Western artistic trends had been carried eastward and synagogues of Worms, Regensburg and Cracow were built upon the same scheme. During the Renaissance, Italy began to export to the whole European continent architects, masons, painters, sculptors, many of whom went to Poland and Russia; some occasionally built or remodeled a synagogue. From the blending of these Italian influences with native elements in the Carpathian region, the Ukraine, Lithuania and White Russia, a Jewish folk art developed, which after the Chmielnicki pogrom (1648) was carried by emigrants from Eastern Europe back to the West.[48] Medieval animal decoration was revived in modest country synagogues of the East in terms of a provincial *baroque.* This was actually a survival of a tradition, some links of which were lost. Folk art has a long memory. In this Eastern European synagogue decoration we meet the biblical leviathan, the *behemot,* the hieratic eagle, the fabulous snake of medieval descent, the unicorn familiar from Hebrew illuminated manuscripts in the West as well as from Christian art, the four animals from *Pirke Abot,* and the view of the restored Jerusalem. Regardless of the origin of these pictorial devices—from peasant folk art, imported Oriental textiles, engravings and woodcuts from West and East—the common source of this imagery was the prayer book, with its traditional symbolism.

In a period, then, when Jewish art in central Europe stagnated, a new wave of folklore and artistic conceptions from the East was driven to Moravia, Hungary and farther westward down to the Fuerth region where, scattered in villages and townlets, lived the remnant of German Jewry.

In the seventeenth century there emerged the free republic of Holland, whereto Jews, Sephardic and Ashkenazic, flocked seeking refuge from religious persecution.[48a] Amsterdam superseded the Italian centers of Hebrew printing, and it was again through the medium of the book that Jewish art received its new stimulus.

The Marranos from Portugal, who in Holland returned to their old faith, had a more liberal conception of art, and because of their higher living standard there was among them a certain need for outer display. Family portraits belonged to the amenities of life; and we see Jews portrayed by Dutch artists.

Jewish artists soon began to attempt portraiture also, and it was characteristic of their background that their first attempts in portraiture were intended for books. Thus, in the seventeenth century appear author portraits, designed and sometimes engraved as well by Jews for frontispieces. To be sure, these were portraits of scholars and community leaders. We would hardly expect portraits of women or children in such a dignified and serious company. However, Aaron Chaves, much ahead of his time, designed in the second half of the seventeenth century a portrait of Daniel Levi Barrios with his wife, son and daughter, which was to be appended to a poetical paraphrase of the Bible written by Barrios.[49] The portrait was allegorical and the text was only a version of the Bible; nevertheless, the Portuguese community of Amsterdam refused to give its approbation to the publication of the book.

The Ashkenazim were even more particular about portraits. The portrait of Rabbi Zebi Ashkenazi in the eighteenth century had to be drawn clandestinely, without the rabbi's knowledge. His son, Rabbi Jacob Emden, had serious misgivings about this portrait. He also disapproved of the portrait medal cast for Eleazar Shmelka, the Ashkenazic rabbi of Amsterdam.[50] As late as 1837 Rabbi Akiba Eger in Posen had to be portrayed clandestinely.[51] However, there was a great demand for portraits of prominent rabbis. Whether Ádamus Wagner's portrait of Rabbi Jonathan Eybeschuetz (d. 1767), signed and dated 1770, was painted after a drawing from life we do not know. The portrait was exhibited in the Akiba Eger Exhibition in Berlin in 1937.[52] The well-known engraving is a slightly modified version of that portrait. Among others the engraved portrait of Rabbi Ezekiel Landau (d. 1793) should be mentioned. Engravings were later superseded by lithographs. The Jewish Museum in

Berlin had one of the largest collections of portraits of rabbis and scholars, some of considerable artistic value.

The Sephardic community in Amsterdam may be regarded as having practically initiated that type of portraiture among Jews, although some attempts had already been made in Italy. After all, Salom Italia, who engraved portraits of J. J. A. Leon Templo [Jacob Jehudah Leone][53] and of Manasseh ben Israel, came to Holland from Italy. In Amsterdam there was a larger field and a greater demand to tempt an artist.

The Ashkenazic community of Amsterdam, more concerned with religious needs, produced a new illustrated Haggada which was to play a considerable part in the development of Jewish folk art. Compiled for the Ashkenazic and Sephardic ritual, this Haggada was published in 1695 under the patronage of Moses Wesel, an Ashkenazic Jew. The engravings were picked from the immense work of Matthaeus Merian of Basel, who had illustrated a Luther Bible and other popular publications.[54] Children particularly delighted in the many-figured and lively pictures, and it is noteworthy that for Goethe and Heine the Merian pictures were associated with the most cherished childhood memories. However, Heine knew them only from his Haggada—a handwritten and hand-painted version of the Amsterdam Haggada. He never suspected their origin. It is worth reading what he says about those lovely pictures, in his *Rabbi of Bacharach*. Executed in 1723 by Moses Judah Loeb, son of Benjamin Wolf Broda from Trebitsch, Moravia, this Haggada was dedicated to Lazarus von Geldern, Heinrich Heine's great-grandfather.[55] (The Haggada was in the possession of Dr. Heinz Frank in Amsterdam, a refugee from Cologne, when I saw it in 1936.)

The von Geldern Haggada is one of the numerous versions of the Amsterdam print, produced in the eighteenth century. The artists hailed mostly from Moravia, Bohemia and Hungary. In simplifying the composition of the scenes, Judaizing the facial types and costumes, these artists added a popular, provincial flavor to the pictures. Never blindly copying their model, they often introduced scenes or traits of their own invention, thus expanding the picture cycle and adapting it to the tastes and fashions of their own generation. Therefore, those eighteenth-century versions of the Amsterdam Haggada, neatly copied on parchment and illustrated with brightly gouache miniatures, have to be evaluated on their own merit. They offer a remarkable attempt to depict the "Jewish scene." They are in fact the first Jewish genre pictures created by Jewish artists, domestic interiors enlivened with a pot of flowers on the window sill and a bird in the cage, showing charming women, lovely children, men, old and young, gathered around a table, scenes not borrowed from Merian nor necessarily original inventions, yet ably compiled and sometimes exquisitely painted.

With these self-taught, obscure, provincial painters the puritanic spell was broken and Jewish art was at last liberated from its limitations imposed by history rather than "Law."

The painters born on the threshold of the nineteenth century,[56] the miniature-portrait painter Jeremias David Alexander Fiorino of Kassel, the well-known Moritz Oppenheim who was active in Frankfort, and Eduard Magnus, born in Berlin, all have something of the sweetness and lyricism of the Haggada painter of the eighteenth century, despite their formal training, the different background and broader outlook. Their subjects may be Jews or non-Jews; the painters do not engage in any ambitious projects likely to involve them in conflicting situations.

With closer participation in the cultural life of their countries, however, Jewish artists began to join groups organized to carry out definite ideological programs, such as the German Nazarene group in Rome, adherence to which brought about the conversion of the painter brothers, Johannes and Philipp Veit, grandsons of Moses Mendelssohn. Eduard Bendemann, who painted biblical compositions in the classicist vein, also realized soon that he needed a larger audience than Jews could offer and acted accordingly.

The problem of the Jewish artist was that of a man who cannot find an outlet for his activities within his ethnic group and sees himself drawn to the more powerful national audience. At least in Germany, this meant, in the first half of the nineteenth century, desertion of the ancestral faith.

In Austria, Hungary, Poland and Russia things matured more slowly, and serious conflicts could be more easily avoided. In the second half of the century, we meet in these countries an art which caters to the tastes of a cultivated Jewish middle class. This art was dedicated to the Jewish motif, which, as the century wore on, lost most of its lyrical character and struck a more bitter accent.

It is indicative of the social awareness of the promoters of Jewish art in Eastern Europe that a pupil of the sculptor Mark Antokolski, the late Boris Schatz, set out to found in Palestine a school of arts and crafts, the Bezalel School at Jerusalem. The idea of reactivating artistic crafts, metal and woodwork, rug weaving, embroidery and penmanship, had much in common with the program of William Morris. Characteristically, the work of Abel Pann, the outstanding painter of the Bezalel group, was close in style to that of the English Pre-Raphaelites. Whatever the merits of the individual artists associated with the Bezalel movement, they laid the foundation for a freer and more creative art in the future.

A Sephardic Jew, Camille Pissarro, a native of the Antilles, became in the seventies, in Paris, the first exponent among Jews of an experimental type of art, a member of a small group of pioneers which coined its own vocabulary.

Some people may see the significance of the impressionist movement started by Pissarro and his friends in the deheroization of man and the devaluation not only of "studio nudes," but of subject matter in general; others may see that significance in the abandoning of the academic principles of composition and the revolutionizing of painting techniques.

To the Jewish artist this movement meant a release from the sense of inferiority, from the constant awareness of his modest artistic heritage. Here at last was an art which did not claim a noble ancestry; it was a democratic art fitting into modern society, and an art in which the Jew was given a fair chance of achievement. And he accomplished a good deal.

The generation that holds the field now, and which made its first appearance during the First World War, has found a stronger and more universal response than any previous generation. The Jewish artist, like the Jewish writer, addresses himself in our time to the world, to all men. And it would appear that with art surrendering its claim to divinity and exclusiveness, the fight is actually won—for it was this claim to divinity which the Second Commandment had fought.

NOTES

[1] G. E. Wright, "How did early Israel differ from her neighbors?" in *Biblical Archaeologist*, VI, No. 1 (Feb. 1943), pp. 6 ff.

[2] W. F. Albright, *From the Stone Age to Christianity* (Baltimore, 1940), p. 206.

[3] J. W. and G. M. Crowfoot, *Early Ivories from Samaria* (London, 1938), p. 12.

[[3a] Cf. William Foxwell Albright, "The Biblical Period," this work, Vol. I, pp. 29-33.]

[4] E. B. Tylor, "The winged figures of the Assyrian and other ancient Monuments," *Proceedings of the Society of Biblical Archaeology*, June, 1890, p. 391.

[5] Ernst Cohn-Wiener, *Die juedische Kunst* (Berlin, 1929), Fig. 23.

[6] G. Dalman, *Arbeit und Sitte in Palaestina* (Guetersloh, 1939), VI, 107 ff.

[7] M. Gruenbaum, *Gesammelte Aufsaetze zur Sprach- und Sagenkunde,* ed. Felix Perles (Berlin, 1901), pp. 202-203.

[8] H. T. Obbink, "Jahwebilder," in *Zeitschrift fuer die Alttestamentliche Wissenschaft und die Kunde des nachbiblischen Judentums* (Giessen, 1929), Vol. 47, p. 267.

[9] G. E. Wright, "Solomon's Temple Resurrected," in *Bibl. Arch.*, Vol. IV, No. 2 (May, 1941), p. 28.

[10] J. W. and G. M. Crowfoot, *op. cit.,* pp. 18 and 24.

[11] W. H. Beyer and H. Lietzmann, *Die juedische Katakombe der Villa Torlonia* (Berlin, 1930), plate 28 and p. 44 where erroneously described under No. 27.

[12] *Ibid.,* plate 26a; see also p. 44.

[13] Erno Munkácsi, *Miniatuermuevészet Itália koenyvtáraiban, heber Kodexek* (Budapest), publication of the Jewish Museum, n.d., Plate VI. 18. The codex was previously in the Derossiana in Vienna and is described in Hans Tietze, *Die illuminierten Handschriften der Rossiana in Wien-Lainz* (Leipzig, 1911), pp. 110-111.

[14] Rachel Wischnitzer-Bernstein, *Symbole und Gestalten der juedischen Kunst* (Berlin, 1935), pp. 27-31, fig. 20.

[15] *Idem.*, "The Messianic Fox," in *Review of Religion*, Vol. V, No. 3 March, 1941, p. 260, plate I.

[16] Robert Bruck, *Die Malereien in den Handschriften des Koenigreichs Sachsen* (Dresden, 1906), pp. 219-225, fig. 138. The manuscript is summarily described without any attempt at interpreting the illustrations.

[16a] Cf. Albright, *op. cit.*, pp. 47 ff.]

[16b] Elias Bickerman, "The Historical Foundations of Postbiblical Judaism," this work, Vol. I, pp. 95 ff.]

[17] H. F. Pearson, C. H. Kraeling, M. Crosby, J. J. Obermann, A. Pagliaro and C. C. Torrey, *Excavations at Dura-Europos*. Report of Sixth Season, Preliminary Report on the Synagogue at Dura (New Haven, 1936).

[18] R. Wischnitzer-Bernstein, "The Conception of the Resurrection in the Ezekiel Panel of the Dura-Synagogue," in *Journal of Biblical Literature*, Vol. LX, No. 1 (March, 1941), pp. 43-55; *idem*, "The Samuel Cycle in the Wall Decoration of the Synagogue at Dura-Europos," *Proceedings of the Amer. Acad. for Jewish Research*, XI (1941), 85-103. For a more detailed discussion of the Dura synagogue paintings see the writer's book *The Messianic Theme in the Paintings of the Dura Synagogue* (Chicago, 1948), with bibliography, pp. 117-124. See also W. G. Kuemmel, "Die aelteste religioese Kunst der Juden," *Judaica*, II, 1 (Zurich, April, 1946), pp. 1-56; A. Grabar, *Martyrium, Recherches sur le culte des reliques et l'art chrétien antique*, 2 vols. (Paris, 1946, Plates, 1943); H. Riesenfeld, *The Resurrection in Ezekiel XXXVII and in the Dura-Europos Paintings* (Upsala Universitets Arsskrift, 1948).

[19] R. Krautheimer, *Mittelalterliche Synagogen* (Berlin, 1927), pp. 68 ff., figs. 14 and 15.

[20] E. L. Sukenik, *Ancient Synagogues in Palestine and Greece* (London, 1934), pp. 28-31, fig. 5.

[21] *Ibid.*, pp. 31-35, fig. 8.

[22] Wischnitzer-Bernstein, "The Sabbath in Art," in A. E. Millgram, *Sabbath, The Day of Delight* (Philadelphia, 1944), pp. 324-327, fig. 19; for a discussion of gold glasses cf. *Idem*, "Die Messianische Huette in der juedischen Kunst," *Monatsschrift fuer Geschichte und Wissenschaft des Judentums*, XXX, 5 (Breslau, 1936), pp. 381 ff.

[23] For the interpretation of the meaning of the Zodiac motif see Karl Lehmann, "The Dome of Heaven," in *Art Bulletin*, College Art Association of America, Vol. XXVII, No. 1, (New York, 1945), pp. 1-27.

[24] J. N. Epstein, (ed.), *Tarbiz*, (Hebrew), Vol. III, No. 19, pp. 15 ff. (Jerusalem, 1931-1932). Cf. also Sukenik *op. cit.*, p. 27.

[25] Vladimir Stassof and David Gunzburg, *L'Ornement Hébreu* (Berlin, 1905). (Plates with summary description.)

[26] Leopold Loew, *Graphische Requisiten und Erzeugnisse bei den Juden* (Leipzig, 1870-1871), Pt. I, p. 34. See also Alfred Freimann, *Responsa of Maimonides* (Jerusalem, 1934) 20 and p. 19.

[27] Sefer Hasidim, (ed. Berlin) 709. Quoted in D. H. Mueller and J. von Schlosser *Die Haggadah von Sarajevo*, with appendix by David Kaufmann, "Zur Geschichte der juedischen Handschriften-Illustration" (Vienna, 1898), p. 257.

[28] Loew, *op. cit.*, p. 33; *Germania Judaica*, I. Elbogen, A. Freimann and H. Tykocinski (eds.) (Breslau, 1934), Vol. I, pt. 2, pp. 289-290.

[29] *Germania Judaica, op. cit.*, p. 293.

[30] *Ibid.*, p. 290.

[31] David Kaufmann, "Art in the Synagogue," in *Jewish Quarterly Review*, IX, 264, (London, 1897).

[32] Carl Brisch, *Geschichte der Juden in Coeln und Umgebung aus aeltester Zeit bis auf die Gegenwart* (Cologne, 1879), I, 39; see also *Germania Judaica, op. cit.*, p. 199.

[33] Loew, *op. cit.*, p. 17.

[34] *Ibid.*, p. 34; Bruno Italiener, *Die Darmstaedter Pessach Haggadah* (Leipzig, 1927), p. 18,

[35] Wischnitzer-Bernstein, "The Messianic Fox," *op. cit.*, p. 263.

[36] Rachel Wischnitzer, "Illuminated Haggadahs," in *J.Q.R.*, Vol. XIII, No. 2, p. 206 (London, 1922).

[37] Mueller and Schlosser, *op. cit.*, plate fol. 2.

[38] Wischnitzer, "Une Bible Enluminée par Joseph ibn Hayyim," in *Revue des Études Juives,* Vol. LXXIII, 146, p. 166. (Paris, 1921).

[39] Samuel Berger, "Les Bibles Castillanes," in *Romania*, XXVIII, 522 (Paris, 1899).

[40] Max Golde, "Die synagogale Kunst im Mittelalter," in *Menorah*, V. 571-584 (Frankfort am Main, 1927).

[[40a] Cf. Cecil Roth, "The European Age in Jewish History (to 1648)," this work, Vol. I, pp. 243 ff.]

[40*] Wischnitzer, "Les Manuscrits à Miniatures de Maimonide," *Gazette des Beaux-Arts*, VI, pér. T. XIII, 869 (Paris, July-August, 1935), pp. 49 ff.

[41] Wischnitzer-Bernstein, "Studies in Jewish Art," in *J.Q.R.*, N. S., Vol. XXXVI, No. 1, pp. 58-59 (Philadelphia, 1945).

[[41a] Cf. above, Alexander Altmann, "Judaism and World Philosophy: From Philo to Spinoza," pp. 86-88.]

[42] Kaufmann, "Art in the Synagogue," *op. cit.*, pp. 264, 265, 266.

[43] *Ibid.*, p. 258.

[44] Illustrated in E. L. Sukenik, *The Ancient Synagogue of Beth Alpha* (Jerusalem, 1932), figs. 36 and 37.

[45] Kaufmann, *loc. cit.*

46 *Ibid.*, pp. 255 ff.

47 *Ibid.*, p. 266.

48 Some aspects of these eastward and westward trends were discussed in: E. Lissitzky, "The Synagogue of Mohilev," in *Rimon* (Hebrew), III, 9-12 (Berlin, 1923); *idem,* in *Milgrom,* (Yiddish) III, 9-13 (Berlin, 1923); E. Toeplitz, "Wall Paintings in Synagogues of the XVII and XVIII Centuries," in *Rimon, op. cit.,* pp. 1-8; *idem*, in *Milgrom, op. cit.,* pp. 1-7; *idem,* "Malerei in den Synagogen" (Besonders in Franken), in *Beitraege zur juedischen Kulturgeschichte* III, 3-16 (Frankfort am Main, 1929). See also Wischnitzer, "Mutual Influences between Eastern and Western Europe in Synagogue Architecture from the 12th to the 18th Century," in *YIVO Bleter* (Journal of the Yiddish Scientific Institute), Vol. XXIX, No. 1, pp. 3-51 (New York, 1947). *Idem.,* in English, in *YIVO Annual,* II-III, 1947-1948, pp. 25-68. G. K. Loukomski, *Jewish Art in European Synagogues* (London, 1947).

[**48a** Cf. Cecil Roth, "The Jews of Western Europe (from 1648)," this work, Vol. I, pp. 262-263.]

49 F. Landsberger, "New Studies in Early Jewish Artists," in *Hebrew Union College Annual,* XVIII, pp. 304 ff., fig. 7 (Cincinnati, 1944).

50 Loew, *op. cit.,* p. 39.

51 A. Kronthal, "Juedische Bildnismaler der Posener Biedermeierzeit," in *Jahrbuch fuer juedische Geschichte und Literatur,* XXX, 214-215, (Berlin, 1937).

52 *Akiba Eger Ausstellung* (Catalogue by R. Wischnitzer-Bernstein and E. Pessen, Jewish Museum, Berlin) Hanukkah, 1937, No. 31.

53 *Encyclopaedia Judaica,* X, p. 792. "Leon Templo, Jakob Jehuda Arje ben Abraham (1603-1675) owed his name, Templo, which he transmitted to his descendants, to his model of the Temple of Solomon which caused a sensation in its time and stimulated a whole literature."

54 Wischnitzer-Bernstein, "Von der Holbeinbibel zur Amsterdamer Haggadah," in *Monatsschrift fuer Geschichte und Wissenschaft des Judentums,* Vol. LXXV, Nos. 7 and 8, pp. 1-18 (Breslau, 1931). For Van Dyck's influence on Jewish illustration: *Idem,* "The Esther Story in Art," in Philip Goodman, *The Purim Anthology* (Philadelphia, 1949), pp. 234 ff.

55 Elizabeth Moses, "Juedische Kult-und Kunstdenkmaeler in den Rheinlanden," in *Rheinischer Verein fuer Denkmalpflege* (Duesseldorf, 1931), I, 99-200.

56 For a survey of modern Jewish art see Karl Schwarz, *Die Juden in der Kunst* (Vienna and Jerusalem, 1936, 2nd ed.); *idem, Ha-Umanut Ha-Yehudit Ha-Hadashah Beeretz Yisrael* (Jerusalem, 1941); Franz Landsberger, *A History of Jewish Art* (Cincinnati, 1946). Helen Rosenau, *A Short History of Jewish Art* (London, 1948); for discussion of modern synagogue architecture, Wischnitzer-Bernstein, "The Problem of Synagogue Architecture," *Commentary,* III, 3 (New York, March, 1947), pp. 233-241.

BIBLIOGRAPHY

For technical reasons, and in order to point out the more recent concerns in Jewish art studies, works cited in the footnotes have not been listed in this expanded bibliography.

AMEISENOWA, ZOFJA, "Animal-headed Gods, Evangelists, Saints and Righteous Men," *Journal of the Warburg and Courtauld Institutes*, XII (1949), pp. 21 ff.

————, "Bestiarius w Biblji hebrajskiej z XIII go wieku," *Miesiecznik Zydowski*, III (1933), pp. 79 ff.

————, *Biblja Hebrajska XIV go wieku Krakowie i jej dekoracja malarska.* Cracow, 1929.

————, "Das messianische Gastmahl der Gerechten in einer hebraeischen Bibel aus dem XIII. Jahrhundert," *MGWJ*, LXXIX, 6 (November/December 1935), pp. 409 ff.

————, "Some Neglected Representations of the Harmony of the Universe," in *Essays in Honor of Hans Tietze 1880-1954* (New York, 1958), pp. 349 ff.

————, "Eine spanisch-juedische Bilderbibel um 1400," *MGWJ*, LXXXI, 2 (March/April 1937), pp. 193 ff.

————, "The Tree of Life in Jewish Iconography," *Jour. of the Warburg Inst.*, II (1938-1939), pp. 326 ff.

AVI-YONAH, MICHAEL, "The Ancient Synagogue of Ma'on (Nirim). The Mosaic Pavement," BEAS, III (1960), pp. 25 ff. See also Levy, Shalom.

————, *Mosaic Pavements in Palestine.* Oxford University, 1935.

————, *Oriental Art in Roman Palestine.* Rome, 1961.

————, and SCHAPIRO, MEYER, *Israel: Ancient Mosaics.* New York, 1960.

BICKERMAN, ELIAS J., "Sur la théologie de l'art figuratif à propos de l'ouvrage de E. Goodenough," *Syria*, XLIV, 1-2 (1967), pp. 131 ff.

————, "Symbolism in the Dura Synagogue," *The Harvard Review*, LVIII, 1 (January 1963), pp. 27 ff.

BLOCH, PETER, "Siebenarmige Leuchter in christlichen Kirchen," *Wallraf-Richartz Jahrbuch*, XXIII (1961), pp. 55 ff.

BOECHER, OTTO, "Die alte Synagoge zu Worms," *Der Wormsgau*, XVIII (1960).

BOEHM, GUENTER, "Raices Judias de la pintura cristiana," *Boletin de la Universidad de Chile*, Nos. 71-72 (November/December 1966), pp. 90 ff.

CANTERA BURGOS, FRANCISCO, *Sinagogas españolas.* Madrid, 1955.

COHEN, BOAZ, "Art in Jewish Law," *Judaism*, III, 2 (Spring 1954), pp. 165 ff.

DIRINGER, DAVID, *The Illuminated Book* (London, 1967), pp. 147-161.

GLUECK, NELSON, "The Zodiac of Khirbet El-Tannur," *Bull. Am. Sch. Or. Res.*, No. 126 (April 1952), pp. 5 ff.

GOLDMAN, BERNARD, "The Question of a Judaic Aesthetics in Ancient Synagogue Art," *Journal of Aesthetics and Art Criticism*, 1961, pp. 295 ff.

————, *The Sacred Portal*. Detroit, 1966.

GOLDSCHMIDT, ERNST D., *et al.*, *The Bird's Head Haggadah*. Jerusalem, 1965.

GOODENOUGH, ERWIN R., *Jewish Symbols in the Graeco-Roman Period*. 12 vols. New York, 1953-1965.

GRABAR, ANDRÉ, "Le thème religieux des fresques de la synagogue de Doura (245-256 après J. C.)," *Revue de L'Histoire des Religions*, CXXIII (1941), pp. 143 ff., and CXXIV (1941), pp. 5 ff.

GUTMANN, JOSEPH, "The Haggadic Motif in Jewish Iconography," *Eretz-Israel* (Jerusalem, 1960), pp. 16-22.

————, "Jewish Elements in the Paris Psalter," *Marsyas*, VI (1954), pp. 42 ff.

————, "The Jewish Origin of the Ashburnham Pentateuch Miniatures," *JQR*, N.S. XLIV (1953-1954), pp. 55 ff.

————, "The 'Second Commandment' and the Image in Judaism," HUCA, XXXII (1961), pp. 161 ff.

————, "Wedding Customs and Ceremonies in Art," in *The Jewish Marriage Anthology*, edited by P. and H. Goodman (Philadelphia, 1965), Chap. 12, pp. 175 ff., 347 ff.

HANFMANN, GEORGE M. A., "The Eighth Campaign of Sardis (1965)," *Bull. Am. Sch. Or. Res.*, No. 182 (April 1966), pp. 2 ff.

ITALIENER, BRUNO, *Die darmstaedter Pessach Haggadah*. 2 vols. Leipzig, 1927-1928.

KAMPF, AVRAM, *Contemporary Synagogue Art*. New York, 1966.

KATZ, ELIAS, and NARKISS, BEZALEL, *Machsor Lipsiae* (Leipzig, 1964), pp. 9 ff., 85 ff.

KITZINGER, ERNST, *Israeli Mosaics of the Byzantine Period*. New York, 1965.

KRAELING, CARL H., *The Synagogue*. The Excavations at Dura-Europos, Final Report VIII, Part 1. New Haven, 1956.

KRETSCHMAR, GEORG, "Ein Beitrag zur Frage nach dem Verhaeltnis zwischen juedischer und christlicher Kunst in der Antike," *Festschrift fuer Otto Michel zum 60ten Geburtstag*, edited by Otto Betz (Leiden, 1963), pp. 295 ff.

LAMBERT, ELIE, "La synagogue de Doura-Europos et les origines de la mosquée," *Semitica*, III (1950), pp. 67 ff.

LANDSBERGER, FRANZ, Articles on Hebrew illuminated manuscripts, iconography, and ceremonial objects, HUCA, XV, XVI, XVIII-XXIX, XXXI (1940-1960).

————, "The Illumination of Hebrew Manuscripts in the Middle Ages and Renaissance," in *Jewish Art*, edited by Cecil Roth. Tel-Aviv, 1961.

LEVY, SHALOM, "The Ancient Synagogue of Ma'on (Nirim)," BEAS, III (1960), pp. 6 ff. With contributions by L. Y. Rahmani, A. S. Hiram, J. Dunayevski, M. Avi-Yonah, S. Yeivin.

MAYER, LEON A., *Bibliography of Jewish Art*. Edited by Otto Kurz. Jerusalem, 1967.

————, "Jewish Art in the Moslem World," in *Jewish Art*, edited by Cecil Roth. Tel-Aviv, 1961.

MESNIL DU BUISSON, R. COMTE DU, "L'Inscription de la niche centrale de la synagogue de Doura-Europos," *Syria*, XL (1963), pp. 303 ff.

———, *Les Peintures de la synagogue de Doura-Europos, 245-256 après J. C.* Rome, 1939.

METZGER, MENDEL, "The Earliest Engraved Italian Megilloth," *Bulletin of the John Rylands Library, Manchester*, XLVIII (1966), pp. 38 ff.

———, "Les illustrations d'un manuscrit hébreu du nord de la France (1278-1340 environ)," in *Mélanges René Crozet* (Poitiers, 1966), p. 1237.

———, "The John Rylands Megillah and Some Other Illustrated Megilloth of the XVth to XVIIth Centuries," *Bulletin of the John Rylands Library, Manchester*, XLV (1962), pp. 148 ff.

———, "Quelques caractères iconographiques et ornamentaux deux manuscrits hébraïques de Xe siècle," *Cahiers de Civilization Médiévale*, I (1958), pp. 205 ff.

———, "A Study of Some Unknown Hand-painted Megilloth of the XVIIth and XVIIIth Centuries," *Bulletin of the John Rylands Library, Manchester*, XLVI (1963), pp. 84 ff.

———, "Two Fragments of a Spanish XIVth Century Haggadah," *Gesta*, VI (1967), pp. 25 ff.

METZGER, THÉRÈSE, "Note sur le motif de la poule et des poussins dans l'iconographie juive," *Cahiers Archéologiques*, XIV (1964), pp. 243 ff.

Monumenta Judaica. 3 vols.: *Exhibition Catalogue, Handbuch, Fazit*. Cologne, 1964.

NAMENYI, ERNEST, "The Illumination of Hebrew Manuscripts After the Invention of Printing," in *Jewish Art*, edited by Cecil Roth (Tel-Aviv, 1961), pp. 1423 ff.

———, "La miniature juive au XVIIe et au XVIIIe siècle," *Revue des Etudes Juives*, CXVI (1957), pp. 27 ff.

NARKISS, BEZALEL, "Bibliography of Mordecai Narkiss," *Eretz-Israel*, VI (1960), pp. 5 ff.

———, "Medieval Illuminated Haggadot," *Ariel*, No. 14 (1966), pp. 35 ff.

NARKISS, MORDECHAI, "An Italian Niello Casket of the Fifteenth Century," *Journal of the Warburg and Courtauld Institutes*, XXI, 3-4 (1958), pp. 288 ff.

———, "The Oeuvre of the Jewish Engraver Salom Italia," *Tarbiz*, XXV (1956); English summary, XXVI, 1, p. v ff.

———, "The Origin of the Spice Box Known as 'Hadass,'" *Eretz-Israel*, VI (1960); English summary, p. 40.

———, "The Snuff-Shovel as a Jewish Symbol," JPOS, XV (1935), pp. 14 ff.

PIECHOTKA, MARIA and KAZIMIERZ, *Wooden Synagogues*. Warsaw, 1959.

ROSENAU, HELEN, "Contributions to the Study of Jewish Iconography," *Bulletin of the John Rylands Library, Manchester*, XXXVIII, 2 (1956), p. 466.

———, "The Jonah Sarcophagus in the British Museum," *Journal of the Archaeological Association*, 3d series, XXIV (1961), pp. 60 ff.

———, "Notes on the Illumination of the Spanish Haggadah in the John

Rylands Library," *Bulletin of the John Rylands Library, Manchester,* XXXVI (1954), pp. 468 ff.

————, "Problems of Jewish Iconography," *Gazette des Beaux-Arts* (July 1960), pp. 5 ff.

————, "Some Aspects of the Pictorial Influence of the Jewish Temple," *Pal. Explor. Fund Quar. State.,* LXVIII (1936), pp. 157 ff.

————, "The Synagogue and Protestant Church Architecture," *Journal of the Warburg and Courtauld Institutes,* IV (1941), pp. 80 ff.

————, "Textual Gleanings in Jewish Art," *Cahiers Archéologiques,* XIII (1962), pp. 39 ff.

ROTH, CECIL, "An Additional Note on the Kennicott Bible," *The Bodleian Library Record,* VI (1961), pp. 659 ff.

————, "The 'Chair of Moses' and Its Survivals," *Pal. Explor. Quar.* (1949), pp. 100 ff.

————, "Jewish Antecedents of Christian Art," *Journal of the Warburg and Courtauld Institutes,* XVI (1953), pp. 24 ff.

————, "The John Rylands Haggadah," *Bulletin of the John Rylands Library, Manchester,* XLIII (1960), pp. 131 ff.

————, "An Illuminated Hebrew Scroll of Esther from China," *Oriental Art,* I (1948-1949), p. 176.

————, "A Masterpiece of Medieval Spanish-Jewish Art: The Kennicott Bible," *Sefarad,* XII (1952), pp. 351 ff.

————, "Messianic Symbols in Palestinian Archaeology," *Pal. Explor. Quar.* (1955), pp. 151 ff.

————, "New Notes on Pre-Emancipation Jewish Artists," HUCA, XVII (1942-1943), pp. 499 ff.

————, *The Sarajevo Haggadah.* Text by Cecil Roth. New York, 1963.

———— (ed.), *Jewish Art: An Illustrated History.* Tel-Aviv, 1961.

ROTH, ERNST, "Der Buchmaler vom Trienter Judenprozess," *Israelitisches Wochenblatt fuer die Schweiz* (April 1, 1966), pp. 27 ff.

————, "Das Wormser Machsor," in *Die alte Synagogue zu Worms,* edited by Ernst Roth (Frankfurt a. M., 1961), pp. 217 ff.

SCHEIBER, ALEXANDER, *Die Kaufmann Haggadah.* Introduction by Alexander Scheiber. Budapest, 1957.

SCHUELER, IRMGARD, "A Note on Jewish Gold Glasses," *Journal of Glass Studies,* VIII (1966), pp. 48 ff.

SMITH, MORTON, "Goodenough's Jewish Symbols in Retrospect," JBL, LXXXVI, 1 (March 1967), pp. 53 ff.

————, "The Image of God: Notes on the Hellenization of Judaism, with Especial Reference to Goodenough's Work on Jewish Symbols," *Bulletin of the John Rylands Library, Manchester,* XL (1957-1958), pp. 473 ff.

SONNE, ISAIAH, "The Paintings of the Dura Synagogue," HUCA, XX (1947), pp. 255 ff.

————, "R. Wischnitzer. The Messianic Theme in Paintings of the Dura Synagogue," review in *The American Journal of Archaeology,* LIII, 2 (June 1949), pp. 230 ff.

————, "The Zodiac Theme in Ancient Synagogues and in Hebrew Printed

Books," *Studies in Bibliography and Booklore*, I, 3 (1953-1954), postscript 1 2, p. 82.

SQUARCIAPINO, MARIA FLORIANI, "La sinagoga di Ostia," *Bollettino d'Arte del Ministero della Pubblica Instruzione*, IV (October/December 1961), pp. 326 ff.

———, "Die Synagoge von Ostia Antica nach der zweiten Ausgrabungskampagne," *Raggi, Zeitschrift fuer Kunstgeschichte und Archaeologie*, V (1963), pp. 13 ff.

SUKENIK, ELEAZAR L., "The Ancient Synagogue at Yafa," BEAS, II (1951), pp. 6 ff.

———, "The Samaritan Synagogue at Salbit," BEAS, I (1949), pp. 26 ff.

Synagoga. Juedische Altertuemer. Handschriften, und Kultgeraete. Catalogue of an Exhibition of Jewish Antiquities, Manuscripts, and Ceremonial Objects. Frankfurt a. M., 1961. Exhibition first shown in 1960 at Recklinghausen, West Germany.

TAMMUZ, BENJAMIN (ed.), *Art in Israel*. Israel, 1963.

URBACH, E. E., "The Rabbinical Laws of Idolatry in the Second and Third Centuries in the Light of Archaeological and Historical Facts," *Israel Exploration Journal*, IX (1959), pp. 149 ff. and 228 ff.

WEITZMANN, KURT, "Die Illustration der Septuaginta," *Muenchener Jahrbuch der Bildenden Kunst*, 3d series, III-IV (1952-1953), pp. 96 ff.

WERNER, ALFRED, "Jewish Artists of the Age of Emancipation," in *Jewish Art*, edited by Cecil Roth (Jerusalem, 1961), pp. 539 ff.

WISCHNITZER, MARK, *A History of Jewish Crafts and Guilds*. New York, 1965.

WISCHNITZER, RACHEL, "Alfred Rubens. A History of Jewish Costume," review in *Judaism*, XVI, 4 (Fall 1967), pp. 50 ff.

———, *The Architecture of the European Synagogue*. Philadelphia, 1964.

———, "Arnold Whittick. Eric Mendelsohn," review in *Journal of the Society of Architectural Historians*, XVII, 3 (Fall 1958), pp. 35 f.

———, "Avram Kampf. Contemporary Synagogue Art," review in *Journal of the Society of Architectural Historians*, XXVI, 1 (March 1967), pp. 78 f.

———, "Bernard Goldman. The Sacred Portal," review in JSS, XXIX, 3 (July 1967), pp. 185 f.

———, "The Beth Alpha Mosaic," JSS, XVII, 2 (April 1955), pp. 133 ff.

———, "The Egyptian Revival in Synagogue Architecture," PAJHS, XLI (1951), pp. 61 ff.

———, "Erwin R. Goodenough. Jewish Symbols in the Greco-Roman Period, XII vols.," reviews in *In Jewish Bookland*, the Jewish Book Council, November 1954, May 1955, April 1957, February 1959, September 1964, and October 1966.

———, "Ezra Stiles and the Portrait of Menasseh ben Israel," *American Jewish Historical Society Quarterly*, LI, 2 (December 1961).

———, "Gleanings. The Zeena U-Reena and Its Illustrations," in *N. M. Gelber Jubilee Volume* (Tel-Aviv, 1963), pp. xxxv ff.

———, "The Meaning of the Beth Alpha Mosaic," *Bulletin of the Israel Exploration Society*, XVIII (1954), pp. viii ff.

————, "The Moneychanger with the Balance, a Topic of Jewish Iconography," *Eretz-Israel*, VI (1960), pp. 23 ff.

————, "Passover in Art," in *The Passover Anthology*, edited by Philip Goodman (Philadelphia, 1961), Chap. 16.

————, "Rembrandt's So-called 'Synagogue' in the Light of Synagogue Architecture," in *The Abraham Weiss Jubilee Volume* (New York, 1964), pp. 129 ff.

————, *Synagogue Architecture in the United States*. Philadelphia, 1955.

————, "Thomas U. Walter's Crown Street Synagogue, 1848-49," *Journal of the Society of Architectural Historians*, XIII, 4 (December 1954), pp. 29 ff.

————, "The Unicorn in Christian and Jewish Art," *Historia Judaica*, XIII (1951), pp. 141 ff.

CHAPTER 6

THE CONTRIBUTION OF THE JEWS TO MEDICINE

By Arturo Castiglioni

It is very difficult to consider Jewish medicine a chapter with a character all its own in the history of medicine in general.[1a] Our sources for Jewish medicine in antiquity are few and rare. There are available no medical writings which go back to ancient times; there is not even a collection of medical prescriptions or medical stories such as we have for the Egyptians and the Babylonians. The two works that are the sources for the study of Jewish history, the Bible and the Talmud, are chiefly books of laws in which medical subjects are dealt with only incidentally, only in so far as they concern the legislator. In the Talmud some laws on medical matters or problems are discussed, but always from the religious, moral or legal point of view, and evidently medical men have not at all or rarely been consulted. The Rabbis had some general knowledge of medicine, and this was the basis for their judgment or their views.

Jewish medicine of antiquity, at least what has come down to us in the texts of the sacred books, was dominated by the theocratic principle that governed the moral, social and political life of the people. It is easy to understand that this small people, which for centuries was subject to terrible wars, conquests and the influence of mighty neighbors, should in the evolution of its medicine also reveal the results of these circumstances. Unlike Egyptian or Greek medicine, therefore, Jewish medicine cannot be described as something distinctly itself. The first Jewish physicians of whose literary activity we know (seventh or eighth century c.e.) belonged to the world of Arab culture and wrote generally in Arabic, and the most ancient medical work in Hebrew is a collection of prescriptions by the Jewish physician, Sabbatai ben Abraham Donnolo, who lived in Italy in the tenth century and wrote also a mystical commentary on the Book of Creation.

It is even more difficult to speak of Jewish medicine in the period after the destruction of the Temple,[1b] when the bulk of the Jewish people lived in exile. A decisive influence in their medicine was surely the essential character of their religion, and the law which constitutes its basis. This influence is manifest even in the evolution of the thought and activity of the physician, of the hygienist, of the scholar. But the great evolution in medical science, the shift in the Greek schools from magic and dogmatic medicine to clinical medicine and the revolutionary changes in medical doctrine and practice in recent times were not brought about by Jewish scholars; nor did they play any characteristic role in this evolution. The science and scientific activity of the Jews became a part, sometimes more, sometimes less important, of the cultural life of the people in whose midst they lived. Single great scholars accomplished remarkable work, single schools had an important part in the education of scholars and practitioners; it is, however, impossible to say that these scholars or these influences derived from a special character of the Jewish people or of the Jewish mind, and as such stimulated definite action in one or another direction. For many centuries the Jews were concentrated in the Mediterranean countries. Here their medicine had its most important development. A remarkable period of this development is connected with the Arab conquest of the Mediterranean countries. The Jews were the great intermediaries of the Mediterranean; for centuries all commercial goods as well as the treasures of literature and science passed through their hands. The Jewish physicians were philosophers and subtle reasoners, able practitioners, expert diagnosticians and excellent students of botany and pharmacology. They won most important positions at the courts and as teachers, and from this time originate the fame they enjoyed and the role they played in the schools of the Renaissance, especially in Italy, France and Spain. In the following centuries, however, the battle of the European Jews against persecution made their participation in scientific activities difficult and often impossible.

With the emancipation of the Jews in many European countries and the progressive internationalization of science, Jews became more active in medicine and other sciences but no longer did their work have a peculiar character. In later times Jewish scholars held a prominent place as teachers and practitioners, and they made an important contribution to scientific progress. But this contribution cannot be distinguished from that of other great scholars with whom the Jews were in constant contact and from whom they adopted the fundamental concepts and systems of medicine.

We believe, therefore, that this chapter, which attempts to survey the role the Jews played in the history of medicine, may be divided into four parts. The first will be devoted to the medicine of the Bible and Talmud; the second, to the evolution of medicine among the Jews in the Middle Ages and their influence on Arabic medicine; the third, to the role Jewish scholars played in the schools of the pre-Renaissance and Renaissance periods; and finally, a short account of medicine among the Jews in the modern period.

It is not our intention to write the history of the great physicians and scholars and to give their biographies: this has been done in many works at different times and from different points of view. We shall try as far as possible to trace the history of the ideas, the evolution of medical thought, either as it was influenced by the Jews or as it exerted its influence on them, and to give a picture of the role the Jewish scholars and practitioners played in the history of medical science.

The fundamental concept that distinguished the medicine of biblical Israel from that of all other ancient peoples is this: Scripture declares it as a basic doctrine that the One God is the source of life and health; He is also, however, the source of all disease, which comes as a punishment and reproof. "I kill, and I make alive; I have wounded, and I heal" (Deut. 32:39). The animistic concept, the belief in malignant demons, universally accepted among peoples in protohistoric times, was suppressed and all magical practices were forbidden. This is the principle clearly expressed in all canonic books.

The Jewish concept of pathology reveals, however, the belief in a supernatural cause. Humbert states correctly that the origin of disease was attributed by the Jews equally to the Will of God, or to human malediction, or to a fault committed by ancestors (as in the threat of Divine punishment up to the third and fourth generations). As defenses against the hostile influence of individuals, prayers and spells were used. Sigmund Mowinckel and Adolphe Lods have shown that many of the invocations of the Psalms are to be regarded as simple incantations, and that such curses as "Let their eyes be darkened that they see not . . . Let them be blotted out of the book of the living" (69:24, 29) are procedures analogous in their form and scope to the magic preserved in the Assyro-Babylonian texts. According to the earliest narratives, it is not always the One God Who strikes. The plague is carried by an angel of God, who strikes 185,000 Assyrians in one night (II Kings 19:35). The "destroyer" smites the firstborn of Egypt (Ex. 12:23) and the "adversary," one of the *Bene Elohim*, inflicts malignant ulcers on Job. Angels and malignant demons appear here and there in the sacred books; one of these demons devours the limbs of the dead (Job 18:13).

The concept that tends to attribute chief importance to the blood and a preponderant role in general to the humors is of Sumerian origin. In Scripture, too, will be found the influence of the Egyptian pneumatic concept, that the spirit is the center of life (see Gen. 7:22 "in whose nostrils was the breath of the spirit of life").

In the development of the Jewish concept there is a manifest tendency and practical necessity to concentrate authority and power in the hands of the priestly caste, not because the priests are believed to possess by themselves the power of healing but because they are the interpreters or intermediaries of the will of the One God.

Note the fundamental difference from the medicine of other peoples.

The Jewish priest never plays the role of a physician; he gives his advice according to the religious Law and can help with his prayers. He may be, and really is, an adviser and an expert friend, but he never believes or boasts that he is a healer. When King Asa consulted physicians instead of calling for the help of God through His priests he was promptly punished: he "slept with his fathers" (II Chron. 16:12, 13).

According to this conception it is to God that the sick appeals for the cure of his ills; before Him man prostrates himself to invoke salvation. From the belief in the healing power of God followed the duty to obey all Divine precepts with a scrupulousness no less thorough than that of other nations in their use of magical prescriptions, and to carry out rules of sanitation with the same exactness and fervid faith that had to accompany all religious practices. This was the cause for the rapid development of sanitary legislation, what we may call the first codification of hygienic regulations, among the Jews.

In this recognition of a supreme Divine law and in the abolition of magic beliefs and practices lies the importance of the monotheistic concept for the evolution of medicine in Israel. All the medical practices described in ancient Egyptian and Babylonian texts are originally magic practices, though they may sometimes be rooted in experience; they belong to the religious rites of strange gods and are, therefore, forbidden to the people of Israel. Medicine is poorly represented in early Jewish literature because whenever the magic medicine of Babylonia and Egypt appeared in ancient Judea it was rigorously proscribed and suppressed. Nevertheless, it cannot be denied that in Israel, as among others, some of these practices persisted through the centuries, and it is interesting to see the traces of these practices in the biblical literature. In Scripture, however, they appear under a different aspect: they are made compatible or at least not in conflict with the monotheistic concept.

Traces of magic are evident in the following few examples: The snake was worshiped throughout the Orient as a healing god and was the object of a widespread magic cult; in the Bible he appears in the stories of the Garden of Eden and the brazen serpent. The persistence of this cult is proved by the fact that the serpent had to be destroyed by King Hezekiah to prevent its worship. The Babylonian "Sabbath" is quite likely connected with the magic concept familiar to all Oriental peoples of the unlucky number seven and its multiples. Circumcision was practiced among many primitive peoples and it can probably be explained as an attempt to substitute some bloody rite for human sacrifice. The story of Abraham and Isaac in Gen. 22 is surely connected with the substitution of animal for human sacrifice. Circumcision was prescribed also in Egypt, but only for the priests and upper classes. In Judaism, however, as is repeatedly affirmed in the biblical text, the entire people are regarded as priests, regardless of caste or class; all regulations therefore are imposed equally upon everyone.

The belief in the action of malignant demons (masculine, *shedim*, feminine, *lilit*) which cause insanity, sore throat, asthma and many other ills was prevalent among the Jews. The application of pieces of parchment bearing biblical verses or exorcistic formulae was supposed to aid recovery. A man of God could transfer leprosy from one person to another (II Kings 5:27); with a number of charms the priest could "dry up the thigh and swell the stomach" of the sinful woman after he had made her drink the water in which had been immersed a curse written on a piece of parchment. In epidemics one could obtain relief by sacrificing the sinful person (II Sam. 21:5-6); the prophet Elijah (I Kings 17:21-22) brought a dead child back to life by breathing into its mouth, a rite similar to a Babylonian practice. The proceedings described in Leviticus 14 and the ceremony of the blood of the paschal lamb are founded on analogous practices elsewhere.

In the course of time, after the general acceptance of monotheism, all these beliefs, traditions and customs were absorbed into and filtered through the moral and legislative system of Judaism and the theocratic principle definitely governed the moral, social and political life of the people and the evolution of its medicine. Thus the use of the phylacteries (*tephillin*) and the *mezuzot*, originally ancient apotropaic rites, assumed the character of a religious law of moral importance.

The concept of purity is of eminent importance in biblical legislation. Physical purity is put on a par with moral purity, and it is not admitted that heart and mind can be pure without cleanliness of the body. The aim of Jewish religious precepts, to which the hygienic regulations belong, is purity before God. Hygienic regulations were imposed on the people by law with the authority characteristic of Divine maxims and in the form of religious ceremonies. Some of these regulations existed also in Egypt and in Babylonia, where they had a magic character; but in the Bible the religious distinction between pure and impure is a standard for everyday life. Whoever becomes impure (*tame*) for whatever reason, whether he had committed an evil deed or had contracted a contagious disease, or had touched a corpse, could become pure (*tahor*) with the help of exactly prescribed practices in which bathing was of the greatest importance. The hygienic law of impurity after contact with corpses, of women during and after the menstrual period, of those affected with gonorrhea and leprosy, arise from a purely religious concept. This originally mystic apparatus is important and soon assumes a symbolic character. David prays to God: "Wash me thoroughly from mine iniquity, and cleanse me from my sin" (Ps. 51:4). The sinner is told: "For though thou wash thee with nitre, and take thee much soap, yet thine iniquity is marked before Me" (Jer. 2:22).

This makes it amply clear that the practice of purification signified to the common mind also a cleansing of oneself from the sin of moral transgression. The well-known passage in the Psalms, "I will wash my hands in innocency" (26:6), takes on symbolic significance, and later the purifying bath is transformed into the symbolic baptism.

No Jew could enter the Temple without being pure, that is to say, without having first taken a bath if he had been in contact with impure persons or things or had done anything which made his body impure. Even before reading the Law, which was regarded as a daily duty for every Jew, a bath had to be taken. The same rite was prescribed after every ejaculation.

The people of Israel did not have professional physicians, although an empirical medicine flourished among the Jews as everywhere else. In ancient times there was no physician (*rophe*) even on such occasions as that of embalming Jacob's body. For embalming, Joseph called physicians from Egypt. That is why we can derive only fragmentary information on medical cures and medicines from the Bible. The prophets appear to have acted in some cases as wonder-healers, but it is evident that their healing activity was closely connected with an intense moral and religious suggestion.

Later we find mention of physicians and we learn that they enjoyed great esteem. Jesus, the son of Sirach (180 B.C.E.), says, "Honor the physician according to thy need of him with the honor due unto him because verily the Lord hath created him." The physician is always considered as the intermediary, working with the help and carrying out the Will of God.

The Jewish physician who appears in the pages of the Talmud is not a specialist like the Egyptian medical men of whom Herodotus speaks. The physician of the Talmud prescribes cures for internal diseases, but he is also a surgeon who binds the patient on the table and has with him a bag which contains his instruments. He is able to heal wounds with herbs, to give dietetic prescriptions and to give the patient a potion (*samme deshinta*) for inducing sleep during the operation (Baba Mezia 83b). He opens an abscess and, we are also told, is able to open the skull with a trephine to operate on the brain and to close the wound with the skin of a squash (Tosefta Ohalot 2.6). Amputation of limbs and of gangrenous parts is performed. The physician is expert in the treatment of fractures and it is expected that he be ready to work with knife, plasters, bandages and internal remedies alike.

Gynecological or obstetrical interference of physicians was not admitted,[1c] but midwives (*meyalledet*) played an important role. Some of them are quoted in the Bible; for instance, at the delivery of Rachel (Gen. 35:17) and of Tamar (Gen. 38:28). In the Mishna the midwife is called *hakama*, the "wise woman," like the *sage femme* of the French. Embryotomy was also to be performed by a midwife if a surgeon could not be reached, but not by a pagan because she might kill the child.

Unlike other legislations, the Jewish law holds the physician responsible only if he has intentionally hurt his patient, not if an error occurred. This is commented upon by Pardo, quoted by Preuss, with the observation that "if the physician should be made responsible for every mistake nobody would follow this profession. The judgment and punishment are reserved to God."

There is a clear distinction in the Talmud between the physician, *rophe*, and the bloodletter (*umman*). The latter was considered a worker and had a very low social position. The Talmud regards him unfavorably: he can never become a leader of a community nor take part in the election of king nor High Priest. It may be noted that the profession is despised also among the Arabs. Circumcision, the most frequent surgical operation, was generally practiced by the physician or by a specialist who was called *mahola*, later *mohel*. Circumcision was a religious act of fundamental importance; it was, however, prescribed that children who were sick or bleeders should not be circumcised.

The anatomical knowledge in biblical and talmudic literature was derived only from occasional inspection of corpses and from the examination of the internal organs of slaughtered animals in order to determine their condition. That human dissections should have been practiced in ancient times is very unlikely. The fear of hurting a corpse (*niwwul met*) was certainly the most important reason making dissection impossible. Not even exhumation and inspection of the corpse was permitted. For the same reason embalming was forbidden. A similar attitude is responsible for the custom once general in Egypt of throwing stones at the embalmer as a punishment, after he had performed his work. It is, however, told of the pupils of Rabbi Ishmael (about 100 C.E.) that they boiled the corpse of a prostitute who had been condemned to death, in order to learn what was the number of bones in the human body (B. Bekorot 45a). This method of treating bones seems to have been usual in antiquity, and was expressly forbidden by Pope Boniface VIII in 1301.

In his scholarly work, Preuss has given an exhaustive summary of talmudic anatomy. We may only say briefly that the esophagus, the larynx, the trachea, the lungs, meninges and the genital organs are described, and the spleen, kidneys, liver, heart and intestines are often mentioned. Blood constitutes the vital principle; muscles are referred to as *basar* (flesh) and the tendons as *giddim*. The body was thought to have 248 bones and 365 tendons. One bone called *luz*, placed somewhere in the vertebral column, was believed to be the nucleus from which the body would be reconstructed at the resurrection of the dead. This ossicle, which was said to be indestructible, was searched for by the anatomists of the Middle Ages without success.

It may be noted that, according to the texts, the liver, the origin of the blood, is the most important organ and the center of life. The heart is not the center of the circulation, but the seat of the soul (Aristotelian doctrine). The anatomical and physiological information about the brain is very poor. During sleep, the brain, they believed, could be removed without breaking any bones, through the nose or, according to the Talmud, through the auditive channel.

The importance of dreams was generally accepted. R. Eleazar stated, "There is no dream without significance," and R. Hisda said, "A dream which is not interpreted is like a letter which is not read." In general the opinion of the teachers is against this interpretation of dreams which, however, are given prominent place in the Bible and Talmud. Very interesting is a statement by R. Joshua b. Hananja that all dreams can be realized according to their interpretation and that for any dream there are not less than twenty-four interpretations which may be correct.

The popular view of etiology of diseases was analogous to that of the Babylonians and Egyptians. The belief in the stars was widespread as was the belief in the influence of the evil eye (*ayyin ha-ra*), which also is probably of Babylonian origin, and is widespread in our times, too, especially among the Mediterranean peoples.

It was generally believed that a mortal disease lasted five days. In therapy the incantation (*lahash*) played an important part, but it was considered part of the occult practices of which no sign can be found in the Talmud. Amulets and charms were very much in use and were not forbidden, probably because this practice was too deeply rooted in the traditional belief of the people. What we know of the spread of epidemic diseases in biblical and later times proves that the idea of contagion, its dangers and the need to overcome them by isolation was well known to the Semitic peoples. In the story (I Sam. 5:1-2) of the capture of the Ark of the Covenant by the Philistines, who carried it to the temple of Dagon, is found the description of an epidemic of bubonic plague (their punishment for the desecration), and when the Philistines decided to return the Ark they offered at the same time a symbolic gift of five golden emerods and five golden mice to the God of Israel. Here is remarkable evidence of the importance attributed to rodents in the spread of the plague in very ancient times. In another epidemic (II Kings 19:35) we are informed of the mortality caused when the angel of the Lord killed 185,000 of Sennacherib's soldiers (705-681 B.C.E.). In the story of this pestilence, which is referred to by Herodotus (II, 141), the rat also plays an important part. In fact, according to Egyptian tradition, the Assyrians were decimated by the god Ptah, who was represented in the temple of Thebes with a rat in his hand. It is probable that the importance attributed to animals as transmitters of disease also had a magic origin.

Leprosy received considerable attention in the biblical books. The Hebrew word for leprosy is *tsaraat*. The number of writings on this subject and of commentaries on the thirteenth chapter of Leviticus, where the diseases are described, is so great that we may easily believe that many discussions took place in order to identify the disease. All the descriptions of the symptoms and of the sanitary measures justify the conclusion that leprosy is meant. Preuss closes his study on the subject with the statement that it is at least a probable identification: we have to admit, however, that the term was often used for other clinical phenomena such as psoriasis, eczema and various inflammations of the skin, perhaps even syphilis. The person suspected of being a leper was brought to the priest; if he found that the *nega*, the affected place, was white and appeared to be deeper than the surrounding skin, he declared that it was really *tsaraat* and that the patient was impure. Note that the symptomatic signs here quoted are the same that the Arabian physicians, especially Avicenna, describe as characteristic of leprosy. It is the white sign, *morphoea alba*, which is recognized as such plus the fact that the hair on the spot turns white.

Among the other more frequent diseases in biblical times were dysentery, dropsy, apoplexy, and mental diseases like Saul's. That certain venereal diseases were common in Judea is apparent from the strict hygienic regulation for those with an "issue" (gonorrhea?). According to certain interpreters, the biblical account of the plague of Baal-Peor should be regarded as the story of a syphilis epidemic as a result of the Hebrews' visit to the brothels of the Midianites. The terrible disease killed twenty-four thousand people. This interpretation, however, is not at all sufficiently proved.

Other diseases like *shehim* (universal eczema), the disease of King Hezekiah (pharynx abscess?), the *baale raatan* (leprosy) are difficult to identify. The information about their symptoms, their course and their recovery is neither clear nor the same in the different accounts; only hypothetical suppositions, therefore, can be advanced.

The sect of the Essenes, which was formed about 150 B.C.E.,[2a] deserves to be mentioned. The Essenes were Jews who lived a monastic life; they included the *Therapeutae* and *Hemerobaptists*, and it seems that the former particularly practiced medicine in some mild form of suggestion. Some believe that the name "Essene" is derived from the Aramaic *Asa* (he healed), corresponding to the Greek Therapeutae. In the therapy of the Essenes prayers and pious formulae were very important and we may compare this medicine with the Christian conventual medicine which arose in the Middle Ages at the time of the foundation of the monasteries.

The Essenes were considered saints, wonder-healers who cured by faith and by words. They practiced medicine in order to perfect the soul and make it more accessible to Divine truth and Divine health. By conjuration they drove hostile spirits out of the patient's body. The Mishna (Bekorot 4:4) refers to Teudas, who was acquainted with conditions in Alexandria as a worthy physician, and Josephus (De Ant. Jud. VIII, 2:5) describes the cure of a possessed person in the presence of the Emperor Vespasian by Eleazar, an Essene. A root allegedly recommended by King Solomon and endowed with healing properties was introduced into the nose of the sick man. The Essene pronounced the name of the wise king and a magic formula and the patient recovered. The laying on of hands was practiced and amulets were used.

It is interesting to note that in the Talmud some animal products, in some kind of primitive opotherapy of magical origin, are prescribed. A man bitten by a mad dog was given the omentum of the dog to eat; parts of the liver and the spleen of animals were prescribed for diseases of that organ.

From many biblical passages it is clear that the art of the apothecary was not unknown to the ancient Hebrews. In Ex. 30:22-26 we read: "The Lord spoke unto Moses, saying, 'Take thou also unto thee the chief spices, of flowing myrrh five hundred shekels, and of sweet cinnamon half so much, even two hundred and fifty, and of sweet calamus two hundred and fifty and of cassia five hundred, after the shekel of the Sanctuary and of olive oil a hin. And thou shalt make it a holy anointing oil, a perfume compounded after the art of the perfumer.'"

Mandrake also was a very popular remedy among the ancient Hebrews and it was generally believed to be useful in promoting conception (Gen. 30:14). Nitre was employed as a cleansing agent and oil was used to dress wounds, bruises and sores (Is. 1:6). Many remedies, especially ointments, are referred to by Roman authors as being used by Jews.[3]

Jewish philosophers and physicians participated actively in the flourishing science of Alexandria and, at the time of the Ptolemies, enjoyed a great popularity. The Greeks were then inclined to admire these strange people and to accept them in the schools, in the public discussions, and in the professions; but in the first century C.E. anti-Semitism began to manifest itself and in the Christian empire it took on the form of a social persecution, despite the fact that Julius Caesar and the early Roman emperors followed the policy of the Hellenistic princes to patronize the Jews and grant them full liberty. Jews adopted Greek as their mother tongue and Jewish students inherited the intellectual legacy of Greece.[4a] The inner conflict of the Jewish-Hellenistic intellectual world is reflected in the work of Philo.[5a]

Biblical-talmudic literature permits us to trace the evolution of medical thought among the Jews from fundamental magical beliefs and conceptions common to all primitive peoples to an empirical and religious medicine. How great the influence of Greek medicine was is difficult to determine. The Talmud, as already observed, is a collection of discussions and of laws and their interpretation but not of medical doctrines. We may, therefore, pass only a general judgment on the practice of medicine and believe that the Jewish physicians of those days accepted the diagnostic rules and therapeutic means prescribed by Greek medicine, but did not care too much for the clinical doctrines or the theoretical scientific explanations that were the characteristic elements of Greek science. Jewish physicians acknowledged the facts, but were cautious and skeptical in adopting doctrines which appeared to them heterodox from the point of view of their strong religious faith, whose central belief was expressed by the words of Divine revelation, "I am the Lord, that healeth thee" (Ex. 15:26).

In his memorable speech at the International Medical Congress in Rome (1894) on "Morgagni and Anatomical Thought," Rudolf Virchow said: "In the Middle Ages the Jews and the Arabs certainly had a definite influence on the progress of medical doctrine. Recent discoveries have brought to light Hebrew manuscripts which demonstrate with how great a diligence and scholarship the Jewish physician of the Middle Ages was active in the preservation and development of medical thought."

The role played by the Jews during the Arab conquests of the Mediterranean is an impressive one in the history of the Middle Ages and the pre-Renaissance.[6a] In contact with the Arabs, among whom they were respected physicians, teachers and counselors, Jews were perhaps the only aliens able to understand the language and the psychology of the people whose victorious banners flew over southern Europe for six centuries. The Jews enjoyed complete freedom in their professional and intellectual activity. They became the advisers of sultan and caliph and once more played the historic role to which they seemed destined by the geographical position of their native country, and by their constant relations with different races and creeds as a result of war, persecution, dispersion and exile. These events had surely given the Jews their peculiar orientation of thought, for they had to adjust themselves to different conditions, laws and customs, and to adopt or reject new beliefs. Theirs was the passionate desire to seek out the true and the best everywhere, as far as possible to placate hostile powers and conciliate opposing opinions. They were, or tried to be, according to the biblical prescription, the seekers and teachers of truth, always fighting with others and themselves for their beliefs. They were acquainted with Greek philosophy and medicine and had felt deeply the influence of the Alexandrian schools. To the Arabs, a people of warriors and fanatic believers whose contact with Western civilization was a violent one at the outset, the Jews gave the first lessons in classic philosophy and science.

At first not only difference in religion but also difference of language was the chief difficulty in the evolution of a Jewish medical literature. The Jews in the Diaspora used Hebrew in their writings, but always needed new words for their scientific vocabulary. These they took from the language of the country they inhabited; and thus the glossaries or dictionaries arose. Later, however, when the Jews in exile forgot the Hebrew language, or used it only in their prayers and in their religious studies, it was necessary for the teacher and scholar who had to address a larger public to write in the language of the country; hence the fact that for the most part Jewish physicians, among them the most illustrious like Maimonides, wrote their medical works in Arabic.

In the evolution of Arabic medicine, the study of classical medical authors went hand in hand with philosophy, and both subjects were entirely free from any religious influence. Thanks to the meticulous researches of Moritz Steinschneider, we now know how great was the service of Jewish translators to science. In their hands was the light of ancient scientific knowledge and by adding it to Arabic culture they saved Greek science for the Occident. The most important classical writings in philosophy, astronomy, mathematics and medicine were translated from Greek into Arabic. Hardly fifty years after the conquest, a Babylonian Jew translated a medical work from Syrian into Arabic.[7] In the latter half of the seventh century Masarjawaih translated many medical texts. These were later retranslated by other Jewish scholars from Arabic into Hebrew and Latin. The activity of Jewish physicians among the Arabs had a decisive influence on the progress not only of Arabic but, later, of Western medicine also.

Although the bulk of Jewish Arabic scholarship consisted of translation from and assimilation of Greek works, it did far more than that. They not only transmitted ancient knowledge, but also contributed to the creation of new knowledge.

The most remarkable Jewish medical writers were Isaac Israeli (850-950 C.E.) and Moses Maimonides (1135-1204). The first was physician to the Caliph Obaid Allah and wrote philosophical works on the elements. According to Harry Friedenwald, Israeli's medical works were the greatest contributions of Arabic Jewish physicians. His full name was Abu Yakub Ishak ibn Suleiman al Israeli, and his works, soon translated into Hebrew and Latin, had widespread fame. He was known among the Arabs as Israeli, in the Western medical world as Isaac Judeus. His works were translated into Latin by Constantinus Africanus, the learned monk who was said to be of Jewish origin. Israeli's most famous books, which are frequently referred to as classics, and which served as textbooks at the school of Salerno, were the books on Urine and Fever, the Opera Isaaci Judaei *"medicorum monarcha,"* were published in Latin in Lyons (1515).

Moses Maimonides (Abu Imram Musa ibn Maimun), born in Cordova in 1135, fled to Fez in 1148 because of the persecutions by the Almohades; later he went to Palestine and finally to Cairo, where he settled in 1165 and soon became famous as philosopher and physician. He was the physician of Saladin and his son, and head of the Jewish community of Egypt; he died in 1204 and was buried in Tiberias. As George Sarton says, his influence was far reaching in space and time. He occupied a prominent place among the great thinkers of the Middle Ages and the forerunners of scientific medicine. That he was the greatest exponent of a new trend of thought is shown by the influence of his work on Albertus Magnus and Thomas Aquinas. He practiced medicine with intelligent observation of his patients, with love and faith, and strictly followed the moral precepts of the Bible. His fame as a healer is still a living tradition throughout the Orient. Even today his synagogue in Cairo is considered an especially sacred shrine, the sick go there to pass the night in order to speed their recovery. And to his tomb at Tiberias, on the shore of the Sea of Gennesaret, a pilgrimage of the sick takes place even at the present time. Many places in different countries enjoy similar fame, but this is the only case in history where the physician himself is regarded, after his death, as a wonder-healer.

This is not the place to estimate the importance of Maimonides as philosopher and religious writer.[8a] We may only say that his profound comprehension and fervid admiration of the scientific achievements of the Greek philosophers and physicians, and, on the other hand, his firm belief in the teachings of the Law, led him to attempt a conciliation between Aristotle and the Bible. This is evident also in his medical works, in his fight against astrology and superstition, in his deep understanding of the importance of a psychological therapy, in his high conception of the duties of the physician. To understand and with a free mind to discuss new currents of thought without abandoning the laws and the traditional beliefs of the Jewish people caused perpetual conflict in the soul of Jewish scholars at all times. In his stupendous activity as commentator of the sacred books, as revered judge in all religious problems, and at the same time as teacher and physician, Maimonides followed the example of the prophets and the great Rabbis. In the evolution of scientific thought in the Mediterranean, which was the center of civilization for twenty centuries, the work of Moses Maimonides had a decisive influence.

Among the distinguished medical translators we may mention the following: Moses ibn Tibbon (*c.* 1283), a Provençal physician who translated many works of Maimonides and Rhazes; Nathan Ha-Meati of Cento (Italy), who lived in Rome (1229-1283) and translated, among other books, the *Canon* of Avicenna and the *Aphorisms* of Hippocrates with the *Commentaries* of Galen. Hasdai ibn Shaprut, minister to the caliph of Cordova (*c.* 960), with the aid of a Greek monk translated Dioscorides into Arabic.

Faraj ben Salim was one of the most prominent translators of the thirteenth century. He was very likely connected with the school of Salerno, and must have been in close touch with Charles of France, who ruled Sicily from 1266 to 1285. The Latin translation of the medical work by the Arabic Ali ibn Jazla, which was published in 1532, was dedicated to the king. Faraj was one of the first Jewish doctors to translate from the Arabic directly into Latin. (One of the most popular translators was Gerard of Cremona, who put into Latin the *Canon* of Avicenna [a book which vied in popularity with Aristotle's and Galen's works] and the treatise on surgery by Abulcasis, which was widely read in the Occident until the end of the Renaissance.) The influence of Jewish physicians in Spain and their activity in the schools of southern France (Montpellier), perhaps also in the school of Salerno which many Jewish students attended, was of far-reaching importance.

During the Middle Ages, when dogmatism and Scholasticism hampered the evolution of Western medicine, there occurred an interesting development in Jewish medicine. On the one hand, in certain circles mysticism began to be cultivated with a renewed vigor, and in the *Zohar*, the mystic's Bible, so to speak, appeared its most significant expression. Elsewhere in the present work, the nature of the *Zohar* is discussed.[9a] For our immediate purpose, however, and from one point of view, the work may be described as a mystic-medical book. According to the *Zohar*, the soul, invisible and imperceptible, has its seat above the cortex and governs life through the organs which are divided into two regions separated by a "heaven," the diaphragm. Through channels the Divine grace flows to all parts of the body, but the function of the organs ceases when sin stops the flowing of grace. Different pulses are described and mystically connected with the four elements. A supreme importance is attributed to generation: mysticism and the erotic are closely connected, and each organ receives mystic significance.

Another form of mystic medicine originated in the traditional trust of the devout in the counsel of holy men whose sayings have been preserved for centuries by pious Jews in the East and by the Hasidim. These mystical tendencies were not without influence on Jewish medicine: they introduced the medicine of the so-called wonder Rabbis, who were the revered advisers and medical counselors. Their cures, however, were generally limited to moral or hygienic prescriptions and to the use of certain prayers, formulae or cryptograms. The work of the wonder-healers flourished whenever superstition or belief in the occult was rampant. Generally their medical system was of only the mildest sort; its suggestive therapy was often educational, always fantastic, but certainly not dangerous.

Medicine among the Jews in Eastern Europe, especially in Poland, followed the same mysticism up to our time. In a book published by Jacob Koblenz (Offenbach, 1788) many wonder remedies are recommended, among them incantation with formulae in Hebrew and Yiddish. Throughout the Middle Ages certain prayers and biblical passages were very popular as remedies. The Psalms were often prescribed as cure. In the *Shimmush Tehillim*, which was often printed, we find passages which have to be recited to hasten delivery, passages for protection against eye diseases, against fever. Psalm 22:21 was believed to be especially efficacious against dogbite.

In 1720 a book, *Toledot Adam*, was published whose authors were said to be Elia baal Shem, Joel baal Shem and Simha Rofe; the work contains a great number of cabbalistic prescriptions. The name *baal Shem* was given to those who were believed to be cabbalistic wonder-healers. The most famous of them was the "Besht," Israel baal Shem Tob, the founder of modern Hasidism. It is evident that a continuous line leads from the mystic therapy of the Essenes to the therapeutic system of the wonder practices popular in the East up to the present.

In the schools of the Mediterranean countries, especially in Italy and France, Jewish physicians had always played an important role. The condition of the Jews in the Middle Ages had been one of great hardship and persecution, their activities were restricted; nevertheless, they had maintained an almost continuous line of medical practitioners. Friedenwald, who has written an interesting chapter on this period of Jewish medicine also, says that the history of the Jews in the Diaspora has been the longest in Italy, lasting over more than two thousand years. Already by the end of the fourth century c.e. the Jews had attained great prominence and many of them were official physicians, *archiatri*. Thereafter many church councils forbade Christians to call upon Jewish physicians or be medically treated by them.

However, many exceptions were made. In 1220 Pope Honorius III took under his papal protection Azzachus Avembenist of Barcelona, Jewish court physician to the king of Aragon. Pope Martin IV had at his court a Jewish physician who was a pupil of Rabbi Nathan of Montpellier and his example was followed by many Popes. The attitude of the Popes toward the Jew varied at different times, but in general we can say that the Jewish physicians continued in their prominent position.

In the thirteenth and fourteenth centuries Jewish physicians enjoyed the protection of the rulers and great fame even in Catholic Spain. One of these physicians was Judah Alfachar (d. 1235). He had the title of *Nasi* (Prince) at the court of Ferdinand III in Toledo, and held an important position not only as physician, but also as collector of revenues. Another was Sheshet Benveniste, physician and diplomat at the court of Aragon, with the same position and title. José Orabuena (fourteenth century) was the physician of the king of Navarre and for a long time the treasurer of the court. Both Samuel and Judah ibn Wakar were physicians who enjoyed the confidence of the ruling family.

In many Italian cities, especially in Ferrara, Mantua, and Genoa, many Spanish and Portuguese refugees were received and many Jewish physicians granted the privilege of practicing medicine.

The part that Jewish scholars and teachers played in the old schools is an important one. According to Theodor Puschmann, medicine was probably taught in the ancient Jewish academies of Tiberias, Sura and Pumbedita;[10a] in general, however, medicine was learned by a student serving as apprentice to a physician. Sometimes schools of higher learning grew out of a private undertaking. Dr. Harry Friedenwald quotes a prospectus, published in 1564, by David Provençal and his son Abraham, for a Jewish university to be established in Mantua where not only the sacred laws, but also Latin, logic, philosophy and mathematics were to be taught. Both father and son were physicians. It is not known whether this project was realized, but we do know of an early Jewish school in Paris where medicine was taught; in the fourteenth century, it is said, this school rivaled the university. Many medieval rabbis were physicians as well. The Gaon Hai in his *Moral Admonitions*, about 1000 C.E., urged the study of medical writings.   There were teachers who had a large number of pupils and conducted private schools in which medicine also was taught.

The school of Salerno plays an important role in the history of medical teachings. Salvatore De Renzi tells the well known story of its foundation by four physicians: a Greek, a Latin, an Arab and a Jew (Elinus), each teaching in his own language. This is almost certainly a legend, but it is probably founded on ancient tradition. The Jews played an important part in medical education at this time; Donnolo, who practiced medicine in the tenth century, enables us, as George Sarton says, "to realize how the so-called school of Salerno gradually came into existence. Such men as Donnolo created in southern Italy that focus of medical syncretisms and eventually of medical teaching."

Among the Salernian teachers Benvenutus Grassus (Grapheus) deserves to be mentioned. His book on ophthalmology, translated into English by Casey Wood of Chicago, was very much studied and commented upon in the ancient universities. Benvenutus is believed to have come from Jerusalem and is described by Sarton as the most famous non-Moslem oculist of medieval times. Julius Hirschberg believes that he was Jewish, and in a Parisian codex his name reads *"Biem Venu Raffe."* This name, Hirschberg observes, is very likely only a slight change from the Hebrew *Ha-Rophe*.

His book, *De oculis eorumque egritudinibus et curis*, was the most popular Latin textbook on the subject, as is shown by the number of copies which have been preserved in Latin, English, French and Provençal (twenty-two manuscripts and eighteen printed editions). It also had the distinction of being the first printed book on ophthalmology (Ferrara, 1474). Benvenutus makes frequent reference to his own anatomical studies on the structure of the eye, and his books constituted a notable advance over the work of the Arabic authors. For five hundred years it was regarded as the classical text on ophthalmology.

Salernian uroscopy found in Isaac Judeus, whom we mentioned above, its classic master. According to his book, the urine was carefully examined for color, density and content. For deducing some extremely important conclusions, the different kinds of clouds and precipitates which form after standing for a time were observed. Though this method had no diagnostic value, it was employed for centuries.

In France, in many cities near the Spanish border, where the influence of the Arabic-Jewish physicians was more deeply felt, there were Jewish schools where medicine was taught. Rashi (Rabbi Solomon ben Isaac, 1040-1105), born in Troyes, famous commentator of the Talmud, had a remarkable influence on scientific thought. At Lunel there was a flourishing medical school where Judah ibn Tibbon taught. These schools certainly had an influence on the University of Montpellier, which was perhaps as old as Salerno and for many centuries a leading medical school. Jean Astruc (1684-1766), who studied medicine in Paris and wrote a history of the medical school of Montpellier, stressed the importance of the Jewish participation in the early years of the university.

The first Jewish teacher of Montpellier, Jacob ben Makir ibn Tibbon (Prophatius Judeus), who lived from 1236 to 1304, was, according to Astruc, regent of the university for a long time. Among the outstanding Jewish doctors at Montpellier were the five doctors of the Saporta family, the first of whom, Luis, came from Lerida in Spain, lived first in Arles, then in Avignon, and became professor at the faculty in Montpellier (1506-1529). He was Charles VIII's physician and died at the age of 106. His great-grandson Jean was graduated in 1572 and became professor in 1577 and vice-chancellor in 1603. The Saportas were Marranos[11a] and for this reason were not admitted to municipal office. Friedenwald has suggested that Jean Astruc was also of Jewish origin. It is in any case interesting that the tradition of Jewish instructors and their influence on the development of medical studies at Montpellier survived so long. In the hall of the faculty there is a plaque in honor of Nathan ben Zechariah, master of the medical school in the thirteenth century.

After the Spanish victories and with the end of Arab domination in the Mediterranean, during the renaissance of art and science, the great migration of the Jews began. Among the Jews expelled from Spain were physicians and these now went to the Orient, especially to Constantinople, and to Italy and France.[12a]

The first universities were founded at the end of the thirteenth century; they were under the permanent supervision and control of the Catholic Church, and in 1431 the Council of Basel decreed that no Jew should receive a university degree. However, in many cases Jews were admitted as students to the medical schools, obtained a degree, and sometimes also were permitted to lecture.

With the Bull of Pius IV (1565), it was decided that no Jew should be admitted to any examination for the doctorate. The Venetian Senate, however, eager to protect freedom of learning and teaching at Padua, named a procurator who had the power to grant the degree regardless of the candidate's religion. The non-Catholics had recourse to the Counts Palatine, who had obtained the privilege of conferring academic degrees from the emperor. In 1616 the Venetian Senate decreed the foundation of a collegium which conferred degrees by authority of the Venetian state. Padua had the largest number of Jewish students, not only from Italy, but from foreign countries. Ismar Elbogen, in his article on Padua in the *Jewish Encyclopedia*, says that from 1517 to 1619 eighty Jews obtained the medical degree at Padua, and that in the next century there were about 150. At other universities, *e.g.*, in Rome and Ferrara and Siena, Jewish medical students were admitted and received their degrees.

This is not the place to enumerate all the Jewish physicians who had a part in the history of the ancient universities. Some names should be given, however, particularly those whose works were very popular in the medical literature of the Renaissance and are still considered remarkable contributions to medical progress.

Most interesting was Amatus Lusitanus, born in Castello Branco, Portugal. His parents were Marranos. He studied medicine in Salamanca, went back to Lisbon and later left Portugal for Antwerp. His reputation was so great that he was invited by Duke Hercules d'Este II to occupy the chair of medicine at the University of Ferrara (1540-1547). He lectured on Hippocrates and Galen, enjoyed the friendship of colleagues and scholars and participated in the dissections performed by the famous anatomist Canano. He later went to Ancona, where he finished his first *Centuria* in 1549. Amatus was often called to other cities as consultant; in May, 1550, he was invited to Rome to treat the newly elected Pope Julius III and later to attend the Pope's nephew, the ruler of Ancona. He spent several months in Rome and was very successful. In April, 1551, he finished his *Centuria II*, which was dedicated to Cardinal d'Este. In May, 1551, he dedicated his translation of Dioscorides to the Senate of Ragusa, where he wished to be appointed as city physician. His life was extremely adventurous, and it may be cited as an example of the persecution and the restrictions of Jews and Marranos at this time. In 1555 Pope

Paul IV was elected, and new decrees were promulgated forbidding Jewish physicians to treat Christian patients and ordering the yellow badge for all Jews. The Inquisition began its ruthless program, a great number of Marranos were arrested and subjected to torture, many burned at the stake. The house of Amatus was broken into and all valuables, including books and manuscripts, were looted.

Amatus repaired to Pesaro, where the Duke of Urbino was very friendly toward the refugees; from there he went to Ragusa, where his fame was soon established. But the persecution was not yet ended. In 1558 he left Ragusa for Salonica, where he found a large practice, and wrote the *Centuria VII*. It is believed that he died in 1568 of the plague that was raging in the city. His great work, the translation and comments on Dioscorides, was published in 1553 and contained many criticisms of the book by Matthioli, a famous pharmacologist, who replied to the criticisms in a violent way.

The medical writings of Amatus are interesting chiefly because they cite a great number of case histories, followed by discussion in the form of a dialogue between himself and other scholars. In therapy Amatus stressed the importance of proper diet and general hygiene; he describes more than twenty surgical cases and made an important contribution to the surgical treatment of empyema. He reveals in all his work an extensive knowledge of medical literature and a fine power of observation. He was emphatic in his opposition to superstition and magical treatment. In the history of the discovery of the valves of the veins, Amatus, who worked in Ferrara with the famous anatomist Canano, played an important part.

Another of the great physicians in the medicine of the Renaissance was Abraham ben Samuel Zacutus, also known as Diego Rodrigo, born in Salamanca about 1452. After the expulsion of the Jews from Spain he fled to Portugal and later to Tunis, where he was taken prisoner. He was not only a well-known physician, but also an author of astronomical and historical works of which the *Almanach Perpetuum* and the *Astrolabe* are the best known. It is certain that Vasco da Gama, the first navigator who made the voyage around the Cape of Good Hope, and had a long consultation with Zacuto before leaving, utilized his books during the navigation.[13a]

His great-great-grandson, well known under the name of Zacutus Lusitanus, born in Lisbon in 1575, took the doctor's degree in Salamanca in 1596 and went to Amsterdam in 1625. He published two interesting books of medical history, but he was considered chiefly as a great clinician. He was one of the first to describe blackwater fever, and made an important contribution to the knowledge of syphilis. His *Opera Omnia* were published in Lyons in two large volumes (1642-1644) and were dedicated to Louis XIII of France.

Jewish physicians were among the pioneers in the East Indies. The most illustrious of this group was Garcia da Orta, born in the last years of the fifteenth century in Elvas, Portugal. He studied medicine in Salamanca, then became professor of logic in Lisbon and in 1534 finally sailed for India. He lived in Goa, where he carried on extensive study of medicinal herbs. His work, *Colloquios dos simples e drogas e cousas medicinae de India*, appeared in 1563 and was immediately recognized as the first and most important contribution to the knowledge of Indian flora. The *Colloquios* had a great influence on the study of tropical medicine and of pharmacology. Da Orta's life was one of great affliction: he was tried as a Marrano by the Inquisition, but judgment was pronounced twelve years after his death. In Portuguese literature he is recognized as a most distinguished representative of the natural sciences.

To the same group of medical pioneers in the East Indies belongs Cristoval d'Acosta, a Marrano who was born in Mozambique in about 1515. He embarked for India in 1568 and stayed there four years. He devoted himself to botanical studies and tried to complete the work of his predecessor, Garcia.

Of medical importance in the sixteenth and seventeenth centuries was the family de Castro, of Spanish and Portuguese origin. Many physicians belonged to this family, the first, and one of the most distinguished, being Rodrigo de Castro (1550-1627). He was the author of a book on gynecology, *De Universa Muliebrium Medicina* (Cologne, 1603), which went through many editions.

One of the physicians in this family deserves special mention. Orobio de Castro, born in Portugal in 1620, studied philosophy and medicine in Seville, became professor of philosophy and later took up medical practice. He was very well known and had a large family. He was denounced to the Inquisition by a servant, who had been whipped for stealing, and was thrown into prison and tortured. The story of his suffering, quoted by Friedenwald, is found in the history of the Inquisition by Philipp van Limborch, who had it from Orobio's own mouth: "A linen garment was put over his body and drawn so very close on each side that it almost squeezed him to death. When he had overcome this torture and persisted in his refusal to confess, they tied his thumbs so very tight that the blood spurted out from under the nail." The whole procedure was repeated for a long time and always with new instruments. Finally he was condemned to perpetual banishment. He left Spain, went to Toulouse and then to Amsterdam, where he publicly reverted to Judaism, took the name Isaac and became one of the leaders of the community.

From the Renaissance up to modern times, that is, to the epoch of the Emancipation,[14a] Jewish physicians practiced medicine all over Europe, as we have seen, in great numbers and often with success; however, everywhere, with the exception of Italy, they were persecuted and interrupted in their activity. Some acquired great fame and were also physicians and counselors to kings and princes; sometimes they also had important positions and special privileges; but these were always exceptional cases. In general their life was insecure and it was not possible for them to have an important part in research and in teaching because admission to the great hospitals, the medical schools and general practices was either entirely forbidden or permitted only sporadically for short periods and under the protection of some enlightened ruler.

In the seventeenth century, when religious struggles were raging in Germany, the Italian universities were the only ones where Jewish students could obtain the doctor's degree. For a long time Padua was the school to which they came from all countries of Europe. The first Jewish student, a certain Bonacosa, was inscribed in Padua's medical school in 1255. Elijah Delmedigo (1460-1497) was one of the first among the famous Paduan professors; he taught also in Florence and Perugia. But it was in the sixteenth or seventeenth century that Jews from Germany, Austria and Poland flocked in great numbers to the university. For two centuries all Jewish doctors permitted to practice in Germany and Austria held their degrees from Padua.

It was only in 1782, after the so-called Act of Tolerance by the Emperor Joseph II of Austria, that Jewish students were admitted to the Austrian universities and as candidates for the doctor's degree in the medical schools. However, even when other German universities—such as Giessen, Halle, Goettingen—opened their doors to the students it was very difficult for them to be admitted to the academic profession. Jewish doctors were often referred to as "Italian doctors" because most of them had studied in Italy, and it was only at the beginning of the nineteenth century that a change occurred, that they were free to practice and were given the opportunity to become assistants and professors at the universities.

In the nineteenth century, when emancipation of the Jews was proclaimed after the French Revolution, Jewish students began to attend universities in ever-increasing numbers, and their love for medical studies became intense. Although medical students and professionals faced all kinds of hardship, which made it difficult and sometimes impossible for a Jewish scholar to attain a chair at a university, many distinguished scholars appeared in every branch of medical science.

It is not the purpose of this chapter to list the names of all the eminent physicians who exerted a decisive influence on medical progress. We wish merely to call to the attention of the reader the fact that some specialties, such as immunology, clinical medicine, otology, ophthalmology and psychiatry, seem to be the fields in which the talents of Jewish scholars were particularly noteworthy. In all branches of medicine, however, we find Jews who are prominent.[15a] Especially in the German and Austrian universities there was a growing number of Jewish teachers and students during the era of Enlightenment. In the first part of the nineteenth century three outstanding scientists contributed to the progress of clinical medicine; Moritz Heinrich Romberg (1795-1873), the founder of modern neuropathology who became professor in Berlin in 1838, Robert Remak (1815-1865), professor in Berlin (1859), the founder of microscopic anatomy of the nerves, and Ludwig Traube (1818-1876), who ranks among the greatest clinicians of the period.

Jacob Henle (1809-1885) was among the most famous teachers at German universities. Already in 1840 he postulated the existence of micro-organisms as the cause of contagious diseases. Hermann Lebert (1813-1878), professor in Zurich (1853) and Breslau (1859), was among the first to use the microscope for pathologic-anatomical investigations. One of the greatest clinicians and brilliant teachers of the Vienna school was Heinrich von Bamberger (1822-1888), who taught in Vienna (1872) and was the teacher of Edmund von Neusser. His textbook on diseases of the heart is considered classic. Ludwig Lichtheim (1845-1928), professor in Berlin and Koenigsberg, first described subcortical aphasia, which is named after him; Ottomar Rosenbach (1851-1907) was called to Berlin in 1893 and described the reflex neurosis named after him, as well as the sign of Rosenbach.

Oscar Minkowski (1858-1931) was the founder of modern metabolism research to which Adolf Magnus-Levy (b. 1865) brought an outstanding contribution. Georges Hayem was professor of clinical medicine in Paris (1893-1911) and first described the blood platelets (1878).

In psychiatry Joseph Breuer (1842-1925) was, with Sigmund Freud (1856-1940), the founder of the revolutionary doctrine of psychoanalysis: certainly one of the most famous scientific teachings of the nineteenth century. Cesare Lombroso (1836-1909) gave a new impulse to the study of delinquency and his doctrine has had a mighty influence on legislation in modern times. Abraham A. Brill (1874-1948) of Columbia University was the advocate of psychoanalysis in America and contributed to the development of the doctrine.

In pediatrics Edward Heinrich Henoch (1820-1910) and Heinrich Finkelstein (b. 1865) were leaders in the progress of modern pediatrics in Germany; Max Kassowitz (1842-1913) did basic work on hereditary syphilis and rickets; Bela Schick (b. 1877) is universally known for research in the fields of diphtheria and scarlet fever. The pioneer of pediatrics in America was Abraham Jacobi (1830-1919), and among prominent American pediatricians are men like Isaac Arthur Abt (b. 1867), professor at Northwestern University; Abraham Levinson, with his studies on cerebral spinal fluid; Henry Koplik (1858-1927), the founder of a

Children's Pavilion at the Mt. Sinai Hospital in New York, discoverer (1896) of the initial spots in measles (Koplik spots); and Alfred Fabian Hess (1875-1933), with his splendid studies on rickets and scurvy.

Among the founders of modern neurology were Moritz Benedikt (1835-1920) and Moritz Rosenthal (1833-1889) of Vienna. Emil Redlich (1865-1930) discovered the pupillar phenomenon that is named after him. Otto Marburg (b. 1874) of Vienna and New York, pathology of the nervous system, Arnold Pick (1851-1924), with his investigations of the anatomy of the brain, and Ludwig Edinger (1855-1918) are considered among the most eminent research workers and teachers in this field. Hermann Oppenheim (1858-1919) of Berlin was the first to give attention to post-traumatic neurosis.

In dermatology and syphilology the names of the founders of the Viennese school of dermatology, Ferdinand von Hebra (1816-1880) and Moritz Kaposi (Kohn) (1837-1902) immediately come to mind. Paul Gerson Unna (1850-1929), professor in Hamburg, won great fame through his anatomical and biochemical works in the field of skin pathology.

Among the great surgeons of the nineteenth century Anton Woelfler (1850-1917), a pupil of Billroth, was the first to perform gastroenterostomy (1881). To the Vienna school belong also Robert Gersuny (c. 1844-1924) and Julius Schnitzler (1865-1939). James Israel (1848-1926) in Berlin was a leader in urologic surgery and in this field Otto Zuckerkandl (1861-1921) was an outstanding teacher. Mario Donati (b. 1879), professor of surgery at the University of Milan, is generally recognized as the leading surgeon in Italy.

Among the most distinguished gynecologists were Ernst Wertheim (1864-1920) and Joseph Halban (1870-1939), and more recently Bernhard Zondek (b. 1891), whose name became famous through the Aschheim-Zondek reaction (1927).

Among the great ophthalmologists are the names of Hermann Cohn (1838-1906), professor in Breslau, and Harry Friedenwald (b. 1864) of Baltimore who is well known also for his splendid work in medical history. A leader of scientific otology was Adam Politzer (1835-1920), professor in Vienna, founder of a famous school to which disciples came from all over the world. The best known among the pupils of the Vienna school were Heinrich Neumann (1873-1939) and Robert Bárány (b. 1876), professor at Upsala. Among the prominent representatives of laryngology are Karl Stoerk (1832-1899) of Vienna and his pupil M. Hajek (1861-1941), a brilliant surgeon who accomplished a fundamental work. Sir Felix Semon (1849-1921) occupied an important rank among English laryngologists.

Modern physiology was enriched by the work of Rudolph Heidenhain

(1834-1897), Moritz Schiff (1823-1896) of Frankfort, professor in Florence, and Jacques Loeb of Chicago (1859-1924). Among the great research workers in general and experimental pathology were Salomon Stricker (1834-1898), professor of experimental pathology in Vienna, and Arthur Biedl (1869-1938), professor at the German university in Prague, whose book on endocrinology (1910) is of fundamental importance. The revolutionary current of thought that upset the fundamental conceptions in therapy was determined by three great scholars: Carl Weigert (1845-1904), Paul Ehrlich (1854-1915) and August von Wassermann (1866-1925). Weigert introduced new staining methods and wrote a new page in the history of the pathology of the tissues; Ehrlich discovered the doctrine of immunobiological relations and was the founder of chemotherapy with the introduction of Salvarsan (1910) in the therapy of syphilis, marking a new era in the history of the struggle against that disease. Wassermann's work on toxins and antitoxins was one of the most important contributions to the science of immunity. The reaction that is named after him made his name famous. Still another, Fernand Widal (1862-1929), is well known for the reaction of typhoid fever (1896).

In 1908, together with Metchnikoff, Ehrlich received the Nobel Prize. Robert Bárány received it in 1945, and Otto Meyerhof in 1923 for his work on the physiology of the cell. In 1930 the prize was awarded to Karl Landsteiner of the Rockefeller Institute in New York for his discovery of the blood groups, and in 1931 to Otto Warburg for his work on the respiratory ferment. Otto Loewi of Graz, and now of New York, received the prize in 1936 for his outstanding work in biochemistry.

In the field of the history of medicine two great Jewish scholars did very important work as teachers and leaders: Charles Singer (b. 1876)[16a] of London published a great number of studies on the history of medicine in antiquity and the Middle Ages, and was the leader of the modern English medical historical school, and Max Neuburger (1868–1955), professor of the history of medicine in Vienna, then in London, brought a new impulse to historical studies with his classic book on the history of medicine, with the foundation of the institute for the history of medicine in Vienna, and with a great number of historical works illustrating the relation between the great school of Vienna and the progress of medicine in other countries.

The consequences of the spread of anti-Semitism in the past decade and its terrifying development after the rise of Hitler in Germany, and of the occupation of so great a part of Europe by the victorious Nazi armies, are well known. Jewish professors and physicians who in all the occupied countries had held prominent positions were jailed or exiled; the activity of the medical schools in Germany, in Poland, in France, in Italy and in the Balkan countries was halted; the books of the Jewish scholars were burned. It was a fight which threatened to destroy freedom of science and of opinion, but for many reasons it concentrated first on the Jews, their lives and their activities as professionals and teachers. The end of the war with the victory of the United Nations has changed the situation, but the loss is irreparable. The work that was accomplished by Jews in the European countries was destroyed or wiped out. At the same time, however, what had occurred in the Middle Ages was repeated. The persecuted Jews found a haven partly in Palestine, where scientific medicine began to rise and flourish, partly in other countries, especially in the United States. Just as in the Renaissance Jewish scholars and physicians found a shelter in Italy and the possibility of learning and teaching in the Italian universities, so during World War II a great number of them came from Germany and the occupied European countries to the United States and began here the reconstruction of their life and of their work.

Once more, as in ancient times, during the struggles in the Mediterranean countries and the Arab conquests, the Jewish scholars have been the intermediaries of scientific thought between the East and the West and have upheld freedom of teaching and of learning.

To summarize, then: The evolution of medical thought among Jews followed the line of development to be observed among other peoples, from mystic and magic to empiric and sacerdotal, with this important difference, that the moral and ethical influence of monotheism always predominated in Judaism. The moral and sanitary laws assumed the character of religious prescriptions, and it was among the Jews that hygienic laws were imposed and accepted with the authority of divine commands.

Despite long centuries of persecution in various countries, in two great epochs, during Arab supremacy in the Mediterranean and the Renaissance in certain cities and under certain conditions, the study and practice of medicine flourished. This development of medical studies culminated in the nineteenth century after the Emancipation. In certain periods and regions, particularly in the Orient where Jews were segregated and hounded, the intensive cultivation of traditional mystical beliefs led to a development of medicine like that of the Essenes, the cabbalists, the Hasidim. Note, however, that even when magical practices are suggested and accepted as an escape from misery, as an expression of hope in supernatural salvation, this magic is always practiced with words and scripts, with formulae and sayings, and never degenerates into cruel or obscene acts—a rather frequent and sometimes characteristic phenomenon among other peoples. The mystic medicine of the Jews always had a metaphysical, I might say a literary, character; it involved essentially a subtle discussion and interpretation of words and letters, symbolic signs and numbers. There is not a trace of black magic and its attendant practices in the history of Jewish occult, suggestive medicine.

The history of medicine among the Jews reflects the history of the Jewish people, its sufferings, its struggle for liberty and religious freedom. In this distress the Jews return to the pure virtue of the faith that heals, and which represents the highest and last hope of sufferers. What contri‑ bution the Jews made to the science and practice of medicine was made through the centuries by thousands and thousands of believers, of scholars, of martyrs, of teachers and of humble practitioners, obedient to the moral law that constitutes the basis of the Jewish religion. They were inspired by a passionate desire for knowledge and longing for the truth. The Jews have been called the People of the Book: they have been in medicine as in many fields of intellectual activity diligent scholars, great searchers and learned teachers, able to command the respect and the esteem of their pupils and their patients even during the most difficult conditions of their own lives.

NOTES

[1a Throughout this chapter there is material on persons also mentioned below in Charles Singer, "Science and Judaism," Chap. 7.]

[1b Cf. Judah Goldin, "The Period of the Talmud (135 B.C.E.-1035 C.E.), this work, Vol. I, pp. 145 f.]

[1c The Talmud often refers to children born by Caesarian section, *i.e.*, the law that forbids circumcision of such a child on the Sabbath.]

[2a Cf. *ibid.*, pp. 120-121.]

3 Celsus, Lib. V., 19-22.

[4a Cf. Elias J. Bickerman, "The Historical Foundations of Postbiblical Ju‑ daism," this work, Vol. I, p. 95.]

[5a Cf. above, Alexander Altmann, "Judaism and World Philosophy: From Philo to Spinoza," pp. 68 f.; see also Ralph Marcus, "Hellenistic Jewish Litera‑ ture," this work, Vol. II, pp. 73 f.]

[6a Cf. Cecil Roth, "The European Age in Jewish History (to 1648)," this work, Vol. I, pp. 231-233.]

7 Steinschneider, M., *Arabische Literatur*, Introd.

[8a Cf. Altmann, *op. cit.*, pp. 83 ff.]

[9a Cf. Abraham J. Heschel, "The Mystical Element in Judaism," this work, Vol. II, Chap. 5.]

[10a Cf. Goldin, *op. cit.*, pp. 184 ff.]

[11a Cf. Roth, *op. cit.*, p. 245.]

[12a Cf. Singer, *op. cit.*, pp. 242 ff.]

[13a Cf. Anita Libman Lebeson, "The American Jewish Chronicle," this work, Vol. I, p. 487.]

[14a Cf. Cecil Roth, "The Jews of Western Europe (from 1648)," this work, Vol. I, p. 273.]

[15a Cf. Singer, *op. cit.*, pp. 264 f.]
[16a Cf. Singer, *op. cit.*]

BIBLIOGRAPHY

The most exhaustive treatise on the history of Jewish medicine is the book of Julius Preuss, *Biblisch-Talmudische Medizin* (Berlin, 1911), which is up until now the most authoritative work on this subject. The history of Jewish hygiene has been dealt with accurately by Max Grunwald (ed.), *Die Hygiene der Juden (mit Bibliographie)* (Dresden, 1911). Mystic medicine of the Cabbalists has been studied by Karl Preis, *Die Medizin in der Kabbala* (Frankfort, 1928). An important contribution to the history of Jewish physicians in ancient times and in the Middle Ages has been made by Harry Friedenwald, *The Jews and Medicine* (Baltimore, 1944, 2 vols.), in which the author throws light upon the work of great scholars, translators, and research workers. An account of the development of ancient Jewish medicine is summarized in Maurice B. Gordon, "Medicine among the Ancient Hebrews," in *Isis* (Bruges, 1941), Vol. 33, Pt. 4. For the history of circumcision see J. Almkvist "Zur Geschichte der Circumcision," in *Janus* (Leyden, 1926), Vol. 30:86, 152, and D. Schapiro, "La Péritomie; étude générale et particulière," in *Janus* (1923), Vol. 27:161, 241, 259 and 1924, 28:120, 193. On the conception of pathology see Adolphe Lods, "Les idées des Israélites sur la maladie, ses causes et ses remèdes," in *Beihefte zur Zeitschrift fuer die Alttestamentliche Wissenschaft,* 40 (Giessen, 1925), pp. 181-193. The prescriptions for contagious diseases have been studied by E. W. G. Masterman, "Hygiene and Disease in Palestine in Modern and in Biblical Times," in *Palestine Exploration Fund, Quarterly Statement* (London, 1918), pp. 13, 56, 112, 156, and 1919, p. 27; also Georg Sticker, *Vorgeschichtliche Versuche der Seuchenabwehr und Seuchenausrottung* (Zurich, 1924). Among the older historians whose works deserve to be consulted, see Thomas Bartholin, *De Morbis Biblicis miscellanea medica* (Frankfort, 1672), and Richard Mead, *Medica sacra* (Amsterdam, 1749). Other subjects of Jewish medicine have been treated by L. Kotelmann, *Die Ophtalmologie bei den alten Hebraeern* (Hamburg und Leipzig, 1910); Max Neuburger, *Die Medizin im Flavius Josephus* (Vienna, 1919); Ludwig Ventianer, *Asaph Judaeus* (Strassburg, 1916-1917, 2 vols.). On the plague see Otto Neustaetter, "Where did the Identification of the Philistine Plague (I Sam. 5 and 6) as Bubonic Plague Originate?" reprint from *Bulletin of the History of Medicine* (Vol. XI, No. 1, Baltimore, 1942, pp. 36-47). The subject of the ritual food prescription among the Hebrews has been studied by S. I. Levin, and E. A. Boyden, *The Kosher Code of the Orthodox Jew* (Minneapolis, 1940).

POSTSCRIPT

By Harry A. Savitz, M.D.

The advances and significant discoveries made in modern medicine in recent years have been greater than those of the previous two thousand years. In the field of therapeutics there is no parallel in a period of the past to compare with the achievements of modern medicine. In this advance Jews have played a most significant role in all branches of the field of medicine. The number of Jewish physicians who have been awarded the much-coveted Nobel prize is striking evidence of the role they have played. According to the medical historian Sussman Muntner, Jews have received more than 30 percent of all the Nobel prizes given in medicine and biology. In 1967 the Nobel prize went to George Wald, professor of biology at Harvard University since 1948. In 1959 Arthur Kornberg received the Nobel prize for his work in genetics. On December 15th, 1967, it was announced that a Stanford University scientific team headed by Kornberg had artificially produced in the laboratory the active, infectious inner core of a virus. This opens the way to great advances in genetics.

Other Jewish Nobel laureates in medicine in recent years include Sir Joseph Erlanger (1873-   ), professor at Washington University, in 1944, for his work in neurology; Ernst Boris Chain (1906-   ), biochemist at Oxford, in 1945, for his part in the discovery of the curative properties of penicillin; and in 1946, Herman Joseph Muller, professor at Indiana University, for his work in genetics, stressing the hereditary effects of x rays on genes. In 1950 Tadeusz Reichstein (1897-   ), who was born in Poland and later became head of the department of organic chemistry at the University of Basel, was the recipient of a Nobel prize for discoveries relating to hormones of the adrenal cortex. In 1952 Selman Abraham Waksman (1888-   ) received the award for his discovery of streptomycin, the first antibiotic effective against tuberculosis. Fritz A. Lipman received the award in 1953 for his studies on living cells.

Jewish physicians have distinguished themselves as research workers and discoverers of new weapons to fight old diseases. Jonas Edward Salk (1914-   ) developed an injectible vaccine as a prophylactic against poliomyelitis and thereby kindled the hope that other virus diseases may also be vanquished. An earlier worker, who earned a permanent niche in the annals of medical history, was Waldemar Haffkine (1860-1930). He produced prophylactic vaccines against cholera and plague and founded the research laboratory in Bombay which is now known as the Haffkine Institute. Simon Flexner (1863-1946) discovered the dysentery bacillus (Flexner bacillus) and in 1908 originated an antimeningococcus serum used in the treatment of cerebral meningitis.

In the field of hematology and related areas the contributions of Jewish physicians are many. Raphael Isaacs (1891-1965), of the Michael Reese Hospital in Chicago, discovered (with C. C. Sturgis) the therapeutic effect of dessicated stomach (venticulin) in pernicious anemia. Edwin Joseph Cohn (1892-1953), professor at Harvard Medical School, by his method of fractionation of human plasma, isolated a concentrate known as the Cohn fraction. Alexander S. Weiner (1907-   ), of Brooklyn, New York, with K. Landsteiner made the important discovery of the Rh factor, and Phillip Levine (1900-   ), a native of Russia, discovered with Landsteiner the blood factors M, N, and F. In 1941 he also discovered the cause of erythroblastosis fatalis, a disease of the newborn. Reuben L. Kahn (1887-   ), of Ann Arbor, Michigan, originated the Kahn test for syphilis in 1921. In 1966 the Albert Lasker award went to Sidney Farber of Boston (1904-   ), for progress in his twenty-year battle to control leukemia in youngsters.

Substantial contributions in the field of otology have been made by two Jewish physicians practicing in New York. Julius Lempert, in 1941, described modifications of the endaural fenestration to benefit the hard of hearing, and more recently Samuel Rosen has achieved notable success with his technique for stapes-mobilization surgery, which has restored hearing to large numbers of patients.

In addition to the number of Jewish physicians who have distinguished themselves as great clinicians, diagnosticians, or consultants, one must recognize the significant number of research workers who have further advanced the frontiers of the medical sciences. They have been teachers of medicine as well and have helped to develop new generations of physicians and research workers. Their number is legion, but a few names will serve as illustration of some who were, in a sense, the top of a pyramid with a broad base of physicians of eminence. In this group was Emmanuel Libman (1872-1946) of the Mt. Sinai Hospital in New York. His fame rests on his outstanding skills in the field of pathology, his broad clinical experience, and his detectivelike clinical observations. Another great clinician, research-worker, and teacher was Soma Weiss (1899-1942), physician-in-chief, Peter Bent Brigham Hospital, and Hersey Professor at Harvard Medical School, of whom Walter B. Cannon said, "There in term all too short, he left a standard of stimulating leadership which, through future years, will be looked upon as a model." The late Samuel Levine (1891-1966), professor at Harvard Medical School, renowned cardiologist and keen clinician, outstanding teacher, achieved fame extending beyond the boundaries of this country. He was the recipient of many awards, including the second annual Distinguished Teachers award granted by the American College of Cardiology. In 1954 a chair in medicine at Harvard was endowed in his honor. Another notable physician, teacher, and research worker is Charles K. Friedberg (1905-   ), of Mt. Sinai Hospital in New York, whose textbook on diseases of the heart is the bible of cardiology to many physicians.

It has been characteristic of history that suffering and persecution have led Jews to migrate from one country to another. It is perhaps the bit of good in the mass of adversity that brought a wealth of Jewish medical talent to the United States in the twentieth century. George Klemperer (1865-1946), a great clinician who was forced to leave his native Germany, contributed an important textbook, *An Outline of Clinical Diagnosis*, which has run through twenty editions. From Prague came Bruno Kisch (1890-1966), who became associated with Mt. Sinai and Elmhurst City hospitals and with Yeshiva University, where he was medical director as well as professor of physiology and, subsequently, professor of philosophy and the history of science.

Jews in general and Jewish physicians in particular have always had a keen interest in psychology and psychiatry. A number of great rabbis of the past were good psychologists and made use of this ability to the great advantage of their flocks. There have been remarkable contributions in this field by Jewish physicians.

Sigmund Freud (1865-1939) was the "Columbus of the unconscious mind." His discoveries have shaken the complacent conventions of Western civilization. According to Stefan Zweig, "They may seem simple and self-evident—the fact is, however, that they have altered all the standards of our mental dynamics." Freud's theories changed mental pathology from the visual to the auditory plane (listening to the patient's neuroses). Freud introduced the will-to-pleasure principle. Alfred Adler (1870-1937) stressed the role of the will-to-power in his individual psychology, and Victor Frankel introduced another new idea, the "will-to-memory," and a new method of treatment which he called logotherapy. One of the first physicians to use shock therapy was Nathan Savitsky (1902-1953), an erudite scholar who was a consultant neurologist to Hillside Hospital, neuropsychiatric consultant to Lebanon Hospital, and director of neuropsychiatry at the Morrisania City and Seton hospitals.

The Jewish physician, conscious of the many contributions to medicine by Jews and feeling kinship with them, has developed an acute historical sense. As a result of this, we have a number of Jewish physicians who have made contributions to medical history. Arturo Castiglioni (1874-1953), author of the preceding chapter, was professor of medical history at Padua and later was invited by Yale University to be professor of history of medicine. He was an eminent humanist and a great Renaissance scholar. Judah Lob Katznelson (1847-1917), while living in Russia, wrote a book in Hebrew on medicine in the Talmud. Julius Preus of Berlin wrote a book in German which is now considered a classic, *Biblisch-talmudische Medizin* (Berlin, 1911). Victor Robinson (1886-1947) devoted many years to the history of medicine—he was a gentle Boswell to the great physicians. He authored more than a dozen books and edited the thirty-volume *Historia Medicinae*. Solomon R. Kagan of Boston wrote many biographical sketches and also published a book of Jewish contributions to medicine in America. An outstanding medical historian is Sussman Muntner of Israel, who, in addition to editing many volumes of Maimonides' work, has written a great deal on medical history. He feels that the Jewish medical genius can flow if the Jewish physician of today feels a sense of kinship with the great Jewish physicians of the past.

There is a further contribution to medicine made by Jews in the role they have played in the establishment of many Jewish medical institutes, hospitals, and medical schools in this country, where large numbers of physicians are continually grinding out the notable results of their diligent research. A few of the outstanding institutions founded by American Jewry are the Mt. Sinai Hospital of the City of New York, organized in 1852 and now with a medical school of its own; the Michael Reese Hospital of Chicago, the National Jewish Hospital in Denver, and the Beth Israel Hospital in Boston, which was organized in 1927. The Albert Einstein College of Medicine of Yeshiva University in New York is beginning to take its place among the best medical schools in our country.

A striking contribution of the Jews to medicine in recent years is being made in the Middle East by the Israelis. They are building their country with a great university, two medical schools, and the famous Weizmann Institute. Israel has become one of the foremost medical centers in the Middle East. Numerous experiments and investigations are in process and great projects have been undertaken, many of which have already brought benefit to Israel and to many other new nations. In 1959 William A. Laurence, science editor of *The New York Times*, delivered a lecture in which he said, "I have been watching cancer research in this country, as well as in Europe, for many years, and I'm here to tell you that the work done at the Department of Experimental Biology at the Weizmann Institute is the equal of any in the world, and probably more imaginative than most of the cancer research going on in this country." Not only does the Law come out of Zion and the word of God from Jerusalem, but there also comes a continuous stream of medical progress for the benefit of all mankind.

Addendum

FARBER, SIDNEY, *Medical World News*, November 25, 1966.

KAGAN, SOLOMON R., "The Influence of the Jew on Modern Medicine," in *The Hebrew Impact on Western Civilization*, edited by D. D. Reese. New York, 1951.

LAURENCE, WILLIAM A., "Science in Israel," a lecture given at the Theodor Herzl Institute, March 1958. Published by the Weizmann Institute of Science, Tel-Aviv, 1958.

LIBMAN, EMMANUEL, *Journal of the Mt. Sinai Hospital*, January 1947.

OSTER, SIR WILLIAM, "Israel and Medicine," *Menorah Journal*, I, No. 3 (1915).

ROSEN, S., "An Assessment of the Technique of Stapes Surgery," *Journal of the American Medical Association*, 178:1144-6 (December 1961).

SAVITSKY, NATHAN, *The Journal of Nervous and Mental Diseases*, November 1953.

SAVITZ, HARRY A., "Waldemar Haffkine, Pioneer in Vaccine-Therapy," *Medical Leaves*, IV (1942), p. 130.

———, "Medicine as an Intellectual Outlet of the Jew," *College of Jewish Studies*. Chicago, 1965.

SUSSMAN, MUNTNER, "Jewish Contributions to Medicine," *Hebrew Medical Journal*, XII (1966).

WEISS, SOMA, *In Memoriam 1899-1942*. Cambridge, Mass., 1942.

ZWEIG, STEFAN, *Mental Healers*. New York, 1932.

CHAPTER 7

SCIENCE AND JUDAISM

By Charles Singer

1. THE GREEK FOUNDATIONS OF SCIENCE

Science has been defined as a search for judgments on which *universal* assent is attainable. Nevertheless, despite this universal element, there is a relation between science and certain particular phases of civilization. The association of science with Judaism is a special case of a general rule, for only in certain periods in the millennia of Jewish history and only in certain localities has there been scientific development. Association of science with Judaism has never been worldwide. In considering these special occurrences we must often dwell on individual achievements; yet much more significance should be attached to those aspects of Jewish thought which have favored the growth of scientific ideas. For this consummation we must await an adequate sociological history of the human vehicles of Judaism.

The first step toward the scientific attitude must be the realization that Nature works in regular and ascertainable ways. Barbarous men, children, even animals, show trust in Nature. They behave as though confident that day will succeed night, that the moons will wax and wane, that summer heat will follow winter cold, that the processes of life will run in certain cycles. But to accept Nature's ways is very different from seeking systematically to know her ways. That form of inquiry appears only late and is always exceptional. It is first clearly discernible among the Greeks of the sixth century B.C.E. Without some consideration of science among them its course among the Hebrews cannot be intelligible.

The Greeks, it has often been remarked, had no sacred writings. The forwardness of their science contrasts with the backwardness of their religion. At a very early stage they concluded that the world is subject to laws that are ever further discoverable. This was the *scientific idea*. Their science and ours grew out of it.

Before the close of the sixth century B.C.E. Greek thinkers were seeking universal applications of conceptions derived from their science. They distinguished as a universal principle *physis*, a word which survives in *physics*, *physiology*, *physical*, and *physician*. Physis meant at first growth or development, the essential element of all existence. This, it was seen, always follows definite rules, notably those of development and dissolution, coming into being and passing away, generation and corruption. By transference physis came to be regarded as this rule of change itself, and so something near to what we now call a *natural law*.

As knowledge grew, natural laws were traced more widely. Men tried to discern what lay behind them. It was inevitable that some should see in these laws a common active element. Physis was thus given an independent existence. It was, in fact, more or less personified. Had the religion of the Greeks grown with their other activities, physis would perhaps have reached the rank of a god.

The change in intellectual outlook initiated by Socrates (470-399 B.C.E.) was as fundamental as the spiritual revolution heralded by the Unknown Prophet of the last chapters of Isaiah. Socrates was skeptical as to the validity of all human knowledge, and his thought turned away from physical philosophy. His predecessors, concentrating on the physis of the sensible universe, had developed a system of physics. But his interest, like that of the Hebrew prophet, was in conduct. Seeking guidance for right conduct he concluded that man's soul partook of the Divine. He rejected the whole structure of the physicists and regarded as futile all attempts "to pursue knowledge for its own sake"; instead he stressed "practical wisdom" (*phronesis*), leading to right action. It was *phronesis* against *physis*. Phronesis also tended to personification under various names.

From the conflict between the followers of the Socratic revolution and the physical philosophers arose the main streams of Greek thought. One of them leads on to Plato and to the *doctrine of ideas*. Its ultimate development was the complete indifference to worldly happenings of certain later "Neoplatonists." The physical philosophy, on the other hand, often assumed dogmatic forms, as with the followers of Epicurus (342-270 B.C.E.), the title in Rabbinic writings for the most refractory type of paganism. It is significant that both the Neoplatonic and Epicurean schools ultimately became inimical to science, while neither was friendly to current religion. The development of both science and religion is thus historically associated with other systems of thought which chose a middle way. For science this was the path of Aristotle and his successors which drew heavily on the physical philosophers. For religion it was that of the great Judeo-Christian system of thought, which borrowed not a little from Neoplatonism.

"That nothing," says Aristotle in his *Metaphysics*, "comes to be out of that which is not, but everything out of that which is, is a doctrine common to nearly all the natural philosophers." Only if this is so is investigation of the material universe worth while. Such a view would have found itself in immediate conflict with a religion that had reached the coherent and vocal level of that of the Hebrews. As it was, the inevitable clash among the Greek-speaking peoples was deferred until their philosophy was confronted with Judeo-Christian thought.

But within the philosophic realm itself there was from the first a tension. As this increased it burst its bonds and ultimately brought ancient philosophy to an end. In a world in which, to use the phrase of Lucretius (*c.* 60 B.C.E.), "nothing is ever begotten of nothing by divine will," it must be that all things act by rules inherent in everlasting matter. What, then, is left that is our real conscious selves?

The question was variously answered. Christians and Jews, as well as those who hovered between the creeds of these, were in agreement in giving the answer—"man's immortal soul." But the Stoic, the most "religious" of the philosophic schools, could, like the Epicurean, only reply with the saintly emperor, Marcus Aurelius (C.E. 121-180): "Thou hast subsisted as part of the whole. Thou shalt vanish into that which begat thee, or rather thou shalt be taken again unto its Seminal Reason, by process of change." Such thinkers could take little interest in Nature. In our day men learn Nature's ways to control her, but that time was not yet. Epicurus would have us know only so much about her as would remove all fear of supernatural interference. Stoic and Epicurean alike show a flagging scientific curiosity. Men were weary of the world. Why seek to know more of Nature, the pitiless, the tyrannical, the irresistible machine? It is better to forget her demonic majesty. We are on the brink of the "Dark Ages." Let us return, then, to the Hebrews and their ideas on Nature.

2. THE BIBLICAL CONCEPT OF NATURE

The earlier parts of the Old Testament know nothing of natural law. Natural events, and especially the more dramatic and destructive, thunder and whirlwind, drought and flood, plague and famine, reveal God expressing Himself. "The voice of the Lord is upon the waters: the God of Glory thundereth" (Ps. 29:3). Even in a less anthropomorphic setting natural events are still acts of Him:

> Who hath measured the waters in the hollow of His hand,
> And meted out heaven with the span,
> And comprehended the dust of the earth in a measure,
> And weighed the mountains in scales . . . ?
> I form the light, and create darkness;
> I make peace and create evil;
> I am the Lord that doeth all these things.
>
> （Is. 40:12, 45:7 *c.* 540 B.C.E.)

Such a work as Job of the fourth century B.C.E. shows a definite development. The author dwells on the wonder and intricacy of the rules by which God governs His world. *His* world! If Job does not comprehend them, how can he hope to grasp their purpose?

> Dost thou guide the heavens to know the laws,
> Dost thou establish the dominion thereof in the earth? (Job 38:33.)

These laws are invoked as proof of the power, wisdom and goodness of God, for exactly the same reason as in the famous *Bridgewater Treatises* of more than two thousand years later. The recognition of the natural laws in Job is an echo of the main preoccupation of Greek thinkers when the book was being written.

In the later "Wisdom literature," the contact with Greek thought has become quite evident.[1a] The general features of physical philosophy have been grasped and the concept of the relation of God to the material world has become modified. The laws of nature are now administered by the elusive Wisdom (*Hokmah*) or the awesome Word (*Memra*).

The gracious form of the one or the stern features of the other are almost as difficult to discern as those of *Physis*, whom they both in part resemble. Wisdom has divine attributes, being omniscient and omnipresent. "She reacheth from one end of the world to the other and ordereth all things aright" (Wisdom 8:1). The Word is specially responsible for the catastrophic events. "While all things were in silence . . . Thine Almighty Word leaped down from heaven as a fierce man of war and brought Thine unfeigned command as a sharp sword and filled all things with death" (Wisdom 18:12-16).

This new turn of thought has become self-conscious and polemic. It is set against Greek physical philosophy, wherein various "first principles" had been adopted. Thales proposed "water," Heraclitus "fire," Pythagoras the "circling stars," Anaximenes "air," other philosophers a subtle world essence, or *pneuma*, "winds," while astrological science, coming in from Babylonia, claimed the actual complex mathematical order of the heavenly bodies as the motive power of all things. The Wisdom of Solomon, written by an orthodox Jew in Alexandria about 100 B.C.E., inveighs against all these:

> Surely vain were all men in their natures,
>   and without perception of God
> Who could not, from the good things that are seen,
>   know Him that is.
> Neither by giving heed to the works
>   did they recognize Him who hath wrought them,

But either fire [Heraclitus], or wind [the Pneumatists]
    or the swift air [Anaximenes],
Or circling stars [Pythagoras], or raging water [Thales],
    or the lights of heaven [the astrologers]
They deemed the gods which govern the world.

(Wisdom 13:1-2)

3. NATURE IN LATER JEWISH AND JUDEO-CHRISTIAN THOUGHT

Much of the pseudepigraphic and apocalyptic literature written by Jews of the later pre-Christian or first post-Christian centuries shows the same tendency. This may be traced in the Book of Jubilees, the Apocalypse of Baruch, the Book of Enoch, and the New Testament Book of Revelation.

That this movement, even under philosophic guidance, became indifferent to or contemptuous of scientific spirit is shown by the Alexandrian Jewish thinker Philo, contemporary of Jesus. His trend was Neoplatonic and away from the study of phenomena. He represents a separation of religious Judaism from an interest in phenomena. Judaism and physical philosophy have diverged completely.[2a]

Philo was a conscious "philosopher" in the Greek sense. He betrays this in several ways not found in earlier Jewish writings. The biblical record and Rabbinic doctrine treat God as a separate and very personal existence outside the world, which He had produced by definite acts and continues to guide. But the God of the Hellenist Philo is without emotions or attributes and consequently without name—changeless, imperceptible by man, self-sufficient, simply existent. This God of the Platonic idea could not act upon the world, or create or guide it, though He might set it going once and for all. The old Hebrew view was as incompatible with that of Philo as with that of the Stoics.

Under these circumstances Philo resorted to a new form of an old device. He introduced an existence between God and the world. Physis, Phronesis, Wisdom, the Word (*Memra*) were previous attempts. Philo's device was the Logos. They have now become a regular pantheon! Any of them must turn men's thoughts away from phenomena. Logos and the Memra have other parallels in Rabbinic literature and their further development appears clear enough in the Gospel of St. John, in Acts and in other New Testament works. Science cannot live at close quarters with any of these divine emanations. Judeo-Christian thought lost interest in Nature and her phenomena.

There was yet a further reason for the "flight from phenomena" in later Jewish as in early Christian thought. Since the Socratic revolution some Greek thinkers had regarded the material universe as essentially without worth. They opposed *Nous*, mind, Soul or Spirit to *Hyle*, Brute Matter. The idea of the worthlessness of the material world could be made to fit Hebraic doctrine and the biblical story of the Fall of Man. The view could and did thus enter Jewish and Judeo-Christian thought. Though Philo, like other early Jewish and Judeo-Christian writers, seeks to avoid the conclusion that the world is evil, his efforts, like theirs, are not very successful. His claim, like theirs, is verbal, not real. The "sins of the flesh" became a theological commonplace which passed over naturally, along with the *Logos*, into Christian thought. It is a main theme of apocalyptic literature, Jewish, Christian and intermediate.

Paul's teaching was greatly influenced by this idea, which he extended to include a physical basis of sin. "We know that the Law is spiritual; but I am carnal, sold into the power of sin" (Rom. 7:14). Christianity thus followed Judaism in turning away from phenomena, if for an allegedly different reason. Paul does not conceal his contempt for Greek physical philosophy. It is not so much false as trivial and irrelevant and, before the fearful issue of salvation, therefore impious.

Another common Judeo-Christian thought emphasized this contempt. The end of the world was at hand. Now in much Greek physical philosophy this world is one of a long series. Its end is but the beginning of another like to it, re-formed from its "elements." But in the Judeo-Christian conception the end of the world must involve the destruction of the elements themselves. "The day of the Lord will come as a thief. At that time the heavens will pass away with great violence and the *elements* will be dissolved with heat, and the earth and the works that are in it will be burned up" (II Pet. 3:10) [author's italics]. With that in mind who could regard phenomena? Belief in an imminent Messiah was as deadly for science as was the apocalyptic vision. The combination of the two was instantly fatal. "The day of the Lord" rang the death knell of Greek science. We see it most dramatically in that Jewish work in the New Testament known as Revelation. Judaism, having approached the scientific view of the world, led or escorted Christianity in a retreat therefrom. Opportunity for reunion was not to come again to Judaism for a thousand years and to Christianity for longer.

4. NATURE IN RABBINIC THOUGHT

Thus Jewish thought for the first nine centuries of the Christian era is almost entirely devoid of the scientific element.[2b] A certain amount of calendarial debate and discussion on well-worn lines of the physical bases of purity rules covers most of the area. Many have vainly searched the Talmud for evidence of scientific interest or scientific method. The excursions have been unfruitful. Those who have written on science and medicine in Rabbinic literature have merely shown that such studies have left some faint trace on Jewish life in talmudic times. What they have *not* shown is that science took any part, either integral or incidental, in Rabbinic *thought*. It could not have been otherwise. The basic conception of Torah is that every phase of knowledge must be brought into relation with or drawn from an existing and accepted system. Science can exist and even flourish *by the side of* any thought-world, religious, mystic, even magic, but it cannot exist *within* any world but its own. Any attempt to force it to do so is rapidly fatal to it. While science could and later did develop in the same civilization as Torah, it could not and did not take root in a mind or a culture already fully occupied by that concept. A quotation on natural law from the Talmud itself illustrates this incompatibility or rather impossibility:

"*Give ear, ye heavens* (Deut. 32:1). God said to Moses, 'Say unto Israel; Consider the heavens which I made to serve you, Have they ever failed in their duty? [*lit.*, changed their nature.] Does not the sun rise in the east and give light to the inhabitants of the earth? It rises and sets with regularity (Eccl. 1:5), nay, more, it rejoices in doing its Creator's will (Ps. 19:5).' *And let the earth hear My mouth's words (Ibid.).* 'Consider the earth which I created for your service. Has it ever changed its nature? Have you ever sown wheat, and has it yielded barley? Or does the cow not thresh and plough? or the ass not bear his load and walk? Does not the sea observe the limits which I have assigned to it? (Jer. 5:22). If *these* have not changed their nature, these which, unlike you, were created neither for profit nor for loss; if, unlike you, when they do well, they receive no reward, if when they sin, they are not punished: they have no care for their sons and daughters, yet these have not changed their nature: but you if you do well, you receive reward, if you do evil, you receive punishment, and you have care for your sons and daughters. How much more ought you in no wise to change your characters? [*i.e.*, from good to bad, in view of Deut. 32:5, 'You have corrupted yourselves.']' "[3]

Nature, as thus represented, elicits no curiosity and commands no more affection than a machine. There is no hint of the infinite variety and beautiful complexity of the physical world, still less of its exploration as a continual delightful adventure. No scientific interest could be evinced by those whose lives were passed within the talmudic universe of discourse. Scores of Greek names occur in the Talmud, but not one is of a man of science. Even Aristotle is unmentioned. Saadia Gaon (882-942), founder of Rabbinic philosophy,[4a] who had read some Aristotelian works in Arabic, avoids naming him. The discussion of secular science was for many centuries resisted by Rabbinic authority.

Philosophy and science ultimately obtained entry into Israel via Islam.

Christendom was some two hundred and fifty years behind Israel and received the gift largely through Israel. Science, having reached Israel, was certainly seized upon and developed with astonishing vigor. Medicine was followed with particular zeal and success. On this point certain observations should be made on which we shall need to enlarge later.[5a] First, in the Middle Ages science among Jews was almost confined to the Mediterranean area. Second, in Spain, where science first and mostly flourished among Jews, science obtained a foothold before talmudic studies came fully to occupy the Jewish intellect. Third, Jewish devotion to medicine can be explained partly as surrogate for Jewish interest in conduct, partly as a way of livelihood for those interested in science, partly as a result of social pressure which excluded Jews from other professions. There is, in fact, hardly a Jewish scientific personality before the nineteenth century that did not practice medicine.

The question remains why within Judaism scientific interest declared itself only on certain occasions. These were (a) within Islam and neighboring countries from the tenth to the thirteenth century with a trailing off into a mainly translatory period from the thirteenth to the fifteenth; (b) as part of the Marrano incident in the sixteenth century and (c) in northwestern Europe for about a hundred years from shortly before the mid-nineteenth century. The answer must cover not only these phenomena but also certain others, notably the substantial absence of the scientific element within Judaism at other times and places, the late entry of science into the Jewish orbit, the intensity of Jewish application to certain sciences, and the character of the non-Jewish cultures associated with the three main scientific outbursts among the Jewish people. Discussion of these matters is best deferred till the incidents themselves have been reviewed.

5. Hebrew-Arabic Science

Until the ninth century scientific interest is hardly encountered in Jewish writings. Only the Egyptian astronomer Masha alla ("What God wills," c. 770-820), known to Latins as Messahalla, has left any impression on later ages. He was the first Jewish man of science (if he was a Jew) to write in Arabic. There is little evidence that before him Jews were especially prominent even in medicine. The great scientific movement within Judaism arose as part of the renaissance of learning in the Arabic-speaking world.

The Arabic language was cultivated by Jews as a consequence of the Saracen conquests. From the mid-ninth century it was familiar to all who dwelt in Moslem lands. Arabic writing rapidly replaced Aramaic, which from about 300 c.e. till that time had been used for both secular and sacred purposes. For centuries scientific works were written by Jews in

Arabic. Yet while Jews spoke Arabic throughout the Islamic world they did not everywhere develop science. The overwhelming Jewish interest was talmudic throughout the Asiatic Arabic-speaking world. Science took no root there. But the Talmud did not effectively reach the West till the tenth century and by then science was established among the Jews of Tunis and Egypt and was appearing in Spain.

In Spain, Arabic continued in general use among Jews, even in the Christian zone, till the end of the twelfth century. Spanish Jews preserved some living acquaintance with the language till the fourteenth century. Even then, when Arabic had ceased to be spoken by Spanish Jews, it was still used for learned purposes by Western Jewish scholars. But from the beginning of the thirteenth century, the output of original literature in Arabic by Jews ceased to have value. Original scientific works in Hebrew, however, continued to appear, while Jews were actively translating into Latin from both Arabic and Hebrew until the sixteenth century.

We must not expect in the Hebrew-Arabic scientific literature that vast variety and range associated in the twentieth century with the word "science." The experimental and the biological sciences were absent from the whole Western medieval scheme, both Latin and Arabic. In effect we meet but three kinds of works that can be called scientific: (a) cosmological, passing into philosophy, (b) mathematical often associated with astronomy and astrology, and (c) medical with rare excursions into biology.

Science of its very nature tends to become superannuated. The cosmology of the Middle Ages is now an interesting fossil that has left some quaint remains in our language. But our own mathematical and medical systems are natural outgrowths of the mathematical and medical systems of the Latin Middle Ages, which were in their turn not only influenced by the Hebrew-Arabic material but were actually founded and based upon it and extended very little beyond it. The transmission of this material and its development were largely the work of Jews. Indeed, it is fair to present medieval European mathematics and medicine as special developments of the Hebrew-Arabic system. The cosmological systems of the Latin Middle Ages also bear constantly the impress of Jewish thoughts.

6. The Kairouan School, Ninth and Tenth Centuries

Of the departments in which Jews have attained distinction, medicine comes first. The ancient Jewish contribution to hygiene, both social and individual, has often and rightly been stressed. But, although highly important, it was not made by the scientific method or presented in the scientific spirit. Therefore, it does not concern us here. But during certain periods from the ninth century Jews have contributed to scientific medicine to a degree out of all proportion to their numbers.

This phenomenon is first observable in Tunis under a local dynasty that ruled from Kairouan for more than a century from 800. One of these sultans invited to his capital the Egyptian Jewish (?) physician Isaac ibn Amram (d. 908). His writings show a definite scientific interest. He had Jewish pupils and a most distinguished Jewish successor, Isaac ben Solomon Israeli (*c. 855-c. 955*), Isaac Judeus of the Latins. He is the first Jewish scientific figure whose life course is known.

Isaac Judeus, like Isaac ben Amram, who was perhaps his teacher, was born in Egypt and like him may have received direct some remnant of the Greek scientific tradition of Alexandria. He practiced as an oculist in Egypt where he served the sovereign. Later at Kairouan he was physician to several of its rulers. A Moslem historian describes him as a man of the loftiest character and worthy of the highest respect, for, though much occupied about the court, he was quite indifferent to wealth and personal advancement. He lived childless and unmarried—a most unusual thing among medieval Moslems or Jews—and died at over a hundred.

This able and saintly man wrote many philosophical treatises. That *On Definitions* introduced some of the favorite terms of the Latin Scholastics which they adopted from it. Isaac's larger philosophic work expounds Aristotelian physics. Beside these he wrote *On Diet, On Urine, On the Pulse, On Simples,* and above all his great book *On Fevers.* This last, perhaps the best clinical treatise of the Middle Ages in any language, was widely read until the seventeenth century.

Isaac's medical works early influenced the Latin West. His pupil's pupil was Constantine the African, who began life in a Jewish environment at Kairouan. When that city was sacked by the Bedouins in 1057 he made his way to Sicily. There he became the Oriental secretary of the Norman invader, Robert Guiscard, who afterward conquered Salerno, in the shin of Italy. At Salerno, alone in Christian Europe, there was the remnant of a medical school in the reawakening of which Jews had some part. Constantine spent the last ten years of his life as a monk at Monte Cassino, turning into Latin the writings of Isaac and of one of Isaac's pupils. They were the first Arabic medical works to be translated into Latin and introduce the long supremacy of Hebrew-Arabic medicine in Latin Europe.

Isaac's *On Fevers* was, for centuries, the constant companion of every European physician and was, in fact, one of the most genuinely useful in his library. Isaac's work influenced the Persian Avicenna (987-1037), whose vast *Canon of Medicine* was and is extremely popular among the Arabic-speaking peoples. Through it certain of Isaac's views can be traced throughout the world, for the *Canon* was early translated into every literary language, and several times into Hebrew.

The centuries from the tenth to the twelfth are the flowering time of the scientific movement within western Islam. In this Jews had a large share. Science had come to Spain in the ninth century, when the life of Spanish Jews was still isolated from that of their fellow countrymen. The entry of Jews into science opens, as might be expected, with medicine.

7. THE IBERIAN SCHOOL, TENTH TO TWELFTH CENTURIES

Of medical writings of classical antiquity the most popular, during the first Christian millennium, was that *On materia medica* of the Asiatic-Greek Dioscorides (first century c.e.). In 948 the Byzantine emperor sent to the Spanish caliph a finely illustrated manuscript of this work. Since no one in Spain knew Greek the caliph asked the emperor for an interpreter. In 951 he sent him a learned monk Nicholas who gave open instruction in Greek at Cordova to many physicians and scholars. Among them was the Andalusian Jew, Hasdai ibn Shaprut (915-970).[6a] He joined Nicholas in translating the Dioscorides manuscript into Arabic. These two were thus the first Westerners to introduce Greek writings directly to the Arabic-speaking world. Their version of Dioscorides still circulates in the Orient.

Ibn Shaprut was a man of great and varied activity. The shift of the Jewish intellectual center from Babylonia to Spain came in his time and was largely his work. He is the first of the brilliant Jewish scientific school that lasted till the thirteenth century. He was also instrumental in establishing talmudic study in Spain (*c.* 945).

A member of the scientific school initiated by Hasdai was another Andalusian—Jonah ibn Biklarish ("man of Biclar" or Valleclara) of Almeria. About 1080 he produced a dictionary of drugs in Syriac, Persian, Greek, Latin and "vulgar barbarian" (Spanish). It is the earliest of its kind. Jonah was one of the first Jewish scholars to learn Latin, which, it must be remembered, took with Christians the place of Hebrew with Jews. His knowledge of Greek probably reached him in a direct tradition from his fellow countryman and coreligionist ibn Shaprut.

A very different figure was Jonah's contemporary, Moses Sephardi. He was born in 1062 at Huesca in Aragon, then in Moslem hands. In 1096 Pedro I recovered it for the Christians and it became the Aragonese capital. Pedro was succeeded in 1104 by his brother Alfonso to whom Moses became physician. In 1106 Moses was baptized as Petrus Alfonsi (Alfonso's Peter), Alfonso being godfather. He wrote two astronomical works and another which makes a plea for astronomical observation. Alfonsi visited England, became physician to Henry I, and was intimate with Walcher, prior of Malvern, an ardent astronomer. In 1120 Walcher issued a work which introduces the use of degrees, minutes and seconds and contains certain exact observations. All are in the Arabic manner and had evidently been learned from Alfonsi. This represents the first impact of Arabian learning in England.

A figure as important for Jewish culture as Hasdai ibn Shaprut was the

Catalan Abraham bar Hiyya (d. *c.* 1150), known to the Latins as Savasorda, that is, *Sahib al schurta,* "chief of the police," which was his office. Until his time the Sephardic and the Ashkenazic Jews had been almost isolated from each other. They were in geographical but not social contact on the frontier between Catalonia and Provence. In 1112 these territories came under one ruler. Thus Savasorda could contact the Provençal Jews, among whom Arabic was unknown. To them he opened secular studies by translating Arabic scientific works into Hebrew. He was the first Arabic speaker to prepare works specifically for a non-Arabic speaking audience. Writing always in Hebrew, he and his successors gave to that language a special interpretive value which it retained for centuries. His chief scientific work was an encyclopedia of mathematics, astronomy, optics and music. In it he wrote: "I have not entered on this work of my own wish or for my own honor, but because in all the land of France there is no book on these sciences in the holy tongue. Therefore I have summarized what follows from the Arabic." A treatise by him on practical geometry (1116) was translated into Latin by his friend Plato of Tivoli (1145) as the *Liber embadorum*. It is the first introduction of Arabic trigonometry and mensuration to the Latin West and contains the oldest table of chords in a Latin work. It made a special impression on Leonardo of Pisa, the ablest mathematician of the Middle Ages, who embodied large sections of it in his *Practical Geometry* (1220).

Savasorda also left a treatise *On the Form of the Earth* which was turned into Latin and French. He wrote in 1123 the first Hebrew treatise devoted to the calendar and also Hebrew astronomical tables based on Ptolemy. His *Scroll of the Revealer* is an extensive treatise on the courses of the stars, treating Arabic astronomy with understanding and acuteness. In it he concludes that the Messiah will come in 1358! Savasorda, with his Christian friend, Plato of Tivoli, translated at Barcelona a whole series of Hebrew and Arabic works into Latin (1133-1145). The most important of them was Ptolemy's *Quadripartitum*.

The famous Abraham ibn Ezra (1092-1167), poet and scholar, was born in Toledo. In 1140 his life was devastated by the conversion of his son to Islam. Thenceforth he led a wandering life, first in Italy, where he composed many works, and then in Provence, where he was enthusiastically received. In 1158 he went to London, where he wrote an account of the intellectual state of the Jews in England. After much journeying he died at Calahorra in northern Spain. He has permanent importance as a forerunner of biblical criticism, and Spinoza derived much from him. Ibn Ezra seconded Savasorda in translating Arabic writings into Hebrew, thus opening secular literature to his coreligionists and especially to the Ashkenazim outside Spain. His wanderings helped to distribute manuscripts of his works.

Among Abraham ibn Ezra's scientific achievements is the introduction into Hebrew science of a decimal system of numeration with place value for the integers. This he did through his commentary on al-Kwarizmi's tables (Narbonne, 1160). He made certain other real additions to mathematics. Several of his astrological treatises became extremely popular. Among the works that he translated into Hebrew from Arabic were two treatises on astrology by Messahalla (Lucca, 1148). Incidentally, ibn Ezra provides some important information as to the passage of the decimal place-value system from Indian to Arabic mathematics.

The advent of Latin translations of Arabic scientific works aroused the emulation of Latin Christians. A number sought a knowledge of Arabic. All worked with Jewish aid. The pioneer was Adelard of Bath (c. 1090-1150) who visited both Spain and the Sicilies. His great achievement is the Latin translation of the astronomical tables of al-Kwarizmi. They included a table of sines and, with Savasorda's Liber embadorum of about the same date, introduced Arabic trigonometry to the Latin world. Adelard also made a version of Euclid. His popular Natural Questions is a compendium drawn from Arabic sources and largely from a debased "Aristotelian" work. The French-Jewish scribe Berachiah Ha-Nakdan (Benedictus Punctator), who was in Oxford in 1194, translated it from Latin into Hebrew. It was the first work so treated. This Hebrew version has since been translated into English. Parts of it have thus passed from Greek into Syriac, from Syriac into Arabic, from Arabic into Latin, from Latin into Hebrew and from Hebrew into English!

Throughout the medieval period the Latin West was eagerly seeking the treasures of Arabic learning. Jews, as translators and interpreters, played an overwhelming part in this effort. The best known of the native Spanish translators was Johannes Hispalensis, whose Arabic name, ibn Daud (ben David), was corrupted by the Schoolman into Avendeath (c. 1090-1165). He was born at Toledo, soon after that city fell into Christian hands (1085). He translated a whole host of astronomical and astrological works, among them those of Albumasar (786-886) of Bagdad, of Omar ibn al-Farrushan (d. c. 932) the Persian, of Thabit ben Kurra (826-901) the "Sabian" of Harran, of Messahalla (d. 815) the Jew of Egypt, of Messahalla's pupil Albohali (d. 835), of Alfraganus (d. c. 880) of Fargan in Transoxania, and the Centiloquiam of Ptolemy (c. 180). Avendeath provided an appreciable proportion of the mathematical, astrological and astronomical works in the medieval Latin library.

Notable among Avendeath's versions was the pseudo-scientific, pseudo-Aristotelian Secretum secretorum. This extremely popular work he prepared for a Spanish queen. There are copies and variants in hundreds of manuscripts in many languages, Hebrew included. It influenced serious scholars, and Roger Bacon wrote a commentary on it.

Most important of Avendeath's translations is the Liber Algorismi de practica arismetrica. This is an elaboration by Avendeath of an elaboration by a Moslem writer of the work of the Persian Muhammad ibn Musa al-Kwarizmi (fl. *c.* 830). In it our so-called *Arabic* numerical notation, in which the digits depend on their position for their value, is fully used in a Latin work for the first time. It is professedly based on Hindu knowledge. The "Arabic" numerals displace the clumsy Latin forms. The method was but slowly accepted. The whole of modern mathematics may be said to date from this translation but incorporation into our system was hardly complete until the sixteenth century. The word *algorism*, used in the Middle Ages for what we now call arithmetic, conceals the name al-Kwarizmi, *i.e.*, "the man of Khiva."

The most active translator from the Arabic was Gerard of Cremona (1114-1187). As a young man he came to Toledo to acquire Arabic that he might read Ptolemy's *Almagest*. He remained for life and superintended the translation of no less than seventy-one works, many, such as the *Canon of Medicine of Avicenna*, of great length. He worked with a whole school of Arabic-speaking Jews and Christians. They translated many scientific works by Jews such as Messahalla and Isaac Judeus. Perhaps the oddest work from his school is that of "Alchandrius." It is an astrological treatise which contains a number of Hebrew words. It seems based on a very early pre-Arabic original showing remnants of the ancient classical astrology. It may be the earliest scientific work of Jewish origin.

8. MAIMONIDES. SECOND HALF OF THE TWELFTH CENTURY

Contemporary with the twelfth-century Jewish movement in science in Spain and the West there was in Africa a comparable activity, for which Jews were almost entirely responsible. Several were physicians to the caliphs and published genuine clinical observations—a very unusual thing at that time. The letter of one to Saladin (d. 1193) has survived. Incomparably the most important of this school was the great thinker Maimonides, with whom Jewish philosophy culminates.

Moses ben Maimon, called Maimonides (1135-1204), was born at Cordova, and educated by a learned father and Arabic masters. When he was thirteen Cordova fell to the fanatical Almohades. Maimonides fled and, after wandering in Spain, Morocco and Palestine, settled in Cairo (1155) where he passed the rest of his life. He was a very successful physician and was attached to the court. His works, both medical and philosophical, became widely known, not only among Arabic-speaking peoples, but also among the Latins and Jews. He used Arabic for nearly all his writings.

Maimonides held that there can be no conflict between truths discerned by reason and those inculcated by revealed religion. The former are to be sought primarily in the Aristotelian writings, the latter in the Torah. He was convinced that both written and oral Torah contain philosophical material which harmonizes with Aristotle. We can here discuss neither his philosophical nor his religious views,[7a] but we are concerned with his presentation of the structure of the world. This had a share in determining both Latin and Jewish beliefs. With certain closely similar schemes it provided the framework within which alone medieval science could develop. It is set forth in his *Guide for the Perplexed*.[8a]

The universe in the Maimonidean-Aristotelian system is spherical, with earth fixed in the center, and the heavens revolving round it. The matter of our world is composed of the four elements, *earth, air, fire* and *water*. These, however, are not seen in their pure form on our imperfect globe. Each has in it an admixture of the other three. The three lighter elements tend to range themselves in concentric hollow spheres around the spherical earth. *Earth* being heaviest is naturally lowest, that is, at the center. Remove it from the center and its natural motion is in a straight line toward its own place, that is, downward toward the center; hence gravity. *Water* is next heaviest; its natural place is just above earth; like earth it tends toward the center. Above the water, which laves earth's surface, is the hollow sphere of *air*, concentric with that of earth and water. The natural motion of air is opposite to that of earth and water, straight outward, that is, upward, toward the circumference of the world. It cannot, however, go beyond the sphere of the lightest and purest element *fire*. The natural place of this is outside the other elements but like air it tends outward, that is, upward. Fire, too, forms a hollow sphere, the *Empyrean*.

All things formed by combination of the elements in this our lower world are subject to generation and decay. While nothing here is permanent, there is yet no annihilation, for all material change is but recombination of the four elements. Causes of all this generation and decay are the motions of the heavenly bodies that occupy spheres outside the sphere of the outermost element. Lowest of these heavenly bodies is the moon, next the other planets, next the fixed stars. The heavenly bodies are composed of a fifth substance, something purer than the elements, namely, the *quintessence* or *ether*. Heavenly bodies differ from things composed of the four elements in that they are not subject to generation, save at the Creation, or to decay, save at the final consummation and then at God's will. Their only change is *movement*, but this movement differs from that of things in our lower world and notably of the elements there. These have their natural movement of falling or rising in straight lines, but the heavenly bodies circle eternally round the center, for the circle is the perfect figure. They are set in a series of concentric transparent spheres which revolve and carry them in their movement:

> For ever singing as they shine
> The Hand that made us is Divine.

The world thus pictured is finite in time as well as in space. God Himself set the outermost sphere in motion, or rather is the eternal cause of its motion. Similarly each of the many circular motions, of which the composite movements of the heavenly bodies are the resultant, is produced by its own proper mover, which is pure form or spirit. Hence the absurdity of astrology, for it is these spirits, acting under God, that cause the movements of the stars and not *vice versa*.

One aspect of the physics of Maimonides affected scientific development. Maimonides perceived that the difference between belief in an eternal and belief in a created world may ultimately be resolved into a difference between belief in impersonal mechanical law, as an explanation of the universe, and belief in an intelligent being acting with a particular design. Maimonides admits that Aristotle's resolution of all motions below the lunar sphere in terms of an impersonal mechanical law is successful. It is in the outer spheres that Aristotle fails, though we need not follow Maimonides into details of his failure. Yet, since outer and inner spheres are intimately connected, failure in explaining the one involves failure in the other. The mechanistic view of the world, which excludes free will, miracle and efficacy of prayer, must, he claims, therefore be rejected.

For the mechanistic hypothesis Maimonides substitutes the intelligent purpose and design so dear to the heart of Galen (130-200 c.e.), physician to the philosopher-emperor Marcus Aurelius (121-180 c.e.). With the works of Galen, Maimonides, as a physician, was very familiar. For Maimonides, as for Galen, *design*—God's plan—is expressed in *natural law* and continues to be directed by intelligence. That there were rules of wide application in nature Maimonides fully realized; that these rules depended for their working on certain underlying series of events he also accepted. But ultimately these rules depended, he held, on the action of an intelligence working to intelligible ends. By avoiding the enormous claims of Galen that these ends were wholly known or immediately discoverable by man, he leaves far more room for scientific discovery than does Galen and far less room for the comparable claims of astrology.

The actual scientific efforts of Maimonides do not compare in profundity with his philosophic studies. They can, perhaps, hardly be expected to exhibit great originality—a quality to which his age attached a negative value—but they do nevertheless reveal him clearly as a highly competent, sensible, trusted and effective physician. He knew no Greek and relied entirely on Arabic versions of Galen and Aristotle and on Arabic writers who in their turn relied on Galen and Aristotle. His medical writings have exercised much influence on both Eastern and Western medicine. It is reasonable to claim for them that they kept Hebrew-Arabic medicine sane and levelheaded. Most of his medical works have been translated into both Hebrew and Latin.

Maimonides must have been a very busy man. He thus describes his day's work in a pleasant letter written in 1199, a vivid picture of the life of the best type of medieval physician:

I dwell at Fostat but the sultan at Cairo; these places are two Sabbath days' journey [about one mile and a half] from each other. My duties to the sultan are very heavy. I have to visit him daily early in the morning; and when he or any of his children, or inmates of his harem, are indisposed I dare not leave Cairo, but must spend most of the day in the palace. If any of the royal officers fall sick, I must attend them. Hence I usually go to Cairo very early in the day, and can hardly return to Fostat until afternoon. Then I am tired and hungry. I find the antechambers filled with people, Jews and Gentiles, nobles and common people, judges and bailiffs, a mixed multitude, awaiting my return.

I dismount from my animal, wash, and beg my patients to bear with me while I eat, the only meal I take in the day. Then I attend to my patients, write prescriptions and directions for them. Patients come in and out till nightfall, and sometimes, I assure you, until two hours and more in the night. Sometimes I converse with and prescribe for them while lying down from sheer fatigue, and when night falls I am so exhausted that I can scarcely speak.

Thus none converse with me [on religious matters] except on the Sabbath. Then the whole congregation, or at least most of them, come to me after the morning service, when I advise them as to the work of the week. We study together a little until noon, when they leave. Some return and read with me after the afternoon service until evening prayers. Thus I spend the days. I have related to you only a part of what you would see if you were to visit me.

Late in the twelfth century Maimonides received an inquiry from the Rabbis of Provence asking his views on astrology. He replied in Hebrew that he regarded it as superstition. This attitude was rare in the Middle Ages, for astrology then stood for rationalism. Astrology was therefore often condemned as impious but seldom for the reasons that Maimonides gave. Though he wrote no work on astronomy, his views on the subject can be traced in his other works. They were conservative, rejecting the doctrine of epicycles as contrary to the view of Aristotle.

Almost exactly contemporary with Maimonides was ibn Ruschd (1126-1198) of Cordova, Averroës of the Latins. He held the office of a judge but studied and practiced medicine. He was a Moslem and his writings earned him the bitter enmity of orthodox Moslems, just as those of Maimonides were long abhorrent to orthodox Jews. Averroës had immense influence on Jewish thought.[9a] The opponents of Averroës regarded him as a Judaizer. The general contents of his writings were similar to those of Maimonides though his opinions were very different. The works of Averroës, like those of Maimonides, were almost immediately translated into Hebrew. The widely read Latin versions of Averroës were rendered not from Arabic but from Hebrew. Averroan works and doctrine were forbidden in the universities and regarded by the church as presenting the utmost spiritual danger.

9. PROVENÇAL AND SICILIAN TRANSLATORS, THIRTEENTH CENTURY

The end of the twelfth century and the death of Maimonides (1204) saw the close of the brilliant period of Spanish and Egyptian Jewish science. There were several important figures in the centuries to come though none to measure by Hasdai ibn Shaprut, Abraham bar Hiyya and Maimonides. Nevertheless, the demand for translations from Arabic and Hebrew increased with the development of the universities. Jews played the main part in providing these. Why, then, did their original output fall in quality and quantity?

The full answer is complex but the major factors are plain enough. The thirteenth century was the great period of foundation of universities. Those at Palencia, Valladolid, Salamanca, Lerida and Coimbra in the Iberian Peninsula and, outside it, Paris, Montpellier, Salerno, Bologna, Padua, Naples, Rome, Oxford and Cambridge all began effectively in the thirteenth century. From all these Jews were excluded. As the learned output of the universities rose, that of the Jews fell in relative importance. Jews were thrown back on their own resources. Moreover, the Inquisition was established in Spain and the position of Spanish Jews was steadily deteriorating.[10a] The Jews of Provence and Italy were losing such hold as they had on the Arabic language. Outside the Mediterranean area secular science had hardly reached any Jewish group. Among the Ashkenazim, outside France and Italy, talmudic studies remained all-absorbing. The Golden Age of Jewish science was over.

Prominent among the translators of the Silver Age were members of the Provençal family Bene Tibbon of Spanish origin. Samuel ben Judah ibn Tibbon (c. 1160-1232) of Lunel and Marseilles[11a] introduced Aristotle to Hebrew readers by his Hebrew version of the *Meteorology* from the Arabic. He made it at sea during a voyage from Alexandria (1212). He also rendered a commentary on Galen, but he is chiefly remembered for his diffusion of the Maimonidean philosophy in the West and his development of the Hebrew philosophical language.

Jacob Anatoli (c. 1194-1256) of Marseilles was a disciple and son-in-law of this ibn Tibbon. The Emperor Frederick II invited him to Naples (1231), where he possibly met Thomas Aquinas and certainly Michael Scot. Anatoli turned the work of Averroës into Hebrew and thus took the first step toward Averroistic heresy among both Jews and Latins. Equally influential was the help that he gave to Michael Scot (d. c. 1235) to render into Latin a conflation of the great biological works of Aristotle, the first work of ancient biological science that became available to the West.

In the same region and period there worked the Sicilian Moses Farrachi (Ferrachius). He was specially employed as one of a band of Jewish translators by Charles of Anjou (1220-1285). His great achievement is his Latin version (*c.* 1275) of the enormous *Liber continens*, a medical work by Rhazes (d. 932). Another Jewish Sicilian translator, Moses of Palermo, was engaged by Charles to learn Latin. He afterward translated a veterinary work from Arabic.

The most active of all the translators from Arabic into Hebrew was Moses ben Samuel ibn Tibbon of Marseilles. In addition to Aristotle's philosophical works, he translated many mathematical and medical treatises including Geminus's *Introduction to Hipparchan Astronomy* (Naples, 1246), Euclid's *Elements* (Montpellier, 1270) and Theodosius of Bithynia's *Spherica* (Montpellier, 1271), medical works by a pupil of Isaac Judeus 1259), Rhazes's *Antidotary* (1257), Avicenna's *Canticum* (1260), and many others.

10. CASTILIAN AND ARAGONESE ASTRONOMERS AND CARTOGRAPHERS, THIRTEENTH CENTURY

In Spain there were some noteworthy translations from Arabic in the thirteenth century. Alfonso X of Castile (1252-1284), called "the Wise," came to the throne when the transference of Eastern thought was very active. He directed the translation of some of this material into the vernacular and so influenced the development of the Spanish language. He was himself an author, interested in philosophy and astronomy, and employed a number of Jewish translators. The most remarkable scientific work of his reign was the so-called *Alphonsine tables*. These lists of planetary movements are the basic documents of modern astronomy and continued in repute for centuries. They were prepared under the wise king's direct command between 1262 and 1272 by two learned Jews of Toledo, Judah ben Moses Cohen, a physician, and Isaac ben Sid, a synagogue precentor. They are based on the tables of a Cordovan astronomer of the eleventh century and the last edition for practical use appeared at Madrid in 1641! They were consulted by Kepler and Galileo. The tables on which they were based were themselves rendered into Spanish by another Jewish translator for Alfonso X.

The preface of the Alphonsine tables tells that, since computed positions often differ from those observed, the king had collected instruments and directed observations to be taken at Toledo. The writers, Moses Cohen and Isaac Hazan, therefore observed the sun for him through an entire year, particularly at the equinoxes and solstices, and at the middle of the signs of Taurus and Scorpio, Leo and Aquarius. They also observed conjunctions of planets both with each other and with fixed stars, and took observations of lunar and solar eclipses. Both authors produced many other important astronomical, mathematical and mechanical works in Spanish, and constructed many astronomical instruments.

Alfonso's patronage of learning was copied by his neighbors, the monarchs of Aragon. The Jew Astruc Bonsenior of Barcelona was secretary and interpreter to King Jaime I of Aragon (1208-1276) in his campaigns. His son Judah Bonsenior became interpreter to Alfonso III (reigned 1265-1291) and Jaime II (reigned 1291-1327). In 1287 Alfonso III took him on his expedition to Minorca. In 1294 Jaime II arranged that he review the translation into Spanish of all Arabic business documents.

A scientific department in Aragon that was largely officered by Jews was that of mapmaking. For Aragonese merchants sailing books of the Mediterranean known as *portolani* were prepared. These contained descriptions of coasts, harbors, anchorages and so forth. Toward the end of the thirteenth century they began to be provided with charts. The *portolano maps* give the outline of the Mediterranean and have the directions of and distances between different ports. The best were made in the island of Majorca, where an important school of Jewish mapmakers sprang up. They relied largely on the Arabic geographers.

At Las Palmas in Majorca the Jew Cresques drew up in 1375 the first map that set forth the discoveries of Marco Polo. This was sent as a gift from the king of Aragon to Charles VI of France. Cresques long continued his cartographical activities. In 1419 he was summoned to Portugal by Prince Henry the Navigator (1394-1460), to assist in establishing an astronomical observatory.

11. Rise of North Italian School, Thirteenth Century

By the mid-thirteenth century the two original gates of entry of Arabic science into Europe—the Spanish Peninsula and the Sicilies—were ceasing to function. In the former, organized into Christian kingdoms, the vernaculars Catalan, Castilian and Portuguese began to be used even for learned purposes. The cultural and political importance of the Sicilies was waning. The universities of north Italy and France had determined the intellectual centers of gravity. Islam was in retreat in the West, and at its heart had sustained the irreparable blow of the Mongol invasion and sack of Bagdad (1227). The great period of translation from the Arabic was past although the process continued for centuries. Yet the prestige in Europe of Arabian science was still undiminished. Padua had become an important medical school, linked to Venice, the portal of Eastern trade, and Paduan learning had stamped itself on the philosophical and medical thought of Italy and soon spread to Montpellier.

Jews were numerous at Padua and there one of them, Bonacosa, made
the first important north Italian contribution to the library of Arabic-Latin
medical translations, the *Colliget* (Arabic *Kulliyyat, i.e.,* "General [med-
ical] rules") of Averroës (1264). It was long studied at Padua and the
last edition appeared there in 1560. It was translated twice into Hebrew.

Another product of the Paduan Jewish school was a Latin translation
from the Hebrew version of the *Theizir* (Arabic *Taysir, i.e.,* "Aid to
health"), of the Spanish Moslem, Avenzoar (d. 1162), written for his
friend Averroës. It was widely read in Hebrew, whence it was turned into
Latin by the Jew Jacob of Capua, an immigrant from the south. He also
rendered into Latin from Hebrew the *Hygiene* of Maimonides, and a book
of Indian stories, the so-called *Kalilah wa-Dimmah*. This collection became
extraordinarily widespread, largely through Jewish agency. It is said to
have been translated into thirty-eight languages and to have passed into
about one hundred and eight editions. The English version was derived
from the Spanish, which was taken from Latin, which was taken from
Hebrew, which was taken from Arabic, which was taken from Pehlavi,
which was taken from Sanskrit!

Another strange document of the Paduan school is the most popular
of all the medieval books on remedies, the *Canones generales* of "Mesue."
This is the name of a well-known Arabic medical writer, but the book is a
compilation from the Hebrew. At the end of the thirteenth century one
Samuel ben Jacob of Capua, son of the above, composed this drug list, or
part of it, in Hebrew. From this the Latin version was prepared. It became
very popular and was printed scores of times, the last occasion being in
1581. It was the chief pharmaceutical work of the Renaissance and has
influenced the modern pharmacopoeias, including that of England.

A translator who links north Italy with north Spain and south France
was Abraham ben Shemtob of Tortosa, whose father, Shemtob ben Isaac of
Marseilles, was a well-known translator into Hebrew from Arabic. In 1290,
with the Christian Simon Cordo of Genoa, Abraham produced in Latin the
popular drug list associated with the name of *Serapion junior*. This
mysterious figure is unmentioned by the Arabic historians. He was invented, perhaps by Cordo and Abraham, to cover a work of miscellaneous
Arabic and Hebrew origin. *Serapion* was frequently printed. It, too, has
influenced the modern pharmacopoeias. The partnership between Cordo
and Abraham Shemtob produced several other medical translations.

12. French Christian and Jewish Hebraists, Thirteenth and Fourteenth Centuries

In southern France, Jews were particularly active in the practice of
medicine, notably at Avignon. There were many Jewish physicians at

Montpellier, which had been a medical center since the early twelfth century. In the thirteenth century it received a new medical tradition from Bologna and Padua. In 1263 John of Brescia, who had migrated to Montpellier from Bologna, collaborated with the Jew Jacob ben Makir in translating from Arabic into Latin certain important astronomical tables.

This Jacob ben Makir (d. 1308) was born at Marseilles, studied at the great talmudic seminary in Lunel, married the daughter of Moses ben Samuel ibn Tibbon and practiced actively as a physician at Montpellier. After assisting John of Brescia he busied himself in presenting the philosophy of Maimonides in Hebrew. He is best known for a Hebrew work that he wrote in 1288 on the astronomical quadrant, into which he introduced certain improvements. The form he advocated was known as the "Jewish quadrant" (*quadrans judaicus*). This important work was turned into Latin no less than three times, on the first occasion by an Englishman, who was making a stay at Montpellier about the year 1308, and on the second occasion about 1314 by the Christian Hebraist Armengaud of Montpellier. The well-known surveying instrument usually called *Jacob's staff* is probably named after this Jacob ben Makir. The first description of it that we have is, however, by his countryman and coreligionist Gersonides. An *Almanach* of Jacob ben Makir was used by Dante in the *Divina Commedia*.

Jacob ben Makir made many translations of scientific works from Arabic into Hebrew, such as Euclid's *Elements* and Alhazem's *Astronomy*, the works of Autolycus and of Menelaus *On the Sphere*, and Aristotle's *De partibus animalium* and *De generatione animalium* in the version of Averroës. His work was appreciated in both Latin and Hebrew circles and he is quoted by Copernicus and Kepler.

With Jacob ben Makir is associated the equally accomplished Christian Hebraist and physician Armengaud Blasius of Montpellier (d. 1314). He rendered many Hebrew works into Latin including writings of Maimonides. He was always helped by Jacob ben Makir or by his pupils. In 1305, while at Barcelona in attendance on Jaime II of Aragon, he occupied his spare time in Latinizing from the Hebrew the very curious *Cantica* of Avicenna and the medical work of Maimonides *On the Treatment of Poisoning*. His reliance on Hebrew rather than Arabic for these works exemplifies a widespread practice in the Scholastic ages. The reciprocal relationship of Jacob ben Makir and Armengaud is typical and was much commoner in the later Middle Ages than appears on the surface.

In 1305 Armengaud was displaced in his attendance on Jaime II by Arnald of Villanova (1235-1311), than whom few medieval figures would give a better opportunity to a romantic writer. Arnald, after a youth of hardship, studied at Naples and Salerno, traveled in Italy, Sicily, France and Spain and taught at Montpellier. Both there and at Barcelona he was associated with Armengaud. He was one of the earliest European alchemical writers and he also wrote voluminously on philosophical subjects in a heretical vein. He had some knowledge of both Hebrew and Arabic, and had ample access to those who had such knowledge. He was medical adviser to the papal court both at Rome and at Avignon, was employed as ambassador on more than one special mission, and he ended a very eventful life at sea. He translated from the Arabic a work of Avicenna on the heart and from the Hebrew a work of Avenzoar on diet. Both were effected with Jewish help. On the other hand, Arnald's own works were much read in Hebrew into which language about ten of them were translated.

By the second half of the thirteenth century activity in translation from Arabic had spread northward, and had reached Paris and Flanders. The earliest patron of these northern translators of whom we have tidings was the Fleming, Henri Bate (c. 1244-1310), a disciple of Albertus Magnus (1206-1280) at Paris. He was intimate with William of Moerbeke (d. 1285), the translator from the Greek employed by Thomas Aquinas (1227-1274). Bate received an ecclesiastical benefice at his birthplace at Malines in 1273. Next year a French Jew, one Hayyin, translated into French works of Abraham ibn Ezra in Bate's house at Malines. These influenced Bate's later writings, notably a treatise on the astrolabe, produced in 1274 on William of Moerbeke's suggestion. Bate later went to . Italy and translated other works of ibn Ezra at Orvieto (1281 and 1292). Other works of ibn Ezra were translated by the heretical Paduan professor Peter of Abano (1250-1318), one of the most picturesque of the Scholastics whose natural death saved him from a more violent one, for his body was exhumed and burned.

During the first half of the fourteenth century the French Jews displayed much philosophic and scientific activity. The leading representative of this movement is Levi ben Gerson, known as Gersonides (1288-1344).[12a] He lived at Avignon and Orange, and is important in the general history of philosophy and especially for the thought of Spinoza. He was a courageous man of outstanding scientific ability, but as a writer Hebrew was his only medium. The extent, variety and depth of his knowledge bear testimony to the qualities and possibilities of medieval Hebrew literature.

Gersonides was an enthusiastic Aristotelian, who fearlessly interpreted what he regarded as the view of his master in opposition alike to current Judaism and to the Averroism of the schools. He regarded himself as a complete rationalist and his philosophy was largely banned by his own people. His work that most stirred the world in which he lived was astronomical. A passage from it dealing with "Jacob's staff" was translated into Latin in 1342 during his lifetime by order of Pope Clement VI as *The Instrument That Reveals Secrets*. Later the whole work was Latinized. It demonstrates the falseness of the current view that all the heavenly bodies move round the same center. It thus in a sense leads on to Copernicus. It deservedly enjoyed a high reputation and was still esteemed in the seventeenth century, when Kepler was at pains to secure a copy. Kepler quotes Gersonides several times and refers to three separate works by him.

Mention should perhaps here be made of the very important French Hebrew fourteenth-century writer Hasdai Crescas. He had nothing to say on science in the modern sense but he is philosophically important as opposing Aristotle as represented by Maimonides. Thus he anticipates the reaction against Aristotle that later introduced the scientific movement to the Latin world.[13a]

13. DECLINE OF HEBREW-ARABIC SCIENCE, FIFTEENTH AND SIXTEENTH CENTURIES

In the later fourteenth century the long decline of the Jewish scientific intellect began. The political and social conditions of Jews were steadily deteriorating, culminating with the expulsion from Spain, Sicily and Sardinia in 1492. Yet it was long before the Hebrew-Arabic element that had already entered Latin thought began to lose importance. The main philosophical reading of the West continued to be affected by Hebrew-Arabic literature far into the time of printing, and even to the seventeenth century. In this connection it must be remembered that the revival of Greek learning affected science much later than literature and philosophy.

Among the later Jewish translators of the period of decline, mention should be made of Elijah Delmedigo (1463-1497) of Padua. A good Hebrew, Latin and Italian scholar and a physician as well, he applied himself to philosophy and took part in the activities of the university. Padua, alone among the universities, occasionally granted a medical degree to Jews and that from as early as 1409. Among Elijah Delmedigo's students was Pico della Mirandola (1463-1494), at whose request some of his translations were undertaken. Delmedigo's writings are mostly Latin renderings of various treatises by Averroës. He also produced original philosophical works. He differs from Pico in having a strong bias against cabbalism.

In contrast to Delmedigo is Judah Verga of Lisbon, where he died under torture in 1490. He was a cabbalist but his secular work was of an exclusively scientific nature. Among his scientific writings, which are all in Hebrew, is a description of an astronomical instrument which he invented to determine the sun's meridian. The account of it was written at Lisbon about 1457.

It may seem strange that cabbalistic and scientific learning should occur in the same individual. In fact, however, this was often the case. Thus Guglielmo Raimondo of Girgenti, who was converted to Christianity in

1466, and later became a bishop, had both these interests. From him we have a translation of an astronomical work of the Arab mathematician Alhazen of Basra (965-1038). The dedication cites the Talmud and ibn Ezra. About 1477, Raimondo also prepared a number of eclipse tables.

A similar combination of interests was exhibited by Paolo Ricci, a converted Jew of German origin who acted as physician to the Emperor Maximilian. He translated cabbalistic treatises from Hebrew and later became professor of medicine at the University of Pavia. He is mentioned favorably by Erasmus. In 1519 he issued the only edition that we possess of the medical treatise of the Spanish physician, Albucasis (1013-1106).

Bonet de Lattes was of a family from Lattes near Montpellier and he himself was from Carpentras. He achieved an excellent reputation for himself as a physician and was medical attendant to two successive Popes, Alexander VI (d. 1503) and Leo X (d. 1513). In 1493 in a work dedicated to Pope Alexander VI he described in Latin an astronomical instrument for taking solar and lunar altitudes and thus determining the hour. It gained much popularity. A pleasing description of Bonet, his house, his instruments and his mode of life has been left by a Christian scholar who visited him at Rome (1507). Some remains of this house were recovered half a century ago.

By the sixteenth century translation of scientific works into Latin directly from the Arabic had ceased, but translation into Latin from Hebrew continued, mostly in the spirit of the New Learning. The last of the Jewish translators who can rightly be termed medieval, Jacob Mantino (d. 1549), was also connected with Padua. He was born in Spain, whence, on the Expulsion, his parents brought him as an infant. He studied philosophy and medicine at Bologna and Padua, and devoted most of his life to translation into Latin. He settled in Venice and attracted the attention of Clement VII as well as that of many scholars. His eventful life was marked by office as physician to Pope Paul III and by disputes with the Messianic visionary, Solomon Molko (1500-1532).

Mantino rendered into Latin from Hebrew works of Averroës, Gersonides, Maimonides and Avicenna. He is best remembered, however, as editor of the monumental standard Latin edition of Averroës published at Venice in 1552, soon after his death. It was the basis of the Averroistic philosophical school that flourished among Christians and Jews at Padua well into the seventeenth century and had some distinguished exponents. William Harvey (1578-1657), discoverer of the circulation of the blood, was affected by it. The ultimate representative of the medieval Hebrew-Arabic movement in Italy was the Averroist, Cesaro Cremonini (d. 1637), professor of philosophy at Padua till his death.

The decline of what we may call the Hebrew-Arabic-Latin scientific movement is contemporary with the advent of a Jewish element in the new

"Renaissance" of science. The movement was short lived. It is illustrated by the careers of two Jewish astronomers, Abraham Zacuto and Joseph Vecinho who were involved in the explorations of Vasco da Gama and Columbus. So far as Hebrew-Arabic science in the Iberian Peninsula is concerned, theirs is a swan song.

Abraham Zacuto (1450-1510) taught astronomy at the universities of Salamanca and Saragossa. Leaving Spain he settled in Lisbon as astronomer to John II. He was consulted on the expedition of Vasco da Gama, whose vessels were fitted with astrolabes designed by him and provided with improvements that he introduced. In 1473, while still at Salamanca, Zacuto wrote in Hebrew a *Perpetual Almanac*. This was translated into both Latin and Spanish by his pupil Vecinho and issued in 1496 at Leiria in Portugal by a Jewish printer. Manuscript copies of it were carried in the fleets of Vasco da Gama, Cabral, João de Nova, and Albuquerque.

This Joseph Vecinho was also in the service of John II of Portugal, who sent him to the coast of Guinea to measure the solar altitude. When the plan of Columbus for Western exploration was laid before King John he submitted it to a committee of five, of whom Vecinho was chief. The other members were the Bishop of Ceuta, the court physician, the German cartographer Martin Behaim, and a Jewish mathematician named Moses. The committee reported against the expedition but Columbus retained a high respect for Vecinho and wrote in the margin of one of his books: "In the year 1485, the king of Portugal sent Master Joseph, his physician and astronomer, to determine the altitudes of the sun throughout Guinea, all of which he performed. He reported to the king, in my presence, that he found the Island of Idols near Sierra Leone to be exactly five degrees distant from the equator. Afterward the king often sent to Guinea and other places, and always found the results accord with those of Master Joseph." In another marginal note Columbus states that during voyages to Guinea he had taken solar altitudes of the sun, which always agreed with those of Vecinho.

Columbus (1446-1506) had, in fact, much intercourse with Jewish men of science and was acquainted with Zacuto as well as with Vecinho. Almost the first financial assistance that he secured was from the Jewish statesman and Bible commentator, Isaac Abrabanel (1437-1508), and in his will Columbus left a legacy to a Lisbon Jew. At least five Jews accompanied him on his first expedition, especially as interpreters. The first landing was effected on October 15, 1492, and on November 2, Columbus sent out his first expedition on American soil. It consisted of two men, one the Jew Luis de Torres. Torres was one of the first Europeans to tread American soil and the first to experiment with the effects of tobacco, using himself as guinea pig. He settled and died in Cuba.

Many have thought that Columbus was himself of Jewish origin and there is much to support that view. One point that might be made is that Columbus, though born and bred in Genoa, never employs an Italian word in any of his documents. Spanish is the only vernacular that he uses. This language was and is the lingua franca of Mediterranean Jews. For a Genoese to write only Spanish would in itself suggest a Jewish origin.

This is perhaps the place to mention the remarkable figure of Pedro Nunes (c. 1492-1577). He was born of a Marrano family in Portugal and studied medicine at Lisbon and mathematics at Salamanca. He went to the East Indies as an official in 1519 but was soon recalled as professor of philosophy at Lisbon. In 1529 he became cosmographer royal. In 1544 he was called to the chair of mathematics at Coimbra. Nunes devoted himself to investigation of figures and lines on spheres other than "great circles." He is a founder of scientific navigation and his *Treatise on the Sphere* (Lisbon, 1537) and *On the Art and Science of Navigation* have an assured place in the history of cartography. He himself escaped the direct attentions of the Inquisition but his grandchildren paid the penalty.

14. THE MARRANO EPISODE[14a]

In the world of intellect the persecution of Jews in Spain had certain surprising implications, some of which have been insufficiently recognized. Toward the end of the Jewish Iberian period there was, especially in Portugal, a remarkable number of Jewish writers touched by the spirit of the New Learning. The works of Judah Verga (d. 1490), Abraham Zacuto (d. 1510) and Joseph Vecinho (d. c. 1495) were the swan song of Jewish science in the Peninsula. With the migration their tradition was continued by such men as Elijah Delmedigo (d. 1497), Abraham de Balmes (1423-1523) and Jacob Mantino (d. 1549). But from then onward Jewish science, outside medicine, is mute until the nineteenth century. No important Jewish name appears in scientific literature, except in medicine, for nearly three centuries. The revival is not then with the Sephardim but with the Ashkenazim of Central Europe. This very fact adds significance to the immense number of physicians of the Marrano migration.

For much of the sixteenth, seventeenth and even the eighteenth centuries an astonishingly high proportion of important physicians of Europe was of Marrano descent. The phenomenon needs explanation, which is not yet perhaps fully forthcoming. Many factors may be suggested. Doubtless it was an advantage to possess the full clinical tradition of the Hebrew-Arabic medical system. Social pressure certainly left few avocations open to foreign refugees. Perhaps the mental detachment that comes of insecure social position may not be without its uses to the medical observer. Surely a natural channel of the Jewish tradition will always be humane social service. Assuredly it was no small thing to acquire early a respect for learning. Moreover, the minds of the Marranos were free in a sense in which those of professing Jews were not, for their very circumstances and history implied release from Rabbinic limitations.

There is something to be said for all these as factors of the intellectual outburst, which was almost exclusively among those of Sephardic and Iberian origin. The period coincides with the movement of the center of gravity of the Latin intellect from the Mediterranean area to the northwest. Thither the Marranos largely followed it. The northern Ashkenazim, however, were still in a pre-Scholastic stage. They were neither in a social nor an intellectual position to develop secular studies and there is no significant scientific figure among them before the nineteenth century. The determining elements in the outburst of Marrano intellectual activity will be a matter of opinion. The general situation bears resemblance to that of the Jews of Central Europe during the past hundred years. A culture hunger is aroused by the breakdown of the Rabbinic environment. This is most easily satisfied by the rising enthusiasm for science in a changed social milieu. The New Learning of the sixteenth century was to the Marranos what the New Science was to central European Jewry.

In both cases importance must be attached to the freeing of the mind from talmudic preoccupation. This sounds like a truism since a mind preoccupied by any line of thought obviously cannot at the same time admit another line. But it is a special feature of talmudic preoccupation that it tends to occupy the whole area of thought as do few other studies; for the Talmud is not only a subject of study, it is a habit of thought, a cast of mind, a way of life. The practical test lies in the historic record. Very few if any talmudists have made contributions to science. Why should this be? The answer must be in terms of Jewish sociology or psychology where it cannot be followed in this place.

It is difficult to give a picture of the medical activity of Marranism as a whole. It represents no definite school. The groups with which we are concerned are almost entirely disconnected. It is precisely this division among themselves that prevented the Marranos from developing a separate religion and so from having a history in any proper sense. But an account of the lives of a score of Marrano physicians over these three hundred years reveals the impetus of a remarkable intellectual movement working itself out until it becomes extinct in the nineteenth century. Not all the figures here selected are of great medical eminence. Some are selected as helping to complete the patchwork picture of the Marrano intellect. Some, too, were not Marranos themselves but descendants of Marranos.

Belonging to the first generation of the migration were two physicians bearing the name Leo, whose widely different careers illustrate the diversity of the Marrano activities. The better known was Leo Hebreus or Judah Abrabanel (c. 1470-1535), son of the famous statesman Isaac

Abrabanel. In 1492 his son was taken from Leo and baptized and he himself was expelled from Spain. He practiced in Naples and was physician to the successive kings of the "Sicilies." That realm being invaded, he sought a home successively at Venice, Corfu and Genoa, where his famous *Dialogues of Love* was written (1502) for his friend the philosopher Pico della Mirandola. Leo was a Neoplatonic dreamer and his work is a discussion between *Sophia*, Wisdom, and *Philo*, Love. Despite its esoteric character it contains matter of medical interest and Leo's medical services were always highly esteemed. The book is an Italian classic. It was printed nineteen times in the sixteenth century and has been translated into many languages, including Hebrew and English.

The other Leo, less known to fame, was a pioneer in a different sense. He was of Venice, and ventured to Russia in 1490 in the train of an ambassadorial mission to Moscow, the first Western European medical man to enter Russian territory. He was called to treat a local prince, who unfortunately died. The physician was accordingly executed and Russia had naturally to wait some time for her next Western medical adviser.

Francisco Lopez de Villalobos (1472?-1549) was one of the very few great physicians who remained in sixteenth-century Spain. His surname is that of a place near Zamora but it is uncertain whether he was born there or at Toledo. He studied at Salamanca, was much occupied about the court of King Ferdinand (1509-1516) and of the Emperor Charles V (1518-1542), retiring at the age of seventy. He came early under suspicion of the Inquisition and was incarcerated for eighty days but managed to clear himself. He was forced on later occasions to be a witness to the burnings of heretics. Villalobos has a definite place in the history of medicine. He provided the clearest early account of syphilis in the form of a poem published at Salamanca in 1498. He wrote other important medical works which are still of interest.

Dionysius Brudo (c. 1470-c. 1540), son of a medical man, occupied an excellent post as physician to the crown in Lisbon. He was a controversialist on bloodletting, the method of which was a subject of violent debate at the time. In 1534, despite his eminence, he found reason to leave suddenly for Antwerp and a pension from the crown ceased to be paid him. His Jewish sympathies had been discovered. His son Manuel Brudo is said to have declared himself a Jew at Venice. Manuel practiced in England for a time about the year 1540. A work by him on the treatment of fevers (Venice, 1544) was widely read. It contains many references to his English cases and his English experiences and to English customs.

Although not medically important, one of the more remarkable of the Marrano physicians was another member of the London Marrano group, Hector Nunez (c. 1520-c. 1595). He was born at Evora, graduated at Coimbra, came to England about 1550 and joined the minute colony of Judaizing Marranos in London of whom there were about a hundred.

He became their leading spirit during the reign of Catholic Mary (1553-1558), despite the rigidly anti-Jewish attitude of her husband, Philip of Spain. Hector had widespread connections in the government and continued to enjoy the confidence of Elizabeth's great ministers, Burleigh and Walsingham. He was the first Jew or Marrano to be admitted as a fellow of the Royal College of Physicians (1554). He was esteemed within the college, holding the title of censor in 1562 and 1563. The college books show that he was still living in 1589 but that he was not then in England.

The most striking medical figure of the sixteenth century was the Belgian professor at Padua, Andreas Vesalius (1514-1564), founder of the study of anatomy. For both of his anatomical works (1538 and 1543) he had Jewish assistants. He speaks of the chief of these in the most cordial way as his friend and guest. He needed their help to explain to him the meaning of Arabic and Hebrew anatomical terms.

Of the medical men of the sixteenth century few were better known in their own time than Juan Roderigo who usually called himself Amatus Lusitanus (1511-1568).[15a] He was born at Castello Branco in Portugal, son of Marrano refugees from Spain. He took a medical degree at Salamanca and practiced for a while in Lisbon. About this time complaints were raised in the Cortes that almost all physicians and apothecaries were "New Christians," that is, Marranos. There was much truth in this. Anticipating the entry of the Inquisition into Portugal (1536) Amatus left for Antwerp. There he established a reputation based partly on his *Index to the Remedies of Dioscorides* (1536). In 1540 he was called to the chair of medicine at Ferrara, then one of the most tolerant places in Europe. It was a center for anatomical study, a subject entirely neglected in Spain and Portugal. At Ferrara he performed a considerable number of dissections and witnessed more. He was invited to become court physician in Poland and town physician in Ragusa. Owing to some miscalculation concerning the latter he moved to Ancona (1547), where he carried on a very successful practice and wrote the first of his seven *Centuriae* (1549) of medical observations. This was issued at Rome in 1551 during a long visit there. In 1555 decrees issued by the new Pope, Paul IV, placed restrictions on medical practice by Jews and Marranos. A number in Italy were arrested by the Inquisition and twenty-four burned at the stake. Amatus fled first to Pesaro and then across the Adriatic to Ragusa. Finally he reached Salonica, 1558. There he wrote his *Centuria VII* (1561) and died some years later.

Amatus wrote an important book on *materia medica* (Venice, 1552) that contains many original botanical observations. The works by which he is rightly remembered, however, are his *Centuriae*. These are clinical records of actual cases, the first major collection of the kind ever made, and are of great historic and scientific importance.

Garcia da Orta (1498-1568) was one of the most distinguished medical men of the sixteenth century. He studied at the universities of Salamanca and Alcalá. In 1534 he sailed for India and settled finally at Goa. He was the pioneer of the study of tropical diseases and one of the fathers of botanical science. His valuable and interesting *Colloquies on the Simples and Drugs of India* (Goa, 1563) was the first book printed in that country. It is still consulted as the earliest authority on the subject. Da Orta traveled much in India and his observations were outstanding. One of his famous sayings expresses the true spirit of science: "In Spain I would never have dared to affirm anything contrary to the Greeks and particularly to Galen, but in India, free from convention, in the midst of luxuriant vegetation, it matters little what Dioscorides, Pliny, Avicenna and Galen have said. Do not frighten me with them. I have seen." What was in effect an illustrated edition of Da Orta's book was produced in 1578 by another Marrano, Cristoval d'Acosta.

Many of Garcia da Orta's relatives suffered from the Inquisition and his sister was burned at the stake in the year of his death. In 1580 the Inquisition found that he was a Jew and ordered his remains to be burned. He had been dead for twelve years.

Continuity of medical tradition in a Marrano family is illustrated by the Saportas. The Catalonian Luiz Saporta was born at Lerida (*c.* 1460-1565). After nine years of medical practice there he left for Provence and started practices first at Arles, then at Avignon, and then at the ancient university town of Montpellier. He did much military service, received many signs of royal approval and is said to have died at Marseilles, age 106. His son Louis Saporta II (*c.* 1490-*c.* 1580) took his degree at Montpellier and practiced at Toulouse, where he acquired a great reputation, dying at the age of ninety. His son Antoine Saporta (*c.* 1510-1573) was born at Montpellier, took his medical degree there in 1531, became professor of medicine there in 1540, dean in 1551 and chancellor in 1566. His son Jean Saporta (*c.* 1550-1605) also became professor there (1577) and later vice-chancellor (1603).

Rodrigo de Castro (1546-1627) came of a well-known Marrano medical family, many members of which, including his own brother, suffered from the Inquisition. He was born at Lisbon, educated at Salamanca and practiced first at Evora and then at Lisbon. He earned a great reputation and was offered a post in India to continue the work of Garcia da Orta. He decided, however, to leave Portuguese territory, fearing the inquiries of the Holy Office. He settled in Hamburg about 1590 and there became one of the most respected and sought-after physicians in northern Europe, being called upon to attend a number of sovereigns and high notables. De Castro's own reputation was greatly increased by his steady refusal to leave his post in plague-time. About the beginning of the seventeenth century the very small band of Marranos in Hamburg began openly to profess the Jewish religion. Official sanction was given to their residence in 1611. De Castro wrote two books of considerable medical importance, one the earliest original modern treatise on gynecology and the other on the relation of the doctor to the state. He had two sons who also were physicians.

At the end of the sixteenth century the grand dukes of Tuscany sought to attract a higher type of professor in reorganizing the University of Pisa. One of their captures was a young man named Galileo Galilei. For the medical department distinguished Marranos were available. Among those secured was Estevão Rodrigues de Castro (1559-1637), a native of Lisbon. He was a prolific writer who made pioneer observations in pathology. A gifted teacher, he was called in 1615 to Padua, the leading medical school of the time. He was followed at both Pisa and Padua by Antonio Rodrigues da Fonseca (d. 1632), another native of Lisbon and also a voluminous writer, whose achievement lay in having helped to check the practice of excessive bleeding.

Abraham Zacuto (1575-1642) the Portuguese (Lusitanus) came of a long line of physicians, perhaps the longest on record, for his great-grandfather of the same name was already the third of his line. Our Zacutus was born at Lisbon, studied at Salamanca and Coimbra and took his degree at Siguenza. After practicing for thirty years (1596-1626) in his native town with noteworthy success, he was forced to flee and headed for Amsterdam. He joined the Jewish congregation there and at once began a long and voluminous series of publications which ended only with his death. Zacutus was a strong medical conservative. Although he had passed beyond the "Arabist" phase he was obstinately Galenist in the mood of the previous generation. Living till almost the middle of the seventeenth century this attitude was certainly backward but he was nevertheless an excellent clinical observer. His work on the infectious diseases is still occasionally consulted and he was one of the first to describe the deadly blackwater fever.

A physician who is immortalized for adventitious reasons is Dr. Ephraim Hezekiah Bueno (d. 1665). He came of a Spanish family that included many physicians. His father, Joseph Bueno, arrived in Amsterdam from Bordeaux, where he had taken a medical degree, and was a doctor of good repute. Ephraim was very friendly with Manasseh ben Israel, whose first work he published, but he will always be remembered by the delightful picture of him by Rembrandt known as "The Jewish Doctor." His features represent the best Spanish type, with gentle, pitiful, sadly thoughtful eyes; a typical Sephardi. Beneath the contemporary engraving by Lyrius is inscribed, "A second Avenzoar, distinguished in medicine and a pupil of a distinguished father." He was a kind and charitable man, an efficient doctor and a good son of the synagogue.

John Lumbrozo (d. 1665) was a refugee from Portugal to Holland. Thence in 1656 he came to palatinate of Maryland, where he practiced medicine with much success. In 1663 he secured letters of denization. He was the first Jewish inhabitant of Maryland of whose faith there is documentary evidence. One of the earliest trained practitioners there, he was probably the earliest ex-Marrano to practice medicine in the territory of what is now the United States. His career is of interest in relation to the development of religious toleration in Maryland. After two years of undisturbed quiet as a recognized Jew, as a consequence of his own indiscretion zealots obtained his arrest for "blasphemy," that is, for denying the doctrine of the Trinity. He was released under the general amnesty proclaimed a few days later by the Protector, Richard Cromwell.

Balthasar Orobio de Castro (1620-1687) was the child of Marrano parents living in Seville. He studied at Alcalá and became a teacher of philosophy at Salamanca. Later he studied medicine and practiced successfully at Seville, attending relations of the king. He was denounced by a servant to the Inquisition as an adherent of Judaism, but persistently denied the truth of this through two years of imprisonment and torture. In view of his later history it is evident that this treatment turned him toward Judaism in at least the sense that it turned him against Christianity. On his release he left Spain (1663) and became professor of medicine at Toulouse. Finally he migrated to Amsterdam (1666), where he embraced Judaism openly. There he practiced medicine until his death. He is known chiefly for his theological writings and for his friendship with Spinoza. His wife died at Amsterdam in 1712. Members of his family continued to be victims of the Inquisition far into the eighteenth century. An Orobio de Castro was writing medical works at Amsterdam toward the end of the nineteenth century.

Fernandez Méndez (c. 1645-1725) was born in Portugal and was graduated from Montpellier in 1667. He reached London in 1669 and became physician in attendance on Queen Catherine of Braganza (d. 1705). In 1687 he was admitted a fellow of the Royal College of Physicians. He married a lady of the migration, a Jewess, and a child was born to them in the royal palace of Somerset House. He was one of those in attendance on Charles II in his last illness. There is no reason to suppose that Mendez was a man of any special medical ability. The fact that the queen should choose this ex-Marrano illustrates the poorness of non-Jewish medical personnel in Portugal. The great tradition of Marrano medicine was itself petering out.

Daniel da Fonseca (1667-c. 1745) was born in Portugal. His grandfather had been burned as a Marrano and his father escaped as one when Daniel was only eight years old. He was baptized, brought up in the Catholic faith and entered the priesthood, nevertheless secretly adhering to the Jewish religion. This being suspected, he fled to France, where he studied medicine. He then made his way to Constantinople, where he openly embraced Judaism, practiced medicine, successfully obtained the confidence of high officials and showed himself consistently pro-French and anti-Austrian. He was appointed physician to the French embassy and later to the sultan himself. He retired about 1730 to Paris, where he spent his last years in the delightful society of the salons, a friend of Voltaire, who regarded him as the only Jewish philosopher.

Samuel Nunez (c. 1680-c. 1750) was a Marrano physician of great distinction who was born in Lisbon, where he was educated and practiced in high circles. He was denounced to the Inquisition, however, and he and his family were imprisoned. His services were in such demand that he was released but had to submit to the permanent residence in his house of two officers who would make certain that he did not relapse into Judaism. He succeeded in persuading the captain of an English ship to take his family and himself to England secretly. There they joined other Marranos and a small party of German Jews. They set sail in 1733 for Georgia. Despite attempts to prevent them from settling, most of them, protected by Oglethorpe, were able to remain, Nunez among them. He became a substantial landowner and was an ancestor of Mordecai M. Noah.

Jacob de Castro Sarmento (1691-1761) was born at Braganza, studied at Evora and Coimbra, taking his medical degree in 1717. He left his country to escape the Inquisition, settled in 1720 in London, was admitted to the Royal College of Physicians in 1725, became a fellow of the Royal Society in 1729 and of the college in 1739. He was one of the earliest advocates in England (1721) of the protection against smallpox by "variolation," that is, by inoculation with a mild form of the disease (to be distinguished sharply from vaccination, which came into use eighty years later). It is possible that he may have brought the idea with him from Portugal as he did a preparation of quinine, which he introduced. He published in Portuguese in London a work of some importance on mineral substances used in medicine (1731-1758). He openly professed Judaism and equally openly corresponded with Jesuits on scientific matters. He always retained his connections with Portugal and translated Newton's works into Portuguese. He left the synagogue in 1758.

Of the later Marranos perhaps the most important scientifically was Jacob Rodrigues Pereira (1715-1780). He was born in Spain of Marrano parents. On his father's death his mother was in danger of denunciation to the Inquisition. She and her son fled, settled in Bordeaux and embraced Judaism. From about 1737 on, the young man devoted himself to the experimental study of deaf-mutes. He thus slowly elaborated a method of teaching them to speak and gradually his method was accepted. His achievements have been generally acknowledged in modern times and his scientific reputation now stands very high. His interest in deaf-mutes was inherited by his great-grandson.

It would be very easy to extend this description of the pageant of Marrano life with a whole series of romantic figures. It would be equally easy to include in our illustrative list many scores of physicians distinguished in their day but short of eminence. Again the series might be made to include many theologians or other thinkers who, in the Jewish manner, had practiced for a time as physicians or had medical degrees. But by the mid-eighteenth century the Marrano impetus was failing. The migration had ceased. The Iberian Peninsula had become, as it remains, the most backward and illiterate region of Western Europe. The Marranos themselves were largely absorbed in the general population. The Jewish people of the eighteenth century, whatever their interest in the sociologist and social historian, provide little for the historian of science.

15. A HUNDRED YEARS OF CENTRAL EUROPE

The role of Jews in the drama of modern scientific progress has been noteworthy in several Western countries. In central Europe it has been overwhelming and a discussion of the entire situation would be interminable. Here the consideration of the historical elements must suffice, omitting contemporary figures. Moreover, in order to keep within reasonable limits, we must confine ourselves, for the most part, to the German-speaking region. In that area Jews have played an ever-increasing part in intellectual life. Something must, therefore, be said of the history of Central European science, which is, in effect, German science. Furthermore, the German-speaking area is the effective center of the modern Jewish people. It is true that by the beginning of the twentieth century the relative importance of the German language and of German culture from the Jewish standpoint was rapidly declining. Nevertheless, Germany remained, until the rise of Nazism, the center of Jewish intellectual life.

A characteristic of German cultural history is the lateness of its scientific development. The great scientific movement of the sixteenth, seventeenth and eighteenth centuries, beginning in Italy, spread to northwestern Europe. For a long time the German area was little affected by it. There were a few eminent early German scientists but no outstanding school of scientific thought in a German environment. The real German scientific contribution was scarcely begun until the end of the eighteenth and did not reach impressive proportions until the nineteenth century. The first important native school of scientific thought was the mathematical, astronomical and physical movement linked with the great names of Karl Friedrich Gauss (1777-1855), and Wilhelm Eduard Weber (1804-1891) and associated largely with Goettingen.

Both this tardy arrival and rapid development are rendered partially understandable by the history of the universities and of the technical industries of Germany. German scientific technique has, like German learning, always been in the hands of university professors. The brilliant amateur, so frequently a figure in French and English science, has seldom appeared on the German scene. On the other hand, a significant role has been played by the "doctoral dissertation," a feature always greatly stressed in German university life. Until well into the nineteenth century German custom demanded that these dissertations, like lectures, be formal and in Latin. When this tradition, with its associated turgid absurdities, was finally abandoned, the system so developed as to provide German professors with what were, in effect, considerable staffs of trained but unpaid assistants. The officers of German universities have always been under state control and, given judicious state support, it was easy for a professor to introduce a high degree of organization into research.

Neither institutes nor organizations create science. Men of science are unique and beyond all valuation. Looking back upon the history of science as a whole, taking into consideration the proportion of people in Europe who use the German tongue, the high state of their material culture, and realizing that a large proportion of German scientific writings are products of non-German or part-German influences, it may fairly be said that Germans have been distinctly less successful than several other peoples in producing creative work of the first rank. But the situation in the second half of the nineteenth century had special features. Much of the significant scientific advance in German in that period was related to skilled co-operative effort. There are phases in the development of the sciences for which a high degree of organization is especially favorable. Such a phase was traversed for certain sciences between the years 1860 and 1920. It happened to coincide with the industrialization of Germany. The rise of industrialism and the development of great scientific institutes were of mutual assistance, notably from 1882 to 1907, when the extremely able Friedrich Althoff reigned tyrannically in the Prussian Ministry of Education.

In the later nineteenth century private benefaction in the United States, England and France had not yet enabled research to be organized on anything like the scale that we see today [1946]. Moreover, universities in these countries shunned industrial contacts, sometimes even depreciating the sciences. Hence the German universities had advantages in certain disciplines. In Germany many scientific departments, ably officered and with numerous highly trained and well-disciplined staffs, were in a position to concentrate directly on specific problems to a degree unknown elsewhere. All this fitted the state-directed industrialization under the Prussian hegemony, some of the profits from which were skillfully diverted to the needs of fundamental research. The development of scientific interests among Jews in Germany must be considered with this background in mind.

The nineteenth- and twentieth-century outburst of Jewish intellect reveals both contrasts and parallels to that of the earlier Marrano episode. In contrast it was almost entirely among Ashkenazim, for Sephardic activity has progressively waned. Its external accompaniments were those liberating, liberalizing, humane forces that both produced and emerged from the French Revolution. The atmosphere of this emancipation was totally different from the extreme Catholic nidus that bred the Iberian Marranos. Moreover, the political emancipation of Jews in central Europe resulted, and was designed to result, in their assimilation to the normal social environment.[16a] This, too, was quite unlike the designedly extrusive process of the Spanish and Italian Inquisitions. Furthermore, the Emancipation coincided with and was partly dependent on a general recession of the power of the churches.

Despite these differences in origin, the two movements had analogous features. Both arose among people in whom the breakdown of talmudism had left the tension produced by a spiritual vacuum. It is not remarkable that in the resulting cultural hunger the intellectual products should bear traces of this. The Marranos, like their later counterparts, carried some residue of the old Jewish culture and, like them, they had not quite completely absorbed the culture of their environment. The double maladjustment, not so great as to constitute a spiritual conflict of the gravest kind, was yet enough to give an independence of approach, a philosophic detachment to the entrant into the newly accessible scientific field. This was certainly an advantage. An impartial outlook is a significant part of the equipment of the man of science. The circumstances that may induce it are worthy of further attention from the social psychologist.

It is not easy to depict the rise of science as a part of the history of western European Jews. Science, in the modern sense, is truly no part of their heritage. How could it be rooted in the history of a people to whom the renaissance of literature and of learning, of art and of science, had brought nothing except heavier bonds? The Renaissance has little place in Jewish history. On the other hand, the development of science itself cannot be said to be distinctive of any people. How could it be, since science is, of its nature, universal? It is neither Jewish nor Christian, neither national nor racial, but a product of a particular philosophic outlook. If we use language exactly we cannot speak at all of Jews or of Judaism in science. We do so in this place only by making several elipses and assumptions.

As with the Marrano episode, we can thus but present an imperfect panorama, emphasizing here and there those activities in which Jews have especially distinguished themselves. And even for such a partial account of the part that Jewish individuals have played in science it is necessary to correlate the record with that of the admission of Jews to universities.

In the sixteenth century the only university to which Jews had any easy access was Padua. In the seventeenth, Leyden began to take its place both in scientific eminence and in the freedom with which religious tests were waived. This great Dutch school achieved even greater prominence in the eighteenth century. In the central European universities professing Jews could hardly obtain admission until the mid-nineteenth century, while important posts, and notably full professorships, were almost entirely denied to them until well into the twentieth century. In the ancient English universities it was not possible for a Jew even to take a degree until the passing of the Universities Test Act in 1871.

Under these circumstances there arose in the German-speaking countries a movement closely resembling Marranism. Among nineteenth-century Jews, as among Christians, only a small proportion were "believers" in any profound sense. Many, both of Jewish and of Christian parentage, to whom religion meant little, found the formal profession of Christianity no unbearable strain on the conscience. In all countries, but especially in the Germanic, facile "converts" passed readily enough into the prevailing formal Christianity. Naturally they carried with them some elements of their traditional habits of thought. Of such persons it may be said that, except for the fact that their environment was happier and safer, their spiritual outlook did not and does not differ vastly from that of the earlier Iberian Marranos.

But while these German Marranos differ in some respects from their neighbors of non-Jewish origin, these differences did not and do not unite them. They have no common outlook. These nominal Christians of Jewish origin represented, and still represent, no organized or effective movement. As with the Iberian Marranos, their separateness was the result of external pressure rather than of internal force. This absence of internal force, this failure of and even resistance to organic development, has been the real basis of the Jewish tragedy. Even Jewish nationalism is basically of external origin, part of the nationalist pandemic that has swept the world for a century. Moreover, the withering of the religion, the only possible unifying element in the Jewish intellectual revival, happened to be contemporary with certain scientific developments. Jewish emancipation coincided with an era of enormous scientific advance, the result of extreme fragmentation in the scientific field resulting from the natural product of increasingly complex techniques. As with the finest craftsmanship, the very exercise of technique provided an outlet for self-expression. The frustrated and culture-starved German Marranos eagerly occupied this new field. They gave to it a certain spiritual significance that they drew from their half-forgotten religious heritage.

There is another and contrasting side to this scientific movement corresponding to the natural variety of character found in every social aggregate. Those of the reflective type sought immediate substitutes to fill the religious gap. They rapidly became part of the philosophic movement at the German universities. With this we are hardly directly concerned, except for the significant effect it had on the scientific movement itself. In fact, some of the greatest Jewish exponents of science in the early nineteenth century were men of the widest scientific grasp. Let us glance at the effects on Jews of these new sources of inspiration.

Before World War II Jews formed roughly one per cent of the population of Europe, which was roughly five hundred millions. But the Jewish five millions was far from evenly distributed. In the Iberian Peninsula it was next to nothing. In Scandinavia it was about one-tenth of one per cent. In parts of Russian and Rumanian territory it was a hundred times as much. The special area of Jewish intellectual success, though not of density of Jewish population, was German-speaking. In that region Jews formed about one in a hundred of the entire population. To a lesser extent Italian-speaking Europe, with a Jewish population of about one in a thousand, presented similar phenomena. These were less marked in the French- and English-speaking worlds. For obvious reasons Jewish intellectuals played hardly any part in the old Russian Empire and Rumania. Jewish scientific development was thus confined to a relatively small part of the European area in which Jews were settled.

These phenomena are capable of comparatively simple historical and demographic explanation. Jewish activity in the scientific realm has been particularly notable in the mathematical and medical fields. Mathematics relies less on apparatus and on organization than do other departments of science. In its development the solitary worker is less handicapped than in most departments. Those debarred from normal social, literary and scholastic contacts naturally throw themselves into this most abstract discipline. Jewish addiction to medicine again requires little explanation. Its pursuit is in the full Jewish tradition. Moreover, the social developments of the time and the constitution of the universities made it simpler for Jews to enter this than any other profession.

But when all is said there remains an essential something that is a real source of wonder. A people scattered, disunited, numerically less than one of the smallest nations of Europe, has for a century provided from an effective German-speaking population of some two millions an ever-increasing proportion of the best scientific exponents in central Europe and Italy. Put the matter numerically and in the roughest way. In pre-Nazi Germany Jews formed about three-quarters of one per cent of the population. Of distinguished German mathematicians, physicists and medical researchers, they provided something like thirty times their due proportion, for at least twenty-five per cent of these were Jews. In Italy, where the Jewish population was only one per thousand, Jewish intellectual supremacy was even higher in certain departments. Well above fifty per cent of the distinguished Italian mathematicians were Jews.

We turn to glance at some individual achievements in the different sciences, beginning with mathematics.

Karl Jacobi (1804-1851), son of a Jewish merchant of Potsdam, was the first prominent German mathematician of Jewish origin and among the greatest mathematicians of modern times. A prolific writer and able teacher, he profoundly influenced the entire realm of mathematical thought of his age; there is hardly a branch upon which he did not leave an imprint. His greatest contribution was his development of the theory of elliptic functions. Very important was his work on the theory of numbers and of determinants and, especially, of functional determinants ("Jacobians"), of the calculus of variations, of differential equations and of the theory of mechanics. In the last two fields his achievements form the basis of modern mathematical physics.

Jacobi's pupil Leopold Kronecker (1823-1891) of Liegnitz in Silesia entered the business world but by the time he reached his early thirties had saved enough to give all his energies to mathematics. He became the recognized leader of the "Berlin school." His chief work was on the theory of numbers. His theory of equations was based on the idea of the theory of groups of Galois. Kronecker tried to "arithmetize" the whole of mathematics.

Among the greatest mathematicians of all time, whose ideas revolutionized the whole area of mathematics, was Georg Cantor (1845-1918). Though born at St. Petersburg, he was of German origin, speech and culture and spent nearly the whole of his life in Germany. Despite the greatness of his achievement he was a tragic figure. Misunderstood by his contemporaries and exhausted by the struggle to defend his views, he passed into depression mounting to insanity. It would be hardly possible to overestimate the value of his idea of sets or aggregates, which is fundamental to the study of the philosophical foundations of mathematics. Of prime importance, too, is his notion of transfinite numbers by which he overcame the *horror infiniti* of his predecessors. The notations of the so-called "transfinite cardinal numbers," represented by the Hebrew symbol א, remains his monument. The whole of modern analysis and theory of functions is based on Cantorian principles and his activity marks a period in the history of mathematics.

A distant relation to his namesake was the German scholar Moritz Cantor (1829-1920) who wrote an unsurpassed history of mathematics and organized much research in the subject.

At the age of eighteen, Hermann Minkowski (1864-1909) of Alexotas in Lithuania submitted his solution of a problem in the theory of quadratic forms to the Academy of Sciences at Paris. It earned the Grand Prix des Sciences Mathématiques. He became a professor at Goettingen, long a leading mathematical center. His introduction of the new notion of geometrical illustration into the theory of numbers created the so-called "Geometry of Numbers" and made his reputation international. No less important were his works relating to the new mechanics of Albert Einstein. His name must always be connected with the scientific revolution of the theory of relativity of time and space.

Felix Klein (1849-1925) was the recognized head of the Goettingen "universalists." He was a model professor both as teacher and as organizer of research. During the last forty years of his life his was the foremost mathematical influence in Germany. His many-sidedness is especially noteworthy. He held that all the various geometries should be regarded from the standpoint of the theory of groups. He was a very able propagator of Georg Friedrich Bernhard Riemann's theory of functions and his own researches in allied departments are of lasting value. A strong adversary of one-sided specialization, he dealt with all the branches of mathematics, seeking to link them more closely and to treat them as a unit. Klein played an important part in the planning and editing of the famous *Mathematical Encyclopedia*, and its success is largely due to his fascinating personality.

In addition to such men, whose genius is admittedly of the highest rank, there were and are scores of very eminent German-Jewish mathematicians whose distinction cannot yet be estimated. It is not possible here to list even their names. Of special interest, however, is Emmy Noether (1882-1936), the very gifted daughter of the well-known mathematician Max Noether (1844-1922). She was one of the most brilliant modern algebraists and perhaps the ablest woman mathematician since Hypatia. Through her numerous works she gave a new direction to the theory of algebraic fields, initiated by Evariste Galois and developed by Richard Dedekind and Kronecker. She laid down the foundations of the theory of ideals, of great importance in modern algebra. Expelled by the Nazis, she found refuge in the United States, where she died soon after her arrival.

Luigi Cremona (1830-1903), one of the outstanding Italian mathematicians, was the founder of the modern "synthetic" geometry. The "Cremona transformation" has proved of importance. In addition to this achievement, he was a senator and minister of education. Another Italian, Vito Volterra (1860-1940) was largely instrumental in the creation of a new branch of mathematics, the theory of integral and differential equations. He stands among the great mathematicians of modern times. Tullio Levi-Civita (1873-1942) died in the Vatican during World War II, having been dismissed in 1938 from his professorship in accordance with the Fascist anti-Jewish policy. With Gregorio Ricci (Curbastro) he laid the foundations of absolute differential calculus. This, as Einstein has recognized, made possible the formulation of the mathematical theory of general relativity. Levi-Civita's work in mechanics and theoretical astronomy is no less valuable. Gino Loria (1862-1954) has contributed greatly to the theory of curves and is of the highest distinction as a historian of mathematics. Federigo Enriques (1871-1945) earned great regard as a mathematical philosopher. There have been several other eminent modern Italian-Jewish mathematicians. When one recalls that only one Italian in a thousand is a Jew, the contemporary existence of at least five eminent Italian-Jewish mathematicians is, in itself a matter, of note.

Several of the most prominent figures in French mathematics have been of Jewish origin. The most notable are Georges Halphen (1844-1889), Paul Appel (1855-1930) and Jacques Hadamard (1865-   ). In general Jewish eminence in mathematics have been a special feature of the German scene. In the English-speaking world, however, a mathematician of the first rank was James Joseph Sylvester (1814-1897). As a loyal Jew he was unable to take a degree at Cambridge and still less to hold a fellowship. Nevertheless, he adorned the chair of mathematics successively at London, at the Royal Military Academy, Woolwich, at Johns Hopkins and at Oxford. In brilliance of conception, in acuteness of penetration, in fluency and richness of expression, Sylvester has had few equals among mathematicians of any age or nationality. At an earlier date Benjamin Gomperz (1779-1865) of London, though occupying no official position, helped to lay the foundation of modern vital statistics.

Success in astronomy usually demands official status and Jews, especially in the German zone, have thus been more handicapped than in mathematics. Nevertheless, there have been among them some able exponents of astronomical science.

One of the greatest of all astronomers, Sir William Herschel (1738-1822), was born at Hanover, his family being of remoter Jewish origin, and settled early in England. His discovery of the planet Uranus in 1781 brought him immortality. He conducted valuable researches on double stars, nebulae and star clusters and is the founder of modern stellar astronomy. His theory of the general structure of the universe still holds the field. His sister Caroline (1750-1848) was his very able research assistant, detecting some remarkable nebulae and many comets. His son Sir John (1792-1871) has a rank among astronomers second only to his father.

Wilhelm Beer (1797-1850), brother of the well known Parisian musician Giacomo Meyerbeer, having secured a competence in business, devoted himself to astronomy. With Needler he produced a great chart of the moon which marked an epoch in works of its kind. The Viennese Maurice Loewy (1833-1907) settled in Paris and with the support of Urbain Jean

Joseph Leverrier made researches on comets and on the photosphere of the sun. He became president of the French Academy of Sciences and, as so often, German loss was the world's gain. Samuel Oppenheim (1856-1928), a Moravian, president of the Astronomical Society of Vienna, was a master of astronomical calculations. His writings are devoted to the motion of stars, double stars and calculation of orbits of comets.

Despite the early death of Karl Schwarzchild (1873-1916)—the result of service in the German army during World War I—he was one of the greatest astronomers of his day. As a schoolboy he published two articles on determination of orbits. In later years he originated in photographic photometry a new method depending on measurement of density of star images. He introduced the use of a color index for stars, which has yielded information on their spectral types and surface temperatures, and is well remembered for his *Goettinger Aktinometrie*, a catalogue of 3,500 stars completed in accordance with his newly invented method. No less influential have been his mathematical study of star movements and of the structure of the solar system and his contributions to physical theory, especially in optics.

A German-Jewish astronomer who had a remarkable career was Hermann Goldschmidt (1802-1866) of Frankfort. After years in his father's warehouse he migrated in 1836 to Paris, where he earned distinction as a painter. In 1847 he turned to astronomy and in 1852 discovered a minor planet which he called Lutetia, the ancient name of Paris. He continued his researches and revealed the presence of fourteen previously unknown asteroids. Of Jewish origin also was Adolf Marcuse (1860-1930), who made numerous astronomical expeditions and, like Fritz Cohn (1866-1921), was director of the Royal Observatory at Berlin. German-Jewish astronomers who worked in Switzerland were Adolf Hirsch (1830-1901) of Neuchâtel, remembered for his services to the International Commission for Measurement of the Earth, and Rudolf Wolf (1816-1893) of Zurich, the accepted historian of astronomy.

Experimental physics, even more than astronomy, is dependent on that free access to a laboratory which only university status can provide. Nevertheless, many Jews have distinguished themselves in this field. The earliest was Moritz Jacobi (1801-1874), brother of the great mathematician. He was an architect but devoted much attention to the electrical deposit of metals, or electroplasty. The first Jew elected to the Prussian Academy of Sciences was Peter Riess (1805-1883), who devoted himself to the study of frictional electricity. But during the second half of the nineteenth century the number of German-Jewish physicists became so large that we can mention only a few of fully recognized distinction.

Eugene Goldstein (1850-1930) of Gleiwitz (Silesia) was one of the most skillful experimental physicists of modern times. His name is especially associated with the discovery of gamma rays. Great scientific men cannot be arranged in order of merit. Yet it is safe to say that Heinrich Hertz (1857-1894) is among the ten physicists of most influence during the past hundred years. He wrote little during his short life but every line was significant. He measured the length and velocity of electromagnetic waves and showed that they are the result of transverse vibration and are subject to reflection, refraction and polarization, like those of light and heat. He demonstrated that electromagnetic oscillations are propagated with the same velocity as light and finally demonstrated the electromagnetic nature of light. He adumbrated the principles of wireless and of X rays. It is pitiful to recall that Hertz's pupil, successor and literary executor, Philipp Lennard, himself a recipient of the Nobel Prize, shamed his old age by devoting himself to violent anti-Jewish Nazi propaganda directed largely against the teacher whose works he had edited and whose biography he had written.

Outstanding work in solar physics was done by Ernst Pringsheim (1857-1917) of Breslau. Certain other of his investigations led naturally to the quantum theory later enunciated by Max Planck.

Lise Meitner (1878-) of Vienna is among the small band of great women physicists of whom Madame Curie is the best known. Like hers, Lise Meitner's name is connected with radioactivity. She is especially remembered for her discovery in 1918, along with Otto Hahn, of the element protoactinium with atomic number 91. Her name will always be connected with the development of the theory of atomic energy.

Jews played a large part in the development of the classical physics of the nineteenth century. It may fairly be said that their contributions to the physics of the twentieth century based on relativity have been overwhelming in proportion to their numbers. The mention of Albert Einstein, Niels Bohr, James Franck, Ludwig Hertz must suffice. At the time of the Nazi seizure of power the general development of theoretical physics was greater at Goettingen than in any other university in the world. The dismissal of teachers under the "Aryan" edicts left the two great institutes of physics in that university almost entirely depopulated.

Few Jewish physicists distinguished themselves in the classical period outside the German zone. The most eminent was probably the American Albert Michelson (1825-1919), whose parents were driven from Germany when he was two years old. Between 1879 and 1882 Michelson made measurements of the velocity of light. In 1886, along with Edward Williams Morley, he made experiments on the relative motion of ether and matter, showing that the ether within a transparent medium is carried forward when it moves, but at a lesser velocity. In 1887 he had suggested the wave length of sodium light as a standard unit. This was put into effect in a very delicate experiment performed by him in Paris in 1892.

Since this unit depends only on the properties of vibrating atoms it is probably one of the most constant dimensions in nature. In 1900 he showed that spectral lines are tripled when the radiations emanate in a magnetic field. Michelson was the first American to be awarded the Nobel Prize.

Jews have perhaps been less successful in the practical development of physical principles than in investigating the fundamental properties of matter. In other words, they have excelled more in pure than in applied science. Nevertheless, there have been some very eminent inventors among them.

Siegfried Marcus (1831-1897) of Mecklenburg, a very gifted and versatile inventor, produced the first electrical instrument for regulating temperature and the first effective means of estimating earth movements. He is, however, particularly remembered as father of the internal-combustion engine, of which he constructed a model in 1864. By 1875 he had made a practical engine which he was able to drive in the streets of Vienna, where it was still preserved in 1937. The scheme of lighter-than-air dirigibles was first developed by the German David Schwarz, who built his first airship at St. Petersburg in 1892. His patents were afterwards purchased from his widow by Count Zeppelin.

Philip Reiss (1837-1874), born in poverty near Frankfort, began experiments on hearing apparatus in boyhood which ultimately developed into what was in effect a telephone (1861). This was exhibited in 1864. It was on his principle that Alexander Graham Bell and Thomas Edison perfected their device (1876). Emil Berliner (1851-1929) of Hanover settled in the United States in 1870 and there developed several inventions, among them the microphone.

Hermann Aron (1845-1913) was professor at the Artillery School at Berlin and developed an effective electrometer (1888). Leo Arons (1860-1919) was a picturesque figure who was dismissed from his post at Berlin University (1899) because of his Socialist sympathies. He did much to advance the practical applications of electricity. Notably he invented the first mercury vapor lamp (1896). Gabriel Lipman (1845-1921) of Luxembourg passed his scientific life in Paris, where he held a chair of physics. His development of color photography earned him a Nobel Prize in 1908.

Arnold Berliner (1862-1939) was put to death by the Nazis. A man of extraordinary scientific versatility, he rendered great services to German science as editor for many years of *Naturwissenschaften*, a journal for the general exchange of scientific views.

Chemistry was for long largely extra-academic. Thus Jews had opportunities that were denied them in physics. An early Jewish arrival in the chemical field was Heinrich Magnus (1802-1879), a pupil of Berzelius at Stockholm and of Gay-Lussac in Paris. He made many technical contributions of importance, perhaps the most significant being his determination of the coefficient of expansion of gases. He described a large number of new compounds, one of which, his "green salt" (a platinum-ammonia compound), is still known by his name. He ultimately became rector of Berlin University.

Charles Gerhardt (1816-1857) of Strasbourg was a pupil of Justus von Liebig and did most of his scientific work in Paris. He has a distinguished place in the history of chemistry, for his name is associated with the doctrines of valency and of chemical equivalents. He developed the molecular theory and made the first effective classification of organic compounds.

There is nothing more remarkable in the history of modern Germany than the rise of her chemical industry. Without this she could not have become a great power. There were so many and such able chemists of Jewish origin associated with this process that it is safe to say that without them her industrial development would have been impossible.

Adolf Frank (1834-1916) was the founder of the potash industry of Germany. He instituted the first potash factory (1861) at Stassfurt near Magdeburg, obtaining it from the local mineral deposit. Until then potash had been extracted from ashes burnt in or under pots, hence the name. With the Polish Jew, Nikodem Caro (1871-1935), he took the first step toward the nitrogen-fixation industry by forming calcium cyanide from nitrogen and calcium carbide. This industry was to be epochal not only for Germany but for the world.

Equally important for German economic development was Adolf von Bayer (1835-1917), professor at Munich whose mother was a Jewess. Just as Frank founded the German heavy chemical industry so did Bayer found that of fine chemicals. He was one of the foremost organic chemists of his day, the discoverer of the phthalein class of dyes (1874) and the first to synthetize indigo (1878). Synthetic indigo came entirely to take the place of the natural product. His patents passed to the Badische Anilin und Soda Fabrik, which formed the nucleus of the giant I. G. Farbenindustrie. Other patents absorbed by that combine were those of Heinrich Caro (1834-1910) of Poznan, the discoverer of methylene blue and of many other aniline dyes and of Carl Liebermann (1842-1914) of Berlin, who made important discoveries among the aniline compounds. German chemical industry was, in fact, substantially based on Jewish genius and Jewish enterprise.

The name of Victor Meyer (1848-1897) of Berlin is one of the greatest in the history of organic chemistry. At Heidelberg he was the favorite pupil and personal assistant of Robert Wilhelm von Bunsen. He succeeded Friedrich Woehler at Goettingen (1882) and Bunsen (1889) at Heidelberg, where he died by his own hand. His comprehensive researches on nitro compounds of the fatty series, upon isonitrous compounds and upon thiophene are among the most remarkable of the nineteenth century. The method he devised for estimating vapor density has become standard.

To give an account of all the German chemists of Jewish origin would be to write an appreciable part of the history of German chemistry from about 1860 onward. There have also been many distinguished Jewish chemists outside the German zone, but only a few can be mentioned here.

Henri Moissan (1852-1907) of Paris is remembered for several achievements. He succeeded in isolating fluorine, long a main problem in chemistry. He invented the electric furnace for very high and steady temperatures, which is known by his name. He demonstrated the nature of the diamond by producing it artificially.

Another brilliant chemist was the Englishman Raphael Meldola (1849-1915). He made the first oxazine dyestuff (Meldola's blue, 1879) which has become important for cotton dyeing, and worked much on naphthalene and azo compounds. He was very versatile, took much interest in biology, was a friend and correspondent of Charles Darwin and experimented with the coloration of animals.

A rather special place is occupied by Edmund Lippmann (1857-1942) of Vienna. He was the leading authority on the chemistry of sugars and the sugar industry and introduced the strontium process into sugar refining. He extended his researches into the history of the subject and finally became an authority on its alchemical aspects.

The name of Fritz Haber (1868-1934) will always be associated with the opening up of new industrial possibilities by a practical method of nitrogen fixation, the "Haber process" for the synthetic production of ammonia. It proved of the utmost importance to Germany's supply of nitrates both for agricultural and for military purposes. Nevertheless, in 1933 he was forced by the Nazis to leave Germany. This great benefactor of his country died in exile while Germany made war with the processes he had invented.

Richard Willstaetter (1872-1942) of Karlsruhe, a very great biochemist, discovered several forms of chlorophyll in plants. He demonstrated relationships between this green coloring matter and the red coloring matter in the blood of animals. He also produced the anesthetic avertin.

Mineralogy, as a science, has few exponents but among them the most distinguished were several who were Jewish. The first of them, the Parisian Armand Lévy (1794-1841), who spent many years in England, was a skilled mathematician and did much to introduce mathematical notation into crystallography. Harry Rosenbusch (1836-1914) of Heidelberg became head of a new school that dealt with the microscopy of minerals. Auguste Michel Lévy (1844-1911) of the Collège de France and of the French geological survey was among the founders of the modern science of petrography. Edward Suess (1831-1914), born in London, son of a German merchant, was long professor of geology in Vienna. His monumental *Face of the Earth* (1885) has been translated into many languages and gone into many editions. Many tendencies in modern geology have stemmed from it. Victor Goldschmidt (1853-1933), for many years a professor in Heidelberg and afterwards at Oslo, was one of the greatest exponents of crystallographic science. He introduced the binocular goniometer. His monumental work summarized the knowledge of the subject and his home became the recognized meeting place of the crystallographers of the world. His son succeeded him as professor of crystallography at Oslo.

Turning to biology, it might be thought that age-old urbanization of Jews would deprive them of interest in what were primarily countrymen's subjects. That this has not proved to be the case is doubtless due to the fact that the traditional Jewish attitude toward medicine has always involved contact with the problems of living things. In fact, since the German universities have been opened to them Jews have always been prominent in biology.

The name of Nathaniel Pringsheim (1823-1894) is especially connected with the study of algae. He demonstrated the reproductive processes of many kinds and showed that they were exhibited in an alternation of sexual and asexual generations (1856), both of which he elucidated. He produced a classic work on the life of the fern (1862) and later turned to plant physiology, doing much to explain the action of chlorophyll (1874). He subsequently demonstrated that light itself may have a lethal effect on plants (1879).

Ferdinand Cohn (1828-1898) of Breslau, a pupil of Johannes Mueller, was a peculiarly skilled microscopist particularly interested in the minute fungi. As author of the first monograph on bacteria he is the father of bacteriology. He rendered a great service by his encouragement of an unknown young man, Robert Koch (1843-1910). The latter's demonstration of the relation of anthrax bacteria to the disease was publicized by Cohn (1876); it contained the first evidence of the production of a specific human disease by a known species of bacteria.

Perhaps the most influential botanical teacher of the nineteenth century was Julius Sachs (1832-1897) also of Breslau and professor for many years at Wuerzburg. After applying himself to the study of the structure of forms of plants he turned to physiology and from 1857 became immersed in the problems of nutrition. He became convinced that chlorophyll is not diffused in tissues but is contained only in special bodies, the "chloroplasts." He showed that sunlight plays the decisive role in determining their action in reference to the absorption of carbon dioxide. Further, chlorophyll is formed only in light and, moreover, in different variations of light the process undergoes different degrees of activity. Sachs's researches covered every aspect of botany and he became a kind of botanical dictator.

Edward Strasburger (1844-1912) worked at Bonn, where he laid the foundations of the knowledge of the phenomena of nuclear division (*Mitosis*, 1875), clarifying the relation of nuclear changes to the sexual process. He was an encyclopedic botanist and his textbook is still in common use. Demonstrating that the chromosomes are individually recognizable and traceable from cell to cell (1905-1908), he thus laid the foundations of the modern science of genetics.

Approaching the medical field we are overwhelmed with names. From the beginning of the nineteenth century the number of distinguished Jewish names in the German-speaking countries have progressively increased in this their own traditional field. During the century interest became most intensely focused on the minute analysis of structure and its correlation with function. In this field Jews played a particularly prominent part.[17a]

The earliest influential Jewish figure in this movement was Karl Friedrich Canstatt (1807-1850) of Ratisbon, who made a study of the finer structure of the eye. Perhaps his greatest discovery was his pupil at Erlangen, Robert Virchow, accounted with Henle the founder of modern pathology.

Jacob Henle (1809-1885) of Fuerth near Nuremberg was the greatest German microscopic anatomist of his time and one of the greatest anatomists of all time, comparable only to Vesalius. He was professor of anatomy at Zurich (1840), Heidelberg (1844) and Goettingen (1852). His achievements in his special field were enormous and his work in histology was the first of its kind. He was a most versatile genius, for he was a poet, artist, orator and a very great teacher. And he was in his way a prophet, for he saw, as in a glass darkly, the microbic origin of infectious disease.

Benedikt Stilling (1810-1879), a skilled surgeon, introduced a new technique for the microscopic examination of the nervous system in the manipulation of which he was extremely expert. Structures in the nervous system are still identified by his name. He also instituted important advances in nervous physiology.

Ludwig Traube (1818-1876) of Ratibor worked in Berlin for thirty years, and was a founder of experimental pathology and of the scientific investigation of the action of drugs. He was an outstanding clinician and a particularly successful teacher. Gustav Valentin (1810-1883) of Breslau accomplished much in the physiology of muscle and nerve and in the digestion of carbohydrates. Gottlieb Gluege (1812-1898) of Brakel in Westphalia migrated to France and was thence called to Brussels. He did excellent physiological work, wrote the first treatise of pathological histology (1839-1841), began the study of parasitology and gave the earliest account of the essential cause of trichiniasis.

Robert Remak (1815-1865) of Posen worked in Berlin, where he had a distinguished reputation as a microscopist. His most eminent service was perhaps to demonstrate the true nature of the multiplication of cells. In 1842, long before Pasteur and Koch, using himself as guinea pig, he showed that certain skin diseases are caused by microscopic organisms. He was also a pioneer in electrotherapy.

Moritz Schiff (1823-1896) of Frankfort began as a zoologist and turned afterwards to physiology, which he taught at Florence and Geneva. He was a man of restless energy, almost prophetic insight and infinite originality, who covered too many fields to be a complete master of one. He anticipated Pavlov in the conception of conditioned reflexes, Claude Bernard in that of vasodilator nerves and much later work on the thyroid. He was a pioneer in many aspects of brain physiology and his experiments in the artificial production of diabetes via the nervous system (1856-1859) are classics.

Rudolph Heidenhain (1834-1897) of Breslau is especially associated with the interpretation of secretion in cellular terms. His research projects on the secretion of various organs and his stains and methods of staining are daily recalled in every biological laboratory. Julius Conheim (1839-1884), while professor at Breslau, revealed the true nature of suppuration, proving that the corpuscles of pus are formed from those of the blood. Despite his short life his contributions to pathological knowledge were numerous and very important.

Hugo Kronecker (1839-1914) of Liegnitz in Silesia, professor of physiology at Berne in 1885, distinguished himself particularly by his work on the fatigue and recovery of muscle, by his proof that the heart muscle can pass into a tetanic state and by his investigation of the mechanism of swallowing. He invented many ingenious physiological devices, and he is especially remembered for his demonstration that the heart's motto is "all or none," that is, that it will either contract to its fullest extent or not at all.

Carl Weigert (1845-1904) was perhaps the most eminent microscopic anatomist of the later nineteenth century. He introduced many new methods and was responsible for the highly important technique of bacterial staining which is one of the most valuable aids to modern scientific medicine. He also greatly added to the knowledge of the structure and function of the nervous system.

Elie Metchnikoff (1845-1916) was a Russian half-Jew who worked most of his life in Paris. His most important experiments, begun on the water flea, showed how amoeboid cells act as scavengers in the body, engulfing and digesting solid particles and notably bacteria. He showed that inflammation is accompanied by the gathering of swarms of these scavengers or policemen to the site of the injury.

Oscar Minkowski (1858-1931) brother of the mathematician, demon-

strated the relation between the pancreas and diabetes and thus led to the
study which culminated in the discovery of insulin.

Jacques Loeb (1859-1924) left Germany for America in middle life
and ultimately became head of the department of experimental biology
at the Rockefeller Institute. His research projects were of varied character.
Many of them were designed to demonstrate that much "vital" action can
be explained as response to chemicals or physical stimuli and do not involve the intercurrence of "mind."

These are hardly more than a random sample of those of central
European Jewish origin who made distinguished contributions to nineteenth-century medicine. The mind of any well-informed medical man will
react to the names of the members of this list.

The most characteristic development of modern medicine is the interest
in the vast complexity of the functions and minute parts of the body and
their reactions to its environment and especially to the organisms of
disease and to their products. In this field the Jewish contribution is
overwhelming. There is Alexander Besredka (1870-1940) of the Pasteur
Institute, Ludwig Brieger (1849-1919), who initiated the study of toxins,
Albert Neisser (1885-1916), discoverer of the gonococcus, Albert Frankel
(1848-1916) and Carl Friedlaender (1847-1887), discoverers of the
organism causing lobar pneumonia, Fernand Widal (1862-1929), elucida-
tor of the nature of blood reactions, Paul Ehrlich (1854-1915), the greatest
of biochemists, who made chemotherapy a science, Waldemar Haffkine
(1860-1930), introducer of protection against plague and cholera, Alexander Marmorek (1865-1923), whose serum provides protection against
streptococcal infection, Casimir Funk (1884-   ), one of the discoverers
of vitamins and originator of the name, Ernst Salkowski (1844-1923),
father of clinical pathology.

In the investigation of the functions of the nervous system a high place
is taken by Wilhelm Erb (1840-1921), who introduced electrodiagnosis
by induction, revealed the significance of the knee jerk and, along with his
contemporary Hermann Oppenheim (1858-1910), described many unrecognized pathological conditions.

Anatomy, in the old sense of the term, is regarded as one of the
"completed" sciences. Such significant contributions as were made to it in
the past generations were largely the work of Jews, among them the
Viennese Julius Tandler (1869-1910), last of the great anatomists, and
Emil Zuckerkandl (1849-1910), also of Vienna, whose account of the
structures of the parts of interest to otorhinologists is likely to remain the
standard work of reference.

Space fails even for the names of eminent exponents of clinical practice of
central European origin, but we mention Wilhelm Ebstein (1836-1912)
of Goettingen, and the great authorities on drugs Matthias Liebreich

(1838-1908) of Berlin, Oswald Schmiedeberg (1838-1921) of Dorpat, and Moritz Romberg (1795-1893) of Berlin.

Psychology in its medical applications may be said to be almost a Jewish science. Since our list must be brought to an end we do so with the names of Alfred Adler (1870-1937) of Vienna, Viktor Adler (1852-1918) of Prague, Sigmund Freud (1856-1939) of Vienna, and Bernard Hollander (1864-1934) of London. These men have not only introduced new methods of treatment but they have changed the whole direction of medical thought, practice and education. They have done more, for they have taught us a great deal about ourselves and changed the outlook of modern philosophy.

As one contemplates the galaxy of talent at which we have but glanced, two reflections arise. First, it is a tragedy for the Jewish people that the stream of life and thought that this implies has been broken. The break is more than that of the inevitable death of individuals, for the stock from which they have arisen has ceased to reproduce itself adequately. This is a loss to humanity as well as to the Jewish people. And secondly, it is a tragedy for the German people that, at the urging of a perverted outcast, it has extruded from its body politic a main source, perhaps *the* main source, of its claim to respect from the world of intellect. So far as the products of the intellect are concerned we must write *Germania fuit*, for henceforth German will be a language of secondary importance in the field of learning.

The intellectual future of the Jews themselves must depend, in this writer's opinion, upon many factors that are at present indeterminable, but most of all on one that *is* determinable. We live in a world in which religions and religious sanctions are breaking down. Religion is the one link that can unite the Jewish people. The problem is whether the Jewish religion can or cannot develop in a non-Jewish environment as one of the great world religions. If it can, the future of a special Jewish intellectual atmosphere is secure. If it cannot, Judaism will continue as a fossil fragment of the ancient Syrian civilization and, like other fossils, it will slowly but surely disintegrate.

Notes

[1a Cf. Elias J. Bickerman, "The Historical Foundations of Postbiblical Judaism," this work, Vol. I, pp. 99-101; see also Robert Gordis, "The Bible as a Cultural Monument," this work, Vol. II, pp. 28-33.]

[2a Cf. above, Alexander Altmann, "Judaism and World Philosophy: From Philo to Spinoza," p. 68; see also Ralph Marcus, "Hellenistic Jewish Literature," this work, Vol. II, pp. 73 ff.]

[2b Professor Saul Lieberman, the authority on Judaism in the Hellenic period, finds that "many parallels exist between the rabbinic natural science and that of the Greeks and the Romans of that time" (the first four centuries). He cites discussions of many natural phenomena—botanical, zoological and biological—comparing the concepts of the Rabbis and their contemporary scholars in other cultures. Professor Lieberman concludes that in natural science there were "great similarities between the methods, behavior, practices and notions prevalent among Jews and gentiles alike." However, he cautions that "no definite opinion can be pronounced until all that the Rabbis said about it is collected." See his "The Natural Science of the Rabbis," in *Hellenism in Jewish Palestine*, New York, 1950, pp. 180 ff. The editor of the present work is indebted to Dr. Solomon R. Kagan for questioning the opinion expressed by Dr. Singer.]

[3] *Sifre, Deuteronomy, Haazinu*, 306, f. 131 a. (Quoted from Montefiore and Loewe, *Rabbinic Anthology*, London, 1938.)

[4a] Cf. Judah Goldin, "The Period of the Talmud (135 B.C.E.-1035 C.E.)," this work, Vol. I, pp. 202 ff.; see also Altmann, *op. cit.*, pp. 77 ff.]

[5a] Cf. also above, Arturo Castiglioni, "The Contribution of the Jews to Medicine," Chap. 6.]

[6a] Cf. Cecil Roth, "The European Age in Jewish History (to 1648)," this work, Vol. I, pp. 231-232.]

[7a] Cf. Altmann, *op. cit.*, pp. 83 ff.]

[8a] Cf. Abraham S. Halkin, "Judeo-Arabic Literature," this work, Vol. II, pp. 148-150.]

[9a] Cf. Altmann, *op. cit.*, pp. 85-88.]

[10a] Cf. Roth, *op. cit.*, pp. 246 ff.]

[11a] Cf. Halkin, *op. cit.*, p. 151.]

[12a] Cf. Altmann, *op. cit.*, p. 86.]

[13a] Cf. *ibid.*, pp. 86-87.]

[14a] Cf. Roth, *op. cit.*, p. 245.]

[15a] Cf. Castiglioni, *op. cit.*, pp. 201-202.]

[16a] Cf. Cecil Roth, "The Jews of Western Europe (from 1648)," this work, Vol. I, pp. 273-274.]

[17a] Cf. Castiglioni, *op. cit.*, pp. 204 ff.]

BIBLIOGRAPHY

General Works

For the general scientific background: Charles Singer, *Short History of Science to the Nineteenth Century* (Oxford and New York, 1941, and later editions). For an objective study of Judaism and the Jewish people in world history: A. J. Toynbee, *A Study of History* (abridgement by D. C. Somervell) (Oxford and New York, 1946). For estimate of the contribution of Judaic thought to modern civilization: Edwyn R. Bevan and Charles Singer (eds.), *The Legacy of Israel* (Oxford and New York, 1927, and subsequent editions). For a general account of the contribution of Jews, as distinct from Judaism, Cecil Roth, *The Jewish Contribution to Civilization* (Cincinnati, 1940). Much material is to be found in that mine of well-arranged learning, George Sarton, *Introduction to the History of Science* (Baltimore, 1927).

Specialized Works

For the Rabbinic attitude toward nature: C. G. Montefiore and H. Loewe, *A Rabbinic Anthology*, selected and arranged with Comments and Introduction (London and New York, 1938). The entire Hebraeo-Arabic period with bibliography is treated by Aldo Mieli in *La Science Arabe et son rôle dans l'évolution scientifique mondiale* (Leyden, 1938). The specifically Hebraic aspect of Arabic science is treated with superb comprehensiveness, but for reference only, in Moritz Steinschneider, *Die hebraeischen Uebersetzungen des Mittelalters und die Juden als Dolmetscher* (Berlin, 1889-1893). For the translation of this literature into Latin, etc., Moritz Steinschneider. *Die europaeischen Uebersetzungen bis Mitte des 17 Jahrhunderts* (Vienna, 1904-1905), also only for reference. For the Marrano episode: Cecil Roth, *A History of the Marranos* (Philadelphia, 1941). For the Central European century: Louis Gershenfeld, *The Jew in Science* (Philadelphia, 1934); Ernst Heppner, *Juden als Erfinder und Entdecker* (Berlin, 1913); Felix A. Theilhaber and Ernst Heppner in *Juedisches Lexikon*, Vol. 2, cols. 462-467 (Berlin, 1928); *L'Apport d'Israel à la Civilisation: Conférence donnée à l'Hotel de la Paix, à Lausanne, le 8 fevrier, 1939, sous la Présidence de M. le Prof. Henri L. Miéville*, containing "La Médecine" by Professor Dr. Maurice Muret, and "La Philosophie et les Sciences," by Marcel Reymond (Lausanne, 1939); H. Newman (ed.), *The Real Jew, Some Aspects of the Jewish Contribution to Civilisation* (London, 1925), containing "The Jew and Scientific Research," by S. Brodetsky, "The Jew and Medicine," by Lester Samuels, and "The Jew and Chemistry," by Philip Blackman; Madison C. Peters, *Justice to the Jew* (London, 1899), Ch. VII: "The Jew in the Sciences."

For Medicine

Harry Friedenwald, *The Jews and Medicine* (Baltimore, 1944, 2 vols.), Sidney Osborne, *Germany and Her Jews* (London, 1939), Ch. 3: "The Jews as Physicians"; Ch. 4: "German Jews as Scientists and Inventors." Felix A. Theilhaber, *Schicksal und Leistung, Juden in der deutschen Forschung und Technik* (Berlin, 1931). *Cahiers Juifs*, Alexandria-Paris, Nos. 5-6, September-November, 1933: *L'Apport des Juifs d'Allemagne à la Civilisation Allemande*, contains "Le Progrès des Sciences Naturelles," by Horace Goldie, "Médecine, Chirurgie, Pathologie," by Ernst Fraenkel, "Mathématique, Physique," by Bernard Kwal and "Techniciens et Inventuers," by E. Aisberg. *The Jewish Review*, No. 5, June-September (London, 1933). *The Jewish Contribution to Modern Life and Thought in Germany* contains "The Physical Sciences," by H. Levy; "Applied Science," by F. Adler, and "Medicine," by Samson Wright.

POSTSCRIPT:
THE JEWISH CONTRIBUTION TO ASTRONOMY IN THE MIDDLE AGES

By Bernard R. Goldstein

Science in the Middle Ages has often been viewed as intellectually sterile; some ancient texts were preserved and they were then passed on, more or less intact, to the modern world. In this view, the Arabs were the principal conservers, and Jewish participation was largely confined to the transmission of scientific ideas from the Islamic world to Western Europe. However, as a result of a century of modern research into the history of the exact sciences, especially astronomy, it can now be said that this is grossly overstated and highly distorted. Indeed, the Arab and Jewish contributions include a large number of innovations and improvements as well as the creative use of ancient scientific achievements.

Islamic science began in the late eighth century, and by the early ninth century it far surpassed the scientific level of the immediately preceding era of late antiquity. This renaissance developed from contacts with Greek, Persian, and Hindu cultures, and yet it mimicked none of them. A number of the Islamic scientists of this period were in fact Jews whose literary language was Arabic. It was not until the twelfth century that Jews began to write scientific treatises in Hebrew, and this tradition continued into the sixteenth century. The earliest of these treatises were written in Spain, but in the thirteenth and fourteenth centuries, southern France was the dominant location, and later the vicinity of Constantinople was the scene of these activities. In addition to numerous translations of Arabic treatises, we find many original works that deal with scientific subjects.

In order to write on scientific matters in Hebrew, one created a technical vocabulary and literary style which would be intelligible to someone literate only in Hebrew. Thus, for example, it would not have been satisfactory to borrow a large number of words from Arabic. The process of introducing Islamic science into a new cultural and linguistic milieu took roughly a century, from the middle of the twelfth to the middle of the thirteenth century, and it involved the efforts of both translators and authors who paraphrased previously known material. But once this job was finished, scientific matters could be discussed in Hebrew, as well as in any other language, by an author dependent entirely on Hebrew sources.

We shall be concerned here only with three kinds of texts: translations, treatises in which Islamic science was applied to the problems of the Jewish calendar, and treatises which report original research.

From our point of view translations serve different functions depending on whether or not the original survives. In those cases where we have the original, we are in a position to judge the care and accuracy of the translator and to establish with certainty the equivalence between Hebrew and Arabic technical terms. However, greater interest is aroused when the original does not survive.

1. Among the important witnesses to the early Islamic tradition are the surviving Hebrew versions of Ibn al-Muthannā's commentary (written in the tenth century in Spain) on the astronomical tables of al-Khwārizmī (written early in the ninth century in Baghdad). Neither the original Arabic text of al-Khwārizmī's tables nor of Ibn al-Muthannā's commentary survives. In this commentary Ibn al-Muthannā attempted to explain the Hindu procedures, which underlie al-Khwārizmī's tables, in terms of Greek geometric conceptions unknown to the Hindus. This approach was perhaps natural because the Hindu procedures came to the Islamic world without any coherent explanation of their underlying principles. The topics discussed in this commentary include finding the celestial coordinates of the sun, moon, and planets, the computation of solar and lunar eclipses, and the determination of the time of day from the observed altitude of the sun above the horizon.

It may be of interest that the two Hebrew versions are quite independent and, in general, use different technical terms. Yet, leaving aside the problems of understanding the astronomical content, both versions would have been intelligible to any educated Jew in the Middle Ages, regardless of his knowledge of Arabic.

One of the Hebrew versions, composed by Abraham ibn Ezra (twelfth century), has an introduction which includes a description of the transmission of Hindu science to the Islamic world. It may be summarized as follows:

The first Abbasid khalif (c. 750) had heard of the sciences of the Indians and wished to have some of their books translated into Arabic, for "profane," i.e., nonreligious, sciences were unknown to the Arabs at that time. He was not sure that this was religiously permissible until the angel of dreams assured him of it. He sent for a Jew, and told him to go to Arin (i.e., Ujjain) to bring back an Indian scholar, which by some subterfuge the emissary managed to do. The Jew served as an interpreter between the Indian, Kanka, and the Arab who translated the book of Indian astronomy. Only traditional facts were presented in this book; the reasoning behind them was omitted.

2. There are many medieval treatises in which the Jewish calendar is described, but *The Sanctification of the New Moon* by Maimonides is certainly outstanding. This Hebrew text, composed toward the end of the twelfth century, is divided into three main sections: the calendaric rules that applied while there was a properly constituted court (Sanhedrin) in

Jerusalem; the rules that apply to the fixed calendar in use in his day (and still do today); and the astronomical computation by which the beginning of the month may be determined.

In the first section Maimonides presented a systematic formulation of Jewish law, even though it was no longer practiced (as he had done with many other aspects of Jewish law, *e.g.*, temple ritual). The two basic problems in the Jewish calendar are, first, the determination of the length of the lunar month, which is fixed by the appearance of the new crescent, and second, the determination of the length of the year as twelve or thirteen months so that Passover will occur in the spring. In ancient times, Maimonides reported, the Court resolved the first question by examining witnesses and the second by reconciling three principal criteria: the time of the vernal equinox, the ripeness of the barley crop, and blooming of the fruit trees. Maimonides argued that the members of the Court, who examined witnesses claiming to have seen the new crescent, had at their disposal astronomical calculations by which they could judge their veracity. Although he adduced no evidence to support this contention, he used it to justify the third section of his treatise where he discussed such an astronomical computation.

In the second section, Maimonides carefully listed the arithmetic rules for the determination of the fixed calendar, "a procedure which has been accepted by all the communities of Israel" (XVIII, 11). This information was widely known, and Maimonides did not mention anything unusual here.

From an astronomical point of view section three is of particular significance because the text deals with one of the most difficult problems in ancient and medieval astronomy, the determination of the day on which the new crescent will appear. Although Maimonides did not make any original contribution to astronomy, he clearly demonstrated his acquaintance with the most competent astronomical literature of his day, and this in itself is a real achievement. By making use of Ptolemaic astronomy, with some relatively minor medieval changes, he was able to define the astronomical conditions under which visibility of the new moon is possible and the direction of the horns of the crescent at that time.

3. Levi ben Gerson (1288-1344) is best known for his philosophical and exegetical writings; yet he also made a significant original contribution to astronomy. He was born in Bagnols in southern France, and as far as is known, he spent his entire life in that region, particularly in Orange and Avignon. Levi included his *Treatise on Astronomy* in his great philosophical work, *Wars of the Lord* (*Milḥamōt Adonai*), but because of its length and special character it is not to be found in the manuscripts or printed editions of the rest of the work. This treatise, which contains 136 chapters,

was translated from Hebrew into Latin, and both versions survive only in manuscript form.

In this treatise Levi attacked some of the fundamental principles of Ptolemaic astronomy and suggested several alternatives. It is not meant as an elementary text for students, and thus it is assumed that the reader has some familiarity with medieval astronomical literature. For his renovation of astronomy Levi preferred to rely on his own observations rather than those of the ancients, and for this reason he mentioned ten solar and lunar eclipses and about one hundred other astronomical events that he had observed. In the works of other medieval astronomers, however, contemporary observations are rarely mentioned, i.e., only about 250 observations are recorded in all of the medieval Islamic treatises presently known.

Levi's objections to Ptolemaic astronomy are largely of a technical character. For example, he argued that a consequence of the model for the moon's motion in the *Almagest* is that the moon would appear twice as large in diameter at quadrature (half-moon) as at opposition (full moon); since such a variation is not observed, it follows that Ptolemy's model is false. Levi's objection is valid, for despite the fact that Ptolemy's model accounts rather well for the direction of the moon, it distorts the moon's distance from the earth. In order to correct this fault in theoretical astronomy, Levi produced a model for lunar motion which eliminates this variation in lunar size. He also demonstrated that his model shows better agreement with his observations of the position of the moon than does Ptolemy's model.

Another topic considered in this treatise is the construction and use of an instrument, later known as the Jacob Staff, which Levi tells us he invented. This instrument consists of a ruler with a sliding crosspiece and allows the observer who holds the ruler before his eye to measure the angular distance between two stars or planets.

Levi was aware that some of the Islamic philosophers in Spain objected to Ptolemy's use of eccentrics and epicycles, and he specifically discussed the remarks of al-Bitrūjī (who flourished at the end of the twelfth century) which appear in a treatise translated into Hebrew in 1259. But these Islamic writers had not arrived at a viable alternative, and so they could not displace Ptolemaic astronomy, as Levi indicated quite clearly. On the other hand, he was not aware of the very competent contemporary research in astronomy in the eastern regions of Islam. If we compare Levi's approach with that of Ibn al-Shātir (fourteenth century, Syria),[1] the differences are striking. Both Levi and Ibn al-Shātir noticed that Ptolemaic lunar theory produced too great a variation in the apparent size of the moon. However, to remedy this Ibn al-Shātir constructed a model which cleverly used epicycles, whereas Levi depended upon a complicated eccentric device. Moreover, Ibn al-Shāṭir wished to produce agreement with Ptolemy's observations, whereas Levi preferred to find agreement with his own observations.

There are a number of reasons to believe that Levi's astronomical research was sponsored or supported by Christians. The first few chapters of his *Treatise on Astronomy*, concerning trigonometry and the Jacob Staff, were translated into Latin during his lifetime (in 1342) by Peter of Alexandria (an Augustinian friar) and dedicated to Pope Clement VI, who resided at Avignon. Shortly after Levi died, another treatise of his was translated into Latin by this same friar with the aid of Levi's brother Solomon.[2] In Levi's introduction to his astronomical tables, he says that he was writing them at the request of "many great and noble Christians." [3] A final bit of evidence is that Levi mentions, without naming him, "a distinguished cleric who studied this science [astronomy] with us." [4]

In conclusion, it may be said that a meaningful history of the Jewish contribution to science in the Middle Ages awaits the careful scrutiny of a far larger number of texts than have hitherto been examined. The bibliographical aids are generally available, and it remains the task of scholars to take advantage of them.

NOTES

[1] Cf. V. Roberts, "The Solar and Lunar Theory of Ibn ash-Shāṭir," *Isis,* XLVIII (1957), 428-432.

[2] Cf. L. Thorndike, *A History of Magic and Experimental Science,* Vol. 3 (1934), pp. 309-311.

[3] Cf. British Museum, Ms. *hebr.* Add. 26,921, fol. 12ᵛ.

[4] Levi ben Gerson, *Treatise on Astronomy,* Chap. 100, Bibliothèque Nationale, Paris, Ms. *hebr.* 724, fol. 186ʳ.

BIBLIOGRAPHY

ALTER, G., "Two Renaissance Astronomers: David Gans and Joseph Delmedigo," *Rozpravy Československé Akademie Věd,* LXVIII, No. 11 (Prague, 1958).

BENSAUDE, J., *L'astronomie nautique au Portugal,* 4 vols. Bern-Geneva, 1912-1920.

CANTERA BURGOS, F., "El Judio salamantino Abraham Zacut," *Revista de la Academia de Ciencias de Madrid,* XXVII (1931), pp. 63-309.

———, *Abraham Zacut.* Madrid (1935).

ESPENSHADE, P., "A Text on Trigonometry by Levi ben Gerson (1288-1344)," *The Mathematics Teacher,* LX (1967), pp. 628-637.

GOLDSTEIN, B. R., "The Book on Eclipses of Masha'allah," *Physis*, VI (1964), pp. 205-213.

———, "The Medieval Hebrew Tradition in Astronomy," *Journal of the American Oriental Society*, LXXXV (1965), pp. 145-148.

———, *Ibn al-Muthannā's Commentary on the Astronomical Tables of al-Khwārizmī*. Two Hebrew versions, edited and translated, with an astronomical commentary. New Haven, 1967.

IMMANUEL BEN YAAQOV (BONFILS), *Shesh Kenafayim*. Zhitomir, Russia (now U.S.S.R.), 1872 [in Hebrew].

KENNEDY, E. S. "Al-Khwārizmī on the Jewish Calendar," *Scripta Mathematica*, XXVII (1964), pp. 55-59.

MAIMONIDES, *Sanctification of the New Moon*. Translated from the Hebrew by S. Gandz, with supplementation and an introduction by J. Obermann, and an astronomical commentary by O. Neugebauer. New Haven, 1956.

MILLÁS VALLICROSA, J. M., *Estudios sobre Azarquiel*. Madrid-Granada, 1943-1950.

———, *Estudios sobre historia de la ciencia española*. Barcelona, 1949.

———, *La obra enciclopédica de R. Abraham bar Ḥiyya*. Madrid-Barcelona, 1952.

RENAN, E., "Les écrivains juifs français du XIV siècle," *Histoire Littéraire de la France*, XXXI (Paris, 1893).

SABRA, A. I., "The Authorship of the *Liber de crepusculis*," *Isis*, LVIII (1967), pp. 77-85.

STEINSCHNEIDER, M., *Die hebraeischen Uebersetzungen des Mittelalters*. Berlin, 1893; reprinted, Graz, Austria, 1956.

———, *Mathematik bei den Juden*. Berlin-Leipzig, 1893-1901; reprinted, Hildesheim, W. Germany, 1964.

———, "Mathematik bei den Juden (1551-1840)," *Monatsschrift fuer Geschichte und Wissenschaft des Judentums*, XLIX (1905).

———, *Gesammelte Schriften*, Vol. I. Berlin, 1925.

VERA, F., *Los Judios españoles y su contribucion a las ciencias exactes*. Buenos Aires, 1948.

CHAPTER 8

THE RISE OF THE STATE OF ISRAEL

By Oscar I. Janowsky*

1. INTRODUCTORY

The proclamation of the State of Israel on May 14, 1948, was at once the culmination of earlier developments and the beginning of a new era. A climax was reached in the building of the Jewish National Home, foreign rule was terminated, and the Jews of Israel assumed governmental powers. But the fundamental aims of the preceding period—Jewish immigration, land settlement and economic development, national regeneration and cultural unity—remained substantially unaltered. In large measure, too, the same agencies, men, and political groupings continued to provide leadership. The changes wrought by independence were most significant, but the stabilizing factor of continuity must not be ignored.

Origins of the State of Israel[1a]

The Jews or Hebrews have been identified with Palestine—the Land of Israel—since patriarchal beginnings. For some 500 or 600 years, the entire Hebrew people dwelt in the Land of Israel. Between the eighth and sixth centuries B.C.E., the Diaspora developed, and increasing numbers of Jews lived outside the homeland. But Palestine remained the center of Jewish life during the Second Commonwealth, and throughout that long period Jews in varying numbers continued to return to Palestine from the Diaspora. Even after the Romans sacked Jerusalem and burned the Second Temple in 70 C.E., the Jews of Palestine enjoyed a limited autonomy and continued to exert religious and cultural leadership over the Jews of foreign lands. After the fourth century C.E., persecution sapped the strength of Palestine Jewry and the population dwindled, but the idea persisted that the Jews and the Land of Israel were indissolubly linked to one another. Throughout the Middle Ages, and in modern times, too, small groups of Jews felt the need to "Return to Zion," and came to live in the Holy Land or at least to be buried in hallowed ground.

* I am indebted to Dr. Oskar K. Rabinowicz for suggestions covering the entire chapter, and to the Honorable Haim Cohen of Israel for comments on the section dealing with "Development of State and Government." This acknowledgment, however, does not involve delegation of responsibility.

The lure of Palestine for the Jews endured through the long centuries of dispersion. The land was remembered as the cradle of early peoplehood. There the Jews had been welded into what we call today a nation. National triumphs and catastrophes, perpetuated in religious lore, remained associated with the country. Above all, the religious and literary genius of the Jews had blossomed in the Land of Israel, and it ever remained as the spiritual haven. In prayer and poetic yearning, in synagogue art and group imagery, the Land of Israel symbolized at once the glory of bygone days and the hope of redemption as a people.

This set the stage for the Zionist movement of the late nineteenth and early twentieth centuries. The impulse came from within the Jewish group, primarily in Eastern Europe, where a cultural revival fostered national consciousness. The nationalist ferment among the submerged peoples of the area likewise affected the Jews, and the external pressures of anti-Semitism added a compulsive urge to return to Palestine and rebuild the old homeland. During the 1880's, groups of pioneers began to settle in Palestine, and an organized movement developed to encourage and sustain the settlers.

Theodor Herzl gave dynamic leadership to the incipient Zionist movement. A Zionist Congress was held in Basle, Switzerland, in 1897, and a Zionist Organization was established with the aim of creating "for the Jewish people a home in Palestine secured by public law." An administrative apparatus was set up, an official journal founded, financial instruments established, and Herzl launched diplomatic and personal negotiations which brought Zionism to the attention of governments and public opinion. Herzl's activities were cut short by untimely death, but the Zionist movement endured. Jewish immigration to Palestine continued and by 1914 there were some 85,000 Jews in the country.

The First World War proved decisive in the history of Zionism. On November 2, 1917, the British government issued the Balfour Declaration, pledging to facilitate "the establishment in Palestine of a national home for the Jewish People." Soon thereafter the British conquered the country and, when the war was over, Palestine was administered as a Mandate under the League of Nations, with the United Kingdom as Mandatory or trustee. The Balfour pledge was incorporated in the terms of the Mandate, which recognized "the historical connection of the Jewish people with Palestine" and the right to reconstitute "their national home in that country." Britain was to encourage the immigration and close settlement of Jews on the land; Hebrew (as well as English and Arabic) was to be an official language; and a "Jewish Agency" was to assist and co-operate with the British in the building of the Jewish National Home. The approval of the terms of the Mandate by the Council of the League of Nations gave international sanction to the ideal of a Jewish National Home in Palestine.

These triumphs of Zionism appeared decisive, but they proved insufficient for the realization of a viable Jewish National Home. The fundamental need was large-scale Jewish immigration, which depended on extensive economic development. The latter, however, required governmental powers which the Jews did not possess.

The British wielded the powers of government, but their primary objective was to advance imperial interests rather than Jewish national aspirations. Imperial interests required peace and stability in the Middle East with tractable native populations and governments. If the National Home could be built with Arab acquiescence, British good will would, no doubt, have been assured. But the Arabs opposed the National Home and resorted to rioting and bloodshed. Since suppression threatened to alienate the native population, the British sought to placate the Arabs by restraining Jewish efforts.

The commitments of the Balfour Declaration and the Mandate included safeguards for the Arabs, and the British attempted to steer a course which they regarded as just to both peoples. However, as the Arab-Jewish conflict sharpened, that course veered away from the requirements of the Jewish National Home. The emphasis shifted, and the demands of the Arabs began to outweigh in British policy the positive injunctions to further the Jewish National Home.

The Arabs proved the most formidable obstacle. Their leadership was imbued with the spirit of nationalism, and the masses were aroused to resist Jewish immigration and the entire idea of the National Home. The Jews argued that economic development increased the capacity of the country to absorb Jewish immigration without harm to the Arabs, and they adduced evidence that the latter profited from Jewish efforts. All to no effect. The Arab leadership repeatedly fomented violence, which taxed British patience, not so much with Arab resistance as with Jewish dynamism, which they came to regard as the cause of their difficulties.

In 1936, Arab riots broke out again and soon assumed the character of a national revolt. And in the late 1930's, world events predisposed the British to sacrifice the National Home to real or presumed imperial interests. The challenges of Hitler and Mussolini induced a policy of appeasement in Europe, in the Mediterranean, and in the Middle East. The Arabs, too, were to be appeased by the White Paper of 1939. The latter limited Jewish immigration to a total of 75,000 between 1939-1944, and thereafter the Jewish National Home was to be shut tight even against Jewish refugees, unless the Arabs approved. This was followed by drastic restrictions on land sales to Jews which barred further acquisition of land in 95 per cent of the area of Palestine. In the end, the Arabs were not appeased, but these measures committed the British to the scuttling of the Jewish National Home.

The Second World War taxed the statesmanship of Palestine Jewish leadership. They had no choice but to rally to the support of Britain, for the Nazis were the supreme enemy. However, the brutal enforcement of the White Paper of 1939 led to defiance. When the victims of Nazi terror perished for want of asylum, and when hapless refugees were turned away from the National Home, Palestine Jewry was bitterly resentful. Some elements resorted to terrorism, but among the Jewish population as a whole national discipline held. A threefold policy was evolved: co-operation in fighting the war was offered the British government; illegal immigration was encouraged in defiance of the British authorities; and the desire for a National Home hardened into a demand for statehood.[1]

The Building of the Jewish National Home

The Jews were obliged to expend much effort in defending their policies, in presenting evidence before the numerous British commissions of inquiry, and in pleading their cause in Palestine, England, and elsewhere. But their best energies were devoted to constructive work and, despite all hindrances, remarkable progress was made in the building of the Jewish National Home.

The work of building was guided by various agencies, some of which had the support of non-Zionists. But the most important were the instruments of the world Zionist movement. The leading body was the Zionist Organization, or the Jewish Agency (after 1929), which had the right under the Mandate of advising and co-operating with the British authorities on matters affecting the National Home. It mobilized the support of Jews and others, negotiated with the British, and represented the cause of the National Home before the organs of the League of Nations. The Palestine Executive of this body set up administrative departments which dealt with immigration, agricultural settlement, trade and industry, labor, education, health, and other functions.

The *Keren Hayesod* and the Jewish National Fund were the chief financial instruments. The former raised over £P18,000,000 between 1920-1946 (59 per cent in the United States), and figured in the financing of almost every important effort relating to the building of the National Home. The Jewish National Fund purchased land as the "possession of the Jewish people"; in 1945-1946, it held over 213,000 acres—about 44 per cent of all land owned by Jews.

Numerous other agencies co-operated in the development of the National Home. Baron Edmond de Rothschild of Paris had generously supported the early agricultural settlements, and in the 1920's the Palestine Jewish Colonization Association (PICA) took over his holdings and continued his work. By 1945, the Rothschild and PICA activities had resulted in the acquisition of about 123,000 acres and the founding or support of some forty settlements.

Hadassah, the Women's Zionist Organization of America, concentrated its efforts on public health and medical service, in which it became a major influence in the country. It maintained hospitals and clinics; pioneered in child welfare, nurses' training, preventive medicine, and the care of the tubercular; and co-operated in antimalaria and other health efforts. The Women's International Zionist Organization (WIZO) engaged mainly in the training of pioneer women in agricultural, vocational, and home-making functions.

Business organizations worked with private capital independently of the Zionist bodies. One example was the Palestine Economic Corporation, which participated in financing large undertakings, such as the Palestine Potash Company and the Palestine Electric Corporation. Finally, Palestine Jewry developed numerous agencies, notably the *Histadrut* or General Federation of Labor, which shared in the work of building, and profoundly affected the character of the Jewish National Home. During 1917-1945, the Jews brought into Palestine about £P154,000,000, of which about 29 per cent was secured by "national" and philanthropic agencies, and close to 71 per cent was imported and invested as private capital or brought by immigrants who settled in the country.[2] The Jewish investment in Palestine in thought, energy, and financial means was prodigious, and the achievement was worthy of the effort.

Population Growth and Economic Development. In 1882, when modern Jewish immigration to Palestine began, the Jews were an insignificant minority of some 24,000 who lived on sufferance. During the following sixty-six years, about 550,000 Jews settled in the country; and in 1948, the *Yishuv* was a self-reliant community of about 650,000,[3] imbued with national purpose, conscious of its aims, and determined to see to their realization.

Settlement on the land absorbed the best energies of the Jewish public bodies because Jews had long been city dwellers lacking experience in agricultural work. Land was purchased at high prices, mainly from large and absentee landowners, costly reclamation work was undertaken, and the pioneers were trained in modern methods of cultivation. In 1882, Jews were in possession of less than 6,200 acres; by 1946, some 446,000 acres had been acquired—barely 7 per cent of the country's area, or about 12 per cent, if the Negev is excluded. From five Jewish agricultural settlements in 1882, with a population of about 500, the number of settlements had grown to some 293 by 1948, with a population of about 110,000. When the Mandate came to an end, more than 16 per cent of the Jewish population lived in rural settlements and supplied close to one-half the food supply of the Jewish population of the country.[4]

Urban and industrial growth was equally marked. In 1948, the Jews of Jerusalem (102,000) were about two-thirds of the city's population. Haifa's Jews increased from some 3,000 in 1914 to 66,000 in 1944-1945 (55 per cent of the population). And Tel-Aviv, founded in 1909 as a suburb of Jaffa, became by 1948 an "all-Jewish city" of about 190,000.

Industry in the modern sense was barely known in Palestine before the First World War. Twenty-five years later, industry was an important factor in the economy of the country, and local needs and military requirements during the Second World War accelerated the trend toward industrialization. A few figures will reveal the extent of growth. In 1925, some 536 Jewish industrial establishments (exclusive of handicrafts) operated with less than 5,000 in personnel, about £P1,517,000 in capital investment, and horsepower of 5,733. In 1946, the corresponding figures were as follows: number of establishments, 2,500; personnel, 47,000; value of annual output, £P44,000,000; capital investment (1943), £P20,523,000; horsepower, 167,532. And it was Jewish immigration and the application of Jewish enterprise and capital which effected this radical expansion of industry.[5]

Domestic commerce and foreign trade likewise grew at a rapid rate. During 1923-1945, imports increased eightfold and, while exports lagged far behind imports, the *rate* of increase of exports was nearly twice that of imports. The balance of trade was consistently unfavorable, but the percentage of imports covered by exports rose markedly: in 1923, exports were less than 29 per cent of imports, but by 1945 fully 50 per cent of imports were balanced by exports. And the deficits in foreign trade were covered by capital imports of immigrants, the tourist trade, remittances from abroad, and funds secured by the Zionist agencies. A careful comparative study of the economies of the Middle Eastern countries led Alfred Bonné, Professor of Economics at the Hebrew University, to conclude that "Palestine is the only country presenting, mainly in its Jewish sector, the picture of an economy approaching that of the developed communities of the West."[6]

Distinctive Features of the Jewish National Home. Economic expansion was not uncommon in underdeveloped countries after the First World War. What made Palestine unique was the national and social setting in which the economy functioned. The National Home was not built on cheap labor, its architects were not dominated by the urge for profits, and the financial backers were motivated by national idealism or philanthropy rather than by gain. There was experimentation with co-operative institutions and a widespread conviction that social stability and change must rest on respect for human personality, individual freedom, and democratic processes.[7]

The dominating ideal was national rebirth, and *halutziut*, or dedicated pioneering, the means of its realization. The Hebrew language was revived, so that in 1948 over 75 per cent of Palestine Jewry above two years of age spoke Hebrew, and over 93 per cent of all children aged two to fourteen employed it as their vernacular.[8] The traditional Jewish faith in education was reflected in a far-flung voluntary system which imparted some elementary education to about 90 per cent of the Jewish children, and which expended in 1944-1945 nearly four times the Palestine government's education budget. The Hebrew University and the Haifa Institute of Technology were founded when the National Home was little more than a hope and a half-promise. Adult education in the form of evening courses, lectures, and tours brought knowledge to the isolated settlements as well as the urban centers. And Hebrew culture, the press, the theater, music, and the plastic arts were developed to a high level in two generations by a heterogeneous immigrant population.[9]

Advanced health and welfare services were a distinctive feature of the Jewish National Home. The work of Hadassah has been noted. In addition, Palestine Jewry maintained health organizations, among which *Kupat Holim* (the Sick Benefit Fund of the *Histadrut*) was the most important. The latter was a co-operative welfare agency which was established in 1912 with an initial membership of 150 and grew so rapidly that by 1945 it was serving about 46 per cent of the Jewish population of Palestine. This voluntary agency, and several additional smaller mutual aid associations, performed the functions of health insurance. Members received hospital and medical services, medicines, convalescent facilities, maternity aid, and sickness benefit allowances. The insurance funds were composed of contributions from workers and employers, but the Palestine government furnished neither subsidy nor administrative aid.

The results of Jewish health work were evident in the vital statistics. The death rate among Jews fell from an annual average of 13.70 per thousand during 1922-1925 to 8.08 per thousand during 1936-1940. Infant mortality among Jews was 132.11 per thousand in 1925 and 35.80 in 1945. And the influence of Jewish health measures reached the entire population of Palestine, including the non-Jews.[10]

The unique feature of the Jewish National Home was the social idealism which inspired large segments of the Jewish population. Physical labor—self-labor and toil especially on the land—was idealized as the preferred means of restoring the land and reclaiming the people.[11] Novel forms of group living were evolved in the collective settlements (the *kvutzot* and *kibbutzim*), in which property and income, production and distribution, were socialized. And this was done without compulsion, because human needs rather than preconceived doctrines determined social evolution. Those who preferred less pervasive forms of co-operative living fashioned the Workers Smallholders' Settlement (*Moshav Ovdim*) and the Collective Smallholders' Settlement (*Moshav Shitufi*), which combined individualized family living with varying degrees of collective production, or joined middle-class settlements, where co-operation was limited to joint purchasing, marketing, water supply, and the like. In 1945-1946, there were about 140 *kibbutzim* and *kvutzot* with a population exceeding 40,000; some sixty-two *moshavei ovdim* (population over 17,000), and nine *moshavim shitufiyim* (population close to 900).

The co-operative movement extended also to urban industries, trade, and services. *Tnuvah,* the most successful of the marketing co-operatives, was occupied with the domestic sale of agricultural produce. The export of citrus fruit was handled mainly by co-operatives. Jewish motorized transportation was almost wholly organized co-operatively. Co-operatives were popular in homebuilding, irrigation and water supply, in credit and banking. In 1945, when the Jews numbered less than 600,000, they maintained about 1,000 co-operative societies, with a combined membership of some 350,000 and total resources in excess of £P32,000,000.[12]

The *Histadrut* (General Federation of Jewish Labor) represented most of the elements affected by labor idealism. It was not the only Jewish labor organization, but by far the most important one. Organized in 1920 with an initial membership of 4,400, it grew rapidly, and after 1930 embraced over two-thirds of all gainfully employed Jews.

The *Histadrut* was one of the unique institutions developed in the Jewish National Home. It was a labor organization which included industrial and farm workers, the skilled and unskilled, wage earners, co-operative farmers, "white-collar" workers, and members of the liberal professions. The usual trade union efforts relating to organization, bargaining, and labor conflicts occupied its attention, and it won important concessions in collective bargaining, regulation of employment, insurance against industrial accidents, paid vacations, separation allowances, and the like. However, its functions went far beyond those normally associated with labor organizations.

Through co-operative self-help measures, the *Histadrut* sought to alleviate the effects of illness, old age, and unemployment. *Kupat Holim* (the Sick Benefit Fund) has been mentioned. An unemployment fund was used as a reserve for periods of depression, and assistance was provided for the aged, the invalid, and the dependent. Moreover, the *Histadrut* was involved in the ownership and management of units of production, marketing, transportation, banking, and other economic activities. Finally, it engaged in far-reaching educational and cultural services, conducting a network of schools and sponsoring adult education, book publishing and a labor press, artistic ventures connected with the theater and music, and recreational and sport organizations. Through these and other efforts, the *Histadrut* profoundly affected the character of the Jewish National Home.[13]

Democracy, too, was a distinctive feature of the Jewish National Home. The atmosphere of Jewish Palestine was democratic. Equality was a working principle of social relationships; respect for human personality and for individual differences prevailed; above all, freedom to differ and to express varying points of view was maintained. And voluntarism rather than compulsion governed political, social, and economic life. Jewish Palestine was not a utopia, but diverse elements were able to work together in relative peace in the building of the Jewish National Home.

Development of the Jewish Community

Palestine Jewry was a composite of immigrant groups differing in language, religious observance, social doctrine, and political orientation. But the overwhelming majority felt a sense of community which transcended factional loyalties and responded readily to efforts at representative unity. The first efforts in that direction were voluntary: in 1920 an Elected Assembly was chosen and it designated a National Council (*Vaad Leumi*) which pressed for government recognition. This was achieved under the Religious Communities Organization Ordinance (1926), which sanctioned a considerable measure of semiautonomous government.

Four elections were held for the Elected Assembly during the period of British rule—in 1920, 1925, 1931, and 1944—and each was contested by various parties and factions. The *Mapai* (the Palestine Labor Party) was predominant throughout, controlling 35 to over 50 per cent of the seats in the Elected Assemblies.[14] Other important parties were the middle-class groups, such as the General Zionists and Zionist Revisionists, the *Mizrachi*, and groupings of Oriental Jews.

The Elected Assembly and National Council served primarily as organs of Jewish public opinion, representing the Jewish point of view before the British administration, commissions of inquiry, and the Mandates Commission of the League of Nations. However, during the 1930's, the administrative functions of the National Council increased steadily as it assumed supervisory and financial responsibilities in education, culture, health, and welfare.

The Arabs and the Building of the Jewish National Home

The Jewish National Home was built in the midst of an Arab majority which was inevitably affected by the far-reaching changes. That the Arab population, or at least its leadership, was hostile has been noted, but this hostility was not the result of harmful economic or social effects suffered by the Arabs. On the contrary, they profited, at least materially, from the coming of the Jews.

The Jews bought all but an insignificant fraction of the land they acquired, and the exorbitant prices paid by them[15] enriched the Arabs. Except for some 317 families, Arab cultivators did not become landless as a result of direct land sales to Jews.[16] The Arab death rate and infant mortality declined, and the Arab population of Palestine grew more rapidly than in neighboring countries. Jewish medical and health facilities helped the Arabs, and banks and mortgage companies were available to them. They were encouraged by the example of the Jews to improve farming methods, develop industry, organize co-operatives, combat usury. Their wages were higher, agricultural productivity greater, and per capita national income larger than in neighboring Arab lands.[17]

Moreover, Jews made repeated attempts to promote understanding and co-operation with the Arabs. The *Histadrut* helped in the organization of Arab labor and in the attainment of better working conditions. In the middle 1920's, the *"Brit Shalom"* group, in the early 1940's the *"Ihud"* group, and especially the League for Arab-Jewish Rapprochement, all worked for co-operation. These elements were not numerous, but they included prominent Zionist leaders who exerted considerable influence.[18]

However, the differences between Arabs and Jews were too fundamental to be bridged by these efforts. Estrangement deepened and the two peoples constituted separate and self-contained communities. By the end of the Second World War, the Jews were a vigorous community with a dynamic economy and effective political leadership. The Arabs, too, were organized, determined, and militant. A quarter-century of conflict had reached a critical stage, and decisive events were in the making.

2. FROM NATIONAL HOME TO SOVEREIGN STATE

After the Second World War

The Second World War brought on an uneasy truce between Palestine Jewry and the British. Official Jewish leadership, represented by the Jewish Agency, was centered in Palestine, with David Ben-Gurion as the dominant personality. Its basic position was opposition, not to British rule, but to the policy of the White Paper of 1939—a subtle distinction but an important one. The rescue of Jews from certain death at the hands of the Nazis was the central issue, and when the British refused to tolerate the infiltration of refugees, they met with defiance. So far as official Jewish leadership was concerned, this defiance was limited to illegal immigration; in other matters affecting the war, the British had the co-operation of the *Yishuv*. However, dissident elements were straining against this Jewish policy, and to clarify this factor a glance backward is necessary.

During the Arab revolt of the late 1930's, the *Haganah* (Jewish defense units), an arm of the Jewish Agency, was under restraining orders not to engage in retaliatory terror against the Arabs. The policy was to co-operate with the British, and some 19,000 Jews were enlisted as auxiliary police. The Revisionists, however, organized in 1937 the *Irgun Zvai Leumi* (National Military Organization), which took punitive measures against the Arabs and promoted illegal immigration, employing violence when necessary. By 1938, the *Haganah*, too, was encouraging illegal immigration, and when the White Paper was issued in 1939, its co-operation with the British lapsed. The *Haganah* avoided clashes with the British, but it, too, defied the immigration law. The British retaliated by dismissing and disarming Jewish auxiliaries, and by resorting to mass arrests, collective fines, and elaborate searches for arms. The *Haganah* persisted in the policy of restraint (*Havlagah*), but the reply of the *Irgun* was guerrilla war upon the British.

During the Second World War even the *Irgun* co-operated for a time with the British, but this led to a secession from its ranks and the appearance of the Fighters For Freedom (the Sternists), who continued to employ terror against the Mandatory power. The vigorous reaction of the British, who did not distinguish between degrees of opposition, led to a renewal of *Irgun* terrorism. By 1944, the *Irgun* and the Sternists were in open revolt.

When the World War came to an end in Europe on May 8, 1945, all elements in Palestine were consolidating their positions for the final struggle. The Arab States had become allies by declaring war on Germany and Japan the preceding February, and they had formed the League of Arab States, which warned against any compromise on the issue of Jewish immigration. The Palestine Arabs, too, demanded that the White Paper be enforced.

The mood of the masses of Palestine Jews was one of anxious hope that the policy of the White Paper would be abandoned. This hope was not entirely baseless. The British admitted to Palestine the illegal immigrants who had been interned at Mauritius. A Labor government came to power in London in July, 1945, and the British Labor Party had been emphatically pro-Zionist. The feeling of horror which gripped the world when the enormity of Nazi crimes against the Jews stood revealed encouraged the Jews to believe that the gates of Palestine would not be closed to the remnant which had been snatched from the gas chambers. The White Paper policy could not endure!

In these circumstances the Jewish Agency pursued a twofold policy: it appealed to the humanitarian impulses of public opinion, especially in the United States, to reinforce the demand for the admission of refugees to Palestine; and it defied the White Paper by organizing and promoting illegal immigration. The effect was to focus attention on the dramatic issue of refugee settlement. The survivors of the Nazi extermination camps had no homes to return to, and no state offered them asylum. The Jewish National Home appeared to be the proper place for them.

This policy appeared promising. European governments no longer hindered the movement of Jews toward Palestine, as they had done during the war. American public opinion was aroused: members of Congress and state governors appealed to the President on behalf of the Jews; and later, in

December, 1945, both houses of Congress passed a resolution favoring free Jewish immigration into Palestine and the development of the country as a democratic commonwealth.

In August, 1945, President Truman requested the British government to admit 100,000 refugees (displaced Jews) to Palestine.[19] This embarrassed the British, because the fundamental problems were ignored and the issue narrowed to the moral and humanitarian plea of salvaging victims of brutal persecution. But the admission of 100,000 Jews would mean the violation of the White Paper and a radical departure from accepted policy. This the Labor government was not prepared to do.

Like its predecessors, the Labor government hoped to hold the Middle East with the aid of the Arabs. It therefore agreed to admit no more than 1,500 Jews a month, but to ease the tension it proposed that an Anglo-American Committee of Inquiry examine the entire situation. Apparently it was hoped thus to set the humanitarian problem into its complex political framework. The committee's report appeared in April, 1946, and it recommended, among other measures, the admission of 100,000 refugees to Palestine, the removal of restrictions on land sales, economic development, and the suppression of terrorism and violence.[20] This meant the repudiation of the White Paper, and the Arab States responded immediately by threatening violence. The British government decided to delay action, pending further negotiations with the American government. The White Paper remained British policy.

The delays and disappointments lashed Palestine Jewry to fury. Many months had passed since the end of the war, and the hapless victims of the Nazis still languished in camps. The methods of diplomacy had been tried and powerful friends had interceded, but the British government held fast to the White Paper policy and showed no signs of relenting. To all appearances, the Arab threats of violence were more effectual than the policy of restraint of the Jewish Agency. As hopes for a peaceful solution and faith in moderation withered, violence became inevitable.

The appeal of the terrorist methods of the *Irgun* gained ground. Apparently its appraisal of British intentions had been more realistic. The Jewish Agency still tried to distinguish between disaffection and rebellion, between defiance of and resistance to the White Paper and open warfare on the British administration. It tried to avoid bloodshed by directing *Haganah* attacks not against British personnel but against barriers to illegal immigration. But the failure of diplomacy to achieve results in London, and the indiscriminate reprisals of the military in Palestine, caused some members of the Jewish Agency to waver, especially since it was becoming increasingly difficult to restrain certain leaders of the *Haganah*. The Jewish Agency therefore authorized from time to time co-operation with the *Irgun* in local raids on British installations which hampered illegal immigration.

When the British government declined to admit 100,000 Jews, as recommended by the Anglo-American Committee, the *Haganah* decided on a demonstration of force, in the hope of influencing the British and probably also to reassure the *Yishuv* so that leadership would not fall into the hands of the extremists. In June, 1946, the *Haganah* attacked vital communications, blowing up strategic bridges on the borders and damaging the railway workshops. The British retaliated with mass arrests, including leaders of the Jewish Agency and National Council, widespread house searches for arms, and other repressive measures. This only encouraged the extremists, and in July the Government Offices in the King David Hotel in Jerusalem were demolished by the *Irgun*, with the loss of nearly 100 British, Arab, and Jewish lives. The *Yishuv* was shocked by this outrage, and the Jewish Agency denounced it as a "dastardly crime." Shortly thereafter, condemning other activities of the *Irgun*, the Agency announced that it would root out terrorism.

Skillful leadership on the part of the British might have isolated the terrorists, but the military authorities of Palestine ignored the declaration of the Jewish Agency and met the challenge by reprisals upon the entire *Yishuv*. Tel-Aviv was isolated for several days, a curfew was imposed on all Palestine Jews, many thousands were interrogated, hundreds detained, and the Military Courts imposed death sentences on terrorists. The British security forces became a veritable army of occupation.

The temper of the military was symbolized by an order issued by the commanding general against fraternization with Jews. He condemned the entire Jewish community of Palestine, placed all Jewish homes and business establishments out of bounds, forbade "any intercourse with any Jew," and concluded by assuring the troops that they would thus "be punishing the Jews in a way the race dislikes more than any, by striking at their pockets and showing our contempt for them."

The Jews, not yet recognized as ripe for practical statecraft, were more fortunate in their spokesman than the experienced and stately British Empire. In October, 1947, when bitterness against the British had become even more intense, Ben-Gurion said to the Elected Assembly in Jerusalem,

We have not absolved the Labor Party of its pledges, nor will we, but we shall not entreat it to carry out a new policy against both inclination and ability. Well and good—the British wash their hands of us and depart! Go in peace, we say: we can manage—and at once—if you will just let us be.[21]

The British government in London was not as reckless as the military in Palestine, but it, too, was determined not to yield to Jewish pressure, diplomatic or activist. It sanctioned the deportation of illegal immigrants to Cyprus, which began in August, 1946. This intensified violence which was met with further repression.

About the same time, the so-called Morrison Plan proposed the division of Palestine into Arab and Jewish provinces, with the British in effective control.[22] It was rejected by Arabs and Jews and also by President Truman. Further negotiations with Arabs and Jews followed, but no solution could be found.

By the beginning of 1947, the Palestine conflict had reached deadlock not only as between Arabs and Jews but for the British as well. The Arabs were adamant against any compromise. Jewish opposition in Palestine could not be liquidated without bloody repression, and world opinion would not tolerate that. And American public opinion, unequivocally expressed by President Truman, pressed for action on the admission of refugees. Harassed and impotent, the British Government announced on February 25, 1947, that it would submit the Palestine problem to the United Nations.

It must be noted that this decision did not mean the abandonment of the Mandate. Apparently the aim was to convince the United Nations and world opinion of the soundness of British policy. Assured that the Mandate was unworkable, and that chaos would ensue if they withdrew, the British appear to have expected little more than futile debates in the United Nations, and a new mandate from that body to govern Palestine without the troublesome provisions for Jewish immigration, the Jewish Agency, and the National Home. From present available evidence, one can only assume this conclusion, but the assumption appears warranted by subsequent British actions. At all events, the British remained in Palestine.

Palestine Before the United Nations

The General Assembly met and, after extensive discussions, adopted a resolution on May 15, 1947, constituting the United Nations Special Committee on Palestine (UNSCOP) to investigate the problem and present proposals for a solution. The committee's report, submitted at the end of August, unanimously recommended that the British Mandate be terminated as soon as practicable; that Palestine achieve independence after a short transitional period; that the economic unity of Palestine be preserved; and that in the interval between the end of the Mandate and independence, the governing authorities in Palestine should be responsible to the United Nations. Other recommendations dealt with the Holy Places, the displaced Jews, and with the need for a peaceful transition to independence and democratic government in Palestine thereafter.

On the basic question of Palestine's future, the eleven members of the committee were divided. A majority of seven members proposed partition into an Arab state, a Jewish state, a special regime for the city of Jerusalem under United Nations control, and economic union. A minority of three favored a federal state, with Jerusalem as its capital and autonomous Arab and Jewish provinces. One member abstained from voting on either plan.

The General Assembly convened in September, 1947, and after lengthy debates in committees and in full session adopted the partition plan by a vote of thirty-three to thirteen (with ten absentions) on November 29, 1947. The United States, the Soviet Union, and France voted for partition; the United Kingdom abstained. In approving the partition plan, the General Assembly added two significant provisions, namely: a United Nations Palestine Commission of five states was established to implement the decision, and the Security Council was asked to provide for the enforcement of partition.[23]

The Jews accepted partition. The leadership of the Palestine Arabs defied the United Nations and determined to resist. And the Arab States threatened invasion of Palestine. Under these circumstances, successful and reasonably peaceful implementation might have been achieved if the Palestine Commission had been able to effect a gradual and orderly transfer of authority from the Mandatory power to the Arab and Jewish States; if the Security Council had taken an unequivocal and forceful stand against open warfare; and, above all, if the British government had co-operated or at least refrained from hindering the process of orderly partition. None of these conditions obtained.

The Palestine Commission sought to arrange for the establishment of Arab and Jewish Provisional Councils of Government and for a progressive transfer of administrative authority to itself by taking over areas as the British evacuated them. It planned to supervise the Provisional Councils during the transitional period following the termination of the Mandate, to control military forces, to maintain essential public services, to protect the Holy Places, to delimit frontiers, to divide government assets, and to make preparatory arrangements for economic union. The British government, however, announced that it would co-operate only in a solution acceptable to Arabs and Jews. Since partition did not meet this condition, it declared that the Mandate would be terminated on May 15, 1948, and its troops evacuated in stages soon thereafter.

Moreover, the Palestine Commission was informed that Britain would remain in full control until the end of the Mandate, and that there would be no piecemeal or gradual transfer of authority. While it remained the Mandatory power, Britain refused to facilitate the delimiting of frontiers, the establishment of Provisional Government Councils, the organization of armed militias, or the transfer of any administrative personnel to the Commission. In fact, the Commission was not authorized to enter Palestine until two weeks before the end of the Mandate. Without consulting the Commission, the British also proceeded to dispose of government assets. They blocked sterling balances and excluded Palestine from the sterling area. Such measures invited chaos.

While the United Nations was grappling with the problem, the situation in Palestine deteriorated rapidly. Illegal immigrants continued to arrive and, when apprehended, were forcibly transferred and interned in Cyprus. Terrorism by Jews and reprisals by the military became endemic. A climax was reached in July, 1947, when the ship *Exodus*, with over 4,000 illegal immigrants, was intercepted. The refugees were sent back to France, where they had embarked, and when they refused to leave the ships they were taken to Germany and forcibly interned in a displaced persons' camp.

The partition resolution passed by the General Assembly called on the Mandatory power to evacuate, not later than February 1, 1948, a port and hinterland in the territory of the projected Jewish state in order to facilitate substantial Jewish immigration. The British government declined to comply.

The passage of the partition resolution by the General Assembly was the signal for open fighting between Arabs and Jews in Palestine, and early in 1948 armed Arab bands entered the country from Syria and Transjordan. Casualties were counted in the thousands, and the British either could not or would not maintain law and order, for which they were solely responsible, as they refused to allow the Palestine Commission to intervene.

The Arab States, too, were arming for invasion, and there is no record of any efforts on the part of the British to dissuade or restrain them. In fact, the British continued to supply arms to Arab states in accord with treaty obligations, while they imposed and enforced an embargo on Palestine. And they refused to permit the formation of a Jewish militia. The Arabs could not but conclude that the British would welcome action in defiance of the partition resolution of the United Nations.

Had the Security Council taken a determined stand, open warfare might have been avoided. But the Security Council took no action for nearly three months, and when it did take up the question toward the end of February, 1948, it was evident that the policy of the British had had its effect. After prolonged discussions, a resolution presented by the United States delegation was adopted, calling for another session of the General Assembly to reconsider the question.

The Assembly convened on April 16, 1948, and its committees debated at length a United States proposal for a temporary trusteeship for Palestine until a permanent solution could be found. In the end, this idea failed because the Arabs favored it only if it meant the total abandonment of a Jewish state, the Jews rejected it, and no state other than the United States was prepared to provide armed contingents for its enforcement. On May 14, 1948, this tragic fumbling reached a dramatic denouement. While the Assembly was in plenary session it was announced that the State of Israel had been proclaimed and that the United States had granted it *de facto* recognition. The Assembly then resolved that the Security Council appoint a Mediator to seek peace for Palestine.[24]

The War of Independence

What is known in Israel as the War of Independence began immediately after the adoption of the partition resolution by the General Assembly on November 29, 1947, and ended with the Israel-Syrian armistice on July 20, 1949. It consisted of two distinct phases, marked off by the termination of the Mandate at midnight on May 14, 1948. During the first phase, the British were responsible for law and order, but desultory fighting punctuated the entire period. The Palestine Arabs attacked immediately after the adoption of the partition resolution and were soon joined by irregulars from across the borders. Isolated Jewish settlements were attacked, attempts were made to block vital roads, and fighting flared up in the cities of mixed population, including Jerusalem. After the middle of February, the entire country was affected. Arabs and Jews clashed, vantage points were seized, and truces arranged by the opposing forces, while the British did little to stay bloodshed. In fact, the Arab Legion, a well-armed Transjordan force commanded by British officers, became involved shortly before the termination of the Mandate.

By May 14, 1948, when the State of Israel was proclaimed, the Jews held Haifa, Jaffa, Safed, and Tiberias, most of the roads had been cleared, and numerous Arab villages in the Jewish sector of the country had been occupied. In Jerusalem there was a stalemate: the Arabs held most of the Old City, within the walls; the Jews held most of the New City; but, while some of the surrounding Arab strong points had been taken and supplies pushed through, the road to the coast was blocked and the Jews of Jerusalem were under siege. One thing was clear when the first phase of the war ended—the Jews more than held their own against the Palestine Arabs and the irregulars from across the borders.

The second phase began on May 15, 1948. The Arab States—Egypt, Transjordan, Iraq, Syria, and Lebanon, with auxiliaries from Saudi Arabia and Yemen—invaded Palestine with high expectations of a quick and easy victory. But the Jews, far from being overwhelmed, made notable gains. The north held against the Syrians and Acre (Acco) was taken. The Arab Legion seized the Old City of Jerusalem and cut the coastal road, but the Jews built a new road—the "Road of Valor"—and relieved the New City. The Egyptians were ineffective in the south.

It was the turn of the United Nations to bring the fighting to an end. On May 20, 1948, Count Folke Bernadotte of Sweden was appointed Mediator to help restore peace to Palestine. About the same time, the United States proposed that the Security Council order a cease-fire with a clear threat of sanctions against the recalcitrant party. Israel favored and the Arab States opposed such action. The Soviet Union and France supported the resolution, but the United Kingdom rejected it, and it failed to pass. Instead a mild resolution was adopted calling on Israel and the Arab States to arrange a cease fire. Israel agreed, but the Arab States refused.

On May 29, 1948, a United Kingdom resolution was adopted, calling for a four-week truce and warning that noncompliance would lead to the consideration of enforcement action by the Security Council. This had the desired effect and Bernadotte, the Mediator, succeeded in establishing a four-week truce, beginning on June 11, 1948.

Before the truce expired on July 9, the Mediator and the Security Council requested both parties to extend it. Israel made a favorable reply, but the Arab States refused and fighting was renewed, with Israel scoring further gains. The Council thereupon ordered a cease-fire, indicating that noncompliance would lead to the consideration of sanctions. On July 18, 1948, the second truce went into effect without a time limit.

Clashes continued to occur during 1948-1949, but the truce was invariably restored by the Mediator, supported by Security Council warnings to the adversaries. The Mediator, Bernadotte, was assassinated by Jewish terrorists on September 17, 1948, and the American, Ralph J. Bunche, became Acting Mediator. It was the latter who succeeded in negotiating the armistice agreements between Israel and Egypt (February 24, 1949), Lebanon (March 23, 1949), Transjordan (April 3, 1949), and Syria (July 20, 1949). Demarcation lines were set and Mixed Armistice Commissions, in each case with a chairman from the staff of the United Nations, were appointed to deal with infractions. The agreements were therefore under the supervision of the United Nations.[25]

In sanctioning the armistice agreements, the United Nations recognized the reality of the partition of Palestine. But the partition was the issue of war and not of the conciliatory efforts of the world organization. The United Nations Special Committee on Palestine had proposed a division based mainly on the distribution of population, and had awarded about 3,600 square miles to the Arab state and about 6,400 square miles to the Jewish state. And its proposals for economic union had held out the hope of a viable economy for both Arabs and Jews. The partition resolution of the General Assembly (November 29, 1947) had made some revisions, so that the Arab state was to receive about 4,300 square miles and the Jewish state about 5,700 square miles.[26] The Jews had accepted the change, keeping the door open to a peaceful solution and economic union.

However, the Arabs rejected the proposals for a peaceful settlement and resorted to war, while the British refused to co-operate in the implementation of the decisions of the United Nations. The war and the armistice agreements resulted in the occupation by Israel of territory including Acre, Lydda, Ramleh, Beersheba, and Nazareth, extending its area to about 7,000 square miles. The rest of Palestine was divided: Egypt held the

Gaza strip, and Transjordan seized the remainder despite protests from the other Arab States. In addition, the Jerusalem enclave, which was to have been internationalized, was held in part by Israel and in part by Jordan in defiance of the United Nations.

At this writing, [Spring, 1958] the armistice agreements define the uneasy relation between Israel and the Arab States because the attempts to achieve a political settlement have failed.

Bernadotte, the Mediator, had proposed modifications of the partition plan which abandoned the idea of economic union of the Arab and Jewish states, and which, Israel claimed, would have reduced its territory to some 2,100 square miles.[27] The Arabs were quite willing to receive the additional territory, but they refused to accept the State of Israel which was part of the Mediator's plan. Rejected by both parties, the plan was dropped.

In December, 1948, the General Assembly established the United Nations Conciliation Commission to assist Israel and the Arab States in achieving a final settlement through direct negotiation. No mention was made of the original partition resolution.

The Conciliation Commission made repeated efforts to find the basis for a settlement. Negotiations were held in Lausanne, Switzerland, during 1949 and subsequently at New York, Geneva, and Paris. But the Arab States and Israel could not be brought together in face-to-face negotiations. On the basic issues, too, no agreement could be reached. Israel sought an over-all peace settlement; the Arab States preferred to deal with individual issues, especially with that of the Arab refugees who had fled during the war. On this issue, Israel was ready to readmit a limited number of the refugees as an integral part of a peace settlement, but the Arab States would not agree even in principle to the settlement of refugees in other lands. As to Jerusalem, Israel agreed to international control of the Holy Places but not of the entire part of Jerusalem which it held. The Arab States, not including Jordan, accepted in principle an international regime for Jerusalem, but Transjordan, which held the Old City, rejected the idea. The same deadlock held on the question of boundaries. The Arab States, which had rejected the original partition plan, now sought to secure the cession of the additional territories seized by Israel, but it was not clear that they would accept that as a final settlement. Israel insisted on its *de facto* boundaries.[28]

Thus the Palestine situation remained and remains unsettled to this day. No peace with the Arab States has been achieved, and the armistice agreements define a *de facto* situation. In Jerusalem, too, Israel and Jordan hold their respective segments without the approval of the United Nations. However, Israel was admitted to membership in the United Nations on May 11, 1949, and by that time it had been recognized by fifty-four of the states of the world.[29]

The Flight of the Arabs

The flight of the Arabs from Israel remains to be considered—a startling development which has affected profoundly the State of Israel and the entire Middle East. This phenomenon of mass hysteria may never be fully explained, but available evidence warrants a number of conclusions, or at least reasoned assumptions.

War obviously involves killing, but in modern times the idea of "civilized" warfare has been evolved. This means that combatants may be killed but not tortured or mutilated, and that the civilian or noncombatant population must be protected against outrage, pillage, or murder. Every war has produced its crop of charges of atrocities, particularly against civilians, and some of the charges have undoubtedly been true.

In Palestine, it was especially difficult to wage "civilized" warfare. There was a legacy of bitterness and violence and a tradition of murder and mutilation even of the innocent, as in the Hebron atrocities in the riots of 1929, when more than sixty devout and nonpolitical Jews—men, women, and children—were done to death. Moreover, when disciplined armies are involved, the reckless elements can be held in check, but during the last weeks of the Mandate, Palestine was in a state of anarchy. The British had not permitted the Palestine Commission to supervise the establishment and functioning of Arab and Jewish militias. Fighting was conducted by small bands, some of which could not be controlled. Finally, during the early months of 1948, Arab-Jewish hostilities consisted of raids, reprisals, ambushes along the roads, and other guerrilla tactics. In that situation, the distinction between combatants and noncombatants became as blurred and tenuous as the difference between legitimate military operations and atrocities. When Arabs ambushed a bus and killed its occupants; when the Jews staged a commando raid at night on a village which harbored foreign irregulars; or when a member of either party threw a bomb: were these legitimate measures or atrocities? Charges and countercharges therefore filled the air.

Then came in rapid succession two shocking acts of terror. On April 9, 1948, a band of the *Irgun* attacked Deir Yassin (a village on the outskirts of Jerusalem which had not permitted foreign Arab infiltrators to use it as a base of operations) and massacred some 250 Arab men, women, and children. The Arab response was quick and sharp: on April 13, 1948, a convoy from Jerusalem to the Hadassah hospital and Hebrew University on Mt. Scopus was attacked and seventy-seven doctors, nurses, teachers, and students were massacred. These atrocities quickened the sense of insecurity into panic.

By January, 1948, Arabs in considerable numbers had begun leaving cities such as Haifa and Jaffa. In April, when hostilities were intensified, whole villages were evacuated. But after the massacres of Deir Yassin and the Hadassah-Hebrew University convoy, panic and total flight accompanied occupation by enemy forces. The number of Jews in Arab areas was small—only about 7,000 eventually left. The Arab exodus was a mass flight of hundreds of thousands.

The two massacres, particularly that of Deir Yassin, must therefore be designated a cause of the flight of the Arabs. But it was not the only cause. There is evidence that the Arab leaders stimulated, if they did not actually order, the exodus. An eyewitness learned from Arabs fleeing Tiberias in April that their leaders had ordered them to leave and that they would soon return. The same writer concluded from what he saw in Haifa that the exodus of the Arab civilians was the policy of the Arab leaders.

Apparently the Arab leaders, especially those of the Arab States, expected a lightning war and a quick victory. Evacuation of the Arabs from war areas was considered desirable to allow guerrilla and regular forces greater freedom of action and to arouse war passions in neighboring Arab States. The Arab leaders therefore encouraged fear and panic and, at the same time, gave assurances of a speedy return home. It is significant that 80 per cent of the Moslems and only 50 per cent of the Christian Arabs fled the country.

One conclusion appears incontrovertible. The mass flight of the Arabs came as a surprise to the Jews. Early in April, 1948, before the massacre of Deir Yassin, Ben-Gurion was speculating on the reasons for the flight of Arabs. During the latter part of the month, when the Jews took Haifa, the Jews pleaded with the Arab leaders not to encourage flight, and the *Haganah* distributed leaflets assuring the Arabs equal treatment.[30] As the initial shock passed, however, the Jews ceased to discourage the exodus and even welcomed it.

The State of Israel: Geographical Features

The new state that emerged from the war is a narrow strip on the southeastern coast of the Mediterranean Sea extending irregularly for 260 miles from the borders of Lebanon and Syria in the north to Egypt and the Gulf of Aqaba in the south. It is bounded by 590 miles of hostile Arab borders which cut deep into the heart of Israel. North of Tel-Aviv, the country is only twelve miles wide, and at Elat only nine miles; its greatest width is south of Beersheba—seventy miles. The Mediterranean alone affords free access to the outside world, but even there the Gaza strip of some 125 square miles is under Egyptian occupation.

The total area of Israel is about 8,050 square miles, somewhat smaller than the State of Massachusetts. The Coastal Plain runs along the Mediterranean and extends in varying depths into the interior, and most of Israel's population lives in this region. Eastward the mountains range from Galilee to Sinai, with fertile valleys, notably the Valley of Jezreel, affording good agricultural land for settlement. The Jordan Valley is mostly below sea level. The Negev comprises about half the area of the country. Desert and steppe land until recently, Israel has begun the cultivation of the northern portions, and its potential in minerals and oil holds promise of economic viability for the young state.

The climate in the north and west is of the Mediterranean variety, with warm summers and mild winters. The Jordan Valley, however, is hot and humid in the summer, and the hot days and cool nights of the Negev are reminiscent of the desert. Rainfall is ample in the north and generally also in central Israel. The Negev, however, is dry, and agricultural development in that area depends on piping water from the north. The water resources of the country as a whole are limited. The Jordan River flows for 73 of its 158 miles in Israeli territory, and the Yarkon and Kishon are relatively small rivers. Lake Kinneret (Lake Tiberias) is a large body of fresh water, but the Dead Sea, although rich in minerals, is too salty for agricultural irrigation.

3. THE FIRST DECADE OF ISRAEL: 1948-1958

The Ben-Gurion Era

No single individual has had so profound an influence on the development of Israel as David Ben-Gurion. He was a dominant influence in the molding of the labor movement of Palestine; he led Palestine Jewry during the last decade of the Mandate; he headed the Provisional Government and was the driving force in the War of Independence; his views were a determining factor in the fashioning of the new state and government; and, except for an interval when he voluntarily retired, he has been the unchallenged leader since the establishment of the state.

Ben-Gurion was born in Poland in 1886 and arrived in Palestine in 1906. He received a traditional Jewish education and private instruction in general subjects and languages. For a time, he studied law at the University of Constantinople, and at the age of fifty-five he learned ancient Greek in order to read the classics in the original.

During his formative years in Palestine, Ben-Gurion worked as an agricultural laborer, and participated in the early efforts at trade union organization, self-defense, and co-operative settlement. He was quickly recognized as the leader of the Poale-Zion Party of Palestine, and played a prominent role in the founding of the *Histadrut*, which he served as General Secretary from 1921 to 1933. During the First World War, he helped organize the Jewish Legion and himself served under its colors. And throughout these hectic years, he traveled widely, lectured, and wrote extensively.

By the middle 1930's, Ben-Gurion had attained top leadership in Zionist

counsels. In 1933, he was elected to the Executive of the World Zionist
Organization, and he became its chairman as well as the chairman of the
Jewish Agency Executive in Palestine; these positions made him the effective leader of the Zionist movement. He was the moving spirit behind the
adoption of the "Biltmore Program" (1942), which called for a Jewish
Commonwealth in Palestine, unlimited Jewish immigration, and the formation of a Jewish army. Before the various commissions of inquiry, too,
he represented the Jewish cause with force and dignity.

Ben-Gurion is richly endowed with the qualities of leadership. Possessed
of deep insight and extensive knowledge, he has applied both to the furtherance of a clear-visioned objective—the creation of a secure and prosper-
ous Jewish state, based on a society of workers and rendered viable by
economic development with the aid of modern science and the support of
world Jewry. Jewish immigration and dedicated pioneering (*Halutziut*)
have been and remain the basic principles which he has championed with
fervid eloquence and obstinate devotion.

Ben-Gurion does not argue premises but posits them as self-evident
truths, and he speaks with contagious conviction. But he is no doctrinaire.
He can appraise opposing viewpoints and balance social and economic ideals
against the unyielding facts of a situation. This realism enables him to
compromise in order to achieve the attainable.

Ben-Gurion's achievements are due in no small measure to his unflagging
vitality and indomitable courage and determination. And these qualities
have found expression not only in defiance of the enemy but also in the
stern suppression of evil within his own camp. Finally, although at times
impatient and self-assured, he is immune to the temptation of this age to
impose doctrinaire ideals by violence. His conception of unity is not enforced totalitarian conformity, but co-operation cemented by democratic
processes and the rule of law.[31]

Development of State and Government

The State of Israel (*Medinat Yisrael*) was proclaimed on May 14, 1948,
when Ben-Gurion read the Declaration of Independence at a meeting of
the Council of the People held in the Tel-Aviv Museum. The government
and administration were fashioned gradually in successive stages.

It was noted above that the Jews had developed quasi-governmental
autonomous institutions during the period of the Mandate—the Elected
Assembly with its National Council (*Vaad Leumi*) and the Palestine Executive of the Jewish Agency. These bodies formed the nucleus of the first
Jewish national administration. In November, 1947, a Joint Emergency
Committee was set up, and during the following four months it took measures to counteract the creeping chaos which resulted from the disintegration
of the British administration. Provision was made for the conservation of

food and fuel supplies, for hospital facilities, a broadcasting system, a police force, and similar services; mobilization of persons of military age was begun; and plans were made for the future state. In March, 1948, the Emergency Committee was superseded by a more representative agency. The National Council (*Vaad Leumi*) was reorganized to represent all elements in the Jewish population and reconstituted as the Council of the People—a body of thirty-seven, including the fourteen members of the Executive of the National Council, the twelve members of the Palestine Executive of the Jewish Agency, and eleven deputies of parties and groups not heretofore represented. The new Council, and the executive of thirteen (known as the Administration of the People) which it designated, conducted Jewish affairs until the end of the Mandate. It was the Council of the People which proclaimed the State of Israel.

With the establishment of Israel, the Council of the People became the Provisional State Council, with Chaim Weizmann as President, and the Administration of the People became the Provisional Government, with David Ben-Gurion as Prime Minister. The Provisional Council and Government, which functioned until February 14, 1949, discharged all affairs of state. Its first legislative act was to repeal the legal provisions which had restricted Jewish immigration and land transfers to Jews! Beyond that, it declared in force the existing law, the courts, and the local governments, unless modified by the constituted authorities.

The Provisional Government directed the war, provided for internal security, adopted budgets and imposed taxes, set up administrative agencies and a civil service. It facilitated immigration and took a census of the population of the country (November 8, 1948). It appointed a special committee which approved a draft constitution for submission to the Constituent Assembly. Finally, the Provisional Government made all the legal and administrative arrangements for national elections to the Constituent Assembly, which were held on January 25, 1949. The Constituent Assembly —the *Knesset*—met on February 14, 1949, and inaugurated a permanent government. Chaim Weizmann was elected President of Israel and David Ben-Gurion became Prime Minister of a coalition government.[32]

SYSTEM OF GOVERNMENT

Israel is a democratic parliamentary republic. The Proclamation of Independence declared that the State of Israel ". . . will be based on the principles of liberty, justice and peace as conceived by the Prophets of Israel; will uphold the full social and political equality of all its citizens, without distinction of religion, race or sex; will guarantee freedom of religion, conscience, education and culture. . . ." At this writing, no formal Bill of Rights has been adopted, although the first Cabinet's program, which was approved by the *Knesset* in March, 1949, included as fundamental principles equality of rights and duties for all, including women, freedom of expression, of religious observance, of education and culture, and labor rights in significant detail.[33] Moreover, the safeguards of the Mandatory regime have remained in force, and new legislation has decreed full equality for women and the abolition of corporal punishment and of the death penalty for murder. In actual practice, the principles of democracy, the rule of law, human rights, and fundamental freedoms have prevailed. Representative government based on popular elections and majority rule has functioned effectively. Above all, the rights to differ and to express differing views in speech, assembly, and publication have been observed. The status of the Arab minority will be discussed subsequently.

Israel has no formal written constitution in the sense of a fundamental law which requires, as in the United States, a special process of amendment and which limits the powers of the organs of government. Steps were taken to formulate a written constitution: under the Provisional Government a draft with elaborate provisions for fundamental human rights was prepared and submitted to the First *Knesset*.[34] But it was decided after lengthy debates to allow constitutional law to evolve gradually. The compelling motivations against a formal, written constitution appear to have been the desire to allow the government freedom of action during the formative fluid period, and the practical difficulty of harmonizing the demands of the orthodox elements with those of the anti-clericals. Individual constitutional laws were therefore enacted, equal in legal authority to other laws and subject to change by the ordinary process of legislation.

The structure of government embraces the usual executive, legislative, and judicial branches, with a President, a parliament, a cabinet, and a system of courts. The President is the titular head of the state, who enjoys great public esteem but whose functions are mainly ceremonial and formal. His powers are limited. He convenes the *Knesset*, calls on the outstanding party leader to form a government, and receives the resignation of a cabinet which has lost the confidence of the *Knesset*. He may dissolve the *Knesset* when no new cabinet can be formed.

The President signs all bills passed by the *Knesset*, but he has no veto power over legislation. He signs treaties after ratification by the *Knesset*. He receives diplomatic representatives from foreign powers and names Israel's diplomats and consular agents, but the appointments are first approved by a cabinet minister. All his important official acts require the countersignature of a cabinet minister. He does have two significant discretionary powers. He may pardon offenders and reduce punishments, and he has the authority to consult with leaders of various parties before designating one to attempt to form a cabinet.

The President is elected by a majority vote and secret ballot of the *Knesset* for a term of five years. The first President was Chaim Weizmann, a distinguished scientist, the central figure in the negotiations which secured the Balfour Declaration, and the outstanding leader of the Zionist movement during the period of the Mandate. He was elected on February 16, 1949, and died on November 9, 1952. His successor, chosen on December 8, 1952, and re-elected on October 30, 1957, is Yitzhak Ben-Zvi,[34a] who shared in the building of the National Home as pioneer in self-defense, scholar, leader of the *Histadrut* and, for more than a decade, Chairman of the National Council.

The *Knesset* is the supreme agency of government. It is a one-chamber parliament of 120 members, whose powers are not limited either by formal constitution or by presidential veto or by Supreme Court. It is answerable only to the people, who elect it for a term of four years by direct, equal, and secret ballot, and proportional representation.

As a legislative body, the *Knesset* has functioned after the manner of the British House of Commons, with bills introduced by the government, scrutinized in committees, debated in full session, and passed by majority vote. Debates are limited by allotting time to each party in accord with its representation in the *Knesset*, and filibustering is thus eliminated.

The *Knesset* exercises extensive controls over the executive. The cabinet or government is responsible to it: it cannot be formed without the support of a majority of the *Knesset* and must resign when it fails to command the latter's confidence. The *Knesset* also ratifies treaties, and it supervises the administration of government departments. Ministers and other officials are required to appear before *Knesset* committees and to report on their activities, and special committees conduct searching investigations when necessary. Interpolations or questions are addressed to ministers and their replies are presented to the *Knesset*. Finally, control of the budget reinforces the power of the *Knesset* over the government and administration.

Special provision has been made for close and continuous scrutiny of state financial and economic activities under the aegis of the *Knesset*. A State Comptroller, named by the President on the recommendation of a committee of the *Knesset*, audits accounts and reports to the Finance Committee of the *Knesset* on the legality, economy, and efficiency of the government bodies under his supervision. And it is specially stipulated that the State Comptroller is responsible to the *Knesset* and not dependent upon the government.

The *Knesset* has proved an efficient and effective parliament. Informal in dress and appearance, it has conducted affairs with proper decorum and has shown an independent spirit toward the government.

The cabinet or government is the functioning executive body. The Prime Minister, a member of the *Knesset*, is charged by the President with the responsibility of forming a government, and he negotiates with party leaders on the choice of his colleagues, who may or may not be members of the *Knesset*. When approved by the *Knesset* through a vote of confidence, the government is constituted.

The principles of responsibility and unity govern the cabinet system. Responsibility involves accountability to the *Knesset* and dependence on the confidence of the latter. Unity means collective responsibility of the cabinet: once a decision is made by majority vote, all its members are expected to support it, and open opposition to a cabinet proposal cannot be voiced or indicated except by express permission of a majority of the cabinet. The cabinet system of Israel rests on the coalition of political parties.

The administrative departments of the government follow the pattern of all governments, with several exceptions. There are ministries of defense, foreign affairs, finance, commerce and industry, agriculture, labor, interior, justice, health, social welfare, education and culture, communications, and posts. There is a ministry of police, and the special needs of the country have prompted the establishment of ministries of development and of religious affairs. In addition, the Prime Minister's Office embraces important administrative units, with total personnel exceeding that of a number of the ministries. Among these are the Civil Service Commission, the Central Bureau of Statistics, the Scientific Research Council and institutes of specialized research, the Atomic Energy Commission, broadcasting and press services, a technical assistance liaison office, state archives, and the Government Tourist Corporation.[35]

The judicial branch of the government comprises religious as well as civil courts. The hierarchy of civil courts includes four Municipal and seventeen Magistrates' Courts (including two Juvenile Courts) with minor civil and criminal jurisdiction; three District Courts which hear appeals from the lower tribunals and serve as courts of first instance in major civil and criminal cases; and the highest court of the land—the Supreme Court of seven justices, a president, and a deputy president. The Supreme Court cannot declare unconstitutional laws passed by the *Knesset*, but it can invalidate administrative actions or interpretations of statutes which it regards as contrary to the "rule of law."

The Rabbinical Courts exercise exclusive jurisdiction in marriage and divorce, while in other matters of personal status, such as alimony, probate, and succession, they may act when all parties consent. The ecclesiastical courts of the Christian communities have exclusive authority in marriage, divorce, alimony, and confirmation of wills, and they may judge other matters of personal status with the consent of the parties. The Moslem courts have exclusive jurisdiction in all matters of personal status. The Jews have recourse in these matters to Rabbinical Courts and the Moslems and Christians to religious courts of their respective communities. There are also tribunals for special types of cases, such as rents, profiteering and speculation, and national insurance, and tribal courts for the Bedouins.

The independence of the judiciary is assured by special safeguards against political appointments and by tenure subject only to good behavior. The civil judges and those of the Rabbinical Courts are appointed by the President on the recommendation of Appointments Committees consisting of judges of the Supreme Court, ministers of the government, members of the *Knesset,* and representatives of the Israel Bar Association. The judges of the Moslem and Christian Religious Courts are appointed by the Minister of Religious Affairs in consultation with their respective communities.

The body of law administered by the courts consists of enactments of the *Knesset* and laws inherited from the previous regimes. The latter include Ottoman survivals especially in private and land law, legal provisions which obtained under the Mandate, English common law and equity, rabbinical law, and religious law of the Moslem and Christian communities.[36]

Local government,[37] initiated cautiously during the period of the Mandate, has been extended and democratized since the establishment of the state. Property qualifications for voting have been abolished. The franchise has been extended to women in all local elections. And mayors and vice-mayors, appointed under the British regime, are now elected by the local representative bodies.

At the end of 1956, a total of 154 local authorities were functioning, and their jurisdiction covered about 90 per cent of the population of the country. There were twenty Municipalities of varying sizes, with a population of over 1,065,000; eighty-six Local Councils, with some 335,000 people; and forty-eight Regional Councils, embracing nearly 650 agricultural settlements and about 215,000 people. All these bodies are elected directly by their constituents, but they operate under the close and confining supervision of the Ministry of the Interior.

The functions of the local authorities embrace education and culture, health and sanitation, water works, housing, and other local needs, with special attention devoted to the absorption of new immigrants. The Regional Councils pool the efforts of the villages in public works, antimalaria measures, drainage, and major water works. However, the competence of the local authorities has not as yet been fully defined, and there is considerable variation in the services performed even by the large municipalities. Nor is there a clear division of function between them and the central government. To remedy these and other deficiencies, the Minister of the Interior has appointed an advisory Local Government Council which will, no doubt, assist in the preparation of appropriate legislation.

PARTIES, PARLIAMENTS, AND CABINETS

Political Parties: Since the establishment of Israel, and before that, too, Ben-Gurion's leadership has been exerted through the Israel Labor Party, because political parties are the decisive influence in the government and they permeate all public life in Israel. Local government, trade union affairs, agricultural settlements, co-operative agencies, and numerous other activities reflect party differentiation, and practically every political party conducts some social, economic, or cultural institutions, including youth movements, theaters, athletic clubs, and housing projects. Politics and partisanship are, therefore, never dormant, and ideological loyalties create an atmosphere of intense and zealous rivalry. The clash of economic interests and of social and religious philosophies is reinforced in Israel by the fact that economic, social, and cultural institutions are newly fashioned and susceptible of being molded; that the state itself and the governmental apparatus have not yet achieved permanent form. Hence the anxious desire of every party to attain power in order to stamp its image and ideals on the country and its people.

The present system of government, structured as it is on party loyalties, both reflects the influence of the latter and serves to strengthen their hold on public affairs. Elections to the *Knesset* are based on a system of proportional representation, whereby the citizen votes for a party list rather than an individual. The lists of candidates, up to 120 (the total membership of the *Knesset*), are prepared and numbered in descending order of preference by the central bodies of the parties, and seats in parliament are allocated in accordance with the proportion of votes won by each party list. If a member of the *Knesset* dies or resigns, he is replaced not by the successful candidate in a by-election but by the next name in the order of preference on the party list. Thus a member of parliament represents his party and not a specific constituency. The members of a coalition cabinet, too, are chosen in interparty negotiation, and it is the party rather than the Prime Minister which designates its representatives in the government. As a result, the composition of the *Knesset* and the cabinet as well as programs and policies are controlled by the party organizations.

Israel is a multiparty state, and every one of the Jewish political parties had its origin or early development during the period of the Mandate. The parties reflect the composite character of the population. Emigrants from many lands, the Jews have brought with them differing cultural backgrounds, religious orientations, political conceptions, and social ideals. Many of the European immigrants had made doctrinal commitments and stanch party affiliations in their native lands, and slogans, programs, even party names, were transplanted to the new homeland. The result was a plethora of parties and groupings during the period of the Mandate, and these have persisted under the new state.

The parties represent differences in social doctrine, religious loyalties, economic status, national objectives, and geographical origin. However, these divisive factors are not all-embracing, because some of the parties include subgroups with diverse subsidiary interests. For example, the religious parties are at one in opposing the secular state, but elements within these parties differ on the question of private versus co-operative enterprise. Therefore, the common practice of arranging parties in a political spectrum ranging from right to left or from conservative to radical coloration could be misleading. In the interest of clarity, the most important parties of Israel will be grouped according to the major emphases of their ideologies and programs.

Labor or Socialist objectives are the fundamental tenets of several political parties. The most important and the dominant party in Israel is the *Mapai*, or the Israel Labor Party, which originated in a merger in 1930 of several factions: the *Poale Zion*, a Zionist-Socialist group largely Marxist in orientation; a non-Marxist Zionist-Socialist element, known as the *Hapoel Hatzair* (Young Worker); and an organization of agricultural workers. The philosophy of the Israel Labor Party is social-democratic, but it seeks to attain the Socialist goal primarily through the co-operative ownership of the means of production and distribution rather than through their nationalization. Symbolized by the policies of its leader, Ben-Gurion, and by the achievements of the *Histadrut,* the program of the Israel Labor Party favors political and social democracy and a planned economy which includes state-controlled private enterprise. In foreign policy, it is oriented toward the Western democracies, without definite commitment to the Eastern or Western blocs.

Mapam, or the United Workers Party, was founded in 1948 when three left-wing Socialist elements joined forces. The constituent elements were the *Left Poale Zion*, a strictly Marxist faction which favored Zionism but emphasized the class struggle; another group—*Hashomer Hatzair* (The Young Watchman)—which combined militant socialism with Zionist pioneering; and leftist elements (*Ahdut Haavoda-Poale Zion*), which had seceded from the *Mapai*. The adherents of *Mapam*, like those of *Mapai*, had long labored in the Zionist pioneering movement and in the building of collective and co-operative settlements, and they had been in the forefront of the struggle for independence.

The *Mapam* program, seeking to combine Zionism with Marxism, favors a united Socialist Labor Front, the rapid socialization of the economy, and co-operation with Arab labor. In foreign policy, it has vacillated between a pro-Soviet position and neutralism.

Mapam has proved an unstable union of leftist forces, with the pro-Soviet orientation the chief cause of discord. As a result, the strength and influence of the party have declined. Several of its *Knesset* representatives have gone over to the Communists or to *Mapai*. Others have seceded to form an independent faction—*Ahdut Haavoda-Poale Zion*—which favors neutralism in foreign policy and is outspokenly critical of the Soviet Union.

At the extreme left of the Socialist movement is the Communist Party, a small but vociferous group which echoes faithfully the line dictated by the foreign policy of the Soviet Union.

The "Religious Bloc" has consisted of four parties—The *Agudat Israel* and *Poale Agudat Israel,* and the *Mizrahi* and *Hapoel Hamizrahi.* The *Agudat Israel* represents the uncompromising Orthodox elements which, before the rise of Israel, frowned on Zionist ideology, opposed the Hebrew movement, and held aloof from the organized Jewish community. Since the establishment of the state, it has co-operated in forming various governments, but it still sets its face sternly against all forms of modernism, including woman suffrage. Its positive policy aims to maintain and further strict adherence to Orthodox ritual and traditional religious lore.

The *Mizrahi* has been a religious party within the Zionist movement and it has participated in Jewish national and communal institutions. It is less intransigent than the *Agudat Israel,* accepting woman suffrage, for example, as a concession to the mood of the times. It strives to develop Jewish national life in the spirit of religious tradition.

The *Poale Agudat Israel* and *Hapoel Hamizrahi* are the labor offshoots of the parent parties. Sharing the religious views of the latter, they differ on economic policy: whereas the parent parties favor private enterprise, the labor groups have turned to co-operative endeavors. In 1956, the *Mizrahi* and *Hapoel Hamizrahi* merged into a single party.

Middle-class interests are represented by two strong parties and several minor factions. The General Zionists embrace the secularist and non-Socialist segments of the Jewish population who seek to develop Israel without the constraints of class conflict, social doctrines, or religious-clerical controls. This party played a leading role in the building of the Jewish National Home, and some of the foremost figures in Zionism, including Chaim Weizmann, came from its ranks. In part, its influence has been due to the paramount role played by middle-class elements in the Zionist organizations of various countries, and consequently also in the World Zionist Organization.

The General Zionist Party favors private enterprise with a minimum of government or party interference, and the abandonment of state encouragement of collectivism. It calls for the elimination of party influence in education, public health, labor exchanges, and other national functions. It is oriented toward the Western democracies in foreign policy.

The *Herut* (Freedom) Party is an outgrowth of the Zionist Revisionists and the *Irgun* elements of the Mandate period. Its program, which calls for "a self-supporting national economy, based on initiative, free competition and increased productivity," is strongly anticollectivist and, like the General Zionists, it opposes party influence in education and the social services. Its distinguishing characteristic is the maximalist national position:

it seeks the "reunion of the land of Israel," that is, the inclusion of all of Palestine in the State of Israel.

In addition, there are various minor parties or splinters. The Progressives are an offshoot of the General Zionists who favor co-operation with the moderate labor parties. The *Sephardim* and Yemenites have attempted, with diminishing success, to organize Oriental Jews. Finally, several Arab parties have won seats in the *Knesset* and, although neither Socialist nor prolabor in orientation, they have generally supported the Mapai Party.[38]

Parliaments: Three national elections have been held since the establishment of Israel. The Constituent Assembly—the First *Knesset*—was elected on January 25, 1949. By the end of 1950, the *Knesset* majority which supported the coalition government began to founder over religious issues, and early in the following year Ben-Gurion precipitated general elections, which were held on July 30, 1951. The Second *Knesset* lasted the full term of four years, and on July 26, 1955, the Third *Knesset* was elected.

The table (page 722) presents comparative figures on the three elections —the popular vote and its distribution among the parties, the percentage of citizen participation, and the party strength in each *Knesset*. These figures and the general conduct of the elections suggest a number of conclusions.[39]

First and foremost, the elections reveal that Israel is a functioning democracy, that the vote is taken seriously, and that the electorate is mature enough to shun violence and rely on the ballot to effect desired changes. All the elections have been peaceful, democratic, and free of corrupt manipulation, and the percentage of popular participation has been high— nearly 87 per cent of the eligible voters in 1949, over 75 per cent in 1951, and close to 83 per cent in 1955. This is most significant because the electorate doubled between 1949 and 1955, and large numbers of the new immigrants had never voted before and could hardly have been expected to share effectively in democratic processes. Apparently faith in democratic elections is deep enough in Israel to permeate the masses of politically primitive new arrivals. In this respect at least, large numbers of the new immigration have been assimilated.

The multiplicity of parties has remained a characteristic feature of Israeli elections: twenty-one parties and factions took part in the elections of 1949, and twelve secured seats in the *Knesset*; seventeen party lists contested each of the subsequent elections, and representation in the *Knesset* was secured by fifteen parties in 1951 and by twelve in 1955. However, closer examination will reveal that only six or eight parties really matter, and that splinter groups tend to disappear. In 1949, nine splinter groups polled a combined total of less than 5 per cent of the vote, and three others won only one seat each. Furthermore, nine Jewish splinter parties of 1949 failed to appear in 1951, and two new factions that submitted lists in 1951 failed to elect any candidate to the *Knesset*. The decline of splinter groups

TABLE I

Elections to the Knesset

	1st Election, January 25, 1949			2nd Election, July 30, 1951			3rd Election, July 26, 1955		
	Votes	% of Total	Members	Votes	% of Total	Members	Votes	% of Total	Members
Mapai	155,274	35.7	46	256,456	37.3	45	274,735	32.2	40
Mapam	64,018	14.7	19	86,096	12.5	15	62,401	7.3	9
Ahdut Haavoda-Poale Zion							69,475	8.2	10
General Zionist	22,861	5.2	7	111,394	16.2	20	87,099	10.2	13
(Hapoel Hamizrahi [a]	52,982	12.2	16	46,347	6.8	8	77,936	9.1	11
Mizrahi [a]				10,383	1.5	2			
Agudat Israel [a]				13,799	2.0	3	39,836	4.7	6
Poale Agudat Israel [a]				11,194	1.6	2			
Herut	49,782	11.5	14	45,651	6.6	8	107,190	12.6	15
Israel Communist Party	15,148	3.5	4	27,334	4.0	5	38,492	4.5	6
Progressives	17,786	4.1	5	22,171	3.2	4	37,661	4.4	5
Israel Arab Democrats	7,387	1.7	2	16,370	2.4	3	15,475	1.8	2
Sephardic Oriental Communities	15,287	3.5	4	12,002	1.8	2	6,994	0.8	—
Progress and Work (Arab)				8,067	1.2	1	12,511	1.5	2
Yemenites	4,399	1.0	1	7,965	1.2	1	2,448	0.3	—
Agriculture and Development (Arab)				7,851	1.1	1	9,791	1.1	1
Fighters (Lohamim)	5,363	1.2	1						
WIZO	5,173	1.2	1						
Other Jewish tickets	13,198	3.4	—	4,413	0.6	—	16,133	1.9	—
Other Arab tickets	6,026	1.3	—				4,484	0.5	—
Eligible voters	506,567			924,885			1,057,795		
Total voting	449,095			695,007			876,085		
Canceled votes	5,411			7,515			22,866		
Voting participation	86.9%			75.4%			82.8%		

[a] These four parties presented one list, the "United Religious Bloc," at the 1949 election; they ran on separate lists in the election for the 2nd *Knesset* (7/30/51); and in the 3rd *Knesset* election, the religious parties ran on two lists, one including the *Mizrahi* and *Hapoel Hamizrahi*, and the other the *Agudat Israel* and the *Poale Agudat Israel*.

has been accelerated by the election law of 1951, which denied representation to any party which polled less than 1 per cent of the valid votes cast. One can detect a tendency toward the consolidation of parties along ideological lines, but the present *Knesset* (elected in 1955) still includes three independent labor parties, two religious blocs, and three Arab splinter parties with little, if any, ideological differences.

The election of 1951 indicated a trend toward the more moderate parties: *Mapam* declined, while *Mapai* increased its percentage of total votes; and the General Zionists emerged as the second party in the *Knesset*, with *Herut* reduced to a fraction. The 1955 election, however, appears to have reversed this trend. *Herut* nearly doubled its proportionate following and the General Zionists lost heavily. *Mapam's* decline continued, but *Mapai* lost, too, and the total non-*Mapai* (leftist) labor strength increased. Whether this connotes a trend toward the extremes of the right and left, it is difficult to say. In all likelihood, the election of 1955 registered the disappointment of the new immigrants with the hardships and insecurities of life in Israel, and also general impatience with the government's moderation in the face of border provocation, and with its reliance on the West when the latter was barely friendly. At all events, *Mapai* emerged from every election as the preponderant party in the *Knesset*, with one-third or more of the seats.

Cabinets or Governments. The governments (cabinets) of Israel have been coalitions, reflecting the multiparty composition of the *Knesset*. The Provisional Government (May 15, 1948–March 10, 1949) included all of the important parties (*Mapai, Mapam*, Religious Front, General Zionists, Progressives, and *Sephardim*) except the Revisionists or *Herut*. After the election of the First *Knesset*, however, Ben-Gurion formed a less unwieldy government of *Mapai* and the Religious Front, with representation also of the Progressives and the *Sephardim*. This coalition of the secularist *Mapai* and the clerically-oriented Religious Front created tensions and cabinet crises, but it was repeatedly reconstituted and held together until December, 1952—close to four years. *Mapai* made a number of concessions in religious matters and the Religious Front supported the basic economic and political policies of the Prime Minister and his party.

The success of the General Zionists in the election of 1951, when they emerged as the second largest party in the *Knesset*, foreshadowed a radical shift in the parliamentary and cabinet coalition. The *Mapai* and the General Zionists were both moderate parties, albeit with rival labor and middle-class philosophies and programs. If a compromise could be effected on basic policies, government stability would be immeasurably enhanced, because the two parties commanded a clear majority in the *Knesset*.

The attempt was made, with the understanding that practical measures rather than theory would be stressed, especially economic development to absorb the new immigrants. In December, 1952, a *Mapai*-General Zionists government was formed, with the co-operation also of *Hapoel Hamizrahi* and the Progressives. This coalition held despite secondary crises until June, 1955, when the General Zionists withdrew from the government.

During this period, a momentous change occurred when Ben-Gurion resigned from the government and withdrew from public life (December 7, 1953). Leadership in the government was assumed by Moshe Sharett, an outstanding figure in the *Histadrut* and *Mapai*, a skillful negotiator, head of the Political Department of the Jewish Agency during the period of the Mandate, and the foremost Israeli diplomat who had served as Foreign Minister since the establishment of the state. However, Ben-Gurion's retirement was temporary. He returned as Foreign Minister in February, 1955, and on November 3, 1955, succeeded Sharett as Prime Minister.

The return of Ben-Gurion to power ushered in a third major shift in the composition of the government coalition. The General Zionists had withdrawn in June, 1955, just prior to the election of that year. Their defeat at the polls eliminated them from consideration as a compelling factor in a cabinet coalition. The new government therefore reflected the labor-liberal majority of the Third *Knesset*. It consisted of a five-party coalition: the three labor parties—*Mapai*, *Mapam*, and *Ahdut Haavodah*; the combined *Mizrahi-Hapoel Hamizrahi*; and the Progressives. This has proved a stable combination and, at this writing, it still constitutes the government of Israel. In January, 1958, a crisis developed when one of the parties revealed to the press an important matter under consideration by the cabinet. The Prime Minister, and hence the cabinet, resigned, but it was soon reconstituted, after a firm commitment of all five parties that the secrecy of cabinet deliberations and collective responsibility would be preserved, and that the coalition would hold until the election of 1959.[40]

Coalition cabinets based on a multiplicity of parties are notoriously unstable, as is evidenced by the French Third and Fourth Republics. The Israeli cabinet system, however, has been astonishingly stable. There have been eight or nine major cabinet changes between 1948 and 1958, but only once (in 1951) did a government fall because of an adverse vote in the *Knesset*. The changes have been due mainly to such formal factors as the election of a new *Knesset*, the choice of a new President, and the withdrawal of a Prime Minister. The significant shifts have been three, and each has resulted from a national election: the election of the First *Knesset* resulted in the *Mapai*-Religious Front coalition; the Second *Knesset* produced the *Mapai*-General Zionist bloc; and the Third *Knesset* yielded the labor-liberal government. To be sure, the cabinets have been uneasy coalitions, with all too frequent flare-ups and crises, but that is the nature of peacetime coalitions everywhere. In fact, even where the two-party system prevails, as in England, minor crises are not uncommon when a government lacks an overpowering leader.

Several factors have contributed to the relative stability of the Israeli government. First, the preponderant strength of *Mapai*, with one-third or more mandates in every *Knesset*, has made it the anchor of every cabinet. The predominant influence of Ben-Gurion has served as a stabilizing force, and the usual carry-over of most ministers into reorganized cabinets has enhanced the continuity of policy. Finally, the rigorous discipline of Israeli parties has curbed irresponsible action by individual members of the *Knesset*.

The press of Israel has devoted much attention to the question of parties and coalitions, and Ben-Gurion himself has deplored the fragmentation of the electorate. However, for Israel coalitions are not an unmixed evil. The burden of a Prime Minister would, no doubt, be eased by the solid support of a majority party. But where, as in Israel, differences are ideologically motivated, a two-party system might result in irreconcilable conflicts. Coalitions which make compromises imperative tend to soften differences, thus contributing to national unity. A case in point is the fact that even the unyielding and unco-operative *Agudat Israel* was held in line by participation in the government.

POLITICAL AND SOCIAL REFORMS

During the first decade of independence, the issues which have agitated the public in Israel and occupied the attention of government and parliament have dealt with the consolidation of state institutions and agencies and with the fundamental problems of mass immigration, security, national unity, and economic prosperity. The policies relating to immigration, economic development, the furtherance of welfare, and foreign affairs will be dealt with subsequently. Here the major political and social reforms will be outlined.

The fundamental laws relating to the structure and functions of government—the so-called "small" or "minor" constitution—have been discussed in the preceding section. The system of taxation was reorganized, customs and excise duties were regulated, the effort was made to curb profiteering, and necessary modifications in the law and in legal procedure were introduced, including the abolition of the death penalty, except for treason and for Nazi collaborators. In addition, provision was made for coinage; for the flag, emblem, and seal of Israel and similar appointments of statehood; for passports, visas, and other matters governing relations with foreign countries. Especially important was the Nationality Law of 1952, which declared that Israeli nationality might be acquired through birth, residence, naturalization, and "return," the latter referring to immigrating Jews who were endowed with the "right of *Aliyah*."[41]

The National Defense Army. Apart from the Arab attack, the most formidable challenge to the new State of Israel came from within, and it centered in the issue of a single and disciplined national army. In May, 1948, the Provisional Government issued an ordinance establishing a "Defense Army of Israel," and forbidding the maintenance of "any armed forces outside the Defense Army of Israel." The *Irgun* complied, but with reservations: its members joined the government forces and some of its arms were surrendered; the *Irgun* command, however, was maintained and independent efforts continued to import arms from abroad. In June, 1948, after the first truce had come into effect, the ship *Altalena* arrived off Tel-Aviv with a consignment of arms for the *Irgun,* and the demand that the *Irgun* yield the ship to the government met with defiance. Regarding this as rebellion, Ben-Gurion had the ship wrecked by gunfire and the *Irgun* organization outlawed.

This must have been one of the most difficult decisions in Ben-Gurion's career. The arms and the military personnel of the *Irgun* were desperately needed, for the truce was temporary and the Arab States were preparing for renewed attack. He realized, however, that the *Irgun* challenge was the greater menace, threatening civil war and the loss of the respect of foreign powers for the new state. And this incident affords a superlative illustration of Ben-Gurion's qualities of leadership—the ability to identify and concentrate on the basic issue, the courage to make a difficult decision, and the determination and daring to see it through regardless of immediate consequences.[42]

Another fundamental decision was made about that time, again at the behest of Ben-Gurion. In the early days of the war, the *Palmach* was the pride of Israel's defense. It was a tough and spirited striking force, drawn mainly from the *kibbutzim* and held together by self-discipline and comradeship in arms. Some of the leaders wished to preserve that element as a separate military elite, but Ben-Gurion firmly opposed the plan, and his view prevailed despite the serious opposition of high officers. The forces were reorganized as a national army on the usual model prevailing in democratic countries. Conscription was introduced for able-bodied men and unmarried women, and formal discipline enforced with ranks, officers' quarters, and differential rates of pay. The notion of an ideological elite among the defense forces was abandoned.[43]

National System of Education. During the period of the Mandate there was no compulsory education in Palestine, even on the elementary level, and the Jews maintained and supported a network of schools on an autonomous basis. However, the Jewish schools varied widely in curriculum and orientation, with religious emphasis and labor ideals the chief differentiating factors. The religious schools of the *Agudat Israel* were entirely independent, and the nationally motivated schools were divided into three

types or "trends." The General schools taught (along with the secular subjects) the Bible as national literature and as the repository of national tradition and ideals, but they were regarded as "secular" schools because, as
a rule, they did not seek to instill in the children the urgency of religious
belief or observance. The *Mizrahi* schools emphasized religious instruction,
without neglecting the elementary branches. And the Labor schools, situated mainly in the co-operative settlements, underscored the ideals of labor
and included work in field or shop as part of the curriculum.

The establishment of Israel rendered imperative the co-ordination of
the schools into a national system of education, but the government proceeded with caution. In September, 1949, compulsory and free elementary
education was decreed for all children five to fourteen years of age, and
for adolescents, aged fourteen to eighteen, who did not complete their
elementary education. Provision was made for local rates to cover educational budgets, and responsibility for regular attendance was lodged with
employers (of adolescents) as well as with parents. The trends were recognized by law, and parents were empowered to designate the type of school
to be attended by their children.

The trends were not an artificial improvisation but an outgrowth of the
heterogeneous character of the Jewish population. During the period of
the Mandate, when voluntary effort characterized Jewish education, division along religious and party lines was unavoidable; but once the state
assumed responsibility for elementary education, the trends became an
anachronism. They were costly, necessitating two or more schools in a
locality where one could meet essential needs. They perpetuated partisan
indoctrination when national unity was essential. And they occasioned un-
seemly and harmful competition for the children, especially of the immigrant camps, which in turn threatened the stability of cabinets.

The reform was achieved in August, 1953, when the State Education
Law was passed. The General, *Mizrahi*, and Labor trends were eliminated,
and partisan administrative control as well as selection and training of
teachers lapsed. The setting of standards and supervision was vested in the
Ministry of Education, which has discharged this function in co-operation
with local authorities.

However, the objective has been unity rather than strict uniformity, and
provision has been made for differences. The standard curriculum of the
elementary schools allows for variations in the subjects taught up to 25
per cent of school time. Private schools, too, are permitted to function
outside the state system, provided basic standards are met to the satisfaction of the Ministry of Education. These concessions have afforded the legal
basis for the continued existence of the schools of the ultra-Orthodox
Agudat Israel, the most troublesome obstacle to educational unity. Such
of these schools as accept three-quarters of the standard curriculum receive

a state subsidy, and the remainder are allowed to function independently as private schools. The *Agudat Israel* schools include only a small fraction of the school population (about 4 per cent). For the country as a whole, partisan schooling has begun to give way to a national system of elementary education.[44]

Religion and the State. The American ideal of the separation of church and state does not obtain in Israel, where historical precedent and current conditions have created distinctive needs and imposed religious functions upon the state. The British Mandatory administration and all preceding regimes in Palestine were involved in religious affairs, of which one example was the application of religious law in matters of personal status. The immigration into Israel of masses of devout Oriental Jews called for state aid in matters affecting religion no less than in economic and social requirements. The Moslem, Christian, and Druse minorities required state attention. Finally, the dependence of the government upon the religious parties resulted in concessions which extended state concern with religion.

In Israel, the religious courts are an integral part of the judiciary. Religious Councils deal with public services of a religious nature on the local level, and the state budget assists in providing synagogues for public worship. Non-*kosher* food is banned in the Army messes and in related state institutions. Orthodox women subject to military conscription may be exempted on religious grounds. And the Ministry of Religious Affairs performs administrative and fiscal functions. It administers the moneys paid out of state funds for religious needs and supervises the administration of the religious courts and of other state agencies entrusted with matters involving religion.[45]

In general, it may be said that religion is part of the function of the state in Israel and that religion has figured prominently in politics. However, the attempt has been made to preserve freedom of conscience and freedom of religious observance and nonobservance. The state provides for the citizens who desire a religious way of life, but it does not seek to impose religious observance on nonbelievers. In fact, a large part of the population, including many of the leading officials, are nonobservant in the Orthodox sense of the word. Yet, in some respects, Orthodox practice is imposed on all Jews. Marriage and divorce, for example, are legal only when performed by the recognized Orthodox functionaries.

Women's Rights. In the Middle East, the emancipation of women has been retarded by religion, which has sanctioned their inferior status. During the period of the Mandate, the British authorities made no serious effort to advance women's rights, but the government of Israel has boldly promoted the legal equality of the sexes, despite the vigorous opposition of religious fundamentalists. The right to vote has been extended to women, and civil office is open to them. Under the Equality of Women's Rights Law (1951), women have full power to own and dispose of property, even after marriage, and to effectuate any legal transaction. Discrimination against women in the guardianship of minor children has been eliminated. The conditions for the acquisition of Israeli nationality apply equally to men and women. Equal pay for equal work has been decreed. Even the laws of marriage and divorce have been modified to deprive man of his time-honored privileged position. Child marriage is prohibited, as is the divorce of a woman against her will, unless authorized by a court. And polygamy is a criminal offense.[46]

Israel and World Jewry. Before the establishment of the State of Israel, the building of Palestine had been furthered through the co-operative efforts of the local Jewish population and of large segments of the Jewish communities of various countries. And the Jewish Agency, with consultative power under the British Mandate, served to co-ordinate Jewish constructive efforts. Since political authority was then wielded by the British, and since Jewish activities were in the main of a voluntary nature, the role of the Jewish Agency was acceptable to the Jews, if not always to the British. The rise of Israel, however, rendered necessary a clarification of the relationship of the Jewish Agency to the new state, and this was provided in 1952 by a law which defined the status and functions of the World Zionist Organization and Jewish Agency.

The law states that Israel is "the creation of the entire Jewish people"; that its gates are open to Jewish immigration, and that the World Zionist Organization-Jewish Agency will continue as before to concern itself with immigration and with settlement and absorption projects. Specifically, the State of Israel has recognized the World Zionist Organization "as the authorized agency which will continue to operate in the State of Israel for the development and settlement of the country, the absorption of immigrants from the Diaspora and the co-ordination of the activities in Israel of Jewish institutions and organizations active in those fields."[47]

From this and other laws it is clear that governmental power resides in the constituted authorities which are duly elected by the people of Israel. Jews of other countries are not citizens of Israel unless they choose to migrate thither. Active Zionists, too, are not Israeli nationals unless they settle in that country. However, Jews of other countries who desire to aid in the development of Israel have a function which the State of Israel has recognized. That function is to co-operate in the work of immigration, settlement, and progress of the country so that the immigrants may be properly absorbed. To be sure, the people of Israel, and the State too, expect all Jews to assist immigration and to co-operate in the building of the country. But Israel cannot and does not wield any authority over Jews of other lands. Such assistance as is rendered is entirely voluntary.

In one area—that of religious and cultural life—the Jews of various countries have a close and intimate bond with the Jewish people of Israel. They share with them the fundamentals of religion, a language, over three millennia of Jewish history, customs, ceremonies, and folkways. But this relationship, too, is purely voluntary. The state and people of Israel have no compulsive authority, even in the religious and spiritual sense, over Jews of other countries.

Israel's Population—Policies and Problems

The machinery of government which has been described is fundamentally a means for the attainment of desired ends and, like all peoples, the Israelis have sought to achieve domestic unity, economic prosperity, and national security. Considering the limited resources of the country and the circum-stances surrounding the establishment of the state, these objectives would have been most difficult of attainment even for a settled and stable population. The immigration policy pursued by Israel has rendered infinitely more formidable the obstacles to unity and prosperity, if not to security. That policy has been called the "Ingathering of the Exiles."

THE "INGATHERING"[48]

Mass immigration and its effects have dominated government policy and public life in Israel since the establishment of the state. Immigration into Palestine had been the key to the building of the Jewish National Home from the very beginnings of the Zionist movement and, during the entire period of the Mandate, it had been the paramount issue that divided Jews, Arabs, and British. The admission and absorption of immigrants had become a passion with the Jews, and desperate efforts had been made to bring refugees into the country in the face of obstacles that appeared insurmountable. Once independence endowed the Jews with governmental authority, the gates were thrown wide open, beckoning to all to come and share in the building of the new homeland.

The Declaration of Independence announced that "the State of Israel will be open to the immigration of Jews from all countries of their dispersion." The Law of the Return of July 5, 1950, proclaimed *Aliyah* (immigration of Jews for settlement in Israel) as a right: "Every Jew has the right to come to this country as a settler." And this principle, accepted as an axiom, echoed and re-echoed from the rostrum of the *Knesset*, the press, the radio, and public and private utterances throughout the land. The ringing words of Ben-Gurion in the *Knesset* were characteristic of the mood of the Jews of Israel:

It was for this [mass immigration—the Ingathering of the Exiles] that the State was established, and it is by virtue of this alone that it will stand.[49]

The chief reasons for this passion for immigration are twofold. Many of the Israelis themselves endured homelessness and persecution, and they have felt keenly for their brethren who have languished in refugee camps or lived on sufferance in the midst of unfriendly majorities. In addition, immigration has been regarded as a means of self-preservation. A small people in the midst of vast and hostile Arab populations, the Israelis have feared the overwhelming force of numbers. An increase in the Jewish population enhances the sense of security.

At times the zeal for immigration leads to extravagant hopes that all Jews will settle in Israel, and even to impatience with those who are content to remain in their present homelands. However, sober reality has prevailed, certainly among the leaders, and most Israelis understand that the Jewish masses of the United States, and of other countries, too, do not regard themselves as "exiles" and do not feel the need to migrate to Israel. They even recognize that "at all times *Aliyah* has been a product of Jewish anguish"; that persecution and insecurity as well as vision have motivated emigration of Jews from their native lands. The emphasis of the Ingathering has been upon the Jewish communities which really have suffered "exile" in the sense of insecurity or inferior status. And with respect to these, the policy has been to transport them to Israel en masse, even when Israel is not fully ready to absorb them.[50]

The achievement of the Ingathering has been startling—in many respects, unparalleled in the story of organized human migration. With a Jewish population of about 650,000 at the time of the establishment of the state, Israel has had the dauntless courage to bring into the country nearly 900,000 immigrants in less than ten years! And about 685,000 of the latter arrived in the first three years and eight months of independence! The table (page 732) presents the annual immigration totals.[51]

It is evident from this table that mass immigration continued from the rise of the State of Israel until close to the end of 1951. And during that brief period of about three and one-half years, the most troublesome of the Jewish refugee problems were liquidated. The words "Jews" and "refugees" had become practically synonyms as a result of Nazi terror, and the Western world had been unable or unwilling to provide asylum for the masses of desperate human beings. At the close of the Second World War, the condition of the survivors of the Nazi extermination camps aroused a sense of horror and widespread sympathy for the victims, but that, too, fell short of a solution: large numbers continued to languish in camps with little hope for the future. The State of Israel welcomed the hapless beings, not grudgingly but eagerly, and the displaced persons' camps were quickly emptied of Jews, except for the small "hard core" cases who could not or would not be moved. The Jews ceased to figure as a major refugee problem in Western Europe.

TABLE II

Annual Immigration Since May 15, 1948

Year	Immigration
1948 (May 15-December 31)	101,825
1949	239,424
1950	169,720
1951	174,014
1952	23,408
1953	10,388
1954	17,485
1955	36,327
1956	54,996
1957	71,100
Total	898,687

Cyprus had become a refugee center where the British had interned illegal Jewish immigrants to Palestine. By February 10, 1949, the last Jews had been transported to Israel and the camps closed with festivities in which even the British participated. The surviving Balkan Jews, notably those of Bulgaria, had emerged from the war and the accompanying Nazi savagery destitute and broken in health. The large majority found homes in Israel. The masses of Polish and Rumanian Jews had perished at the hands of the Nazis, and the survivors found their erstwhile homelands intolerable. Those who were allowed to emigrate were transported to Israel.

The Moslem countries of the Middle East and North Africa were reservoirs of refugees. The war between Arabs and Jews in Palestine naturally exposed local Jewish communities in Arab lands to persecution. But that was only the culmination of deeper forces of hostility. For centuries, Jews had been tolerated but despised in Moslem lands because of their difference in religion. In Yemen, for example, medieval conditions had prevailed, with Jews not only relegated to an inferior status but also subjected to gross and humiliating discrimination and intermittent persecution, including ritual murder charges and mob violence. The effects of nationalism in Moslem lands had likewise resulted in economic deterioration for the Jews and in mounting political and legal insecurity. Finally, Nazi-Fascist propaganda, and in some cases anti-Jewish legislation, despoiled the Jews and endangered their lives. Thus, massacres occurred in Libya during 1945, before the Palestine situation became acute. A mass refugee problem was building up, when Israel came to the rescue.

There was a dramatic quality about the Ingathering from the Moslem lands. The Jews of Yemen (some 45,000) and of Iraq (about 123,000) were brought in by airlift, popularly known as "Operation Magic Carpet" and "Operation Ali Baba." This gave the refugees a sense of dignity and human worth. Although totally beggared, they were not just human debris, discarded by their native lands and unwanted elsewhere. They had a sense of belonging, of being wanted and welcomed. They were returning "home."

In many an instance the Ingathering removed practically the entire Jewish population of an area, thus sweeping clean the festering remains of age-old Jewish problems. Practically all the Jews of Yemen, of Iraq, of Libya, and of other countries were transported to Israel. There was an atmosphere of finality about Ingathering. Israel claimed for its own the Jews who were "unwelcome guests" (a Nazi phrase) in certain lands.[52]

However, mass immigration created overwhelming problems in Israel. The cost of transporting destitute multitudes to Israel was high; that of settling and rehabilitating them all but prohibitive. A modification in policy therefore ensued. The ideal of the Ingathering remained, and families or individuals who came of their own accord were assisted. But publicly financed mass immigration was curtailed and limited to such Jewish communities as were subject to pressure or attack. The result was a sharp decline in immigration during 1952-1954. By the middle of 1954, mass immigration was again resumed in response to the urgency of the North African situation, where the national revolt against French rule increased Jewish insecurity.

The economic, social, and cultural absorption of nearly 900,000 persons in less than a decade, and by a community which numbered initially only 650,000 Jews, would have been a formidable undertaking even under the most favorable conditions. In Israel this effort has been made in the face of unyielding obstacles and discouraging perplexities. The resources of the country have been relatively meager. The borders have been continuously disturbed by latent or active hostilities. Constructive economic measures have been hampered by legal restraints, regional boycott, and naked force. And the human material of the new immigration has added a host of special problems.

A brief comparison of the new immigration with that of the Mandate period will reveal the magnitude of the task of settlement and absorption. During the entire period of the British administration, about 484,000 Jewish immigrants arrived in Palestine, whereas nearly 900,000 immigrants were admitted from May, 1948, to the end of 1957. Immigration during the Mandate period was severely limited by a strict definition of the economic absorptive capacity of Palestine. Under the new state, the immediate absorptive capacity of the country has been disregarded: masses of immigrants have been transported to Israel and then the means have been sought to absorb them. Furthermore, prior to 1948 immigration was highly selective; that is, persons with some means were admitted, and those without means were in the main young persons with good employment potential, who received training in economic skills as well as in the Hebrew language and national ideals. The new immigrants have been either destitute displaced persons or Jews who have been obliged to leave property and belongings in their native lands. They have arrived in Israel without capital, without a knowledge of the language, the country, or the national values of their new homeland, and many have been lacking in education and culture, in the modern sense of the words. A large segment of the old immigration was imbued with social idealism, with a passion for labor, especially manual labor; among the masses of new immigrants, work and work standards have not been held in high esteem.[53] The hundreds of thousands who have swept into Israel since the establishment of the state became consumers even before they set foot on Israeli soil. Their participation in production has been a gradual process.

The territorial origin of the immigrants is of considerable importance. Prior to the establishment of Israel (1919-1948), close to nine-tenths of the Jewish immigrants hailed from Europe or other "Western" countries, with Asia and North Africa supplying only about 10 per cent of the total. Since May, 1948, however, a majority of the newcomers have been of Asian or African origin. Invidious comparisons respecting countries of origin are, of course, inadmissible and unsound. But the sociocultural character of the new immigration has complicated the problems of adjustment to the new environment. Lack of technical training, indifference to sanitation and health hygiene, the prevalence of infectious diseases, illiteracy, and a heritage of substandard living in slum areas—these and other difficulties have had to be met and mastered in order to preserve the social, economic, and cultural standards of Israel.

Finally, in transporting to Israel the entire Jewish communities of several Moslem countries, the Ingathering has added to the burdens of the young state. With proper planning, the young and vigorous could be trained to take their place among the gainfully employed in a relatively short time. But along with that element have come also the aged and infirm, the handicapped and the diseased, the mentally and socially maladjusted, the young children and those past middle age whose economic productive capacity has been problematical or long delayed. This is evident in the age distribution of the Israeli population. The census of November, 1948, showed a child population (under 15 years of age) of 28.5 per cent; at the close of 1956, it was 34.2 per cent of the Jews of Israel. In 1948, the component of the Jewish population over 45 years of age was 18.8 per cent of the total; at the end of 1956, it was 23 per cent. The population element which held the greatest promise of economic productivity, that is, the fifteen–forty-four age group, composed of 52.7 per cent of the Jewish population in 1948, and only 42.8 per cent in 1956. And there were other, less obvious considerations. For example, a considerable proportion of the women of the old immigration was gainfully employed, especially in the rural areas, whereas the immigrants from Moslem lands were not accustomed to gainful employment away from home.

In a word, the settlement and absorption of the new immigration have been a colossal undertaking. Many have had to be trained or retrained for gainful employment. Housing has had to be provided for hundreds of thousands, and schooling for a large child population. Medical needs have mounted, health services have been strained, and special efforts have been necessary to acquaint the newcomers with elementary hygiene and sanitation.

The measures taken to cope with the problems of mass immigration have been numerous and varied, but only the main features of the effort can here be outlined. During and immediately after the War of Independence, the immigrants remained in reception camps until housing and employment could be found for them. This was obviously unsatisfactory because the newcomers remained idle and dependent, with little opportunity to help themselves.

In the summer of 1950, the *Maabara* system was introduced. A *Maabara* (plural, *Maabarot*) was a transitional settlement with temporary housing and employment, and the immigrants resident therein were in considerable measure dependent upon their own resources. Some of the *Maabarot* were entirely temporary, set up in an area because of the availability of employment. Others were planned to evolve into permanent settlements as the land or industries were developed to absorb the immigrants. In such cases, the temporary housing was gradually replaced by permanent dwellings. During 1954, still another method—the "Ship to Farm" form of settlement—was inaugurated. Villages were laid out, homes furnished, schools and clinics built, and immigrants taken to the settlements immediately on arrival, where they worked under the supervision of instructors.

However, one must not assume that the process of absorption has worked smoothly. Inevitably, there have been complications, hardships, disappointments, and improvisations. For example, tent settlements are hardly satisfactory in the winter season, and torrential rains have created emergencies which have required the removal of immigrants to better shelter. Yet, somehow, the situation has been kept in hand, and the vast majority of the immigrants have found homes in Israel. The visitor to Israel during the past decade could see the dreary reception camps and the hardly less unsatisfactory *Maabarot*. But he could also see numerous new villages and permanent housing dotting the countryside, with the remains of the temporary settlements still bearing witness to the rapid progress achieved.

The essential point is that the immigrants have not been left to shift for themselves, as has been the practice in many countries of immigration. The government of Israel has sought to guide the process of absorption, and the settled population has endured austerity and hardship to ease the lot of the newcomers. World Jewry has helped generously with funds, for the cost has been stupendous. It has been estimated that, on the average, the cost of transporting and settling an immigrant has amounted to about $3,000.

The result of the Ingathering is evident in the growth of Israel's population. On May 14, 1948, the Jewish population was estimated at 650,000. An incomplete census taken on November 8, 1948, recorded 716,000 Jews and 69,000 non-Jews, in a total of 785,000. By the end of 1957, the population of Israel had grown to 1,975,954, and this total included 1,672,741 Jews and 213,213 non-Jews.[54] The non-Jewish minority, mainly Arabic, calls for special analysis.

THE MINORITY POPULATION

The minority population of Israel consists predominantly of Arabic-speaking Moslems and Christians, with a small group of Druses situated in Galilee and on Mt. Carmel. For convenience, the entire minority population will be referred to as "Arabs."

The census of November 8, 1948, which recorded only 69,000 non-Jews, did not include the Arabs of western Galilee, the Beersheba areas, and the villages of the Sharon. The inclusion of these districts increased the initial Arab population of the new state to an estimated 120,000 at the end of 1948. One year later the Arabs numbered about 160,000, and at the end of 1957 their population was 213,213. The increase was due largely to the Family Reunion Scheme, which allowed relatives to rejoin families, and to infiltrators who returned clandestinely and settled down.

The essence of minority rights relates to the acquisition of nationality; constitutional equality; actual nondiscrimination in political, economic, and social opportunities; and the sharing of social services. In areas of mixed national groupings, special rights affecting religion, language, and culture are likewise of supreme importance if minorities are not to be forcibly denationalized.

As has been noted, nationality is acquired in Israel by birth, residence, naturalization, or immigration. The condition of birth applies equally to Arabs and Jews. Residence has been established by national registration instituted in 1949 or by legal entry prior to July 14, 1952. This has no doubt involved some difficulty for Arabs, but over 90 per cent of the Arabs resident in Israel have acquired Israeli nationality. Immigration does give preferential treatment to Jews: under the Law of the Return, immigrant Jews acquire Israeli nationality automatically, whereas Arab immigration is discouraged and those who do return to Israel must undergo a process of naturalization.

Legal equality has been proclaimed for all regardless of "religion, race, or sex," and this has been implemented in the functioning of democratic government and in the operation of the social services.

At the end of the War of Independence, some 35,000 Israeli Arabs could not return to their homes because these were outside the borders of Israel, because the villages had been settled by Jewish immigrants, or because the government held the area for security reasons or for large-scale development. In such cases, provision has been made for compensation in land or in cash, and the claimants have had recourse to judicial settlement when necessary. At the time of writing, some 80 per cent of the Arab agriculturists own their farms, and agricultural methods and yields have improved markedly as a result of government assistance, including irrigation, loans, and instruction in modern cultivation. Agricultural machinery is being introduced, crops have been diversified, and new crops such as tobacco, cotton, and sugar have been encouraged, and the output per acre has increased. The *Histadrut* and the Ministry of Labor have assisted in the formation of co-operatives, and some thirty-two agricultural marketing co-operatives and twenty-five co-operative wholesale associations function in the Arab villages. These measures and the ready market for farm produce have brought prosperity to the Arab peasants.

The Arabs in industry and in service occupations have profited from the labor legislation which applies equally to all: the work day is limited and a weekly day of rest and paid holidays are enforced. National insurance, too, covers Arabs as well as Jews. Equal pay for equal work obtains for Arabs and Jews in government jobs and public institutions as well as in the Jewish farm communities which employ Arab labor and in the *Histadrut* industrial undertakings. In private industry, the unskilled Arab laborer is at a disadvantage, but the *Histadrut* efforts to unionize the Arab workers have resulted in wage increases which have narrowed the differential in scales of pay.

The government has made loans to Arabs engaged in the fishing industry. Emergency public works and labor exchanges in Arab areas have been provided to care for the unemployed. Roads have been built around Arab villages and towns. Water works have been constructed, as at Nazareth, which now, for the first time in its long history, has water piped into the homes. Vocational training facilities have been set up and government loans advanced to Arabs to enable them to acquire industrial and agricultural skills. The effort has even been made to assist Arabs through evening courses to qualify for the Civil Service.

The health and welfare services of the country are available to and utilized by the Arabs. The government has made grants-in-aid for the maintenance of clinics by Arab local authorities, and it has established a visiting nursing service and mobile medical units for villages without clinics. Anti-malaria work has been extended to all Arab areas, and courses have been organized to train Arab personnel in nursing and sanitation. As a result, the Arab death rate and infant mortality have declined.

Arab education has undergone remarkable progress. Under the British Mandate, 454 Arab schools (in 1946) were maintained for a population of over a million. With the development of the new state, and especially with the enactment of compulsory education, educational facilities have multi-plied. In 1957, there were some 103 Arab villages and eight towns in-habited in whole or in part by Arabs. These were served by 115 Arab state primary schools with 1,064 classes for a population of about 213,000, and a considerable number of the schools are in villages which formerly had none.

The growth in Arab education since the establishment of the state is especially significant. In 1949, only 56 Arab schools functioned with 186 teachers and some 7,400 pupils, whereas in 1957 the 115 schools had 835 teachers (including 243 women) and 28,267 pupils. The over-all per-centage of Arab school-age children attending school, which was 48 per cent during the period of the Mandate, has risen to over 70 per cent of the settled Arab population. The state has also taken steps to improve the quali-fications of Arab teachers. Special in-service and refresher courses have been given, and the higher educational institutions of Israel have, of course, been available to the Arabs. In 1956, an Arab Teachers Training College was opened in Jaffa.

The Arabs have participated in the public life of Israel. Men, and women too, have voted in parliamentary elections in surprisingly high percentages: 79.3 per cent of the qualified voters in the election of 1949, 85.5 per cent in 1951, and 91.2 per cent in 1955. And every *Knesset* has had Arab depu-ties—three in the First *Knesset*, eight in the Second, and eight in the Third. The Arab vote has been divided between independent Arab splinter parties and the general parties of the country. In the election of 1955, close to one-half (about 48 per cent) of the Arab votes were cast for three Arab factions, which elected a total of five deputies. The latter generally voted with *Mapai,* which polled in addition close to 14 per cent of the Arab votes. The predominant party of Israel thus had the support of about two-thirds of the Arab electorate. About 15 per cent of the Arabs voted Communist, and *Mapam* and the General Zionists received appreciable support.

Some progress has also been made in local government among the Arabs. This has been especially difficult because of the lack of experience of the latter in self-government and because of the fear that local government would entail taxation. Under the British Mandate, elementary education and local services had been provided free of charge, and taxation had been minimal. Family feuds have likewise militated against united local efforts. However, local government is functioning in the two all-Arab towns, and some sixteen Arab local councils have been set up. In all, about 40 per cent of the Arab minority have been involved in some measure of local self-government. The Arabs vote eagerly: in elections in 1955 to five local authorities, about 94 per cent of the qualified voters cast ballots. Some of the councils have concerned themselves with water and sewage systems, roads, and electricity and telephone services. But the government has had to supply most of the necessary budgets through loans and grants-in-aid.

The Arabs also enjoy national-cultural rights. The special religious courts with jurisdiction over matters of personal status (marriage, divorce, custody of children, wills, etc.) have been mentioned. In addition, the Arabic language has official status. It is the language of instruction in the state-supported Arab schools, and it is freely used by Arabs in public life. Arabs employ their language in the *Knesset* and its committees and their addresses are immediately translated into Hebrew. Similarly Hebrew speeches in the *Knesset*, simultaneously translated into Arabic, are heard by the Arab members through earphones. At committee meetings, an interpreter sits beside an Arab member and whispers a running translation of the discussion. Proposed legislation, the agenda of meetings, and the main clauses of the budget are available in advance in Arabic translation. The *Official Gazette*, which contains the laws and ordinances of the state, appears in Arabic as well as Hebrew, and in Arab districts official notices appear in Arabic. Finally, coins, banknotes, postage stamps, and the like carry Arabic along with the Hebrew inscriptions.

However, one important disability remains to be noted. Military government has prevailed in certain Arab areas, especially along the borders, with restrictions on freedom of movement, night curfews, and other security regulations. The stringency of the controls has varied with the tension resulting from the activities of armed infiltrators. However, a noticeable relaxation has been evident. During 1957, Druses and Arabs serving in the army were allowed freedom of movement in border areas, and intervillage travel restrictions in Galilee were relaxed for the general Arab population. At one time, there were forty-six "closed areas" in Galilee, but these have been reduced to strictly border regions which affect perhaps 10 per cent of the Arab population of Galilee. In the Negev, too, travel restrictions have been eased.

In summary, it may be said that the Jewish majority and Arab minority have eyed each other with suspicion and even hostility. The Arabs have suffered an unprecedented upheaval, physically and psychologically. War destruction and dislocations have brought economic ruin to many. Family units have been severed; old parties, associations, newspapers, and leaders have vanished; and the entire social fabric has distintegrated. The shock of military defeat and reduction to the status of a minority has been over-whelming. Loyalties of kinship and fears of reprisals, too, have predisposed Arabs to co-operate with infiltrators in acts of sabotage. This has engendered fear and suspicion in the Jewish majority, and security restrictions have further estranged the Arabs.

The Arab States have fanned the smoldering hostility from without, and the Communists have exploited Arab grievances within Israel. The center of Communist strength is in the Arab city of Nazareth. A third of the party membership and party vote is reputed to be Arab, and as much as 35 per cent of the Arab urban vote went to the Communists in 1955. (It was about 15 per cent of the total Arab vote.) All of this is a reflection of Arab hostility to the State of Israel.

Yet the extent of co-operation and accommodation has been most impres-sive. The policies of the government have brought economic prosperity to the Arabs, educational progress, improvement in health, and social better-ment. The major grievances are the Arab refugees, reduction in status to that of a minority, preferential treatment of Jews in immigration, and security restrictions. The progress made in majority-minority relations dur-ing the past ten years has been considerable, but permanent harmonious co-operation will depend on a solution of the refugee problem and on peace with the Arab States.[55]

The Welfare State

The term "welfare state" is generally employed to describe the trend of the twentieth century for the state to become actively involved in the functioning of the economic system in order to ensure maximum economic and social security. Previously the ideal had been "free enterprise," which precluded state intervention and state controls of the economy. The free functioning of economic "laws" had been regarded as the best assurance of general prosperity, and hence of individual security. The maladjustments resulting from industrialization and the disruptive effects of two world wars have rendered necessary state intervention. In some countries, state controls have destroyed democratic liberties, but the Western democracies have attempted to combine varying forms of state control of the economy, and even state planning, with political democracy. Israel, too, has sought to fashion a democratic welfare state.

The ideal of the welfare state is deeply rooted in Israel. It permeated all of the major efforts in the building of the Jewish National Home during and prior to the period of the Mandate. Formerly, however, it found ex-pression in the voluntary activities of the Jews, who did not wield govern-mental power. With the rise of Israel, social security and welfare have become state functions.

The welfare state is evidenced in Israel by the assumption of state and government responsibility for the economic welfare and social and cultural progress of the people. It is sustained by a passion for equality among large sections of the population and a conviction that full employment and a "living wage," health facilities, rest and leisure, education and culture, are human rights; that advanced levels in social services and standard of living must be maintained, if necessary even in defiance of adverse economic realities. The means employed for the realization of the ideal have been direct involvement of the government in economic affairs through ownership or control; planned settlement of the immigrants and planned economic, social, and cultural development; the control of housing; social security legislation and relief and rehabilitation; and measures for health, welfare, education, and culture.

LAND AND LABOR

Land is nationally owned or administered, except for about 10 per cent of the total area remaining in private possession.[56] The rest is held by the state or the Jewish National Fund or the Custodian of Abandoned Property, and parcels are assigned on long-term lease to groups, institutions, or individuals. Private enterprise in agriculture and especially in industry is permitted and even encouraged, but it is subject to government regulation. Moreover, a large segment of the economy—industry, commerce, communication, transport, and finance—is directly controlled by the state through public corporations which are to a considerable extent state-financed and in which management is frequently shared by the government. The government is thus the largest employer and investor, and in addition the *Histadrut* controls at least 20 per cent of the economy through its far-flung enterprises.[57]

In an uncontrolled economy, wages are conditioned by the productivity of labor, but in Israel wage policy is determined largely by the tradition of social idealism and by labor organization, especially of the *Histadrut*. There is, of course, a differential in wages between the skilled and unskilled, but the effort has been made to achieve a single wage scale for particular jobs, even for the untrained Arabs and immigrants. And provision has been made for cost-of-living allowances, seniority rights, paid vacations, and social services.

Special legislation has been enacted setting up machinery for the settlement of labor disputes, without curtailment of the right to strike, and collective agreements in labor relations are encouraged and must be registered with the Ministry of Labor. A state inspection service has been set up and charged with the supervision and promotion of labor safety and vocational hygiene and welfare.

A comprehensive scheme of social security insurance was projected as soon as the United Nations Assembly approved the establishment of a

Jewish State. The first phase was enacted by the National Insurance Law of 1953, which made provision for old age and survivors' benefits, maternity grants, and insurance against industrial accidents. This compulsory insurance covers all inhabitants between the ages of eighteen and sixty-seven, the salaried, self-employed, and nonemployed as well as wage earners. The insurance fund is composed of contributions by employers and employees, with a subsidy from the state treasury. Old age pensions are paid generally at sixty-five for men and sixty for women, but there is encouragement to continue working for an additional five-year period. The pensions are related to the cost-of-living index, so that a rise in prices does not undermine the value of the benefits.

Maternity insurance not only provides the usual payments but also serves as a stimulus for proper medical care. Benefits may be denied for employment outside the home against the advice of a physician, or for noncompliance with medical instructions. Since delivery in hospitals or maternity clinics is directly related to the payment of benefits, 95 per cent of Jewish women utilize such facilities, and even Arab mothers increasingly turn to hospitals and clinics for delivery.

Apart from maternity, the employment of women is regulated by law. The Minister of Labor is empowered to prohibit or restrict their employment in certain industries, and night work is forbidden, save in stated exceptional cases.[58]

National health and unemployment insurance has not as yet been introduced because of financial stringency. But health needs are met by the voluntary insurance schemes, especially the Sick Fund of the *Histadrut*. The unemployed, too, have not been disregarded. The government attempts to estimate in advance anticipated unemployment and provides public works programs to absorb them.

HOUSING

The housing and settlement of immigrants quickly became the government's responsibility, and the latter has also built homes for war veterans and civil servants. In addition, the government has co-operated in low cost housing schemes for the settled population, and it has made loans to housing companies to stimulate building. Since the establishment of Israel, the government has built or assisted in the building of about two-thirds of all housing units. The *Histadrut* and political parties have also subsidized housing projects for their adherents.

Private ownership and construction of housing is permitted but strictly controlled. Tenants of residential and business premises are protected against eviction or arbitrary rise in rentals, and even the state is subject to the same restrictions with regard to its tenants as private owners of property.[59]

RELIEF AND REHABILITATION

Relief and rehabilitation have received a great deal of government attention, with major emphasis upon wounded or handicapped veterans and their families. Provision is made for hospitalization, medical care, convalescence, education and retraining, and housing and pension payments for the seriously disabled.

Mass immigration has imported mass misery, and the government has made an effort to alleviate distress. The Ministry of Public Welfare has maintained the necessary agencies in the *Maabarot*, and it has subsidized over 150 bureaus of local authorities to the extent of 20-90 per cent of their budgets. The assistance has taken the form of material support, medical aid and hospitalization, placement in institutions of the aged, children and mental cases, and counseling in family problems. The effort has been made to train the blind and handicapped for gainful employment, and to rehabilitate physically and mentally defective children and neglected youth. Insurance has been provided for the aged, including those of the minorities, with the government contributing 25 per cent of the cost.

Nongovernment agencies have greatly reinforced the efforts of the government. The Jewish Agency and the *Histadrut* have borne a large share of the burden. Hadassah has continued its extensive medical services, and it has launched a family health program near Jerusalem which combines medical, health, and social service facilities. The Women's International Zionist Organization (WIZO) has rendered valuable aid. And Malben (agency for the care of handicapped immigrants), founded and financed by the American Joint Distribution Committee, has maintained special centers for the handicapped who can do some useful work, as well as institutions for the aged, the chronically ill and disabled, and the mentally afflicted.

The shortage of trained social workers has been a serious handicap, but measures have been taken to cope with the problem. A Social Welfare Institute functions in Jerusalem under the joint supervision of the government and the Hebrew University, and a Social Welfare School is maintained by the Tel-Aviv Municipality with the aid of a government subvention.[60]

PUBLIC HEALTH

The achievements in public health have been truly phenomenal. When the Mandate came to an end, Palestine Jewry enjoyed through voluntary health services standards of health, life expectancy, and an infant mortality rate which compared favorably with the Western world. The mass immigration threatened to undermine these health standards. Many immigrants from the displaced persons' camps and especially from Oriental lands were chronic cases or permanently disabled, needing hospitalization. Typhus, typhoid, diphtheria, filariasis, trachoma, malaria, and other diseases were endemic in the Arab areas of emigration. Yet so effective have been the health measures of Israel that no major epidemic has occurred. The tubercular have been hospitalized, and the incidence of other diseases sharply reduced.

The voluntary agencies have continued their admirable health services, nominally under the supervision of the Ministry of Health. *Kupat Holim,* the Sick Fund of the *Histadrut,* has expanded its facilities, so that it serves about two-thirds of the population. With a budget twice that of the Ministry of Health, it functions in some 600 localities, and maintains fourteen hospitals, fourteen convalescent homes, and over 900 clinics staffed by about 7,800 professional workers, including 1,400 physicians and over 2,200 nurses. The *Kupat Holim* and four smaller sick funds provide voluntary health insurance for about 75 per cent of the population.

Hadassah, the pioneer in health work in Palestine since 1918, has remained a primary influence in Israel. Its medical facilities are paramount in the Jerusalem area, and it has led the way in experimenting with mental health, occupational therapy, and preventive medicine. It has devoted much attention to medical education, co-operating with the Hebrew University in the establishment of the first medical school in the country. Its community health work, mentioned above, is a pioneering venture which supplies at one center preventive medicine and social services as well as curative facilities.

The work of Malben, founded by the American Joint Distribution Committee in 1950, has been noted. Its special sphere of interest has been the handicapped immigrant, with emphasis on the tubercular. Some 18,000 tuberculosis cases have been treated, and extensive rehabilitation has restored many to economic usefulness. Sheltered workshops have been set up for cured tuberculosis patients as well as for the physically handicapped. Malben also maintains homes for some 3,000 aged and indigent invalids. Finally, the *Magden David Adom* (the equivalent of the Red Cross) operates over forty branches and first-aid stations, conducts a blood bank and ambulance service, and campaigns for accident prevention.

The government has supplemented the efforts of the private agencies in all fields of public health, and it has concentrated attention on antimalaria work, sanitation and food hygiene, the control of epidemics through testing and quarantine, the expansion of hospital facilities and public health laboratories, and mother and child care.

The progress achieved by the combined efforts of the government and private agencies can be indicated here only by a few illustrative figures. The number of hospitals has increased from 63 in 1948 to 100 (at the end of 1955); hospital beds from 4,600 to over 12,200, of which 37 per cent are maintained by the government. In 1955, Israel had 3.1 beds in general hospitals per 1,000 population, compared with 5.1 in the United States and 1.2 in Egypt. Mother-and-child-care stations have grown rapidly: at the end of 1954, there were 375; by the end of 1956, the number had increased to 485. The number of licensed physicians was 3,957 (over 20 per cent women) at the end of 1956—the highest proportion of doctors to the population of any country in the world. The proportion of dentists was one per 2,025 inhabitants, again one of the highest in the world. There is a shortage of nurses, but the ratio of 3.3 per 1,000 population is higher than in Norway, Sweden, Poland, and even the United States.

The effects of medical and health work are reflected in the vital statistics of Israel. The birth rate in 1955 was 27.2 per 1,000 among the Jews and 42.78 among the Arabs. (It was 24.9 in the United States, and 44.8 in Egypt.) The crude death rate was 5.77 for the Jews and 8.01 for the Arabs. (In the United States it was 8.2, and in Egypt 19.3.) Life expectancy at birth for the Jewish population has risen from 65.2 years in 1949 to 69.4 for males and 72.1 for females in 1955. The latter figures were close to those of the United States, but in Egypt life expectancy was 35.6 for males and 41.5 for females.

Infant mortality, a good index of public health, affords the best evidence of the successful effort to maintain health standards. In 1947, the last year of the British Mandate, the infant mortality rate among Jews was 29.2 per 1,000 live births. In 1949 the rate leaped to 51.75, but by 1955 it was down to 32.5 for the entire population. (In the United States the rate was 26.6, and in Egypt 128.6.) A breakdown of the Israeli figure for 1955 indicates future possibilities. In the *kibbutzim*, the infant mortality rate was only 18.7, the lowest in the world. In the *Maabarot* and rural settlements, it was high—45.3 per 1,000—but this represented a sharp decline from 1950.[61]

At the time of the establishment of Israel, the health conditions among the Jewish population had risen to a high level as a result of a quarter-century of intensive voluntary effort. Mass immigration from substandard areas threatened retrogression, but energetic measures have obviated the danger. The health of the new arrivals has been improved and the high standards of the settled population maintained. The task has been prodigious and commands further effort, but Israel has remained a health oasis in the bleak Middle East.

EDUCATION AND HEBREW CULTURE

The educational problems posed by mass immigration have been hardly less challenging than those of health. The enactment of compulsory and free elementary education in 1949 and the fashioning of a unified national system of education in 1953 have been noted. These measures have resulted in four categories of schools, namely Jewish State and State-Religious Schools, Jewish Independent (or Unofficial or Recognized) Schools, and Arab Schools. The elementary school enrollment in 1957 was as follows:[62]

	HEBREW SCHOOLS			ARAB-PRIMARY	GRAND
Total	State	State-Religious	Independent	SCHOOLS	TOTAL
285,796	196,178	71,082	18,536	24,659	310,455

Of the total primary school population, 68.6 per cent attend State Schools, 24.8 per cent attend State-Religious Schools, 6.6 per cent attend Independent Schools.

The above figures do not include the children who attend preschool kindergartens, and Christian missionary schools, which are not under government supervision. Furthermore, some 11,800 pupils attend continuation classes. If these are added, the preschool, elementary school, and continuation school population is at least 400,000.

Secondary education is less satisfactory because it is neither free nor compulsory, and because many parents depend upon the supplementary earnings of adolescents. In 1957, the enrollment in academic secondary schools was about 26,000. About one-third of the secondary school pupils receive scholarships or grants, and the government also provides subsidies for teaching equipment and other purposes.

In addition to normal academic education, Israel also provides specialized instruction for relatively large numbers of students. Close to 3,000 students attend high school evening classes. Trade and agricultural schools include 11,000 or 12,000 pupils, and close to 5,000 students are in special schools and classes for the handicapped.

The majority of Israeli schools are coeducational. The elementary curriculum covers eight years and the secondary school four years of intensive study. In addition to the common branches, the course of study includes physical education, agricultural and prevocational work, nature study, arts and crafts, and English. Arabic is taught in 116 Hebrew primary and secondary schools and continuation classes.

The teacher problem has become acute because of mass immigration and because of the lack of qualified Arab teachers. In 1957, there were 4,601 full-time and 9,450 part-time teachers, and the shortage was estimated at 10-15 per cent. To meet the need, over 3,200 students were in training in 1957 in more than twenty-five teachers' colleges and courses, and in addition the School of Education of the Hebrew University has provided specialized and advanced instruction for teachers and other educational personnel.

Higher education and research are maintained on an advanced level in Israel. The Hebrew University is the central institution of higher learning in the country, with an enrollment of 4,373 graduate and undergraduate students (1957-1958), an academic staff of 756, and courses of study and research embracing the humanities, the natural and social sciences, medicine, dentistry and pharmacy, law, agriculture, education, and librarianship. Its standards of scholarship, the renown of members of its faculty, and the high quality of its productive research have won recognition for the Hebrew University as one of the great centers of learning in the world. The state contributes materially to its maintenance budget and the University, in turn, has been a vital factor in the economic and cultural development of the country. The campus on Mt. Scopus became inaccessible after the War of Independence, but the faculty and students carried on in improvised quarters under the most perplexing difficulties. This courage has been rewarded, and a new campus, constructed at Giv'at Ram in Jerusalem, was officially opened in May, 1958. The new campus is already becoming one of the foremost cultural centers of the country.

The Israel Institute of Technology (*Technion*), situated at Technion City on Mt. Carmel, has won an enviable reputation as a school of engineering, architecture, aeronautics, and applied science. Its staff of 427 is engaged in the instruction of 2,021 students (1956-1957) and in extensive research. *Technion* also provides varied facilities for laboratory testing.

The Weizmann Institute of Science at Rehovot has functioned under that name since 1949. It is devoted mainly to advanced research in applied mathematics, nuclear physics, electronics, optics, and the chemical and biological sciences. Its staff of 500 workers includes 150 scientists, some of whom are widely known in scientific circles. The Prime Minister's Office also contains a Scientific Research Council and an Atomic Energy Commission, as mentioned above. The former consists of the leading scientists and engineers and it serves as the consultant body to the government in matters affecting public health and the development and utilization of the country's resources. In recent years, two other universities have been founded, namely, the Bar-Ilan University at Ramat Gan and the Tel-Aviv University, which is developing under the guidance of the Hebrew University. Finally, a large number of talmudic academies devote themselves to religious studies.

Archaeology is pursued systematically in Israel under the supervision of the Department of Antiquities. The latter directs the diggings in co-operation with the Hebrew University and the Israel Exploration Society, and finds are widely discussed in the press and by the general public. During 1956-1957, some forty excavations were in progress in various parts of the country and a partial survey was made of the Sinai Peninsula.

Israel's cultural life is rich and varied, and the government plays a leading role in its advancement. Adult education has received special attention because of the keen desire for learning among all classes of the population, and also because of its efficacy in facilitating the cultural absorption of the new immigrants. The Ministry of Education and Culture organizes thousands of meetings with cultural content each year. Hundreds of lectures (some 900 in 1956-1957) are given under the auspices of the Hebrew University. And other agencies, notably the *Histadrut*, bring popular education to the remotest settlements.

The study of the Hebrew language is central in adult education. The revival of Hebrew was one of the great achievements of the Jewish National Home, and in 1948 over 75 per cent of all Jews above two years of age spoke Hebrew, while more than 93 per cent of all Jewish children aged two to fourteen employed it as their vernacular. The new immigration, however, necessitated renewed efforts because relatively few of the newcomers had command of the language. Of the adult immigrants of 1948-1949, only 0.4 per cent employed Hebrew in daily life, and only about 16 per cent could speak, read, and write Hebrew. As a result, the percentage of Hebrew-speaking Jews in the Israeli population fell sharply: at the end of 1950, less than 60 per cent of those over two years of age and only about 80 per cent of the children between two and fourteen spoke Hebrew. The central and local governments and private organizations have therefore worked strenuously to spread knowledge of the language even as new waves of immigrants have poured into the country. Short-term courses in Hebrew, given to thousands each year, have proved especially effective.

The Ministry of Education and Culture also maintains a Hebrew Language Academy which continues the work of the Hebrew Language Council (*Vaad Halashon*) of the pre-state era. This body decides on questions of grammar, terminology, and other matters affecting the use of Hebrew in daily speech, scholarship, and science, and its publications include a quarterly for language research and popular pamphlets.

Libraries are widespread and popular. The most important by far is the Jewish National and University Library, which had amassed a valuable collection of 500,000 volumes on Mt. Scopus. When the bulk of that collection became inaccessible, the work of replenishment began anew, and persevering efforts have assembled some 450,000 volumes, which will soon be housed in a new library building. In addition, there are some 700 libraries of varying size and degrees of specialization. Even immigrant settlements have been provided with basic libraries. Archives, too, are well organized and regulated by law. There are state archives, Zionist and historical archives, labor archives, military archives, archives of Middle East Jewish communities, and collections relating to personalities such as Weizmann, Jabotinsky, and others.

Books are read avidly in Israel. About 1,000 titles appear every year, three-quarters of them original works in fiction, poetry, and scholarship, and the remainder translations. A twenty-volume *Hebrew Encyclopedia*, now in process of publication, has over 40,000 subscribers. The Bialik Foundation publishes works of lasting value in literature, art, and science, the Rabbi Kook Foundation concentrates on religious literature, and inexpensive paperback books are issued by the *Histadrut* and by others in relatively large editions.

The Jewish population of Israel supports twenty-three daily newspapers, fifteen of them in Hebrew and the remainder in a half-dozen foreign languages. Some 290 periodicals, including fifty government publications, appear in the country, and devote themselves to literature, art, economics, law, youth, etc.

The arts, too, have a wide following in Israel. The Israel Philharmonic Orchestra, founded by Bronislaw Hubermann, gives 135 concerts annually, which are attended by some 19,000 subscribers, and special concerts attract additional numbers. The State Broadcasting Company, the Defense Forces, and the city of Haifa have their own orchestras, and a Music Festival is held every year during Passover at Ein Gev on Lake Kinneret. There are also conservatories, choirs, and chamber music, folk, and ballet groups. The government encourages these activities and takes special pains to further the study of music in the schools.

The theater has achieved a high artistic level. Four co-operative repertory companies—*Habimah*, *Ohel* (a workers' theater of the *Histadrut*), the Chamber Theater, and the *Zira* Theater—gave some 2,500 performances in 1955-1956 before audiences which totaled over 1,000,000. Tel-Aviv is the center of these companies, but performances are given throughout the country and especially in the co-operative settlements. The latter have their own amateur theatricals as well, and so do the schools, the army, and other groups. A special group arranges performances in the immigrant camps.

Arts and crafts are taught in several schools, notably the Bezalel Art School of Jerusalem, founded in 1906. Painters of note have settled in the country, and their works have been exhibited in New York and Paris as well as Israel. The new immigrants have brought art skills in design, embroidery, and jewelry, and the government as well as private organizations have encouraged the preservation and continued practice of these crafts.

Sports are popular in Israel, and the major political groupings have their sports affiliates. But co-operation is achieved through the Israel Amateur Sports Federation, which works with the Ministry of Education and Culture in planning the sports curriculum of educational institutions and in encouraging training and competitive events.[63]

THE CO-OPERATIVE MOVEMENT

The active concern of the Israeli government with economic, social, and cultural life has not discouraged individual or group initiative. On the contrary, the spirit of self-help and voluntarism, deeply rooted among the Jewish pioneers of the country, has gained in range and influence. This is well illustrated by the co-operative movement.

The collective and co-operative agricultural settlements and their urban counterparts developed before 1948 have been outlined in the introductory pages. These and similar group efforts have continued both because of the momentum of the immediate past and because the forces which produced co-operative forms of living—social idealism, the passion for Jewish immigration, the need to absorb the immigrants, and the requirements of defense in a hostile environment—have been and are still at work. However, modifications have appeared in response to changed conditions. Through the Ministry of Labor, the government has furnished continuous supervision of the work of co-operatives. It has promoted education in co-operative administration, assumed the tasks of research and statistical tabulation, and has aided in the settlement of interco-operative disputes. All co-operatives have joined in a General Cooperative Council which serves as an advisory body to the government. The new type of immigration has likewise necessitated compromises in co-operative living.

At the end of 1956, the number of active co-operatives was 2,508, with a membership of some 750,000, which embraced more than one-third of the population of the country. Of this total, about 78 per cent were working-class societies, and three-quarters of the latter were affiliated with the *Histadrut*. It should be noted, however, that more than 20 per cent of the co-operatives are middle-class and other nonworking-class undertakings. As much as one-fifth of the entire economy of the country is organized co-operatively, and in specialized fields the influence is far greater. For example, co-operatives account for about 90 per cent of citrus exports and for the distribution of about 73 per cent of Israel's agricultural produce. Almost all urban and interurban bus transport is in the hands of co-operatives.

More than one-third of all co-operatives (850) are concerned with agriculture. They embrace the collective and co-operative settlements, marketing and processing agencies, and societies for irrigation, mutual insurance, and other agricultural purposes. Co-operation in housing is widespread, with 484 societies; 297 are engaged in industrial production, services, and transportation; 403 are devoted to provident and pension funds; and the remainder deal with credit, mutual assistance, savings, and miscellaneous functions.

The collective agricultural settlements were a distinctive feature of the Jewish National Home before independence was achieved. Since the establishment of Israel, the number of these settlements has increased, as indicated in the following table.[64]

Table III

Growth of Collective and Semi-Collective Agricultural Settlements

Type of Settlement	1946		1956	
	Number	Population	Number	Population
Kibbutz and *Kvutzah*	140 (in 1945)	over 40,000	223	81,300
Workers Smallholders' Settlement (*Moshav Ovdim*)	62	17,099	101	
Immigrant Smallholders' Settlement (*Moshav Olim*)	——	——	182	93,000
Collective Smallholders' Settlement (*Moshav Shitufi*)	9	878	20	3,082

However, the pressures of mass immigration and the shortage of trained manpower have resulted in modifications which have compromised the original ideals of co-operative living. Some of the *kibbutzim* have been obliged to employ hired labor, mainly in construction and in industrial enterprises. The chief difficulty has been with the immigrant settlements. The new immigrants have had no understanding of the ideas and forms of the co-operative, and many have demanded immediate payment for work done. The result has been an ingenious improvisation for the gradual enlightenment of the newcomers. The older *moshavim* have established a special company which supervises the work of the immigrant settlers and pays the latter in wages and a share of the profits. In the first stages, the company absorbs losses, but gradually the new settlers are taught to share in the losses as well as profits. Leadership in these settlements has been provided by experienced members of collectives who have left comfortable homes and pleasant associations and volunteered for the arduous tasks of training the new immigrants.[65]

The collective and co-operative movement has permeated all Israel, but fundamentally it has been a product of the same forces which fashioned the labor movement, notably the *Histadrut*. Some labor elements have championed co-operation as an ideal, as the antithesis to competition, and as the beginnings of a new society in which private enterprise would disappear, and with it the profit motive and "exploitation."

However, the development of the co-operative movement warrants the conclusion that the co-operative commonwealth has been a secondary consideration. The primary purpose of all Jewish efforts in Palestine has been first the building of the Jewish National Home, and more recently the consolidation of the state. And in the process of building, abstract ideals and preconceived doctrines have yielded to the necessities of promoting immi-

gration and facilitating land settlement and urban development in order
to absorb the newcomers. The co-operative movement has been for some
persons an end, a feature of the ideal society of the future. But more emphatically, it has been a means—an effective method of building the commonwealth.

The welfare state is often confused with the regimentation of totalitarian
regimes. Since government plays an active role in economic, social, and
cultural life in both types of social and political organization, the analogy
is drawn. But it ends abruptly. The essence of totalitarianism is compulsion,
regimentation, and the denial of the right to differ. In Israel, however,
democratic processes prevail, differences are freely expressed, and voluntarism permeates the entire social and cultural pattern of life. The state
supervises and works with voluntary associations, but it neither destroys
nor dominates them.

Economic Growth

The Ingathering and the welfare-state policies were undertaken in defiance of economic realities. The known natural resources of Israel in 1948
were meager indeed.[66] Agricultural expansion was dependent upon irrigation, which in turn required costly development of the none too plentiful
water resources of the country. The major Dead Sea works, which constituted the only exploitation of mineral resources prior to 1948, were
occupied and destroyed by the Arabs during the War of Independence.
The development of large-scale industry was hampered by deficiencies in
industrial raw materials and by lack of coal for the generation of power.
If economic considerations had prevailed, the Ingathering would not have
been undertaken and the welfare state would not have endured.

Noneconomic factors have motivated basic Israeli policies,[67] as they did
formerly the building of the Jewish National Home. Jewish homelessness
and persecution and the requirements of national security have produced
the bold and almost reckless policy of unrestricted immigration. Social
idealism and a powerful labor movement have emphasized social welfare
in economic development, so that the wage scale has not been determined
solely by labor productivity and agricultural or industrial progress has not
been measured exclusively by its profitability. In brief, national and social
ideals have fashioned the fundamental objectives of Israeli policies, and
the economy has been employed as a purposive instrument for their realization.

STAGES IN ECONOMIC POLICY

Three stages are well marked in the economic development of Israel,
and the volume of immigration has been the cardinal factor in each. Mass

immigration and extensive but mainly improvised economic activity marked the period from the establishment of the state in May, 1948, to the end of 1951. This was followed by the New Economic Policy during 1952-1954, which achieved greater economic stability. Since 1955 the country has been grappling with conditions and problems similar to those of the first period but not as acute.

During the first three years and eight months of independence (May, 1948 to the end of 1951), about 685,000 Jewish immigrants arrived in Israel—a total exceeding the entire Jewish population of May, 1948. The economic absorption of such a mass, and of the considerable proportion of the older immigrants who were only partly rooted productively in the economy,[68] would have been difficult even under normal conditions and favorable circumstances, neither of which obtained in Israel. The War of Independence, fought during this period, strained the economy of the country, and the failure to achieve peace settlements with the Arab States necessitated further outlays for defense. Boycott by the Arab States likewise affected the Israeli economy adversely by cutting off markets and sources of supply. Finally, the new immigrants were untrained manpower which could not be used with economic efficiency even when employed.

The Israelis attacked these formidable problems with zeal and determination. Between May, 1948, and 1951 the number of agricultural settlements nearly doubled, and the total cultivated area more than doubled, while the irrigated area increased by more than one-third. Large sums were spent in the building of some 168,000 rooms, mainly as housing units for immigrants. The output of electricity, as well as the amount supplied for industrial purposes, more than doubled. Basic industries were established, industrial machinery imported, roads built, and natural resources surveyed and studied for effective utilization. And special legislation was enacted to attract foreign capital. The Law for the Encouragement of Capital Investment (1950) offered exemption from property and local taxes for at least the first five years of an undertaking; it allowed special concessions in matters affecting depreciation and income tax rates; and it held out the opportunity for nonresidents to withdraw annually in foreign currency a maximum of 10 per cent of the investment.[69]

However, the strains of settling masses of immigrants, liquidating a war, building up defense forces, and promoting extensive development projects were too much for Israel's economy. The weaknesses showed especially in inflation and in an unfavorable balance of trade.

The immigrants became consumers as soon as they arrived in Israel, because they had to be supplied with a minimum of food, clothing, and shelter. But the majority arrived without means and did not immediately share in the production of goods. This created an increased demand for the available supply of commodities. Large defense expenditures likewise increased purchasing power without adding to the supply of consumer goods. The long-range program of economic development added to the pressure upon the goods desired for current consumption. Finally, unbalanced budgets, deficit spending, the issue of Treasury Bills, and the expansion of credit created a spiral of inflation, with increased prices, costs, and wages and a decline in the value of the Israeli pound.

The pattern of foreign trade was equally discouraging. Military equipment and economic development were dependent upon foreign sources of supply, and considerable quantities of consumer goods had to be imported to provide for the increased population. But purchasing power at home and inflation curtailed even the meager exports of the country, so that during 1949-1951 exports amounted to only 11 or 12 per cent of the value of imports, and the annual trade deficits increased steadily, reaching a total of some $333,000,000 in 1951. During this period the government attempted to check inflation by means of rationing, price controls, and other direct administrative measures. But these efforts were nullified by black-market operations and by waning public confidence, especially after clothing and footwear rationing was introduced in the summer of 1950. The drought of the following winter aggravated the situation, threatening collapse of the entire currency and price structure.[70] A change in policy became imperative.

The New Economic Policy is generally associated with the official devaluation of the Israeli pound on February 13, 1952. In fact, however, it was more far-reaching, and some of the measures were adopted as early as the spring of the preceding year. The New Economic Policy gradually abandoned direct controls such as rationing and sought to curb inflation and improve the balance of payments by indirect means. The issue of Treasury Bills was stopped and the attempt was made to balance the regular state budget. Credit was restricted and consumption curtailed through the reduction of purchasing power. Basic wages were frozen, except when justified by higher productivity, and a compulsory development loan was levied. These measures helped to reduce imports, and a special exchange rate served to stimulate exports. Above all, immigration dropped from over 174,000 in 1951 to less than 24,000 in 1952, some 10,000 in 1953, and about 17,500 in 1954.

The effects of the New Economic Policy were evident in increased agricultural and industrial production and in the development of local raw materials. Average daily unemployment fell sharply during 1954. The foreign trade deficit fell from $333,000,000 in 1951 to some $198,000,000 in 1954. Greater stability in prices and costs was achieved during 1954, and public confidence was restored.[71]

In 1955, however, noneconomic factors again disturbed the trend toward economic stability. Mass immigration reappeared as a result of disturbances in North Africa. Military expenditures mounted to meet the threat of the arms agreement of Egypt with the Soviet and its satellites in September, 1955, and the Sinai campaign of October-November, 1956, further strained the Israeli economy. Dependence on foreign imports again increased and greater purchasing power intensified inflationary pressures.

ECONOMIC ACHIEVEMENTS

The recurring difficulties have not discouraged the Israeli government or people. Economic planning, building, and development have been pursued with vigor and the achievements since independence have been most impressive, not only in quantitative growth but also in dynamic planning which has discovered hitherto unknown resources, increased the fertility and yield of the soil, and attacked desert and swamp through bold irrigation projects.

Self-sufficiency in agriculture may be a future hope, but the progress made since 1948 has been remarkable. The cultivated area has increased from some 412,000 acres (1,650,000 dunam) in 1948 to about 950,000 acres (3,825,000 dunam) in 1957. The irrigated area has more than tripled, and agricultural machinery has multiplied. The number of tractors, for example, increased from 681 in 1948 to 4,700 in 1956, and that of combines from 261 to 896. As a result, agricultural production has nearly tripled, although only 17 to 18 per cent of the labor force has been employed in agriculture, afforestation, and fisheries. It has been estimated that all local requirements in milk, eggs, poultry, vegetables, and potatoes are now met by Israeli agriculture, and that it supplies two-thirds of the country's food needs.[72]

Water and reclamation are the keys to agricultural development in Israel. From 1948 to 1956 water consumption for agricultural purposes increased more than threefold. In 1955 a sixty-six-inch pipe line went into operation, carrying water from the Yarkon River, north of Tel-Aviv, to the Negev. Other pipe lines are under construction, but the realization of the elaborate Jordan River development plan has been delayed because of Arab obstruction. The draining of the 15,000 acres of swamp land in the Huleh area, north of Lake Kinneret, was completed in 1957.

Industrial development has had to cope with serious obstacles. For example, the Dead Sea potash works were destroyed by the Arabs, and rehabilitation required not only a new plant but a new road from Beersheba to Sodom (the south end of the Dead Sea). Operations, resumed toward the end of 1953, did not really get under way until 1955-1956. Furthermore, industrial raw materials have had to be imported, except for some food products, fertilizers, and the cement, glass, and ceramics industries.

However, progress has been made despite the difficulties. New establishments have been built for the production of steel, pipes, tires and other rubber goods, electrical appliances, paper products, fertilizers, automobile assembly, radios, and other articles. The labor force engaged in industry, mining, and quarrying reached about 125,000 in November, 1955, and the annual output has increased consistently, tripling between 1948-1956. The relative concentration in the various fields of industry is revealed in the following figures on industrial production in 1956: food processing industries, about 24 per cent of the total industrial production; metals and textiles, 12 to 14 per cent each; stone and cement, about 10 per cent; wood, chemicals, clothing, and footwear, 6 to 7 per cent each; printing and paper, mining and minerals, electrical appliances, motor vehicles, machinery, and diamond cutting and polishing, about 2 to 4 per cent each; and rubber products and leather goods, less than 2 per cent each.[73]

Construction, especially for housing, is a major industry. Between 1949 and 1956, over 150,000 housing units comprising more than 460,000 rooms were built. Notable progress has also been registered in transportation and communication, vital for Israel's economy. The railroad system was disrupted by the war and passenger service was not restored until 1950. Since 1948, railway mileage in operation has increased about two and one half times, including an extension to Beersheba. The road network and motorized transportation have been expanded. Civil aviation has grown. The merchant marine has increased from ten to thirty vessels between 1948-1957, and the tonnage from about 14,000 to 136,000. The port of Haifa and the facilities at Tel-Aviv–Jaffa have been modernized and improved, and work has begun on the development of Elat, on the Gulf of Aqaba, as a major port.

Industrial expansion will be vitally affected by the planned exploration and development of natural resources, especially in the Negev. Oil, discovered at Heletz in September, 1955, is already providing about 5 per cent of the country's needs.[74] Phosphates, copper, ceramic clay, and glass sand have been found in large quantities, and exploitation is under way or in preparation. Some iron has beeen discovered in Upper Galilee, and there are indications that the Negev contains other minerals. Notable progress has also been made with industrial crops, such as cotton.[75]

ECONOMIC PROBLEMS

The economic progress of Israel has been striking, but serious problems remain, with the trade gap between imports and exports the most baffling. The table (page 757) summarizes the balance of trade in American dollars.[76]

These figures show that Israel has had a trade deficit since its establishment as a state, and that, after a steady rise in the annual deficit through 1951, it declined considerably from 1951 through 1954. Since 1955, however, the deficit has been rising again, chiefly because of renewed mass immigration and the threat of Egyptian and Syrian arms purchases.

Closer analysis will reveal that Israel has made significant progress in

TABLE IV

Balance of Trade, 1949-1956
(in millions of dollars)

Year	Imports	Exports	Trade Deficit (Excess of Imports over Exports)	Exports as % of Imports
1949	253.1	29.7	223.4	11.7
1950	298.8	36.9	261.9	12.3
1951	379.8	46.8	333.0	12.3
1952	321.1	44.4	276.7	13.8
1953	281.2	59.7	221.5	21.2
1954	286.5	88.1	198.4	30.8
1955	325.0	90.2	234.8	27.8
1956	364.0	107.2	256.7	29.5

its trade balance. Between 1949 and 1956 imports increased by about 44 per cent, but exports multiplied more than two and one-half times. In 1949, exports covered only 11.7 per cent of imports; in 1956, they covered 29.5 per cent of imports. Equally significant has been the change in the nature of the imports and exports. Whereas consumer goods accounted for about one-third of all imports in 1949, they constituted less than one-sixth of the imports of 1956; and raw materials, which were about one-third of the imports of 1949, increased to about one-half in 1956. Exports, too, have undergone a change. Citrus fruit, which provided 63 per cent of all exports in 1949, constituted only 39 per cent of the exports of 1956, although the value of the amount exported doubled. At the same time, the export of industrial products, including diamonds, increased from about 26 per cent to about 52 per cent of total exports.

The annual trade deficits have been covered by American government grants-in-aid and technical assistance, German reparations payments, Israel government bond sales abroad, private foreign investment, and private foreign philanthropy.[77] For a new and underdeveloped country, foreign trade deficits and even indebtedness are neither unusual nor alarming, so long as capital is available from external sources. However, dependence on foreign aid is risky, and Israel has been seeking (with considerable promise, as has been noted) to achieve greater balance in its international trade.

Other economic problems relate to the relative paucity of natural resources, the occupational structure and utilization of manpower, the need of foreign capital to finance development, and the Arab boycott. The planned exploration and development of mineral resources has been mentioned, and the success achieved in raising 30 per cent of the country's cotton needs and 28 per cent of sugar beet requirements holds the promise that the resource base can be expanded.

The manpower problem is largely but not wholly the result of unselective immigration. The distribution of the civilian labor force is given in the following table.

TABLE V

Distribution of Civilian Labor Force in Percentages[78]

Branch of Economy	% of Total	
	November, 1955	June, 1956
Agriculture, forestry, and fisheries	17.6	17.7
Industry, mining, and quarrying	21.5	20.9
Construction and public works	9.3	8.3
Electricity, gas, water, and sanitary services	2.0	2.9
Commerce, banking, and insurance	13.5	12.5
Transportation, storage, and communication	6.6	6.4
Government and public services	21.2	23.2
Personal and recreational services	8.3	8.1
Total	100.0	100.0

It is evident from this table that a low proportion of the labor force is engaged in essential production, especially in agriculture and industry. In part this is due to the lack of training of the immigrant population, which government efforts have not yet been able to overcome, and to the lack of funds for the expansion of productive industries. Intensive training and concentration on production for export remain basic needs for the future.

Finally, stabilization of the Israeli economy requires increased investment from internal sources and a reduction of the gap between exports and imports. The arbitrary reduction of imports would reduce living standards, and the diversion of funds from public services to investment would entail the sacrifice of the ideal of the welfare state. The alternative to such drastic remedies lies in the ability of Israel to secure funds from external sources until resources can be developed and manpower trained.[79]

In summary, it may be said that the economic progress of Israel depends not only on the development of the country but actually upon the creation of essential resources and an effective labor and managerial force. Materials, men, money, and markets are the basic needs. Arable land must be created through irrigation. Potentially available minerals must be found and exploited, and industrial raw materials grown and developed. Managerial skill must be acquired and the mass of immigrants trained into an effective labor force. Savings and foreign capital are necessary for investment, and the cost of production of Israeli goods must be low enough to compete in world markets. And Israel requires peace and security, so that money and manpower will not be diverted to military preparedness and war.

International Relations

Israel's international relations began auspiciously enough. The United States and the Soviet Union were among the first to accord recognition to the new state, and both voted for its admission to the United Nations. Relations with Britain improved rapidly, France was cordial, and diplomatic contacts were soon established with a large majority of the lesser states of the world. Israel was ready to play the role of a small but enlightened state and to make its contribution to international co-operation.

ISRAEL AND THE UNITED NATIONS

Within the United Nations, Israel has participated in the General Assembly and its committees as well as in the Specialized Agencies which deal with world health, education and culture, agriculture, labor, economic and technical assistance, and other matters. It has also made a good record in the ratification of international conventions, including the declaration on compulsory jurisdiction of the International Court of Justice and the Genocide Convention. In 1952, an international symposium on desert research was held in Jerusalem under the auspices of the United Nations Educational, Scientific and Cultural Organization (Unesco). And in the following year, Israel was honored by the election of its representative as a vice-president of the United Nations General Assembly.[80]

On broad international questions, Israel has sought to pursue an independent policy and to keep clear of involvement in the conflict between the Soviet Union and the Western democracies. Characterized successively as "neutrality," "nonidentification," and "independent," this foreign policy has attempted to preserve freedom of judgment and action, without automatic commitments in orientation toward East or West, and without permanent political alignment with either bloc. In this spirit, Israel recognized the People's Republic of China, which the Soviet Union favored, and supported United Nations action against North Korean aggression, which was sponsored by the United States and the West.[81]

However, the early eagerness of Israel to share actively in the efforts of the United Nations to promote international co-operation has waned. The inability of the United Nations to effect a peace settlement in the Middle East has discouraged the Israeli government and people. And the repeated charges directed against Israel have compromised its position in the world organization and compelled concentration of its energies on the defense of its policies. The result has been a progressive withdrawal from active sponsorship of proposals and resolutions that have come before the General Assembly and its committees.

The unresolved issue of Jerusalem has remained an embarrassment to Israel. The General Assembly Resolution of November 29, 1947, had provided for an international regime. The Conciliation Commission, too, favored a form of internationalization, and, while its plan was discarded, a majority of the General Assembly resolved in December, 1949, in favor of internationalization. The Arab States had originally rejected the partition resolution of the General Assembly, including the proposed international regime for Jerusalem, and they had resorted to force in defiance of the United Nations. Subsequently, when Jordan had seized the Old City of Jerusalem, it had refused to accept internationalization.

Israel proposed "functional internationalization," that is, an international regime for the Holy Places but not international government for the entire territory of Jerusalem. In December, 1949, after the General Assembly had declared in favor of an international regime, Israel moved the *Knesset* and the ministries to Jerusalem, and in July, 1953, the Foreign Ministry, too, was lodged in the New City of Jerusalem as the nation's capital.

The General Assembly considered the question again in 1950, but the necessary majority could not be secured either for a proposal relating to the Holy Places or for internationalization. In 1952, another motion reaffirming internationalization failed of adoption.

The issue has thus remained deadlocked. It is significant that the General Assembly has declined to reaffirm internationalization, but in principle the resolution of December, 1949, remains in force. Both Israel and Jordan have failed to comply with that resolution, while the other Arab States have supported internationalization, apparently as a means of embarrassing Israel. It is Israel's view that the issue of Jerusalem no longer centers in the Holy Places, which are located, with few exceptions, in Jordan, but rather in the eagerness of certain governments to placate the Arab States in their quarrel with Israel.[82]

The problem of the Arab refugees has likewise served to compromise Israel's international position. It has been a matter of continuing concern for the United Nations, and funds have had to be raised for the maintenance of the mass of uprooted humanity. All disinterested states would like to see the troublesome problem liquidated, and repatriation has appeared to many as the simplest solution. Israel has argued that the flight of the Arabs was the issue of the fighting which the Arab States had precipitated; that Arab leadership directed or encouraged the exodus; that extensive repatriation in the climate of Arab hostility would undermine its very existence. Proposals have been made for the resettlement of the bulk of the refugees with international financial assistance. But the Arab States have opposed resettlement, and they have made effective use both of the problem and of individual refugees in their protracted conflict with Israel.[83]

ENMITY OF THE ARAB STATES

The Arab States have presented the most formidable obstacle to the consolidation of Israel's international position. They have refused to recognize the existence of Israel and their hostility has hardened into a determination to destroy the new state. To this end, they have pursued a policy of encirclement, noncommunication, economic boycott, and harassment along the borders and in the United Nations.

All of Israel's land frontiers border on Arab territory. These have been sealed off against trade and travel, and even foreigners cannot normally proceed to or from Israel by way of an adjoining Arab state. The Arab States have refused visas to travelers holding a visa for Israel. The effort was made to deny entry into an Arab state to anyone who had or was about to visit Israel, and when Premier U Nu of Burma did visit Israel in 1955, he was obliged to cancel a projected call in Cairo.

The Arabs have refused to have any intercourse with Israel, not only in direct negotiation (except for the Armistice Supervision Commissions) but also in the regional agencies of the United Nations. Several of the Specialized Agencies, including the World Health Organization and the Food and Agricultural Organization, maintain regional offices in Egypt or Lebanon, and the latter have denied access to these institutions to Israeli representatives. The Arabs have also declined to participate in any conference, seminar, or educational institute held under international auspices anywhere in the Eastern Mediterranean if Israel is included. The acquiescence of the international bodies has resulted in the exclusion of Israel from United Nations regional activities. Similarly, the Arabs were successful in barring Israel from the Asian-African Conference at Bandung, Indonesia, in 1955.[84]

The boycott has hampered water development projects. Obstacles were interposed in the drainage of the Huleh swamps, which delayed the completion of the project. It, and the unwillingness of the Arabs to relate water development to refugee settlement, have been important factors in bringing to a halt elaborate irrigation plans for the Jordan River Valley. International financial aid, particularly from the United States, would have benefited the Arabs as well as Israel, but after an auspicious beginning the project has languished.[85]

The Arab boycott of Israel has cut off all direct trade relations and sought to influence foreign firms and governments to shun Israel or face in their turn exclusion from Arab lands. Ships calling at Israeli ports have been blacklisted and denied trade facilities or services in Arab ports. Goods consigned to Israel have been seized. All commercial aircraft serving Israel have been forbidden to fly over Arab territory. Business firms which maintain branches in Israel have been threatened with boycott, and the boycott propaganda has reached out to Jewish firms of neutral countries, regardless of their trade relations or lack of relations with Israel. Saudi Arabia has directed that no Jewish personnel be included among the American forces at the Dhahran air base, and the American government has acquiesced. Israel has contended that the acquiescence of governments in the restrictive measures which affect their nationals and trade has encouraged the Arabs in the far-reaching boycott, which it regards as a menace to peace and hence a violation at least of the spirit of the United Nations charter. It is a fact that when the Arab threats have been ignored or challenged, they have proved hollow. In 1952, when West Germany and Israel were negotiating a reparations settlement, the Arab States threatened Germany with a boycott, but the latter disregarded the propaganda without serious consequences. Similarly, a warning was issued to the airlines in 1954 that they would be barred from Arab countries if any of their planes touched Israel. An effective protest disposed of this threat.

The blockade of Israel has been extended to the Suez Canal and the Gulf of Aqaba. The Constantinople Convention of 1888 clearly stipulates that free passage be allowed all ships through the Suez Canal, even in wartime. But the Canal has been barred not only to all Israeli ships but also to goods consigned to Israel and defined unilaterally by Egypt as contraband. Israel took the matter to the Security Council, which censured the action of Egypt as "unjustified interference with the rights of nations . . ." but the latter has persevered in its policy. In 1954, the Security Council again considered a resolution expressing grave concern over Egypt's failure to heed its previous decision, but the negative vote of the Soviet Union precluded any further action. At the same time, a Soviet veto prevented any decision on the blockade of the Gulf of Aqaba.[86]

Armed clashes along the borders of Israel have proved even more damaging to Israel's foreign relations, and they have, of course, contributed to tension and disturbance in the Middle East. The Armistice Agreements have constituted the legal basis of interstate relations, and Mixed Armistice Commissions have been charged with supervision. An armistice is a temporary condition which generally bridges the gap between war and peace. When it extends over a long period without a peace settlement, conflict is inevitable. Since no peace has been negotiated, the Armistice Agreements have remained in force to the present.

In such a situation, suspicion, anxiety, and misunderstanding would produce border clashes, even if hostility were minimal. On the Israeli borders, the presence of refugees and the enmity of the Arab governments have created a maximum of distrust and conflict. "Infiltrators" have penetrated Israel in small bands and perpetrated theft, sabotage, and murder. Moreover, trained and armed commando units, known as *fedayeen*, have operated chiefly from bases in Gaza and Sinai, attacking border patrols, mining roads, wrecking houses, and engaging in other forms of sabotage. The result has been thousands of charges and countercharges, many of which have been investigated by the Mixed Armistice Commissions. But the latter have been able to do little more than hand down findings in favor of one or the other of the parties. The outrages have continued.

Israel's policy has been to resort to raids in force as reprisal and deterrent. The most serious raid occurred in October, 1953, after the gruesome murder of a Jewish woman and her two children. The Jordanian village, Kibya, was attacked and some fifty-three men, women, and children were killed. The action came before the Security Council and Israel argued that the raid was the result of provocation and border harassment; that hundreds of its citizens, including women and children, had been killed by Arab marauders with the connivance and assistance of the Arab States; that the alternative would be private action by Israeli irregulars. But the Security Council severely censured Israel. Israel was clearly at a disadvantage. Small bands of "infiltrators" or *fedayeen* are difficult to apprehend or to identify with official Arab authorities. They can be disowned and classed as irresponsible irregulars. Moreover, the murder of a few Israeli civilians at a time lacks dramatic appeal. A raid in force, however, involves the constituted authorities, and the innocence of the victims is accentuated. Since Kibya, Israeli reprisals have been directed against military posts and bases, but legally reprisals cannot be tolerated by agencies of the United Nations.[87]

The root of the evil has been the continuance of a precarious armistice and the inability to achieve a peace settlement. And this, in turn, has been largely due to the divided world in which "East" and "West" have sought to use the Middle East in their struggle for power.

THE "EAST-WEST" CONFLICT

The Arab States have been courted by both the Western powers and the Soviet Union. Western Europe is dependent on the oil supplies of the Middle East, and huge investments in oil properties have won the Arabs powerful friends.[88] Moreover, the United States and Great Britain have sought to enlist the Arab States in defensive alliances for the containment of the Soviet Union. Finally, Arab bases are considered essential for the West in the struggle with the Soviets.

The United States has been friendly to Israel and quite generous with economic aid, and Britain and France as well as the United States have sought to maintain stability in the Middle East. On May 25, 1950, the three powers made a declaration opposing an arms race in the region and "the use of force or the threat of force between any of the states in that area."[89] However, the use of the Dhahran airport as an American base was secured from Saudi Arabia in 1951, and the Bagdad Pact of 1955 has depended on Arab States. These have involved the strengthening of the military potential of the latter, and the exclusion of Israel from the defensive alliances of the Middle East has resulted in its isolation. Israel has protested against the arms build-up of the Arab States, and it has sought an effective guarantee of its frontiers. These pleas have remained unanswered.[90]

The Soviet Union has become increasingly hostile to Israel. During 1952-1953, and especially after the infamous Jewish doctors' case, Soviet policy became blatantly anti-Israel and even anti-Semitic, and since then the Arab States have had strong Soviet support against Israel in the United Nations. But it would be an oversimplification to ascribe this development to anti-Semitism.

The Soviet Union has always been hostile to Zionism, but its foreign policy is determined not by ideological considerations but by the exigencies of power politics. It has carved out a sphere of influence in Eastern Europe, in which it brooks no outside interference, but it has recognized no such limitations upon itself beyond its sphere of influence, and it has especially sought to penetrate the Middle East. It favored the establishment of Israel and the termination of the Mandate in order to dislodge the British from Palestine, but Israel could not serve the purposes of Soviet designs upon the Middle East. Israel's early policy of nonidentification with the East or West was not in keeping with the character of a faithful satellite, and its position against aggression in Korea showed that its inclinations were toward the West. Moreover, the Arabs were more numerous, and their sense of grievance against the West could be more easily exploited. The Soviet Union has therefore become the champion of the Arabs against Israel.[91]

By 1955, Israel found itself almost completely isolated. The United States and Great Britain were committed to the Bagdad Pact, from which Israel was excluded. The Soviet Union was openly pro-Arab. And the United Nations, which had approved the establishment of a Jewish State, brought the Palestine war to a close, and admitted Israel into the international organization, was proving unequal to the task of effecting a peace settlement or of preventing economic warfare. Moreover, the Arabs were using the United Nations as a forum for attacks and denunciations of Israel, which it regarded as unjustified. Border attacks and harassments, it felt, were balanced by fine legal formulas rather than viewed as the inevitable consequence of the latent state of war which the Arabs perpetuated. Finally, the maneuvering of the Great Powers created the feeling that Israel was a pawn in a power conflict and might be sacrificed on the altar of appeasement. A mood of pessimism gripped the country, and both people and government reached the conclusion that they could look for assistance neither to the Western democracies nor the United Nations; that they must rely on their own strength to achieve security.[92] The arms deal between Egypt and Czechoslovakia turned this pessimism into bitterness. The Arabs were about to secure the means of making good their threats, and they were freed from the moderating pressures of the West. Israel felt in mortal peril.

THE SINAI CAMPAIGN

During 1955-1956 arms from the Soviet bloc enabled Egypt to effect a military build-up in the Sinai Desert, and by the fall of 1956 a unified military command was formed with Jordan and Syria. Israel regarded these measures as directed against itself, and on October 29, 1956, its army struck and soon cleared the Egyptian forces out of the Gaza strip and Sinai, at the same time lifting the blockade in the Gulf of Aqaba. For their own reasons, British and French forces attacked the Suez Canal area. United Nations action, and United States and Soviet pressure, resulted in the withdrawal of all forces from the occupied areas, but the Sinai campaign had important results for Israel. The Egyptian military preparations in the Sinai Desert were disrupted. A United Nations Emergency Force was established along the Israel-Egyptian border and in the Gulf of Aqaba, which put an end to the *fedayeen* raids and the blockade of the port of Elat. Israel was no longer isolated in the United Nations. And it served notice that it would not submit passively to armed attack or to partition of the Munich variety.[93]

However, the basic issues remain and the Arab States are even more unyielding. Israel is still surrounded by hostile neighbors, and its efforts to build a viable welfare state are still thwarted by isolation in the Middle East and by the threat of world conflict between the Soviet bloc and the West.

NOTES

[1] The most thorough and comprehensive study of Palestine under the British Mandate is *Palestine: A Study of Jewish, Arab and British Policies,* 2 vols., New Haven, 1947. This study was made by I. B. Berkson with the assistance of a group of scholars. It was sponsored by the Esco Foundation for Palestine. J. C. Hurewitz, *The Struggle for Palestine,* New York, 1950, is a thorough scholarly study, and P. L. Hanna, *British Policy in Palestine,* Washington, 1942, is a well-documented account of political developments. On the history of Zionism and its chief leaders, see N. Sokolow, *History of Zionism, 1600-1918,* 2 vols., London, 1919; I. Cohen, *The Zionist Movement,* New York, 1946; J. De Haas, *Theodor Herzl: A Biographical Study,* 2 vols., Chicago, 1927; C. Weizmann, *Trial and Error,* London, 1949. A penetrating analysis of the latter work is given in O. K. Rabinowicz, *Fifty Years of Zionism,* London, 1952. See the texts of the following: The Balfour Declaration, in Great Britain, *Zionism* (Foreign Office

Handbook, No. 162), London, 1920, p. 44; the Mandate for Palestine, in Great Britain, Colonial Office, *Mandate for Palestine* (Cmd. 1785), London, December, 1922; the White Paper of 1939, in Great Britain, Colonial Office, *Palestine Statement of Policy,* May, 1939 (Cmd. 6019), London, 1939; the Land Transfer Regulations, in Great Britain, Colonial Office, *Palestine Land Transfer Regulations,* February, 1940 (Cmd. 6180), London, 1940.
[¹ᵃ See Itzhak Ben-Zvi, "Eretz Yisrael under Ottoman Rule, 1517-1917," this work, Vol. I, Chap. 8.]

² A. Ulitzur, *Two Decades of Keren Hayesod: A Survey of Facts and Figures, 1921-1940,* Jerusalem, 1940, especially pp. 26-27; Hadassah Medical Organization, *Twenty Years of Medical Service to Palestine, 1918-1938,* Jerusalem, 1939, pp. 13-62. D. Gurevich and A. Gertz, *Statistical Handbook of Jewish Palestine, 1947,* Jerusalem, 1947, is an invaluable collection of statistical information. See pp. 192-193, 344, 366-367, 369, 375, 427.

³ See *The Hebrew Encyclopedia* (Hebrew), Vol. VI, Jerusalem, 1957, p. 671. Allowance has been made for some 60,000 who emigrated.

⁴ See *Palestine Review,* January, 1945, p. 161; *Statistical Handbook of Jewish Palestine,* pp. 140, 142, 155, 435; *Palestine: A Study of Jewish, Arab and British Policies,* Vol. I, p. 368, Vol. II, pp. 691-692, 1052; Government of Israel, *Government Yearbook,* 1952, pp. 305, 327; *The Hebrew Encyclopedia,* Vol. VI, p. 837. For a general discussion of agricultural settlement, see A. Ruppin, *Three Decades of Palestine,* Jerusalem, 1936.

⁵ See *Statistical Handbook of Jewish Palestine,* pp. 48, 206-209, 220-223; A. Bonné, *State and Economics in the Middle East,* 2nd ed., London, 1955, pp. 302-303; A. Revusky, *Jews in Palestine,* New York, 1945, chs. VI, VIII; *The Hebrew Encyclopedia,* Vol. VI, pp. 898-902; *Government Yearbook,* 1950, p. 241.

⁶ Bonné, *op. cit.,* p. 222. On the development of trade, see also *Statistical Handbook of Jewish Palestine,* pp. 233-239 ff., 254-259.

⁷ An extended analysis of these factors will be presented in the author's projected work on Israel.

⁸ See *The Hebrew Encyclopedia,* Vol. VI, p. 676.

⁹ See *Statistical Handbook of Jewish Palestine,* pp. 334-341; *Palestine: A Study of Jewish, Arab and British Policies,* Vol. I, pp. 321-324, Vol. II, pp. 698-704. An extensive account of the development of the arts is given in *The Hebrew Encyclopedia,* Vol. VI, pp. 1070-1129.

¹⁰ See *Statistical Handbook of Jewish Palestine,* pp. 84-85, 344-351; *Palestine: A Study of Jewish, Arab and British Policies,* Vol. II, pp. 667 ff.

¹¹ A symbol of labor idealism was Aaron David Gordon (1856-1922), whose writings were published in Hebrew in five volumes. A selection is available in English in his *Selected Essays,* New York, 1938. See, for example, pp. 247-253.

¹² There is an extensive literature on the collective and co-operative movements. See, for example, H. Viteles, "The Cooperative Movement," *The Annals of the American Academy of Political and Social Science,* November, 1932 (Palestine issue), pp. 127-138; *idem,* "The Cooperative Movement in

Israel," *The Hebrew Encyclopedia*, Vol. VI, pp. 943-951; *idem,* "Communitarian Rural Settlements in Palestine," *Year Book of Agricultural Cooperation, 1939*, London, 1939, pp. 133-153; A. Ben-Shalom, *Deep Furrows*, New York, 1937; G. Baratz and others, *A Village on the Jordan*, London, 1954; E. Samuel, *Handbook of the Jewish Communal Villages in Palestine*, 2nd Eng. ed., Jerusalem, 1945; H. F. Infield, *Cooperative Living in Palestine*, New York, 1944; *Statistical Handbook of Jewish Palestine*, pp. 64-65, 178, 406-410.

[13] On social insurance and co-operative activities of *Histadrut*, see I. Kanievsky, *Social Policy and Social Insurance in Palestine* (submitted to 30th Conference of ILO, Geneva, 1947), Tel-Aviv, 1947, ch. VI; General Federation of Jewish Labour in Palestine, *Memorandum Submitted to the Anglo-American Commission of Inquiry*, Tel-Aviv, March, 1946 (mimeographed), pp. 68-74; S. Kurland, *Cooperative Palestine: The Story of the Histadrut*, New York, 1947, Part 3. On *Histadrut* membership, compare the *Histadrut* Executive Committee, *The Histadrut During 1945-1948, Summary Report* (Hebrew), Tel-Aviv, 1949, pp. 392-393; *Memorandum Submitted to the Anglo-American Commission of Inquiry*, p. 9; and *Statistical Handbook of Jewish Palestine*, p. 290.

[14] See M. Burstein, *Self-Government of the Jews in Palestine Since 1900*, Tel-Aviv, 1934, chs. IV-VII; *The Hebrew Encyclopedia*, Vol. VI, pp. 538-540.

[15] For the prices of land, see *The Hebrew Encyclopedia*, Vol. VI, pp. 822-823.

[16] This figure is for the end of 1936. On the "displaced Arabs," see Lewis French, *Reports on Agricultural Development and Land Settlement in Palestine*, Jerusalem, 1931-1932, pp. 59-60 ff.; Great Britain, Colonial Office, *Palestine Report, 1936* (Colonial No. 129), London, 1937, p. 90; *Palestine: A Study of Jewish, Arab and British Policies*, Vol. II, pp. 717-718.

[17] See Bonné, *op. cit.*, p. 304; *idem, The Economic Development of the Middle East*, New York, 1945, p. 126; *idem, Statistical Handbook of Middle Eastern Countries*, Jerusalem, 1944, pp. 59, 119; and *Memorandum Submitted to the Anglo-American Commission of Inquiry*, pp. 21-27, 60-65, 76-77.

[18] For a discussion of Arab-Jewish relations and the idea of binationalism, see *Palestine: A Study of Jewish, Arab and British Policies*, Vol. I, pp. 562-593; Vol. II, pp 1015-1020, 1099-1104, 1158-1177. See also O. I. Janowsky, "Zionism Today: A Clarification," *The Menorah Journal*, October-December, 1943, pp. 227-258.

[19] The text of President Truman's letter to Prime Minister Attlee is in *The Department of State Bulletin*, November 18, 1945, pp. 790-791. For Concurrent Resolution 44, see *Congressional Record*, 79th Congress, First Session, December 17, 1945.

[20] Department of State, *Anglo-American Committee of Inquiry: Report, April 20, 1946*, Washington, 1946, pp. 1-12.

[21] General Barker's order is quoted in J. Kimche, *Seven Fallen Pillars: The Middle East, 1945-1952*, New York, 1953, pp. 42-43. The British government justified Barker's instructions but dissociated itself from "the actual terms" of the letter. See *Parliamentary Debates*, House of Commons, Vol.

426, No. 188, p. 963. Ben-Gurion's quotation is from D. Ben-Gurion, *Rebirth and Destiny of Israel*, New York, 1954, p. 217. For summaries of policies of the *Haganah, Irgun,* and Sternists, and relations among them, see H. Sacher, *Israel: The Establishment of a State,* New York, 1952, pp. 181-194; M. Pearlman, *The Army of Israel,* New York, 1950, ch. 8; B. Litvinoff, *Ben-Gurion of Israel,* New York, 1954, pp. 143-146 and ch. 7, *passim; The Hebrew Encyclopedia,* Vol. VI, pp. 553-562. For the *Irgun* view of the King David Hotel attack, see M. Beigin, *The Revolt: Story of the Irgun,* New York, 1951, ch. XV.

[22] See Great Britain, Colonial Office, *Proposals for the Future of Palestine* (Cmd. 7044), London, 1947, pp. 2-8.

[23] United Nations Special Committee on Palestine, *Report to the General Assembly,* U.N. Doc. A/364, especially pp. 42-65; United Nations, *Official Records of the Second Session of the General Assembly,* Vol. II, November 29, 1947, pp. 1424-1425. For the debates, see pp. 1310-1428. For a detailed analysis, see J. Robinson, *Palestine and the United Nations,* Washington, 1947, chs. IV-XVI.

[24] J. Garcia-Granados, *The Birth of Israel,* New York, 1948, Ch. 25, especially p. 287. For the discussions in the Security Council, beginning with February 24, 1948, and in the General Assembly, see United Nations, Security Council, *Official Records,* 3rd Year, Nos. 16-51, 57-58, 65-67, 69; United Nations, *Official Records of the Second Special Session of the General Assembly,* Vol. I, April 19–May 14, 1948, pp. 9-47. D. Horowitz, *State in the Making,* New York, 1953, pp. 297-304, conveys the dramatic quality and tension of the final vote on the partition resolution. The same author reveals (pp. 232-235) the uncompromising attitude of Azzam Pasha, leader and Secretary-General of the Arab League. L. L. Leonard, "The United Nations and Palestine," *International Conciliation,* October, 1949, pp. 603-786, is an excellent study of United Nations efforts.

[25] Summaries of the military operations are given in Pearlman, *op. cit.,* chs. 9-21; E. O'Ballance, *The Arab-Israeli War, 1948,* London, 1956; *The Hebrew Encyclopedia,* Vol. VI, pp. 569-594. The atmosphere of the period is caught in H. Levin, *I Saw the Battle of Jerusalem,* New York, 1950. The texts of the armistice agreements are in United Nations, Security Council, *Official Records,* Docs. S/1264 (Egyptian-Israeli Armistice, 24 February, 1949); S/1296 (Israeli-Lebanese Armistice, 23 March, 1949); S/1302 (Jordan-Israel Armistice, 3 April, 1949); S/1353 (Israeli-Syrian Armistice, 20 July, 1949). For a juridical analysis of the agreements, see S. Rosenne, *Israel's Armistice Agreements with the Arab States,* Tel-Aviv, 1951. An interesting comment on the United Nations Conciliation Commission is given in J. G. McDonald, *My Mission in Israel, 1948-1951,* New York, 1951, pp. 174-180 ff.

[26] Leonard, *op. cit.,* pp. 737-738, 740.

[27] Great Britain, Foreign Office, *Progress Report of the United Nations Mediator on Palestine* (Cmd. 7530), London, 1948. For a summary of Bernadotte's proposals, see F. Bernadotte, *To Jerusalem,* London, 1951, pp. 235-244.

[28] See United Nations, Conciliation Commission for Palestine, *First Prog-*

ress Report, Doc. A/819, March 15, 1949; *Second Progress Report,* Doc. A/838, April 19, 1949; *Third Progress Report,* Doc. A/927, June 21, 1949; and subsequent reports.

[29] Carnegie Endowment for International Peace, *Israel and the United Nations* (report of a Study Group set up by the Hebrew University of Jerusalem), New York, 1956, p. 50.

[30] See Kimche, *op. cit.,* pp. 209-210, 227-232; Ben-Gurion, *op. cit.,* pp. 228, 237; photostat copies of a British officer's reports, in Pearlman, *op. cit.,* pp. 116-117; Levin, *op. cit.,* pp. 90 ff. Quotations from Arab sources are given in Government of Israel, *The Arabs in Israel,* New York, 1955, pp. 9-12, and extensive excerpts from Arab works are given in Hebrew translation in S. Sabagh (trans.), *Be'eynei Oyev (Through the Eyes of the Enemy),* Tel-Aviv, 1954. See epecially pp. 22-24, 32-33, 48-49, 52.

[31] Litvinoff, *op. cit.,* is a full-length scholarly biography. See also the penetrating account of M. Syrkin, "Ben-Gurion at Seventy," *Jewish Frontier,* December, 1956, pp. 9-12. Selected addresses are available in English in Ben-Gurion, *op. cit.*

[32] On the Provisional Government, see Law and Administration Ordinance, May 21, 1948; Courts (Transitional Provisions) Ordinance, June 30, 1948; and Transition Law, February 16, 1949, in *Laws of the State of Israel,* Vol. I, pp. 7-11, 23-25; Vol. III, pp. 3-4. See also Government of Israel, *Government Yearbook,* 5710 (Hebrew), Tel-Aviv, 1950, pp. 3-10; *The Israel Yearbook, 1950-1951,* pp. 49, 197-198 ff.

[33] For the text, see *Government Yearbook,* 1950, pp. 50 ff. See also *ibid.,* 1956, p. 31.

[34] The text of the Draft Constitution is given in J. Ben-Jacob, *The Rise of Israel,* New York, 1949, pp. 200-217; in J. Dunner, *The Republic of Israel,* New York, 1950, pp. 249-259; in *The New York Times,* December 10, 1948. For the debates in the *Knesset,* see *Divrei Haknesset,* 1st *Knesset,* 113th-117th Sessions, February 7, 13, 14, 20, 1950, pp. 725-746, 766-784, 794-804, 808-828. Ben-Gurion's address on the question of a constitution is available in English in Ben-Gurion, *op. cit.,* pp. 363-380.

[34a Author of Chap. 8 in Vol. I of this work.]

[35] For the system of government and legal structure, see Transition Law of 1949; State Comptroller Law, May 24, 1949; State President (Tenure) Law, December 5, 1951; *Knesset* Immunity Laws, 1951-1952; in *Laws of the State of Israel,* Vol. III, pp. 23-26; Vol. V, pp. 149-152; Vol. VI, pp. 4-6, 45-47; M. Rosetti, "Israel's Parliament," *Parliamentary Affairs,* Vol. VIII (Autumn, 1955), pp. 445-452.

Summary accounts are given in *The Hebrew Encyclopedia,* Vol. VI, pp. 623-633; N. Bentwich, *Israel,* New York, 1952, pp. 94 ff; M. H. Bernstein, *The Politics of Israel,* Princeton, 1957, ch. V, and especially ch. VI on the Civil Service; G. de Gaury, *The New State of Israel,* New York, 1952, *passim;* J. Dunner, *The Republic of Israel,* New York, 1950, ch. VIII; H. Lehrman, *Israel:The Beginning and Tomorrow,* New York, 1951, pp. 12-56; O. Kraines, *Israel: The Emergence of a New Nation,* Washington, 1954, pp. 1-37; S.

Rosenne, *The Constitutional and Legal System of Israel,* New York, 1957, pp. 17-38; L. F. R. Williams, *The State of Israel,* London, 1957, ch. IX.

[36] On the legal structure, see especially *The Hebrew Encyclopedia,* Vol. VI, pp. 633-665; *Government Yearbook,* 5717 (1956), pp. 311-332; B. Akzin, "Codification in a New State," *The American Journal of Comparative Law,* Vol. V, No. 1, pp. 44-77; Y. L. Kohn, "The Emerging Constitution of Israel," in M. Davis (ed.), *Israel: Its Role in Civilization,* New York, 1956, pp. 130-145; Rosenne, *op. cit.,* pp. 1-16.

[37] For the legislation on local government, see *Laws of the State of Israel,* Vol. IV, pp. 177-178; Vol. VI, pp. 21, 63-72; Vol. VII, p. 131; Vol. IX, pp. 54-60. See also *Government Yearbook,* 5716 (1955), pp. 436-438; 5717 (1956), pp. 300-302; and the appropriate sections under "Ministry of the Interior" in the preceding yearbooks. See also R. Shaffar, "Local Government in Israel," in *The Israel Yearbook,* 1952-1953, pp. 319-363; M. Kalir, "Local Government," *ibid.,* 1957, pp. 237-247. Bernstein, *op. cit.,* ch. 12, contains an appraisal based on close study and personal observation.

[38] The salient points of party platforms are given in *The Israel Yearbook,* 1952-1953, pp. 97-101; 1957, pp. 17-24. For a penetrating analysis, see B. Akzin, "The Role of Parties in Israeli Democracy," *The Journal of Politics,* Vol. 17, 1955, pp. 507-545. See also de Gaury, *op. cit.,* pp. 76-90; M. Roshwald, "Political Parties and Social Classes in Israel," *Social Research,* Summer, 1956, pp. 199-218. A good summary of parties during the Mandate period is given in Revusky, *op. cit.,* pp. 194-208.

[39] Central Bureau of Statistics, *Totz'ot Habhirot* (Election Results, 1955), Special Series, No. 51, Jerusalem, August, 1956, Tables I-V, pp. 3-7.

[40] Good accounts of the functioning of the *Knesset* and of cabinet crises are given in *Government Yearbook,* 5711 (1950), pp. 59-65; *ibid.,* 5713 (1952), pp. 51-56; *ibid.,* 5714 (1953-1954), pp. 55-61; *ibid.,* 5715 (1954), pp. 13-21; *ibid.,* 5716 (1955), pp. 16-17 ff.; *ibid.,* 5717 (1956), pp. 35-37 ff.; *ibid.,* 5718 (1957), pp. 51-58; *The Israel Yearbook,* 1950-1951, pp. 65-76; *ibid.,* 1957, pp. 13-17. The cabinet crisis of 1951 affords a good example of Israeli parliamentary government. See *Divrei Haknesset,* 1st *Knesset,* 225th-227th Sessions, February 12-14, 1951, pp. 1037-1110. For the cabinet crisis of January, 1958, see *ibid.,* January 7, 1958, pp. 563-591.

[41] For the Nationality Law, April 8, 1952, see *Laws of the State of Israel,* Vol. VI, pp. 50-53; and for the abolition of the death penalty, *ibid.,* Vol. VIII, p. 63. For other laws dealing with currency, coinage, customs, passports, etc., see *ibid.,* Vol. I, pp. 13, 30-34, 43-44; Vol. II, pp. 58-59, 92-93; Vol. III, pp. 26-27; Vol. VI, pp. 76-77, 159-162.

[42] On the *Altalena* incident, compare Ben-Gurion, *op. cit.,* pp. 251-260, and Beigin, *op. cit.,* chs. XI–XII. The vital importance of national discipline at that time is illustrated in McDonald, *op. cit.,* pp. 17-18.

[43] See Defense Army of Israel Ordinance, May, 1948; Defense Service Law, September, 1949; Defense Service (Amendment) Law, February, 1950; and Reserve Service (Compensation) Law, in *Laws of the State of Israel,* Vol. I, pp. 15-16; Vol. III, pp. 112-118; Vol. IV, pp. 62-64; Vol. VI, pp. 27-32.

[44] See *Laws of the State of Israel,* Vol. III, pp. 125-131 (Compulsory

Education Law, September, 1949); Vol. IV, pp. 91-92, 184-185 (amendments of 1950); Vol. VII, pp. 113-119 (State Education Law, August, 1953).

[45] See *Laws of the State of Israel*, Vol. I, p. 18 (Days of Rest Ordinance, June, 1948); Vol. II, p. 37 (Kasher Food for Soldiers Ordinance, November, 1948); Vol. III, pp. 66-67 (Jewish Religious Services Budget Law, August, 1949); p. 116 (Art. 11 [d] of Defense Service Law, September, 1949); Vol. VII, p. 137 (Art. 8 of National Service Law, August, 1953). On the structure and functions of the Ministry of Religious Affairs, see appropriate sections in *Government Yearbooks*, especially 1950, pp. 188-192, and 1956, pp. 365-371. For a general discussion, see E. Samuel, *Problems of Government in the State of Israel*, Jerusalem, 1956, ch. 8.

[46] See *Laws of the State of Israel*, Vol. IV, pp. 158-159 (Marriage Age Law, August, 1950); Vol. V, pp. 171-172 (Women's Equal Rights Law, July, 1951).

[47] See *Laws of the State of Israel*, Vol. VII, pp. 3-4 (World Zionist Organization-Jewish Agency [Status] Law, December, 1952).

[48] There is a vast literature on the Ingathering, of which only some salient items can be noted. See Law of the Return, July, 1950, in *Laws of the State of Israel*, Vol. IV, p. 114. Examples of official policy are available in the government programs; see *Government Yearbook*, 1950, pp. 50-51 ff.; *ibid.*, 1956, pp. 25-27 ff. The *Government Yearbooks* also provide annual summaries on "Immigration and Absorption." See also appropriate sections in the *Israel Yearbooks*. The best analysis of the demographic aspects of the Ingathering is R. Bachi, "Demography," *The Hebrew Encyclopedia*, Vol. VI, pp. 665-707. For the position of the major political parties, see Note 38 above. L. Eshkol, "How to Absorb 100,000 Immigrants," *The Jerusalem Post*, July 4, 1957, illustrates the more recent preoccupation with mass immigration.

[49] For debates on the need for and significance of the Ingathering, see *Divrei Haknesset*, 1st *Knesset*, 19th, 25th-26th, 28th-29th, Sessions, March 30, 1949, April 26-27, 1949, May 3, 11, 1949, pp. 266-275, 399-404, 409-458, 470-477, 486-500. See also Ben-Gurion, *op. cit.*, pp. 346 ff., 360-361, 386-388, 427-428, 468-471, 492, 495-496.

[50] See, for example, *ibid.*, pp. 347, 396, 468, 470.

[51] The latest figures available at the time of writing are in Government of Israel, Central Bureau of Statistics, *Statistical Monthly of Israel* (Hebrew), Part I, February, 1958, p. 160.

[52] J. Schechtman, "The End of Galut Yemen," *Jewish Affairs*, February 1, 1950, pp. 3-33, is a very good illustration of the Ingathering from one Moslem country and of the conditions that made it necessary. For a popular, human-interest account, see S. Barer, *The Magic Carpet*, New York, 1952. The *JDC Review* contains valuable information on conditions in Moslem and other refugee lands and on mass emigration to Israel. See, for example, the issues of April, 1948, pp. 13–14, 21-22; May, 1948, pp. 29, 32-33; September-October, 1948, pp. 61-63; May, 1949, pp. 13-24; July, 1949, pp. 25-26, 32-34.

[53] A careful survey, however, has revealed that the new immigrant has,

on the whole, adjusted himself better to work and the industrial situation than to the general community. See "Cultural Assimilation and Tensions in Israel," *International Social Science Bulletin* (UNESCO), Vol. VIII, No. 1, 1956, pp. 7-123. See also R. Patai, *Israel Between East and West,* Philadelphia, 1953, especially chs. 7, 10, 11.

 54 *Statistical Monthly of Israel* (Hebrew), Part I, February, 1958, p. 157. See also *Government Yearbook,* 5711 (1950), p. 358.

55 On the Arab minority, see Land Acquisition (Validation of Acts and Compensation) Law, March, 1953, in *Laws of the State of Israel,* Vol. VII, pp. 43-45; G. T. Renner, "Arab Education in the Near East," *Middle Eastern Affairs,* August–September, 1950, pp. 215-224; J. L. Benor, "Arab Education in Israel," *ibid.,* pp. 224-229; *ibid.,* June-July, 1950, pp. 199-200; S. D. Goitein, "The Arab Schools in Israel Revisited," *ibid.,* October, 1952, pp. 272-275; M. Piamenta, "Arabic in the *Knesset,*" *ibid.,* February, 1955, pp. 45-47; A. Zidon, *Haknesset* (Hebrew), Tel-Aviv, 1950, pp. 83-84. For the distribution of the Arab vote in the election of 1955, see *The Hebrew Encyclopedia,* Vol. VI, p. 714. Good summaries of the condition of the Arabs are given in Government of Israel, *The Arabs in Israel,* New York, 1955; D. Peretz, "The Arab Minority of Israel," *The Middle East Journal,* Spring, 1954, pp. 139-154; Bernstein, *op. cit.,* pp. 68-69, 85-86, 298-302; Williams, *op. cit.,* ch. X. See also sections under Ministries of Interior and of Religious Affairs in *Government Yearbooks,* especially 1957, for statistics on education and culture.

56 *The Hebrew Encyclopedia,* Vol. VI, pp. 819-820.

57 Bernstein, *op. cit.,* p. 229.

58 See *Laws of the State of Israel,* Vol. V, pp. 125-133 (Hours of Work and Rest Law, May, 1951); Vol. VIII, pp. 4-35 (National Insurance Law, November, 1953), 175-182 (Labour Inspection [organization] Law, September, 1954); *Government Yearbook,* 5718 (1957), pp. 450-459 (Settlement of Labour Disputes Law, February, 1957, and Collective Agreement Law, February, 1957); see also P. B. Nortman, "Working Conditions and Social Security in Israel," *Middle Eastern Affairs,* May, 1951, pp. 167-179.

59 See *Laws of the State of Israel,* Vol. VIII, pp. 75-89 (Tenants' Protection Law, April, 1954); Vol. IX, pp. 172-183 (Tenants' Protection Law, July, 1955).

60 See *Government Yearbook,* 5718 (1957), pp. 383-388; Bernstein, *op. cit.,* pp. 334-338.

61 On health conditions, see *Government Yearbooks,* especially 5717 (1956), pp. 284-295; 5718 (1957), pp. 181-190; *The Hebrew Encyclopedia,* Vol. VI, pp. 717-728.

62 *Government Yearbook,* 5718 (1957), pp. 172-173.

63 On education and culture, see *Government Yearbooks,* especially 5718 (1957), pp. 172-199; *The Israel Yearbooks,* especially 1957, pp. 201-235. *The Hebrew Encyclopedia,* Vol. VI, pp. 675-679, 983-1129, contains detailed information on education, culture, and especially the arts. H. Gamzu, "The Israel Theatre," *Middle Eastern Affairs,* May, 1952, pp. 150-154; E. Silberner, "Libraries in Israel," *ibid.,* March, 1955, pp. 78-83. For a thorough study of the revival of Hebrew, see R. Bachi, "A Statistical Analysis of the

Revival of Hebrew in Israel," *Scripta Hierosolymitana*, Vol. III, Jerusalem, 1956, pp. 179-247. For the development of higher education, see M. Spiegel and others, *The Hebrew University of Jerusalem*, Jerusalem, 1950; L. Levensohn, *Vision and Fulfillment*, New York, 1950; S. Livny, "Technion—Israel Institute of Technology," *Middle Eastern Affairs*, June-July, 1956, pp. 222-227. On archaeology and excavations, see *Israel Exploration Journal*, published in Jerusalem.

[64] This table is based on State of Israel, Ministry of Labour, *Cooperative Societies in Israel, 1956*, Jerusalem, 1957, pp. 11, 13, 15, and on the listing of all Jewish settlements and their social structure in 1946, in *Statistical Handbook of Jewish Palestine, op. cit.*, pp. 411-426.

[65] On the co-operative movement, see *Cooperative Societies in Israel, 1956*, pp. 3-31; Viteles, in *Scripta Hierosolymitana*, pp. 53-103; S. N. Eisenstadt, "The Social Conditions of the Development of Voluntary Association—A Case Study of Israel," *ibid.*, pp. 104-125; Y. Talmon-Garber, "Differentiation in Collective Settlements," *ibid.*, pp. 153-178. On recent developments in the collectives, see United Nations, *Monograph On Community Settlements and Report of the Survey Mission on Community Organization and Development in Israel*, February, 1954; M. E. Spiro, *Kibbutz: Venture in Utopia*, Cambridge, Mass., 1956; M. Weingarten, *Life in a Kibbutz*, New York, 1955.

[66] See C. Tadmor, "Natural Resources of Israel," *Middle Eastern Affairs*, May, 1954, pp. 154-158; *The Israel Yearbook*, 1950-1951, pp. 79-80.

[67] Bernstein, *op. cit.*, chs. 7-9, presents a realistic analysis of Israel's economy. See also D. Horowitz, "Fundamental Trends in Israel's Economy," *Middle Eastern Affairs*, May, 1952, p. 139.

[68] E. Levy, *Israel Economic Survey, 1953-1954*, Jerusalem, 1955, p. 12.

[69] *Laws of the State of Israel*, Vol. IV, pp. 93-100 (Encouragement of Capital Investments Law, 1950). For the achievements to the end of 1951, compare address of Prime Minister in *Divrei Haknesset*, 2nd *Knesset*, 55th Session, February 13, 1952, pp. 1315-1321, with *Statistical Abstract of Israel, 1956-1957*, pp. 65, 98, and with Levy, *op. cit.*, pp. 17-18.

[70] P. Hartal, "Changes in Living Standards in Israel," *Middle Eastern Affairs*, February, 1953, pp. 37-50; D. Patinkin, "Monetary and Price Developments in Israel: 1949-1953," *Scripta Hierosolymitana*, Vol. III, pp. 25-27; *Statistical Abstract of Israel, 1956-1957*, p. 159.

[71] On the New Economic Policy and its effects, see Levy, *op. cit.*, pp. 18-24 ff., 55 ff.; Patinkin, *op. cit.*, pp. 28 ff.; *Middle Eastern Affairs*, March, 1952, p. 98; August-September, 1952, p. 260; December, 1952, p. 404; January, 1953, p. 32; May, 1953, p. 198; June-July, 1954, p. 244; December, 1954, pp. 406-407.

[72] See *Statistical Abstract of Israel, 1956–1957*, pp. 64, 65, 81, 82, 185; Levy, *op. cit.*, pp. 84 ff.; *Israel: 10 Years of Progress, 1948-1958*, pp. 18-20. On water development, see G. G. Stevens, "The Jordan River Valley," *International Conciliation*," January, 1956, pp. 227-283; *Israel Digest*, May 11, 1956, pp. 1-2; *Middle Eastern Affairs*, August-September, 1955, p. 287.

[73] See *Bank of Israel Bulletin*, No. 7, Jerusalem, 1958, p. 57.

[74] American Israel Corporation, *16th Annual Report*, 1957, p. 9.

[75] On developments in industry and transportation, see *Statistical Abstract*

of Israel, 1956-1957, pp. 91-94,98-99, 108-109, 111-113, 116 ff.; United Nations, *Economic Developments in the Middle East, 1955-1956,* New York, 1957, pp. 32-35; Levy, *op. cit.,* pp. 98-118; M. Orion, "Transportation in Israel," *Middle Eastern Affairs,* May, 1953, pp. 172-179; January, 1950, p. 30; April, 1950, p. 129; November, 1950, pp. 338-339; November, 1955, pp. 355-357; May, 1956, p. 204; February, 1957, p. 86; American Israel Corporation, *Annual Report, 1956,* pp. 4-10. On Israel's national income, see *Bank of Israel Bulletin,* p. 20; Bernstein, *op. cit.,* p. 208.

[76] *Statistical Abstract of Israel, 1956-1957,* p. 159. Compare *Bank of Israel Bulletin,* p. 53, and Bernstein, *op. cit.,* p. 219. The table presents the latest figures of the Central Bureau of Statistics, which has recalculated previous data at the single rate of exchange of £I. 1.800 = $1. For a detailed analysis of the composition of imports and exports, see L. H. and M. D. Keyserling, *Speeding Israel's Progress,* New York, 1957, pp. 37-42.

[77] For an excellent summary of foreign sources of capital, see Bernstein, *op. cit.,* pp. 211-219. On American aid and its effects, see *Israel Economic Forum,* Vol. VII, November, 1955, pp. 10-29; B. W. McDaniel, "American Technical Assistance and Economic Aid in Israel," *Middle Eastern Affairs,* October, 1955, pp. 303-318; "Facts and Figures: United States Aid to the Middle East, 1945–1957," *ibid.,* November, 1957, pp. 385-390.

[78] *Statistical Abstract of Israel, 1956-1957,* p. 185.

[79] See D. Horowitz, *Kalkalat Israel (Israel's Economy),* Tel-Aviv, 1958, pp. 385-399, for analysis of income and standard of living. On the problems of manpower, see E. Ginzberg, *Manpower Utilization in Israel,* Tei-Aviv, August, 1953 (Report to the Government of Israel), pp. 1-47; *idem, Second Report on Manpower Utilization in Israel,* Tel-Aviv, June, 1956, pp. 1-45. On development of natural resources, see Levy, *op. cit.,* pp. 87, 120-124. Good accounts of basic economic problems are given in Bernstein, *op. cit.,* pp. 185-192; D. Horowitz, "The Economic Problems of Israel," *Middle Eastern Affairs,* November, 1956, pp. 373-377.

[80] See *Government Yearbook,* 5713 (1952), pp. 124-125; 150-159; *ibid.,* 5715 (1954), p. 132; B. Akzin, *New States and International Organizations,* Paris, 1955, pp. 49, 67 ff., 84-88; *Government Yearbook,* 5713 (1952), pp. 124-125.

[81] See, for example, addresses of Foreign Minister Sharett in the *Knesset, Divrei Haknesset,* 1st *Knesset,* 103rd Session, January 4, 1950, pp. 429–430 ff.; 161st Session, July 4, 1950, pp. 2057-2058; W. Eytan, "Israel's Foreign Policy and International Relations," *Middle Eastern Affairs,* May, 1951, pp. 155-160; *Israel and the United Nations,* pp. 182-187. This report of a study group set up by the Hebrew University of Jerusalem contains an excellent summary of Israel's attitude on various questions that have come before the United Nations.

[82] W. Eytan, *The First Ten Years: A Diplomatic History of Israel,* New York, 1958, p. 84; ch. 4, *passim;* M. Sharett, address in *Knesset, Divrei Haknesset,* 1st *Knesset,* 101st Session, January 2, 1950, pp. 375-380; A. Eban, *Voice of Israel,* New York, 1957, pp. 31-33, 45-61; *Government Yearbook,* 5711 (1950), pp. 143-145. On United Nations proposals and resolutions, see

United Nations, General Assembly, *Official Records,* Plenary Meetings, 4th Session, December 9, 1949, pp. 606-607; 5th Session, December 15, 1950, p. 684; 7th Session, December 18, 1952, p. 413; *ibid., Resolutions,* 4th Session, September 20–December 10, 1949, p. 25; *ibid.,* 5th Session, Supplement No. 9 (Doc. A/1286), and Supplement No. 18 (A/1367/Rev. 1), pp. 10-11. For Israel's position, see *ibid.,* Plenary Meetings, 4th Session, pp. 598-602. See also P. Mohn, "Jerusalem and the United Nations," *International Conciliation,* October, 1950, pp. 425-471.

⁸³ For Israel's position on the refugee problem, see Eban, *op. cit.,* pp. 33-37, 216-237 (statements of Ambassador Eban before General Assembly on May 5, 1949, and November 18, 1955); Eytan, *op. cit.,* ch. 6.

⁸⁴ See Akzin, *op. cit.,* pp. 135-137.

⁸⁵ See G. G. Stevens, "The Jordan River Valley," *International Conciliation,* January, 1956, pp. 227-283; D. A. Schmidt, "Prospects for a Solution of the Jordan Valley Dispute," *Middle Eastern Affairs,* January, 1955, pp. 1-12; *Israel and the United Nations,* pp. 105-107.

⁸⁶ United Nations, Security Council, *Official Records,* 558th Meeting, September 1, 1951, pp. 1-3; *ibid.,* 664th Meeting, March 29, 1954, pp. 12 ff. See also *Government Yearbook,* 5713 (1952), p. 127; *ibid.,* 5714 (1953-1954), p. 150; *ibid.,* 5715 (1954), p. 125; *ibid.,* 5716 (1955), pp. 184-185; Eban, *op. cit.,* pp. 255-275 (address before the Security Council, October 13, 1956); Eytan, *op. cit.,* pp. 88-104; B. Shwadran, "Egypt Before the Security Council," *Middle Eastern Affairs,* December, 1951, pp. 383-400; E. Ereli, "The Bat Galim Case before the Security Council," *ibid.,* April, 1955, pp. 108-117.

⁸⁷ See United Nations, Security Council, *Official Records,* 642nd Meeting, November 24, 1953, p. 21; *Government Yearbook,* 5713 (1952), p. 126; *ibid.,* 5714 (1953-1954), pp. 149-150; *ibid.,* 5715 (1954), pp. 123-155; *ibid.,* 5716 (1955), pp. 180-186; *ibid.,* 5717 (1956), pp. 237-239 ff.; Eytan, *op. cit.,* pp. 104-117; M. Dayan, "Israel's Border and Security Problems," *Foreign Affairs,* January, 1955, pp. 1-18; B. Shwadran, "Israel-Jordan Border Tension," *Middle Eastern Affairs,* December, 1953, pp. 385-401; M. Pearlman, "Bagdad-Gaza-Bandung," *ibid.,* May, 1955, pp. 145-149. For a pro-Arab view on border clashes, see E. H. Hutchison, *Violent Truce: A Military Observer Looks at the Arab-Israeli Conflict, 1951-1955,* New York, 1956, *passim.*

⁸⁸ B. Shwadran, *The Middle East, Oil, and the Great Powers,* New York, 1955, presents a thorough and well-documented account of the role of oil in Middle East power politics.

⁸⁹ For the text of the Three Power Declaration, see *Middle Eastern Affairs,* June-July, 1950, p. 173.

⁹⁰ See address of Foreign Minister Sharett in *Divrei Haknesset,* 2nd *Knesset,* 496th Session, November 15, 1954, pp. 64-66 ff.

⁹¹ See *Government Yearbook,* 5714 (1953-1954), p. 155; *ibid.,* 5716 (1955), pp. 181-184; *ibid.,* 5717 (1956), pp. 239-240, 249-250; Eytan, *op. cit.,* ch. 7; D. J. Dallin, "Soviet Policy in the Middle East," *Middle Eastern Affairs,* November, 1955, pp. 337-344; I. London, "Evolution of the U.S.S.R.'s Policy in Middle East, 1950-1956," *ibid.,* May, 1956, pp. 169-178, and Soviet policy statements, pp. 188-195.

⁹² See *Israel and the United Nations,* pp. 289-294.

[93] On the Suez-Sinai crisis, see United Nations, General Assembly, *Official Records*, First Emergency Special Session, *Resolutions*, pp. 2-4, and debates in *ibid., Plenary Meetings*, First Emergency Special Session, November 1-10, 1956, *passim; ibid.*, Eleventh Session, November 12, 1956–March 8, 1957, *Resolutions*, pp. 61-62, and debates in *ibid., Plenary Meetings, passim*. See also *Government Yearbook*, 5718 (1957), pp. 247-251 ff.; *Divrei Haknesset*, 3rd *Knesset*, 228th Session, January 23, 1957, pp. 826-829 ff. (Premier Ben-Gurion's address); Eban, *op. cit.*, pp. 276-292 (Address before General Assembly, November 1, 1956). The exchange of notes between President Eisenhower and Prime Minister Ben-Gurion, and between Premier Bulganin and the latter, are given in *Middle Eastern Affairs*, January, 1957, pp. 13-16. The radio-television address of President Eisenhower, February 20, 1957, is given, in *ibid.*, April, 1957, pp. 139-143. On the lifting of the Aqaba blockade, see P. A. Porter, *The Gulf of Aqaba: An International Waterway*, Washington, 1957, pp. 1-18.

BRIEF BIBLIOGRAPHY

AKZIN, BENJAMIN, *New States and International Organization*. Paris (UNESCO), 1955.

BACHI, ROBERTO (ed.), *Scripta Hierosolymitana*. Vol. III (Studies in Economic and Social Sciences). Jerusalem, 1956.

BARATZ, G., and others, *A New Way of Life: The Collective Settlements of Israel*. London, 1949.

BARATZ, JOSEPH, *A Village by the Jordan*. London, 1954.

BARER, SHLOMO, *The Magic Carpet*. New York, 1952.

BEIGIN, MENACHEM, *The Revolt: Story of the Irgun*. New York, 1951.

BEIN, ALEX, *Theodor Herzl*. Philadelphia, 1941.

BEN-GURION, DAVID, *Rebirth and Destiny of Israel*. New York, 1954.

BEN-JACOB, J., *The Rise of Israel*. New York, 1949.

BEN-SHALOM, A., *Deep Furrows*. New York, 1937.

BENTWICH, NORMAN, *Israel*. New York, 1952.

BERNADOTTE, F., *To Jerusalem*. London, 1951.

BERNSTEIN, MARVER H., *The Politics of Israel*. Princeton, 1957.

BONNÉ, ALFRED, *State and Economics in the Middle East*. 2nd ed. London, 1955.

BURSTEIN, MOSHE, *Self-Government of the Jews in Palestine Since 1900*. Tel-Aviv, 1934.

COHEN, ISRAEL (ed.), *The Rebirth of Israel*. London, 1952.

———, *A Short History of Zionism*. London, 1951.

———, *The Zionist Movement*. New York, 1946.

CROSSMAN, RICHARD, *Palestine Mission*. New York, 1947.

CRUM, BARTLEY C., *Behind the Silken Curtain*. New York, 1947.

DAGAN, PERETZ, *Pillars of Israel Economy*. Tel-Aviv, 1955.

DAVIS, HELEN MILLER, *Constitutions, Electoral Laws, Treaties of States in the Near and Middle East*. Rev. ed. Durham, 1953.

DAVIS, M. (ed.), *Israel: Its Role in Civilization*. New York, 1956.

DE GAURY, GERALD, *The New State of Israel*. New York, 1952.

DE HAAS, J., *Theodor Herzl: A Biographical Study*. 2 Vols. Chicago, 1927.

DUNNER, JOSEPH, *The Republic of Israel*. New York, 1950.

EBAN, ABBA, *Voice of Israel*. New York, 1957.

EISENSTADT, S. N., *The Absorption of Immigrants*. London, 1954.

ELATH, ELIAHU, *Israel and Her Neighbors*. New York, 1957.

Esco Foundation for Palestine, *Palestine: A Study of Jewish, Arab and British Policies*. 2 Vols. New Haven, 1947.

EYTAN, WALTER, *The First Ten Years: A Diplomatic History of Israel*. New York, 1958.

FRANKENSTEIN, CARL (ed.), *Between Past and Future: Essays and Studies on Aspects of Immigrant Absorption in Israel*. Jerusalem, 1953.

GAMZU, HAIM, *Painting and Sculpture in Israel*. Tel-Aviv, 1951.

GARCIA-GRANADOS, JOSÉ, *The Birth of Israel*. New York, 1948.

General Federation of Jewish Labour in Palestine, *Memorandum Submitted to the Anglo-American Commission of Inquiry*. Tel-Aviv, March, 1946. Mimeographed.

GINZBERG, ELI, *Manpower Utilization in Israel*. Tel-Aviv, 1953.

———, *Second Report on Manpower Utilization in Israel*. Tel-Aviv, 1956.

GORDON, A. D., *Selected Essays*. New York, 1938.

Great Britain, Colonial Office, *Mandate for Palestine*, Cmd. 1785. London, 1922.

———, *Palestine Land Transfer Regulations*, Cmd. 6180. London, 1940.

———, *Palestine Partition Commission Report*, Cmd. 5854 (Woodhead Report). London, 1938.

———, *Palestine Royal Commission Report*, Cmd. 5479 (Peel Report). London, 1937.

———, *Palestine Statement of Policy*, Cmd. 6019 (White Paper of 1939). London, 1939.

———, *Reports on the Administration of Palestine and Transjordan*. London, 1920-1938.

GROSSMAN, KURT R., *Germany's Moral Debt: The German-Israel Agreement*. Washington, 1954.

GRUBER, RUTH, *Israel To-day*. New York, 1958.

GRUSHKA, THEODORE (ed.), *The Health Services of Israel*. Jerusalem, 1952.

GUREVICH, D., and GERTZ, A., *Statistical Handbook of Jewish Palestine, 1947*. Jerusalem, 1947.

Hadassah Medical Organization, *Twenty Years of Medical Service to Palestine, 1918-1938*. Jerusalem, 1939.

HALKIN, S., *Modern Hebrew Literature*. New York, 1950.

HANNA, PAUL L., *British Policy in Palestine*. Washington, 1942.

Hebrew Encyclopedia, The. Vol. VI. Jerusalem, 1957.

HOROWITZ, DAVID, *Kalkalat Israel*. Tel-Aviv, 1958.

———, *State in the Making*. New York, 1953.

HUEBNER, T., and VOSS, C. H., *This Is Israel*. New York, 1956.

HUREWITZ, J. C., *Diplomacy in the Near and Middle East*. Vol. II. Princeton, 1956.

———, *The Struggle for Palestine*. New York, 1950.

HUTCHISON, E. H., *Violent Truce: A Military Observer Looks at the Arab-Israeli Conflict, 1951-1955*. New York, 1956.

HYAMSON, ALBERT M., *Palestine Under the Mandate, 1920-1948*. London, 1950.

Israel, Government of, *Cooperative Societies in Israel, 1956*. Jerusalem, 1957.

———, *Divrei Haknesset* (Official Records of the *Knesset* in Hebrew). Jerusalem, February 14, 1949, to date.

———, *Government Yearbook*. Jerusalem, 1950-1957.

———, *Iton Rishmi, Moetzet Hamedinah Hazmanit* (Records of the Provisional State Council). Tel-Aviv, May 16, 1948–February 10, 1949.

———, *Laws of the State of Israel* (Official English translation). Jerusalem, Vols. 1-9. This series thus far includes laws enacted during 1948-1956. For subsequent legislation, see *Reshumot, Sepher Hahukkim*.

———, *Statistical Abstract of Israel*. Jerusalem, 1949/1950–1956/1957.

Israel and the United Nations (report of a Study Group set up by The Hebrew University of Jerusalem; prepared for the Carnegie Endowment for International Peace). New York, 1956.

Israel Economist, The: Annual. Jerusalem, 1949/1950–1956/1957.

Israel Yearbook, The. Tel-Aviv, 1950-1951 to 1957.

KALLEN, H. M., *Utopians at Bay*. New York, 1958.

KANIEVSKY, I., *Social Policy and Social Insurance in Palestine*. Tel-Aviv, 1947.

KIMCHE, JON, *Seven Fallen Pillars: The Middle East, 1945-1952*. New York, 1953.

KRAINES, OSCAR, *Israel: The Emergence of a New Nation*. Washington, D. C., 1954.

KURLAND, S., *Cooperative Palestine: The Story of the Histadrut*. New York, 1947.

LAQUEUR, WALTER Z., *Communism and Nationalism in the Middle East*. New York, 1956.

LEHRMAN, HAL, *Israel: The Beginning and Tomorrow*. New York, 1951.

LEVENSOHN, L., *Vision and Fulfillment*. New York, 1950.

LEVIN, HARRY, *I Saw the Battle of Jerusalem*. New York, 1950.

LEVY, EMANUEL, *Israel Economic Survey, 1953-1954*. Jerusalem, 1955.

LITVINOFF, BARNET, *Ben-Gurion of Israel*. New York, 1954.

McDONALD, JAMES G., *My Mission in Israel, 1948-1951*. New York, 1951.

NATHAN, ROBERT; GASS, OSCAR; and CREAMER, D., *Palestine: Problem and Promise*. Washington, 1956.

O'BALLANCE, EDGAR, *The Arab-Israeli War, 1948*. London, 1956.

PATAI, RAPHAEL, *Israel Between East and West*. Philadelphia, 1953.

PEARLMAN, MOSHE, *The Army of Israel*. New York, 1950.

PERETZ, DON, *Israel and the Arab Refugees*. 2 Vols. New York, 1955. Mimeographed.

RABINOWICZ, OSKAR K., *Fifty Years of Zionism*. London, 1952.

———, Herzl, *Architect of the Balfour Declaration*. New York, 1958.

RACKMAN, EMANUEL, *Israel's Emerging Constitution, 1948-1951*. New York, 1955.

REVUSKY, ABRAHAM, *Jews in Palestine*. New York, 1945.

ROBINSON, JACOB, *Palestine and the United Nations*. Washington, 1947.

ROSENNE, SHABTAI, *Israel's Armistice Agreements with the Arab States*. Tel-Aviv, 1951.

ROYAL INSTITUTE OF INTERNATIONAL AFFAIRS, *Great Britain and Palestine, 1915-1945*. London, 1946.

RUPPIN, A., *Three Decades of Palestine*. Jerusalem, 1936.

SABAGH, S., (transl.) *Be'eynei Oyev* (Through the Eyes of the Enemy). Tel-Aviv, 1954.

SACHER, HARRY, *Israel: The Establishment of a State*. New York, 1952.

SAMUEL, EDWIN, *Handbook of the Jewish Communal Villages in Palestine*. Jerusalem, 1945.

——, *Problems of Government in the State of Israel*. Jerusalem, 1956.

SCHECHTMAN, JOSEPH B., *The Arab Refugee Problem*, New York, 1952.

SHWADRAN, BENJAMIN, *The Middle East, Oil and the Great Powers*. New York, 1955.

SOKOLOW, N., *History of Zionism, 1600-1918*. 2 Vols. London, 1919.

SPEISER, E. A., *The United States and the Near East*. Cambridge, Mass., 1950.

SPIEGEL, M., and others, *The Hebrew University of Jerusalem, 1925-1950*. Jerusalem, 1950.

SPIEGEL, S., *Hebrew Reborn*. New York, 1930.

SPIRO, M. E., *Kibbutz: Venture in Utopia*. Cambridge, Mass., 1956.

SYRKIN, MARIE, *Way of Valor, A Biography of Golda Myerson*. New York, 1955.

TAUBER, E., *Molding Society to Man: Israel's New Adventure in Cooperation*. New York, 1955.

ULITZUR, A., *Two Decades of Keren Hayesod (A Survey of Facts and Figures, 1921-1940)*. Jerusalem, 1940.

UNITED NATIONS, General Assembly. *Official Records*.

——, Security Council. *Official Records*.

——, *Monograph on Community Settlements and Report of the Survey Mission on Community Organization and Development in Israel*. United Nations, 1954.

——, Conciliation Commission for Palestine. *Progress Reports, 1949* ff.

——, Department of Economic and Social Affairs. *Economic Developments in the Middle East* (varying titles), 1949/1950–1955/1956. New York, 1951-1957.

——, Special Committee on Palestine. *Report to the General Assembly*, U.N. Doc. A/364.

United States, Department of State, *Anglo-American Committee of Inquiry: Report, April 20, 1946*. Washington, D.C., 1946.

WEIZMANN, CHAIM, *Trial and Error*. London, 1949.

WALLENROD, REUBEN, *The Literature of Modern Israel*. New York, 1956.

WEINGARTEN, MURRAY, *Life in a Kibbutz*. New York, 1955.

WILLIAMS, L. F. RUSHBROOK, *The State of Israel*. London, 1957.

UNESCO, *International Social Science Bulletin*, Vol. VIII, No. 1. Paris, 1956.

ZIDON, ASHER, *Haknesset*. Tel-Aviv, 1950.

CHAPTER 9

JUDAISM AND THE DEMOCRATIC IDEAL

By Milton R. Konvitz

JEWISH AND DEMOCRATIC IDEALS

In this chapter we shall take as the essence of the democratic ideal the belief in equality. An explication of this belief in equality leads to cultural and religious pluralism; to constitutional government, with effective checks on the agencies of government; a wide and equitable distribution of property; universal education and emphasis on reason, rather than superstition and force, as instruments of social control and progress; freedom of speech, freedom of the press, and freedom of assembly.

Just as a sharp distinction must be made between the accidental and the essential aspects of democracy, so the same distinction must be made among the various aspects of Judaism. Judaism, too, has had its highest insights, which, though they may have been conditioned by historical events, deserve perpetuation on their own account. On the other hand, like all other social institutions, Judaism has frequently needed to accommodate itself to the accidents of time and place in ways which did not at all times exhibit its own highest ideals. As in the case of democracy, it is the deeper motivation, the profounder insights, rather than the superficial aspects, that have kept alive Judaism as a way of life and as a philosophy of life.

Living in the middle of the twentieth century, we, of course, face problems radically different from those faced by the prophets thousands of years ago, or by the great Rabbis responsible for the Babylonian and Palestinian Talmuds.[1a] Freedom of speech must mean something sharply different to a people with a press than it did to a people who prohibited reduction of their learning to writing. This means only that the branches of democracy are different; the root is the same: it is the same wherever and whenever people live together in a community, wherever and whenever people constitute a society. The problem of human freedom is always the same: though at one time, to achieve more of it, we must fight a civil war to abolish economic and physical slavery; at another time we must fight to abolish racial distinctions in immigration policy; at one time, to achieve more of freedom, we must carry on a fight for woman suffrage; at another time the fight is against the white primary and the poll tax;

at one time the fight is for freedom to teach Torah in Jabneh; at another time the fight is for freedom to teach the theory of evolution in Tennessee. The scenes change; the characters and the plot are pretty much the same. This does not mean, necessarily, that the history of mankind can be written in terms of the history of liberty. We are not here concerned with the degree of truth in a Crocean philosophy of history. All we mean to say is that, whatever liberty may have meant at different times in the history of mankind, its essential character, as we have stated it, has been always pretty much the same. The struggles have been variations on a theme. The theme has been: human equality and freedom.

THE DEMOCRATIC IDEAL: RACIAL AND NATIONAL EQUALITY

Almost at the outset of our discussion we must face the obvious question of the consistency of the concept of the chosen people with the democratic ideal. How can a people that considers itself elected of God as His special inheritance, find its institutions and ideals consistent with democracy? Some have met the question by a denial that Jews today consider themselves God's chosen people.

This is one answer. Most Jews, however, assert that, when rightly understood, there is no inconsistency between the doctrine of the chosen people and democratic ideals. The doctrine of the chosen people may lead to exclusiveness, physical and spiritual isolation, haughtiness of spirit; but this happens only when the doctrine is adhered to by a person with a narrow heart and mind, who has no real comprehension of the meaning and utility of the doctrine. When taken on a higher ground, it is said, the concept has great value in furthering the ideals of both Judaism and democracy.

An excellent statement of this point of view is to be found in the philosophical writings of Rab Saadia Gaon.[2a] "All creatures are His creatures," said Rab Saadia Gaon, "and we may not say that He has taken to Himself one to the exclusion of the other or to a greater degree than another." For, "if God hath chosen but one man and one city, who would remember the rest of mankind?"

In the same way, said Rab Saadia Gaon, we must consider allusions to God as the God of Abraham, Isaac and Jacob. "For when the Psalmist exclaimed 'O Lord, the portion of *mine* inheritance and *my* cup,' did he alone want to possess the master of the worlds?"

"We hold," said Rab Saadia Gaon, "that He is the God of all mankind" and that "the worth of each man and his lot are equally precious before Him." The doctrine of the chosen people to Rab Saadia Gaon was nothing more than an expression exalting and praising God; for he who feels himself especially touched by God's love describes himself as the recipient of God's grace and special favor. But it carries no implication that God does not stand in the same loving relationship to all men, and that others may not designate that relationship in the same or similar terms.

It is probable that today most Jews accept the doctrine of the chosen people as the Jews' explanation of the possession by them "of a spiritually unique literature and philosophy." The Jews are the chosen people only because God has chosen them from among all peoples to give them the Torah.[3a] The supreme treasure is not the Jewish people but the Torah; and the former are important in God's universal scheme only as the recipients and bearers of this great treasure. Israel was selected and made the custodian of the Torah only so that he might share his inheritance with all other men. It is the duty of Israel to be the model and guide to all nations; but this he can accomplish only by living in accordance with the dictates of the Word of God in the Torah. In brief, Israel was "chosen" only in the sense that he was selected by God to transmit the Torah to all the peoples of the earth—to be a light unto the nations. When the Exile was considered from this standpoint, the Rabbis said that it was not intended as a punishment of Israel, but as an opportunity to spread the Word of God among the nations of the earth: the Jews are deprived of a home and the security it offers because they are God's servants. Viewed in this light, the doctrine of the chosen people offers the Jews no privileges denied to others; on the contrary, it imposes on them a mission, loyalty to which must bring them suffering, humiliation, agonies of pain and death; the Jew must suffer persecution, so that of him one might say in truth: "He is despised and rejected of men; a man of sorrows, and acquainted with grief." In this aspect, the doctrine implies no superiority inherent in the Jewish people, apart from the superiority that is attached to one who is charged with the duty to carry an important message. It is the message and not the messenger that is superior; so that one might speak really of the *Chosen Message* rather than of the *Chosen People*; the people are not endowed with superiority, but charged to be humble; humility, rather than riches or glory, must clothe them.

This interpretation of the concept points away from the particularism that is frequently charged against Judaism, and points to the universalism of which the Prophets were the leading spokesmen. Judaism, then, is a universalistic religious faith. Its truths are not to be kept under lock and key. In the first place, the truths of Judaism are to guide the Jewish people at every step and at every moment: Israel must obey God's law; he must strive to attain the purposes of mankind, as directed by God, *within his own community*. But he must do more: he must strive to attain that purpose in the *entire community of mankind*. If the Jew is particularistic at all, it is only that he wants to make of himself a *worthy* messenger, *one who himself lives by the message he carries*.

Jews, it has been said, are actually "an ethnic group with a universalistic religious faith which transcends the values of a single people but which they are forced to use as an instrument of survival in an alien world." This is the irony of Jewish existence: devotion to a universalistic faith marks the Jews off as a "peculiar" people, a "chosen" people! But God's "covenant" with this people is binding on God only so long as Israel himself observes the letter and spirit of the "covenant." To quote from Reinhold Niebuhr:

> The first religious apprehension of a universal and unlimited moral obligation was achieved in prophetic monotheism, which had its inception in the prophet Amos's conception of a universal history, over which the God of Israel presided as sovereign but of which the history of Israel was not the center and end. Amos thought of the "Holy One of Israel" as a transcendent God who would both use and reject the special mission of Israel in his universal designs and who could taunt his own people with the words, "Are ye not as children of the Ethiopians unto me?"

This is not, I submit, only a Christian's view of the mission of Israel; it is the view of Israel, the view of Israel's prophets. The "chosen people" are not at the center of the world; they are charged with the duty to live by, and transmit, the highest moral ideals, in deep humility and in a spirit of charity. But God's ways are inscrutable; the Torah was written in the words of man, so that man might understand it, but there are errors and sins at every step and in every moment of the life of a mortal man; there is the finiteness of the intelligence, and the contingency of the will. Who, then, knows what is the ultimate truth? or what is the way or the plan of God? All one can do is walk humbly; and if one does this, he may trust that he is walking humbly with his God.

This is what is meant by the doctrine of the chosen people. Admittedly, it is a statement of ideals and not a description of the way Jews live. To live by these ideals would make it very dangerous to be a Jew. But during the past thousands of years many Jews have lived dangerously. The ideal, at any rate, is not an impossible one; and even if it were, it might, from the moral point of view, still be a relevant one.

When men are judged by any empirical test they are not equal: some are richer than others, some wiser, some swifter, some more beautiful. Yet the essence of democracy is equality. Men reject the empirical tests and assert their equality notwithstanding the evidence adduced by their eyes and ears and other senses. "All men are created equal," said Jefferson in the Declaration of Independence; and he had no footnote references to statistical tables by way of documentation. The belief in equality is a transcendental belief, if you wish; it makes an assertion which may be true only in the world of noumena. But no matter: it is the cornerstone of the democratic faith and the essence of moral idealism. "The basis of democratic development," says Harold Laski "is therefore the demand that the system of power be erected upon the *similarities* and not the *differences* between men." Here we have the clue to the problem of democracy: differences are not to be eliminated, for it is good that one man paint better than another, that one woman cook better than does her neighbor, that one surgeon operate better than another; yes, and even that one man legislate better than another. But the system of power (political power, economic and social power) must be based on the similarities and not on the differences between men. The demand for equality manifests itself in many relations: there is the demand for equal suffrage; for economic equality; there must be no privilege by birth; there is the demand for educational equality; there must be equality in participation in the results of social developments and improvements; equality before the law (real and not merely formal equality).

At bottom the democratic faith is a moral affirmation: men are not to be used merely as means to an end, as tools; each is an end in himself; his soul is from the source of all life; a man is born "trailing clouds of glory behind him"; no matter how lowly his origin, a man is here only by the grace of God—he owes his life to no one but God. He has an equal right to pursue happiness: life, liberty and the pursuit of happiness are his simply by virtue of the fact that he is a live human being. He has his place in the sun, and neither the place nor the sun was made by men.

This faith finds its essence in what Henry Michel called the "eminent dignity of human personality." One of the chief sources of this faith is in the wellsprings of Judaism.

It may be possible to arrive at the philosophy of equality within the framework of secular thought, as, *e.g.*, in the systems of John Dewey and Bertrand Russell and in socialist Marxism. Within the framework of a religious system, however, it is probably impossible to arrive at the philosophy of equality in the absence of a belief in ethical monotheism.

For as long as one believes in the existence of a multiplicity of gods, each expressing his own biases and partialities, loving his friends and hating his enemies, and no one supreme god above all others, there is no room provided for accommodation of the beliefs in the fatherhood of God and the brotherhood of man. In ethical monotheism, however, these beliefs are basic. Judaism conceived of God as the creator and ruler of the entire universe: "In the beginning God created the heavens and the earth." He created Adam and Eve, from whom all mankind have sprung. Humanity lives, therefore, in "One World"; one world in every sense of the term; the laws of physical nature are the same everywhere; the laws of human nature are the same everywhere: the heavens and the moral law are the same everywhere.

Not only are the physical laws the same everywhere, but the laws of righteousness too. For God is not only *ehad*, One, but He is God "sanctified in righteousness." He is the judge of all the earth, as Abraham said, and cannot act unjustly. "Thou art not a God who hath pleasure in wickedness; evil shall not sojourn with Thee; Thou hatest all workers of iniquity." God, as the prophet said, wants to loose the fetters of wickedness, to undo the bands of the yoke, to deal bread to the hungry, to cover the naked, to shelter the homeless—He wants to see all this, and more, accomplished—but through the free agency of man.

Implicit and explicit in the ethical monotheism that is Judaism are, then, the beliefs in the fatherhood of God and the brotherhood of man. Thus Malachi cried out: "Have we not all one Father? Hath not One God created us?" Thus is posited the fatherhood principle. But in the same breath the prophet added: "Why do we deal treacherously every man against his brother?" The fatherhood and brotherhood principles go together; they are inseparable: if two men have the same father, are they, then, not brothers?

"God," said the Rabbis, "is on the watch for the nations of the world to repent, so that He may bring them under His wings." When the nations will accept the reign of righteousness, the Kingdom of God will have become established; and God wants this to happen above all else.

The most graphic expression of the fatherhood of God and the brotherhood of man is the statement in the Bible that man was created in the image of God. The Rabbis did not tire of creating homilies on this figurative expression of the oneness of the human family. Thus, R. Joshua b. Levi said: "When a man goes on his road, a troop of angels proceed in front of him and proclaim, 'Make way for the image of the Holy One, blessed be He.'" The following passage from the Mishna is especially revealing of the universalism of Judaism:

Only one single man was created in the world, to teach that, if any man has caused a single soul to perish, Scripture imputes it to him as though he had caused a whole world to perish; and if any man saves alive a single soul, Scripture imputes it to him as though he had saved a whole world. Again, but a single man was created for the sake of peace among mankind, that none should say to his fellow, "My father was greater than your father"; also that the heretics should not say, "There are many ruling powers in heaven." Again, but a single man was created to proclaim the greatness of God, for man stamps many coins with one die, and they are all like to one another; but God has stamped every man with the die of the first man, yet not one of them is like his fellow. Therefore every one must say, "For my sake was the world created."

In another passage there is the same emphasis on the transcendent importance of human life, any man's life:

"By ten sayings the world was created." To teach you that him who fulfills one command, or keeps one Sabbath, or preserves one human life, the Scripture regards as if he had preserved the whole world. And him who commits one sin, desecrates one Sabbath, and destroys one human life, the Scripture regards as if he had destroyed the whole world.

It is related that Ben Azzai quoted the verse from Genesis, "This is the book of the generations of Adam," and remarked that this is the greatest principle in the Torah. The same point was made by Rabbi Akiba but in a different statement. He said that the greatest principle in the Torah is "Love thy neighbor as thyself." Rabbi Tanhuma put the matter in a third way. He said that one should not say to himself, "Because I am despised, so may my neighbor be cursed with me"; for if one acts in this way he despises a being made in the image of God.

In the Talmud the question is raised why man was created a solitary human being, why were there not created several Adams and several Eves at one time? The answer given is this: "So that it might not be said that some races are better than others."

The injunction against shedding blood is repeated frequently in the Bible and in the writings of the Rabbis, and the law was declared that the life of one man may not be sacrificed to save the life of another man. The law is illustrated by the following passage from the Talmud:

A man came to Raba and said, "The prefect of my town has ordered me to kill so and so, or he will kill me." Raba said, "Let him kill you; do you commit no murder. Why should you think that your blood is redder than his? Perhaps his is redder than yours."

In the Midrash it is stated that the falling of rain is an event greater than the giving of the Torah, for the Torah is for Israel only, but rain is for the entire world. According to the Mekilta, however, even the Torah is for the entire world: "The Torah was given in the wilderness and in fire and in water. As these three are free to all the inhabitants of the world, so are the words of the Torah free to all the inhabitants of the world."

Are only the righteous among Israel the elect of God? Not at all; for righteousness, like sin, is the great leveler; the sinners among Israel are no better off than the evil ones among the non-Jews; and the righteous Israelites are not preferred to the righteous among the non-Jews. "The just among the Gentiles are the priests of God," says the Midrash. "I call heaven and earth to witness that whether a person be Jew or Gentile, man or woman, manservant or maidservant, according to his acts does the Divine Spirit rest upon him." Just as the acknowledgment of idolatry is a repudiation of the Torah, so repudiation of idolatry is an acceptance of Torah.

The injunctions in the Bible relating to the treatment of a brother were not construed as being directed only to the treatment of Israelites (though all Israelites are brothers) but of all mankind (for all men are brothers). Thus it was said: "The heathen is thy neighbor, thy brother. To wrong him is a sin." The point is made graphically by the following incident in the Midrash:

Simeon ben Shatah was occupied with preparing flax. His disciples said to him, "Rabbi, desist. We will buy you an ass, and you will not have to work so hard." They went and bought an ass from an Arab, and a pearl was found on it, whereupon they came to him and said, "From now on you need not work any more." "Why?" he asked. They said, "We bought you an ass from an Arab, and a pearl was found on it." He said to them, "Does its owner know of that?" They answered, "No." He said to them, "Go and give the pearl back to him." "But," they argued, "did not Rabbi Huna, in the name of Rab, say all the world agrees that if you find something which belongs to a heathen, you may keep it?" Their teacher said, "Do you think that Simeon ben Shatah is a barbarian? He would prefer to hear the Arab say, 'Blessed be the God of the Jews,' than possess all the riches of the world . . . It is written, 'Thou shalt not oppress thy neighbor.' Now thy neighbor is as thy brother, and thy brother is as thy neighbor. Hence you learn that to rob a Gentile is robbery."

In the same spirit it is said in the Talmud that an idolator who studies the Torah is like the High Priest; that a non-Jew who lives a godly life is like the High Priest. It is related that Rabbi Judah told the Emperor Antoninus that he would have a share in the world to come even though he was a non-Jew; for all men have a share in the world to come as long as they desist from acts of violence. In the spirit of Simeon ben Shatah the Talmud states:

In a city where there are both Jews and Gentiles, the collectors of alms collect both from Jews and Gentiles, and feed the poor of both, visit the sick of both, bury both, comfort the mourners whether they be Jews or Gentiles, and restore the lost goods of both.

The Bible begins the story of man not with the birth of Abraham but with the creation of Adam and Eve; and the Rabbis said that Adam was made from dust gathered by God from the four corners of the earth, so that no people should later be able to say that he was made from the dust gathered only in their own corner of the world. And wherever one turns in the writings of the Jews this motif of equality, the fatherhood of God and the brotherhood of man, appears irresistibly. Thus, at the Passover *seder* a drop of wine is to be spilled from the cup at the mention of each of the ten plagues with which the Egyptians were afflicted, the reason being, say the Rabbis, that one's cup of joy cannot be full as long as there is suffering somewhere in the world. And Purim, when the names of the sons of Haman, as they are hanged, are read in the synagogue, the reader must try to read them all in one breath; for it is painful to consider the torture of even Haman and his sons. Again, at the Passover *seder* the head of the household reads of the drowning of the Egyptian hosts in the Red Sea; and the Rabbis comment on the passage by relating that when the drowning was taking place, angels in heaven commenced to sing the praises of the Lord, but He rebuked them, saying, "My children are drowning, and you would sing!"

These sayings of the Rabbis are in the spirit of Amos, who cried out: "'Are ye not as children of the Ethiopians unto Me, O children of Israel?' saith the Lord. 'Have I not brought up Israel out of the Land of Egypt? and the Philistines from Caphtor, and Aram from Kir?'" (9:7).

So, too, according to Isaiah, The Lord says: "Blessed be Egypt My people and Assyria the work of My hands, and Israel Mine inheritance" (19:25). And when Jeremiah speaks of the afflictions that must be visited upon the sinful people of Moab, he says that God wails: "Therefore will I wail for Moab; yea, I will cry out for all Moab; for the men of Kir-heres shall my heart moan" (48:31). And the Book of Jonah, which occupies so prominent a place in Jewish ritual, relates of God's concern for the salvation of the inhabitants of the city of Nineveh—a city of Gentiles, not of Jews.

It is clear, we believe, that Judaism, or the ethical monotheism elaborated by the Old Testament and the Rabbis, posits as one of its fundamental precepts the equality of all men before God: all men who share righteousness share the grace of God. And righteousness is not considered from the standpoint of ritual observance: works of benevolence, says the Talmud, form the beginning and end of the Torah; or, as Micah expressed the truth:

> Wherewith shall I come before the Lord?
> And bow myself before God on high?
> Shall I come before Him with burnt-offerings?
> With calves of a year old?
> Will the Lord be pleased with thousands of rams,
> With ten thousands of rivers of oil?
> Shall I give my first-born for my transgression,
> The fruit of my body for the sin of my soul?
> It hath been told thee, O man, what is good;
> And what the Lord doth require of thee;
> Only to do justly and to love mercy
> And to walk humbly with thy God (6:6-8).

THE DEMOCRATIC IDEAL:
SOCIAL AND POLITICAL EQUALITY AND FREEDOM

That the ideals of equality and freedom which one finds at the heart of Judaism were not projected merely for "the end of days," but were principles of daily conduct, becomes clear when one examines some of the institutions that are characteristic of Judaism. In their relations with Gentiles the Jews could speak of equality and freedom only as ends to be achieved after a long struggle: both the Jews and the non-Jews will need to realize the nature of righteousness and strive for it together before they lie down together in equality, no one a lion and no one a lamb, but all children of the One Father, brothers who have issued from the same source of life. The ideal was always there; Israel could preserve itself only by loyalty to its universalistic religion; its mission was never to be treated lightly, let alone forgotten; and every opportunity was to be taken advantage of to elicit from the non-Jew a blessing for the One God, and thereby to bring him closer to righteousness. The incident about the pearl found on the Arab's donkey dramatically illustrates the consciousness of the obligation to win adherents for God and His ethical laws. That is what *Kiddush ha-Shem* means. The same awareness of this mission is illustrated by the dictum in the Talmud that to cheat a Gentile is even worse than to cheat a Jew, for besides being a violation of the moral law, such conduct brings Israel's religion into contempt and causes a *Hillul ha-Shem* (a desecration of the Name).

In relations among themselves the Jewish people had an opportunity to give the ideal of equality "a local habitation and a name." The keystone of the Jewish community was the precept that "all Israel are responsible for one another." The Rabbis relate that when Moses summoned all Israel before God, he said, "Your captains, your judges, your elders." But God made him add the words: "all the people of Israel." This passage receives clarification by the statement of the Rabbis that Moses did not stop with "all the people of Israel," but went on to add: "your little ones, your wives, and the stranger that is in thy camp"; for, said the Rabbis, "God's mercies are on male and female alike, on the wicked equally with the righteous, as it says, 'From the hewer of thy wood to the drawer of thy water.' All are equal before God; hence it says, 'All the people of Israel.' " Rabbi Akiba said that even the poorest in Israel are looked upon as freemen who have lost their possessions, "for they are the sons of Abraham, Isaac and Jacob." In other words, all *men* are equal because all are the children of Adam and Eve; all *Israelites* are equal because all are the children of Abraham, Isaac and Jacob—not to mention Adam and Eve.

The hereditary character of the priesthood in ancient Israel[4a] has led to the charge that Judaism recognized a class of privileged persons whose rights were obtained by birth: a hereditary aristocracy. But this is due to a misunderstanding. The priests were not permitted to consider themselves the heads of the community; they were a class whose status was determined by function; they were servants of God in a special sense; but being such servants, they carried obligations rather than privileges. People were not to stand in superstitious fear of them; they had no superior spiritual powers. The Rabbis had freed themselves from almost every trace of sacerdotalism. The priesthood was maintained because the Torah required it; but it was not the priests who blessed Israel; it was God Who bestowed the blessing; the priests were not intermediaries, like angels or saints.

It says at the end of the priestly benediction, "and it is I that will bless them." One might think that if the priests choose to bless the Israelites, then they are blessed, and if they do not choose, they are not blessed. Therefore it says, "And it is *I* that will bless them. *I* will bless my people."

Nor did the Rabbis themselves constitute a privileged caste. Three crowns were recognized, the crown of the Torah, the crown of the priesthood, and the crown of the kingdom.

Aaron was worthy of the crown of the priesthood and obtained it, David was worthy of the crown of the kingdom and obtained it. The crown of the Torah remains, so that no man shall have the pretext to say: "If the crown of the priesthood and the crown of the kingdom were yet available, I would have proved myself worthy of them and have obtained them." For the crown of the Torah is available for all. For God says: "Of him who proves himself worthy of *that* crown, I reckon it to him as if all the three were yet available, and he had proved himself worthy of them all. And of everyone who does not prove himself worthy of the crown of the Torah, I reckon it unto him as if all three crowns were yet available, and he had proved himself worthy of none of them."

The crown of the Torah is not inherited; it was worn by men who earned their living by cobbling shoes, weaving flax or making candles. Ben Azzai said: "If any man humiliates himself for the Torah, eats dry dates and wears dirty clothes, and sits and keeps guard at the doors of the wise, every passer-by thinks him a fool, but at the end you will find that all the Torah is within him"; and if the Torah is within him, he may wear the crown of the Torah. A famous passage in *Pirke Abot* is the following:

This is the way that is becoming for the study of the Torah: a morsel of bread with salt thou must eat, and water by measure thou must drink, thou must sleep upon the ground, and live a life of trouble, the while thou toilest in the Torah. If thou doest thus, "Happy shalt thou be and it shall be well with thee"; happy shalt thou be in this world, and it shall be well with thee in the world to come. Seek not greatness for thy self, and crave not honor more than is due to thy learning; and desire not the table of kings, for thy table is greater than theirs, and thy crown greater than theirs; and faithful is He, the master of thy work, to pay thee the reward of thy labor.

As water is priceless, said the Rabbis, so is the Torah priceless; and as water is free for all, so is the Torah free for all. But the Torah was also compared to wine: as wine cannot keep in vessels of gold and silver, but only in cheap earthenware vessels, so the words of the Torah are preserved only in him who makes himself lowly. "The greater the man," says the Midrash, "the humbler he is." Man, especially one who wears the crown of the Torah, must be as humble as is God Himself; wherever you find the greatness of God, there, too, you will find His humbleness. For "God loves nothing better than humility." Said Rabbi Johanan: "The words of the Torah abide only with him who regards himself as nothing." The Torah was not to be used as an ornament with which one might adorn himself; nor was it to be used as a spade with which to dig; knowledge of the Torah was its own reward; it is only to study the Torah that God created man: study of the Torah is his purpose, his end, his happiness and his reward.[5a] "Do the words of the Torah for the doing's sake; speak of them for their own sake. Do not say: 'I will learn Torah so that I may be called wise, or sit in the College, or gain long days in the world to come.'" Nor may one charge fees for teaching the Torah; for the words of the Torah are free; God gave the Torah free: "he who takes a fee for the Torah destroys the world."

The humility with which the greatest of the three crowns was to be worn is illustrated by the following incident related in the Talmud:

One day, at the close of the fig harvest, Rabbi Tarfon was walking in a garden, and he ate some figs which had been left behind. The custodian of the garden came up, caught him, and began to beat him unmercifully. Then Rabbi Tarfon called out and said who he was, whereupon they let him go. Yet all his days did he grieve, saying, "Woe is me, for I have used the crown of the Torah for my own profit." For the teaching ran: "A man must not say, I will study so as to be called a wise man, or rabbi, or an elder, or to have a seat in the College; but he must study from love. The honor will come of itself."

The Rabbis did not constitute a caste; they generally were not supported by the community but had to carry on a trade or calling from which they might support themselves and their families: "I call heaven and earth to witness," says the Midrash, "that every scholar who eats of his own, and enjoys the fruits of his own labor, and who is not supported by the community, belongs to the class who are called happy; as it is written, 'If thou eat the fruit of thy hands, happy art thou.'" They were teachers, but received no compensation for their teaching; they had to make a living by spending a part of their day in some occupation for which there was a monetary reward: "He who occupies himself with the study of the Torah only is as if he had no God." A man was counseled to spend as little time as possible, however, at his trade or work: only long enough to earn sufficient money to keep body and soul together. It was the duty of everyone to study the Torah at some time during each day: at least two ordinances in the morning and two in the evening; but the more study, the greater the reward (in the world to come). "If a scholar engages in business and is not too successful, it is a good omen for him. God loves his learning and does not want to enrich him." The greatest calumny was to call one an *am ha-aretz*, a boor; to be poor was to be blessed, but to be ignorant was to be cursed. No *"mitzva"* was greater than study: the study of the Torah was superior to all other things—all other things except one: teaching Torah. "He who learns receives but one-fifth of the reward that goes to him who teaches."

It is evident, then, that the crown of the Torah did not carry with it social privileges: the most learned man still needed to continue at his cobbler's bench or carpentry work. On the contrary, it imposed the obligation to teach. The social ideal of Judaism was a community of scholars, where all would be companions. This is what it means to have been created in the image of God: to fulfill the obligation or commandment to study the words of God. This commandment was imposed on *every* Jew equally; it had to be fulfilled by himself, and not by a surrogate.

The schools were commanded not to engage in strife one with the other. Tolerance in scholarly dispute was an obligation. "If a scholar has no *derek eretz* [good taste, refinement], he is lower than an animal." It is related that Rabbah would open his discourse with a jest, and let his hearers laugh a little. For years the schools of Hillel and Shammai[6a] maintained a dispute over a matter of law, finally a Voice descended in Jabneh and cried out: "The words of both are the words of the Living God, but the decision should follow the School of Hillel." It was asked, why, if the words of both are the words of the Living God, was the decision granted to Hillel's school? The reply was: "Because the members of the school of Hillel are amiable of manner and courteous; they teach the opinions of both schools; and furthermore, they always give the opinion of their opponents first." This teaches, said the Rabbis, that whoever abases himself is exalted by God. One was not to assume that the Divine Wisdom rested with him alone and that those who differed from him uttered words of no worth. One was to be a constant fount of tolerance and humility; one must be conscious of the relativity of his own statements even when, or perhaps especially when, the statements related to ultimate truths; for one was always subject to error and sin; all statements of truth were subject to finiteness and contingency. "One says its meaning is this, and another says its meaning is that. One gives such an opinion, his fellow a different one. But they all were given from one shepherd—that is from Moses, who received the teaching from Him who is One and unique in the world." This spirit of tolerance, mutual respect, profound religious humility, is perhaps best expressed in the following favorite saying of the Rabbis of Jabneh:

I am a creature of God and my neighbor is also His creature. My work is in the city and his is in the field. I rise early to my work and he rises early to his. He cannot excel in my work and I cannot excel in his. But perhaps you say, I do great things while he does small things. We have learnt that it matters not whether a man does much or little, if only he directs his heart to heaven.

Judaism is not merely a matter of beliefs and ceremonies, it is a way of life; and the economic aspect of human existence was not a matter of indifference to the prophets and Rabbis. The Bible was not considered a mere theological treatise; it was viewed as a document with the greatest social significance; for in its teachings one could find the ways by which to enter into intimate relation with God, and find joy and freedom in His service; also the ways by which to enter into proper social relations, so that the perfect social order, the kingdom of heaven, might be established on the earth. Today we might be tempted to say that one aim was religious while the other was social; but Judaism would reject the distinction. Judaism recognizes no profane virtues; all virtues are sacred; the social function is as religious as the religious function is social. "Rabbi Judah said in the name of Rab: 'A man is forbidden to eat anything until he has fed his beast.'" Was this considered a religious law or a social law? The distinction would not have been comprehensible to either Rabbi Judah or Rab. In Judaism all duties are divine commands. While several duties appear to be arbitrary, nearly all are expressed in laws which our conscience recognizes as obligatory on free will. Economics and ethics are the same; ethics and religion are the same.

In a word, there was no distinction between the social conscience and the religious conscience. The study of the Torah was chiefly the study of social relations, individual and communal problems. The Torah taught that "if two men claim thy help, and one is thy enemy, help thy enemy first"; and the same Torah taught that "he who gives food to a small child, must tell its mother"; and the same Torah taught that one must permit the poor to glean after the reapers, and that one must not take interest on a loan.

Perhaps it was the experience of the Israelites in Egypt that compelled them to project the ideal of social equality and freedom. For in Egypt they saw that when great wealth and political power are in the hands of the same group, the welfare and happiness of the rest of the people are greatly imperiled. Political and economic power must be spread out among all, with little if any disparity in the distribution. If this is not accomplished, and men are unjustly exploited—used as mere means and not as ends; when it is forgotten that every man bears the image of God—physical, spiritual and social pestilence will spread, and insurrection will follow, shaking the community to its very foundations. Masters cannot exploit their workers and God should not see. The excessive wealth of the masters leads to luxury; derived through injustice, wealth breeds further injustice; luxury corrupts what may have been left untouched by the injustice of exploitation. In the end the system collapses; blind injustice leans against the pillar of its palace and is destroyed with it.

Furthermore, as Charles Foster Kent has well pointed out, the experience of Moses showed him that violence does not avail in correcting industrial evils. The only true method is that which he used:

Education and organization of those industrially oppressed; clear presentation of their claims and rights; patient, persistent agitation in order to educate public opinion; and efficient organization to protect their interests.

The Israelites did not win their freedom merely to duplicate among themselves the system they had rejected. They were to build their own community on a basis of moral idealism, ethical religion and social justice. There was to be in the Promised Land no form of political or industrial oppression; for always the Jews were commanded to remember, at every turn, in every crisis, at every temptation to commit an injustice: "Remember that thou wast a slave in the land of Egypt, and that the Lord thy God brought thee out from there by a mighty hand and an outstretched arm." Future generations, after the exodus from Egypt, were commanded to look upon themselves as though *they*, and not merely their forefathers, had been rescued from the hand of the Egyptian taskmaster. The *freshness* of their freedom was constantly to be before their eyes.

Moreover, they were commanded to remember in humility that it was not by their own strength that they won their freedom, but because God is One Who watches over the poor, the fatherless, the afflicted, the helpless, the outcast: He is a just Judge; He loves justice and mercy and righteousness, and requites evil with evil. God has created a world in which the moral law is as implacable, as impersonal, and as imperative as is a physical law: there is no escape from it.

In ancient Israel the atmosphere was a thoroughly equalitarian one: all were practically equal and free. Each was represented in the council of the clan or tribe.[7a] While slavery was tolerated (it is to be remembered that the United States retained this institution until only three generations ago), the harshness of the master-servant relationship was in many ways mitigated. The biblical fugitive-slave law, unlike the laws passed by Congress before the Civil War, protected the fugitive; for in Deuteronomy it is provided:

Thou shalt not deliver to his master a bondsman that is escaped from his master unto thee. He shall dwell with thee in the midst of thee, in the place which he shall choose within one of thy gates, where it liketh him best; thou shalt not wrong him (23:16-17).

While the institution of private property was recognized, and there were laws against theft, clear recognition was given to the fact that property is fundamentally a social object, that property is subject to social control, that society may direct as to how much property a man may possess, how much of his income he may retain for his own use, for how long a period he may divest himself of title to property allotted to him, and so on. Thus it was provided that "when thou comest into thy neighbor's vineyard thou mayest eat grapes until thou have enough at thine own pleasure . . . when thou comest into thy neighbor's standing corn, thou mayest pluck ears with thy hand . . ." (23:25-26). Among the first laws to protect the rights of laborers are those found in the Bible. The Sabbath was instituted as a social institution, as a day of rest: "in it thou shalt not do any manner of work, thou, nor thy son, nor thy daughter, nor thy man-servant, nor thy maid-servant, nor thine ox, nor thine ass, nor any of thy cattle, nor thy stranger that is within thy gates . . ." (5:14). Wages were to be paid promptly:

Thou shalt not oppress a hired servant that is poor and needy, whether he be of thy brethren, or of thy strangers that are in thy land within thy gates. In the same day thou shalt give him his hire, neither shall the sun go down upon it; for he is poor, and setteth his heart upon it; lest he cry against thee to the Lord, and it be a sin in thee (24:14-15).

The well-off were forbidden to oppress the impoverished citizen:

No man shall take the mill or the upper millstone to pledge, for he taketh a man's life to pledge . . . When thou dost lend thy neighbor any manner of loan, thou shalt not go into his house to fetch his pledge. . . . And if he be a poor man, thou shalt not sleep with his pledge; thou shalt surely restore to him the pledge when the sun goeth down, that he may sleep in his garment, and bless thee (24:6,10,12-13).

Bankruptcy laws were instituted, so that a man shall not be borne down by his debts forever, but shall, instead, have an opportunity for a fresh economic start. "At the end of every seven years shalt thou make a release" (15:1); the creditor shall not exact the debt from his debtor. At the same time, he who hath must not close his heart to the importunities of him who hath not, and say to himself that "the seventh year, the year of release, is at hand" (15:9), and refuse to lend to the poor; for if this happen, God will hear the cry of the poor man, and the rich man will be guilty of a crime. "Thou shalt surely give him and thy heart shall not be grieved when thou givest unto him" (15:10). The owner of the land was not to think that the land was *really* his, to do with as he pleased;

for the land is the Lord's; and the Lord commanded that every seventh
year the land must lie fallow; it must not be abused, lest it become a waste
place, and all the land a dustbowl. A share of a man's income had to be
turned over to the communal authorities for the relief of needy persons.
Even when a man builds a house for himself, he must take into consideration the duties he owes his neighbors; he must make a parapet for
his roof, so that no one will fall from it.

Time and again the prophets cried out against the economic inequalities
that resulted in loss of freedom, injustice and oppression. Men became too
rich and too powerful for their own and the community's good. Such rich
men were declared enemies of the people and the chief sinners against God.
The accumulation of such wealth and the exploitation it entailed were
condemned in the strongest terms possible:

> Because they sell the righteous for silver,
> And the needy for a pair of shoes,
> That pant after the dust of the earth on the head of the poor,
> And turn aside the way of the humble . . .
> And they lay themselves down beside every altar,
> Upon clothes taken in pledge,
> And in the house of their God they drink
> The wine of them that have been fined (Amos 2:6-8).

Amos foretold such as these what their destiny would be:

> Hear this word,
> Ye kine of Bashan, that are in the mountains of Samaria,
> That oppress the poor, that crush the needy,
> That say to their lords, "Bring, that we may feast."
> The Lord God hath sworn by His holiness:
> "Lo, surely the days shall come upon you,
> That ye shall be taken away with hooks,
> And your residue with fish-hooks . . ." (4:1-3).

Isaiah brought severe charges against the oppressors of the common man:

> It is ye that have eaten up the vineyard;
> The spoil of the poor is in your houses.
> What mean ye that ye crush My people,
> And grind the face of the poor? . . . (3:14-15)
> Woe unto them that join house to house,
> That lay field to field
> Till there be no room and ye be made to dwell
> Alone in the midst of the land! (5:8).

Just as Judaism posits the ideals of social equality and economic equality,
so, too, it posits political freedom and equality. Israel was to be a holy
nation, each Israelite was to be a member of "a kingdom of priests, a
holy nation." God alone is ruler over Israel. What need is there of a king?

No one was permitted to make laws for the nation; for God had given His Torah to His people Israel—to every Israelite; there was no room left for a king. Not even David or Solomon[8a] could abrogate the laws of the Sabbath, or of the seventh year, or make oppression of the needy just. Israel was different from all other peoples: its legislation came from God. If a king cannot make laws, of what use can he be? God was the Lawgiver, the Ruler and the Judge. When the Jews asked Samuel to appoint over them a king, he told them of what use a king could be:

"This will be the manner of the king that shall reign over you: he will take your sons and appoint them unto him, for his chariots, and to be his horsemen; and they shall run before his chariots. And he shall appoint them unto him for captains of thousands, and captains of fifties; and to plow his ground, and to reap his harvest, and to make his instruments of war, and the instruments of his chariots. And he will take your daughters to be perfumers, and to be cooks, and to be bakers. And he will take your fields, and your vineyards, and your oliveyards, even the best of them, and give them to his servants. And he will take the tenth of your seed, and of your vineyards, and give to his officers, and to his servants. And he will take your men-servants, and your maid-servants, and your goodliest young men, and your asses, and put them to his work. He will take the tenth of your flocks; and you shall be his servants" (I Sam. 8:11-17).

The Jews never forgot this lesson of Samuel's; even though they took upon themselves the yoke of a kingship, they would not tolerate oppression and despotism. The king was to be a servant of the people and not their master; he was to rule under God and not as a substitute for Him. Thus the Jews became a "rebellious" people; for they would not tolerate a tyrant even if he were of the seed of David. When Solomon died, the northern tribes rose in protest against a perpetuation of oppressive measures by Rehoboam, whom Solomon had nominated as his successor.[9a] It is related that Rehoboam and the Israelites met at Shechem, where he was asked if he would make lighter their yoke. The king took counsel with the old men who had served Solomon, and they said to him: "If thou wilt be a servant unto this people this day, and wilt serve them, and answer them, and speak good words to them, then they will be thy servants forever" (I Kings 12:7). The king would not follow their advice; he "gave no heed to the people." When the Israelites saw that he disregarded their petition, they said to him:

> "We have no portion in David
> Neither have we inheritance in the son of Jesse;
> Everyman to his tents, O Israel" (II Sam. 20:1).

Even if it meant breaking up the kingdom, Judaism's democratic ideals had to be asserted and reasserted. Thus it was throughout Israel's history in Palestine. The people, and sometimes the prophets speaking for the

people, constantly submitted the moral presuppositions of the ruling caste
to scrutiny and re-examination. The freedom of the private moral judgment was always kept alive. When Ahab, misguided by Jezebel, his queen,
showed his disloyalty to the democratic ideals, a popular uprising ended
his dynasty. Elijah spoke for the conscience of Israel.[10a] When Naboth
refused to sell his vineyard to the despotic king, and the king, through
a perversion of justice, had him murdered, Elijah spoke out against the
king, and when the king heard his words, "he rent his clothes and put
sackcloth upon his flesh and fasted, and he lay in sackcloth, and went
softly" (I Kings 21:27). For the king knew that he could reign only
under and within the law; and he was not above the Torah.

And this brings us to our final point, namely, that no people can be free,
no democracy can continue to exist, if the rulers selected by the people do
not consider themselves bound by the law. There must be limitations on
rulers if the individual's rights are to be preserved. The citizen's rights
are measured by the restrictions on government. There must, in other
words, be a constitution which defines clearly how far the government may
go in this matter or that delegated to its authority. Israel had such a
constitution in the Torah. No one was above it. Only under the Torah
could kings rule and judges judge. As God is righteous, so must the king
be; as God defends the weak, so must the king. Only justice is the foundation of a people's happiness and stability. Psalm 72 expresses this thought:

> Give the king Thy judgments, O God,
> And Thy righteousness unto the king's son;
> That he may judge Thy people with righteousness,
> And Thy poor with justice . . .
> May he judge the poor of the people,
> And save the children of the needy,
> And crush the oppressor . . .
> He will have pity on the poor and needy,
> And the souls of the needy he will save.
> He will redeem their soul from oppression and violence . . .

This, in part, is the picture of the ideal king.

Indeed, how could Israel view the status and function of government
otherwise; for does not God Himself govern in accordance with law?
Judaism is a law-centered religious civilization. All that God does, said
Rabbi Akiba,[11a] He does by justice; "the procedure in the heavenly court
is governed by law as in an earthly court." The day has twelve hours, said
Rabbi Judah in the name of Rab, and in the first three God sits and busies
Himself with the Torah! God Himself is bound by the Torah, by His
own laws. He made the world "by law," not arbitrarily. Why, then, should
He not spend His time teaching the Torah to the righteous in heaven?
When Moses went up to heaven, he found God sitting and weaving

crowns for the letters, little flourishes on some letters of the Torah to ornament the Scroll of the Law. The imagination of the Jewish folk could devise no occupation more worthy of God than the writing and study of His own Torah; because Israel found such a delight in the Law: "But his delight is in the law of the Lord; and in His law doth he meditate day and night" (Ps. 1:2). The ordinances of the Lord are to be desired more than gold, yea, than much fine gold; they are sweeter than the honey and the honeycomb. "I have rejoiced in the way of Thy testimonies . . . I will delight myself in Thy statutes." The Lord's commandments apply to every significant act in life; as Rabbi Phineas said, one must think of the commandments when one builds a house, when he makes a door, when he buys new clothes, when his hair is cut, when his field is plowed, when his field is sowed, when the harvest is gathered, "even when you are not occupied with anything, but just taking a walk . . ." And the commandments are for *all* the people to observe: "All are equal before the law. The duty of observance is for all. For the Torah is the 'inheritance of the congregation of Jacob.' It does not say 'priests' or 'Levites' or 'Israelites,' but 'the congregation of Jacob.' " No one can be above the Law—whether he wear the crown of Torah, or the priestly crown, or the royal crown— because all men are equal, all are equally bound by the Law and subject to it, alike at every point; more than this, the world itself is subject to the Law; God made the world in accordance with the Law. Is not then even God Himself bound by the Law? "God created the world by the Torah: the Torah was His handmaid and His tool by the aid of which He set bounds to the deep, assigned their functions to sun and moon, and formed all nature. Without the Torah the world falls." The same Torah sets bounds to man's greed, man's injustice; assigns functions to this man and that, and forms civilization.

Without law there is no freedom. Unless a people meditate on the statutes and delight in the Law, they will not be able to walk at ease; unequal strength will lead to unequal justice; and when justice is dead, said Kant, it is better not to be alive. If Judaism projects a *rechtlichbuergerliche Gesellschaft*, it is to be borne in mind that this law-centered society is also an *ethischbuergerliche Gesellschaft*, for the law is within as well as without; and at the center of the ethico-legal system is the injunction of God: "For unto Me are the children of Israel slaves; they are not slaves unto slaves."

Not all democratic institutions were foreseen by the prophets and Rabbis; such agencies are evolved by societies of men as the need for them is felt to be irresistible even by those who would prevent their emergence. But the spirit, the inner values, the energies of democracy are right at the very heart of Judaism.

NOTES

[1a Cf. Judah Goldin, "The Period of the Talmud (135 B.C.E.-1035 C.E.)," this work, Vol. I, pp. 178-185.]

[2a Cf. *ibid.*, p. 202.]

[3a Cf. Louis Finkelstein, "The Jewish Religion: Its Beliefs and Practices," this work, Vol. II, pp. 482-484.]

[4a Cf. Robert Gordis, "The Bible as a Cultural Monument," this work, Vol. II, pp. 10-11.]

[5a Cf. Finkelstein, *op. cit.*, pp. 473 ff.]

[6a Cf. Goldin, *op. cit.*, pp. 133-137.]

[7a Cf. Gordis, *op. cit.*, p. 23.]

[8a Cf. William Foxwell Albright, "The Biblical Period," this work, Vol. I, pp. 26 ff.]

[9a Cf. *ibid.*, pp. 31 f.]

[10a Cf. *ibid.*, pp. 36 f.]

[11a Cf. Goldin, *op. cit.*, pp. 160-162.]

BIBLIOGRAPHY

The literature on the subject is meager. Following are a number of essays suggested for further reading:

BOKSER, BEN ZION, "Democratic Aspirations in Talmudic Judaism," in *Science, Philosophy and Religion* (Second Symposium), published by the Conference on Science, Philosophy and Religion. New York, 1942.

——, "Rabbinic Judaism and the Problem of Egoism," in *Conflicts of Power in Modern Culture* (Seventh Symposium), ed. by Lyman Bryson, Louis Finkelstein and R. M. MacIver, published by the Conference on Science, Philosophy and Religion. New York, 1947.

BURROWS, MILLAR, "Democracy in the Hebrew-Christian Tradition: Old and New Testaments," in *Science, Philosophy and Religion, op. cit.*

FINKELSTEIN, LOUIS, "The Beliefs and Practices of Judaism," in *The Religions of Democracy*, by Louis Finkelstein, J. Elliot Ross and William Adams Brown. New York, 1941.

——, "Foundations of Democracy—Hebrew Sources: Scriptures and Talmud," in *Foundations of Democracy*, ed. by F. Ernest Johnson, published by The Institute for Religious and Social Studies. New York, 1947.

——, "The Ideal of Religious Liberty—A Jewish View," in *Wellsprings of the American Spirit*, ed. by F. Ernest Johnson, published by The Institute for Religious and Social Studies. New York, 1948.

KAPLAN, MORDECAI M., *The Future of the American Jew*. New York, 1948. Chapter 15 on "Basic Values in Jewish Religion."

A number of pamphlets in the series *Popular Studies in Judaism* published by the Tract Commission of the Union of American Hebrew Congregations and the Central Conference of American Rabbis, Cincinnati, are relevant:

CRONBACH, ABRAHAM, *The Social Outlook of Modern Judaism.*
FELDMAN, ABRAHAM J., *Contributions of Judaism to Modern Society.*
HELLER, BERNARD, *The Jewish Concept of the Chosen People.*
SCHULMAN, SAMUEL, *Jewish Ethics.*
TARSHISH, JACOB, *Judaism and Socialism.*
WITT, LOUIS, *Judaism and Democracy.*

ADDENDUM

BELKIN, SAMUEL, *In His Image.* New York, n.d.
GORDIS, ROBERT, *Judaism for the Modern Age.* New York, 1955.
———, *The Root and the Branch.* Chicago, 1962.
GREENBERG, SIMON, "Intellectual Freedom in the Jewish Tradition," *Conservative Judaism* (Summer 1967).
———, "Judaism and the Democratic Ideal," *ibid.* (Winter 1966).
HIRSCH, RICHARD G., *There Shall Be No Poor.* New York, 1965.
JUNG, LEO, *Human Relations in Jewish Law.* New York, 1967.
KONVITZ, MILTON R., "Judaism and the Pursuit of Happiness," in *The Menorah Treasury.* Philadelphia, 1964.
———, "Many Are Called and Many Are Chosen," *Judaism* (Winter 1955).
———, "Privacy and the Law: A Philosophical Prelude," *Law and Contemporary Problems*, XXXI (1966), p. 272.
LAMM, NORMAN, "The Fifth Amendment and Its Equivalent in the Halacha," *Judaism* (Winter 1956).
———, "The Fourth Amendment and Its Equivalent in the Halacha," *Judaism* (Summer 1967).
LOEWE, RAPHAEL (ed.), *Studies in Rationalism, Judaism and Universalism.* London, 1966. See especially Louis Jacobs, "The Doctrine of the 'Divine Spark' in Man in Jewish Sources"; Raphael Loewe, "Potentialities and Limitations of Universalism in the Halakah"; Kurt Wilhelm, "The Idea of Humanity in Judaism."
RACKMAN, EMANUEL, "Judaism and Equality," in *Equality*, edited by J. Roland Pennock and John W. Chapman. New York, 1967.
SCHECHTER, SOLOMON, "Notes of Lectures on Jewish Philanthropy," *Studies in Judaism*, III (Philadelphia, 1924), p. 238.

CHAPTER 10

THE INFLUENCE OF THE BIBLE ON ENGLISH LITERATURE

By David Daiches

I

It has long been a commonplace among teachers of English in British universities that a proper understanding of English literature is impossible without a thorough knowledge of the Bible and of the Latin and Greek classics. These have been the great twin sources of inspiration for English writers at least from the latter part of the sixteenth century, and to a lesser degree and in a somewhat different way in earlier centuries also. Both these influences operated in a twofold manner: they were used rhetorically, as a teacher of style and literary devices of all kinds, and they also provided a set of stories and ideas which were incorporated, in an infinite number of ways, into the content of the later literature. While the Latin and Greek classics exerted this twofold influence on all the literatures of Europe, it was only in English literature that we find the Bible working similarly in both ways—and this because only in England was there produced a translation of the Bible acclaimed by successive generations as among the very greatest masterpieces of that country's literature. "Among the greatest" is perhaps too mild a phrase, for, while the Authorized Version of the Bible is generally ranked with the works of Shakespeare by literary critics, there can be no question that of the two the Bible has always been the more widely read and the better known among the English people as a whole. The fact, therefore, that the English Bible existed as a great literary work in its own right, as well as constituting a popular source of stories and moral ideas, meant that in England the Bible had a rhetorical, or purely literary, influence in addition to its influence as a rich storehouse of tales and ethical principles. In other European countries the Bible had only the latter kind of influence, for its translation into the vernacular never achieved the position among national literary masterpieces that was achieved by the English translation of the Bible known as the Authorized, or King James, Version.

It is true that in the seventeenth century it is often impossible to distinguish the rhetorical from the ideological influence of the Bible, for familiarity with the diction of the Authorized Version came to be regarded by many as implying an acceptance of certain religious doctrines. There are occasions when the experienced reader can infer from the kind of biblical English used by a writer (for there are many kinds of biblical English) to what particular Protestant sect he belonged. It is also true that in the eighteenth century it is sometimes difficult to distinguish a writer's use of the classics as a source of imagery and other stylistic devices from his acceptance of certain Greek or Roman ideals. In other words, though both the Bible and the classics have two distinct kinds of influence on English literature, there are periods when enthusiasm makes a writer deliberately exhibit one kind to show that he has also been affected by the other. Yet this is true of only certain limited periods, for on the whole it can be fairly said that both the Bible and the classics have had a con-tinuous stylistic influence even in quarters where agreement with the ideas expressed in the models imitated has been of the slightest.

That a Protestant people, encouraged by all the religious controversies of the Reformation to turn to the text of the Bible as their main weapon of attack and defense, should come to know the Bible well is easy enough to understand. But the full extent of the purely *literary* influence of the Bible on English literature can only be explained when we realize the number and variety of literary forms that the Bible contains.[1a] A writer like Milton thought of the Bible both as the fundamental document of his religion and as a collection of literary models comparable on aesthetic grounds with the great classics of Greece and Rome. History, short story, lyric, epic, ode, elegy, tragedy, comedy—these are all displayed in some form in the Old Testament. If we think for a moment of the differences in style and literary form between the simple narrative of Exodus, the lyrical directness of the Psalms (which themselves display a wide variety of poetic expression), the slow-moving, plangent eloquence of the fortieth chapter of Isaiah, the poetic elegies of Jeremiah, the variety of narrative styles shown in the Books of Kings, Ruth, Jonah and Esther, the extraor-dinary quality of the Book of Job (which Milton called a "brief epic")— to mention only a few examples—we can see how the Bible struck the imagination of a generation of writers still wrestling with the problem of literary "forms" and the kinds of style appropriate to different kinds of subject matter. This is what makes the seventeenth century such a pivotal period in English literature; for it was during this century that the struggle was waged with equal intensity both on the religious and on the literary plane. Whereas in many other European countries the religious struggle was fought out on the battlefield, in England it was on the whole a battle fought with texts and pamphlets, and each side produced its triumphs, which include Hooker's *Laws of Ecclesiastical Polity* at the end of the sixteenth century and Bunyan's *Pilgrim's Progress* in the latter part of the seventeenth century—neither of which books could have been written if there had been no English Bible.

It should be remembered that, although it was the acceptance of the Authorized Version as the definitive English translation that made possible the tremendous literary influence of the English Bible, that influence was already beginning to be exerted long before 1611, for the style of the Authorized Version—a style already antique when that translation was made—had been building up for generations, from Tyndale's earliest efforts in 1525, through the work of Coverdale and others for almost a century before the Authorized Version was published. English biblical prose was not born in the seventeenth century: indeed, by the time the Bible of 1611 appeared the people long had fairly fixed ideas of the kind of language appropriate for the English Bible, and they judged—and accepted—the Authorized Version accordingly. Coverdale's Bible, Matthew's Bible, the Great Bible, the Geneva Bible, the Bishop's Bible—each of these versions had played its part in developing biblical English. By 1604, when the Authorized Version was begun, the standard of style had long been set, and the only problem that remained was that of greater accuracy of rendering.

There is another point to be remembered. The achievement of the English biblical style was taking place during the very period when modern (*i.e.*, postmedieval) English literature was entering on its first great phase. When we talk of "the Bible and Shakespeare" (a collocation of a kind possible only in English literature) we are referring to two different kinds of English literary achievement; we are referring also to two contemporary achievements. The Authorized Version was being prepared during the period when Shakespeare was producing his final masterpieces. This was the fine flower of generations of noble experiment with style and language, in both poetry and prose. The fact, therefore, that English Bible translation was fortunate enough to grow up with this great phase of English literature helped both to ensure that it would profit to the utmost from the exciting literary experimentation that was taking place at this time and to produce a counterinfluence from the Bible translation already achieved on the secular literary works being produced. Thus the fanatical attitude of the more extreme Puritan sects to the letter of the biblical text as they understood it was tempered by the simultaneous consideration of the English Bible as a secular document, which contained important lessons for the writer and the literary critic. If this happy conjunction had not taken place, the Puritan suspicion of the arts would have done more damage in England than it actually did. Just as the medieval Church combined sacred and secular activities in the Miracle Plays (which brought the Bible into literature in a very different manner from the way in which it entered literature after the Reformation in England), so the seventeenth-century Puritan was led, often in spite of himself, to an appreciation of literary art even while denouncing the arts as pastimes of the devil. Milton, artist and Puritan, is the great symbolic figure here, but it is also worth considering whether the extraordinary work of Spenser—Platonist, Protestant, and at the same time a "poet's poet"—or the poetry of a Puritan such as Andrew Marvell could have existed were it not for the resolution of Puritanism and aesthetics made possible by English Bible translation. Only in the work of that Greek Puritan, Plato, the poet who denounced poets, is a similar phenomenon to be observed.

2

Before the sixteenth-century English Bible translation had brought the Bible to the people as a literary as well as a religious document, the ordinary Englishman, like his contemporaries all over Europe, had a sporadic knowledge of the Bible from pictures in stained-glass windows, sermons which quoted and elaborated biblical texts, and popular biblical paraphrases. In medieval Europe, therefore, the Bible could be known only for its stories and its doctrine, never for its literary qualities. Even the translations of single biblical texts made by individual members of the clergy in sermons were always made in the preacher's own words, not in the words of such translations as existed. Translations of the Bible did exist in Europe in the Middle Ages, but at least until the end of the fourteenth century they were translations made for individual members of the nobility or by some solitary scholar for his own private use, and they never achieved any circulation. The Church, during this period, took the view that ordinary folk should not read the Bible themselves, but should have appropriate portions of the Vulgate (Jerome's Latin version, the authorized text of the Church) interpreted to them by properly trained experts. "It was not without reason that Almighty God decided that Holy Scripture should be secret in certain places, lest, if it were clearly apparent to all men, it might perhaps be little esteemed and be treated disrespect-fully," wrote Pope Gregory VII to the king of Bohemia in 1179 in a letter refusing the latter's request that his monks might be allowed to recite the divine office in Slavonic. It was this principle that underlay the persecution of sects like the Waldensians in southern France and the Lollards in England, both of which groups advocated the rendering of the Bible into the vernacular so that it could be understood by the people. Innocent III's letter to the archbishop of Metz in 1199 made the same point as Gregory had made earlier. Innocent was concerned with another heretical Bible-reading sect, the "Vaudois," and he expressed the view that "the secret

mysteries of the faith ought not to be explained to all men in all places,"
stating his fear "lest any simple and unlettered person should presume to
attain to the sublimity of holy scripture." In concluding his letter Innocent
asked the archbishop to find out the social and educational status of those
who indulged in vernacular Bible reading, the implication being clear that
permission to read a translation of the Bible would depend on the status
and intentions of the reader. The local applications of this theory (later
embodied in the *Decretal* of Gregory IX and thus becoming of universal
canonical application) made it clear that the clergy as a whole understood
it to imply a general prohibition of biblical translation as such, particularly
when any popular circulation was aimed at.

The Anglo-Saxon church in early medieval England, though it had
formally accepted the Roman discipline at the Synod of Whitby in the
seventh century, never wholly lost those qualities of humanitarian common
sense and quiet individualism characteristic of the Celtic church which had
been originally responsible for the conversion of Britain. The limited but
definite interest in Bible translation in England during Anglo-Saxon times
derives to some extent, perhaps, from these qualities. Bede is said to have
translated the Gospel of St. John into English, though it has not survived.
More definite evidence is the ninth-century *Vespasian Psalter*, which contains the Psalms in Latin together with an Anglo-Saxon "gloss," or literal
word-for-word translation, written above. Such a translation was not, of
course, intended for the general reader: it was to assist the less well
educated of the clergy. The *Paris Psalter*, another Anglo-Saxon version
of the same period—the time of King Alfred—contains a slightly different
Latin text of the Psalms together with an Anglo-Saxon version, in parallel
columns. It is also significant that in the preface to the code of laws drawn
up by King Alfred there is an Anglo-Saxon translation of chapters 20 to
23 of Exodus—the account of the giving of the Law to Moses and of the
Ten Commandments. Anglo-Saxon versions of the Gospels also exist, the
earliest (if we exclude the "glosses") probably dating from the year 1000.

The most famous name in Anglo-Saxon Bible translation is that of
Aelfric, abbot of Eynsham, who is known for his interest in promoting the
translation of the Bible among English scholars. His sermons are full of
biblical texts, translated by himself, and he produced the Anglo-Saxon
Heptateuch, a somewhat abbreviated version of the first seven books of
the Old Testament. Aelfric seems to have been the first English translator
to have made some attempt to achieve an appropriate literary prose style
for his biblical translations.

In an age when the distinction between literature and scholarship was
obscure, and secular literature as a worthy contemporary activity had not
yet achieved recognition, it was inevitable that a high proportion of written
works should be biblical or at least religious. It should be remembered

that by far the great majority of literary works produced in the Middle Ages are religious works. Thus we cannot infer from the Anglo-Saxon record any real "influence" of the Bible on literature, for literature in its modern sense was not yet adequately differentiated from any other activity of "clerks." And when we find numerous paraphrases of Bible stories, such as the Anglo-Saxon poems *Genesis*, *Exodus* and *Daniel*, attributed to Caedmon, we must not forget that these works were produced by the clergy primarily as religious documents and not by secular poets as "literature." The authors of these poems wrote for the instruction and edification of the tiny minority of the population who read them, and not, as the seventeenth-century religious poets wrote, in order to produce works of art which were at the same time religious in content and feeling. It is of course true that many religious documents were not written as "art" though they have later come to be regarded as such. The Bible itself, as the sixteenth- and seventeenth-century English critics were so excited to discover, contains many individual works of literary art, though it is doubtful, to say the least, if they were originally produced as such. But if we are to deal with "influences" at all we must first distinguish the factor that influences from that which is influenced. In an age when writing is the prerogative of the clergy and art is to a large extent (though by no means wholly) a by-product of religion, the question we are discussing becomes chiefly one of terminology.

The position becomes a little clearer in the Middle English period, for an age which produced the medieval lyric, the romances, and the works of Chaucer and his followers can hardly be said to have been without an ideal of secular literature. It is thus possible to make some useful generalizations about the influence of the Bible on English literature from the beginning of the thirteenth century to the middle of the fifteenth. As in Anglo-Saxon times, we have in this period a considerable number of biblical paraphrases, but we also have a variety of secular works which make use of biblical story for purposes of illustration or embellishment and, in addition, some ostensibly religious works which deal with biblical themes in a purely secular manner. There are, too, religious poems such as *The Pearl* which, like the religious poetry of the seventeenth century, were written as works of literary art rather than as religious documents. In the main, however, we are able to say that during this time a general knowledge of biblical story, acquired by the people through nonliterary means, had made it possible for writers to refer to biblical characters in their works with confidence that the significance of the reference would be apparent not only to those who could read the work but also to the much larger number of those to whom the work was read. The more picturesque of the Old Testament stories were frequently so used, sometimes with dramatic effect. While in the Middle Ages, as in later times, the more emotional type of religious poetry drew its inspiration more from the New Testament than from the Old, the Old Testament was the main source for secular writers in search of effective analogies and images, as well as the paraphrasers.

To the medieval Englishman, as to his contemporaries throughout Europe, the Bible was a Latin book[2a]—the Vulgate—and all translations were of course made from the Vulgate, not from the original texts. Neither Hebrew nor Greek was to any extent known in medieval Europe—Greek was acquired in some degree by a few scholars, and the merest rudiments of Hebrew only by the tiny minority of clerics who found Jewish teachers.

It was in the Middle English period that it first became clear that the historical portions of the Old Testament were—at least the earlier parts—fairly widely known and were accepted as authentic history. Thus almost all the medieval histories that are more than chronicles of individual reigns begin with the Creation and accept the Book of Genesis as their starting point. At some stage or other in their narrative these histories link up the story of the nation with which they deal with the biblical account—just as in the romances of this period there is so often a link with Greek and Roman history. The link with the Bible in the medieval histories is in a sense closer than that with the classics in the romances, for the Vulgate was accessible and known, while the texts of Homer and Virgil were known only by repute and even those who referred to these ancient writers had the vaguest ideas of the contents of their works. Indeed, Virgil throughout most of the Middle Ages was known simply as an ancient magician—and this in spite of the fact that his "Messianic" eclogue had long been interpreted by the Church as a prophecy of the coming of Christ and he had therefore won for himself a special place among the classical writers. The "matter of Rome" with which so many of the medieval romances dealt is very difficult to associate with anything found in the Latin or Greek writers, and though the story of Troy haunted the medieval imagination in an almost uncanny fashion, it is not the story that Homer told or Virgil used, but a series of strange, passionate incidents in which figures who are casually mentioned only once by Homer play the dominant parts. But the origins and nature of medieval romance are hardly relevant to this discussion. All we need point out here is that the link between medieval romance and the classics (best exemplified, perhaps, by the characters of Troilus and Cressida and their development up to Chaucer) is less direct than the link between medieval history and the Bible. These medieval histories were almost all written in Latin, however, and cannot be said to be wholly a part of English literature.

The influence of the narrative portions of the Old Testament is thus to be seen in Middle English writing and the Latin works of the period in several ways. Bible characters and events are used for purposes of comparison and illustration. And in the histories biblical events are actually used in the opening portions. There are also paraphrases and glosses of parts of the Bible, including two versions of the Psalms. One might add a less tangible kind of biblical influence, an intense moral feeling about justice and retribution, which one finds in such works as Chaucer's *Pardoner's Tale* and which pervades much of *Piers Plowman*. Such a feeling is directly or indirectly traceable to the Hebrew prophets (though the prophets were little known in the Middle Ages), just as in certain medieval devotional works the influence seems to be that of the Psalms together with parts of the New Testament. But here we come to cases in which we are dealing with the influence of Christianity rather than of the Bible, and this raises questions far beyond the scope of this chapter. There is, however, yet another direct kind of biblical influence noticeable in Middle English literature and conspicuous in such poems as *Cleanness* and *Patience*, in which biblical stories (taken of course from the Vulgate text) are woven almost whole into the narrative. While the function of the biblical stories in these poems is illustrative, the author is not content merely to allude to the story by way of example but proceeds to tell it in his own words. Thus *Patience* illustrates the nobility of that quality by giving a versified version of the story of Jonah.

Finally, before proceeding to say something about actual biblical translations in the Middle English period, we must touch on the most striking of all examples of the use of biblical story in medieval English literature. This is to be found in the Miracle Plays, which, having their origin in antiphonal chants as part of the church service, developed into crude ecclesiastical dramas and finally into full-dress though primitive plays more secular than religious in feeling. The plays as they eventually developed are often lively, if naïve, dramatizations of scriptural story. Some show a boisterous humor and even a flagrant coarseness that testify to the extent to which they had moved away from the spirit of their origins. *Noah and the Flood*, one of the best known, exists in various forms, the version in the Wakefield group being full of lively humor while that in the Chester Cycle contains humorous and realistic details of animal life combined with more serious religious scenes. The famous quarrel between Noah and his wife in the Wakefield *Noah* is a purely original, realistic treatment of an aspect of the Bible story done in contemporary terms. The later the date of these plays the more the elements of humor and realism have ousted the original religious feeling, the mid-fifteenth-century Wakefield Cycle being the furthest advanced on this road. The plays of the late fifteenth-century Coventry Cycle, however, revert to a serious didacticism, drawn almost entirely from the New Testament. The most effective of all the Miracle Plays is the Brome play, *Abraham and Isaac*, a genuinely dramatic version of the biblical story maintaining a high level of serious expression without any contemporary comic relief.

These, then, are the ways in which the influence of the Bible manifested itself in medieval English literature without benefit of any vernacular version. The Bible thus made use of by writers was the Vulgate, a text accessible to all who could read Latin—that is, to the greater number of the relatively large class of "clerks," all of whom were members of the clergy—but inaccessible to the unlearned. The story of the fight for Bible translation, which arose in England in the fourteenth century, shows that even at this period there were forces working for the extension of biblical knowledge among the people. These forces eventually produced a wholly new situation as far as the influence of the Bible on English literature is concerned.

3

The first complete English version of the Bible was the direct result of a challenge to the authority of the Church in matters of practice and doctrine. John Wycliffe, who instigated if he did not actually translate the Vulgate in the early 1380's, was moved by his determination to make the original source document of Christianity available to the people. This attitude, which was to become one of the main elements in Protestant thought, regarded the Bible as the final court of appeal in matters of doctrine. The orthodox view had been that it was the duty of the priests to explain selected scriptural passages in their sermons, relating parts of the Bible story in their own words and adding "the usury of their own minds," i.e., the moral to be drawn. Wycliffe and the movement with which he was associated took the view that the people ought to have direct access to the Bible themselves and ought not to be dependent on the fancy interpretations of preachers—"for some by rhyming, and others by preaching poems and fables, adulterate in many ways the word of God." If the Bible was to be generally accessible, it had to be translated into the vernacular.

We need not here go into Wycliffe's social and theological theories, which led him to formulate his demand for Bible translation and to take steps himself to satisfy that demand. Suffice it to say that Wycliffe and the Lollard movement, which spread many of his ideas, argued for Bible translation that the people might have ready access to the one original source of their religion, and that out of this movement developed the two translations of the Bible from Latin into English associated with Wycliffe's name. The Church opposed the Lollard attitude as it had opposed that of the Waldensians and other groups in Europe who had advocated vernacular Bible translation on a large scale. The Wycliffite translations, like the Lollard movement in general which developed the Wycliffite tradition, remained suspect as heretical, and as late as 1528 Sir Thomas More condemned them as such, though ignorant of their nature. The immediate climax of the controversy about Bible translation was reached in 1408 when the provincial council at Oxford forbade the translation of the text of the Bible into English without specific episcopal license.

The literary quality of the Wycliffite translations is not impressive: the second is better than the first, less literal and wooden, but even it hardly constitutes a great monument of English prose. These two versions, especially the later one, enjoyed a certain popularity, as the number of surviving manuscripts prove, though their popularity cannot, of course, compare with that of later printed Bibles (the Wycliffite versions were made before the age of printing) made after the principle of vernacular translation had been generally accepted.

The Lollard heresy was suppressed at the beginning of the fifteenth century, but the idea that the Bible, as the one original source of Christianity, should be available to the people in their own language did not die. As the criticism of the Church that was eventually to bring about the Reformation spread in England as elsewhere, the demand for Bible translation also grew. The Church shifted its ground somewhat in the face of this growing demand and began to object to the Wycliffite translations because they were erroneous rather than because they made the Bible readily accessible to the public. When Sir Thomas More, for example, was discussing Bible translation in 1528 he made it clear that in his view the Church could only have condemned the Wycliffite versions if they were textually corrupt and contained heretical notes, and he accordingly assumed that these versions did in fact have these faults. Thus there had been a radical shift in orthodox opinion some time before More wrote: earlier, the opinion had been that the text of the Bible should not be made accessible to ordinary people, who were not qualified to interpret it properly, while the later view was that translations for whatever purpose were permissible if they were accurate and contained no heretical notes. This change was the measure of the success of the growing popular demand.

The development of large-scale Bible translation in England is bound up with the development of the Reformation, and the development of the Reformation is in turn inseparable from the growth of the "New Learning." The revival of the study first of Greek and then of Hebrew in the fifteenth century and later made available a critical apparatus for the examination of the original texts of the basic documents of Christianity. This put a new weapon in the hands of the reformers and they lost no time in using it. The work of Reuchlin and Erasmus—who fought obscurantism in the Church without leaving the fold—made the scholarship of the Renaissance available to the zeal of the Reformation, and from this marriage the Golden Age of English Bible translation was born.

The story of that Golden Age has been often told. William Tyndale, profiting by recent developments in Greek and Hebrew studies, began his work on Bible translation from the original texts in 1524 and spent the rest of his life in this activity. He was unable to do his work in England, and for thirteen years worked secretly in exile until he was brought back to England by a trick and burned as a heretic in 1536. Tyndale was an open reformer and attacked not only the abuses of the Church but its doctrine. His zeal for Bible translation was bound up with his interest in Church reformation and his theological ideas; like Wycliffe before him, he wished to have the one original source of Christianity laid open to all. "I defy the Pope and all his laws," Tyndale is said by Fox to have declared, "and if God spare my life, ere many years I will cause a boy that driveth the plow shall know more of the scripture than thou [a 'learned man' to whom he was talking] dost." Tyndale was here echoing words which the humanist Erasmus had uttered earlier in his *Exhortation to the Diligent Study of Scripture,* a work which Tyndale translated.

Tyndale translated the whole of the New Testament and a considerable portion of the Old, and his work is the foundation on which all subsequent English Bible translation is built. Shortly after his death the atmosphere in England grew more favorable to Bible translation. While the rise of humanism and the Renaissance movement in general had put new and stronger weapons in the hands of those who argued in favor of Bible translation, and helped to produce a series of significant changes in European thought and culture, the invention of printing had enabled these changes to develop with unprecedented rapidity and had also made it increasingly difficult for the authorities to prevent the circulation in large numbers of prohibited works. The abuses of the Church, the new attitude to religion that was in part produced by these abuses, the rediscovery of forgotten aspects of the ancient world, the development of a new Greek and Hebrew scholarship and the invention of printing—these were the factors that combined to speed the pace and improve the quality of English Bible translation. At the time of Tyndale's death his victory was already assured.

In England the situation was further helped by the changing political situation. Henry VIII found the Reformation helpful in his personal difficulties, and throughout the many changes in the theory and practice of Church government in England for which he was responsible the cause of the English Bible steadily progressed. In 1530, while strongly condemning Tyndale's translation and prohibiting Bible translation, Henry nevertheless affirmed his intention of providing for an authorized translation when the time was appropriate. Five years later the first complete printed English Bible appeared, the work of Miles Coverdale, a man inspired by the same ideals as Tyndale but milder in his views and more compromising in character. This was not the authorized version for which the English bishops were preparing, but Coverdale assumed that his work would be acceptable to the king. A later edition of Coverdale's Bible, published in 1537, bears the legend: "Set forth with the Kynges moost gracious licence." The main battle had been won, and the 1537 quarto edition of Coverdale's Bible was the first "authorized version" of the Bible in English. Henceforth the fight was to be concentrated not on the right to translate but on the improvement of the translation.

Coverdale's was not an original translation from the Hebrew and Greek but a version derived from later Latin and German versions. Though his style lacked the fine simplicity of Tyndale's, it was smooth and free flowing and contributed substantially to the rhythms of later English renderings. From now on translations followed closely on one another's heels. The same year that Coverdale's first authorized version appeared saw the publication of Matthew's Bible, also "set forth with the King's most gracious licence," and strongly supported by the bishops. Matthew's Bible was a composite version, made up of Tyndale's translation of as much of the Old Testament as he had translated, Coverdale's translation of the remainder of the Old Testament and Tyndale's New Testament. It was this Bible that was the basis for the series of revisions that culminated in the King James, or Authorized, Version of 1611. Its imperfections were freely admitted by the bishops, even though Archbishop Cranmer promoted it as strongly as he could, and the Great Bible, a revision of Matthew's Bible made by Coverdale at the instance of Thomas Cromwell, was published in April, 1540. By this time public Bible reading had become widespread and the readings were often accompanied by scenes almost riotous in their enthusiasm. Thus we find that, while the Great Bible was ordered to be set up in every parish church, provisions were made against the misuse of Bible reading, readers being enjoined not to read "with loud and high voices" or in a disputatious frame of mind, but "humbly, meekly and reverently."

By this time citations of biblical texts in English were freely used to challenge specific practices of the Church. Fox, for example, tells the story of a young man refusing to kneel down before the crucifix and quoting from the Bible in justification, "Thou shalt not make any graven image, nor bow down to it, to worship it." The English Bible was rapidly becoming a familiar part of the ordinary Englishman's intellectual equipment. Further, while in the Middle Ages only the Psalms and the more picturesque narratives were generally known of the Old Testament, from this time on the Hebrew prophets, almost unknown earlier, began to influence men's minds and imaginations.

The Great Bible ran into many editions, but there were continuous suggestions of a further revision. On the death of Edward VI the progress of English Bible translation was temporarily halted. Queen Mary was a

Catholic, and on her accession the printing of vernacular Bibles in England came to an abrupt stop. Many of the Protestants most interested in Bible translation went into exile, and it was at the colony of these exiles at Geneva that the next English translation of the Bible was made. The Geneva Bible, published at Geneva in 1557, was a thorough revision of the Great Bible after the original texts with the help of such other versions and aids to translation as had recently appeared on the Continent. The most accurate and scholarly English translation yet made, the Geneva Bible is not in the direct line of succession of the Authorized Version, though it was fairly heavily drawn upon by the King James translators. On the whole, the Geneva translators sacrificed style to accuracy, and there is a pedantic flavor about the work, particularly noticeable in the spelling of proper names.

The accession of Queen Elizabeth marked a reversion to middle-of-the-road Protestant policy. The Great Bible was once again ordered to be set up in churches (the Geneva Bible, being the work of more extreme Protestants who were considerably to the "left" of Elizabeth's Anglican Church, was not officially recognized). In 1568 the Great Bible was super-seded by a further revision made by a company of bishops, and hence known as the Bishops' Bible. This version was not, however, altogether successful. A combination of the work of different revisers working with little common policy or discipline, it is patchy and uneven, and in accuracy considerably behind the Geneva Bible, which continued to be the most popular translation in England until after 1611. Finally, when James I ascended the throne in 1603 he appointed a company of learned men consisting of the most competent Hebrew and Greek scholars available (excluding, however, those who were definitely antagonistic to the Angli-can Church) to prepare a great new revision. This work, begun in 1604 and completed seven years later, after meticulous and carefully co-ordinated labor, has remained *the* English Bible ever since. There have been more scholarly versions made in the past three-quarters of a century, but none has rivaled the Authorized Version of 1611 in literary quality and none has had the great literary influence of that extraordinary work.

It has often been remarked that the Authorized Version was the work of a syndicate, yet is a total work of art with all the marks of individual genius. This mystery becomes less baffling when we realize that the diction of the English Bible was forged in almost a century's experimentation and was an organic and not a mechanical development. The Authorized Version was the culmination of that development. And when we further realize—as has already been noted—that this development took place during the most brilliant experimental period in the whole history of English literature, we can understand something of what lies behind the diction of this translation.

By the time the Authorized Version appeared the English Bible had been accepted for several generations as the great basic document of English civilization. Theologians, moralists, philosophers, poets, political thinkers and economists turned to it for inspiration, for historical facts, arguments, images, principles and theories. The extent to which the great debate on the nature of political freedom, which raged in England throughout the Civil War and indeed throughout almost the whole of the seventeenth century, drew its inspiration from biblical sources has never yet been fully appreciated by political historians. Anyone who has studied the debates in the Long Parliament and the innumerable pamphlets and tracts of a sociologico-religious or politico-religious nature that fell in a tremendous flood from the printing presses of the period cannot have failed to notice the underlying biblical inspiration. There was an inspiration both in style and in ideas. The various Puritan sects which advocated different types of democratic organization and whose discussions of the nature of liberty contributed more than has yet been conceded to the development of British democratic ideals, were trying to apply biblical principles to the modern world. And though with the Restoration this kind of activity subsided, its effect was by no means lost, and it continued in a milder form throughout subsequent ages. It might further be pointed out that behind the American Constitution and the American Bill of Rights lies the English Bill of Rights of 1689 and all those theories of individual liberty so fiercely debated by Puritan students of the Bible in the seventeenth century and later, given more polished and equable form in the writings of philosophers such as Locke. The influence of the English Bible here will bear much further investigation.

4

We have not mentioned all the English translations made before the Authorized Version, nor have we discussed in any detail the kinds of biblical style developed between 1523 and 1611. A full treatment of these aspects of the subject would require a volume. The main point for our present discussion is that the Authorized Version represents at the same time the culmination of almost a century's work in English Bible translation and one of the greatest literary masterpieces in the language. This twofold aspect accounts in part for the strength of its influence. For a great body of Protestants, both Puritans and Anglicans and, later, a variety of nonconforming sects, the English Bible was the authentic voice of God and could be appealed to, quoted, and directly and indirectly referred to in innumerable ways. Hundreds of biblical texts in the Authorized translation became proverbs and household words in English homes. And though there was a great deal of what their opponents called "canting" among

Puritan quoters of the Bible, among the majority of the people such quotation became a natural embellishment of serious speech. And while the English Bible was working among the people this way and enriching popular speech, which in turn enriched the speech of writers like Bunyan, literary men irrespective of religious belief were assimilating its stylistic riches. The English Bible thus came into English literature both directly and indirectly—indirectly through its influence on popular speech and directly through the conscious utilization of biblical rhythms, images or diction by writers from Milton to Ruskin and beyond.

That this influence was making itself felt before the Authorized Version had become the accepted translation is made clear by the attitude toward the Bible of writers who used other versions. Shakespeare, for example, used the Geneva version, drawing upon it freely for illustration and allusion and taking for granted that his audience would immediately see the references. In this he was typical of a host of writers of his own time and later who often achieved some of their most brilliant effects by such use of biblical sources. The actual vocabulary of the English Bible introduced many new words and familiarized many others which had been in little use previously. Nothing exercises a developing language more effectively than its use in translation. Words and phrases such as "loving-kindness," "tender mercy" (both first introduced by Coverdale), "beautiful" (not found before Tyndale) and numerous others, both gentle and stern, pastoral and passionate, realistic and highly figurative, entered into the English literary language through English Bible translation. The rich imagery of the Song of Songs, the melancholy lyricism of *Kohelet*, the pithy aphorisms of Proverbs—their influence is everywhere in English prose and poetry. In one short piece alone, David's lament for Jonathan, there are half a dozen phrases that have become part of the English language: "how are the mighty fallen," "in their death they were not divided," "swifter than eagles, stronger than lions." One could write a volume on the influence of the Book of Job alone, and a whole treatise on the use of the word "shepherd," both as noun and as verb, deriving from the first verse of Psalm 23. The use of the words prompted by the Bible does not confine itself to the serious use of the original context: the treatise on the use of "shepherd" would have to take up, for example, the ironic and humorous use of the term as applied by Tony Weller to the Reverend Mr. Stiggins in Dickens's *Pickwick Papers*. Too much "canting" by Puritans led to a secondary use of such words, an ironical use which, though only indirectly attributable to the Bible, has had a great deal of influence on English speech and in English fiction.

As far as actual influence on style is concerned, the Psalms, the Prophetic books and the "Writings" had much more influence than the Pentateuch, whose narrative style is extremely primitive (any number of short sentences linked by "and") and whose influence manifested itself through the use of biblical stories rather than through any imitation of rhythm or cadence. But the passionate rhythm of the Hebrew prophets is to be found in much nineteenth-century prose, just as the cadences of the Psalms can be found in both prose and poetry in that century. And as there is some evidence that the translators of the Authorized Version made an attempt to preserve something of the Hebrew rhythm (or what they conceived to be the Hebrew rhythm) in their English rendering, especially in the Prophets, the link with the original text here is more definite than might be thought.

Seventeenth-century English literature is so rich in works showing biblical influence of every kind that it is impossible to deal with this influence in short compass. Though the prose of the period is often more influenced by Latin and Greek models than by the prose of the English Bible, and writers like Robert Burton, Sir Thomas Browne and Jeremy Taylor turned to the classics for their literary inspiration, biblical influence on the poetry of the period and on the controversial tracts on religious and political subjects was continuous. But here, as we have seen, it is difficult to separate religious from purely biblical influence: the two become so intertwined in the religious poetry of the century (and so much of the best poetry of the century was religious) that one cannot isolate the influence of the Bible as a book from that of the Bible as the source document of the Christian religion. Yet in the poetry of George Herbert, for example, there is found that combination of gravity and simplicity which, as a quality of *style*, clearly owes something to English biblical prose. A line like, "But thou shalt answer, Lord, for me," could not have been written if the Psalms had never been translated into English. As a rule it is in those poets whose emotion is more restrained and whose passion is under control that the biblical influence is most clearly discernible: we can see it in Herbert but not in Crashaw, in Vaughan and Marvell more than in Donne. And we can see it in a different sense in the great satires of Dryden, which drew on biblical characters and incidents with a confidence that amounts to nonchalance.

Milton perhaps more than any other English poet was conscious of the twofold value of the Bible—its moral teaching and its literary qualities. Though by no means a typical Puritan, he had the typical Protestant attitude toward the Bible as the final court of appeal for all Christians: "Let them chant what they will of prerogatives, we shall tell them of Scripture; of custom, we of Scripture; of Acts and Statutes, still of Scripture . . ." He also recognized the number of literary forms contained in the biblical writings, and deliberately modeled his own *Paradise Regained* on the Book of Job. A humanist as well as a Puritan, a lover of the Latin and Greek classics as well as the Scriptures, Milton was able to reconcile the religious and the aesthetic aspects of the Bible just as he reconciled classical with biblical imagery. Early Christian practice had long established the tradition of retaining classical gods as Christian devils, and Milton saw the advantages of this combination for poetic expression. As a result, he gives us, from his earliest period, examples of combined biblical and pagan allusions done with complete confidence:

> Peor, and Baalim,
> Forsake their Temples dim,
>> With that twice batter'd god of Palestine,
> And moonèd Ashtaroth,
> Heav'n's queen and mother both,
>> Now sits not girt with tapers' holy shrine,
> The Lybic Hammon shrinks his horn,
> In vain the Tyrian Maids their wounded Thammuz mourn.
>
> And sullen Moloch, fled,
> Hath left in shadows dred,
>> His burning Idol all of blackest hue;
> In vain with cymbals ring,
> They call the grisly king,
>> In dismal dance about the furnace blue;
> The brutish gods of Nile as fast,
> Isis and Orus, and the Dog Anubis haste.
>> —Ode on the Morning of Christ's Nativity—The Hymn

Throughout all of Milton's prose and poetry Bible names and images recur. The fact that his greatest works are on biblical themes makes this the more appropriate. But in general the style as such is influenced more by classical than by biblical models, though in *Paradise Regained* and *Samson Agonistes* he deliberately cultivated a less ornate style closer to at least one kind of biblical style than to that of classical epic.

John Bunyan's use of the Bible was more direct and more naïve than that of Milton. He adopted the Bible's simpler narrative style, making frequent use of the actual language of the Authorized Version. Bunyan's clear prose narrative played its part in the simplification of English prose that went on in the late seventeenth and the early eighteenth century, and thus we can trace some connection between biblical English prose and the prose of Sir William Temple and Joseph Addison, which in turn laid the foundations for generations of later English prose writers.

The growth of hymn writing in the eighteenth century, attributable in large measure to the Wesleyans, did not, as might have been expected, bring the language of the English Bible more and more into English diction, for hymns were by nature nonbiblical—they were the alternative to Scripture reading and biblical paraphrases, using more everyday speech and, often, exhibiting more sentimental attitudes. Even the hymns of William Cowper, often based on specific biblical texts, can hardly be said to be in any sense biblical in their language except for the actual references to the texts used. On the whole, the influence of the English Bible in the eighteenth century took the form of unconscious assimilation of the images and expressions of a familiar text. The direct and conscious influences were almost always classical—and because they were so direct and conscious not always so happy in their results, perhaps, as the less deliberately sought influence of the Bible. At any rate, it is worth remembering that the style of Johnson and Gibbon and the less successful styles of their imitators are classical and not biblical in their inspiration, though, of course, by this time no writer (and least of all Johnson) could have written at length in prose without displaying in his work some of the effects of generations of Bible reading.

"Generations of Bible reading"—the phrase is worth pondering. For the English, perhaps more than any other people in Europe, were Bible *readers*. The Bible was read, both silently and aloud, in innumerable families throughout the country from the late sixteenth century until the late nineteenth, and even today there is much more knowledge of the English Bible among the people of Britain than there is in the United States, in spite of the fact that there are in the latter country whole areas and communities where a lively evangelical tradition has kept Bible reading very much alive. The effect of this continuous Bible reading among the people of Britain was to acquaint all classes with a vocabulary and a number of literary styles (for, as we have noted, the Bible has many styles) that were constantly working on both the spoken and the written English language.

The English poets of the eighteenth and nineteenth centuries drew as naturally on the English Bible for imagery and allusion as if the book had been an original English masterpiece bearing the same relation to later literature as the *Iliad* and the *Odyssey* did to later Greek writing. Some, like Byron, drew deliberately on Old Testament stories and ideas. Among the nineteenth-century prose writers Ruskin was perhaps the most influenced by the Authorized Version. He was brought up to read it regularly, and he more than once testified to the effect this reading had on his literary taste and prose style. Knowing much of the English Bible by heart, he wrote, "it was not possible for me, even in the foolishest times of youth, to write entirely superficial or formal English." Ruskin was also one of those who was profoundly influenced by the ideals of social justice proclaimed by the Hebrew prophets, and in this he was typical of his age, for as the nineteenth century advanced there was a distinct tendency to turn away from those aspects of the Bible which had most influenced earlier writers and to dwell on those books which had been less dwelt on previously. The tendency was, as far as the Old Testament was concerned, away from Law and toward the Prophets. Isaiah, Amos, Hosea and Malachi became more popular than the Pentateuch and the historical books, and their words were often consciously echoed by the increasing number of those who were preoccupied with the problems of social and economic reform. Among English writers and thinkers today this tendency continues to be strong, and there are many who, while turning away from the more specifically theological formulations of religious doctrine, have sought inspiration for a creed of humanistic reform from the passionate and noble utterances of the Hebrew prophets. Among adherents of all religious faiths and of none, the Bible thus continues to exert influence, and to the various kinds of influence the English Bible has had in the past—influence as a source of images and symbols, as a source of literary forms, as a series of models in prose style, as a storehouse of moral and religious ideas— there is now to be added its contribution toward the formulation of a dynamic social philosophy.

Brief though this discussion has been, and few and sketchy as have been the illustrations of the argument, enough has perhaps been said to make clear the extraordinary way in which the Bible has worked in English literature. Because English Protestantism drew equal strength from the humanistic scholarship of the Renaissance and the individualism of the Reformation, insisting equally on broad learning and on the popularizing of the fruits of that learning, the English Bible became at the same time a moral and an aesthetic force. That strange but significant old Hebrew phrase "the beauty of holiness" thus found a new interpretation in the history of English literature, whose development illustrated time and again that wisdom and beauty were bound up with each other. There was a classical ideal at work here too, the Socratic identification of virtue with knowledge and the implied Platonic association of the aesthetic with the moral. In a sense it can be said that the English tradition at its best and most characteristic always tended to interpret the Bible in the light of classical humanism, and thus to avoid pedantry in its view of either. English literature is, on the whole, moral without being didactic and humanistic without being pagan. In the first of these qualities it differs from the German, and in the second from the French. It is not extravagant to see the basis of this English *via media* in the fact that the Bible became known to Englishmen in a book which was regarded at the same time as a great religious and a great literary document. Thus the Puritan read it for its doctrine and fell under its literary spell, and the skeptic read it as a work of art and imbibed its morality. Which of the two profited more is a question that can be debated forever.

NOTES

[1a Cf. Robert Gordis, "The Bible as a Cultural Monument," this work, Vol. II, pp. 36 f.]

[2a Cf. below, Frederick Lehner, "The Influence of the Bible on European Literature," pp. 408-409.]

SELECT BIBLIOGRAPHY

BAIKIE, JAMES, *The English Bible and Story: Its growth, its translators, and their adventures*. London, 1928.

BOWEN, FRANCIS, *A Layman's Story of the English Bible considered in its Literary and Secular Aspect*. New York, 1885.

BUTTERWORTH, CHARLES C., *The Literary Lineage of the King James Bible, 1340-1611*. Philadelphia, 1941.

COOK, ALBERT, S., *Biblical Quotations in Old English Prose Writers*. London, 1898.

——, *The Authorized Version of the Bible and its Influence*. New York, 1910.

DAICHES, DAVID, *The King James Version of the English Bible*. Chicago, 1941.

DEANESLEY, MARGARET, *The Lollard Bible and other Medieval Biblical Versions*. Cambridge, 1920.

GRIERSON, SIR HERBERT, *The English Bible*. London, 1943.

LOWES, JOHN L., "The Noblest Monument in English Prose," in *Essays in Appreciation*. Boston and New York, 1936.

MCAFEE, CLELAND B., *The Greatest English Classic: a Study of the King James Version of the Bible and its Influence on life and literature*. New York and London, 1912.

MCCLURE, JAMES G., *The Supreme Book of Mankind: The Origin and Influence of the English Bible*. New York, 1930.

MCCOMB, SAMUEL, *The Making of the English Bible, with an Introductory Essay on the Influence of the English Bible on English Literature*. New York, 1909.

MOULTON, RICHARD G., *The Literary Study of the Bible*. Boston, 1899.

NOBLE, RICHMOND, *Shakespeare's Biblical Knowledge*. London and New York, 1935.

POLLARD, ALFRED W., *Records of the English Bible*. Oxford, 1911.

SANDS, P. C., *Literary Genius of the Old Testament*. Oxford, 1924.

WESTCOTT, BROOKE F., *A General View of the History of the English Bible* (3d. ed. rev. by W. A. Wright). London and New York, 1905.

WORK, E. W., *The Bible in English Literature*. New York, 1917.

ADDENDUM

FISCH, HAROLD, *Jerusalem and Albion: The Hebraic Factor in Seventeenth-Century Literature*. New York, 1964.

ROSTON, MURRAY, *Prophet and Poet: The Bible and the Growth of Romanticism*. London, 1965.

SCHWARZ, W., *Principles and Problems of Biblical Translation*. Cambridge Univ. Press, 1955.

CHAPTER II

THE INFLUENCE OF THE BIBLE ON EUROPEAN LITERATURE

By Frederick Lehner

It is nothing new to consider the Bible not only as a religious document but also as a great work of literature, an anthology containing historical reports, poetry, short stories, one philosophical drama and illuminated, apocalyptic writings. As literature, it follows the laws of all great literary works: it is a creation of lofty imagination, and it influences writers of the following generations and centuries to appropriate from its content whatever they decisively may feel as new, startling, impressive, stimulating thought and provoking imagination. Indeed, as an anthology of literature, as a source of stories, forms and ideas, the Bible became bread and meat for centuries to come. To be exact, the Bible did not enter the mind of continental Europe as a Jewish document; it became influential as a part of the Old and New Testament, and it took centuries before its specific essence was recognized. First it became a part of the intellectual property through the channels of Christianity.

Thus it was not the Hebrew original—even though the study of the original never was discontinued—it was not even the first Latin translation that created the miracle, that interested nations in Hebrew stories and history and philosophy; it was rather the Latin version of the Hebrew Bible by Jerome (fifth century) that helped the Oriental tales to shine and sparkle in a new setting. At first, of course, its influence was not wide, but when the monasteries sent out missionaries to win over native tribes to Christianity, especially in the eighth, ninth and tenth centuries, the Jewish legends went along with the Christian legends. Soon the Hebrew report about the Creation replaced the report of the Icelandic saga, the story of the tree Yggdrasil. Soon the tragic stories of the Fall, the First Murder, Sodom and Gomorrah, the Flood, the Tower of Babel appeared in many variations, sometimes distorted, more naïve than the original. Then the first epics and plays about Joseph were written, about Moses, Judith, Solomon, Daniel, Susanna and the Elders. Topics and forms abounded. And soon we can perceive several different trends. We can see how topics were discovered and used, how the Psalms became an essential part of the Christian service, how the many apocalyptic dreams in the Bible provoked new utterings and new mystical outbursts, far from the mystical world of Jerusalem.

What could the Bible offer other than what was offered by the other major traditions or legacies of imagination, fiction and folk lore? The four great traditions which influenced and formed European literature in its various manifestations were the Hebrew, the Greek, the Germanic and the Celtic. The Germanic tradition (*Edda*) and the Celtic (*Les Chevaliers de la Table Ronde*) appeared and disappeared again, as well as the Hebrew and the Greek, but they did not have the general appeal, the great and persistent influence on *all* Continental literatures; they did not have the extraordinary and absolute value of the Greek and Hebrew legacies. These two, certainly, were responsible for the spirit of Western civilization; they served as its pillars of beauty and intellectual strength. They formed our world, though in different ways, sometimes alternately, sometimes together, and each according to its special essence, inherent in its spiritual body. If "the governing idea of Hellenism is spontaneity of consciousness,"[1] that of Hebraism is strictness of conscience. Where one legacy stated the problem, the other made it ethical. "It is in the confluence of the Hellenic stream of thought with the waters that flow from Hebrew sources that the main direction of world's progress is to be sought."[2] In this report we are concerned only with one part of the problem. We shall try to observe the influence of the Bible on Continental European literature, to follow this influence, and to analyze its aspects and importance.

Such an influence can be found in many regions and sections of what we call literature. We can easily discover that certain stories, topics, tales of the Bible were taken out of their (religious) context, and told, retold, changed in many curious ways. There is, however, to begin with, the problem of the language itself, a fact that should not be neglected.

In an essay contained in the Oxford *Legacy of Israel*,[3] Laurie Magnus cites good English material to make this point clear. He quotes a poem by Matthew Arnold (*Sohrab and Rustum*) and another poem by Alfred Lord Tennyson (*Ulysses*), and shows rather clearly that, when we analyze their language, the structure of their thoughts, the images and similes, we discover that the Oriental poem by Arnold owes its poetical structure to Greece, while the Greek poem by Tennyson is full of biblical echoes.

This influence of the Bible on the interior construction of a poem, the molding of its expression, the selection of its comparisons, for instance, can be exemplified by the authors of other nations as well: Dante, for instance. In general it can be said that from single words to images, from images to the entire mode of the expression, from expression to topics, philosophy— every kind of influence can be detected in the European languages and literatures. "Sodom and Gomorrah," to cite some examples, the "Tower of

Babel," the "Hueter meines Bruders," "the keeper of my brother," the "calf of gold," a whole world of words, images and ready-made thoughts have remained alive and have been added to the languages of Germanic, Romance and Slavic roots as well. Magnus, in his contribution to the *Legacy of Israel*, proves even more, on the same level. He shows how not only in English, but in other languages as well, "the Hebrew simile has become naturalized." To explain his point he states that the Greek writer compares one element with another, and elaborates the second. The Hebrew simile elaborates the first element as it speaks of it in terms of the second. ("*He* shall be like a tree, *his* leaf also shall not wither.")[4] And the Continent imitates the example.

The historical development of this phenomenon follows a common trend. Often-quoted material influences our thinking to the very expression of thoughts: the Bible, obviously, was often quoted. And as this material found its way to European minds, first mostly through the medium of Latin, the perennial language of the Church, the phenomenon of this influence became genuinely visible only with the Reformation, when Luther's Bible in the German vernacular created the German *Schriftsprache*. This translation and the King James Version[4a] in English-speaking countries and the corresponding efforts in France, in Italy and in Spain popularized the original text and wording of the New and the Old Testament in a tremendously successful and efficient way. The original text became known not only to scholars or priests, not only to educated laymen, but to everyone who could read. And not only certain basic books dealing with scientific topics became afterwards a "Bible" whose pronouncements were law; the Bible itself became a "Bible" in this respect and was consulted, quoted and understood. Let us now proceed to its influence on topics.

The so-called *Wiener Genesis*—the manuscript is of the twelfth century —is the oldest of the many religious poems written in the Austrian Carinthia and based on the Bible.[5] It was written because the Roman Church demanded in its *Breviarium* that the *lectiones* during the time from Septuagesima Sunday to Tuesday after Quadragesima be based on chapters 1 to 14 of Genesis.[6] Thus the poem, as it was preserved for us in the different manuscripts, contained especially two lessons, the Creation and the Fall. (Another chapter, however, added to those two, deals with Cain and Abel, and others with Noah, with Abraham, with Isaac and his sons, and with Joseph in Egypt.) To the same epoch, about 1220, belong two other manuscripts, two epics about Exodus, as described in the first fifteen chapters of the Second Book of Moses.[7] The poem followed the text of the Itala. We have also a separate poem dealing with Moses, a Balaam, two Judiths (mostly to be found among the manuscripts of the Vorau monastery), a *Lob Salomos*, the *Juenglinge in dem Feuerofen*, fragments of a book about the Maccabees, an Esdras, an Isaiah, and a Song of Songs translated in 1276 by Brub von Scombeck, constable of Magdeburg.

These stories and poems taken from the Hebrew Bible were also stories in the medieval tradition. Wherever there was an opportunity to adjust the foreign context to the surrounding European and Christian world, it was done. When the plants of Paradise were described, the poet found his material in the description of a model garden as it was given in Charlemagne's *Capitulare de Villis*.[8] In the *Exodus* we have an elaborate presentation of a medieval army, even the grasshoppers, frogs and flies were enemy armies and described as such. But to summarize, if we take the German epics mentioned above as an example of what happened in all civilized districts of continental Europe, we may correctly conclude that an essential part of the Hebrew Bible was known to every educated man of the twelfth century. But it came to him as a part of the Christian legacy, and the ethical or philosophical content of the Jewish stories was taken purely as a forethought of what was expressed with greater clarity in the Gospels of the New Faith. At any rate, this first approach proved not only stimulating; it was also carried over as a durable element into European literature.

The topics from the Hebrew Bible, of course, were not only chosen by the monks in Austria and Franconia, who described them in hymns or epics or songs. In France, too, the Bible attracted creative minds. If we follow the report given by Bédier and Hazard, we learn that translations of parts of the Bible in prose or in verse, poems taken from this or that chapter of the Scriptures were done in the twelfth century.[9] There are translations of the Psalms, the first of them in the first half of that century; there is a version in verse of Genesis (by Everat for the Comtesse Marie de Champagne) from 1190. In the same year the Hebrew and the New Testament were put into verses by Herman de Valenciennes; and other attempts of this kind followed. And here and there in Europe the *fratres* imitated the French and German example.

In the twelfth century, however, another type of literature, *the drama*, also discovered the treasures hidden in the Hebrew Bible. The oldest drama written in French dates from the twelfth century. It is called *Représentation d'Adam*[10] (author unknown), and again we are back to our topic. This *mystère*, as the religious tragedies were called, presents first the *Paradis terrestre*, then the Temptation and the Fall of Adam and Eve. We see the murder of Abel, after which the prophets parade by and announce the arrival of the Messiah. It is a lively play, and really dramatic, truly medieval and truly French, especially in the scenes of the temptation. This play, however, was only a beginning. The end of the development can be found in the *Cycle de l'Ancien Testament*, a compilation into one great work which was made in the course of the second half of the fifteenth century.[11] The opus is composed of fifty thousand verses. This play was performed in Paris in 1542 by the *Confrères de la Passion* in the Hôtel de Flandres, and proved to be a great success. *"L'entrée coûtait deux sous par personne; et une loge, trente sous pour toute la durée de la représentation qui remplit environ vingt séances."*[12] But this tradition was stopped by the Arrêt du Parlement de Paris (November 17, 1548), which banned *all* religious plays from the stage, including the *Mystère du Vieux Testament*. Nevertheless, it was not very long before the specific value of the topic overcame the ban, and the colorful and thrilling stories of the Bible reappeared on the stage, this time no more as *mystère* nor as *moralité*, but as plots of Renaissance tragedies, climaxed in *Les Juives* by Robert Garnier (1580) and in *Esther* by Jean Racine (1688-1689). Before we proceed to describe this change and new life, however, we have to see what happened in other European countries, especially in Spain.[12a]

In the Iberian Peninsula there was no parliament that forbade the performance of religious plays. The great flowering of these plays was never interrupted by decree. Unfortunately, we do not know too much about their beginnings. But we do know that in the first half of the sixteenth century Diego Sanchez wrote a *Farsa de Salomón*, a *Farsa de Isaac*, a *Farsa de Abrahám, de Moysén, del Rey David*, topics chosen again because of their "close symbolic relationship to Christ's sacrifice."[13] In the second half of the century Micael de Carvajal wrote a *Tragedia Josephina* which deals with the sale of Joseph by his brothers, with his stay in Egypt and the death of Jacob. The most important document, however, is the great Codex at the Biblioteca Nacional (1550-1575) containing ninety-six religious plays, twenty-six of which deal with material taken from the Hebrew Bible.[14] If we look into details, two of these plays treat Adam, one treats Cain and Abel, three deal with Abraham, four with Jacob, two with Joseph and three with Moses, the lawgiver. The ratio is, as we see, twenty-six to ninety-six; that is to say, one-fourth of the entire corpus was taken from the Hebrew Bible, which proves how useful the plots seemed to be for dramatists, and how well they lent themselves to the special treatment of playwrights. We find here, for instance, an *Aucto de los hierros de Adán*, and an *Aucto de la lucha de Jacob con el ángel*, or an *Aucto de la deposório de Moysén*, an *Aucto del rey Nabucdonosor cuando se hizo adorar*, an *Aucto del sueño de Nabucdonosor*, religious plays with familiar topics. And here, too, the subjects correspond to the *lectiones* in Septuagesima, Sexuagesima and the Quadragesima season of the Catholic service, as we had observed when we looked into the epics of the German Middle Ages. And at the time when the religious epic in Central Europe began to lose its appeal, when the religious drama reached its climax in

Spain with Lope de Vega and Calderón de la Barca, the religious epic found its most perfect fulfillment in Italy; the Bible proved again to be a stimulating force demanding respect, offering stories, characters and philosophical insight even into the modern life of the fourteenth century.

If we follow Vossler in his *Medieval Culture*,[15] which is an introduction to Dante and his times, we are soon convinced that the great Italian poet considered the Bible not only a religious document. It was not only Divine truth for him; it was Divine poetry as well. The *Divine Comedy* may be called a summary of the ethical, religious and aesthetic tendencies of the Middle Ages ("the voice of ten silent centuries"). Thus we find in it all the features that belong to such a representation. And the Bible meant for Dante not only the specifically Christian, but the Hebrew Scriptures as well. We find here indeed an extreme reverence for the word and the letter of the Hebrew legacy, we find an almost jealous effort to extract from the pictures in the biblical stories and from their poetic contents more or less general philosophical concepts. We find also that Dante deduced from them moral commandments, and we find mystical significance. It is again Vossler who points out the tremendous influence of the language of the Bible in Dante's work.[16] He shows how Dante's memory was full of biblical reminiscences and pictures. And, true, the Bible is the most-quoted book in his writings. "He [Dante] had it in his head and heart better than many professional clerics."[17] Dante took over unchanged whole sentences, figures, comparisons, similes, especially in his early works. In the *Divine Comedy* this method, this *hantise*, reached its climax. Dante presents the whole cast of the Bible; he presents Adam and Eve, Cain and Abel, Abraham, Rachel, Rebecca, Sarah, Isaac and Esau, Jacob and his sons, the kings, the prophets, the Maccabees, Esther, Ruth, and so on. He presents Cain in the first part of the poem, in *Inferno*, then he lifts him up into *Purgatorio* and we meet the sinner finally even in *Paradiso*, Dante's heaven. But this lavish use of heroes, patriarchs, personages from the Hebrew Bible must not obscure the fact that here again the Jewish men and women are taken from the Christian Bible, of which the Old Testament is a part. Their presence has to be justified. Dante does this very soon, in the beginning of the poem. He crosses a rather Greek landscape in order to enter the Inferno, and among the first people he meets there are the great persons belonging to Jewish antiquity. They are to be found in the first Circle already, in the Limbo, or the borderland of the Unbaptized.[18] It is true, admits Dante, that they have their merit, but to have merit is not enough so long as you have not been baptized. Thus we meet the shades of the First Parent, of Abel, of Noah and Moses, of Abraham, David, Israel with his father and his children and Rachel. If anything is comforting in this picture it is this: we meet them in good company, for soon after them we see Homer, the sovereign poet,

Horace, Ovid, Lucan, Plato, Socrates, Orpheus, Hippocrates and Saladin.
And when Dante uses some striking picture taken from the Hebrew Bible,
Jacob's dream, for example, he soon shapes the tale into a new form, and
the ladder into heaven becomes a representation of contemplative monas-
ticism. But the beginning of the poem is pure Jeremiah. There is the
wilderness in which we find ourselves, "midway upon the journey of our
life"; there is the lion out of Jeremiah's forest ("which will slay them");
there is the wolf of Jeremiah of the evening ("which will spoil them");
there is the leopard ("which shall watch over their cities") and "everyone
that goeth out thence shall be torn to pieces." A good example of the
method Dante used to transform the biblical picture and text is given
in the passage quoted by Vossler to prove the same point. Of the mysterious
tree in Paradise, he says:

Two shoots from this plant first appear on the sixth cornice of the Purga-
torical mountain: first, as actual means of punishments, second, as magical
mouthpieces of moral admonition and warning. Thirdly, we find on the sum-
mit of the mountain the tree of knowledge itself, as a comprehensive allegory,
full of philosophic, ethical, and political instruction. All the transformations
from sensuous materialization to moralizing, and even to intellectualizing,
are here passed through, and according to its needs the Biblical tree receives
the most varied and marvelous environment.[19]

Dante, however, not only quoted and transformed the Bible and transplanted its content into the ideas and symbols of the medieval world. His
work reveals also that in his soul there slumbered a more deeply rooted
affinity with that part of the biblical tradition which comes from the
Prophets. He starts with Jeremiah, as we saw. He possessed not only
the voice but also the spirit of a prophet himself.[20] This "inward genuineness" was certainly one of the reasons why Dante often attained a real
prophetic style of his own

which is both classic and thoroughly Florentine, wherein the Hebrew elements acquired fresh and eloquent life and were all but recognizable. The
single sermon of wrath, *Ahi serva Italia, de dolore ostello,* suffices to convince
us that the Old Testament prophets' language of moral indignation is the
mightiest of all artistic treasures which the Bible bestowed upon our poet.[21]

In Chapter 1 we meet the four apocalyptic beasts of Jeremiah. In the
fourteenth canto of *Inferno* we have Nebuchadnezzar's dream. In *Purgatorio* 29 we meet Ezekiel, in *Paradiso* 15, Isaiah. They certainly live in
Dante's work, as stimulants and even more. In his *Divine Comedy*, then,
the influence of the Bible reached its climax, as far as the medieval approach
is concerned. But with Dante and some minor disciples the trend to quote
the Hebrew Bible, to transform its stories and to interpret them so that
they might prove the events in the New Testament, also came to an end.

The reason for this change has to be sought in the general development religion went through in the sixteenth century, when the Renaissance introduced Luther's Reformation and Protestantism as its religious counterpart. Not only in Germany, but in France and England also, the ideas of Protestantism proved to be a liberating force.

Through the Reformation the Bible became common property and the new era of its influence can now be detected. Especially in German-speaking countries, where Luther's translation was a sensational event, the social group of the *Buerger* could now read the story of the Creation, of Joseph and of Moses in the vernacular. In the mind of Luther the different tales of the Bible did not have the same value, so that he in a sense overlooked their importance for writers and poets. Thus he was enthusiastic about the Fifth Book of Moses, but he was less interested in the Book of Proverbs. The reason for this is obvious. The *Liber Proverbium Salomonis* is for him *"ein schoenes Buch, denn darim sieht man, wie es in der Welt zugeht"* (a beautiful book, for one can see in it what the world looks like). Further, he disliked the Books Ezra, Judith and Tobias, while Job again was classified as a *"sehr gutes Buch."*[22]

At any rate, his translation proved to be influential and stimulating, even more than his remarks in letters or in his *Tischreden*, although these remarks also opened the way to deeper understanding and appreciation. And to those who believed that the Old Testament was entirely superseded by the Gospels, he answered in clear language: "Ob aber jemand wollte vorgeben, das alte Testament sei aufgehoben und gelte nicht mehr . . . antworte ich: Das ist nicht so . . ." (If someone should think the Old Testament discarded and of no further value, I say: It is not so.)[23] There was no religious epic of importance, however, in the sixteenth century, and it took almost two hundred years before Protestantism in Germany dared to follow the English example given by Milton. Only as late as 1748 was Klopstock ready to publish the first part of his *Messiah*. The reason for this is easy to detect. The people could now read the thrilling stories in the vernacular, and there was no immediate need to rewrite them as tales or poems. The drama, on the other hand, was strongly influenced through Luther's translation and also by his remarks. Translation included not only the Greek but the Hebrew of the Bible. The dramatists, however, ostensibly preferred the Jewish tradition, as these stories could easily be adapted to modern sixteenth-century life.

In France, as we have seen, the presentation of medieval religious plays was forbidden by law; the ban struck also the *mystère* of the Old Testament. In Spain, on the other hand, the Golden Age of the drama, of Lope de Vega and Calderón de la Barca (who used very few tales from the Hebrew Bible), kept the Bible more than ever on the stage. But these authors closely followed the medieval tradition in which the Old Testament had to "prove" the New. In Germany now, through Luther, and after him without interruption, the dramatists of the laymen's *Buergerspiele* and the writers of the laymen's school theater, in colleges and universities, with enthusiasm and almost incredible haste, appropriated the rich material offered to them by the Bible in the vernacular. All reports show conclusively that now, as no outspoken religious purpose stood behind the undertaking, and nothing had to be proved but moral, ethical issues, the authors of the *Schuldrama*, of the *Buergerspiele*, preferred the colorful tales of the Hebrew Bible to all the other material at their disposal. It is almost unbelievable, notes one authority, to observe what material was taken as a pretext for a drama. The Fall, of course. Then the first murder, the story of the Patriarchs, Moses, the Judges, Susanna and the Elders, the three men in the fiery furnace, the golden calf. In these dramas, certain characters had become typical of certain problems: passionate and criminal love appeared in Joseph; the mad passion of old men for a young woman was depicted in Susanna; harmonious life in the bosom of the family was presented in Rebecca, in Tobias. But there were also Judith and Holofernes, and another Joseph by a Dutch educator, and another Susanna in German and Latin. In brief, after Luther the dramatists preferred the biblical stories above all; they liked the interesting plots as they found them in the new translation of the Old Testament. The Hebrew Bible became secularized.

But there is also another reason why Luther is featured in this report. He translated not only prose and the historical parts of the Bible, he also translated the Psalms and contributed thereby to a renewal of Hebrew poetry.

His translations of certain psalms were not the first. We have already mentioned French attempts to put Hebrew poetry into the vernacular. From the tenth century we have a free Bavarian translation (or adaptation) of Psalm 138, a poem written in the *althochdeutsch* vernacular. No other part of the Bible was taken over so completely and so uniformly as the Psalms: from the beginning they were a part of the Christian service. What Luther added was a new, strong and productive emphasis, a new evaluation of this part of the Bible. And the genuine poetical feeling of his translation in the vernacular transformed certain Hebrew songs (Psalm 46:6: "Eine feste Burg ist unser Gott . . .") into German poems of unusual brilliance. That is to say, before Luther the songs in the Church (including the *Stabat Mater* and the *Dies Irae*) were influenced by Solomon's psalms. Luther brought the tradition closer to the Bible when he tried his hand at Psalms 2, 14, 46, 67, 124, 128, 130. And there was Clément Marot in France, who published a very successful, but poor translation of the Psalms (1541, *Trente Psaumes de David;* 1543, *Cinauante Psaumes*). The Huguenots especially praised him for his work, for the songs *"qu'ils entonnaient en marchant au combat."* The Huguenots needed a hymnbook. This explains the vogue, the immense success of the book. But it was read by the Catholics also. And, according to Bédier, the courtiers at the court of Navarre and the court of France hummed the *Chants de David*, even though the Sorbonne banned the translation. Thus it became a part of the Protestant liturgy, it deeply influenced the development of French poetry in the following centuries, and was followed by another translation, that of Théodore de Bèze (1563). The Catholics soon tried to compete: Le Baïf's attempt dates from 1578. And there were the German Protestant and Catholic poets in the seventeenth century following his example. A new sphere of influence remained active.

The very program of French classicism—the next trend in modernism—seemed to exclude biblical topics; Greek costumes (more than Greek thoughts and philosophy) outlawed all else. All the more, therefore, is it interesting to see how the Jansenist Jean Racine came back to the Bible when he wrote *Esther* for Madame de Maintenon's school for girls in Saint-Cyr. In *Esther* the play follows the Bible closely, except for the smoother, less bloody ending of the French tragedy. It is a hymn to Israel, and not merely superficially, for it owes its plot as well as its style and philosophy to Hebrew tradition. It is true, the *chœur des Israélites* is a chorus in the manner of Greek tragedy. It follows the tradition and the purpose of Greek drama, but the philosophy and the wording come from the Hebrew legacy, from the Psalms. And when we analyze this chorus we find, for instance, the very words of Psalm 121. But the *Esther* of Racine shows still another interesting change. The biblical story is related to prove its own objective, its own philosophy, not—as in the Middle Ages—to prove Christianity. The process of secularization has gone so far that there is not the slightest allusion to another religion. The play is, furthermore, the perfect amalgamation of Greek form and Hebrew content. The king in the play, however, is Louis XIV.

In the eighteenth century, the Protestants, that is to say, Klopstock, Bodmer, Herder and Goethe, lead us to another and different sphere of influence. The reasons for this change are rather complex. As we saw, there was a readiness to reinterpret the Bible, a readiness that came from Luther and the Reformation. But there was also the influence of Jean Jacques Rousseau, whose social philosophy found its way even into the field of literature. The *"retour à la nature"* in literature meant indeed a new flowering of folklore, of original poetry and ideas, an attitude which soon was used in respect to the Hebrew Bible. Rousseau was—in the beginning—less successful with this idea in France than in Germany. The German disciples of Rousseau—Herder above all, and with him the outstanding disciple of Herder, namely Goethe—looked at Hebrew folk lore with new eyes. They were no longer interested in the Bible as a religious document (overcoming thereby the Middle Ages, and Luther too), they discovered in the secularized text the loftiest piece of "original" literature. Goethe was so much enchanted by the Bible, so strongly influenced by its stories and ideas, that he asked his father's permission to study Hebrew in order to be able to read the Bible in the original. Remarks about his interest in the Hebrew text abound in his work. The *Jahrmarktsfest in Plundersweilen* includes a playlet dealing with Haman, Mordecai and Esther. In *Dichtung und Wahrheit*, his autobiography, sixty-year-old Goethe expresses rather extensively and in clear words how deeply he is and was influenced by the Bible, meaning the Hebrew text. The same can be said about certain paragraphs in the novel *Wilhelm Meisters Lehrjahre*. The influence continued the older the poet and thinker himself grew, as we can see in the appendix to the *Westoestlicher Divan*, where Goethe's admiration for the Hebrew contribution is expressed. The debt to a great influence reached its climax in the greatest drama the poet conceived. The final stage of Faust's life and his death is clearly developed after the greatest model in the Bible, after Moses' last years and death. The lawmaker Faust closely follows the lawmaker Moses in his last experiences, and the end of Faust's life and his salvation is certainly influenced by the Bible on the highest, the spiritual, level.

All over Europe they soon followed Goethe, even in France where the Age of Enlightenment drove religion underground. A student of details and catalogues will easily find how strong was the influence of the Bible on the French writers, poets and dramatists in the nineteenth century. He has only to search the work of Chateaubriand, Lamartine, Alfred de Vigny, Victor Hugo. The characters, whom Chateaubriand borrowed from the Bible, are no more the *belles infidèles* of Robert Garnier or Racine; they are taken from the Bible itself. The words of the young Eudore in *Les Martyrs* come directly from the Song of Songs: *"Que vous êtes belle, mon amie . . . que la myrrhe et l'aloès couvrent votre lit embaumé!"* And finally, according to a subtle remark of the French poet, André Spire, *"la découverte de la valeur de la Bible par Chateaubriand fut l'origine d'une profonde transformation de la langue littéraire française."*[24] And Lamartine writes: *"Lorsque mon âme enthousiaste ou pieuse ou triste, a besoin de chercher un écho à ses enthousiasmes, à ses piétés, ou à ses mélancholies . . . je n'ouvre ni Pindare, ni Horace, ni Hafiz . . . j'ouvre les psaumes et j'y prends les paroles qui semblent sourdre des siècles et qui pénètrent jusqu'au fonds de l'âme des générations."* And in his tragedy *Saul*, and in other works of inspiring importance, Lamartine rediscovered the lyrical *élan* of the prophets: *"La Providence divine est toujours présente, la pitié pour les pauvres et les déshérités, les appels des opprimés à la miséricorde et à la pitié de Dieu."*[25] And Alfred de Vigny left six biblical poems among the thirty he wrote.

Thus, a student of literary influences will find biblical themes, quotations from biblical material, interpretations of certain tales, biblical similes, images and characters in the works of Michelet, Quinet, Lamennais, James Darmesteter (*La Légende Divine*), Leconte de Lisle. He will discover the unbroken influence of a great legacy in the poems and works of French symbolists, Remy de Gourmont (*Lilith*), Gustave Kahn, Edouard Dujardin. In Germany—where the harvest is less abundant than in France—he will find Hebbel's *Judith*, Gutzkow's *Koenig Saul* and Otto Ludwig's *Makkabaeer*, to mention only writers and plays of great importance.

In France the twentieth century witnessed the *Saül* of André Gide, a play sparkling with intellect; so, too, we have *Judith* by Jean Giraudoux, where the biblical story lends itself to a brilliant play of sophisticated spirit. We have *Samaël* by André Spire, a serious philosophical fantasy. And we have *La première famille* by Jules Supervielle, a biblical farce, surrealist in style, full of that *esprit gaulois*. We have tragedy, comedy, farce. The great Viennese Jewish dramatist and poet, Richard Beer-Hofmann, published his biblical tragedies (*Jaakobs Traum, Der junge David*), which enjoyed great success. Stefan Zweig wrote his *Jeremias*. We could point furthermore to the influence of Hebrew poetry—I mean the Psalms—on two French Catholic poets, Péguy and Claudel. But there I should first mention the influence of the Psalms on the *vers libre* of Walt Whitman, and on other forerunners of Claudel. At any rate, we hear an echo from Solomon in the *Grandes Odes* of Claudel, in his dramas, and in the *Mystère d'Eve* by Charles Péguy.

Thus we have reached the climax of a development which began with an old French play, an old German epic. The old sacred story is employed not merely for its narrative, as in the period before Luther; it is adopted not only as a form convenient for moderns. Its potentialities as a symbolic frame for a twentieth-century idea or problem are discovered. We turn, therefore, to Thomas Mann's *Joseph* novel. What could a writer of the twentieth century find in the Bible? In a former work Thomas Mann had described successfully the rise and fall of a nineteenth-century bourgeois family; in another novel he described the intellectual, moral and political situation of Europe before the 1914 war. His style was patterned after the style of Goethe, dramatist, novelist and poet of the eighteenth and the early nineteenth century, and his world was seen with the eyes of a naturalist, that is to say, with the eyes of a man who reveals even romantic feelings as "natural" as possible; and his imagination found its expression and its symbols in the intellectual language of a modern twentieth-century thinker. What could he find in the Bible? Well, in a later work he intended to describe, above all, the problems of the twentieth century. He looked around for some *durable* material in which to express his ideas. And as he looked he could find no more adequate a frame for his picture than the one he discovered in the Bible: the adventures of young Joseph, Joseph in Egypt, Joseph the Provider. The reason for this choice was, of course, not superficial; it was a special and inescapable one. In his own words: "The selection of the Old Testament subject was certainly not mere accident." He found in the story of Joseph and his brothers something which could not be expressed in another material, which could not be presented through another symbol, in the same defiant spirit, with the same convincing clearness. The defiant spirit states: "To write a novel of the Jewish spirit was timely, because it seemed untimely,"[26] a remark which reveals more of the author's mood than of his search for a creative theme. And Thomas Mann knows this as well as we do. As a creative spirit he has to follow his own rules, his own inner law. Therefore, he adds to his first statement, that he did not intend to write a hymn of a tradition, a political tract or a religious essay. He was influenced by a great legacy, he was overwhelmed by it, but he was not sold to it. Thus his story follows the report in Genesis, in Thomas Mann's own words, only "with semijocular faithfulness, and often it reads like an exegesis and amplification of the Torah, like a Rabbinical Midrash," and "all that is Jewish, throughout the work, is merely foreground, only *one* style element among others, only one stratum of its language . . ."[27] But even if we do not overlook the self-imposed limitation expressed in these words, we see that such an approach to the original story, to the original spirit of the sacred text, has never been undertaken or dared before. The *Wiener Genesis* was a Hebrew report, but did not show Jewish spirit at all; and Racine's *Esther* celebrated in a Jewish story the glory of King Louis XIV. The Jewish spirit was only the setting, the décor, the costume in those works. Here we discover that it is at least one stratum of its language. And when Thomas Mann was asked what "made [him] turn to this remote, out-of-the-way subject and induced [him] to transform the biblical legend of the Egyptian Joseph into a broad cycle of novels," he answered that he was "delighted" when he read the original, which means that his imagination was caught by the text. Then, "a preliminary probing and productive searching began in [his] mind as to what it would be like to renew and reproduce this charming story in fresh narrative with all the modern means."[28] This final success and reawakening of a centuries-old story would not prove very much if this reawakening were a single fact. Thomas Mann, however, helps us here, too, when he reveals how "almost immediately, these inner experiences [mentioned above] significantly associated themselves with the thought of a tradition: the thought of Goethe, in fact, who relates in his memoirs *Truth and Fiction* how he, as a boy, had dictated the Joseph story to a friend and, in doing so, had woven it into a broad narrative . . ." As an explanation of this youthful and premature adventure, the sixty-year-old Goethe observes, "This natural story is highly amiable, only it seems too short, and one is tempted to carry it out in all its details." And it seems also to be revealing of the attitude of a twentieth-century man who is influenced by the Bible.

"As a man," confesses Thomas Mann, "and as an artist, I must somehow have been in readiness to be productively attracted by such subject matter, and my Bible reading was not mere chance." This readiness has to be explained more elaborately.

The various stages of life have different inclinations, claims, tendencies of taste—as well as abilities and advantages. It is probably a rule that in certain years the taste for all purely individual and particular phenomena, for the *individual case,* for the "bourgeois" aspect, in the widest sense of the word, fades out gradually. Instead, the typical, the *eternally human, eternally recurring, timeless,* in short, the *mythical steps into the foreground of interest.* For, after all, the typical is already the mythical, in so far as it is pristine pattern and pristine form of life, timeless model and formula of old, into which life enters by reproducing its traits of the unconscious.[29]

How far we have come! To take an illustrious example: the Jewish story of Joseph and his brothers appeared and reappeared again and again, as stimulating form and thought-influencing material in European—French, Spanish, German and Italian—literature. It was an epic in the twelfth century in Germany; a play in the thirteenth century in France and Spain; its characters appeared in Italian and Portuguese works of literature; it was a *moralité* in the Germany of the Protestant Reformation, then again (Goethe), and finally an opera and a ballet and a novel. In brief, it was a sacred story in the original text and became a symbol of humanity in the provisional present form.

By this the circle is rounded again. The Bible, a religious work, has proved its inspiring value in the field of literature, too, as an influence on language, images, thought, as a storehouse for fairy tales, moral stories, ethical legends, as a model for new forms in poetry, and as a gold mine for mythical symbols. Its lasting charm has worked on the greatest occasions—in the *Divine Comedy,* in the *Esther* of Racine, in Goethe's *Faust,* in Mann's *Joseph*-novel—as a genuine, sparkling and influential source of inspiration.

NOTES

[1] E. R. Bevan, and C. Singer (eds.), *The Legacy of Israel,* p. 504.
[2] *Ibid.,* pp. 540 f.
[3] *Ibid.,* p. 483.
[4] *Ibid.,* p. 486.

[4a Cf. above, David Daiches, "The Influence of the Bible on English Literature," p. 400.]

5 P. Piper, *Die geistliche Dichtung des Mittelalters*, pp. 87 ff.

6 *Ibid.*, pp. 91-191.

7 *Ibid.*, p. 194.

8 *Ibid.*, p. 12.

9 J. Bédier and P. Hazard, *Histoire de la littérature française illustrée*, I, 4.

10 L. Petit de Julleville, *Le Théâtre en France*, p. 3.

11 *Ibid.*, p. 19.

12 *Ibid.*, p. 71.

[12a For the development in English literature cf. Daiches *op. cit.*]

13 J. P. Crawford, *Spanish drama before Lope de Vega*, pp. 41 ff.

14 *Ibid.*, pp. 142-147.

15 *Medieval Culture*, II, 99.

16 *Ibid.*, II, 100.

17 *Ibid.*, II, 100.

18 Dante, *Divine Comedy* (Inferno, canto IV).

19 K. Vossler, II, 103.

20 Dante, canto I.

21 Vossler, *op. cit.*, p. 104.

22 *Luthers Werke* (ed. Buchwald), VII, pp. 191, 195.

23 *Ibid.*, VII, 241.

24 *Pour la Victoire*. New York, March 13, 1943.

25 *Ibid.*, quoted by André Spire.

26 Thomas Mann about his *Joseph*-novel (printed report of a lecture delivered at the Library of Congress), p. 17.

27 *Ibid.*, p. 18.

28 *Ibid.*, p. 5.

29 *Ibid.*, p. 7.

BIBLIOGRAPHY

BEDIER, JOSEPH, and HAZARD, PAUL, *Histoire de la littérature française illustrée*. 2 vols. Paris, 1923-1924.

BEVAN, EDWYN R., and SINGER, CHARLES (eds.), *The Legacy of Israel*. Oxford, 1927.

CRAWFORD, J. P. WICKERSHAM, *Spanish drama before Lope de Vega*. Philadelphia, 1937.

PETIT DE JULLEVILLE, LOUIS, *Le Théâtre en France*. Paris, 1923.

PIPER, PAUL, *Die geistliche Dichtung des Mittelalters*. Berlin, 1888. Vol. 3.

ROTH, CECIL, *The Jewish Contribution to Civilization*. Cincinnati, 1940.

VOSSLER, KARL, *Medieval Culture*, An Introduction to Dante and his times. 2 vols. New York, 1929.

I THE JEWS: THEIR HISTORY

II THE JEWS: THEIR RELIGION AND CULTURE

LIST OF ABBREVIATIONS

Am. Jour. Sem. Lang.
    American Journal of Semitic Languages
Annual Am. Sch. Or. Res.
    Annual American Schools of Oriental Research
Antt.
    Antiquities, Josephus
Archiv f. Orientf.
    Archiv fuer Orientforschung
ARN
    Abot of Rabbi Nathan
AZA
    Ahavah Zedakah Ahdut (B'nai B'rith Youth Organization)
b.
    ben (son of)
B.
    Babylonian Talmud
B. B.
    Baba Batra
B. C. E.
    Before the Common Era
BEAS
    The Hebrew University, Jerusalem, *Bulletin (Louis M. Rabinowitz Fund) for the Exploration of Ancient Synagogues*
Beih. Zeits. Alttest. Wiss.
    Beihefte zur Zeitschrift fuer die Alttestamentliche Wissenschaft
Bell. Jud.
    De Bello Judaico, Josephus
Ber. Saechs. Akad. Wiss.
    Berichte ueber die Verhandlungen der saechsischen Akademie der Wissenschaften
Bull. Am. Sch. Or. Res.
    Bulletin American Schools of Oriental Research
Bull. de l'Inst. Français d'Archéol. Orient.
    Bulletin de l'Institut Français d'Archéologie Orientale

Bull. Jew. Pal. Explor. Soc.
　　Bulletin of the Jewish Palestine Exploration Society
C. Ap.
　　Contra Apionem, Josephus
C. E.
　　Common Era
CCAR
　　Central Conference of American Rabbis
CJFWF
　　Council Jewish Federations and Welfare Funds
cod.
　　codex
Comp. Rend. Acad. des Inscr.
　　Comptes-Rendus de l'Académie des Inscriptions
De Abr.
　　De Abrahamo, Philo
De Ant. Jud.
　　Antiquitates Judaicae, Josephus
De Cher.
　　De Cherubim, Philo
De Conf.
　　De Confusione Linguarum, Philo
De Congr.
　　De Congressu Eruditionis Gratia, Philo
De Dec.
　　De Decalogo, Philo
De Ebr.
　　De Ebrietate, Philo
De Fuga
　　De Fuga et Inventione, Philo
De Gig.
　　De Gigantibus, Philo
De Mig. or De Migr.
　　De Migratione Abrahami, Philo
De Mut.
　　De Mutatione Nominum, Philo
De Op.
　　De Opificio Mundi, Philo
De Plant.
　　De Plantatione, Philo
De Post.
　　De Posteritate Caini, Philo
De Praem.
　　De Praemiis et Poenis, Philo

De Sacr.
  De Sacrificiis Abelis et Caini, Philo

De Somn.
  De Somniis, Philo

De Vita Contempl.
  De Vita Contemplativa, Philo

Dion. Halic., *De. Thuc.*
  Dionysius of Halicarnassus, *On Thucydides*

Ec. Hist.
  Ecclesiastical History, Eusebius

Enn.
  Ennead, Plotinus

Ep.
  Epistulae Morales ad Lucilium, Seneca

Epist.
  Epistles, Horace

Eur.
  Euripides

Gen. R.
  Genesis Rabbah

Harv. Theo. Rev.
  Harvard Theological Review

Heracl.
  Heracles, Euripides

HIAS
  Hebrew Sheltering and Immigrant Aid Society

HICEM
  Combination of HIAS—Hebrew Sheltering and Immigrant Aid Society ICA—Jewish Colonization Association, Emigdirect

HUCA
  Hebrew Union College Annual

ICA
  Jewish Colonization Association

JBL or *Jour. Bib. Lit.*
  Journal of Biblical Literature

J. D. C.
  American Jewish Joint Distribution Committee

JE
  Jewish Encyclopedia

JPOS
  Journal of the Palestine Oriental Society

JQR or *Jew. Quar. Rev.*
  Jewish Quarterly Review

JQR N.S. *Jewish Quar. Rev.* N.S.
    Jewish Quarterly Review New Series
JSS
    Jewish Social Studies

J. W. B.
    Jewish Welfare Board
Jour. Near East Stud.
    Journal of Near Eastern Studies
Jour. Pal. Or. Soc.
    Journal Palestine Oriental Society
Jour. of the Warburg Inst.
    Journal of the Warburg Institute
Ket.
    Ketubot
Lam. R.
    Lamentations Rabbah
Leg. All.
    Legum Allegoria, Philo
Lev. R.
    Leviticus Rabbah
Mas. Soferim
    Masseket Soferim
MGWJ
    Monatsschrift fuer Geschichte und Wissenschaft des Judenthums
n.d.
  no date
N.F.
    Neue Folge (new series)
N.S.
    New Series
n.s.D.
    new series, D.
ORT
    Organization for Rehabilitation and Training
OSE
    World Union for the Protection of the Health of the Jews
PAJHS
    Publication of the American Jewish Historical Society
Pal. Explor. Quar.
    Palestinian Exploration Fund Quarterly
Pal. Explor. Fund Quar. State.
    Palestinian Exploration Fund Quarterly Statement
Parm.
    Parmenides, Philo

Quis Rer.
  Quis Rerum Divinarum Heres, Philo
Quod Deus
  Quod Deus Sit Immutabilis, Philo
Quod Omn.
  Quod Omnis Probus Liber Sit, Philo
R.
  Rab or Rabbi
Rev. études juiv.
  Revue des Etudes Juives
R.S.P.C.A.
  Royal Society for the Prevention of Cruelty to Animals
s.a.
  sociedad anonima (corporation)
Shab.
  Shabbat
SI
  Studies of the Research Institute for Hebrew Poetry (Hebrew)
Sifre Deut.
  Sifre on Deuteronomy
Sifre Num.
  Sifre on Numbers
Sitz. Heidelberger Akad. Wissen.
  Sitzungsberichte der Heidelberger Akademie der Wissenschaften
Sitz. Preuss. Akad. Wissen.
  Sitzungsberichte der Preussischen Akademie der Wissenschaften
U.J.A.
  United Jewish Appeal
U.P.A.
  United Palestine Appeal
Yer.
  Yerushalmi
Zeit. Alttest. Wiss.
  Zeitschrift fuer die Alttestamentliche Wissenschaft
Zeit. Deutsch. Pal. Var.
  Zeitschrift des Deutschen Palaestina Vereins
Zeits. Deutsch. Morg. Ges.
  Zeitschrift der Deutschen Morgenlaendischen Gesellschaft
Zeits. Neutest. Wissen.
  Zeitschrift fuer die Neutestamentliche Wissenschaft
Z.O.A.
  Zionist Organization of America

INDEX

Persons, places, and subjects omitted from the index due to limitations of space may be
located by reference to the main subject, *e.g.*, to locate a chemist, look under *Science*; an
author, look under *Literature*. Publications are in general not indexed by title but by author.
Names containing *bar, ben ibn, ha-,* etc., are indexed by the first word of the compound.
Persons and publications cited in Notes or Bibliographies have not all been indexed.
Before May, 1948, references are to *Palestine*; after that date to *Israel, State of*.

Aaron ben Elijah, 80
Aaron of Lincoln, 1
Aaron of London, 1
Abba Saul, 59
Abot, see Pirke Abot
Abrabanel, Isaac, 87, 241
Abrabanel, Judah (Leone Ebreo), 87, 99,
  243-44
Abraham, 45-46
Abraham, O., 147
Abraham bar Hiyya (Savasorda), 83, 227 f.
Abraham ben Shemtob, 236
Abraham ibn Daud, 83 f.
Abraham ibn Ezra, 82, 96, 227-28, 271
Abravanel, *see* Abrabanel
Abt, Isaac Arthur, 205
Abulafia, Moses, 134
Acco (Ptolemais), Palestine, 162
Acosta, Cristoval d', 203, 246
Acquittance, starr of, 6 f., 9-13
Adler, Alfred, 213, 267
Adler, Guido, 147
Adler, I., 151
Adler, Viktor, 267
Aelfric, 392
Agada, *see* Haggada
Agudat Israel, 306, 311 ff.
Ahab, 384
Ahdut Haavoda, 305, 310
Ahrayut, 14-15
Akiba, Rabbi, quoted, 372, 375, 384
Albalag, Isaac, 86
Albert Einstein College of Medicine, 214
Albo, Joseph, 87, 97
Alexander, Samuel, 66
Alexandria, Egypt, 66, 193
Alfachar, Judah, 198-99
Alfonso X, 234-35
Aliyah, 316 f.
Altalena, S.S., 312
Amatus Lusitanus (Juan Roderigo), 201-2,
  245
America, *see* United States
American Jewish Joint Distribution Com-
  mittee, 329 f.
Ammonias Saccas, 74
Amos, 155, 374, 382
Amr ibn Sach'l, 134
Amsterdam, Holland, art, 171-72

Anatoli, Jacob, 86, 233
Anav, 60
Anglo-American Committee of Inquiry,
  287 f.
Anthropomorphism, 68-69
Anti-Semitism, 1st century, 193
  in Soviet Union, 350
Anusim, *see* Marranos
Appel, Paul, 257
Aqaba, Gulf of, 348, 351
Aquinas, Thomas, 86, 89
Arab Legion, 292
Arab States, 278, 284-86, 290-96, 312, 322-
  26, 346-49
Arab Teachers Training College, 324
Arabia, Hebrew-Arabic science, 223-26, 239-
  42
  Jewish influence on medicine, 194-98
  see also Moslems
Arabic-Judaic scientific literature, 223-25
Arabut, 8
Archevolti, Samuel, 169 f.
Aristotelianism, 80-81, 83-85, 217
Arnald of Villanova, 237-38
Aron, Hermann, 260
Arons, Leo, 260
Arragel, Moses, 167-68
Art, 154-74
  Amsterdam, 171-72
  Biblical period, 154-61
  Middle Ages, 165-68
  modern, 173-74
  Renaissance, 168-71
  State of Israel, 335
  synagogue, 162-67, 170
Asa, 187
Ascoli, Italy, 169-70
Asher ben Yehiel, Rabbi, 12
Ashkenazi, Zebi, 171
Ashkenazim, and art, 171 f.
Ashtaroth (Astarte), 154
Asmakta, 17 f.
Assyria, 156 ff.
Astarte (Ashtaroth), 154
Astruc, Jean, 200
Auer, Leopold von, 145
Austria, literature of, 410-11
  17th-19th centuries, 204
Authorized Version, Bible, 388-90, 399-406